urban environmental

management

CONTRIBUTING AUTHORS

Francesca Alexander

Richard N. L. Andrews

Andris Auliciems

Brian J. L. Berry

Douglas Billingsley

Mark Blacksell

Berndt von Boehm

P. H. Bowden

David E. Boyce

Ian Burton

Richard C. Clelland

Richard Cooley

Merrill Eisenbud

V. Fisher

A. Myrick Freeman III

Marshall I. Goldman

James E. Hackett

Evelyn B. Harner

Elizabeth H. Haskell

Robert H. Haverman

John Hewings

Richard J. Hickey

Frank E. Horton

Nancy B. Hultquist

S. Ishikawa

James F. Johnson

Robert W. Kates

Helmut E. Landsberg

Lester B. Lave

Luna B. Leopold

David Lowenthal

Leo Marx

Marvin Mikesell

Lewis W. Moncrief

George B. Morgan

Guntis Ozolins

Donald H. Pack

James T. Peterson

Georges Sabagh

Myra Schiff

Joseph Schofer

John R. Sheaffer

Chris Taylor

Elbert C. Taylor

Peter D. Tyson

Maurice D. Van Arsdol, Jr.

Martin Wachs

Geoffrey Wall

Walter E. Westman

M. Gordon Wolman

Kenneth R. Woodcock

J. P. Wyatt

urban environmental management
planning for pollution control

AN ORIGINAL TEXT WITH INTEGRATED READINGS

BRIAN J. L. BERRY
University of Chicago

FRANK E. HORTON
University of Iowa

prentice-hall, inc., englewood cliffs, new jersey

Library of Congress Cataloging in Publication Data

BERRY, BRIAN JOE LOBLEY,   comp.
  Urban environmental management.

  Bibliography: p.
  1. Environmental protection. 2. Pollution.
  3. Cities and towns—Planning. I. HORTON, FRANK E.,
joint comp. II. Title.
TD170.B49   301.31   74–1315
ISBN   0–13–939611–X

© 1974 by Prentice-Hall, Inc.
Englewood Cliffs, New Jersey

10 9 8 7 6 5 4 3 2

Printed in the United States of America

PRENTICE-HALL INTERNATIONAL, INC., *London*
PRENTICE-HALL OF AUSTRALIA PTY. LTD., *Sydney*
PRENTICE-HALL OF CANADA LTD., *Toronto*
PRENTICE-HALL OF INDIA PRIVATE LIMITED, *New Delhi*
PRENTICE-HALL OF JAPAN, INC., *Tokyo*

contents

v

CHAPTER **7**

CHAPTER **8**

CHAPTER **9**

CHAPTER 10

noise pollution
and abatement strategies   283

CHAPTER 11

environmental pollution
and human health   295

CHAPTER 12

governmental programs affecting
environmental quality   341

preface

The realization that a companion volume to *Geographic Perspectives on Urban Systems* was both needed and timely emerged soon after that book had seen the light of day. In *Geographic Perspectives* we dealt with urban geography from the highly circumscribed social-scientific view of that field, at the very time that the "new environmentalism" was gaining strength as a national movement and a disciplinary perspective, placing further pressures on the field to become increasingly policy oriented. Several books appeared in rapid succession, beginning to probe the physical geography of the city and problems of environmental pollution. But none took the next step of exploiting the discipline's particular concerns with location, spatial relationships and the mutual interdependencies of man and nature, its comprehension of the complexity of ecological explanations, and its skill at spatial analysis and interdisciplinary synthesis. We felt there was a need and an opportunity.

Should we write a totally new volume, or, consistent with *Geographic Perspectives*, draw together the best of the writings of others into an integrated synthesis? We chose the latter path and acknowledge our total debt to the fifty authors who were willing to allow us to blend their contributions into a single text. The Guide to the Readings (pp. xiii–xv) and an introductory footnote to each chapter indicate whose work is included and where it is incorporated. Whereas we selected and edited for flow, balance, and consistency, we have attempted to retain the core of each author's contribution in his own style and sequence.

A number of people have been of great help to us in our task. In particular, we want to acknowledge our debt to John S. Adams, Donald C. Dahmann, James S. Gardner, Charles P. Kaplan, Marvin W. Mikesell, and M. Gordon Wolman. In addition, we would like to thank the Environmental Studies Division of the

Environmental Protection Agency and its director, Peter House, for support and assistance. Project R-801419, "Land Use Forms and the Environment," currently being undertaken under a contract between EPA and The University of Chicago, has provided a variety of insights and raised a whole series of questions about the base level of understanding required for such research that we have tried to address in this book, as well as tables that help fill some of the gaps in the previous literature. The full report of the research project will be published at the same time as this book in the Department of Geography Research Series, The University of Chicago.

BRIAN J. L. BERRY
FRANK E. HORTON

guide to the readings

This book is a text with integrated readings. Selections from a variety of studies have been edited and, with the permission of their authors and editors, combined into a single manuscript. The materials included in each chapter are listed below. Numbers in parentheses are the pages of this book on which selections begin. In addition, use is made throughout the book of the reports of the Council on Environmental Quality: *Environmental Quality, 1970; Environmental Quality, 1971; Environmental Quality, 1972.* Washington, D.C.: U.S. Government Printing Office.

Materials are quoted in the Introduction from:

Elizabeth H. Haskell, *Quality of the Urban Environment: The Federal Role.* Washington, D.C.: The Urban Institute, Working Paper 102–106, May 1970. (2)

David Lowenthal, Ian Burton, Richard Cooley, and Marvin Mikesell, "Report of the AAG Task Force on Environmental Quality," *The Professional Geographer,* Vol. 25 (1973), 39–47. (5)

Chapter 2 includes selections from:

Lewis W. Moncrief, "The Cultural Basis for our Environmental Crisis," *Science,* Vol. 170 (October 30, 1970), pp. 509–512. (9)

Marshall I. Goldman, "The Convergence of Environmental Disruption," *Science,* Vol. 170 (October 2, 1970), pp. 37–42. (11)

Leo Marx, "American Institutions and Ecological Ideals," *Science,* Vol. 170 (November 27, 1970), pp. 945–952. (12)

Maurice D. Van Arsdol, Jr., Georges Sabagh, and Francesca Alexander, "Reality and the Perception of Environmental Hazards," *Journal of Health and Human Behavior,* Vol. 5 (1964), pp. 144–153. (12)

Robert W. Kates, "The Perception of Storm Hazards on the Shores of Megalopolis," in

David Lowenthal, *Environmental Perception and Behavior*, Department of Geography Research Paper No. 109, University of Chicago, 1967. (20)

Much of Chapter 3 is drawn from:

Helmut E. Landsberg, "Man-made Climatic Changes," *Science*, Vol. 170 (December 18, 1970), pp. 1265–1268. (33)

Peter D. Tyson, "Urban Climatology: A Problem of Environmental Studies." Johannesburg: Witwatersrand University Press, 1970. (39)

James T. Peterson, *The Climate of Cities: A Survey of Recent Literature*. Durham, N.C.: National Air Pollution Control Administration, 1969. (40)

Luna B. Leopold, *Hydrology for Urban Land Planning—A Guidebook on the Hydrologic Effects of Urban Land Use*. Washington D.C.: U.S. Government Printing Office, 1968 (Geological Survey Circular 554). (63)

Selections are included in Chapter 4 from:

Donald H. Pack, "Meteorology of Air Pollution," *Science*, Vol. 164 (November 27, 1964), pp. 1119–1127. (86)

George B. Morgan, Guntis Ozolins, and Elbert C. Taylor, "Air Pollution Surveillance Systems," *Science*, Vol. 170 (October 16, 1970), pp. 289–295. (96)

Andris Auliciems and Ian Burton, *Perception and Awareness of Air Pollution in Toronto*, Working Paper Series No. 13, Natural Hazard Research Series, University of Toronto, 1970. (99)

Andris Auliciems, Ian Burton, John Hewings, Myra Schiff, and Chris Taylor, "The Public Use of Scientific Information on the Quality of the Environment: The Case of the Ontario Air Pollution Index," paper presented to the International Geographical Congress, Montreal, 1972. (108)

Chapter 5 materials are included from:

Ian Burton, Douglas Billingsley, Mark Blacksell, and Geoffrey Wall, "A Case Study of Successful Pollution Control Legislation in the United Kingdom," paper presented to the International Geographical Congress, Montreal, 1972. (124)

Kenneth R. Woodcock, *A Model for Regional Air Pollution Control Cost/Benefit Analysis*, TRW Systems Group, McLean, Virginia 22101 (prepared under Contract PH 22–68–60, U.S. Environmental Protection Agency). The report can be obtained from the National Technical Information Service, U.S. Department of Commerce, 5285 Port Royal Road, Springfield, Va. 22151 (accession number PB 202 353). (128)

Chapter 6 draws from:

Nancy B. Hultquist, "Water Pollution as an Aspect of Dynamic Urbanism," Technical Report No. 4, Institute of Urban and Regional Research, University of Iowa, Iowa City, Iowa, 1971. (169)

M. Gordon Wolman, "The Nation's Rivers," *Science*, Vol. 174 (November 1971), pp. 905–918. (173)

Selections in Chapter 7 are integrated from:

Federal Water Quality Control Administration, *Delaware Estuary Comprehensive Study*, Preliminary Report and Findings, Philadelphia: FWQCA, July 1966. (204)

Walter E. Westman, "Some Basic Issues in Water Control Legislation," *American Scientist*, Vol. 60 (November-December 1972), pp. 767–773. (228)

A. Myrick Freeman III and Robert H. Haveman, "Residual Charges for Pollution Control: A Policy Evaluation," *Science*, Vol. 177 (July 1972), pp. 322–329. (237)

Chapter 8 relies upon:

James F. Johnson, *Renovated Waste Water*. Department of Geography Research Paper No. 135, University of Chicago, 1971, pp. 3–23 and 160–166. (247)

Materials are included in Chapter 9 from:

John R. Sheaffer with Berndt von Boehm and James E. Hackett, *Refuse Disposal Needs and Practices in Northeastern Illinois*. Chicago, Ill.: Northeastern Illinois Planning Commission, 1965.

The second part of Chapter 10 is based upon:

Martin Wachs and Joseph Schofer, *A Systems Analyst View of Noise and Urban Planning*, Discussion Paper Series No. 14, Center for Urban Studies, University of Illinois at Chicago Circle, 1970.

Materials reprinted in Chapter 11 are drawn from:

S. Ishikawa, M.D., P. H. Bowden, M.D., V. Fischer, M.D., and J. P. Wyatt, M.D., "The 'Emphysema Profile' in Two Midwestern Cities in North America," *Archives of Environmental Health*, Vol. 18 (1969), pp. 660–666.

Lester B. Lave, "Does Air Pollution Shorten Lives?" Paper prepared for the Committee on Urban Economics Summer Conference, University of Chicago, September 10–11, 1970.

Richard J. Hickey, David E. Boyce, Evelyn B. Harner, and Richard C. Clelland, "Ecological Statistical Studies Concerning Environmental Pollution and Chronic Disease," *IEEE Transactions on Geoscience Electronics*, Vol. GE8 (October 1970), pp. 186–202.

Selections are included in Chapter 12 from:

Richard N. L. Andrews, "Three Fronts of Federal Environmental Policy," *Journal of the American Institute of Planners*, Vol. 37 (July 1971), pp. 258–266.

Merrill Eisenbud, "Environmental Protection in the City of New York," *Science*, Vol. 170 (November 13, 1970), pp. 706–712.

urban environmental

management

CHAPTER *1*

introduction

Perhaps the most important idea to emerge in recent decades with respect to man's use and abuse of his environment is the realization that man lives in a virtually closed resource system, "spaceship earth"—a natural environment with essentially fixed dimensions in terms of mass-energy and assimilative-regenerative capacity. Whatever has been and will be produced, consumed, and ultimately discarded within this resource system is still here and will continue to be, in one form or another. The question is whether the size and regenerative capacity of the natural environment are large and responsive enough to allow sustained economic growth and population expansion in cities and effluent accumulations around them without seriously impinging on health and other demands in the short run, and on growth itself in the long run. There is clear evidence in major metropolitan regions that the answer is a resounding no; externalities, particularly negative effects, grow increasingly pervasive as population expands and economic growth is left to unregulated market forces.

This presents clear challenges to the traditional economic theory of resource use and allocation, which was built on the presumption that virtually everything of value is suitable for private ownership with little or no spillover to other persons, households, or firms when the private

Materials are quoted in the introduction from:
  Elizabeth H. Haskell, *Quality of the Urban Environment: The Federal Role*. Washington, D.C.: The Urban Institute, Working Paper 102–106, May 1970. Begins on page 2.

  David Lowenthal, Ian Burton, Richard Cooley, and Marvin Mikesell, "Report of the AAG Task Force on Environmental Quality," *The Professional Geographer*, Vol. 25 (1973), 39–47. Begins on page 5.

property is put to use by its owner. The competitive market was visualized as a mechanism through which mutual gains could be maximized by individual negotiations and choices. But it is now clear that the pure private-property concept applies satisfactorily to a rapidly narrowing range of natural resources and economic activities. Common property resources, for which it is impossible to assign private property rights, loom ever larger in decisions and choice because it is exactly in such resources—air, watercourses and oceans, landscapes, complex ecosystems—that overuse and accumulating spillovers are threatening the viability of the system as a whole. It is exactly in such cases that lack of a proper pricing mechanism produces misallocations.

In the market economy, prices play a major and valuable role in the allocation of resources to the uses that will be of highest value. On the other hand, degradable environmental resources—the commons, our community resources—are now outside the scope of the market system. Many strategies for direct control of pollution at its many sources or for imposing residuals charges on those who discharge effluents into the environment are now being applied, experimented with, or proposed. Residuals charges, for example, are designed to raise the costs of discharging harmful wastes to the environment, to lead to the curbing of those discharges, and ultimately to reduce the damages they cause, thus in theory extending the corrective powers of the market to the commons.

But since our understanding of complex environmental systems is in a very early stage of development, our ability to design effective control strategies that do not do more damage than the problems they are supposed to correct is limited indeed. We simply know very little about what works and what does not. This book therefore will review some of what we know about the impact of urbanization on environment, the nature and consequences of environmental pollution, and the range of control,

policing, and pricing strategies available to urban policymakers. We believe that many of these issues are fundamentally geographical, involving man's relation to nature and problems of spatial allocation and misallocation, and so we approach the problem as geographers, extending our previous work on the social and economic geography of cities to an explicit consideration of the physical interface.

We know that, physically, cities can be regarded as organisms with their own special metabolism. This special metabolism has two origins: *structurally*, it has heat-holding capacities without parallel in the natural environment; *functionally*, it concentrates and consumes unprecedented amounts of energy (fuel, food) in small areas. According to Abel Wolman the daily input-output energy ratios per 1,000,000 urban inhabitants in a developed country are roughly of the dimensions described in Table 1.1.

TABLE 1.1

Metabolism of a city of one million

Input (*fuel*)		Output (*waste*)	
Water	625,000 tons	Sewage	500,000 tons
Food	2,000 tons	Solid wastes	2,000 tons
Fuel:		Particles	150 tons
coal	3,000 tons	Sulfur dioxide	150 tons
oil	2,800 tons	Nitrogen oxides	100 tons
gas	2,700 tons	Carbon monoxide	450 tons
motor	1,000 tons		

SOURCE: Abel Wolman, "The Metabolism of Cities," *Scientific American*, vol. 213, no. 3 (September 1965), p. 180.

As a consequence of daily metabolic activity of this magnitude, and of the accumulation of the outputs of residuals, urban America becomes increasingly dirty, noisy, poisoned, paved, crowded, monotonous, and stripped of its greenery, wetlands, and wildlife. This beleaguered condition is a matter of growing importance to public policy, for as the quality of the environment deteriorates, so does the quality of life. Deteriorated air, water, and land restrict desired human uses of the environment for recreational, agricultural, domestic, and industrial purposes. Health, social, and economic problems result, for man is a creature of the biosphere, the air/water/land capsule which supports life on earth. While these conditions affect all parts of the nation to some degree, they are primarily urban problems, generated and suffered most in the intensely used urban environment.

It is easy to become an alarmist about the growing magnitude of the environmental crisis and its likely results. Every major river system, the Great Lakes, even coastal waters are polluted by growing wastes from homes, industry, agriculture, mineral extraction, power plants, and watercraft. Municipal sewage returns are now about 5,300 billion gallons a year, and each year over 13,000 billion gallons of waste water is discharged by manufacturing industry. Patterns of pollution match urban/industrial configurations, with the most intense problems occurring in the North Atlantic and Great Lakes states. Close behind are the water-quality problems of the Ohio region and the Upper Mississippi, California, South Atlantic Gulf, and Texas Gulf regions. With pollution, the price of water goes up, additional waste treatment is necessary, and recreation and fish and wildlife habitats diminish.

Similarly, to some degree every community over 50,000 has an air pollution problem, and over 43 million Americans live in those larger cities that have "major" air pollution problems. Most of the gaseous wastes are generated while converting fossil fuels into energy in cars, homes, power plants, buildings, and factories. Burning solid wastes creates air pollutants. Acids, phenols, odors, and heat also contribute to the damaging of human health and safety and the destruction of property and plant life.

To continue the sad litany, garbage, rubbish and other solid wastes—over 360 million tons a year—are generated by household, commercial, and industrial activities in and around urban areas. That amounts to more than ten pounds each day for every man, woman, and child in the United States. The collection and disposal of these wastes not only tax the environment but on the average rank third in municipal budget expenditures. Economical land disposal sites are nearly exhausted around many large cities, and nearly all present disposal practices result in noxious odors, are unsightly, and pollute air and water, often presenting health and safety hazards. Pesticides and fertilizers permeate the soils, and radioactive wastes are a threat to land quality. Five hundred new chemicals are added each year to the 500,000 to 600,000 compounds already on the market. Many of these come to rest in the environment with unknown environmental effects.

As daily urban activity runs its course, cities jangle with transport, construction, industrial, and other noises of modern technology, causing physiological and psychological illness. Street and airport noises often exceed levels that under continual exposure produce hearing loss. Meanwhile, the growth of urban areas means that about one and one-half million acres of open land every year are built up for suburban housing, industrial sites, commercial enterprises, and other urban uses—about 50 percent more than a decade ago. Highways use much of this land. Today, America's 3,600,000 square miles of land surface are covered with 3,700,000 miles of streets and roads, or more than one mile of street for every square mile of land. In downtown Los Angeles two-thirds of the land is devoted to parking lots and streets. There are few surviving greens, greenbelts, or wedges in American cities.

As more land is paved, trees are cut, and wetlands are drained, the natural flow of water from sky to land to sea and back again is altered. Rains and melting snow that once were absorbed by soil and vegetation, replenishing supplies, now increasingly run off; floods and droughts increase while groundwater supplies diminish. At the same time swamps and marshes are often filled in and built on, destroying temporary storage areas. Then storm sewers must be built to artificially channel waters out to sea or to the river, and new water supplies must be sought to compensate for the loss of natural supplies.

Some scientists fear that cumulative human impacts of these kinds on natural systems may trigger disasters that could dwarf the current health, economic, and social problems that have been the focus of postwar urban policy. Science and technology wield more power than ever before to manipulate natural processes, but science still has very little understanding of the effects of man's actions on the thin band of air, water, and soil which supports life on earth. A large measure of guesswork and extrapolation, therefore, is involved in today's predictions—which foresee consequences ranging from major earthquakes, which might result from excessive stress on fault lines and in earthquake zones, to altered wind patterns and atmospheric content that would change the world's climate and vegetation. For example, some scientists believe global temperature may be decreasing, because the sun's rays are blocked by particles in the air. A serious change could cause another ice age. Still others believe that the earth's temperature is warming because of increased carbon dioxide in the atmosphere—an increase of about 14 percent over the past 100 years. Carbon dioxide, the theory goes, captures and holds the sun's energy on the earth's surface, like heat in a greenhouse. A significant warming of the continent could cause the ice cap to melt, flooding coastal cities. In any case, with the added waste heat from power plants, water temperatures may rise significantly over the next few years, which ecologists fear may change whole aquatic life patterns. It is also thought that chemical poisoning or lead pollution of the oceans may destory the plankton essential to photosynthesis which produces much of the world's oxygen supply.

Taken together, water, air, trees, and open land perform many basic functions for the human community: they supply water, moderate climatic extremes, prevent erosion and floods, provide food and shelter, fuel and fun, as well as disperse wastes, noise, and dust. But there are limits to changes that can safely be absorbed. If man destroys bacteria involved in the nitrogen cycle, from which every organism builds its proteins, life on earth will cease. The same is true for the cycles of oxygen, sulfur, and carbon. The balances of prey and predator are also important to man, because a broken link in natural food chains might seriously affect his own food supplies.

Exactly when the destruction of natural systems becomes irreversible is still unknown. It appears to be different for each natural system and the elements of each system. The delayed reaction of ecological changes further complicates this natural phenomenon. The full effects of present changes on the natural world may not materialize for generations. Once they occur, however, it may well be too late for repairs, even with vast amounts of money, technology, and determination.

Apprehensions of environmental disaster of major dimensions go back more than a century to George Perkins Marsh's book *Man and Nature*. But few took his warnings seriously. Since the 1960s, however, complacency has given way to alarm as perceptions of environmental deterioration have increased. A new environmental movement has emerged, and with it a new personality: the ecoactivist. As a consequence of the resulting pressure, environmental quality has become a central issue in national policy. The far-reaching Environmental Policy Act of 1969, for example, established the Council on Environmental Quality and instructed all Federal agencies to include an impact statement as part of future reports or recommendations on actions significantly affecting the quality of the human environment. Section 102(2) (C) defines the impact statement as follows:

SEC. 102. The Congress authorizes and directs that, to the fullest extent possible: (1) the polices, regulations, and public laws of the United States shall be interpreted and administered in accordance with the policies set forth in this Act, and (2) all agencies of the Federal Government shall—

(A) utilize a systematic, interdisciplinary approach which will insure the integrated use of the natural and social sciences and the environmental design arts in planning and decision-making which may have an impact on man's environment;

(B) identify and develop methods and procedures, in consultation with the Council on Environmental Quality established by title II of this Act, which will insure that presently unquantified environmental amenities and values may be given appropriate consideration in decision-making along with economic and technical considerations;

(C) include in every recommendation or report on proposals for legislation and other major Federal actions significantly affecting the quality of the human environment, a detailed statement by the responsible official on—

    (i) the environmental impact of the proposed action,

    (ii) any adverse environmental effects which cannot be avoided should the proposal be implemented,

    (iii) alternatives to the proposed action,

    (iv) the relationship between local short-term uses of man's environment and the maintenance and enhancement of long-term productivity, and

    (v) any irreversible and irretrievable commitments of resources which would be involved in the proposed action should it be implemented.

Prior to making any detailed statement, the responsible Federal official shall consult with and obtain the comments of any Federal agency which has jurisdiction by law or special expertise with respect to any environmental impact involved. Copies of such statements and the comments and views of the appropriate Federal, State, and local agencies, which are authorized to develop and enforce environmental standards, shall be made available to the President, the Council on Environmental Quality, and to the public as provided by section 552 of title 5, United States Code, and shall accompany the proposal through the existing agency review processes;

(D) study, develop, and describe appropriate alternatives to recommended courses of action in any proposal which involves unresolved conflicts concerning alternative uses of available resources;

(E) recognize the worldwide and long-range character of environmental problems and, where consistent with the foreign policy of the United States,

lend appropriate support to initiatives, resolutions, and programs designed to maximize international cooperation in anticipating and preventing a decline in the quality of mankind's world environment;

(F) make available to States, counties, municipalities, institutions, and individuals, advice and information useful to restoring, maintaining, and enhancing the quality of the environment;

(G) initiate and utilize ecological information in the planning and development of resource-oriented projects; and

(H) assist the Council on Environmental Quality established by title II of this Act.

The requirements and implications of the environmental impact statements are clearly far-reaching and fundamental, and they point to a basic need for new and better-organized knowledge than has heretofore been available. Further, a broad range of activities will continue to be called for if the concern of the Environmental Policy Act is to be translated to productive action. There is a requirement for new applications of already-existing knowledge of the physical, chemical, and biological processes going on in the biosphere. There are further requirements for new knowledge of these fundamental processes.

Of prime importance is knowledge of how life forms convert matter and energy, occupy space, and co-exist in a delicate balance with each other and their environment. Those "systems sciences" which can deal with the connections between things and with ways in which interacting parts are kept in balance must be brought to the forefront of the efforts directed towards solving environmental problems.

One of these systems sciences, which treats the environmental interactions of life forms at all levels, is called *ecology*. Another, which deals in particular with man himself and the ways he has changed the earth in building his systems of life support, resource conversion, land occupance, and amusement, is called *geography*. In this volume we proceed from the vantage point of geography, with its particular strengths of synthesis, comprehension of complexity of explanations, familiarity with using broad ranges of data, and explicit concern with location and spatial relationships and with the mutual interdependencies of man and nature.

Geographers are self-selected, often because of their curiosity about and ability to handle a wide range of scholarly approaches. Geographical training generally fosters these traits and expands the range of accessible insights and materials. This is especially true for interactions between man and environment, for which geographers are apt to assume that any subject matter may be germane and must be taken into account more or less systematically.

The wide range of often conflicting insights that geographers normally acquire, together with the profession's past experience with simplistic explanations—notably environmental determinism—makes most geographers reluctant to accept single-factor propositions about cause-and-effect relations. Already sensitive to the need for complex and multiform explanations, geographers bring to environmental problems, which are usually less simple and less easily resolved than they seem, a necessary breadth of overview. The inability of any single discipline to formulate, let alone answer, some of the basic environmental problems suggests a need for the synthesizing, holistic approach long and successfully developed in geography.

Such environmental understanding is apt to require enormously diverse kinds of information, ranging from the location and dispersal mechanisms of specific chemical agents, for example, to the attitudes and behavior of individuals and groups stemming from their images of such agents. More than most other scholars, geographers are early exposed to and trained in a variety of data-gathering techniques, from field observations and laboratory analyses to interviews and questionnaires, from historical, archival, and library sources to attitudinal surveys, from cartographic and statistical analyses to descriptive and holistic syntheses. It is, of course, a rare geographer who is competent to

handle all such techniques; indeed, not many geographers are well trained in most of them. What is significant, though, is that geographical education presupposes the potential utility of any or all such techniques. Geographers are usually willing to recognize the value of evidence drawn from fields in which they themselves lack expertise. Catholicity and eclecticism of this nature are invaluable in many problems of environmental understanding and action.

Interest and training alert most geographers to features of spatial distribution and diffusion, both as to environmental factors and information and as to value systems bearing on those factors. Environmental situations and human assessments both vary from place to place. Too often, laymen and other scholars assume that problems of environmental quality—e.g., pollution—are everywhere essentially similar. Yet environmental constraints vary enormously, not only from region to region but because nations and cultures emphasize a wide range of different environmental issues. One or another type of environmental amenity may seem particularly crucial; productivity and settlement patterns may play a more or less determinative role; environmental quality, if conceptually isolated at all, may be measured in terms of tradeoffs against other social satisfactions. Similarly there are variations in the degrees to which people accept or reject disjunctions between ideal and real environmental conditions, between abstract values and actual conditions, between landscapes of an imagined past and those of a projected future. Moreover, nations and cultures employ unlike modes of education and communications for the diffusion of environmental innovations and utilize diverse economic and political organizations to cope with environmental problems. Modes of resolving conflict over resource use and environmental degradation will depend, for example, on the extent to which resources are viewed as private or common property, on styles of social and community interaction networks, and on proneness to polarize or to compromise conflicts of use and interest. The nature of geographic training is to produce sensitivity to and capacity to analyze such facets of regional variation.

More than most other professions, geography is aware of the complexity of the man–nature interface. Geographers examine landscapes and see them, to varying degrees, as both "natural" and "cultural"; they avoid sharp dichotomies between these realms. And geographers are constantly reminded that the physical environment is felt and responded to through screens of perception and cognition—screens that deserve to be studied along with environment and man.

We hope to represent these distinctive aspects of geographical training, insight, and habit in this volume by demonstrating the insights and capacities in environmental analysis of one systems science, geography, articulating the policy implications of these insights, and extending the perspectives of urban geography to include systematic concern for the physical environment of cities. Since our purposes are thus both interdisciplinary and disciplinary, we begin in Chapter 2 with (1) an exploration of the changing framework of ideas about man and nature and the differences in intellectual stance regarding man's relationships to environment from one part of the world to another, and (2) environmental psychology, involving questions of perception and man's attempts to adjust his activities to natural hazards and environmental risks. We proceed in Chapter 3 to such matters as the energetics of the biosphere and, within this, the impact of urbanization on environment, focusing in particular on the climate and hydrology of cities. The next chapters explore in some detail the nature of air, water, land, and noise pollution and the management of air, water, and land resources in urban ecosystems. Several different planning and evaluation methodologies are exemplified. Thereafter, we turn to questions of environmental pollution and human health. The book concludes with an overview of governmental programs affecting environmental quality at the federal, state, and local levels.

CHAPTER *2*

environmental beliefs
and perceptions

A particular set of environmental beliefs may lie at the root of the current environmental crisis: the traditional laissez-faire attitude to environment that is rooted in the expansionary philosophies of industrial cultures. Another set of such beliefs, which assumed a particular form in the early conservation movement and has achieved more recent recognition in the form of modern ecology, has been instrumental in highlighting the many manifestations of the environmental crisis and producing the first concerted attempts to develop coherent national policies for environmental protection. The nature of these differing belief-systems must be understood, because their adherents perceive the world in different ways, have different goals and priorities, and propose contrasting solutions to environmental problems.

CLASSICAL ENVIRONMENTAL ATTITUDES

Social science started on the American scene with a mechanistic, evolutionary model of man

This chapter includes selections from:

Lewis W. Moncrief, "The Cultural Basis for our Environmental Crisis," *Science*, Vol. 170 (October 30, 1970), pp. 509–512. Begins on page 9.

Marshall I. Goldman, "The Convergence of Environmental Disruption," *Science*, Vol. 170 (October 2, 1970), pp. 37–42. Begins on page 11.

Leo Marx, "American Institutions and Ecological Ideals," *Science*, Vol. 170 (November 27, 1970), pp. 945–952. Begins on page 12.

Maurice D. Van Arsdol, Jr., Georges Sabagh, and Francesca Alexander, "Reality and the Perception of Environmental Hazards," *Journal of Health and Human Behavior*, Vol. 5 (1964), pp. 144–153. Begins on page 12.

Robert W. Kates, "The Perception of Storm Hazards on the Shores of Megalopolis," in David Lowenthal, *Environmental Perception and Behavior*, Department of Geography Research Paper No. 109, University of Chicago, 1967. Begins on page 20.

which was supportive of laissez-faire environmental exploitation. Derived from Herbert Spencer's extensions of Darwin's ideas, this model contained explicit notions of man's relation to nature. Darwin had limited his discussion to biological phenomena, organizing the argument in *The Origin of Species* about four principal propositions: (1) new species continually appear; (2) these new species evolve from older species; (3) evolution of new species is a result of natural selection; (4) natural selection depends upon the continued availability of variations in species, from which the "unfit" are eliminated. The behavior on which natural selection is based was held to be a competitive struggle among individuals for the limited resources of different environments. Environmental variations were taken as "givens" outside the competitive process. The organisms obtaining enough resources to survive, reproduce, and flourish were thought to be of a "superior" order, because they had demonstrated their competitive ability. Superior organisms could, it was argued, pass on to next generations that quality that permitted successful survival, through the principle of inheritance. In turn, the inheritance principle was thought to lead towards successively more ideal forms of environmental adaptation, for competition favored those organisms adjusting best to environmental variations.

Industrialization in a frontier world had already given credibility in America to the idea of an individualistic struggle to survive and to the system of laissez-faire economics. American social science thus accepted quite readily the notion of "social Darwinism," in which biological evolutionary processes were wedded to conservative economic and social ideologies and to exploitative attitudes to environment. The most forthright expression of these ideas is to be found in the work of a sociologist, William Graham Sumner.

In his book *Folkways* (1906, 1959), Sumner examined social customs and interpreted their emergence as the environmental adaptation of highly developed organisms. The work of science, he thought, was to formulate the laws of this adaptive process—division of labor, cooperation, competition, and so on—laws that were already accepted as principles of laissez-faire economics. His idea was that these were laws of nature, outside human intervention. The calculus of forces at work in evolution was formulated in these laws and furnished an interpretation of the social process, defining human social evolution through laws of social adaptation.

Having discovered the social laws, man's task, according to Sumner, was to conform to them and avoid legislative action which might disrupt them. Since these laws determined the successful course of human adaptation, they provided the guidelines for society's progress. Sumner's famous dictum "Stateways cannot change Folkways" was formulated against this theoretical background; it referred to the long-range opposition of what he perceived to be laws of nature to legislative activity that sought, for example, to restrain competition. Man may try to disrupt the social laws, causing society untold damage, he argued, but the natural laissez-faire order will ultimately prevail. The laws of classical economics were understood in this way and obeyed with a devotion which would have done honor to the medieval church. One outcome was the exploitative attitude to resources and environment that remains the conservative economic stance to this day.

Relation to Judeo-Christian Doctrine

Some, notably L. White, Jr. (1967), argue that there is an even more deep-seated and fundamental source for the exploitative attitude that has prompted much of the environmental crisis in Western Europe and North America: the Judeo-Christian tradition, which conceives of man as superior to all other creatures, possessing everything else for his own enjoyment and endowed with a God-given right to use, exploit, modify, and "perfect" the environment in any way he sees fit, using whatever scientific and technological power is at his disposal. White's simple model may be diagrammed as follows:

I ⟶ II ⟶ III

Judeo-Christian tradition   Science and technology   Environmental degradation

An elaborated version developed by Moncrief (1970) explicitly identifies the role played by industrialization and urbanization:

I ⟶ II ⟶ III ⟶ IV

Judeo-Christian tradition

(1) Capitalism (with the attendant development of science and technology)

(1) Urbanization (2) Increased wealth (3) Increased population (4) Individual resource ownership

Environmental degradation

In both of these formulations the underlying role thought to be played by religion in man-to-man and man-to-environment relationships is that of establishing a very broad system of allowable beliefs and behavior and of articulating and invoking a system of social and spiritual rewards for those who conform and of negative sanctions for individuals or groups who approach or cross the pale of the religiously unacceptable.

To the Judeo-Christian tradition, the second model adds the specific effects of democratization and industrialization. In the West two significant revolutions that occurred in the eighteenth and nineteenth centuries completely redirected its political, social, and economic destiny. The French Revolution marked the beginnings of widespread democratization. In specific terms, this revolution involved a redistribution of the means of production and a reallocation of the natural and human resources that are an integral part of the production process. In effect new channels of social mobility were created, which theoretically made more wealth accessible to more people.

At about the same time, but over a more extended period, another kind of revolution was taking place, primarily in England. This revolution amplified by several times the productive capacity of each worker. It also became feasible to produce goods that were not previously producible on a commercial scale.

Later, with the integration of the democratic and the technological ideals, the increased wealth began to be distributed more equitably among the population. In addition, as the capital-to-land ratio increased in the production process and the demand grew for labor to work in the factories, large populations from the agrarian hinterlands began to concentrate in the emerging industrial cities. The stage was set for the development of the conditions that now exist in the Western world.

With growing affluence for an increasingly large segment of the population, there developed an increased demand for goods and services. The by-product of this affluence was waste from both the production and consumption processes. The disposal of that waste was further complicated by the high concentration of heavy waste producers in urban areas. Under these conditions, the volume of such wastes was far greater than the system could absorb and purify through natural means, and the inevitable consequence was serious environmental pollution.

This general sequence took on particular forms in North America, where national policy from the outset was designed to convey ownership of the land and other natural resources into the hands of the citizenry. Thomas Jefferson was perhaps more influential than anyone else in crystalizing this philosophy in the new nation. It was his conviction that an agrarian society made up of small landowners would furnish the most stable foundation for building the nation. This concept, continuously supported up to the present, clearly explains how the natural resources of the nation came to be controlled not by a few aristocrats but by many citizens, and thus how the decisions that ultimately degrade the environment are made not only by corporation boards and city engineers but by millions of individual property owners, each pursuing his own self-interest.

The problem of diffused decision-making combined with the attitudes of the frontier. To many frontiersmen, particularly small farmers, many of the natural resources that are now highly valued were obstacles rather than assets. Nature had to be conquered. Forests needed to be cleared for farming, marshes drained, rivers controlled. Wildlife often represented not only a food source but a competitive threat. Sod was considered a nuisance—to be burned, plowed, or otherwise destroyed to permit "desirable" use of the land. America is thus the archetype of what happens when democracy, technology, urbanization, capitalistic mission, and antagonism (or apathy) toward natural environment are blended.

Convergence of Environmental Disruption in the U.S.S.R.

The forces of democracy, technology, urbanization, increasing individual wealth, and an aggressive attitude toward nature have all contributed directly to the environmental crisis now being confronted in the Western world. However, the convergence of environmental disruption in other ideological contexts, such as the U.S.S.R., call into question whether the Judeo-Christian tradition need be invoked as a necessary precondition for environmental disruption.

In Russia, pollution had been thought to be impossible on ideological grounds. It was thought that if all the factories in a society were state-owned, the state would insure that the broader interests of the general public would be protected (Goldman, 1970). Each factory would be expected to bear the full costs and consequences of its operation. No factory would be allowed to take a particular action if it meant that the public would suffer or would have to bear the expense. In other words, the factory would not only have to pay for its *private costs*, such as expenses for labor and raw materials; it would also have to pay for its *social costs*, such as the cost of eliminating the air and water pollution it had caused. It was argued that, since the industry was state-run, including both types of costs would not be difficult. At least that was what was assumed.

Soviet officials continue today to make such assumptions. B. V. Petrovsky, the Soviet Minister of Public Health, finds environmental disruption in a capitalist society perfectly understandable: "The capitalist system by its very essence is incapable of taking radical measures to ensure the efficient conservation of nature." Implicitly he assumes that the Soviet Union can take such measures. Therefore, it must be somewhat embarrassing for Nikolai Popov, an editor of *Soviet Life*, to have to ask, "Why, in a socialist country, whose constitution explicitly says the public interest may not be ignored with impunity, are industry executives permitted to break the laws protecting nature?"

Behind Popov's question is a chronicle of environmental disruption as serious as almost any in the world. Any depressing report of an incident in the United States can be matched by a horror story from the U.S.S.R. For example, there have been hundreds of fish-kill incidents in both countries. In the U.S.S.R., effluent from the Chernorechensk Chemical Plant near Dzerzhinsk killed almost all the fish life in the Oka River in 1965 because of uncontrolled dumping.

Air resources, too, are misused in the U.S.S.R. Although the Russians at present produce less than one-tenth the number of cars produced in the United States, most Soviet cities have air pollution. In the hilly cities of Armenia, the established health norms for carbon monoxide are often exceeded. Similarly Magnitogorsk, Alma Ata, and Chelyabinsk, with their metallurgical industries, frequently have a dark blue cap overhead. Like Los Angeles, Tbilisi, the capital of the Republic of Georgia, has smog almost six months of the year. Nor is air pollution limited to hilly regions: Leningrad has 40 percent fewer clear daylight hours than the nearby town of Pavlovsk.

The central problem in Soviet resource conservation and environmental protection is one that is equally common in capitalist economies—that of economic expediency (Pryde, 1972). Pollution abatement and careful resource husbandry cost quite a lot of money, whether in dollars or in rubles. Rapid industrialization has been the paramount objective of the U.S.S.R. for the past half century. There is a finite amount of development capital in the Soviet state budget (which is always balanced), and funds spent on environmental concerns are unavailable for industrial expansion. The owners of the industry or factory may be different from those in the United States, but the motivation of the comptroller is the same.

At the individual factory level the overriding goal is to fulfill the annual (or five-year) production plan. If this is accomplished, raw-material waste and pollution tend to be disregarded. As an editorial in the government paper *Izvestiya* said in 1968, there is "the still prevalent belief that increased output of goods compensates for and glosses over the moral and material losses. Victors are not judged."

Thus pollution-control facilities that appear in the plans often are not constructed. After World War II the need to rebuild industry as fast as possible perhaps justified a certain inattention to pollution and to inefficient natural-resource exploitation. But twenty years later the malady still persists.

Even though economies differ, many if not all of the usual economic explanations for pollution in the non-Communist world hold for the Soviet Union. The Russians, too, have been unable to adjust their accounting system so that each enterprise pays not only its direct costs of production for labor, raw materials, and equipment but also its social costs of production arising from such by-products as dirty air and water. If the factory were charged for these

social costs and had to take them into account when trying to make a profit on its operations, presumbly factories would throw off less waste and would reuse or recycle their air and water. However, the precise social cost of such waste is difficult to measure and allocate.

In addition, almost everyone in the world regards air and water as free goods. Thus, even if it were always technologically feasible, it would still be awkward ideologically to charge for something that "belongs to everyone," particularly in a communist society. For a variety of reasons, therefore, air and water in the U.S.S.R. are treated as free or undervalued goods. When anything is free, there is a tendency to consume it without regard for future consequences.

Thus, if the study of environmental disruption in the Soviet Union demonstrates anything, it shows that the Judeo-Christian tradition is not the primary cause of environmental disruption, but industrialization under conditions in which environmental resources are undervalued. This suggests that state ownership of all the productive resources is not a cure-all. The replacement of private greed by public greed is small improvement. Current proposals for the solution of environmental degradation seem no more advanced in the U.S.S.R. than they are in the United States. One thing does seem clear, however: unless the Russians change their ways, there is little reason to believe that a strong centralized and planned economy has any notable advantages over other economic systems in solving environmental disruption.

CONSERVATION, ECOACTIVISM, AND THE PASTORAL TRADITION

That American attitudes toward environment have been dominantly exploitative is unquestioned, and this has led many young Americans to demand a basic change in "the system." But Marx (1970) notes that there has always been a countervailing literary tradition in

America. In this pastoral stream of thought, ideas of the interdependency of man and nature were, if not stressed, at least implicit. These ideas provide, for those seeking it, an intellectual base for today's ecoactivism.

Anyone familiar with the work of the classic American writers (such as Cooper, Emerson, Thoreau, Melville, Whitman, and Mark Twain) is likely to have developed an interest in ecology. One of the first things associated with each of these writers is a distinctive, vividly particularized setting (or landscape) inseparable from his conception of man. Partly because of the special geographic and political circumstances of American experience, and partly because they were influenced by the romantic vision of man's relations with nature, all of the writers mentioned possessed a heightened sense of place. Yet words such as *place, landscape,* or *setting* scarcely can do justice to the significance these writers imparted to external nature in their work. They took for granted a thorough and delicate interpenetration of consciousness and environment. In fact it now seems evident that these gifted writers had begun, more than a century ago, to measure the quality of American life against something like an ecological ideal.

The influence of this assessment on national policy has not been apparent until recently, however, because ecological thinking has been obscured by the more popular "conservation movement." This movement developed in the 1890s, when it was perceived that natural resources might indeed not be inexhaustible. Writers and outdoorsmen such as John Muir and Gifford Pinchot created a consciousness among Americans that the frontier had somehow vanished, that the buffalo were gone and the redwoods following fast, and that the present generation had an obligation to posterity to hand down the natural environment with adequate resources for the future.

The conservation movement gained ground essentially as a wilderness preservation movement, in which a partnership evolved between certain amateurs and the groups they created—the Audubon Society, the Isaac Walton League, the Sierra Club, the various wildlife societies, the Boone and Crockett Club, and major government agencies including the Fish and Wildlife and Forest Services. Sportsmen, naturalists, and property owners formed a coalescing force. Pinchot and Muir influenced Theodore Roosevelt. Senators such as Harry Hawes and Frederic Walcott played their part in the creation of migratory waterfowl preserves, and the Migratory Bird Treaty Act of 1915 introduced the concept of federal regulation of hunting.

But from the beginning the movement attracted people with enough time and money to enjoy the outdoor life: sportsmen, naturalists (both amateur and professional), and of course property owners anxious to protect the sanctity of their rural or wilderness retreats. As a result, the conservationist cause came to be identified with the special interests of a few private citizens. It seldom, if ever, has been made to seem pertinent to the welfare of the poor, the nonwhite population, or, for that matter, the great majority of urban Americans. The environment that mattered most to conservationists was the environment beyond the city limits. In this view, and consistent with the conservative exploitative mind, nature is a world that exists apart from, and for the benefit of, mankind.

The contemporary ecological perspective is different from that of the conservationists, returning to the fundamental premises of the pastoral literature. Its philosophic root is the secular idea that man (including his works—the secondary, or man-made, environment) is wholly and ineluctably embedded in the tissue of natural process. The interconnections are delicate, infinitely complex, never to be severed.

This perspective focuses on the concept of ecosystems, defined by Tansley as "functioning interacting systems composed of one or more living organisms and their effective environments, both physical and biological." The description of an ecosystem may include its spatial relationships; inventories of its physical features, its habitats and ecological niches, its organisms, and its basic reserves of matter and energy; the nature of its income (or input) of matter and energy; and the behavior or trend of its entropy level.

From the ecosystem concept we derive naturally the idea that the biosphere must be considered for all purposes a closed system, save that it depends on continual energy inputs from the sun. In this system air, land, and water are functionally interacting elements among themselves, and with man and his works, in mutually interdependent energy-exchange systems. Therefore, the traditional view that dilution or diffusion is the solution to pollution is misconceived, because this simply reflects the transfer of pollutants from one place and/or environmental medium to another.

The traditional regulatory approach to environmental control in the United States has involved setting "standards" beneath which pollution is thought to be tolerable. If conditions exceed the standards set, the "solution" is to seek some attenuating treatment that pushes the "problem" beneath the threshold of unacceptability once again. But, consistent with the ecosystems view, many treatments simply transfer the problem: air-pollution control devices, for example, discharge effluents into water bodies; burning of solid wastes results in air pollution; improper landfills create health hazards. Little is known about the manifold interactions of pollutants and environmental factors, as for example when reduction of sulfur dioxide as a source of air pollution increases the probability of photochemical smog. Clearly, much needs to be known in a multivariate systems context about the relations of urbanization, industrialization, and environment if effective pollution-control strategies are to be designed.

Equally, just as environmental problems interact, the ecosystem concept points out that the effects do likewise. The synergistic effects of the various problems can be grouped under the elusive term, but very real condition, called the "quality of urban life." Added together, the problems of pollution, noise, loss of open space and amenities create inconvenience, loss of time and productivity, and a sense of tension and unease for those who must live with these conditions.

THE PROBLEM OF PERCEPTION

Urban inhabitants seldom observe natural systems at work, and thus the majority tend to act as if the classical view of independence of man and nature obtained, rather than recognizing the interdependency of ecosystems. Significant gaps continue in the knowledge of wastes sources, the effects of wastes on air, water, or land, and the impact of various forms of pollution, singly or in combination, on people, plants, and other aspects of the physical environment. Considerable honest difference of opinion exists over the amount of improvement in air, water, or land quality that will result from a given investment in a package of waste controls or even one control element. And even when people are aware that their decisions to use and manipulate resources will contribute to environmental problems, they make these choices anyway, because the environmental impact of the choice is external to their decision. Pollution is often the major externality to a great number of municipal, industrial, and individual decisions. Dump the untreated wastes in the river or air. They flow away, downstream or downwind. The costs accrue to others: the downstream town that must increase its treatment of municipal or industrial water, the individual who wants to swim in the river, or the commercial fisherman whose catch is destroyed. It does not pay an individual, economically, to stop polluting unless the whole community stops.

Decisions, in addition, even when internalized, are made to degrade the environment on an incremental basis. The daily, individual decision which degrades the environment is an increment that has no noticeable effect on the total urban area. Open land disappears a few square yards at a time. A river basin is polluted by hundreds of towns and industries and farms. The air of an urban area is fouled by millions of cars, buses, and trucks, power plants and incinerators. The man who decides to drive to work instead of taking public transportation argues that just one more car on the highway will make no difference. Often he has no alternative. While that one decision does not substantially affect air pollution, tens of thousands of similar conclusions result in unacceptable air and noise pollution from ground transportation.

The effect of multiple individual decisions and behavior is to produce an impact of urbanization in the environment that rapidly accumulates to massive dimensions. In turn, the modified and polluted environment affects man's economic and social activities and his social well-being. But the relation between environment and behavior is indirect, expressed through screens of cognition; cause and effect are separated by complex perceptual filters. Men act on the basis of what they *perceive* things to be. Likewise, men's psychological well-being is determined by perceptions of what things are, rather than what scientific analysis demonstrates them to be.

Perception of Environmental Hazards

Little is known about the complex subject of environmental psychology, and particularly about the presence of hazards in city neighborhoods and perception of these hazards by residents of different socioeconomic backgrounds. One of the few exceptions is an analysis by Van Arsdol et al. (1963) undertaken in Los Angeles, which concentrated on those hazards thought to be inimical to individual health—air pollution, air traffic noise, brush fires, floods, and earth slides.

Governmental business organizations provided crude environmental hazard information to the investigators. Oxidant level data were obtained which reflected the photochemical nature of Los Angeles air pollution. A four-category "smog scale" was established; cutting points on the scale were indicative of levels at which there were changes in reported physiological symptoms associated with exposure to smog. Data on air traffic noise were obtained from airports in the Los Angeles area and were defined by a three-point scale specifying noise decibels of areas under usual flight patterns. Four levels of brush-fire hazards were determined as based on the Pacific Fire Rating Bureau fire insurance subcharge rates. Flood rates were designated by the Los Angeles and Orange County Flood Control Districts as sections in which water had "ponded" or was in sufficient depth to damage property by silt deposition during major rain storms. Earth-slide areas were described as those for which the Los Angeles and Orange County Engineer's offices had reported earth slippage during recent years. Data for all hazards were allocated to census tracts.

In the analysis of the perception of the hazards, attention was focused on the manner in which "reality," measured by the presence of hazards within a neighborhood or census tract, was related to individual perception, taking into account a series of social characteristics. To accomplish this, an area probability sample of all housing-unit residents in the Los Angeles metropolitan area was constructed and respondents from 300 of the 1403 census tracts in the area were interviewed in the summers of 1961 and 1962. A 90.2 percent response rate, or 981 interviews, were obtained for occupied housing units in 1961. In 1962, 43 housing units were vacant but interviews were completed with 824 or 87.8 percent of the then occupied units. The 1962 sample, which was used in the research, did not reflect units added to the metropolitan area housing inventory in the one-year interval between the interview dates, but it is representative of the 1962 population for housing units occupied in 1961.

Criterion measures of the level of perception of the five environmental hazards were obtained by asking respondents whether or not the hazards constituted a "serious" or "not serious" problem in their neighborhood and in their county of residence.

Independent variables influencing neighborhood perceptions were considered to be presence or absence of the hazards in the county of residence of the respondents as well as a series of variables including socioeconomic status, family structure, dwelling-unit type, race, age and sex. In addition to population composition, there was also a concern for the manner in which urban life might have influenced environmental perception, as indicated by respondents' neighborhood evaluations, and integration with a normative system, indicated by a measure of anomie. Age of head of household was dichotomized at age 35 and over in order to reflect the presence or absence of young children expected on the basis of the family life cycle. Socioeconomic status of the head of the household was measured by the Duncan-Riess Index, housing-unit type was defined by residence in a single- or multiple-family unit; family structure was described with respect to membership in a "complete" or "incomplete family"; and neighborhood satisfaction was interpreted by analyzing respondents' reactions to their neighborhoods of residence.

Table 2.1 gives the percentage of the sample living in neighborhoods characterized by the presence of environmental hazards and describes the perception of hazards in neighborhoods of residence when hazards were present or absent. With the exception of brush fires, *a smaller proportion of the sample perceived the hazards than lived in neighborhoods with the hazards present.* Smog was the most frequently perceived hazard in residence areas. A higher percentage of the Los Angeles population was exposed to smog than to any other hazard, and smog was the most critical hazard for perception, whether respondents lived in the hazard areas or not. Chi-square tests of independence, as reported in Table 2.2, showed that, with the exception of flood, there was an association between the presence and perception of the hazards at the .01 level of significance. In this respect, the pattern of smog reality and perception is similar to that for other hazards.

Given the demonstrated reality-perception relationships between all hazards except flood, an attempt was made to account for these relationships in terms of a series of independent variables which were utilized as controls. A simple analysis of interaction among categorical variables was used to evaluate the effects of the control variables upon the reality-perception relation-

TABLE 2.1

*Distribution of environmental hazards and respondents' perceptions of hazards:
Los Angeles standard metropolitan statistical area, 1962[a]*

Hazard	Total Respondents	Sample in Hazard Area		Hazard Perceivers		Hazard Present Hazard Perceivers		Hazard Absent Hazard Perceivers	
		No.	Percent[b]	No.	Percent[b]	No.	Percent[c]	No.	Percent[c]
Smog	800	416	52.0%	225	28.1%	162	38.9%	63	16.4%
Air traffic noise	792	156	19.7%	96	12.1%	42	26.9%	54	8.5%
Brush fire	795	30	3.8%	49	6.2%	9	30.0%	40	5.2%
Earth slide	787	43	5.5%	30	3.8%	8	18.6%	22	2.8%
Flood	780	125	16.0%	33	4.2%	8	6.4%	25	3.8%

[a] Percentages do not add to 100.
[b] Percentages based on total.
[c] Percentages based on hazard perceivers.

TABLE 2.2

Environmental hazards—reality-perception relationships, controlling for county perception:
Los Angeles standard metropolitan statistical area, 1962

Hazard × Neighborhood Perception × County Perception	X^2	ϕ	Q	Significance	Interaction
Smog × neighborhood perception	49.16	0.25	0.53	.001	
Smog × neighborhood perception × perceived in county	50.00	0.29	0.56	.001	Yes
Smog × neighborhood perception × not perceived in county	1.67	0.10	0.59	No	
Noise × neighborhood perception	39.98	0.60	0.22	.001	
Noise × neighborhood perception × perceived in county	18.75	0.15	0.59	.001	Yes
Noise × neighborhood perception × not perceived in county	.55	0.08	0.53	No	
Fire × neighborhood perception[a]	21.43	0.16	0.77	.001	
Fire × neighborhood perception × perceived in county	35.29	0.27	0.79	.001	No
Fire × neighborhood perception × not perceived in county	0.09	0.19	0.66	No, $Z = 1.90$	
Slide × neighborhood perception[a]	18.71	0.15	0.76	.001	
Slide × neighborhood perception × perceived in county	11.62	0.18	0.74	.001	Yes
Slide × neighborhood perception × not perceived in county	5.10	0.82	0.11	No, $Z = 3.0$	
Flood × neighborhood perception	0.91	0.22	0.02	No	No
Flood × neighborhood perception × perceived in county	1.74	0.02	0.26	No	
Flood × neighborhood perception × not perceived in county	0.47	0.24	0.03	No	

[a] Z test used due to small cell frequencies.

ships. Hazard data were dichotomized according to recorded presence or absence of hazards in a census tract, and perceptions were dichotomized according to whether the hazards were perceived as "serious" or "not serious." In addition, data used for the control variables—sex, age, socioeconomic status, family type, dwelling-unit type, race, neighborhood satisfaction, and anomie—were dichotomized. The chi-square test of independence, at the .01 level of significance, was used to establish the overall relationship between the perception of a given hazard and its recorded presence. The degree of association between the reality of the hazard and its perception was specified by a Q and a phi coefficient. The Z test for differences between proportions was used when the chi-square expected or observed cell frequencies were less than five or ten, respectively.

After reality-perception relations were determined, control variables were introduced to determine whether they changed the original association. For each comparison, two four-fold contingency tables were constructed. It was then established if the original reality-perception relationship changed when the control variable was introduced. If the chi-square or Z test differed between the subclasses—that is, was significant for one of the two contingency tables and not for the other—the result was interpreted as indicating that there was interaction between the control variable and the original reality-perception association. If interaction was found, the control variable was considered to influence the reality-perception relationship. Tests for brush fires and earth slides were inconclusive, owing to the small portions of the sample residing in areas affected by these hazards.

Table 2.2 illustrates the mode of data analysis. For smog, a statistically significant relationship was found between reality and perception. The reality-perception relationship was significant for county smog perceivers but was not significant for respondents not perceiving smog in the county. The differences in significance between county smog perceivers and nonperceivers was interpreted as indicating that county smog perception influenced the reality perception relationship for smog, with county perceivers being more likely to perceive neighborhood smog than county nonperceivers. To summarize Table 2.2, interaction was found for smog, noise, and slide but not for flood, and results were indeterminate for fire. The perception of smog, noise, and slide in the county was then taken as influencing the reality-perception relationships. Table 2.3 further indicates that respondents generalized

TABLE 2.3

Relationship between neighborhood and county hazard perception: Los Angeles standard metropolitan statistical area

Hazard	X^2 (1 d. f.)	Q	ϕ	Significance
Smog	71.42	0.898	0.300	0.001
Noise	165.82	0.904	0.466	0.001
Brush fire	19.75	0.804	0.160	0.001
Earth slide	24.06	0.835	0.179	0.001
Flood	42.69	0.875	0.237	0.001

between the perception of the hazard in the neighborhood and the county, since for smog and each other hazard a significant chi-square was obtained.

Relationships between reality and perception of hazards controlling for population characteristics are summarized in Table 2.4. The sex of respondents did not influence reality-perception relationships. Age influenced these relationships only in the case of slides, where subjects over 35 years of age were more likely to perceive the hazard than were younger respondents. Socioeconomic status influenced the reality-perception relationship for slides, with high-status respondents being more likely to perceive the hazards than low-status respondents. A similar finding for fire and slide was found with respect to family type, with hazards being perceived more often by respondents from broken

than from complete families. Dwelling-unit type exerted no influence on the reality-perception relationship. Race influenced reality-perception relationships for smog and air-traffic noise, with whites being more likely to perceive the hazards than nonwhites.

These generally negative results indicate that the social structure, defined in terms of the above measures, did not consistently differentiate the extent to which there was an association between hazard reality and perception. The finding with respect to race and perception was not necessarily in disagreement with the similarity of the distribution of smog and ethnic populations. It may be that, while nonwhites are concentrated in smog areas, the intrusion of social hazards in such areas and the preoccupation of such populations with other social problems may have obscured their perception of environmental hazards.

Table 2.4 also presents reality-perception relationships influenced by social-psychological characteristics of respondents. There was an interaction effect for reality and perception of smog, airplane noise, brush fires, and slides while controlling for neighborhood satisfaction. For each of these relationships, the more satisfied respondents were more likely to perceive the hazards than dissatisfied respondents. Anomic or eunomic class placement did not influence the relationships except in the case of brush fires, where the small number of respondents precluded definitive results. Thus, while integration into the social structure as measured by the anomie instrument did not alter the reality-perception relationships, reality-perception was affected by neighborhood satisfaction. In general, smog operated much like the other hazards in influencing the relations of reality and perception for both social-psychological and social-structure variables.

These findings do suggest some leads concerning the relations of environmental hazards to social organization and the culture of the city:

TABLE 2.4

Reality-perception relationships controlling for sex, age, socioeconomic status, family type, dwelling-unit type, race, neighborhood satisfaction and anomie: Los Angeles standard metropolitan statistical area[a]

Control Variable	Hazard	Interaction	Direction
Sex	Smog × neighborhood perception	No	
	Air traffic noise × perception	No	
	Brush fire × neighborhood perception	No	
	Earth slide × neighborhood perception	No	
	Flood × neighborhood perception	No	
Age	Smog × neighborhood perception	No	
	Air traffic × neighborhood perception	No	
	Brush fire × neighborhood perception	No	
	Earth slide × neighborhood perception	Yes	Subjects 35-plus perceive hazard
	Flood × neighborhood perception	No	
Socioeconomic status	Smog × neighborhood perception	No	
	Air traffic × neighborhood perception	No	
	Brush fire × neighborhood perception	No	
	Earth slide × neighborhood perception	Yes	High SES perceive hazard
	Flood × neighborhood perception	No	
Family type	Smog × neighborhood perception	No	
	Air traffic × neighborhood perception	No	
	Brush fire × neighborhood perception	Yes	Broken family perceive hazard
	Earth slide × neighborhood perception	Yes	Broken family perceive hazard
	Flood × neighborhood perception	No	
Dwelling-unit type	Smog × neighborhood perception	No	
	Air traffic × neighborhood perception	No	
	Brush fire × neighborhood perception	No	
	Earth slide × neighborhood perception	No	
	Flood × neighborhood perception	No	
Race	Smog × neighborhood perception	Yes	Whites perceive hazard
	Air traffic × neighborhood perception	Yes	Whites perceive hazard
	Brush fire × neighborhood perception	No	
	Earth slide × neighborhood perception	No	
	Flood × neighborhood perception	No	
Neighborhood satisfaction	Smog × neighborhood perception	Yes	Satisfied perceive hazard
	Air traffic × neighborhood perception	Yes	Satisfied perceive hazard
	Brush fire × neighborhood perception	Yes	Satisfied perceive hazard
	Earth slide × neighborhood perception	Yes	Satisfied perceive hazard
	Flood × neighborhood perception	No	
Anomie	Smog × neighborhood perception	No	
	Air traffic × neighborhood perception	No	
	Brush fire × neighborhood perception	Yes	Eunomic perceive hazard
	Earth slide × neighborhood perception	No	
	Flood × neighborhood perception	No	

[a] Results on brush-fire and earth-slide hazards are only tentative, owing to the small proportion of population living in these areas.

1. In Los Angeles the health hazards of smog and air traffic noise are widely diffused. Smog is more concentrated in areas of older housing than in areas of recent construction. On the other hand, economic hazards of brush fire, flood, and slide appear to be a precursor of urban development in that they are associated with the conversion of raw land to urban uses.

2. When the focus is shifted from the reality to the perception of hazards, there is a direct relationship between the variables for smog, airplane noise, brush fires, and earth slides. Smog is the most ubiquitous of the observed environmental hazards in Los Angeles, and when compared with the other hazards, was the most important for hazard perception. Yet no consistent findings were observed for the influence of social-structure variables upon reality-perception relationships. It may be that environmental hazards of the type described are part of the accepted difficulties of life for some urban subpopulations. Nonwhites, for example, who tend to be more concentrated in health-hazard areas, do not perceive smog and airplane noise to the same degree as the white population. Moreover, it was found that being bound to middle-class norms, as indicated by responses to an anomie scale, did not influence relationships of reality and perception. Anomie was not related to smog perception, yet anomic individuals were found more frequently in smog areas. These findings suggest that measures of social position when applied to individuals do not consistently influence reality-perception relationships.

3. Respondents' evaluations of neighborhood in terms of expressed overall satisfaction did affect the way in which reality was perceived. Data are not available with which the internalized symbolic environment of the individual can be related to the perception of external environmental hazards. It may well be, however, that these hazards are perceived in the context of assumptions that urban populations make about the immediate spatial context of their lives. In this respect, there may be selective perception of environmental hazards incorporated into a preexisting experiential organization. Such an organization may well be independent of socioeconomic characteristics and integration into the social life of the metropolis.

4. While smog is more often present and perceived in the metropolitan area, it is not a unique hazard as far as population perceptions are concerned. Reactions to smog appear to be similar to reactions to other urban annoyances. In Los Angeles, environmental hazards appear to be systematically related to the characteristics of urban subarea populations, when measurements are made on a census-tract basis. The reactions of metropolitan population to hazards, however, are not systematically influenced by the selected measures of their individual placement in the social structure. While individual and areal variables do not necessarily have the same meaning, this hiatus does require an explanation.

Two lines of further investigation are suggested in order to deal with this problem. First is an examination of the profiles of those respondents who did or did not perceive hazards when they were recorded as present or absent. Descriptions of perceivers and nonperceivers classified as accurate or inaccurate in their perceptions should provide more information concerning the role of the symbolic environment in hazard perception. Second, we can introduce techniques to account for the joint effects of individual and areal variation as related to hazard perceptions. Given the mosaic of subworlds present in a metropolitan area, the developmental and population characteristics of such areas must be controlled in order to more specifically delimit the immediate context of experience as it may influence hazard perception.

*The Context of Experience
in Hazard Perception*

A considerable body of recent hazard research attempts to resolve some of the questions outlined above: to delimit the context of experience as it influences hazard perception. One example by Kates (1967) looks at the coastal-storm hazard along the outer shore of Megalopolis. The outer shore of Megalopolis consists of 1300 miles of sand bar, bluff, and tidal marsh. On the 20 percent of this frontage that is developed, air photos reveal over 125,000 man-made structures within ten feet of sea level. The people who live and work in these structures share a common orientation to the ocean and are in turn subject to a set of natural hazards posed by the onshore movement of wind and water powered by the impressive energy of atmo-

sphere and ocean. The degree to which these hazards are recognized by those who locate adjacent to the shore is a critical element in growing national concern with the rising toll of storm damages and with public pressure for increased protection, relief, and insurance against wave and associated wind damage.

Fifteen sites along the coast from North Carolina to New Hampshire were chosen for intensive study by Kates (Figure 2.1). These sites are diverse in settlement, in regional location, and in subjection to natural hazard. They include urbanized areas with a coastal orientation, small

FIGURE 2.1. Location of Study Sites

settlements and fishing ports, seasonally occupied recreational areas, and coastal areas devoid of permanent human occupance.

At each site, excluding the empty shore, a sample of permanent residents, seasonal home owners, and commercial managers was selected for interviews. All respondents were potentially subject to some hazard of tidal inundation from coastal storms, but 15 percent had ground-floor elevations higher than the previously recorded maxima of flooding. The interviews were designed to explore existing hypotheses of human adjustment to natural hazard and to delineate individual hazard perceptions.

Understanding of human adjustment to hazardous natural environments had previously been derived from flood plains, but the observations were reinforced by other research, notably by anthropologists. Their studies suggest that adjustments to natural hazards are common in most societies and at all levels of technological skill. However, the level of adjustment is often suboptimal—that is, fewer and weaker steps are taken than are required to minimize the effects of the natural hazard while permitting maximum use of resources associated with that hazard.

The causes of suboptimal behavior are complex and manifold. Natural hazards include a variety of extreme or rare geophysical events. They are not easily amenable to the prevailing calculus of risk based on relative frequency, and it is difficult, even with technical-scientific expertise, to specify an optimal set of adjustments. Even were such specifications theoretically feasible, to make use of them would require a range of information beyond the capacity of the ordinary individual residing or working within a hazard area. Finally, the pattern of decision-making that leads to suboptimal choice seems to be inherent in the human condition.

People are, in Simon's terms, either *satisficers*, content with suboptimal solution, or, as the traditionalists suggest, *optimizers* who, saddled with ignorance and ill fortune, aspire to, but never reach, the ideal response. A choice between these models of man may always elude the investigator, but it is possible to study how men elect to order their uncertain environments. Ignorance and ill fortune can be operationally defined in terms of individual experience of hazard and the extent of damage suffered. It can be determined what men do or would do about hazard and compare their responses with some technical standard of what men *could* do. Variations in behavior and perception between areas of different magnitudes of hazard and uncertainty, and between natural hazards of different types, can be compared. The coastal data illustrate one such set of relations—that between past and present storm experience and anticipations of the future course of events.

The relation is fundamental to the study of decision-making. In technical terms, future expectation is the specification of a set of outcomes. Based on these perceived sets of outcomes, actions may or may not be taken to reduce damage. How are these outcomes formulated, on what are they based, and whence do they derive?

The specification of storm hazard cannot come solely from scientific and technical knowledge. Even in this area evidence is woefully inadequate. Climatology, meteorology, oceanography, and coastal geomorphology all seek to define significant elements of the land-sea interface. There is no shortage of description, but meaningful measurements—meaningful in terms of human occupance—are lacking.

It is certain that major damage-causing storms will affect the coast of Megalopolis in the future. But it cannot be stated with precision the type of storm to be feared, the frequency of its recurrence, the degree of its magnitude, the likely area of run-up. The past experience can be recorded, but despite the long familiarity of man and sea, information is rudimentary. The most destructive storm of the recent past, that of March 6–7, 1962, was born off Florida, passed northward to devastate the mid-Atlantic coast

over a fetch of upwards of a thousand miles—
and then, without warning, under clear skies
and with a calm sea, sent swells a thousand miles
south to batter the Florida coast again.

One survey has identified classes of storms
significant for human occupance from 1935–64
by 25-mile sectors from 1935 to 1964. Over the
study area, there averaged three storms per 25
miles in the first decade, six storms in the second
decade, and seventeen in the third decade. Has
there been a phenomenal rise in storm occurrence, or is the increase the result of improved
reporting of storms, or of more intensive occupance of low-lying areas—lending new significance to storms that would earlier have passed
unnoticed?

It is against this background of the common
occurrence of coastal storms, combined with
great temporal and spatial uncertainty about
their specific characteristics, that the knowledge
and experience of residents should be viewed.

Almost all the respondents had some knowledge of storm hazard (Table 2.5). Only three
evinced ignorance that storms occur along their
stretch of coast. Two-thirds of them recalled
being aware of the hazard when they first settled there, and 90 percent had experienced a
storm during their period of occupance. Fifty
percent had suffered some water damage and
many more had suffered wind damage. Conscious perception of at least some degree of
natural hazard is generally more widespread
than popular accounts suggest, but an excep-
tionally high proportion of coastal dwellers
display such awareness. Comparable studies on
riverine flood plains reveal far less knowledge
of hazard.

This reflects the distinctive locational orientation of coastal respondents. It is the adjacent sea
that attracted them to their location. The coastal
dweller, attracted to the sea for recreation or
commerce, becomes keenly aware of its varied
states. Even the seasonal visitor, who usually
sees the sea only in its more placid moods,
seems to share this heightened awareness. On
the coast, the daily variation of tide reminds us
of the sea's potential for changing its level.
And boating, bathing, and water sports, with
their sensitivity to weather, provide additional
familiarity with phenomena and so contribute
to this awareness.

But this appreciation of the force of storm
and tide does not carry over into a realistic
assessment of the future. As Table 2.6 shows,

TABLE 2.5

Information and future expectations of coastal respondents

Present Hazard Information	Expectation of Future Hazards (Percent of Respondents)				
	No Storms or Damage Expected	Storms and Damage Uncertain	Storms Expected but No or Uncertain Damage	Storms and Damage Expected	Total
No knowledge	0.8	—	—	—	0.8
Knowledge	2.2	2.4	4.3	0.8	9.7
One experience	6.5	5.7	8.4	9.4	30.0
Two or more experiences	4.6	8.7	22.7	23.0	59.0
TOTAL	14.1	16.8	35.4	33.2	99.5
(Number of respondents)	(52)	(62)	(131)	(123)	(368)

TABLE 2.6

Interpretation and future expectations of coastal respondents

Present Interpretation of Hazards	Expectation of Future Hazards (Percent of Respondents)				Total
	No Storms or Damage Expected	Storms and Damage Uncertain	Storms Expected but No or Uncertain Damage	Storms and Damage Expected	
I. Respondents do not share in the common knowledge of storms	0.9	—	—	—	0.9
II. Respondents share in the common knowledge of storms but:					
a. Deny the common image of storms	2.1	0.3	0.6	0.3	3.3
b. Think storms are unique	5.3	4.0	—	—	9.8
c. Think storms are repetitive and also think:					
1. They are personally excluded	3.7	0.9	0.3	—	4.9
2. Storms are decreasing in time or space	1.2	—	1.5	0.3	3.0
3. Storm trend cannot be ascertained	—	2.7	16.2	12.8	31.7
4. Storms are constant in time or space	0.6	0.9	20.1	21.6	43.2
5. Storms are increasing in time or space	—	—	0.3	2.4	2.7
TOTAL	14.3	8.8	39.0	37.4	99.5
(Number of respondents)	(47)	(29)	(128)	(123)	(327)

even though 90 percent of the respondents had experienced storms, only two-thirds expected storms in the future. And although half of them had suffered some damage in the past, only a third expected a future storm to entail damage for themselves.

Expectations of future outcomes cannot be understood on the basis of simple awareness of the past; such expectations arise out of a process called interpretation. Knowledge and experience of real events in the world are personalized and distorted by preconceptions of *uniqueness* and *repetitiveness*. These concepts are presented in Table 2.6, which classifies respondents on the basis of their replies to structured and unstructured questions about storms. From these verbal clues can be derived the categories of interpretation.

Most respondents interpret storms as repetitive events, and many of them feel that the repetition is in some fashion constant: "Just the process of nature in this area for storms to come every year"; "We get storms, with serious ones at about ten-year intervals." For others, storms are increasing, owing either to the action of man— "They are shooting those rockets up on Wallop's

Island"—or to a perceived migration of hurricane tracks—"They are running up the coast." The spatial pattern may be reversed; some perceive it as "the cycle goes from North Carolina to Florida." These respondents all see storms as decreasing in frequency or intensity.

For a fair number of other respondents, storms are either unique or unknowable: "The 1962 storm was a freak"; "Nature is too unpredictable." And for a very few, hazard is denigrated or even wished away by semantic magic: "We never have any bad storms"; "We might have a couple of hurricanes, but not a storm." The coastal resident who interprets a storm as a freak, unique event, gains no sense of direction from his experience; his future expectations are based on uncertainty and on a desire to deny hazard.

But quite different interpretations of the course of nature may lead to similar expectations. Some respondents who view the repetition of storms as an ordered event derive comfort from their supposed cyclical frequency: "We get storms once in ninety years, we're not due for another." If a major storm occurs and an individual escapes serious damage, the net impact frequently reinforces feelings of security. Storms might be expected in the future, but they will not affect *me*. Similarly, elderly retired couples, although aware of storm hazard, may feel secure from them. Storms seem to them to be spaced far enough apart to assure them of security during their few remaining years.

These interpretations help to explain the gap between actual experience and future expectation. They help to answer the puzzling question as to why people continue to place themselves in areas of high hazard. They show how common experiences are individually interpreted so as to enhance the security of expectations. They suggest something of the way men think about natural phenomena.

Members of the technical-scientific community have by training been prepared to accept a high degree of uncertainty in their scientific work, if not in their private lives. They strive to order the unknowns of natural phenomena but are prepared to accept the unexplained and to await tomorrow's knowledge. The respondents, intelligent and articulate lay people, react to uncertainty in a fundamentally different way, by making events knowable, finding order where none exists, identifying cycles on the basis of the sketchiest of knowledge or folk insight, and, in general, striving to reduce the uncertainty of the threat of hazard. Or conversely, they deny all knowability, resign themselves to the uniqueness of natural phenomena, throw up their hands in impotent despair and assign their fates to a higher power. In such ways their subsequent actions are not related to the environmental hazard itself but to their filtered perceptions of it. As we shall see in subsequent chapters, if they respond in this way to purely natural hazards, their perceptions of and responses to environmental changes produced by complex interactions, but ultimately resulting from accumulated actions by many individuals, including their own, are even more ambiguous.

CHAPTER *3*

environmental effects

of urbanization

We have argued that industrial urbanization, economic growth, and modern technology are the root causes of environmental pollution when individuals are not called to account for their effluents. What are the precise ways in which urbanization causes environmental disruption? The answer is to be found in the ways in which the organized complexity of natural ecosystems is affected by the introduction of massive new inputs of energy, for such ecosystems are best viewed as arising out of the need to organize natural energy exchange in different ways.

In this chapter we turn to a consideration of the energetics of the biosphere and the ways in

which highly distinctive urban climates and hydrologic regimes have resulted from the increased energy released by modern cities and by the paving of natural surfaces.

ENERGETICS OF THE BIOSPHERE

The biosphere is the arena within which the energy-transfer systems operate. The idea of the biosphere was introduced in 1875 by the Austrian geologist Edward Suess, when he concluded a book on the Alps with a chapter on the "envelopes" of the earth. It was brought into general

Much of this chapter is drawn from:
  Helmut E. Landsberg, "Man-made Climatic Changes," *Science*, Vol. 170 (December 18, 1970), pp. 1265–1268. Begins on page 33.
  Peter D. Tyson, "Urban Climatology: A Problem of Environmental Studies," Johannesburg: Witwatersrand University Press, 1970. Begins on page 39.

  James T. Peterson, *The Climate of Cities: A Survey of Recent Literature* (Durham, N.C.: National Air Pollution Control Administration, 1969). Begins on page 40.
  Luna B. Leopold, *Hydrology for Urban Land Planning—A Guidebook on the Hydrologic Effects of Urban Land Use.* Washington D.C.: U.S. Government Printing Office, 1968 (Geological Survey Circular 554). Begins on page 63.

scientific usage in 1926 by the Russian mineralogist Vladimir Ivanovitch Vernadsky. Vernadsky defined the biosphere as the terrestrial envelope in which life exists sandwiched between the depths of the earth and the extremes of space. It excludes those parts of the earth's surface that are too dry, too hot, or too cold to support metabolizing agents without man's technical intervention.

Three special features characterize the biosphere: (1) it is a region in which liquid water can exist in quantity; (2) it receives continuing external energy inputs from an external source, the sun; (3) within it, there are interfaces between the liquid, solid, and gaseous states of matter.

All three conditions appear critical to the support of life. First, all actively metabolizing organisms consist largely of elaborate systems of organic macromolecules dispersed in an aqueous medium. Second, the energy source on which all terrestrial life depends is the sun. The energy of solar radiation can enter the biological cycle only through the photosynthetic production of organic matter by chlorophyll-bearing organisms. These organisms are confined to the part of the biosphere that receives solar radiation by day and are limited to the depths to which gravity may carry them and their excreta. Finally, the energetics of the biosphere depend upon the photosynthetic reduction of carbon dioxide to form organic compounds and molecular oxygen. Photosynthesis produces the atmosphere, free water, and bodies of organisms. Some of the latter, when buried, create organic carbon and fossil fuels—but these are an accidental consequence of a fundamental exchange process in which oxidation of matter produces carbon dioxide and energy useful for growth and reproduction. However, oxidation at the solid-liquid boundary may be affected by the presence or absence of a variety of other elements: nitrogen, phosphorus, sulfur, sodium, calcium, potassium, zinc, lead, iron, copper, and so on, and so a variety of subsidiary exchanges are also necessary for the support of living systems in the biosphere. All biologically important materials must undergo cyclical changes in *exchange systems* so that after utilization they are put back, at the expense of solar energy, into a form in which they can be reused. The rate at which this happens may be quite variable.

Energy Exchange

All energy on earth ultimately derives from the sun; its availability thus varies from one part of the globe to another according to variations in receipt of solar radiation. The prime variable is latitude; hence the broad distinction between polar, temperate, and tropical climates. However, both the atmosphere and oceans redistribute incoming solar energy and thus serve to modify the severe climatic variations that would arise if the climate of each area were simply a function of the incoming short-wave radiation and the counterbalancing outflow of long-wave radiation.

Of the incoming solar energy, approximately one-third is reflected back by the atmosphere and is lost in space. One-half reaches the earth's surface and is absorbed as heat. In the ocean, wave motion redistributes this heat in a fairly thick surface layer, whereas conduction in the soil affects only a thin skin of the land surface. Thus, diurnal temperature variations are much greater on land than at sea.

The remaining fifth of the solar energy is absorbed by the atmosphere, some by upper atmosphere oxygen and ozone and the balance at lower levels by water vapor, dust, and water droplets in the clouds. In turn, energy available in water vapor is taken upward from the earth, mixed in the atmosphere, and ultimately replaces energy lost from the upper atmosphere by radiative cooling.

Convection occurs in both the atmosphere and oceans—in the former because of heating from the earth beneath, and in the latter because of incoming solar energy. The convection currents, in turn, are responsible for the main features of the earth's climatic zones. A course in weather and climate provides the basic understanding of these processes.

Yet other energy cycles arise in the biosphere. The energy that sustains all living systems is solar energy as fixed by photosynthesis and then radiated as heat. It has been estimated that only one-tenth of one percent of solar energy is fixed in photosynthesis, yet this is sufficient to produce both food for man and the energy that runs the life-support systems of the biosphere, namely the earth's major ecosystems: the forests, grasslands, oceans, marshes, estuaries, lakes, rivers, tundras, and deserts.

Half the energy fixed in photosynthesis is used immediately in respiration. Some is stored and enters two kinds of food chains, those of grazing and of decay. In both cases the stored energy may be held in reserve for considerable periods before being transferred to the consuming population. In most food chains there is some constant percentage of energy entering any given population that can be transferred to the next level in the chain without serious disruption of either (e.g., 10–20 percent of the energy entering herbivores can be transferred to carnivores, and so on).

In chains of decay, if all available oxygen is consumed prior to total elimination of the dead matter, other products arise, such as methane, alcohols, hydrogen sulfide. One problem of the rapid increase of man and the elimination of many herbivores, thus degrading food chains, is that much energy that would otherwise have been used for respiration by plants or animals or transferred upward in the food chain is shifted instead to the chain of decay. Nutrients then flow more abundantly, for example, from land to water; scavenger webs in water bodies become overloaded; the oxygen dissolved in water is used up and metabolism shifts from an aerobic form to anaerobic respiration; organic matter accumulates; methane and hydrogen sulfide

output increases, and the total environment degrades.

Oxygen Exchange

Oxygen accounts for about one-quarter of the atoms in living matter. Organic substances stored by plants combine carbon, hydrogen, and oxygen in various ways and are produced by photosynthesis in which light energy reacts carbon dioxide with water to yield organic substances. In aerobic respiration, oxygen serves as a hydrogen acceptor, and water is produced. In anaerobic fermentation, however, oxygen carriers become saturated with hydrogen and until more oxygen is introduced, the organic molecules must serve as the hydrogen acceptor.

In the early period of development of life on earth, anaerobic processes dominated. However, the evolution of multicellular organisms was associated with aerobic respiration, and this in turn produced the oxygen accumulation in the atmosphere. The basic equation is

$$CO_2 + H_2O + \text{energy} = CH_2O + O_2.$$

Most of the carbohydrates reoxidize back to CO_2 and H_2O, but to the extent that carbon is stored in the earth, equivalent oxygen exists in the atmosphere and in oxidized sediments; there is an essential carbon-oxygen balance in the earth.

A major question arises out of the impact of man, for by burning fossil fuels, paving formerly green land, and polluting continental shelves, he reduces free oxygen levels and increases CO_2. Counterbalancing this, by irrigation he introduces photosynthesis to formerly semiarid areas. But on the other hand, by drawing down ground-water supplies, he increases flow into the sea. The full range of these effects is unknown. Modest increases in CO_2 might enhance free oxygen accumulation; higher levels might produce a "greenhouse effect," raising temperatures; burning of fossil fuels might increase atmospheric reflection of solar radiation and reduce temperatures. Speculation abounds, but analysis is skimpy, as we shall see in a moment.

The Carbon Cycle

The carbon cycle is critical to these speculations. It arises from the continuous interactions of living organisms and their physical and chemical environments, involving the equally continuous processes of creation, transformation, and decomposition of carbon compounds. The "engine" is that of photosynthesis, in which

$$CO_2 + 2H_2A + light \longrightarrow$$
$$CH_2O + H_2O + 2A + energy$$

The term $2A$ generally can be written O_2, for in most cases water is involved, but in the case of bacteria it may be sulfur or some other organic radical. Plant growth, thus, uses free oxygen in water and air to unlock energy stored by photosynthesis, releasing carbon dioxide, in a process of respiration. Carbon dioxide, in turn, is used to fix energy through photosynthesis, and carbon fixed by the same process is ultimately returned to the atmosphere through decomposition of dead organic matter.

HUMAN PROCESSES
IN THE BIOSPHERE

Throughout most of his existence on earth, man supported himself as another species with its own niche in the biosphere, functioning within the context of natural energy cycles. He began to shape the biosphere to his own ends when he began to domesticate plants and animals. Natural cycles were modified by systematic grazing, by cultivation, and by burning. In some cases, overgrazing and plowing in semiarid areas have led to extensive denudation. Elsewhere, poorly drained lands have been drained and brought into cultivation. Extensive forests have been cleared and deserts irrigated.

Application of chemical fertilizers has increased yields, and chemical control of diseases, insects, and weeds has had marked effects.

The major environmental impacts, however, have been consequences of the new industrial technologies as man has moved into cities supported by new forms of energy production and use. Before 1800, the power available to human societies was limited to solar energy that had only recently been radiated to the earth. The forms were in animal or human power, burning of materials of animal or vegetable origin, or use of moving air or falling water. The essence of the industrial revolution was to unlock supplies of fossil fuels, the stored solar energy of previous millions of years.

The release of these fuels has disturbed the delicate carbon-oxygen balance of the atmosphere. Burning of coal and oil thus involves not only the consumption of a nonrenewable resource and the possibility of major energy crises within this century; it also involves increasing carbon dioxide emissions, alongside carbon monoxide, the sulfur oxides, hydrocarbons, nitrogen oxides, and particulate matter. Between 1860 and 1960 the carbon dioxide content of the earth's atmosphere grew by 14 percent from 290 to 330 parts per million. Predictions are that the concentration will reach 400 ppm by A.D. 2000.

Some feel, as a consequence, that man may be changing global climates. The First Annual Report of the Council on Environmental Quality reported that man's activities can potentially affect climate in at least seven ways. He can increase the carbon dioxide content of the atmosphere by burning fossil fuels. He can decrease atmospheric transparency with aerosols (tiny solid or liquid particles floating in the air) from industry, automobiles, and home heating units. He can decrease atmospheric transparency by introducing dust (particles larger than aerosols), primarily through improper agricultural practices. He can alter the thermal properties of the stratosphere (upper atmosphere) with water from the combustion of jet fuels. He can change the ability of the earth's surface to reflect solar radiation back into space through urbanization, agriculture, deforestation, and reservoirs. He can alter the rate of transfer of thermal energy and momentum between the oceans and atmosphere by spilling oil on the water's surface. Such oil films on the ocean come from incomplete combustion or spills from sources such as vessels and drilling towers. Let us look at each of these in turn, and then set them within the framework of what is known about natural climatic changes, before examining the specific creation of urban climates and hydrologic regimes.

Carbon Dioxide—An Earth Warmer?

The atmosphere's energy, which determines weather and climate, is derived primarily from visible solar radiation absorbed by the earth's surface and atmosphere. The absorption of that energy tends to raise the temperature at the surface. The earth's surface maintains its thermal balance (keeps from overheating) by radiating energy back to space at longer wavelengths. Carbon dioxide in the atmosphere absorbs incoming visible radiation, but in amounts too small to have any appreciable effect on the radiation reaching the lower atmosphere and the earth's surface. However, carbon dioxide is virtually opaque to some long-wave radiation that is emitted by the earth's surface. Thus, when carbon dioxide concentrations increase, heat loss through radiation from the surface is reduced, producing a "greenhouse effect."

Attempts have been made to calculate carbon dioxide effects on the average surface temperature. One investigator calculated that atmospheric carbon dioxide content increased at a nearly constant rate from the nineteenth-century level of about 290 ppm to 330 ppm in the late 1950s. This increase—about 14 percent—could

have caused the temperature rises observed with instruments during the first 40 years of this century.

But findings indicate that as increasing fossil-fuel consumption raises carbon dioxide output, a lesser percentage of it is retained by the atmosphere, and a larger portion is absorbed by the oceans. Only about half the carbon dioxide produced by fossil fuels from 1958 to 1960 remained in the atmosphere. During the five years from 1966 through 1970 less than 40 percent of manmade carbon dioxide has stayed in the atmosphere. Other calculations also show that the effect of carbon dioxide on temperature may have been overestimated.

A detailed series of observations by Swedish, Scripps Institute of Oceanography, and ESSA scientists shows that from 1958 to 1970 the carbon dioxide concentration in the atmosphere increased from 312 to 320 ppm—an average annual jump of 0.7 ppm. This rate, if continued, would double man-made carbon dioxide accumulations in the atmosphere in about 23 years. Yet the bulk of carbon dioxide has entered the atmosphere at a time when the earth's surface temperature was falling rather than rising. Thus, the heating effects of carbon dioxide are apparently being counteracted by natural fluctuations or by other human activities.

Any attempt to extrapolate the future effect of carbon dioxide on climate therefore must be uncertain because the fraction that will enter the ocean is unknown. If 60 percent of the emissions of carbon dioxide remains in the atmosphere and there is a 5 percent yearly growth of fossil-fuel consumption, then by 1990 there would be about 400 ppm in the atmosphere. If this were not offset by other activity, then the earth's average surface temperature would increase by 1.4°F. On the other hand, if 40 percent of the artificially produced carbon dioxide enters the atmosphere and the present 4 percent growth of fossil-fuel consumption continues, then a level of 400 ppm will not be reached until about the year 2010.

The maximum amount of carbon dioxide that man might introduce into the atmosphere can be determined by estimating the total available fossil fuels. One estimate puts the maximum available coal at about 7.6 thousand billion (7.6×10^{12}) metric tons. This is about twice the coal resources established by geological mapping. Estimates of petroleum resources vary considerably. Some researchers estimate that approximately 2 thousand billion (2×10^{12}) barrels of oil are ultimately recoverable, while others appear to favor the somewhat lower figure of 1.35 thousand billion (1.35×10^{12}). If these fossil fuels were burned, they would produce about 3.3 million trillion (3.3×10^{18}) grams of carbon dioxide. If one-half of that carbon dioxide were added to the atmosphere and there were no compensating effects, then the earth's average temperature would increase by about 2° to 3°F. Such a rise, if not counteracted by other effects, could in a period of a few decades lead to the start of substantial melting of ice caps and flooding of coastal regions.

Particle Pollution—An Earth Cooler?

A human activity which may accelerate temperature drops—and thus help compensate for any carbon dioxide-generated temperature rise—is the injection of small particles into the atmosphere.

Certain kinds of industrial processes emit cloud-condensation nuclei (small particles around which raindrops can form). This affects the frequency of fog and low cloud layers, which in turn influence the radiation that reaches the earth from the sun. Forest fires also produce cloud-condensation nuclei (from dust and ashes) plus large quantities of heat and water vapor. Large-scale burning of forest refuse and accidental forest fires, which are particularly common in the western states (but less prevalent than in the past), might modify climate and weather over large regions in this way. The net effect depends on the abundance, size, distribu-

tion, and altitude of the particles. Some investigators estimate that a decrease of atmospheric transparency of only 3 or 4 percent could lead to temperature reduction of 0.7°F. Another study shows that the addition of 1 percent in the world's average low cloud cover lowers temperatures by 1.4°F. This is almost three times the decrease measured in the last two decades. On the average, about 31 percent of the earth's surface is blanketed by low clouds. If this figure were to reach 36 percent (and there is no evidence at the present time that it will), the temperature would drop about 7°F. That would bring the earth's temperature very close to that required for a return of an ice age.

Increases of fog and low clouds when open country is turned into urban areas are well documented. But it is not known whether there has been any increase of global cloud cover. With satellites, data are now obtained fairly routinely of clouds above oceans. But data are often incomplete, because high clouds prevent satellite observation of lower clouds.

One study concludes that a major part of the variation is due to fine-grained particles introduced into the stratosphere (upper atmosphere) by volcanic eruptions. The calculations are based on estimates of the total debris associated with volcanic explosions, an assignment of 1 percent of this total to stratospheric dust, and an assumption of a 14-month lifetime for the stratospheric dust. All these numbers can be questioned. But if they are correct, it would appear clear that dust from volcanoes overshadows that from urban and agricultural pollution.

Thus, there exists no proof that urban, industrial, and agricultural pollution is the principal cause of the recent global cooling trend. But it is significant that the apparent changes of atmospheric transparency caused by volcanic dust may be sufficient to bring about cooling of the earth's atmosphere. If pollution were significantly responsible, then the world would face an important problem of man-made global climate modification. Atmospheric pollution has increased markedly, and at present there still are no acceptable means of impeding its growth on a global scale.

Vapor Trails—Do They Change the Weather?

Altering the water content of the high atmosphere can upset the earth's radiation balance. Water vapor, like carbon dioxide, can absorb outgoing infrared radiation. In solid form, as ice crystals, it can also block incoming solar radiation. A rise of the stratospheric water-vapor content from 2 to 6 ppm would increase the earth's average surface temperature about 0.9°F. Aircraft add water from combustion of jet fuel. Before 1958, essentially no jet fuel was consumed by domestic airlines in the United States; in 1970, jet fuel was being used by U.S. domestic airlines at a rate of 7 billion gallons a year. Below the stratosphere, water vapor dilutes quickly. The amount added by airliners is small compared with water naturally present at these altitudes. But above the stratosphere, water vapor stays, on the average, for about 18 months because it mixes only slowly with the lower atmosphere. Most commercial jets fly below the stratosphere. But supersonic jets will travel in the stratosphere at altitudes of 60,000 to 70,000 feet. Assuming that water vapor stays in the stratosphere for an average of 18 months, 500 supersonic transports operating 7 hours per day could increase the water vapor content of the stratosphere over a hemisphere by 0.2 ppm if it were uniformly distributed.

These changes appear small. But they augment natural fluctuations. For reasons not yet understood, the water-vapor content of the stratosphere rose from 2 ppm million in 1964 to about 3 ppm in early 1970. Artificially produced water vapor can accelerate that natural growth trend.

There is also evidence that jets contribute to high clouds. Observations at Denver indicate that from 1950 to 1958, on the average, about 8 percent of the sky was covered by high clouds when there were no lower cloud layers. From 1965 to 1969 about twice that portion of the sky was covered by high clouds. Similar observations have been recorded at Salt Lake City. Both cities are on heavily traveled air routes, although there may be other contributing factors. The long-term climatic consequences of such high-cloud-cover increases are still unknwon.

Man and the Thermal Budget

The mean annual difference between solar radiation absorbed by the earth and long-wave radiation reflected from earth into space is about 68 watts per square meter. Most of this net energy surplus is used for the evaporation of water, heating of the atmosphere, and other meteorological processes. A tiny part, less than 1 percent, is used in the photosynthesis of green plants. It is thus turned into a relatively stable form of chemical energy.

Man's activities add slightly to the earth's "thermal budget." Heat generated by industrial, residential, and automotive sources supplement solar radiation. Averaged over the earth's surface, at present man is producing only little more than one ten-thousandth of the net radiation gain of the atmosphere. This is much too little to influence climate on a large scale, but it certainly alters the local climate of cities, as we shall see in a moment.

Energy Output—Disappearing Ice Cap?

In a primitive society, energy utilization consists mostly of the food consumed by the individual. This corresponds to a power output of about 100 thermal watts per person. The world average—including primitive and technologically advanced regions—is somewhat more than 1000 thermal watts per person. In the highly industrialized United States, energy consumption is equivalent to 10,000 watts for each individual. If world population grows to 5 billion and if the worldwide average of energy use increases to 10,000 watts per person, man-made energy input into the atmosphere will reach almost one-hundredth that of the natural net radiation balance over land areas. If energy consumption continues to increase at the present rate of 4 percent per year, then in 200 years artificial energy input into the atmosphere will equal one-third of the natural radiation balance. This level would be reached in only 100 years with a 10 percent yearly increase. These numbers are highly significant because an increase of a few tenths of 1 percent in the radiation balance, if long sustained, would cause polar ice to disappear completely unless other natural or man-made changes compensated for the energy gain.

The combined effect of carbon dioxide pollution and heat pollution is strongly in the direction of warming the earth's atmosphere. Particle pollution tends to lower the earth's temperature. Which pollution effect will ultimately dominate? Will we indeed drown or will we freeze? Despite firm predictions by some ecologists, we do not know the answers. Careful monitoring and extended research are required if we are to manage our global climate wisely. These questions may become critical in the future.

Raising the Albedo

Researchers have calculated that a unit increase in the earth's albedo (reflective surface characteristics) will cause a decrease in average surface temperature of 1.8°F. Thus, man-made changes of the albedo at the earth's surface, if large enough, can cause substantial changes in climatic conditions. Densely built-up regions have a higher albedo than forests and cultivated soils. Deserts, some of which may stem from man's activities, have a much higher albedo than grass-covered fields.

Proliferation of urban areas and highway systems may increase the earth's average surface albedo. The net effect of the change on climate is not understood, because changes in albedo are usually accompanied by alterations in the surface roughness of the earth. These alterations affect the rate at which the surface can exchange heat and momentum with the atmosphere by winds and other turbulent processes. These changes can also affect weather and climate.

Oil on the Water

Effects of oil films on the ocean surface are still poorly understood. With their vast stores of thermal energy, the oceans act as balance wheels to climate. The atmosphere exchanges energy with the ocean through radiation and mechanical processes. The strength of the mechanical interaction associated with air moving over a wave-roughened surface depends on the surface roughness of the water and the velocity and regularity of the wind. Very thin oil films can alter this interchange by reducing turbulence, evaporation, and the radiation emission of the surface.

But it is still unknown whether oil pollution contributes significantly to climatic change.

NATURAL CLIMATIC CHANGES

There is much that is ambiguous in the preceding speculation. As Landsberg (1970a) has noted, the earth's atmosphere has been in a state of continuous slow evolution since the formation of the planet. Therefore it is very dangerous to interpret a short-term trend as a sign of impending catastrophe. Because of differences in the absorptive properties of different atmospheric constituents, the energy balance near the surface has been undergoing parallel evolution. Undoubtedly the greatest event in this evolution has been the emergence of substantial amounts of oxygen, photosynthetically produced by plants. The photochemical development of ozone in the upper atmosphere, where it forms an absorbing layer for the short-wave ultraviolet radiation and creates a warm stratum, is climatically also very important, especially for the forms of organic life now in existence. But for the heat balance of the earth, carbon dioxide (CO_2) and water vapor, with major absorption bands in the infrared, are essential constituents. They absorb a substantial amount of the dark radiation emitted by the earth's surface. The condensed or sublimated parts of the atmospheric water vapor also enter prominently into the energy balance. In the form of clouds they reflect incoming short-wave radiation from the sun and hence play a major role in determining the planetary albedo. At night, clouds also intercept outgoing radiation and radiate it back to the earth's surface.

Over the past two decades Budyko (1969) has gradually evolved models of the global climate, using an energy-balance approach. These models incorporate, among other important factors, the incoming solar radiation, the albedo, and the outgoing radiation. Budyko's calculations suggest that a 1.6 percent decrease in incoming radiation or a 5 or 10 percent increase in the albedo of the earth could bring about renewed major glaciation.

The theory that changes in the incoming radiation are a principal factor governing the terrestrial climate has found its major advocate in Milankovitch (1969). He formulated a comprehensive mathematical model of the time variations of the earth's position in space with respect to the sun. This included the periodic fluctuations of the inclination of the earth's axis, its precession, and the eccentricity of its orbit. From these elements he calculated an insolation curve back into time and the corresponding surface temperature of the earth. He tried to correlate minima with the Pleistocene glaciations. These views have found considerable support in isotope investigations, especially of the $^{18}O/^{16}O$ ratio in marine shells deposited during the Pleistocene. Lower ^{18}O amounts correspond to lower temperatures. Budyko and others raise some doubts that Milankovitch's theory can explain glaciations but admit that it explains some temperature fluctuations. For the last 1700

years there is also evidence that the ^{18}O content of Greenland glacier ice is inversely correlated to a solar activity index based on auroral frequencies. Again, low values of ^{18}O reflect the temperature at which the precipitation that formed the firn fell.

The fluctuations of externally received energy are influenced not only by the earth's position with respect to the sun but also by changes in energy emitted by the sun. Extraterrestrial solar radiation fluctuates with respect to spectral composition, but no major changes in total intensity have yet been measured outside the atmosphere. The occurrence of such fluctuations is indicated by a large number of statistical studies, but ironclad proof is still lacking. Such fluctuations are of either long or short duration. They have been tied to the solar activity cycle. Inasmuch as details are yet unknown, their effect on climate is at present one factor in the observed "noise" pattern.

The Climatic Seesaw

It was only a relatively short time ago that instrumental records of climate first became available. Although broad-scale assessments of climate can be made from natural sources, such as tree rings or pollen associations, and, in historical times, from chronicles that list crop conditions or river freezes, this is tenuous evidence. But a considerable number of instrumental observations of temperatures and precipitation are available for the period from the early eighteenth century to the present, at least for the northern hemisphere. These observations give a reasonably objective view of climatic fluctuations for the last two and a half centuries. This is, of course, the interval in which man and his activities have multiplied rapidly. These long climatic series are mostly from western Europe, but recently a series for the eastern seaboard of the United States has been reconstructed from all available data sources. In this series Philadelphia is used as an index location, since it is centrally located with respect to all the earlier available records.

Figures 3.1 and 3.2 show the annual values for temperature and precipitation for a 230-year span; there are some minor gaps where the data were inadequate. These curves are characteristic of those for other regions, too. In particular they reflect the restlessness of the atmosphere. Many analysts have simply considered the variations to be quasi-random. Certainly, they do not reflect any pronounced one-sided trends. However, there are definite long or short intervals in which considerable one-sided departures from a mean are notable. On corresponding curves representing data for a larger area that encompasses most of the regions bordering the Atlantic, the major segments are those for the late eighteenth century, which was warm; the nineteenth century, which was cool; and the first half of the twentieth century, in which there was a notable rising trend. This trend was followed by some cooling in the 1950s and 1960s.

In the precipitation patterns, "noise" masks all trends, but we know that during a period in the

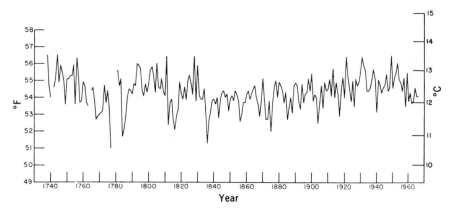

FIGURE 3.1. Annual temperatures for the eastern seaboard of the United States for the period 1738 to 1967—a representative, reconstructed synthetic series centered on Philadelphia.

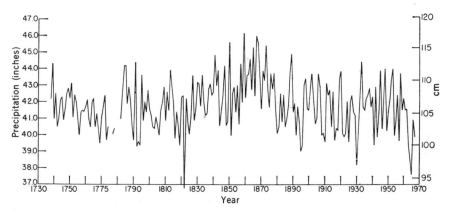

FIGURE 3.2. Annual precipitation totals for the eastern seaboard of the United States for the period 1738 to 1967—a representative, reconstructed synthetic series centered on Philadelphia.

middle of the last century there was considerably more precipitation than there is now. For shorter intervals, spells of drought alternate with high precipitation. Sometimes, for small areas, these can be quite spectacular. An example is the seasonal snowfall on Mount Washington, in New Hampshire; there the snowfall increased from an average of 4.5 meters in the winters of 1933–34 to 1949–50 to an annual average of 6 meters in the period 1951–52 to 1966–67. Yet these values should not be taken as general climatic trends for the globe, or even for the hemisphere.

Even if we take indices that integrate various climatic influences, we still cannot make categorical statements. Glacier conditions are typical in this group of indices. For example, the glaciers on the west coast of Greenland have been repeatedly surveyed since 1850. In consonance with temperature trends for lower latitudes, they showed their farthest advances in the seventh decade of the nineteenth century and have been retreating ever since. This pattern fits the temperature curves to the 1950 turning point, but, although glaciers in some regions of the world have been advancing since then, this is by no means true of all glaciers. The question of whether these changes reflect (i) relatively short-term temperature fluctuations, or (ii) alterations in the alimenting precipitation, or (iii) a combination of these two factors remains unanswered.

Many of the shorter fluctuations are likely to be only an expression of atmospheric interaction with the oceans. Even if external or terrestrial impulses affect the energy budget and cause an initial change in atmospheric circulation, notable lag and feedback mechanisms involving the oceans produce pulsations which, in turn, affect the atmosphere. The oceans have a very large thermal inertia, and their horizontal motions and vertical exchanges are slow. Namias (1968) has investigated many of the fluctuations of a few years' duration. He concluded, for example, that drought conditions on the eastern seaboard of the United States in the 1960s were directly affected by the prevailing wind system and by sea-surface temperatures in the vicinity but that the real dominant factor was a wind-system change in the North Pacific. Such teleconnections (relations among conditions in distant parts of the globe) complicate interpretations of local or even regional data tremendously.

The worldwide effect of changes in the Pacific wind system is obvious from Namias's estimate that accelerations and decelerations cause large-scale breaks in the regime of sea-surface temperatures. These seem to occur in sequences of approximately five years and may cause temperature changes of 0.5°C over the whole North Pacific. Namias estimates that this can cause differences of 8×10^{18} grams in the annual amounts of water evaporated from the surface. The consequences for worldwide cloud and rain formation are evident. It is against this background that we have to weigh climatic changes allegedly wrought by man.

Carbon Dioxide

The fact that the atmospheric gases play an important role in the energy budget of the earth was recognized early. Fourier, and then Pouillet and Tyndall, first expressed the idea that these gases acted as a "greenhouse." After the spectrally selective absorption of gases was recognized, their role as climatic controls became a subject of wide debate. The capability of CO_2 to intercept long-wave radiation emitted by the earth was put forward as a convenient explanation for climatic changes.

Arrhenius (1908) made the first quantitative estimates of the magnitude of the effect, which he attributed mainly to fluctuating volcanic activity, although he also mentioned the burning of coal as a minor source of CO_2. The possibility that man-made CO_2 could be an important factor in the earth's heat balance was not seriously considered until Callendar (1938) showed evidence of a gradual increase in CO_2 concentration in the earth's atmosphere. But it was Plass

(1956) who initiated the modern debate on the subject, based on his detailed study of the CO_2 absorption spectrum.

The crucial question is: how much has CO_2 increased as a result of the burning of fossil fuels? It is quite difficult to ascertain even the mean amount of CO_2 in the surface layers of the atmosphere, especially near vegetation. There are large diurnal and annual variations. Various agriculturalists have reported concentrations ranging from 210 to 500 ppm. The daily amplitudes during the growing season are about 70 ppm. Nearly all early measurements were made in environments where such fluctuations took place. This, together with the lack of precision of the measurements, means that our baseline—atmospheric CO_2 concentrations prior to the spectacular rise in fossil fuel consumption of this century—is very shaky. Only since the International Geophysical Year have there been some regularly operating measuring points in polar regions and on high mountains and reliable data from the oceans which give some firm information on the actual increase.

The best estimate places the increase in atmospheric CO_2 since 1860 at 10 to 15 percent. This is hardly a spectacular change, but the rate of increase has been rising, and various bold extrapolations have been made into the twenty-first century. Much depends on the sinks for CO_2, which at present are not completely known. At present concentrations, atmospheric O_2 and CO_2 stay in approximate equilibrium, through the photosynthetic process in plants. It is estimated that 150×10^9 tons of CO_2 per year are used in photosynthesis. A corresponding amount is returned to the atmosphere by decay, unless the total volume of plant material increases. This volume is one of the unknowns in the estimates of CO_2 balance. Perhaps satellite sensors can give some bulk information on that point in the future.

The oceans are a major sink for CO_2. The equilibrium with the bicarbonates dissolved in seawater determines the amount of CO_2 in the atmosphere. In the exchange between atmosphere and ocean, the temperature of the surface water enters as a factor. More CO_2 is absorbed at lower surface-water temperatures than at higher temperatures. It has already been shown that surface-water temperatures fluctuate over long or short intervals; most of these ups and downs are governed by the wind conditions. The interchange of the cold deep water and the warm surface water through downward mixing and upwelling, in itself an exceedingly irregular process, controls, therefore, much of the CO_2 exchange. Also, the recently suggested role of an enzyme in the ocean that facilitates absorption of CO_2 has yet to be explored. Hence, it is quite difficult to make long-range estimates of how much atmospheric CO_2 will disappear in the oceanic sink. Most extrapolators assume essentially a constant rate of removal.

Even the remaining question of how much the earth's temperature will change with a sharp increase in the CO_2 content of the atmosphere cannot be unambiguously answered. The answer depends on other variables, such as atmospheric humidity and cloudiness. But the calculations have been made on the basis of various assumptions. The model most widely used is that of Manabe and Wetherald (1967). They calculate, for example, that, with the present value for average cloudiness, an increase of atmospheric CO_2 from 300 to 600 ppm would lead to an increase of $2°C$ in the mean temperature of the earth at the surface. At the same time the lower stratosphere would cool by $15°C$.

At the present rate of accumulation of CO_2 in the atmosphere, the doubling of the CO_2 would take about 400 years. The envisaged $2°C$ rise can hardly be called cataclysmic. There have been such worldwide changes within historical times. Any change attributable to the rise in CO_2 in the last century has certainly been submerged in the climatic "noise." Besides, our estimates of CO_2 production by natural causes, such as volcanic exhalations and organic decay, are very inaccurate; hence the ratio of these natural effects to anthropogenic effects remains to be established.

Dust

The influence on climate of suspended dust in the atmosphere was first recognized in relation to volcanic eruptions. Observations of solar radiation at the earth's surface following the spectacular eruption of Krakatoa in 1883 showed measurable attenuation. The particles stayed in the atmosphere for five years. There was also some suspicion that summers in the northern hemisphere were cooler after the eruption. The inadequacy and unevenness of the observations make this conclusion somewhat doubtful. The main exponent of the hypothesis that volcanic dust is a major controller of terrestrial climate was W. J. Humphreys (1940). In recent years the injection into the atmosphere of a large amount of dust by an eruption of Mount Agung has renewed interest in the subject, not only because of the spectacular sunsets but also because there appears to have been a cooling trend since. The Mount Agung eruption was followed, in the 1960s, by at least three others from which volcanic constituents reached stratospheric levels: those of Mount Taal, in 1965; Mount Mayon, in 1968; and Fernandina, in 1968. Not only did small dust particles reach the stratosphere, but it seems likely that gaseous constituents reaching these levels caused the formation of ammonium sulfate particles through chemical and photochemical reactions. The elimination of small particulates from the stratosphere is relatively slow, and some backscattering of solar radiation is likely to occur.

As yet man cannot compete in dust production with the major volcanic eruptions, but he is making a good try. However, most of his solid products that get into the atmosphere stay near the ground, where they are fairly rapidly eliminated by fallout and washout. There is evidence that there has been some increase in the atmospheric content of particles less than 10^{-4} centimeter in diameter. The question is simply: what is the effect of the man-made aerosol? There is general agreement that it depletes the direct solar radiation and increases radiation from the sky. Measurements of the former clearly show a gradual increase in turbidity, and the same increase in turbidity has been documented by observations from the top of Mauna Loa, which is above the level of local contamination. From these observations the conclusion has been drawn that the attentuation of direct solar radiation is, in part at least, caused by backscattering of incoming solar radiation to space. This is equivalent to an increase in the earth's albedo and hence is being interpreted as a cause of heat loss and lowered temperatures. But things are never that categorical and simple in the atmosphere. The optical effects of an aerosol depend on its size distribution, its height in the atmosphere, and its absorptivity. These properties have been studied in detail by a number of authors.

It is quite clear that most man-made particulates stay close to the ground. Temperature inversions attend to that. And there is no evidence that they penetrate the stratosphere in any large quantities, especially since the ban, by most of the nuclear powers, of nuclear testing in the atmosphere. The optical analyses show, first of all, that the backscatter of the particles is outweighed at least 9 to 1 by forward scattering. Besides, there is a notable absorption of radiation by the aerosol. This absorption applies not only to the incoming but also to the outgoing terrestrial radiation. The effectiveness of this interception depends greatly on the overlapping effect of the water vapor of the atmosphere.

Yet the net effect of the man-made particulates seems to be that they lead to heating of the atmospheric layer in which they abound. This is usually the stratum hugging the ground. All evidence points to temperature rises in this layer, the opposite of the popular interpretations of the dust effect. The aerosol and its fallout have other, perhaps much more far-reaching, effects, which are discussed below. Suffice it to say here that man-made dust has not yet had an effect on global climate beyond the "noise" level. Its effect is puny as compared with that of volcanic eruptions, whose dust reaches the high stratosphere, where its optical effect, also, can be appreciable. No documented case has been made for the view that dust storms from deserts or blowing soil have had more than local or regional effects.

Dust that has settled may have a more important effect than dust in suspension. Dust fallen on snow and ice surfaces radically changes the albedo and can lead to melting. Davitaya (1965) has shown that the glaciers of the high Caucasus have an increased dust content which parallels the development of industry in eastern Europe. Up until 1920 the dust content of the glacier was about 10 milligrams per liter. In the 1950s this content increased more than twentyfold, to 235 milligrams per liter. So long as the dust stays near the surface, it should have an appreciable effect on the heat balance of the glacier. There is fairly good evidence, based on tracers such as lead, that dusts from human activities have penetrated the polar regions. Conceivably they might change the albedo of the ice, cause melting, and thus pave the way for a rather radical climatic change—and for a notable rise in sea level. There has been some speculation along this line, but, while these dusts have affected microclimates, there is no evidence of their having had, so far, any measurable influence on the earth's climate.

The possibility of deliberately causing changes in albedo by spreading dust on the Arctic sea ice has figured prominently in discussions of artificial modification of climate. This seems technologically feasible. The consequences for the mosaic of climates in the lower latitudes have not yet been assessed. Present computer models of world climate and the general circulation are far too crude to permit assessment in the detail necessary for ecological judgments.

All of the foregoing discussion applies to the large-scale problems of global climate. On that scale the natural influences definitely have the upper hand. Although monitoring and vigilance are indicated, the evidence for man's effects on global climate is flimsy at best.

THE CLIMATE OF CITIES

This conclusion does not apply on the local scale of cities, however. By far the most pronounced and locally far-reaching effects of man's activities on microclimate have been in cities, as Peterson (1969) and Tyson (1970) have shown. Tyson demonstrates that urban modification of the atmospheric environment occurs in a variety of ways.

The first is by an alteration in the nature of the effective surface: the replacement of the natural surface of soil, grass, and trees by the artificial multiplicity of urban surfaces of brick, concrete, glass, and metal all occurring at different levels above the ground. These artificial materials change the nature of the reflecting and radiating surfaces, the heat exchange near the surface and the aerodynamic roughness of the surface.

Second, towns and cities may generate enormous amounts of heat artificially. At certain times of the year in mid-latitude cities, artificial heat input into the urban atmospheric system by combustion and metabolic processes may approach or even exceed that derived indirectly from the sun. For example, in Hamburg the average production of heat from coal combustion has been estimated as 40 cal/cm^2, whereas radiation from sun and sky on a winter day amounts to only 42 cal/cm^2.

Third, the composition of the atmosphere over cities is significantly altered by the emission of vast amounts of gaseous and solid pollutants into the air. Table 3.1 provides a summary of the major changes in local climate produced by cities, drawn from the pioneering work in the field by H. Landsberg (1961). The most dramatic effect is the creation of the urban heat island,

TABLE 3.1

Climatic changes produced by cities
(after Landsberg, 1961)

Element	Comparison with Rural Environs
Temperature:	
Annual mean	1.0° to 1.5°F higher
Winter minima	2.0° to 3.0°F higher
Relative Humidity:	
Annual mean	6 percent lower
Winter	2 percent lower
Summer	8 percent lower
Dust particles	10 times more
Cloudiness:	
Clouds	5 to 10 percent more
Fog, winter	100 percent more
Fog, summer	30 percent more
Radiation:	
Total on horizontal surface	15 to 20 percent less
Ultraviolet, winter	30 percent less
Ultraviolet, summer	5 percent less
Wind speed:	
Annual mean	20 to 30 percent lower
Extreme gusts	10 to 20 percent lower
Calms	5 to 20 percent more
Precipitation:	
Amounts	5 to 10 percent more
Days with less than 0.2 inch	10 percent more

which serves in particular as a trap for atmospheric pollutants (Figure 3.3).

Recent research has focused on such questions as the effect of city size on heat-island magnitude. Small cities and even small building complexes have been shown to create nocturnal heat islands, and urban-rural differences in temperature have been shown to depend strongly on local microclimatic conditions. In studies of the vertical distribution of temperature over a city, such phenomena as multiple elevated inversions and a downwind urban heat plume have been observed, as in Figure 3.4. Finally, additional research on the determination of meteorological parameters important for heat-island formation has shown that the size of urban-rural temperature differences is highly correlated with the suburban low-level temperature-lapse rate.

Although the recent investigations of relative humidity agree with those shown in Table 3.1, such studies now consider absolute humidity as well. Chandler (1965, 1967a) adequately summarizes the results of such papers. The relative humidity of towns has been shown to be almost always lower than that of adjacent rural areas, whereas urban-rural differences of absolute

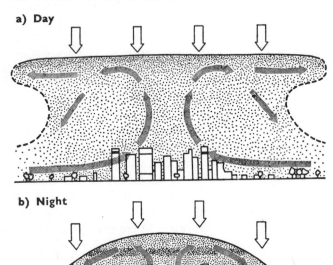

a) Day

b) Night

FIGURE 3.3. Schematic diagram to show the vertical extent of urban heat and pollution domes and the associated city-induced local air circulations that can occur in the absence of strong gradient winds (after Tyson, 1970).

s2

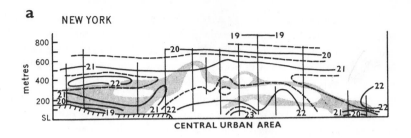

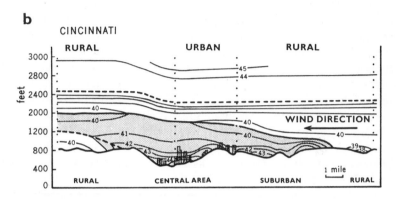

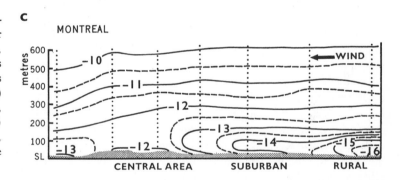

FIGURE 3.4. Vertical temperature distribution (a) over New York on July 16, 1964, 0407–0612 EST, shaded layers indicate elevated inversions (after Bornstein, 1968); (b) over Cincinnati on May 23, 1967 (after Clarke, 1969); (c) over Montreal on March 7, 1969 at 0700 EST (after Oke and East, 1971).

humidity show no such clear-cut relationship. Although weak, a general tendency for drier air is apparent within the city, the frequencies of occurrence of urban vapor pressures above and below those of the country are almost equal.

The conclusions in Table 3.1 on dust-particle concentrations and the occurrence of fog also are generally valid. However, some recent evidence suggests that the frequency of very dense fog in the city center is less than that in outlying regions, possibly because of warmer urban temperatures. Other studies have shown the visibilities are improving in some cities, probably as a result of local efforts at air-pollution abatement.

Recent solar-radiation investigations have substantiated Landsberg's results on the subject. Additional papers have been devoted to urban-rural contrasts, and such aspects as vertical variation of the attenuation of solar radiation and hours of bright sunshine over a city have also been studied.

A modification of Landsberg's results for wind speed may be indicated by the results of a recent study by Chandler (1965). His limited data sample showed that when regional wind speeds were relatively low, speeds over London were higher than those over the countryside, and that fewer calms occurred over the city than over the country. The critical value of wind speed (which determined whether urban or rural winds were faster) usually was between 4 and 5 m/sec^{-1}, though it varied with time of day and season. New work on direction of wind flow has indicated that when conditions are conducive to heat-island formation the wind flow converges toward the city.

Precipitation research has been greatly expanded since the publication of Landsberg's articles. Precipitation patterns around several cities with dense rain-gauge networks have been studied, and small increases were usually found downwind of the cities. Changnon's paper (1968) on the La Porte, Indiana, anomaly, which recorded large increases of precipitation and of days with thunderstorms and hail, has indicated the size of the possible precipitation increase that can result from man's activities. A new research effort has been directed at determining the effects of the many dust particles produced by a city on the development and growth of clouds. Such studies hope to show whether dust particles, which serve as condensation and ice nuclei, act to inhibit or promote rainfall and in what concentrations they are most effective.

Temperature Distribution and the Heat Island

Of all the urban-rural meteorological differences, those of air temperature are probably the most documented. That the center of a city is warmer than its environs, forming a "heat island," has been known for more than a hundred years and continues to receive considerable attention in the literature. Many aspects of a heat island have been studied, such as possible reasons for its occurrence; diurnal weekly, and seasonal variations; relation to city size; and dependence on topography.

The fact that a city is warmer than its environs is seen most readily in a comparison of daily minimum temperatures. As Landsberg (1956) pointed out, such comparisons often show temperature differences of 10°F and occasionally differences as great as 20°F. However, since nocturnal temperatures depend on topography, a fraction of these differences, sometimes a large fraction, can often be ascribed to terrain features.

Numerous measurements of urban heat islands have been made, frequently by use of automobiles to obtain many observations within a short period. An example of a London temperature survey associated with clear skies, light winds, and anticyclonic conditions is presented in Figure 3.5 (Chandler, 1965). This figure shows certain features common to most heat islands. The temperature anomalies are generally related to urban morphology. The highest temperatures are associated with the densely built-up area near the city center; moreover, the degree of warming diminishes slowly, outward from the city's heart, through the suburbs and then decreases markedly at the city periphery (Figure 3.6). The effect of topography is also evident in this example. Urban warming is reduced along the Thames River, in the smaller nonurbanized valleys, and near the city's higher elevations.

Steep temperature gradients at a city's edge have been measured during clear, calm conditions at Hamilton, Ontario (Oke and Hannell, 1968), and Montreal, Quebec (Oke, 1968). These investigators found temperature changes of 3.8 and 4.0 °C/km^{-1}, respectively, which they regarded as typical values for moderate to large cities.

Some recent studies have indicated that the mean annual minimum temperature of a large city may be as much as 4°F higher than that of surrounding rural areas. Chandler (1963, 1966) reported on two studies of London, which showed differences of 3.4 and 4.0°F in mean minimum temperatures at urban and rural sites.

FIGURE 3.5. Minimum temperature distribution in London, May 14, 1959, in °C with °F in brackets (from Chandler, 1965).

FIGURE 3.6. The pronounced outer perimeter (broken line) of London's urban heat island on the night of June 3–4, 1959 (after Chandler, 1965).

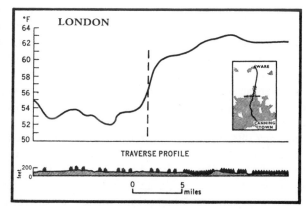

The first study was based on data from 1921 to 1950 for several stations in and around London; the second compared 1959 data for one downtown and one rural location and applied a correction for the difference in elevation at the stations. In another study, Woollum (1964) and Woollum and Canfield (1968) presented data for several stations in the vicinity of Washington, D.C., for a 20-year period; mean minimum temperatures for each season were approximately 4°F higher in downtown areas than in outlying regions.

Although the city heat island as indicated by minimum temperatures can be readily detected year-round, the investigations in London by Chandler (1963, 1966) and in Reading, England, by Parry (1966) indicated that the greatest temperature differences occur in summer or early autumn. Woollum (1964) also found that the mean differences between the warmest and coldest stations of his network were greatest in fall and summer, but that the greatest extreme differences between these stations occurred in winter (see also Landsberg, 1956).

The heat island of a city can be detected during the day but much less readily than during the evening. The slight daytime temperature differences observed are often difficult to distinguish from those due to the effects of topography. In some instances daytime city temperatures may even be lower than those of the suburbs. For example, Landsberg (1956) presented one year of data from city and airport observations in Lincoln, Nebraska, a location essentially free from complicating terrain factors. Daily maxima in the cold season showed little difference between the two sites. During the warm season, however, the airport was more frequently warmer than the downtown site. Such results are not the rule, however, and Landsberg also points out cases of daily maxima that are higher in the city. Similar examples have been given by Chandler (1963, 1966); his data showed that the annual average maximum temperatures of London were 0.6 and 1.1°C higher than those

in the outlying areas. Munn et al. (1969) also readily detected a daytime heat island at Toronto, Canada, using daily maximum temperatures.

A recent report by the Stanford Research Institute (Ludwig, 1967; Ludwig and Kealoha, 1968) presents perhaps the most comprehensive documentation of urban daytime temperatures to date. The authors made about twelve auto traverses each at San Jose, California; Albuquerque, New Mexico; and New Orleans, Louisiana, during daytimes in the summer of 1966. Although the temperature anomalies resulting from topographical influences in these cities were greater than those from the heat island, the downtown areas were approximately 0.5°C warmer than the suburbs despite the effects of topography.

In the summer of 1967 SRI extended the study to Dallas, Fort Worth, and Denton, Texas (population 35,000), where they made 20, 4, and 2 surveys, respectively. When the 1966 and 1967 data were combined with data from three surveys each at Minneapolis, Minnesota, and Winnipeg, Canada (Stanford U. Aerosol Laboratory, 1953a, 1953b, 1953c), and one at London, the investigators found that for these 67 cases the city's warmest part near the downtown area averaged 1.2°C above the typical areas of its environs, with a standard deviation of about 1.0°C. This average value is higher than that observed by other studies, and Ludwig and Kealoha pointed out two possible reasons why investigations of the daytime heat island may underestimate its magnitude. First, they noted that at ground level the highest temperatures of a city do not occur in the central area of tall buildings but rather near that part of the downtown area with "densely packed three- to five-story buildings and parking lots." Second, they noted that temperatures observed at surburban airports were higher than those of a true rural environment, either grass-covered or forested.

The diurnal and seasonal heat-island variations discussed above are illustrated in Figure 3.7 taken from Mitchell (1962). This figure shows

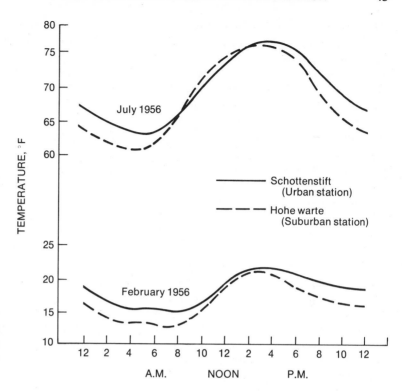

FIGURE 3.7. Diurnal variation of temperature in Vienna for February and July for both an urban and a suburban station (from Mitchell, 1962).

hour-by-hour monthly averages of temperature at an urban and a suburban site in Vienna, Austria. The temperature of the city is higher at night during both February and July, but this urban-rural difference is greater in July. In the daytime, however, the city-rural temperature differences are small during July and consistently small and positive during winter.

The average annual temperatures of a city and its environs, calculated from the daily maxima and minima, also reflect the presence of the urban heat island. Table 3.2 (Landsberg, 1960) lists the

TABLE 3.2

Annual mean urban-rural temperature differences of cities, °C

Chicago	0.6	Moscow	0.7
Washington	0.6	Philadelphia	0.8
Los Angeles	0.7	Berlin	1.0
Paris	0.7	New York	1.1

average annual urban-rural temperature differences for several large cities. To this can be added the average value for London of 1.3°C based on the two studies by Chandler (1963, 1966). Although Woollum and Canfield (1968) do not state a specific number for the mean annual urban-rural temperature differences of Washington, D.C., their recent data for that city indicate that it should be at least 1.0°C, after consideration of the elevation changes of more than 200 feet within the area.

Several urban studies have considered the effect of city size on the magnitude of the heat island. For example, Mitchell (1961, 1962) showed that during this century most major U.S. metropolitan areas have been both expanding and warming. The amount of warming is well correlated with city growth rate. Dronia (1967) compared temperature trends from 67 paired locations around the world, each pair representing an urban and a rural site, usually separated by several hundred kilometers. He found that in the first five decades of this century the urban areas warmed by 0.24°C more than the rural locations. Similarly, Lawrence (1968) noted that from the late 1940s to early 1960s mean daily minimum temperatures at the Manchester, England, airport increased by about 2.0°F relative to nearby rural stations as the urban area expanded beyond the airport. Landsberg's paper (1960) gave 30 years of data for Los Angeles and San Diego, which showed that as the difference in population between those cities increased so did the difference between their mean temperatures.

The relation between city size and urban-rural temperature difference is not linear, however; sizeable nocturnal temperature contrasts have been measured even in relatively small cities. For example, in more than 20 surveys of Palo Alto, California (population 33,000), Duckworth and Sandberg (1954) found that the maximum temperature difference of the survey area was 4 to 6°F. Hutcheon et al. (1967) measured the temperature distribution in Corvallis, Oregon (population 21,000), on two occasions and noted a definite heat island, with maximum temperature differences of 13 and 10°F. Sekiguti (1964) observed a heat island in Ina, Japan (population 12,000). Finally, a heat-island effect resulting even from a small, isolated building complex after sunset has been detected (Landsberg, 1968). In contrast, during the two daytime surveys at Denton, Texas, Ludwig and Kealoha (1968) reported no appreciable difference in the maximum temperatures at the center of town and at its outskirts.

Although general relationships have been developed between heat-island magnitude and some parameter representing city size, be it area, population, or building density, Chandler (1964, 1966, 1967b) has emphasized that the heat-island magnitude at a given location often depends strongly on the local microclimatic conditions. He noted (1968) that data from several English towns showed the strength of the local heat island to be strongly dependent upon the density of urban development very near the observation point, sometimes within a circle as small as 500 meters radius. During nights with strong heat islands, the correlation between the heat island and building density was usually greater than 0.9.

Investigators need detailed knowledge about the vertical distribution of temperature near urban areas to accurately determine the dispersion of pollutants. In three recent investigations, one over New York City (Davidson, 1967; Bornstein, 1968), one over Cincinnati (Clarke, 1969), and one over Johannesburg, S. Africa (Tyson et al., 1972), helicopters have been used to measure the three-dimensional, nocturnal temperature patterns over a city. Besides recording multiple elevated inversions over New York City, Davidson and Bornstein observed that a ground-based inversion was present over the outlying areas, while over the city temperatures were generally higher than those over the countryside from the surface up to about 300 meters. At heights around 400 meters temperatures over the city were generally lower than those of the surrounding area. This finding is similar to those of Duckworth and Sandberg (1954), who noted a "crossover" of the urban and rural temperatures on about half of their wiresonde data.

Clarke has studied vertical temperature distributions in Cincinnati both upwind and downwind of the city. Figure 3.8 shows an example from one of his surveys. On clear evenings, with light consistent surface winds, he found a strong surface-based inversion upwind of the urban area. Over the built-up region, lapse conditions occurred in the lowest 200 feet, while downwind of the urban area a strong inversion was again observed at the surface. Above this inversion, weak lapse conditions prevailed, which Clarke interpreted as the downwind effect of the city. This "urban heat plume" was detectable by

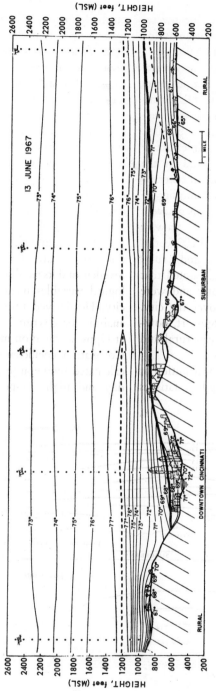

FIGURE 3.8. Cross section of temperature (°F) over metropolitan Cincinnati about an hour before sunrise on June 13, 1967. The heavy solid line indicates the top of the urban boundary layer and the dashed lines indicate a temperature discontinuity with less stable air above. Wind flow was from left to right (from Clarke, 1969).

vertical temperature measurements for several miles in the lee of the city. The findings for Johannesburg are reported in Figure 3.9.

Other authors have investigated the vertical distribution of nighttime urban temperatures with tower-mounted instruments. DeMarrais (1961) compared lapse rates in Louisville between 60 and 524 feet with typical rural profiles. During the warm half of the year, while surface inversions were regularly encountered in the country, nearly 60 percent of the urban observations showed a weak lapse rate and another 15 percent showed weak lapse conditions above a superadiabatic lapse rate. Munn and Stewart (1967) instrumented towers at 20 and 200 feet in central Montreal, suburban Ottawa, and a rural location near Sarnia, Canada. They noted that inversions occurred more frequently and were stronger over the country than over the city. Both DeMarrais, and Munn and Stewart, however, found little difference between rural and urban daytime temperature profiles.

In another study of the vertical distribution of temperature, Hosler (1961) compiled statistics on the frequency of inversions based below 500 feet above station elevation for selected United States localities and discussed the dependence of these data on season, cloud cover, wind speed, time of day, and geographic location. Since he used radiosonde data, which are usually taken at an airport on the outskirts of a city, his results are generally representative of suburban locations and thus underestimate the inversion frequencies of rural sites and overestimate those of cities.

In addition to city size the magnitude of the urban heat island has been shown to depend upon various meteorological parameters. An early study of this type was made by Sundborg (1950), who investigated the relation between the temperature difference between Uppsala, Sweden, and its rural surroundings and meteorological variables measured at the edge of the city. He derived two equations by regression analysis for daytime and nighttime conditions at Uppsala, based on more than 200 sets of data. Correlation coefficients between observed and calculated temperatures were 0.49 and 0.66 for day and night, respectively. At night, wind

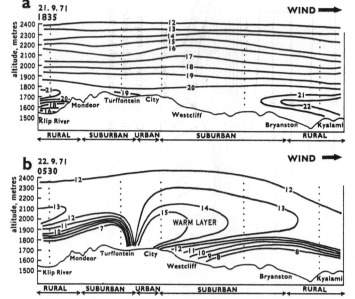

FIGURE 3.9. Vertical temperature structure in a north-south section over Johannesburg on the night of September 21–22, 1971. Temperatures are in °C; wind direction at 0530 was southerly with a speed of 6.0 m/sec^{-1} at an altitude of 1600 and 6.0 m/sec^{-1} at 2400 m; skies were clear.

speed and cloud cover were the most important variables for determining the heat island magnitude.

Chandler (1965) made a similar study based on temperature differences of daily maxima and minima at city and country sites for London and meteorological data observed at London airport. The multiple correlation coefficients for the four equations are 0.608, 0.563, 0.286, and 0.114 for nighttime (summer and winter) and daytime (summer and winter), respectively, an indication that the equations are much better estimators for nocturnal than for daytime conditions. The magnitude of the heat island was shown to depend on wind speed and cloud amount at night, whereas no meteorological variables were found to be particularly significant during the day.

Ludwig and Kealoha (1968) estimated the the magnitude of a city's heat island by using the near-surface temperature-lapse rate, which was usually measured in the environs of the city or at a radiosonde facility of a nearby city. They found this single variable to be highly correlated with the heat-island magnitude, thus providing a simple, accurate method for predicting urban-rural temperature differences. These investigators compiled data from 78 nocturnal heat-island surveys from a dozen cities and estimated the heat-island magnitude by subtracting a typical rural temperature from the highest temperature in the city's center. Examples of their results, stratified by city population, are as follows:

$$\Delta T = 1.3 - 6.78\gamma$$
$$\text{population} < 500,000; \quad (1)$$
$$\Delta T = 1.7 - 7.24\gamma \quad = 500,000 \text{ to } 2 \text{ million}; \quad (2)$$
$$\Delta T = 2.6 - 14.8\gamma \quad > 2 \text{ million}; \quad (3)$$

where the lapse rate, γ, is the temperature change with pressure ($°C/mb^{-1}$)—i.e., a surface-based inversion is represented by negative γ. Correlation coefficients between ΔT and γ for the three cases are -0.95, -0.80, and -0.87, and the root-mean-square errors are ±0.66, ±1.0, and $\pm0.96°C$, respectively. Thus, the resulting equations of this example will usually predict ΔT to within $\pm2.0°C$.

Another meteorological parameter that influences heat island development is wind speed. When the regional wind speed is above a critical value, a heat island cannot be detected. Table 3.3, taken from Oke and Hannell (1968), summarizes several reports on the relation between city population (P) and this critical wind speed (U). Log P and U are highly correlated (0.97), and their relationship is described by the regression equation:

$$U = -11.6 + 3.4 \log P. \quad (4)$$

The authors used this equation to estimate the

TABLE 3.3

Critical wind speeds for elimination of the heat island effect in various cities

City	Author	Year of Survey	Population	Critical Wind Speed, m/sec⁻¹
London, England	Chandler (1962a)	1959–61	8,500,000	12
Montreal, Canada	Oke, et al.[a]	1967–68	2,000,000	11
Bremen, Germany	Mey	1933	400,000	8
Hamilton, Canada	Oke, et al.[a]	1965–66	300,000	6–8
Reading, England	Parry (1956)	1951–52	120,000	4–7
Kumagaya, Japan	Kawamura	1956–57	50,000	5
Palo Alto, California	Duckworth, et al.	1951–52	33,000	3–5

[a] Unpublished.

smallest-sized city that would form a heat island. When $U = 0$, equation (4) yields a population of about 2500. Although they had no data to test this estimate, they recognized that the scatter of their data points increased at the smaller populations and that sometimes even small building complexes produced measurable heat-island effects.

Landsberg (1970c) demonstrates the latter using air and infrared surface-temperature measurements. An example is given in Figure 3.10. The observations represented by the curves of Figure 3.10 were made in a paved court enclosed by low-level structures which were surrounded by grass and vegetated surfaces. On clear, relatively calm evenings the heat island develops in the court, fed by heat stored in the daytime under the asphalted parking space of the court and the building walls. This slows down the radiative cooling process, relative to cooling from a grass surface, and keeps the air that is in

contact with the surface warmer than that over the grass.

The heat island expands and intensifies as a city grows, and stronger and stronger winds are needed to overcome it. Although it is most pronounced on calm, clear nights, the effect is still evident in the long-term mean values.

The location of the highest city temperatures also depends on local meteorology. Munn et al. (1969) noted that at Toronto, Canada, the position of the daytime heat island was strongly influenced by the regional and lake breeze windflow patterns of the area and was often displaced downwind of the city center.

It is generally accepted that two primary processes are involved in the formation of an urban heat island, both of which are seasonally dependent (see, for example, Mitchell, 1962). First, in summer the tall buildings, pavement, and concrete of the inner city absorb and store larger amounts of solar radiation (because of

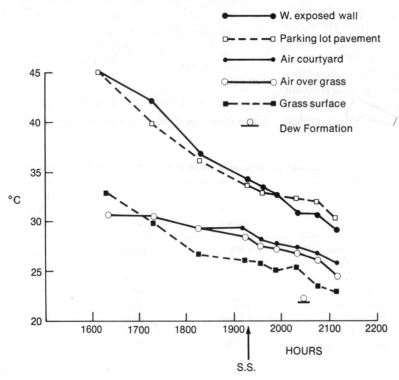

FIGURE 3.10. A typical example of microclimatic heat island formation in incipient urbanization. The top two curves show radiative temperatures of wall and parking lot pavement on a clear summer evening (August 6, 1968). The two middle curves show air temperatures (at elevation of 2 meters) in the paved courtyard and over an adjacent grass surface; from sunset (s. s.) onward, the courtyard is warmer than the air over the grass. The bottom (dashed) curve gives the radiative temperature of grass. The symbol at 2030 hours indicates the start of dew formation.

their geometry and high thermal admittance) than do the vegetation and soil typical of rural areas. In addition, much less of this energy is used for evaporation in the city than in the country because of the large amount of runoff of precipitation from streets and buildings. At night, while both the city and countryside cool by radiative losses, the urban man-made construction material gradually gives off the additional heat accumulated during the day, keeping urban air warmer than that of the outlying areas.

In winter a different process dominates. Since the sun angle at mid-latitudes is low and lesser amounts of solar radiation reach the earth, man-made energy becomes a significant addition to the solar energy naturally received. Artificial heat results from: combustion for home heating, power generation, industry, transportation, and human and animal metabolism. This energy reaches and warms the urban atmosphere directly or indirectly, by passing through imperfectly insulated homes and buildings. This process is most effective when light winds and poor dispersion prevail.

Many authors have investigated the magnitude of man-made energy in metropolitan areas. In two often-cited older studies for Berlin and Vienna (see Kratzer, 1956), the annual heat produced artificially in the built-up area equalled one-third (for Berlin) and one-sixth to one-fourth (for Vienna) of that received from solar radiation. More recently, Garnett and Bach (1965) estimated the annual average man-made heat from Sheffield, England (population 500,000), to be approximately one-third of the net all-wave radiation available at the ground. Bornstein (1968) reported results from a similar study of densely built-up Manhattan. During the winter the amount of heat produced from combustion alone was two and one-half times greater than that of the solar energy reaching the ground, but during the summer this factor dropped to one-sixth.

Projection of energy rejection into the next decades leads to values we should ponder. One estimate indicates that in the year 2000 the Boston-to-Washington megalopolis will have 56 million people living within an area of 30,000 square kilometers. The heat rejection will be about 65 calories per square centimeter per day. In winter this is about 50 percent, and in summer 15 percent, of the heat received by solar radiation on a horizontal surface. The eminent French geophysicist J. Coulomb (1970) has discussed the implications of doubling the energy consumption in France every ten years; this would lead to unbearable temperatures. It is one of a large number of reasons for achieving, as rapidly as possible, a steady state in population and in power needs.

In addition to the two seasonal primary causes of heat islands, other factors are important year-round. The "blanket" of pollutants over a city, including particulates, water vapor, and carbon dioxide, absorbs part of the upward-directed thermal radiation emitted at the surface. Part of this radiation is reemitted downward and retained by the ground; another part warms the ambient air, a process that tends to increase the low-level stability over the city, enhancing the probability of higher pollutant concentrations. Thus, airborne pollutants not only cause a more intense heat island but alter the vertical temperature structure in a way that hinders their dispersion.

Reduced wind speed within an urban area, a result of the surface roughness of the city, also affects the heat island. The lower wind speeds decrease the city's ventilation, inhibiting both the movement of cooler outside air over the city center and the evaporation processes within the city.

Tag (1968) used a numerical model of the energy balance at the atmosphere-ground interface to investigate the relative importance of albedo, soil moisture content, soil diffusivity, and soil heat capacity on urban-rural temperature differences. The author found that during the day the lower city values of albedo and soil moisture caused higher urban temperatures, whereas the higher diffusivity and heat capacity of the city surface counteracted this tendency. At night, however, the relative warmth of the city was primarily the result of the higher urban values of soil diffusivity and heat capacity.

Humidity and Visibility

Even though little research has been done on humidity, the consensus of urban climatologists is that the average relative humidity in towns is several percent lower than that of nearby rural areas, whereas the average absolute humidity is only slightly lower in built-up regions. The main reason to expect differences in the humidity of urban and rural areas is that the evaporation rate in a city is lower than that in the country because of the markedly different surfaces. The countryside is covered with vegetation, which retains rainfall, whereas the floor of a city is coated with concrete, asphalt, and other impervious materials that cause rapid runoff of precipitation. Although the city's low evaporation rates result from the shortage of available water and the lack of vegetation for evapotranspiration, some moisture is added to urban atmospheres by the many combustion sources.

Variations of relative humidity within metropolitan areas resemble those of temperature, since the spatial temperature changes of a city are significantly greater than those of vapor pressure. Thus, because of the heat island, relative humidities in a city are lower than in the suburbs and outlying districts. The humidity differences are greater at night and in summer, corresponding to the time of greatest heat-island intensity (Chandler, 1967a). Other studies have yielded similar findings. Sasakura (1965), reporting on one year of data from Tokyo, showed a value in the suburbs that concurs with Landsberg's average figure. Chandler (1965) also found a 5 percent difference in the relative humidity of a downtown and a rural site near London. In other work (1962b, 1967a) he has presented nocturnal relative humidity profiles across London and maps of spatial distribution for Leicester, England. These show the dependence of relative humidity variations on the form of the city's heat island, which in turn depends upon the density of the built-up complex. Typical humidities of 90 to 100 percent were noted in rural areas during conditions favorable to heat-island formation, whereas in the heart of the city humidity values were approximately 70 to 80 percent. Because of the temperature dependence, when the magnitude of the heat island was small, the urban-rural humidity differences were also small.

Although Chandler (1965) found that the mean annual vapor pressure in London was slightly lower (0.2 mb) than that at a nearby rural location, he (1962b, 1967a) frequently observed that at night the urban absolute humidity was higher than in the outlying regions. Furthermore, variations of humidity within the city often directly corresponded to building density, especially when the meteorological conditions were conducive to heat-island formation.

Humidity levels and visibility are closely related. One situation, based on visibility data at Leeuwarden on the Netherlands coast, indicated that for similar relative humidities the visibility was much lower when the wind was from the continent (with high concentrations of condensation nuclei) than when the wind was from the sea (with low concentrations of nuclei). An example of the relationship between air pollution and visibility has been given by Georgii and Hoffman (1966), who showed that for two German cities low visibilities and high concentrations of SO_2 were highly correlated when low wind speeds and low-level inversions prevailed. McNulty (1968) pointed out that between 1949 and 1960 the occurrence of haze as an obstruction to visibility at New York City increased markedly as a result of increased air pollution.

As part of his general summary Landsberg (1956) presented visibility data from Detroit Municipal Airport (6 miles from downtown) and the Wayne County Airport (17 miles from town). During conditions conducive to the formation of city smogs (winds of 5 miles per hour or less) visibilities less than one mile were observed an average of 149 hours per year at the Municipal Airport but only 89 hours at the rural site. The cause of these low visibilities was listed as smoke in 49 of the observations at the Municipal Airport but in only 5 at the County Airport; most of the occurrences of low visibility were during the late fall and winter. Landsberg (1960) summarized urban-rural fog differences

by noting that metropolitan areas had 100 percent more fog in winter and 30 percent more in summer. In another study, Smith (1961) compiled the number of occurrences of visibilities less than $6\frac{1}{4}$ miles for locations throughout England in the afternoon, the time of least likelihood of fog (Figure 3.11). He found that industrial areas reported low visibilities on two to three times more days than did the rural areas.

Although fog generally occurs more frequently in metropolitan areas, this is not true for very dense fog. Chandler (1965) attributed the high

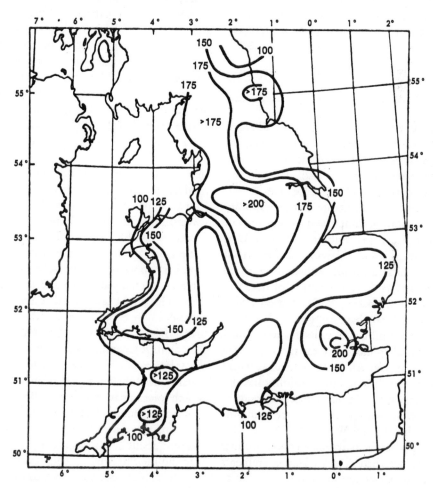

FIGURE 3.11. Average number of days per year with afternoon visibilities less than $6\frac{1}{4}$ miles in England and Wales (from Smith, 1961).

frequencies of fog within a city to atmospheric pollution and relatively low wind speeds, but the extra warmth of a city often prevents the thickest nocturnal fogs from reaching the densities reported in the outlying districts. Table 3.4,

TABLE 3.4

Fog frequencies in London

	Hours per Year with Visibility Less Than			
	40 m	200 m	400 m	1000 m
Kingsway (central)	19	126	230	940
Kew (inner suburbs)	79	213	365	633
London Airport (outer suburbs)	46	209	304	562
Southeast England (mean of 7 stations)	20	177	261	494

presented by Chandler from data of Shellard (1959), shows the estimated hours per year of various density fog in the city center. These same general relationships were also detected by Brazell (1964) using similar London data.

A few recent reports indicate that the visibility in many locations has improved during the last two decades. The better visibilities of major U.S. cities have been associated with local efforts at air-pollution abatement and substitution of oil and gas for soft coal in production of heat (see Holzworth, 1962; Beebe, 1967). Brazell (1964) and Freeman (1968) have suggested that London's improved visibility may be due to enforcement of the air-pollution ordinances of 1954 and 1956. Similarly, Atkins (1968) and Corfield and Newton (1968) found that visibility has also improved near other English cities as a result of air pollution legislation. In another study of London, Commins and Waller (1967) compiled data showing that the particulate content of that city's atmosphere had decreased. Measurements from downtown London showed that the average smoke concentration from 1959 to 1964 was 32 percent lower than that from 1954 to 1959.

Visibility is not improving in all United States cities. A study by Green and Battan (1967) has shown that from 1949 to 1965 the frequency of occurrence of poor visibility at Tucson, Arizona, definitely increased and was significantly correlated with that city's population.

Radiation

The blanket of particulates over most large cities causes the solar energy that reaches an urban complex to be significantly less than that observed in rural areas—a major consequence of air pollution. The particles are most effective as attenuators of radiation when the sun angle is low, since the path length of the radiation passing through the particulate material is dependent on sun elevation. Thus, for a given amount of particulates, solar radiation will be reduced by the largest fraction at high-latitude cities and during the winter. Landsberg (1960) summarized the average annual effect of cities on the solar radiation they received as follows: the average annual total (direct plus diffuse) solar radiation received on a horizontal surface is decreased by 15 to 20 percent, and the ultraviolet (short-wavelength) radiation is decreased by 30 percent in winter and by 5 percent in summer.

De Boer (1966) based a recent study on this topic on two years of global solar radiation measurements at six stations in and around Rotterdam. The study showed that the city center received 3 to 6 percent less radiation than the urban fringe and 13 to 17 percent less than the country. Chandler (1965), also reporting on the solar energy values in the heart of smoky urban areas, observed that from November to March solar radiation at several British cities was 25 to 55 percent less than in nearby rural areas. In addition, the central part of London annually received about 270 hours less of bright sunshine than did the surrounding countryside because of the high concentration of atmospheric particulates.

Further emphasizing the dependence of the

transfer of solar radiation on the air's smoke content, the study of Mateer (1961) showed that the average annual energy received in Toronto, Canada, was 2.8 percent greater on Sunday than during the remainder of the week. Moreover, the Sunday increase during the heating season, October through April, was 6.0 percent but was only 0.8 percent in all other months.

The investigations of atmospheric turbidity by McCormick and Baulch (1962) and McCormick and Kurfis (1966), which were based on aircraft measurements of the intensity of solar radiation, provided data on the variation of solar energy with height over Cincinnati. These authors observed that pollutants over the city, which often had a layered structure and were dependent on the vertical temperature profile, significantly reduced the amount of solar energy that reached the city surface. In addition, they discussed changes of the vertical variation of turbidity (or solar radiation) from morning to afternoon, from day to day, and from clean air to polluted air. Roach (1961) and Sheppard (1958) have also studied attenuation of solar radiation by atmospheric dust particles. They concurred that most radiation scattered by these particles is directed forward and thus attenuation of total solar radiation is primarily due to absorption. Roach estimated that over "heavily polluted areas" absorption of solar energy by the particles was of sufficient magnitude to cause atmospheric heating rates in excess of 10°C per day. A discussion of optical properties of smoke particles is presented in a report by Conner and Hodkinson (1967).

The introduction of smoke controls in London during the mid-1950s has afforded an opportunity to check the radiation-smoke relation. Monteith (1966) summarized data on particulate concentration and solar energy at Kingsway (central London) for the years 1957 to 1963. During this time smoke density decreased by 10 $\mu g/m^{-3}$ while total solar radiation increased by about 1 percent. The average smoke concentration of 80 $\mu g/m^{-3}$ at Kew (inner suburbs) represents an energy decrease of about 8 percent, and in the center of town, where smoke concentrations average 200 to 300 $\mu g/m^{-3}$, the income of solar radiation was about 20 to 30 percent less than that in nearby rural areas. Similarly, Jenkins (1969) reported that the frequency of bright sunshine in London also increased in recent years after implementation of the air-pollution laws. During the period 1958 to 1967 the average number of hours of bright sunshine from November through January was 50 percent greater than that observed from 1931 to 1960.

Measurements of ultraviolet radiation in downtown Los Angeles and on Mt. Wilson (Nader, 1965) showed its dependence on the cleanliness of the atmosphere. Attenuation of ultraviolet radiation by the lowest 5350 feet of the atmosphere averaged 14 percent on no-smog days; when smog was present, attenuation increased to a maximum of 58 percent. Reduced values of ultraviolet radiation in Los Angeles were also measured by Stair (1966). He presented an example in which the effect of smog was to decrease the amount of ultraviolet radiation received at the ground by 50 percent, and he also noted that on "extremely smoggy days" the decrease may be 90 percent or more.

Wind Speed and Direction

The flow of wind over an urban area differs in several aspects from that over the surrounding countryside. Two features that represent deviations from the regional wind flow patterns are the differences in wind speeds in city and country and the convergence of low-level wind over a city. These differences occur because the surface of a built-up city is much rougher than that of rural terrain—exerting increased frictional drag on air flowing over it—and because the heat island of a city causes horizontal thermal gradients, especially near the city periphery. The excess heat and friction also produce more turbulence over the urban area. These general ideas were discussed by Landsberg (1956, 1960); he stated that the annual mean surface wind speed over a city was 20 to 30 percent lower than that over the nearby countryside, that the speed of extreme gusts was 10 to 20 percent lower, and that calms were 5 to 20 percent more frequent. Since then several investigations have refined and expanded the studies summarized by Landsberg. Readers interested in a comprehensive and detailed review of wind flow over a city are directed to a paper by Munn (1968).

A difficulty in estimating urban-rural wind differences is the selection of representative sites within the city from which to take measurements. Most observations of urban wind flow have been taken either from the roofs of downtown buildings, usually several stories high, or from parks or open spaces, whereas very few data have been obtained at street level in the city center, where most human activity occurs. However, these conventional measurements are generally representative of the gross wind flow patterns over a city, and as long as their limitations are recognized they can be useful for urban-rural comparisons.

Although recent reports have concurred that the average wind speed within a city is lower than that over nearby rural areas (Frederick, 1964; Munn and Stewart, 1967; Graham, 1968), the study reported by Chandler (1965) for London shows significant variation from this general rule. Although his analysis is based on only two years of data, it indicates that differences in urban and rural wind speeds depend on time of day, season, and wind speed magnitude. Some of these relations are brought out in Table 3.5 (taken from Chandler, 1965), which summarizes the mean wind speeds at London Airport (on the fringe of the city) and indicates their excess over the values recorded at Kingsway (in central London). The data show that when the regional wind speeds are light (typically at night) the speeds in downtown London are higher than those at the airport, whereas when wind speeds are relatively high, higher speeds

are recorded at the airport. This is evident in comparison of the daytime and nighttime wind speeds given in Table 3.5.

TABLE 3.5

Average wind speeds at London Airport and differences from those at Kingsway, m/sec^{-1}

	0100 GMT		1300 GMT	
	Mean Speed	Excess Speed	Mean Speed	Excess Speed
December–February	2.5	−0.4	3.1	0.4
March–May	2.2	−0.1	3.1	1.2
June–August	2.0	−0.6	2.7	0.7
September–November	2.1	−0.2	2.6	0.6
Year	2.2	−0.3	2.9	0.7

Chandler (1965) attributes this diurnal variation of urban influence to the diurnal differences of regional wind speed and atmospheric stability. At night when surface winds are relatively calm, the stability is much greater in the country, where inversions are common, than in the metropolitan area, where lapse conditions may prevail. This relative instability in the city, combined with the greater surface roughness, enhances turbulence and allows the faster-moving winds above the urban area to reach the surface more frequently; thus at night the average city wind speeds tend to be greater than those of the country. During the day, however, with faster regional winds, the frictional effect of the rough city surface dominates the turbulence effect, and lower wind speeds are observed within the built-up area.

The critical value of wind speed that determines whether the urban winds will be faster or slower than those of the country is highest during summer nights and during both day and night in winter (about 5.0 to 5.5 m/sec^{-1}). These are times of relatively high atmospheric stability. The lowest values of critical speed (about 3.5 m/sec^{-1}) occur during summer and fall days. Moreover, the magnitude of the decrease in urban wind speeds is greatest during spring days and least during spring nights.

Chandler (1965) summarized the wind-speed statistics for London by noting that the annual average urban and suburban speeds were lower than those of the outlying regions but only by about 5 percent. However, the annual differences between wind speeds in the center of London and in the outlying areas were somewhat greater. For these locations, when speeds were more than 1.5 m/sec^{-1} the average difference was about 13 percent, whereas for speeds greater than 7.9 m/sec^{-1} the mean difference was only 7 percent. In summer, little difference between average city and rural wind speeds was evident. Light regional winds (1.5 m/sec^{-1} or less), which increase in speed over the city, occur more frequently in summer and compensate for the occurrences of strong rural winds, which decrease over the city. Finally, in contrast to the earlier figures reported by Landsberg, the London data showed that fewer calms and light winds occurred in the city center than in rural regions.

Past research on the direction of wind flow over urban areas has been primarily concerned with detecting and measuring a surface flow in toward the urban complex. It has been surmised for some time that if a city is warmer than its environs, the warm city air should rise and be displaced by cooler rural air. However, this inflow is weak and occurs only in conjunction with well-developed heat islands, which in turn are dependent on certain meteorological conditions. Since direct measurements of the inflow require a coordinated set of accurate observations, few such investigations have been made.

Pooler (1963) analyzed wind records from the Louisville local air-pollution study and determined that there was indeed a surface inflow of air toward the city. This inflow was the dominant feature of the surface windflow pattern when the regional winds were weak, a situation that could result, for example, from a weak large-scale pressure gradient. Georgii (1968)

reported on urban wind measurements in Frankfort/Main, Germany. During clear, calm nights an inflow toward the city center was detected, with a convergent wind velocity of up to 2 to 4 m/sec^{-1}. He also noted that when the large-scale surface geostrophic wind speed reached 3 to 4 m/sec^{-1} a local city circulation was prevented from becoming established, although the increased roughness of the city was still affecting the wind regime.

Measurements of the wind flow around an oil refinery in the Netherlands have been reported by Schmidt (1963) and by Schmidt and Boer (1963). Although the area involved (4 km^2) was much smaller than that of a moderate-sized city and the heat produced by the refinery per unit area was considerably greater than that of a city, the general relationships are of interest. A cyclonic circulation occurred around the area, with convergence toward the center. Furthermore, ascending air was detected over the center of the area, with descending currents over the surroundings. The greatest vertical velocities measured in the vicinity of the maximum heat production were about 15 cm/sec^{-1}.

Vertical wind velocities were obtained from low-level tetroon flights over New York City by Hass et al. (1967) and Angell et al. (1968). They observed an upward flow over densely built-up Manhattan Island and a downward motion over the adjacent Hudson and East Rivers. They ascribed this flow pattern to the urban heat island, to the barrier effect of the tall buildings, and to the relatively cool river water. Low-level convergence over a city has also been detected by Okita (1960, 1965), who applied two novel techniques. For one study he utilized the fact that rime ice formed on the windward side of tree trunks and the thickness of the ice was proportional to wind speed. For the other (Figure 3.12) he observed the smoke plumes from household chimneys. By observing these features around the periphery of Asahikawa, Japan, he deduced the local wind flow patterns and determined that when the large-scale wind

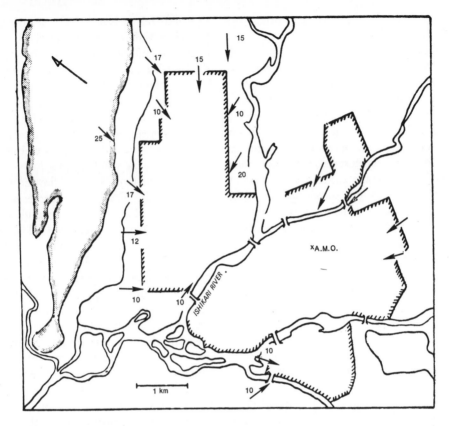

FIGURE 3.12. Direction of wind flow around Asahikawa, Japan, February 26, 1956, as deduced from formation of rime ice on tree branches (from Okita, 1960).

flow was weak there was a convergence over the city.

As a final consideration of urban wind flow, Chandler's observations (1960, 1961) on the periphery of London and Leicester are of interest. Chandler noted that when a well-developed nocturnal heat island formed with a strong temperature gradient near the edge of the built-up area, winds flowed inward toward the city center, but the flow was not steady. Rather, movement of cold air from the country toward the city occurred as pulsations, the strongest winds occurring when the temperature gradient was strongest.

Precipitation

A city also influences the occurrence and amount of precipitation in its vicinity. For several reasons an urban complex might be expected to increase precipitation. Combustion sources add to the amount of water vapor in the atmosphere, higher temperatures intensify thermal convection, greater surface roughness increases mechanical turbulence, and the urban atmosphere contains greater concentrations of condensation and ice nuclei. Since no continuous, quantitative measurements of these various parameters have been made in conjunction with the few urban precipitation studies, the relative significance of these factors is not easy to establish. Landsberg (1956, 1959) gave several European examples of urban rural comparisons and concluded that the amount of precipitation over a city is about 10 percent greater than that over nearby country areas. More recent studies have shown that his conclusion may be an oversimplification and that the greatest positive anomalies occur downwind of the city center.

The effects of cities on precipitation are difficult to determine for several reasons. First, very few rural areas remain undisturbed from their natural state. Second, there is a lack of rain gauges in metropolitan areas, especially instruments with long-term records and uniform exposure throughout the record. Third, many cities are associated with bodies of water or hilly terrain, and these also affect the patterns of precipitation. Finally, the natural variability of rainfall, particularly the summer showers of mid-America, further complicates the analysis of urban-rural precipitation differences. An example of the difficulty of rainfall analysis is the study of Spar and Ronberg (1968). They observed that the record from Central Park, New York City, showed a significant decreasing trend of precipitation of 0.3 inch per year from 1927 to 1965. This trend was not substantiated by data from other nearby sites; at Battery Place, the nearest station, a small rainfall increase was observed during the period.

A very striking example of the effect of the Chicago urban region on local precipitation has been documented by Changnon (1968a). He showed that at La Porte, Indiana, some 30 miles downwind of a large industrial complex between Chicago and Gary, Indiana, the amount of precipitation and the number of days with thunderstorms and hail have increased markedly since 1925. Furthermore, the year-to-year variation of precipitation at La Porte agrees generally with the data on the production of steel and number of smoke-haze days at Chicago (Figure

3.13). During the period from 1951 to 1965 the positive anomalies at La Porte were 31 percent for precipitation, 38 percent for thunderstorm days, 246 percent for hail days, and 34 percent for days with precipitation greater than 0.25 inch. These results are summarized in Table 3.6. Changnon concluded that these observed differences were a real effect of the industrial area and that they represent the general size of precipitation increase that is possible as a result of man's activities. However, because of the effect of Lake Michigan and its associated lake breeze in channeling the pollutants around the south end of the lake toward the La Porte area and inhibiting dispersion, the large differences detected in this study probably are not representative of American cities in general.

Changnon (1961, 1962, 1968b, 1969) has summarized precipitation data for several other midwestern cities and detected positive increases, but not nearly as pronounced as those at La Porte. In St. Louis, Chicago, Champaign-Urbana, Illinois, and Tulsa, Oklahoma, the city precipitation was 5 to 8 percent higher than the average of nearby rural stations. At St. Louis and Champaign-Urbana the rainfall maxima were downwind of the urban center. The increase of 5 percent at Chicago proper represents a relative maximum over the city and is distinct from the higher precipitation rates downwind of Chicago at La Porte. Spatial data were not available for Tulsa. Table 3.6 (from Changnon, 1968b) shows that the percentage precipitation increase is greater during the cold season and that increases in the warm season result from more days of moderate rain and thunderstorms.

Authors do not totally agree on the distribution of precipitation over cities. The rainfall minimum over the Missouri half of metropolitan St. Louis detected by Changnon (1968b) was also noted by Feig (1968), who observed that a map of isohyets of annual precipitation over the eastern United States showed that minimum precipitation areas occur around most

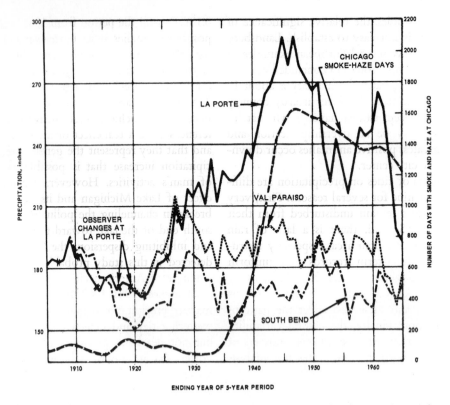

FIGURE 3.13. Five-year moving totals of precipitation at several Indiana stations and smoke-haze days at Chicago (from Changnon, 1968a).

TABLE 3.6

Summary of urban area increases in precipitation and related conditions (Expressed as a percent of rural values)

	Chicago	La Porte	St. Louis	Tulsa	Champaign–Urbana
Annual precipitation	5	31	7	8	5
Warmer half-year precipitation	4	30	a	5	4
Colder half-year precipitation	6	33	a	11	8
Rain days ≥ 0.01 or 0.1 inch					
Annual	6	0	a	a	7
Warmer half-year	8	0	a	a	3
Colder half-year	4	0	a	a	10
Rain days ≥ 0.25 or 0.5 inch					
Annual	5	34	a	a	5
Warmer half-year	7	54	a	a	9
Colder half-year	0	5	a	a	0
Annual number of thunderstorm days	6	38	11	a	7
Summer number of thunderstorm days	13	63	21	a	17

a Data not sufficient for comparison.

cities having no obvious geographic influences. The annual precipitation pattern at Washington, D.C. (Woollum and Canfield, 1968), also shows low values downtown along the Potomac River, with the greatest amounts of precipitation on the north to northwest side of town and with relative maxima in both the eastern and western suburbs (Figure 3.14). On the other hand, Dettwiller (1968) has indicated that the effect of a city is to increase precipitation. He showed that from 1953 to 1967 the average rainfall in Paris was 31 percent greater on weekdays than on Saturdays and Sundays.

Another reason for believing that more precipitation falls over metropolitan districts is that heavy thundershowers sometimes occur over an area that roughly coincides with the urban complex (Staff, 1964; Chandler, 1965; Atkinson, 1968). However, it is always difficult to determine whether a thundershower was a natural event or whether the city actually influenced it in any way.

Although it is hard to determine the relative importance of the several urban factors that affect precipitation, the extensive studies by Changnon (1968b) led him to the following conclusions about the city-precipitation relationship. Two factors were probably most effective in enhancing precipitation at La Porte— high concentrations of ice nuclei from nearby steel mills and added heat from local industrial sources. Because of the high frequency of noc-

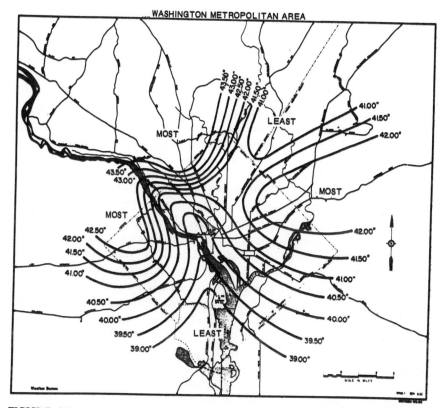

FIGURE 3.14. Mean annual precipitation (inches) over the Washington, D.C., metropolitan area (from Woollum and Canfield, 1968).

turnal thunderstorms and hailstorms at La Porte, he concluded that the thermal and frictional effects were probably the most significant. In addition, the precipitation maximum associated with Champaign-Urbana, an area with little industry and a minimum of nuclei sources, also indicated that the thermal and frictional factors could produce significant differences.

Many recent studies have concentrated on measuring condensation and ice nuclei and determining their possible influence on cloud development and precipitation. Measurements showing that cities are an important source of nuclei were reported by Mee (1968). Typical concentrations of cloud droplets and condensation nuclei at the convective cloud base near Puerto Rico were 50 cm^{-3} in the clean air over the ocean, about 200 cm^{-3} over the unpolluted countryside, and from 1000 to 1500 cm^{-3} immediately downwind of San Juan. Abnormally high concentrations were detected for at least 100 miles downwind of the city. In another study, Squires (1966) pointed out that measurements of condensation nuclei over Denver showed that the concentrations of these nuclei produced by human activities were similar to the natural concentration there. Moreover, Telford (1960), Langer (1963), and Langer et al. (1967) observed that industrial areas, and in particular steel mills, are good sources of ice nuclei. Finally, Schaefer (1966, 1968a) and others (Morgan, 1967; Morgan and Allee, 1968; Hogan, 1967) have shown that lead particles in ordinary auto exhaust form effective ice nuclei when combined with iodine vapor.

Even though cities are generally recognized as good sources of nuclei, the net effect of such nuclei cannot be definitely determined. For example, a few ice nuclei added to supercooled clouds may enhance rainfall, a principle used by commercial cloud seeders. On the other hand, rain that falls from warm clouds is dependent on a number of large drops within a cloud so that coalescence may be effective. If large numbers of condensation nuclei are introduced into a warm cloud, many small drops will form and thus rainfall may be inhibited (Gunn and Phillips, 1957; Squires and Twomey, 1960).

Many examples in the literature show that rainfall can be artificially increased, whereas only a few show decreases. Fleuck (1968) statistically analyzed results of the Missouri seeding experiments by the University of Chicago group and concluded that seeding of clouds in that area suppressed precipitation. In addition, reports of an investigation of the trend of rainfall in eastern Australia (Warner and Twomey, 1967; Warner, 1968) concluded that as the amount of smoke from burning sugar cane in the area increased during the past 50 years, rainfall correspondingly decreased by 25 percent. Therefore, an accurate determination of the effect of a city on precipitation in its neighborhood requires knowledge not only of the number and type of nuclei being introduced by the city but also of such factors as the concentration of natural nuclei and vertical temperature profiles over the city.

Recent findings have further documented Landsberg's statement that it is becoming increasingly difficult to find undisturbed rural areas with which to compare cities to determine urban-rural meteorological differences. Both direct (Schaefer, 1968b) and indirect (Gunn, 1964; McCormick and Ludwig, 1967; Peterson and Bryson, 1968; Volz, 1968) measurements have shown that the particulate content of the atmosphere, even in remote areas, is increasing as a result of greater human activity.

Two other precipitation elements of interest are hail and snowfall. Changnon's study (1968b) of the La Porte anomaly found that from 1951 to 1965 the number of hail days was 246 percent greater than that of surrounding stations. Results from similar investigations at other midwestern cities were not definitive. Landsberg (1956) cited a few instances in which snowfall over an urban area was lighter than that at nearby rural locations, presumably because of higher temperatures over the cities. Potter (1961) found similar results for Toronto and Montreal, Canada.

Research Needs

It is clear that a large volume of research has been conducted showing the affects of cities on local climates. But several topics need exploration in the future. Few studies have been made of the vertical structure of the urban atmosphere, which includes such features as the variation with height of temperature, wind flow, pollutants, and radiation. More such information is needed for a better understanding of the transport and diffusion of pollutants over metropolitan areas. Likewise, additional urban wind measurements are needed at a variety of sites with different exposures, to delineate the fine structure of wind flow throughout a city.

Several aspects of urban-rural radiation differences should be further investigated. In several studies of the effects of a polluted atmosphere on ultraviolet radiation in Los Angeles, the effects were found to be significant. Observations from other cities are now needed to show the amount of attenuation of ultraviolet radiation at different locations. Similarly, studies should be conducted to determine the net effect of a polluted city atmosphere on the total radiation balance of a city, including visible and thermal infrared wavelengths, since net radiation comprises a major fraction of a city's energy budget. In particular, urban-rural differences of infrared radiation should be measured to determine whether reduced values of solar radiation at the city surface resulting from atmospheric pollution are compensated for by an increase in infrared energy.

A cause-and-effect relationship between a city and precipitation has not yet been found. Although several factors are believed to be important, the role of anthropogenically produced dust particles is of special interest. The influence of these particles on the physics of precipitation and the optimum concentration for modifying precipitation have not yet been determined. Also, investigations should be undertaken to ascertain whether city-induced precipitation anomalies of a size similar to that at La Porte, Indiana, are widespread or whether this example is primarily the result of local influences, such as Lake Michigan.

Further research should be directed toward determining exactly upon which parameters urban-rural temperature differences depend. For example, the relative importance of the type and density of local buildings and gross city size on the temperature at a given city location has yet to be definitely established. Similarly, the local cooling produced by parks and greenbelts and the extent of this cooling into nearby neighborhoods should be measured. Such information would be useful in city planning and land-use studies, for example.

Finally, these two questions should be investigated: How far downwind does a city influence climate, and to what extent does a city in the tropics modify its climate? The former question has implications in larger-scale studies of inadvertent weather modification; the latter is important since nearly all research in urban climatology has been done at cities in temperate climates.

HYDROLOGIC EFFECTS OF URBAN LAND USE

Alongside the creation of particular climates, urbanization also affects hydrology, largely through changes in land use. Leopold (1968) records four interrelated but separable effects of land-use changes on the hydrology of an area: changes in peak flow characteristics, changes in total runoff, changes in quality of water, and changes in the hydrologic amenities. The hydrologic amenities are what might be called the appearance or the impression which the river, its channel and its valleys, leaves with the observer.

Runoff, which spans the entire regimen of flow, can be measured by number and by characteristics of rise in streamflow. The many rises in flow, along with concomitant sediment loads, control the stability of the stream channel. The two principal factors governing flow regimen are the percentage of area made impervious and the rate at which water is transmitted across the land to stream channels. The former is governed by the type of land use; the latter is governed by the density, size, and characteristics of tributary channels and thus by the provision of storm sewerage. Stream channels form in response to the regimen of flow of the stream. Changes in the regimen of flow, whether through land use or other changes, cause adjustments in the stream channels to accommodate the flows.

The volume of runoff is governed primarily by infiltration characteristics and is related to land slope and soil type as well as to the type of vegetative cover. It is thus directly related to the percentage of the area covered by roofs, streets, and other impervious surfaces at times of hydrograph rise during storms.

A summary of some data on the percentage of land rendered impervious by different degrees of urbanization is presented by Lull and Sopper (1966). Antoine (1964) presents the data on the percentage of impervious surface area in residential properties listed in Table 3.7.

The percentage decreases markedly as size of lot increases. Felton and Lull (1963) estimate in the Philadelphia area that 32 percent of the surface area is impervious on lots averaging 0.2 acre in size, whereas only 8 percent of the surface area is impervious on lots averaging 1.8 acres.

As volume of runoff from a storm increases, the size of flood peak also increases. Runoff volume also affects low flows because in any series of storms the larger the percentage of direct runoff, the smaller the amount of water available for soil moisture replenishment and for groundwater storage. An increase in total runoff from a given series of storms as a result of imperviousness results in decreased groundwater recharge and decreased low flows. Thus, increased imperviousness has the effect of increasing flood peaks during storm periods and decreasing low flows between storms.

The principal effect of land use on sediment comes from the exposure of the soil to storm runoff. This occurs mainly when bare ground is exposed during construction. It is well known that sediment production is sensitive to land slope. Sediment yield from urban areas tends to be larger than in unurbanized areas even if there are only small and widely scattered units of unprotected soil in the urban area. In aggregate, these scattered bare areas are sufficient to yield considerable sediment.

A major effect of urbanization is the introduction into channels of effluent from sewage disposal plants, and often of raw sewage. Raw sewage obviously degrades water quality, but even treated effluent contains dissolved minerals not extracted by sewage treatment. These minerals act as nutrients and promote algae and plankton growth in a stream. This growth in turn alters the balance in the stream biota.

Land use in all forms affects water quality. Agricultural use results in an increase of nutrients in stream water both from the excretion products of farm animals and from commercial fertilizers. A change from agricultural use to residential use, as in urbanization, tends to reduce these types of nutrients, but this tendency is counteracted by the widely scattered pollutants of the city, such

TABLE 3.7

Impervious surface area related to residential lot size

Lot Size of Residential Area (sq ft)	Impervious Surface Area (percent)
6,000	80
6,000–15,000	40
15,000	25

as oil and gasoline products, which are carried through the storm sewers to the streams. The net result is generally an adverse effect on water quality. This effect can be measured by the balance and variety of organic life in the stream, by the quantities of dissolved material, and by the bacterial level. Unfortunately, data describing quality factors in streams from urban versus unurbanized areas are particularly lacking.

Finally, the amenity value of the hydrologic environment is especially affected by three factors. The first is the stability of the stream channel itself. A channel, which is gradually enlarged owing to increased floods caused by urbanization, tends to have unstable and unvegetated banks, scoured or muddy channel beds, and unusual debris accumulations. These all tend to decrease the amenity value of a stream.

The second factor is the accumulation of artifacts of civilization in the channel and on the flood plain: beer cans, oil drums, bits of lumber, concrete, wire—the whole gamut of rubbish of an urban area. Though this may not importantly affect the hydrologic function of the channel, it becomes a detriment of what is here called the hydrologic amenity.

The third factor is the change brought on by the disruption of balance in the stream biota. The addition of nutrients promotes the growth of plankton and algae. A clear stream, then, may change to one in which rocks are covered with slime; turbidity usually increases, and odors may develop. As a result of increased turbidity and reduced oxygen content desirable game fish give way to less desirable species. Although lack of quantitative objective data on the balance of stream biota is often a handicap to any meaningful and complete evaluation of the effects of urbanization, qualitative observations tend to confirm these conclusions.

Runoff and Peak Flows

Basic hydrologic data on both peak flow and volume of runoff may be expressed in terms of the characteristics of the unit hydrograph—that is, the average time-distribution graph of flow from a unit or standard storm. The unit hydrograph shows the percentage of the total storm runoff occurring in each successive unit of time. The standard storm may be, for example, a typical storm which produced one inch of runoff (Figure 3.15). Such data are derived from the study of individual storms and the associated runoff graphs measured at gauging stations.

One factor stating the relation between the storm and the runoff is lag time. This is defined as the time interval between the center of mass of the storm precipitation and the center of mass of the resultant hydrograph. Lag time is a function of two basin parameters—the mean basin slope and the basin length. These factors empirically correlate with lag time if expressed in the form of the basin ratio (basin length L divided by the square root of the mean basin gradient, s). This basin ratio is also related to drainage area. As drainage area increases, the basin length increases and the average value of slope generally decreases. Thus, natural basin characteristics can be translated into flood-flow characteristics.

Lag time may be materially altered by the effects of urbanization on the basin surface. Water runs off faster from streets and roofs than from natural vegetated areas. This tends to decrease the lag time. The construction of artificial channels, especially storm sewers, also decreases lag time. As the time required for a given amount of water to run off shortens, the peak rate of runoff (flood peak) increases.

In addition to the basin ratio and lag time, the regimen of a stream, however, can be described in many other ways, including flood frequency, flow duration, mean annual flood, discharge at bankfull stage, and frequency of bankfull stage. This is evidenced in past studies of the effects of urbanization on the hydrology of an area. Many different techniques of relating rainfall to runoff have been used, along with various parameters to measure the degree of urbanization.

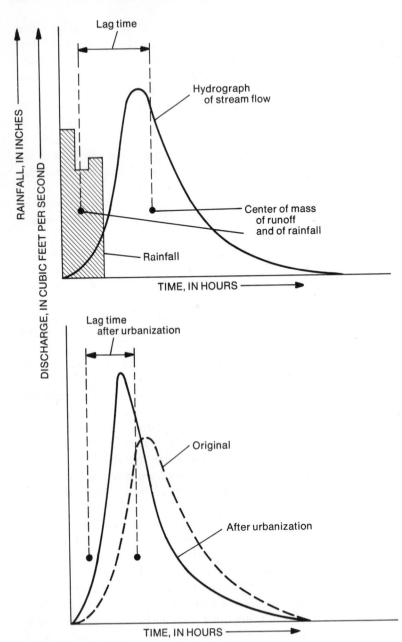

FIGURE 3.15. Hypothetical unit hydrographs relating runoff to rainfall, with definitions of significant parameters.

In order to evaluate our present knowledge, it is necessary to express the results of these studies in some common denominator.

Two forms of presentation will be used. The first is a slight modification of a method previ-

ously used by several investigators, especially D. G. Anderson (1968) and L. D. James (1965). The percentage of an area sewered is plotted against the percentage of the area rendered impervious by urbanization; isopleth lines (lines of equal value of the ratio) on the graph show the ratio of peak discharge under urbanized conditions to the peak discharge under rural or unurbanized conditions. Such a graph will be different for different drainage area sizes and for different flow frequencies.

The second method utilizes a relationship between the degree of urbanization and the frequency at which the original channel capacity would be exceeded.

Table 3.8 is an interpretation and summary of

TABLE 3.8

Increase in discharge as a result of urbanization in a one-square-mile area[g]

Percentage of Area Served by Storm Sewerage	Percentage of Area Made Impervious			
	0	20	50	80
0	1.0	1.2[a]	1.8[a]	2.2[a]
		1.3[b]	1.7[b]	2.2[b]
		1.3	1.6	2.0
20	1.1	1.9[c]	1.8	2.2
		1.4	—	—
50	1.3	2.1[d]	3.2[a]	4.7[a]
		2.8[a]	2.0	2.5
		3.7[e]	—	—
		2.0[f]	2.5	4.2[c]
		1.6	—	—
80	1.6	1.9	—	3.2
100	1.7	3.6[a]	4.7[a]	5.6[d]
		2.0	2.8	6.0[a]
		—	—	3.6

[a] Anderson (1968).   [d] Carter (1961).
[b] Martens (1966).   [e] Wiitala (1961).
[c] Wilson (1966).   [f] Espey, Morgan, and Masch (1966).
[g] Discharge is mean annual flood; recurrence interval is 2.3 years. Data are expressed as ratio of discharge after urbanization to discharge under previous conditions. Data from James (1965) have no superscript.

the effects of urbanization on peak discharges based on previous studies. Results of the studies were interpreted and extrapolated to a common denominator of one square mile, a practical unit of size for planning.

Carter (1961) developed a technique that fol-

lowed the reasoning previously used by Snyder (1938) and that showed lag time as a function of basin characteristics. For 20 streams in the vicinity of Washington, D.C., Carter developed this relation for natural basins, for partly sewered, and for completely sewered basins. As in most studies the difficulty comes in translating these descriptive terms to quantitative measures of urbanization. From data presented by Carter, values were read for a basin ratio of 0.12 representing a one-square-mile area having an estimated length of 1.2 miles and an average slope of 100 feet per mile. It was further assumed that in Carter's study "partly sewered" is equivalent to 50 percent sewered and 20 percent impervious. These conditions provide some of the data shown in Table 3.8

As an indication of the change in impervious area resulting from urbanization, Harris and Rantz (1964) showed that an area near Palo Alto, Calif., changed from 5.7 percent to 19.1 percent impervious in a 10-year period.

One of the most complete analyses of urbanization effects was made by D. G. Anderson (1968) in his study of the urbanization in Fairfax County, Va., near the metropolitan complex of Washington, D.C. Anderson's analysis follows the procedure suggested earlier by Carter but included a larger array of data from 64 gauging stations. Anderson closely confirmed the conclusions of Carter, but he carried the analysis further in a plot of the ratio of peak discharge to the mean annual flood for different percentages of basin imperviousness and for flood flows exceeding the mean annual flood. For Table 3.8, data from Anderson's study were read directly from his graph at the 2.33-year recurrence interval and expressed two separate conditions of sewerage. The first condition was expressed as "main channels natural, upstream drainage sewered"; this was assumed to be 50 percent sewered. The second condition was expressed as "completely sewered drainage basin"; this was assumed to be 100 percent sewered.

Wiitala (1961) presented data on urbanized

versus rural conditions for a medium-sized watershed in Michigan. His data were translated into a ratio of peak discharges, and it was assumed from his report that the urbanized condition represented 20 percent impervious area and 50 percent sewered area.

Martens (1966) reported on three small drainage basins in and near Charlotte, N.C. Using flood-frequency curves from long-term records at gauging stations in the state, he constructed a graph similar to that of Anderson—that is, ratio to mean annual flood for various degrees of basin imperviousness. As before, the difficulty lies in ascertaining the relation of Martens's urbanized condition to the degree sewered. In reading from Martens's graph for recurrence interval 2.33 years, it is assumed that the conditions he discussed include no sewerage and represent changes in impervious area only.

Wilson (1966) presented data on flood frequency for four drainage basins of 1.1 to 11.2 square miles near Jackson, Miss. He presented his analysis in the form of discharge of mean annual flood plotted against drainage area, and he interpolated lines to represent the percentage of the basin having storm sewers and improved channels. It is assumed that his description "20 percent of basin with storm sewers and improved channels" would be equivalent to 20 percent impervious and 20 percent sewered. Similarly, his value of 80 percent was assumed to be 80 percent sewered and 80 percent impervious.

Espey, Morgan, and Masch (1966) analyzed runoff data from urban and rural areas in Texas. Data from this study were used corresponding to a basin length of 5,500 feet and a slope of 0.02. It was also assumed from the authors' description of the area that "urban" could be expressed as 50 percent sewered and 20 percent impervious.

James (1965) analyzed runoff data from a 44-square-mile basin south of Sacramento, Calif., within which 12 square miles had been urbanized. From the basic data on flow, he obtained empirical coefficients used to route a series of synthetic flows by using a mathematical model expressed as a digital computer program. The results were plotted in a series of curves which separated the effects of flood frequency, drainage area, and degree of urbanization. Though the derived curves do not present field data, they also were incorporated into Table 3.8.

Thus in Table 3.8 are compiled, with certain necessary assumptions, the data for seven published and unpublished references which report measurements of the effect of urbanization on peak flow. Although interpretations were necessary to express the degree of urbanization in quantitative terms, there is considerable agreement among the data.

Data from Table 3.8 have been transposed into the graph shown in Figure 3.16. The ratios of peak discharge of urbanized to rural areas are presented for different percentages of sewerage and impervious area; lines of equal values of the ratio are drawn through the data. Briefly, these data show that for unsewered areas the differences between 0 and 100 percent impervious will increase peak discharge on the average 2.5 times. For areas that are 100 percent sewered, peak discharge for 0 percent impervious will be about 1.7 times the mean annual flood and the ratio increases to about eight for 100 percent impervious areas. Figure 3.16, then, reduces the basic data to the same units applicable to a one-square-mile drainage basin and to the mean annual flood.

A basin produces big flows from large and intense storms and smaller flows from less intense but more frequent storms. The great or catastrophic event is rare, and the storm of ordinary magnitude is frequent. These events can be arranged in order of magnitude and counted. For example, all discharge events exceeding 400 cfs (cubic feet per second) can be tabulated from the record at a stream-gauging station and arranged in order of magnitude; the values in the array can be plotted as a discharge-frequency curve. This has been done for the gauging station on West Branch Brandywine Creek at Coates-

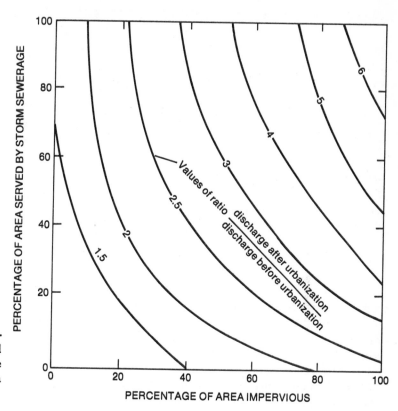

FIGURE 3.16. Effect of urbanization on mean annual flood for a one-square-mile drainage area (based on data from Table 3.8).

ville, Pa., for 9 years of record (Figure 3.17). The theory and practice of constructing such flow-frequency curves is well known. The plotting position or frequency often used is defined as

$$R = \frac{n+1}{m},$$

where R is the recurrence interval in years, n is number of years of record, and m is the rank of the individual event in the array.

Note in Figure 3.17 that the largest flow in the 9-year record was nearly 10,000 cfs. The number 50 printed on the graph means that there were 50 flows equal to or exceeding 500 cfs. Once a year, on the average, a discharge value of about 900 cfs will be equaled or exceeded.

A slightly different result would be obtained if, instead of using the peak flow for each storm, we included in the array only the largest flow in each year. The principle involved is similar. The arithmetic mean of the peak flows for the nine annual events is the "average annual flood." The statistics of this array are such that the recurrence interval of this average annual flood is the same regardless of the length of record, which specifically is 2.3 years. That is to say, a flood of that magnitude can be expected to be equaled or exceeded on an average of once in 2.3 years, or 10 times in 23 years.

Studies of river channels have shown that rivers construct and maintain channels which will carry without overflow a discharge somewhat smaller than the average annual flood. In fact the recurrence interval of the bankfull stage in most rivers is a flow having a recurrence interval of about 1.5 to 2 years.

Urbanization tends to increase the flood potential from a given basin. The channel then will

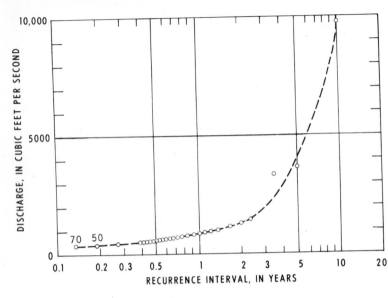

FIGURE 3.17. Flood-frequency curve for partial-duration series, West Branch, Brandywine Creek at Coatesville, Pa., based on data for 1942, 1944–1951.

receive flows which exceed its capacity not just once in 1.5 to 2 years on the average but more often. It is now proposed to estimate how much more often and to indicate the effect of this increased frequency on the channel itself.

Taking the East Branch of Brandywine Creek as an example, the flow-frequency curve can be constructed for a typical subbasin having a one-square-mile drainage area. Figure 3.18(a) shows the relation of average annual flood to drainage area, and Figure 3.18(b) shows the flood-frequency curve for annual peaks for basins in the Brandywine area.

From these curves a discharge-frequency relationship is developed for a drainage area of one-square-mile. The average annual flood is read from Figure 3.18(a) as 75 cfs, and Figure 3.18(b) is used to construct the frequency curve in Figure 3.19 pertaining to a one-square-mile basin marked "unurbanized."

The arithmetic for the construction of the curve is recorded in Table 3.9.

The curve marked "unurbanized" in Figure 3.19 is constructed on semilogarithmic paper from the data listed in the third and fourth columns of the preceding table. The ordinate is the discharge, and the lower abscissa is the recur-

TABLE 3.9

Flood recurrence interval-discharge relationships

Recurrence Interval of Annual Flood[a] (years)	Ratio to Mean Annual Flood[b]	Discharge[c] (cfs)	Recurrence Interval Duration Series[d] (years)
1.1	0.55	41	0.40
1.5	.75	56	.92
2.0	.90	68	1.45
2.3	1.0	75	1.78
5	1.45	110	4.50
10	1.9	145	9.50

[a] Only the highest flood each year.
[b] From Figure 3.18(b).
[c] Obtained by multiplying ratios by 75 cfs from Figure 3.18(a) for a drainage area of 1 sq mi.
[d] All peaks during the year. The values in this column are mathematically related to those in the first.

rence interval in the duration series. An auxiliary scale gives the average number of floods in a 10-year period (calculated as 10 years divided by the recurrence interval). Thus, the flow expected to occur once in 10 years would be about 145 cfs and the fifth largest would be 75 cfs. The latter would also be the average value of the

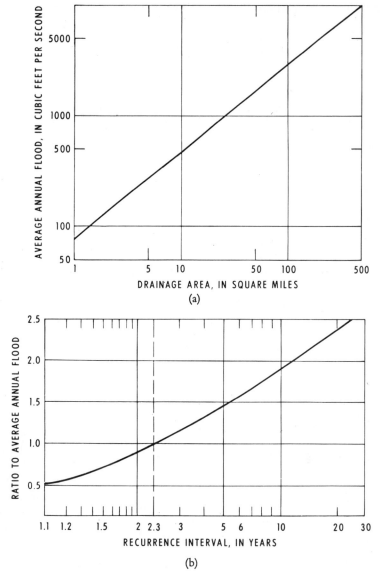

FIGURE 3.18. Regional flood-frequency data for the Brandywine Creek basin, Pennsylvania: (a) relation of average annual flood to drainage area, (b) flood-frequency curve for annual peaks.

largest flows each year during the 10-year record and thus would be the "average annual flood." It would plot, therefore, at an abscissa position approximately at the 2.3-year recurrence interval.

The effect of urbanization on the average annual flood is shown in Figure 3.19, which displays the increase in average annual flood for different degrees of urbanization as measured by the increase in percentages of impervious area and area served by storm sewers. For convenience these are tabulated in Table 3.10.

The average annual flood of 75 cfs was then multiplied by these ratios and plotted as shown in Figure 3.19 at the 2.3-year interval. These values form the basis of a series of frequency

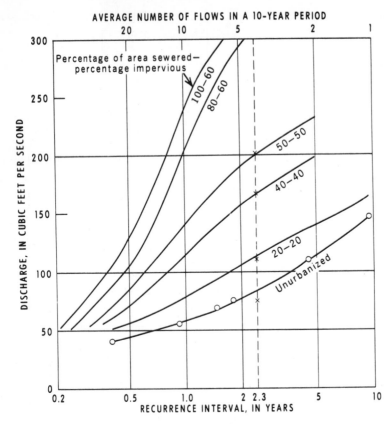

FIGURE 3.19. Flood-frequency curves for a one-square-mile basin in various states of urbanization.

TABLE 3.10

Average annual flood related to impervious area

Percentage of Area Sewered	Percentage of Area Impervious	Ratio to Average Annual Flood
0	0	1.0
20	20	1.5
40	40	2.3
50	50	2.7
80	60	4.2
100	60	4.4

curves for combinations of sewered area and impervious area. The shapes of the curves are guided by the principle that the most infrequent floods occur under conditions that are not appreciably affected by imperviousness of the basin.

The most frequent flows are therefore increased by smaller ratios than would be the average annual flood. Also, the most frequent flows are decreased in number because low flows from an urbanized area are not sustained by ground water as in a natural basin. The curves representing urbanized conditions therefore converge at low-flow values.

Obviously the frequency curves in Figure 3.19 are extrapolations based on minimal data and require corroboration or revision as additional field data become available.

The flood-frequency curve under original (unurbanized) condition passes through a value of 67 cfs at a recurrence interval of 1.5 years. At bankfull condition natural channels generally can carry the flow having that recurrence interval. If one assumes that this flow approximates the capacity of the natural channels, the intersection of the estimated curves for different degrees of urbanization with the discharge value of 67 cfs can be used to estimate the increase in number of flows equal to or exceeding natural channel capacity. An auxiliary scale is shown at the top of Figure 3.19 to facilitate this.

For example, under natural conditions it is expected that a 10-year record would show about seven flows equal to or exceeding 67 cfs, or channel capacity. But if the average annual flood were increased 1.5 times (from 75 to 112 cfs) corresponding to 20 percent sewered and 20 percent impervious, the new frequency curve indicates that 14 flows of 67 cfs or greater would occur in a 10-year period, or a twofold increase in number of flows. Similarly, the ratio of number of flows exceeding bankfull capacity was read from the intersection of the other curves in Figure 3.19 with the ordinate value of 67 cfs to obtain the ratios plotted in Figure 3.20.

Figure 3.20 shows that with an area 50 percent sewered and 50 percent impervious, for example, the number of flows equal to or exceeding bankfull channel capacity would, over a period of years, be increased nearly fourfold.

Urbanization tends to increase both the flood volume and the flood peak. But the increase can be compensated so that the discharge through channels downstream is maintained to any degree desired within the range which existed prior to urbanization. It is obvious that reservoir storage is installed on a river in order to reduce the magnitude of peak discharge by spreading the flow over a longer period. Channels themselves provide temporary storage and act as if they were small reservoirs. Overbank flooding onto the flat flood plain is a way that natural rivers provide for temporary storage and thus decrease flood peaks downstream. This effect of storage has been fully investigated and described (for example see Leopold and Maddock, 1954, especially pp. 36–49).

The provision of flood storage upstream, then, will decrease flood peaks and compensate for the increase caused by urbanization. This storage could take many forms including the following:

1. Drop inlet boxes at street gutter inlets.
2. Street-side swales instead of paved gutters and curbs.
3. Check dams, ungated, built in headwater swales.
4. Storage volumes in basements of large buildings receiving water from roofs or gutters and emptying into natural streams or swales.

FIGURE 3.20. Increase in number of flows per year equal to or exceeding original channel capacity (one-square-mile drainage area), as ratio to number of overbank flows before urbanization, for different degrees of urbanization.

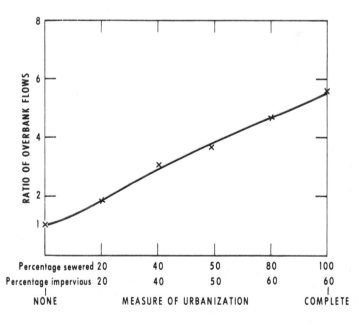

5. Off-channel storage volumes such as artificial ponds, fountains, or tanks.
6. Small reservoirs in stream channels such as those built for farm ponds.

Various types of storage volumes could be used simultaneously in various mixes. The effectiveness depends on the volume of storage relative to the volume of inflow during a storm peak period.

Sediment Production

The basic data available for analyzing the effect of urbanization on sediment yield, though sparse, have been summarized to some extent in the literature. Especially valuable is the report by Wolman (1964), who not only summarized the data obtained from sediment sampling stations in streams in the eastern United States but also studied the sediment yield from building construction activities. Sediment yields from ur-

banized or developing areas ranged from 1000 to more than 100,000 tons per square mile per year.

It should be recognized that sediment yield per square mile decreases with increasing drainage area; nevertheless it is apparent that unurbanized drainage basins yield, on the average, 200 to 500 tons per square mile per year. These figures are slightly higher for the farmed Piedmont lands, which may be expected to produce a sediment yield of 500 tons per square mile per year, such as the Watts Branch basin near Rockville, Md.

The data on urbanized areas studied by Wolman are plotted in Figure 3.21 together with data from suspended load sampling stations of the U.S. Geological Survey as summarized by Wark and Keller (1963).

In Figure 3.21 three bands or zones are labeled A, C, and UC. Wolman and Schick (1967) differentiated the following types

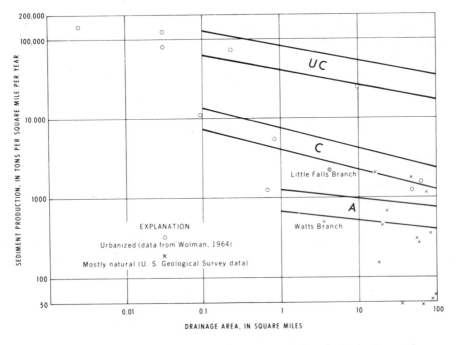

FIGURE 3.21. Annual sediment production per square mile for urbanized and natural areas. Zones: A, agricultural; C, under construction; UC, under construction and undiluted.

of activity: A, agricultural or natural; C, undergoing building construction, but highly diluted before reaching channels; and UC, undiluted sediment yields delivered to stream channels from construction sites.

They found that when building sites are denuded for construction, excavations are made, and dirt is piled without cover or protection near the site, the sediment movement in a rill or stream channel is very large in terms of tons per year immediately downhill from the construction site. If the channel contains little water except during storms (an ephemeral stream), there is no chance for dilution; during storm flow the sediment movement is great. If the construction debris gets into perennial channels, or for other reasons is distributed along a channel or dispersed over a wide area, the dilution lowers the yield per square mile per year. Thus, Wolman and Schick drew the distinction between agricultural, construction, and construction-undiluted.

For very small areas, Wolman (1964) said, "Because construction denudes the natural cover and exposes the soil beneath, the tonnage of sediment derived by erosion from an acre of ground under construction in developments and highways may exceed 20,000 to 40,000 times the amount eroded from farms and woodlands in an equivalent period of time."

Figure 3.21 shows the data as a relation between annual sediment yield per square mile and drainage basin size. The usual suspended load station is on a basin of more than 10 sq mi in area. Seldom is urbanization complete for basins of this size. Figure 3.22 diagrams the sequence of change schematically.

The data measured or estimated by Wolman (1964) in small urbanizing, developed or industrial areas show clearly that the sediment yield is larger by 10 to 100 times that of rural areas. Guy and Ferguson (1962) observed an increase of 250 times in an area near Kensington, Md.

To illustrate the difference in sediment samples obtained during storm flow, actual data for two stations are shown in Figure 3.23. The sediment rating curve, which is a plot of the discharge at any moment in time against the concurrent rate of sediment transport, gives an indication of the order of magnitude of the increase in sediment production from developed, as against rural, areas. The sediment rating curves in Figure 3.23 are for stations near Washington, D.C. Watts Branch drains an area primarily used for farming, though urban influences have

FIGURE 3.22. Schematic sequence: land use, sediment yield, and channel response from a fixed area (from Wolman, 1967).

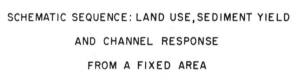

SCHEMATIC SEQUENCE: LAND USE, SEDIMENT YIELD

AND CHANNEL RESPONSE

FROM A FIXED AREA

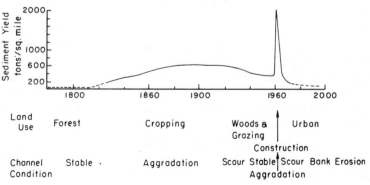

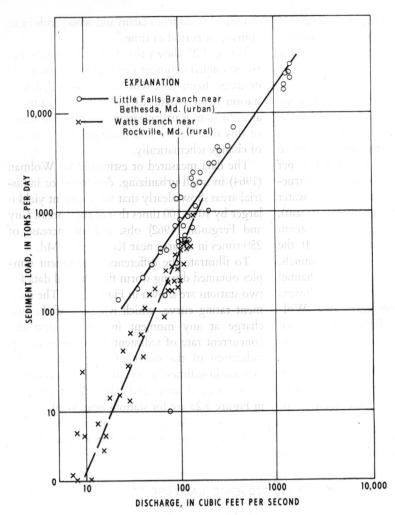

FIGURE 3.23. Relation of sediment yield and discharge for an urban and a rural or unurbanized area.

recently extended into the basin. Little Falls Branch near Bethesda drains a nearly completely urbanized community, consisting of Bethesda and parts of Chevy Chase, Md.

Note that the sediment rating curves tend to converge at high discharges. One might suppose that at those discharges the urbanized areas are actually contributing no more sediment than the unurbanized ones. This is not the case, however, owing to the fact that as a result of urbanization, the number of high flows increases materially. Because most of the sediment during the year is carried during periods of high flow, the result is

that urbanized areas yield on the average larger sediment loads than the unurbanized ones.

The difference in drainage basin size between Watts Branch (3.7 sq mi) and Little Falls Branch (4.1 sq mi) is not alone sufficient to explain the larger discharges in the latter basin. For about the same number of sample storms, note that Little Falls Branch data include discharges varying from 20 to 1500 cfs. In contrast, Watts Branch data (unurbanized) include flows ranging from 7 to 150 cfs. At least some of this difference is probably due to the effect of urbanization on increasing peak flow from a storm of given size, as discussed earlier. The two basins are only 10 miles apart and storms are comparable.

Keller (1962) compared the sediment rating curves for Northwest Branch of Anacostia River near Colesville, Md., a relatively unurbanized basin, and the Anacostia River basin near Hyattsville, Md., which is partly urbanized. He found the sediment production to be about four times greater in the urbanized area.

Most sediment carried by a stream is moved by high flows. In Brandywine Creek, for example, about 54 percent of the total sediment transported annually by the river (drainage area 321 sq mi) is carried by flows that occur, on the average, about 3 days each year.

In Table 3.11, a comparison is made between

TABLE 3.11

Sediment yields in two Maryland streams

	Drainage Area (sq mi)	Tons per Year	Tons per Year per sq mi
Watts Branch in Rockville, Md. (rural)	3.7	1,910	516
Little Falls Branch near Bethesda, Md. (urban)	4.1	9,530	3,220

sediment yield from Watts Branch, a rural landscape, and Little Falls Branch, an urban one. These basins are of the size and type represented in East Branch Brandywine Creek.

Sediment production is importantly related to land slope. Using multiple correlation techniques for a large variety of data from experimental watersheds, Musgrave (1947) developed a multiple correlation in which the rate of erosion is found to be proportional to the 1.35 power of land slope and to the 0.35 power of the slope length. The same conclusion had been derived theoretically by Horton (1945) and verified by comparison with the percentage of area eroded in the Boise River basin, Idaho. Sediment yield, therefore, is more highly sensi-

tive to land slope than to length of slope but is positively correlated with both.

Some idea, however, can be obtained of the difficulty in keeping steep slopes stable after the original vegetation has been disturbed, particularly during construction. If, for example, land slopes of 5 and 10 percent are compared, the doubling of the slope would increase the erosion rate by 2.3 times.

Increased slope length does not have such a large effect on erosion rate. Doubling slope length would increase the erosion rate by only 22 percent.

Because a slope of 10 percent drops 10 feet in a 100-foot horizontal, temporary storage in the form of depressions which might hold silt would be nearly absent. For land slopes above 10 percent, stream channels also would tend to be nearly devoid of areas or depressions which could hold up sediment during its passage downhill. From a practical standpoint, therefore, a figure of about 10 percent probably would be a physical and economic limit beyond which construction would be especially harmful insofar as sediment production is concerned. Any such limiting slope, however, would have to be determined by detailed economic studies.

Wark and Keller (1963) related the average annual sediment discharge in the Potomac River Basin to percentage of forest cover and, separately, to the percentage of land in crops. Average annual sediment yield increased from 50 to 400 tons per square mile per year, or eightfold, as forest cover in the basin declined from 80 percent to 20 percent. Sediment yield increased from 70 to 300 tons per square mile per year, or fourfold, as land in crops increased from 10 to 50 percent.

It has been pointed out in the comparison of sediment rating curves for urban versus rural areas that the rating curves do not appear to be as much different as the values of sediment yield on an annual yield basis. It has been mentioned that a slight increase of sediment concentration can make a large difference in total annual sediment yield, owing to the fact that urban areas produce a larger number of high flows. If the number of flows above bankfull stage is increased by urbanization, the banks and bed of a channel in erodible material will not remain stable, but the channel will enlarge through erosion. Computation indicates the seriousness of this factor.

For example, assume that a channel is capable of carrying 55 cfs at bankfull stage. In the Brandywine area this represents a channel draining a basin slightly less than one square mile in area. The channel necessary to carry 55 cfs at bankfull stage would probably have a velocity of slightly less than 2.5 feet per second and would be about 2 feet deep and 11 feet wide. As indicated in Figure 3.17, urbanization might cause a flow of this frequency to increase 2.7 times, or 150 cfs. If this channel had to adjust itself to carry a flood of 150 cfs at bankfull stage, it is estimated that the new velocity would be about 2.5 feet per second, and the necessary depth and width would have changed respectively to about 3 feet and 20 feet. In other words, this stream would deepen about 50 percent and increase in width a little less than twice its original size. If such erosion took place through at least one-fourth mile of channel length in a drainage basin of one square mile, the amount of sediment produced by this erosion would be 50,000 cubic feet. At 100 pounds per cubic foot, this amounts to 2,500 tons.

This amount can be compared with the mean annual sediment yield for Watts Branch, an unurbanized area near Rockville, Md. Annual sediment yield of Watts Branch is 516 tons per square mile. Thus, the channel erosion alone under the assumptions made would produce as much sediment as 5 years' usual production from an unurbanized area of the same size. Therefore, not only does construction activity have the potential of increasing sediment loads many thousands of times while urbanization is in progress, but the result of the urbanization through

its increase in peak flow would produce large amounts of sediment from channel enlargement as well. This emphasizes the need to provide temporary storage far upstream to counteract the tendency of urbanization to increase the number and size of high flows.

Water Quality

There is little doubt that as urbanization increases, particularly as industrial use is made of land and water, the quality of water decreases. There are two principal effects on water quality. First, the influx of waste materials tends to increase the dissolved-solids content and decrease the dissolved-oxygen content. Second, as flood peaks increase as a result of the increased area of imperviousness and decreased lag time, less water is available for groundwater recharge. The stream becomes flashier in that flood peaks are higher and flows during nonstorm periods are lower.

A study on the Passaic River at Little Falls, N.J., by Anderson and Faust (1965) provides quantitative data on the effect of urbanization and industrialization on water quality. Seventeen years of data for the flow and chemical quality of the 760-square-mile drainage basin were analyzed. Between 1950 and 1963, diversions of water for domestic and industrial supplies increased more than 30 percent. Returns of waste waters into the basin became as much as 10 percent of the water withdrawn. Analysis of the data showed that at relatively low discharge the dissolved-solids content increased about 10 ppm (parts per million) between 1948 and 1955 but increased 75 ppm between 1955 and 1963. That is, during the period of greatest population growth the dissolved-solids content increased nearly 40 percent in a period of 8 years.

A long-term change in the average content of dissolved oxygen was also noted. Between 1950 and 1964 the dissolved-oxygen content dropped from an average of 78 percent of saturation to 62 percent of saturation. Further, the analysis demonstrated that these average changes in water quality occurred in all seasons of the year.

An aspect of population growth not generally appreciated is the large segment of population using septic tanks for disposal of sewage. In a given area this segment often becomes large before community water and sewerage systems are built. For the planner it should be important to know how septic-tank installations can affect water quality in streams and in the ground. In the upper East Branch of Brandywine Creek, a basin of 37 sq mi, the population in 1967 was 4,200. As of that date, there were no community water or sewerage systems; all the population was served by individual wells and septic tanks. Population projections indicate that the basin will have 14,000 persons by the year 1990. During the initial part of this projected growth at least, the number of wells and septic tanks can be expected to increase materially.

The soil, containing as it does a flourishing fauna of microorganisms, tends to destroy or absorb pathogenic bacteria. Effluent draining from the seepage field of a septic tank tends therefore to be cleansed of its pathogens. McGauhey and Krone (1954) showed that the coliform count was reduced by three orders of magnitude in moving from an injection well a distance of 50 feet through sand and gravel. In 100 feet the count was reduced to a small number. As for rate of movement, Mallmann and Mack (1961) showed that bacteria introduced into a permeable soil by a septic-tank seepage field moved 10 feet in 2 days and 20 feet in 3 days and appeared in a well 30 feet away after 10 days.

Both the rate and effectiveness of the process of pathogen reduction depend on the type of soil, as has been summarized by Olson (1964), who emphasized that position of the ground-water table is a critical factor in the transmission of pollutants.

Studies by Wayman, Page, and Robertson (1965) of the changes in primary sewage effluent through natural materials in conditions of saturated flow showed that "most soils removed over 90 percent of the bacteria from sewage within a few feet of travel . . . (but there was) severe clogging in the finer-grained soils." They found, however, that "dissolved solids moved through the columns (of soil) virtually unaffected . . . ."

The same authors report on infiltration of polluted river water through sandy loam. "ABS (synthetic detergent) and coliform bacteria are significantly reduced by infiltration through the unsaturated zone; dissolved solids do not seem to be removed . . . . Once a pollutant gets into the ground water (saturated flow) little additional change in removal of ABS or dissolved solids, even for movement over extensive horizontal distances, is to be expected. This result is in agreement with the data . . . for flow of sewage effluent through various soil columns (saturated flow)."

The data are not definitive regarding the minimum distance a septic-tank seepage field should be separated from a stream channel, but the application of data cited above with general principles does indicate some tentative rules of thumb which might be useful to the planner. A perennial stream represents the intersection of the saturated zone (water table) with the earth's surface. The observations indicate that, for soil cleansing to be effective, contaminated water must move through unsaturated soil at least 100 feet. Owing to the gentle gradient of the water table near the perennial stream and the fact that seepage water moves vertically as well as toward a nearby channel, it would seem prudent that no septic tank should be as close to a channel as about 300 feet, if protection of the stream-water quality is to be achieved. The distance should probably be greater from a perennial than from an ephemeral channel. (An ephemeral stream contains flowing water only in storm periods.) In general, it might be advisable to have no source of pollution such as a seepage field closer than 300 feet to a channel or watercourse.

Even this minimum setback does not prevent

the dissolved materials (nitrates, phosphates, chlorides) from enriching the stream water and thus potentially encouraging the proliferation of algae and otherwise creating a biotic imbalance.

The only detailed study of the effect of urbanization of water temperature is that of E. J. Pluhowski (1968), some of whose results are summarized here. He chose five streams on Long Island for detailed analysis and found that streams most affected by man's activities exhibit temperatures in summer from 10° to 15°F above those in an unurbanized control. Connetquot River, the control stream, flows through one of the few remaining undeveloped areas of central Long Island. Temperatures in reaches most affected by ponding, realignment, or clear cutting of trees are significantly higher in summer, but winter temperatures are 5° to 10°F colder than those observed in reaches unaffected by man.

Solar radiation is the predominant factor in the energy balance determining a stream's thermal pattern. The more solar energy a stream absorbs, the greater its temperature variation diurnally as well as seasonally. By greatly increasing the surface area exposed to the sun's radiation, the construction of ponds and lakes has profoundly affected stream temperature regimens. On Long Island, Pluhowski found that ponds having mean depth of about 2 feet or less substantially increase downstream diurnal temperature fluctuations, whereas ponds deeper than 2 feet exhibit a dampening effect on daily temperatures. For example, during the period October 31 to November 2, 1967, the mean daily range of temperatures at Swan River, in south-central Long Island, varied from 9°F in a reach immediately below a shallow pond (mean depth, 0.5 foot) to 3°F below Swan Lake (mean depth, 3 feet). In reaches unaffected by man's activities, the mean daily temperature fluctuation was about 4°F.

Under natural conditions, less than 5 percent of the streamflow on Long Island originates as direct surface runoff. With the conversion of large areas of western Long Island from farmland to suburban use during the last 20 years, the proportion of streamflow originating as surface runoff has increased sharply. As a direct consequence, streams most affected by street runoff may exhibit temperature patterns markedly different from those observed in streams flowing through natural settings. During the period August 25 to 27, 1967, a series of heavy rainstorms overspread Long Island. Throughout this period, temperatures at each of the five observation sites on Connetquot River showed little day-to-day change. In contrast, temperatures in the upper reaches of East Meadow Brook, which drains highly urbanized central Nassau County, increased steadily in response to the relatively warm street runoff. Pluhowski found that by August 27, water temperatures had risen 10° to 12°F above prestorm levels and were 15°F higher than concurrent temperatures in the control stream.

CHAPTER *4*

the nature of air pollution

We should now turn to a more detailed discussion of urban environmental pollution and management, beginning in this chapter with air pollution. It is, of course, wrong to view air pollution as a new phenomenon. John Evelyn (1661) railed against the pall of smoke above seventeenth-century London:

> Whilst these [chimneys] are belching forth their sooty jaws, the City of London resembles the face rather of Mount Etna, the Court of Vulcan, Stromboli, or the suburbs of hell, than an assembly of rational creatures, and the Imperial seat of our Incomparable Monarch . . . the weary traveller, at many miles distance, sooner smells, than sees the city to which he repairs. This is that pernicious smoke which foils all her Glory, super-inducing a sooty crust or fur upon all that it lights.

Since the dawn of the industrial revolution, urban residents have endured levels of smoke pollution that would be held intolerable today. In the last half of the nineteenth century, a surprising number of aroused citizen groups protested the smoke-laden air of London. But their protests were lost in the overwhelming

Selections are included in this chapter from:
Donald H. Pack, "Meteorology of Air Pollution," *Science*, Vol. 164 (November 27, 1964), pp. 1119–1127. Begins on page 86.

George B. Morgan, Guntis Ozolins, and Elbert C. Taylor, "Air Pollution Surveillance Systems," *Science*, Vol. 170 (October 16, 1970), pp. 289–295. Begins on page 96.

Andris Auliciems and Ian Burton, *Perception and Awareness of Air Pollution in Toronto*, Working Paper Series No. 13, Natural Hazard Research Series, University of Toronto, 1970. Begins on page 99.

Andris Auliciems, Ian Burton, John Hewings, Myra Schiff, and Chris Taylor, "The Public Use of Scientific Information on the Quality of the Environment: The Case of the Ontario Air Pollution Index," paper presented to the International Geographical Congress, Montreal, 1972. Begins on page 108.

orientation to industrial development at any price. Progress in the United States was no more heartening. Chicago and Cincinnati passed smoke-control laws in 1881. By 1912, 23 of the 28 American cities with populations over 200,000 had passed similar laws. But still there was little dent made in air pollution.

In the 1930s, 40s, and 50s smoke pollution reached its zenith in the United States, especially in eastern and midwestern industrial cities. The public outcry against these conditions resulted in the enactment of improved smoke-pollution legislation, its partial enforcement, and a visible improvement in the air of some industrial cities. These local control efforts focused primarily on cutting down smoke from fossil fuels, particularly coal. The fortunate advent of diesel engines in place of steam locomotives and the increased use of gas as a fuel for space heating also helped cut back air pollution in that era.

However, air pollution turned out to be more complex. When the citizens of Los Angeles began to complain of smog, few people suspected that air pollution was a great deal more than just smoke. Los Angeles used virtually none of the fuels primarily responsible for the smoke problems of cities elsewhere; yet smog appeared and worsened. The first breakthrough in developing broader understanding came when Dr. Arie J. Haagen-Smit of the California Institute of Technology finally pinpointed the principal sources of photochemical smog in Los Angeles: hydrocarbons and nitrogen oxides from automobile exhausts. As Dr. Haagen-Smit recalls, the City of Los Angeles' decision to attack the smog problem dated from a report made in 1947 by Raymond R. Tucker, who as an investigator of air-pollution problems played a major role in the battle against smoke in St. Louis and subsequently became the mayor of that city. His report on Los Angeles enumerated the sources of pollution attributable to industry and to individuals through the use of automobiles and the burning of trash. The report recommended immediate control of known

sources of pollution and a research program to determine if any other things in the air should be controlled.

Largely on the basis of the Tucker report, and with the aid of civic groups, the *Los Angeles Times* started a campaign to inform and arouse the public about smog. As a result that state's legislature in 1948 passed a law permitting the formation of air-pollution control districts empowered to formulate rules for curbing smog and endowed with the necessary police power for enforcement of the rules. Los Angeles County created such a district the same year. Figure 4.1 shows the problems they were fighting.

The district began by limiting the dust and fumes emitted by steel factories, refineries, and hundreds of smaller industries. It terminated the use of a million home incinerators and forbade the widespread practice of burning in public dumps. These moves reduced dustfall, which in some areas had been as much as 100 tons per square mile per month, by two-thirds, bringing it back to about the level that existed in 1940 before smog became a serious problem in the community. That achievement should be measured against the fact that since 1940 the population of Los Angeles and the number of industries in the city have doubled.

Although the attack on dustfall produced a considerable improvement in visibility, the typical smog symptoms of eye irritation and plant damage remained. The district therefore undertook a research program to ascertain the origin and nature of the substances that caused the symptoms. One significant finding was that the Los Angeles atmosphere differs radically from that of most other heavily polluted communities. Ordinarily polluted air is made strongly reducing by sulfur dioxide, a product of the combustion of coal and heavy oil. Los Angeles air, on the other hand, is often strongly oxidizing. The oxidant is mostly ozone, with smaller contributions from oxides of nitrogen and organic peroxides.

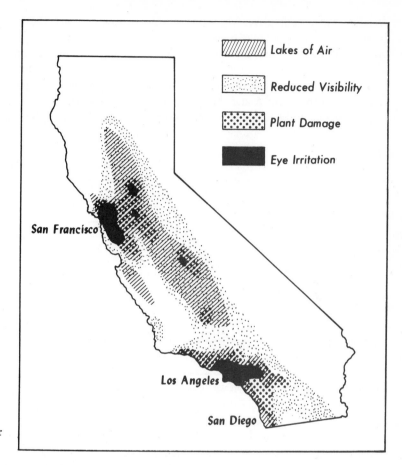

FIGURE 4.1. Extent of air
pollution in California.

During smog attacks the ozone content of the Los Angeles air reaches a level 10 to 20 times higher than that elsewhere. Concentrations of half a part of ozone per million of air have repeatedly been measured during heavy smogs. To establish such a concentration directly would require the dispersal of about 1,000 tons of ozone in the Los Angeles basin. No industry releases significant amounts of ozone; discharges from electric power lines also are negligible, amounting to less than a ton a day. A considerable amount of ozone is formed in the upper atmosphere by the action of short ultraviolet rays, but that ozone does not descend to earth during smog conditions because of the very temperature inversion that intensifies smog. In such an inver-

sion warm air lies atop the cold air near the ground; this stable system forms a barrier not only to the rise of pollutants but also to the descent of ozone.

Exclusion of these possibilities left sunlight as the only suspect in the creation of the Los Angeles ozone. The cause cannot be direct formation of ozone by sunlight at the earth's surface, because that requires radiation of wavelengths shorter than 2,000 angstrom units, which does not penetrate the atmosphere to ground level. There was a compelling reason, however, to look for an indirect connection between smog and the action of sunlight: high oxidant or ozone values are found only during daylight hours. Apparently a photochemical reaction was taking place when one or more ingredients of smog were exposed to sunlight—which is, of course, abundant in the Los Angeles area.

In order for a substance to be affected by light it has to absorb the light, and the energy of the light quanta has to be sufficiently high to rupture the chemical bonds of the substance. A likely candidate for such a photochemical reaction in smog thus was nitrogen dioxide. This dioxide is formed from nitrogen oxide, which originates in all high-temperature combustion through a combining of the nitrogen and oxygen of the air. Nitrogen dioxide has a brownish color and

TABLE 4.1

Estimated emissions of air pollutants, United States, 1969

Source of Emission	Carbon Monoxide	Particulates	Sulfur Oxides	Hydro- carbons	Nitrogen Oxides	Total
	Millions of Tons per Year					
Transportation (primarily automobiles and trucks)	111.5	0.8	1.1	19.8	11.2	144.4
Fuel combustion in stationary sources (space heating, power plants)	1.8	7.2	24.4	0.9	10.0	44.3
Industrial processes......................	12.0	14.4	7.5	5.5	0.2	39.6
Solid-waste disposal	7.9	1.4	0.2	2.0	0.4	11.9
Miscellaneous	18.2	11.4	0.2	9.2	2.0	41.0
Total	151.4	35.2	33.4	37.4	23.8	281.2

SOURCE: U.S. Council on Environmental Quality, *Second Annual Report*, 1971, p. 212.

TABLE 4.2

Selected particulate constituents as percentages of gross suspended particulates (1966–67)

	Urban (217 Stations)		Proximate (5)		Nonurban Intermediate (15)		Remote (10)	
	$\mu g/m^{3a}$	%	$\mu g/m^{3a}$	%	$\mu g/m^{3a}$	%	$\mu g/m^{3a}$	%
Suspended particulates..............	102.0		45.0		40.0		21.0	
Benzene soluble org.	6.7	6.6	2.5	5.6	2.2	5.4	1.1	5.1
Ammonium ion	0.9	0.9	1.22	2.7	0.28	0.7	0.15	0.7
Nitrate ion	2.4	2.4	1.40	3.1	0.85	2.1	0.46	2.2
Sulfate ion	10.1	9.9	10.0	22.2	5.29	13.1	2.51	1.8
Copper	0.16	0.15	0.16	0.36	0.078	0.19	0.060	0.28
Iron	1.43	1.38	0.56	1.24	0.27	0.67	0.15	0.71
Manganese	0.073	0.07	0.026	0.06	0.012	0.03	0.005	0.02
Nickel	0.017	0.02	0.008	0.02	0.004	0.01	0.002	0.01
Lead	1.11	1.07	0.21	0.47	0.096	0.24	0.022	0.10

SOURCE: Thomas B. McMullen, *Comparison of Urban and Nonurban Air Quality*, presented at 9th Annual Indiana Air Pollution Control Conference, Purdue University, Oct 13–14, 1970, Table 4, p. 7.
a Unit of measure: $\mu g/m^3$ = micrograms per cubic meter.

absorbs light in the region of the spectrum from the blue to the near ultraviolet. Radiation from the sun can readily dissociate nitrogen dioxide into nitric oxide and atomic oxygen. This reactive oxygen attacks organic material, of which there is much in the unburned hydrocarbons remaining in automobile exhaust. The result is the formation of ozone and various other oxidation products. Some of these products, notably peracylnitrates and formaldehyde, are eye irritants. Peracylnitrates and ozone also cause plant damage. Moreover, the oxidation reactions are usually accompanied by the formation of aerosols, or hazes, and this combination aggravates the effects of the individual components in the smog complex.

The answer to the puzzle of the oxidizing smog of the Los Angeles area thus lay in the combination of heavy automobile traffic and copious sunlight. After Haagen-Smit's discovery, photochemical smog was at first thought to be a phenomenon amplified by local weather conditions and limited to Los Angeles. Today, however, most major cities are afflicted to some degree by photochemical smog, as well as by many other forms of air pollution, about which more recent research has gradually provided information, understanding, and awareness.

POLLUTANTS AND THEIR SOURCES

A list of twenty-four different types of air pollutants and what is known about their sources, effects, and current abatement and control methods is provided in the appendix to this chapter. Of these twenty-four, five main classes are now regularly monitored in the United States by a comprehensive network of surveillance stations; it has been found that they alone account for more than 280 million tons of pollutants pumped into the air each year.

Table 4.1 indicates the sources of this pollution. Transportation—particularly the auto-

mobile—is clearly the greatest source of carbon monoxide, hydrocarbons, and nitrogen oxides. On the other hand, power plants contribute most sulfur oxides, and industry the particulates. Transportation outweighs the others, however: it accounts for 42 percent of all pollutants by weight. Further, as Tables 4.2, 4.3, and 4.4 show, the pollution concentrations are greatest in urban areas and increase with increasing size of city, urban densities, the amount of heavy industry, and automobile concentrations. Thus, air pollution is for the most part a phenomenon of urban living that occurs when the capacity of the air to dilute the pollutants is overburdened. Population and industrial growth and a high degree of dependence on the motor vehicle cause new gaseous and particulate emissions to complement, interact with, and further complicate the traditional sources of soot and smoke.

TABLE 4.3

Values for pollutant concentration versus population class (1969–70)

Class Number and Population Class	Concentration			Number of Sites
	TSP[a]	SO²	NO²	
1. Nonurban	25	10	33	5
2. Urban < 10,000..	57	35	116	2
3. 10,000	81	18	64	2
4. 25,000	87	14	63	2
5. 50,000	118	29	127	9
6. 100,000	95	26	114	37
7. 400,000	100	28	127	17
8. 700,000	101	29	146	9
9. 1,000,000	134	69	163	2
10. 3,000,000	120	85	153	2
Slope	9.152	6.103	12.109	
Intercept	41.467	0.733	44.000	
r^2	0.748	0.590	0.719	
t Statistic	4.874	3.392	4.526	

SOURCE: The Mitre Corp., MTR-6013, p. 70. Time span—second half of 1969, first half of 1970. Cited in Council on Environmental Quality, *Environmental Quality, Second Annual Report*, 1971, pp. 215 and 243. Regressions: Pollutant concentration on population class number (1 through 10).
[a] TSP: Total suspended particulates.

TABLE 4.4

*Regression results for mean pollutant levels
related to set of explanatory variables*

Dependent Variable (Geometric Mean of Pollutant Listed) and Explanatory Variable	Coefficient	t Value	R^2
Particulates			
Constant	51.55	—	0.26
Log SMSA population	22.94	3.10[a]	
January temperature	−0.54	1.67[b]	
Iron and steel production workers (000)	0.66	2.41[a]	
Nitrates			
Constant	0.664		0.34
Log SMSA population	0.816	1.93[b]	
Central-city density (000)	−0.127	3.44[a]	
Total central-city gasoline sales, in million dollars..	0.011	3.38[a]	
Sulfates			
Constant	5.84		
Central-city density (000) ..	0.53	5.01[a]	0.48
Nonferrous metals production workers (000)	0.81	3.26[a]	

SOURCES: Regression equations estimated in a study by Hoch (1972). Pollution data obtained from U.S. Public Health Service, National Air Pollution Control Administration, *Air Quality from the National Air Surveillance Network—1966 edition*, Durham, N.C., 1968. Measures on pollutants were obtained as follows: particulates for 1966, Table 7, pp. 34–40; nitrates for 1965, Table 18, pp. 62–66; sulfates for 1965, Table 20, pp. 69–73. The 76 cities employed had observations for all three pollutants. Central-city density as of 1960 from U.S. Bureau of Census, *1960 Census of Population*. SMSA population for 1966 estimated as 0.4 (1960 population) + 0.6 (1970 population). 1960 population from *1960 Census of Population*. 1970 population from U.S. Bureau of Census, Advance Population Reports. Manufacturing production workers from U.S. Bureau of Census, *1963 Census of Manufactures, Vol. III, Area Statistics*, Washington, 1966. Central-city gasoline sales from *County and City Data Book, 1967*.
[a] Significant at 0.05 level.
[b] Significant at 0.10 level.

THE METEOROLOGY OF AIR POLLUTION

Many of the control measures outlined in the appendix seek to prevent pollutants from reaching the atmosphere. The more traditional approach to air-pollution control is "dilution through diffusion" in the atmosphere—i.e., simply letting air pollution blow away—a solution depending upon the meteorology of air pollution.

The layer of air (about 10 kilometers thick) which is readily available for the dilution of pollution represents an enormous reservoir, about 5×10^{18} cubic meters. Atmospheric diffusion is ultimately accomplished by the wind movement of pollutants, but the character of the sources of pollution requires that this action of the wind be taken into account in different ways.

The sources can be conveniently grouped into three classes: point sources, line sources, and area sources. In practice, the first two classes must be further divided into instantaneous and continuous sources.

The instantaneous point source is essentially a "puff" of material created or ejected in a relatively short time, as by a nuclear explosion, the sudden rupture of a chlorine tank, or the bursting of a tear-gas shell. The wind of immediate importance is, of course, that occurring at the place and time at which the pollutant is created. Since the wind is highly variable, the initial direction of movement of the puff is also variable and difficult to predict. In addition, dilution of a puff source is a very strong function of time after its release. At first, the small-scale fluctuations of the wind cause it to grow rather slowly, and the larger-scale wind variations simply carry it along on erratic paths. But as the puff grows, larger-scale motions can get a "hold" on it to tear it apart and dilute it more rapidly. Thus, the unique feature of the instantaneous point source is its increasing dispersion rate with time, whence the necessity to consider successively larger scales of meteorological phenomena in calculating its spread.

Continuous point sources (the smoke plume from a factory chimney, the pall from a burning dump) are the most familiar, the most conspicuous, and the most studied of pollution sources. The meteorology of the continuous source must take into account the time changes of the wind at the point of emission. The behavior of a plume from a factory chimney is very much like that of water from a hose being played back and forth across a lawn. It is evident that if the hose is steady the same area will be continually exposed to the water. But if the hose (wind) moves back and forth in an arc, the water (pollution) will be distributed over a wider area, hence the concentration will be less. For a truly continuous source there are other changes of great importance—primarily the diurnal and seasonal cycles.

The isolated line source is less common and therefore of less general interest, with two important exceptions: heavily traveled highways and the swath of chemicals emitted by cropdusting apparatus. In both these examples, if the line of pollutant is uniform and is long enough, the dispersion of the pollution must be attained in only two dimensions: along the wind and in the vertical. If the line source is a continuous one, as might be the case of a freeway in rush hours, spreading in the downwind direction becomes ineffective (at a particular downwind location), so that only the vertical dimension is left to provide dilution. This behavior of the continuous line source has been exploited by meteorologists in field experiments with controlled tracers to permit the detailed study of vertical diffusion, uncomplicated by effects in the other two coordinates.

The area source can vary enormously in size. It may be distributed over several square kilometers, as in an industrial park, over tens or hundreds of square kilometers, exemplified by the "megalopolis" along the eastern seaboard of the United States. These area sources usually include combinations of all the single-source configurations. A large city will include many thousands of home chimneys, thousands of factories and shops, hundreds of kilometers of streets, open dumps, burning leaves, evaporating fumes from gasoline storage or from cleaning plants and paint factories, and everywhere the automobile. The weather problem of the city area source becomes, in the aggregate, quite different from that of a single source. Here we are concerned not with the increasing rate of wind dispersion with increasing scale, or with the behavior of wind with time at a single point, but rather with the replenishment rate of the air over the city. We must consider the total movement of a large volume of air as it "ventilates" the city. Anything that reduces this ventilation rate, whether it be the confining effect of surrounding mountains or the reduced velocities of a slow-moving anticyclone, is of concern.

In the construction of cities man has modified the weather, as we saw in the previous chapter. The volume of effluent injected into the air has reduced the solar radiation. The absorption characteristics of cement and asphalt instead of grass and trees create urban "heat islands." These effects must be considered in the meterology of urban air pollution.

The atmosphere disperses pollutants because, like the sea, it is in constant motion, and this motion is always turbulent to some degree. There is as yet no fully accepted definition of turbulence, but empirically it can be described as random (three-dimensional) flow. There is as yet no complete explanation for the complexities even of controlled wind-tunnel turbulence, hence it is not surprising that the understanding of turbulent diffusion in the atmosphere has progressed largely through empirical treatments of controlled tracer experiments. It is not possible to condense turbulent-diffusion theory to a few paragraphs, so in what follows only the conclusions will be used. Instead, we will turn directly to a discussion of vertical and horizontal turbulent diffusion and atmospheric transport, as a basis for appreciating some of the features of air pollution meteorology.

Vertical Turbulent Diffusion

To all intents and purposes rapid atmospheric diffusion in the vertical is always bounded: on the bottom by the surface of the earth and at the top by the tropopause. The tropopause—the demarcation between the troposphere, where temperature decreases with altitude, and the stratosphere, where the temperature is relatively constant or increases with altitude—is lowest over the poles, at about 8 kilometers, and highest in the tropics, about 20 kilometers. The detection of radon products throughout the troposphere is conclusive evidence of the eventual availability of the full depth of the troposphere for vertical dispersion, since the radon source is exclusively at the earth's surface. Utilization of this total vertical dimension can take place at very different rates, depending on the thermally driven vertical wind. These rates are intimately related to the vertical temperature

profile. On the average (and if we neglect the effects of the phase change of water in the air), enhanced turbulence is associated with a drop in temperature with height of 10°C per kilometer or greater. (This is the dry adiabatic rate.) If the temperature change with height is at a lesser rate, turbulence tends to be decreased, and if the temperature increases with height (an "inversion"), turbulence is very much reduced. See Figure 4.2.

The temperature profile, particularly over land, shows a large diurnal variation. Shortly after sunrise the heating of the land surface by the sun results in rapid warming of the air near the surface; the reduced density of this air causes it to rise rapidly. Cooler air from aloft replaces the rising air "bubble," to be warmed and rise

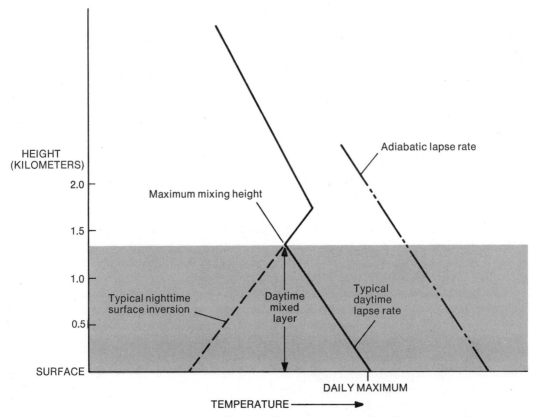

FIGURE 4.2.   Schematic representation of the effect of vertical temperature gradient on atmospheric mixing.

in turn. This vigorous vertical interchange creates a "superadiabatic" lapse rate—a temperature decrease of more than 10°C per vertical kilometer—and vertical displacements are accelerated. The depth of this well-mixed layer depends on the intensity of solar radiation and the radiation characteristics of the underlying surface. Over the deserts this vigorous mixing may extend well above three kilometers, while over forested lake country the layer may be only one or two hundred meters thick. Obviously, this effect is highly dependent on season; in winter the lesser insolation and unfavorable radiation characteristics of snow cover greatly inhibit vertical turbulence.

In contrast, with clear or partly cloudy skies the temperature profile at night is drastically changed by the rapid radiational cooling of the ground and the subsequent cooling of the layers of air near the surface. This creates an "inversion" of the daytime temperature profile, since there is now an increase in temperature with height. In such a situation the density differences rapidly damp out vertical motions, tend to reduce vertical turbulence, and stabilize the atmosphere. The longer hours of winter darkness favor the formation and maintenance of inversions. In the polar regions, in areas relatively unaffected by storms, inversions of 20°C or more may persist for weeks. Under such extreme circumstances, vertical mixing is very slow and the surface layers of the atmosphere can almost be considered as decoupled from the air above. Such a situation may also occur in middle altitudes, but—surprisingly—winter is not the time of most intense and persistent surface-based inversions. The greater frequency and intensity of large-scale storm systems, with their higher wind speeds and extensive cloud cover, tend to prevent the frequent formation of this very stable situation. It is in autumn, with its combination of relatively long nights and fewer storms, that inversions are most frequent and persistent.

Two other temperature configurations, on very different scales, have important effects on vertical turbulence and the dilution of air pollution. At the smaller end of the scale, the heat capacity of urban areas and, to a lesser extent, the heat generated by fuel consumption act to modify the temperature profile. The effect is most marked at night, as was seen in the previous chapter; heat stored by day in the buildings and streets warms the air and prevents the formation of the surface-based temperature inversion typical of rural areas. Over cities it is rare to find inversions in the lowest 100 meters, and the city influence is still evident 200 to 300 meters above the surface. Although the effect even for the largest cities is probably insignificant above a kilometer, this locally produced vertical mixing is quite important. Pollution, instead of being confined to a narrow layer near the height of emission, perhaps only 100 meters in thickness, can be freely diluted in more than double the volume of air, the concentrations being reduced by a similar factor.

On a much larger scale the temperature profile can be changed over thousands of square kilo-. meters by the action of large-scale weather systems. In traveling storm systems (cyclones) the increased pressure gradients and resulting high winds, together with the inflow of air into the storm, create relatively good vertical mixing conditions. On the other hand, the flat pressure patterns, slower movement, and slow outflow of surface air in high-pressure cells (anticyclones) result in much less favorable vertical mixing. This is primarily due to the gradual subsidence of the air aloft as it descends to replace the outflow at the surface. During this descent the air warms adiabatically, and eventually there is created a temperature inversion aloft inhibiting the upward mixing of pollution above the inversion level. As the anticyclone matures and persists, this subsidence inversion may lower to very near the ground and persist for the duration of the particular weather pattern. This pattern is typically associated with the beautiful weather of "Indian summer," but it has also been associated with all the major air-pollution disasters

(Donora, Pennsylvania, in 1948, London in 1948, 1952, and 1962, and others).

The action of mechanical turbulence in the vertical requires rather less discussion. It is obvious that if a moving mass of air reaches an obstacle it cannot penetrate, it must go over or around the obstacle. If the obstacles are numerous (blades of grass, rows of trees, or streets of buildings) the air will be constantly rising and falling. Thus, vertical mechanical turbulence is the response to the roughness of the underlying surface and has the most effect in the first few hundred meters above the surface.

Horizontal Turbulent Diffusion

The most important difference between the vertical and horizontal dimensions of diffusion is that of scale. In the vertical, rapid diffusion is limited to about ten kilometers. But in the horizontal, the entire surface of the globe is eventually available. Even when the total depth of the troposphere is considered, the horizontal scale is larger by at least three orders of magnitude, and the difference, say during a nocturnal inversion which might restrict the vertical diffusion to a few tens of meters, is even greater since the lateral turbulence is reduced less than the vertical component. Mechanically produced horizontal turbulence is, on a percentage basis, much less important than the thermal effects; its effects are of about the same order of magnitude as the vertical mechanical effects.

The thermally produced horizontal turbulence is not so neatly related to horizontal temperature gradients as vertical turbulence is to the vertical temperature profile. The horizontal temperature differences create horizontal pressure fields, which in turn drive the horizontal winds. These are acted upon by the earth's rotation (the coriolis effect) and by surface friction, so that there is no such thing as a truly steady-state wind near the surface of the earth. Wind speeds may vary from nearly zero near the surface at night in an anticyclone to 100 meters per second under the driving force of the intense pressure gradient of a hurricane. Perhaps the absolute extreme is reached in the thermally driven vortex of a tornado, where speeds of 200 meters per second or more (they have never been accurately measured) may occur. The importance of this variation, even though in air pollution we are concerned with much more modest ranges, is that for continuous sources the concentration is inversely proportional to the wind speed. Consider a source emitting one unit of pollution per second in a wind of one meter per second. If the wind increases to two meters per second, the volume of air passing the source is doubled; hence the concentration is halved. It is not quite so simple for multiple emissions in a large area source, but the variation of wind speed is still a fundamental factor in the dilution of air pollution.

The variation of turbulence in the lateral direction is perhaps the most important factor of all and certainly one of the most interesting. In practice this can best be represented by the changes in horizontal wind direction. We have the basic wind currents of the globe—the polar easterlies, the mid-latitude westerlies, the easterly trades of the subtropics, and so on. These are manifested in the semipermanent pressure systems with a superposition of traveling cyclones and anticyclones. Within each of these systems, which may be several thousand kilometers across, the wind is not steady but is varied by the temperature contrasts between ocean and land, mountain and plain, city and field. These create local land-sea breezes, up- and downslope flows, and even in special cases rural-to-city drifts of air. The situation is succinctly described in a parody of a verse by Swift attributed to the meteorologist L. F. Richardson: "Great whirls have little whirls, that feed on their velocity; and little whirls have lesser whirls, and so on to viscosity."

The net effect of these systems is a constantly

varying wind direction. Within a few minutes, the wind may fluctuate rapidly through 90 degrees or more. Over a few hours it may shift, still with much short-period variability, through 180 degrees, and in the course of a month it will have changed through 360 degrees numerous times. Over the seasons, preferred directional patterns will be established depending upon latitude and large-scale pressure patterns. These patterns may be very stable over many years, thus establishing the wind climatology of a particular location.

The emitted pollution travels with this ever-varying wind. The high-frequency fluctuations spread out the pollutant, and the relatively steady "average" direction carries it off—for example, toward a suburb or a business district. A gradual turning of direction transports material toward new targets and gives a respite to the previous ones. Every few days the cycle is repeated, and over the years the prevailing winds can create semipermanent patterns of pollution downwind from factories or cities.

Atmospheric Transport

It is convenient to distinguish the turbulent diffusion of pollution from the bulk transport of pollution away from its source. In fact, the statistical theories of diffusion speak of a steady mean flow and the turbulent fluctuations about this mean. This separation, however, is very dependent on the time and space scale of interest. Five hours of southwest wind may become only statistical fluctuations about a mean monthly northwesterly flow, which is in turn a portion of the annual wind-frequency distribution. Nevertheless, this division of wind behavior into turbulent fluctuations and mean flow is of practical value, because it permits the use of average wind statistics (the mean flow) to describe the "ventilation" of an area. Certain features of the physiography and meteorology of particular areas can seriously reduce this trans-

port or ventilation. Two of the most effective mechanisms for this reduction are topographical barriers and semipermanent subsidence inversions.

Topographical barriers are best described by examples. The semicircular ring of hills and mountains around the Los Angeles Basin slows the flow of air in and out of the area and acts to form a catch basin for pollutants. On a much larger scale, the Great Basin of Utah and Nevada functions in the same way, particularly in winter, providing a huge bowl which can contain a stagnating air mass with very light winds of variable direction. The narrow valleys of western Pennsylvania also act to slow the flow, but in this instance air movement is constrained to follow the contours of the valley, so that the natural variability of the wind is largely ineffective and pollution repeatedly follows the same path. Again on a larger scale, the San Joaquin Valley of California has much the same effect. The persistent surface fogs of the winter season attest to the reduced air transport in the surface layers of air in this area.

The semipermanent inversion is a feature of west coasts of continents throughout the world; Africa, the Iberian Peninsula, South America, and the southwestern coast of the United States all have this typical vertical-turbulence lid created by the subsidence associated with the semipermanent high-pressure areas of the eastern subtropical oceans. If, as in the case of southern California and Chile, there is also a mountain barrier, the meteorological stage is set for man and his technology to create a persistent air-pollution problem.

Applications of
Air-Pollution Meteorology

A military weapons system—in this instance the use of gas in World War I—led to the early quantitative meteorological studies on the dilution of pollutants by the atmosphere. Application to military technology has continued and has provided much valuable information for application to more general and widespread civilian problems.

The major American effort in the meteorology of air pollution began with the Manhattan Engineering Project and the construction of the Hanford Works in the state of Washington. A group of meteorologists, under the direction of Phil E. Church of the University of Washington, set the pattern by measuring, in detail, the variations, wind speed, and direction throughout the Hanford area, and used a 125-meter instrument tower to measure vertical wind and temperature profiles. This early program was followed by similar efforts at the National Laboratories at Brookhaven, Oak Ridge, and Argonne, at the National Reactor Testing Station, and at the Nevada Test Site. Other nuclear sites have had similar meteorological studies.

As understanding of the diffusion process has become more exact, meteorological information has been used more frequently in the design of experiments involving the release of radioactivity, both in order to optimize safety and to increase the efficiency of the experiment. Knowledge of the seasonal and diurnal frequency of necessary wind directions and trajectories helps in scheduling experiments so as to minimize weather delays. Knowledge of the existing meteorology during experiments is often indispensable for the correct evaluation of test results.

On a much larger scale, knowledge of global circulation patterns, long-range diffusion, and atmospheric removal processes, part of it gained by using the radioactive debris of previous tests as wide-ranging meteorological tracers, has permitted accurate forecasts of the time and space distribution of global fallout to be expected in various parts of the world.

Still another use of air-pollution meteorology is in the analysis of an accident, particularly in the determination of the amount of material released. In the two major reactor accidents that have occurred, one at Windscale, England, in 1957 and the other at the National Reactor Testing Station in 1961, perhaps the best estimates of the amount of radioactivity released to the air were obtained by calculating the diffusion equations backward, from the observed concentrations through the existing meteorological conditions to the source strength.

The information thus developed facilitates one of the most important uses of air-pollution meteorology: the planning of the location of pollution sources in relation to sensitive areas (people, animals, and vegetation). Proper site selection makes possible the use of the average features of the weather to minimize the effects of air pollution. Preplanning can be applied to problems of all sizes—choice of location for a rendering plant, selection of a site for a nuclear or coal-fired power plant, urban industrial zoning. The meteorology involved can be as simple as determing the direction of the most prevalent wind or so complex as to require three-dimensional wind statistics, temperature profiles to several kilometers, and data about air trajectories for tens of kilometers from the site. The most efficient solutions must take into account not just meteorology alone, but the entire process, including the economics.

Meteorology and
Urban Air Pollution

In the applications previously discussed, the pollution source is usually discrete, readily identifiable, and, with sufficient effort, amenable to individual study and analysis. In fact, most diffusion theory and experiment have been directed to such sources. These problems are important and will remain so. Air-pollution meteorology is being increasingly applied, however, to the growing problem of urban air pollution, and here the number and variety of pollution sources prohibit individual study. Indeed, one of the major sources, the automobile, does not even stay put. Another complication and one of the most interesting features of this entire problem is that, while in the short term the meteorology of diffusion shows great variation and pollution emissions stay relatively constant, over periods of several years it is the meteorology that becomes stable and the pollution sources that vary.

To deal with these factors, two different approaches have been used. For the short term— and to answer such questions as: What is the statistical distribution of pollutant concentrations? Do different pollutants behave differently in the atmosphere? What are the effects of pollution on weather?—the meteorologist has inverted the problem; instead of calculating the field of concentration from a known source (source-oriented approach), he examines the measured field of concentration and the concurrent weather, and through standard statistical techniques relates the two (receptor-oriented approach). This technique has produced interesting results concerning the atmospheric "half-life" of pollutants, the seasonal variability of pollution, the role of sunlight in the production of photochemical smog, and the reduction of

solar radiation in cities, to mention only a few examples.

In fact, one of the most recent applications of meteorology completely ignores the source. Several years ago the Weather Bureau, on the basis of a statistical evaluation of the concurrent relation of high air-pollution values and large-scale meteorology, found that persistent high values of air pollution were associated with large areas of light wind, at the surface and aloft (slow horizontal ventilation), and sufficient atmospheric stability to inhibit vertical motion. See Figures 4.3 and 4.4. These conditions are most often associated with a slowly moving or stagnant anticyclone; hence the designation of this condition as a "stagnation" model.

In 1963, after several years of successful testing, the Weather Bureau began issuing "Air Pollution Potential Forecasts" for the United States when meteorological conditions satisfy the stagnation model and are expected to persist for at least 36 hours. These are area forecasts and are currently limited to situations where at least

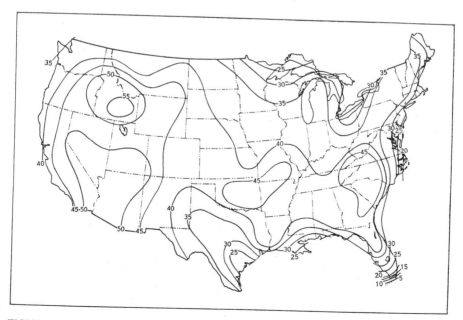

FIGURE 4.3.   Average percentage of hours of low-level inversions per day in the fall season.

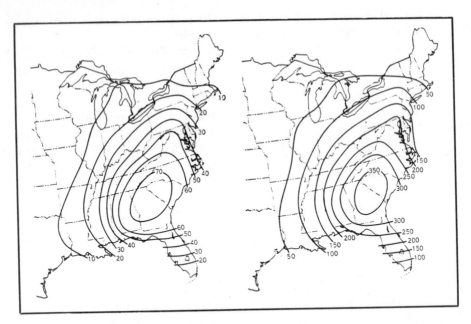

FIGURE 4.4. Frequency of large-scale slow dilution (stagnating anticyclones). Isopleths at left are average number of occurences of stagnation "cases"—4 days or more—in the period 1936–1960. Isopleths at right are average number of days of stagnation in the same period.

90,000 square kilometers are affected. This limitation is necessary because of the significant role played by very local meteorological variations (such as sea breezes or mountain-valley winds) and local pollution emissions, neither of which can be adequately predicted from the large-scale meteorology. In particular the designation "Pollution Potential" is required. If a stagnation area occurs in the Great Plains (as has happened), the air-pollution levels should be very different from those in a similar weather pattern over the industrialized Atlantic States (and they have been). These forecasts, by making advance preparation possible, provide unique opportunities for examining high pollution levels through medical studies, special sampling programs, and so on. Eventually they may contribute to the reduction of pollution levels through control of emissions during these unfavorable periods.

Other applications require a "source-oriented"

viewpoint for answers to the questions: What is the origin of this particular pollutant? What are the effects of new pollution controls? Given a specific growth rate, what are the likely future concentrations of pollution? In this approach the sources within a city might be grouped into, for example, industrial, domestic, transportation; then subdivided according to constituents— sulfur dioxide, carbon monoxide, and so on; and further divided by allocation to specific geographical areas. One of the most promising developments of recent years has been the success of mathematical models of urban diffusion, which can accept such source information and calculate the field of urban pollution concentration.

The initial field test of such a model was carried out in Nashville, Tennessee, in conjunction with an intensive program of pollution measurements and medical surveys conducted by the Public Health Service and Vanderbilt

University. Citywide concentrations of sulfur dioxide were computed for periods as short as two hours, and these values were summed to obtain average daily levels. The model, which incorporated an SO_2 "half-life" and rated all the sources within a 2.5-square-kilometer source area as if they were centered in the middle of this area, was not very sophisticated meteorologically, although it did, by virtue of the two-hour time step, allow for diurnal variability. Crude as this first attempt at prediction was, it gave results that were very similar to the observed values and that in fact had a smaller variability than the sampling values with which the computations were compared. Source inventories are under way which have enabled refinement of the model to be made in other locations. At the same time additional measurements of the diffusion within cities and studies of the best way to measure city ventilation rates will enable the meteorological portion of this and other models to be more sophisticated and more realistic. This work was performed, as one would expect, on a high-speed computer. As in so many other scientific problems, the required calculations (about 10^6 for the 24-hour average concentration field) became feasible only with such assistance.

The use of mathematical models for computer solution appears to promise much in the quantitative determination of pollution concentrations and the evalaution of control strategies, as we shall see in Chapter 5. As we learn more about the meteorology of cities and the distribution of pollutant emissions, it may be possible to predict expected concentrations routinely and to take into account the changes in the patterns that would occur if the emissions were changed. The auto-exhaust pollution from the Sunday-driver pattern could be differentiated from that of the weekday rush-hour regardless of the variation in the atmospheric dilution. On a larger scale, it is expected that computer-produced "Air Pollution Potential Forecasts" will replace the present techniques, which require both manual

data analysis and personal judgment, and will extend both the time period and detail of these forecasts.

Future Problems

Much remains to be learned about how the atmosphere acts to dilute materials and eventually to rid itself of them. The problem is particularly acute within cities, since there now exists no adequate model to describe, in quantitative terms, the movement of air through such a complex structure as an entire city, and since most industrial pollution originates within the city itself. In the near future a major effort will be required to determine the cumulative effect on air purity of the complex of cities that are expanding and combining to create the megalopolis. Here the problem requires consideration of weather patterns over several days and hundreds of kilometers, if we are to determine the extent to which pollution from "foreign" sources 100 to 500 kilometers upwind adds to the locally emitted pollution. On this scale, chemical interactions of pollutants and their "half-lives," the effects of sunlight and humidity, the effects of depletion of pollutants due to deposition, and so on, must be known. None of these problems appears to defy practical solution, but a program of research, probably culminating in extensive, long-range tracer experiments, will be required.

In the longer, and larger, view perhaps the most important future problem is to achieve better understanding of the geochemistry of atmospheric pollutants. It has been pointed out that there are probably no undisturbed atmospheric conditions left in any of the mechanized areas of the world. The possible "greenhouse" effect of carbon dioxide is not known precisely. Sulfur is emitted to the atmosphere in ever-increasing amounts, but we know neither its fate nor its rate of addition with any precision. A careful, long-term program of measurement, probably of global extent, of the most important pollutants, additional research to increase our understanding of the self-cleansing mechanisms of the atmosphere, and more knowledge about the relation between air pollution and climate are required if we are to safeguard the air reservoir in which we live and breathe.

AIR-POLLUTION SURVEILLANCE SYSTEMS

Surveillance of air pollution is an integral and very important part of the total control effort. The data derived from atmospheric monitoring and emission measurements are required throughout the various stages of the abatement effort. Atmospheric surveillance efforts serve to identify the pollutants emitted to the air, to establish their concentrations, and to record their trends and patterns. Subsequently, after air quality and emission standards have been legislated, surveillance systems may be used to evaluate the progress being made in meeting standards, and to facilitate direct enforcement activities including the activation of emergency control procedures during episodes of high air pollution.

The surveillance problem is complex because, given suitable conditions, many of the primary pollutants (those gases and particulates that are emitted directly from sources) will participate in reactions in the atmosphere that produce secondary pollutants such as those found in photochemical smog. One example of the production of secondary pollutants is the combination of water vapor with acid anhydrides to produce an acid aerosol that is corrosive. Particulates may provide a substrate for such atmospheric reactions or may contain metallic catalysts. Solar energy, primarily the ultraviolet portion of the spectrum, accelerates these reactions.

Concentrations of pollutants are extremely variable from one city to another and also within a given urban area. The relative intensity and spatial configuration of sources, the topography,

and the meteorology of an area affect pollutant concentrations. Zones of heavier pollution in each city are caused by the clustering of major sources of air pollution—that is, traffic-congested central business districts and industrial sectors. In cities characterized by good ventilation, emissions are dispersed more rapidly than in cities that are surrounded by hills or where the winds are low and temperature inversions are frequent. Even areas with typically good dispersion can occasionally suffer pollution episodes when a stagnant high-pressure air mass persists.

Surveillance

The first national air surveillance system was implemented in 1953 when the Public Health Service, in cooperation with state and local health departments, set up air sampling stations in seventeen communities. Samples were collected primarily to permit the determination of total airborne protein. In addition, they were analyzed for total suspended particulates, organic matter soluble in benzene and acetone, and several inorganic pollutants. At present EPA is collecting air-quality data for the pollutants listed in Table 4.5. Table 4.2, it will be recalled, presented some typical average concentrations of some of these pollutants for the period from 1966 to 1967.

Present-day surveillance of the nation's air quality is a cooperative effort involving local, state, and federal air-pollution control agencies. There are over 7,000 sampling stations, with some 14,000 samplers, located throughout the United States. They range in complexity from simple static sampling devices to continuous sampler-analyzers that record the concentrations of numerous gaseous air pollutants. Most of these sampling stations are located in major metropolitan areas.

The surveillance conducted by state and local air-pollution control agencies is directed toward enforcement activities. Aerometric data are used to appraise concentrations of specific pollutants

TABLE 4.5

Atmospheric pollutants currently being measured by Environmental Protection Agency

Elements	Radicals
Antimony	Ammonium
Arsenic	Fluoride
Barium	Nitrate
Beryllium	Sulfate
Bismuth	
Boron	*Others*
Cadmium	Aeroallergens
Chromium	Asbestos
Cobalt	β-Radioactivity
Copper	Benzene-soluble organic
Iron	compounds
Lead	Benzo[a]pyrene
Manganese	Pesticides
Mercury	Respirable particulates
Molybdenum	Total suspended particulates
Nickel	
Selenium	*Gases*
Tin	Carbon monoxide
Titanium	Methane
Vanadium	Nitric oxide
Zinc	Nitrogen dioxide
	Pesticides
	Reactive hydrocarbons
	Sulfur dioxide
	Total hydrocarbons
	Total oxidants

to determine whether they exceed the standards, to provide direct control actions, to determine ambient air quality in nonurban areas of a region, and to provide air-quality data during air-pollution episodes. These surveillance systems are primarily designed to sample for pollutants for which criteria documents have been issued—that is, total suspended particulates, sulfur dioxide, carbon monoxide, total oxidants, and total hydrocarbons. The placement or location of sampling stations within the surveillance network must be such that ensuing data can be gainfully employed to meet the following objectives: (1) stations must be oriented to define air quality in heavily polluted areas; (2) stations must be oriented to define air quality in heavily populated areas; (3) stations must be located to provide areawide representation of ambient air quality; (4) stations must be oriented with respect to the source category or source, or both, to provide feedback relative to the effectiveness of adopted control strategies.

The federal monitoring system provides a uniform data base throughout the country against which all other air-quality data can be verified; this system measures pollutants that are expensive or unusually difficult to analyze, identifies and quantifies new or newly recognized pollutants, conducts research in measurement techniques, and demonstrates the impact of pollutant emissions on the air quality of both urban and nonurban areas.

Instrumentation

Solid-state or advanced sensors that have sensitivity, specificity, and reliability are urgently needed and would overcome the problems that now exist with present wet chemical methods. In addition, new techniques will be needed as the air-pollution control effort is expanded to encompass the less abundant and newly recognized air pollutants. Examples of some of the pollutants for which adequate or economical instrumentation and analytical techniques are not yet available include asbestos, pesticides, mercury, odors, and selenium. It is important that measurement methods be capable of providing information for averaging times consistent with established air-quality standards.

A variety of sampling devices are currently being used to evaluate ambient air quality. Table 4.6 illustrates the general classes and their applicability. Mechanized samplers are the most generally used in surveillance systems to collect integrated samples in the field. The most common of these devices is EPA's high volume (Hi-Vol) sampler, which collects particulates on glass-fiber filters. Analysis of these samples provides information on concentrations of total suspended particulates, trace metals, and other organic and inorganic pollutants. In addition to

TABLE 4.6

Classification of air-pollution sampling techniques

Type	Use	Specificity	Common Averaging Time	Relative Cost	Required Training of Personnel	Remarks
Static						
Settleable particulates (dustfall)	Mapping and definition of special problem areas	Total settled particulates and general classes of pollutants	1 month	Collection, low; analysis, high	Collection, low; analysis, moderate	Well-equipped laboratory required for analysis only for definition of problem areas where a chemical analysis will pinpoint a particular source. Sensitive to temperature, wind, and humidity.
Sulfation devices	Mapping and general survey for sulfur dioxide	Responds to oxides of sulfur, hydrogen sulfide, and sulfuric acid	1 month	Collection, low; analysis, high	Collection, low; analysis, moderate to high	
Mechanized						
Hi-Vol	Integrated quantification of suspended particulate	Total suspended particulate and multiple specific pollutants	24 hours	Moderate	Moderate	Detailed chemical analysis of Hi-Vol and gas samples requires sophisticated laboratory, trained chemists; cost is high.
Gas sampler	Integrated quantification of gases	Sulfur dioxide, nitrogen dioxide, ammonia, total oxidants, aldehydes, and other gases	24 hours	Moderate	High	
Spot tape sampler	Relative soiling index	Unknown	2 hours	Low	Low	Provides only a rough, relative index of particulate soiling.
Automatic						
Gas	Continuous analysis of gaseous pollutants	Single gas or group of related gases	Continuous; sample integration usually 1 to 15 minutes	Moderate to high	Moderate to high	Continuous measurements allow use of any desired averaging time by computation. Accuracy is generally much better than other methods. Calibration is simplified. Data are available instantaneously.
Particulate: soiling (automatic tape)	Continuous analysis of soiling rate	Unknown	Continuous; sample integration usually 1 to 15 minutes	Moderate	Moderate	

Cost basis: low, 0 to $500; moderate, $500 to $2000; high, above $2000. Personnel training: low, maintenance level; moderate, technician; high, experienced technician or professional with professional support staff.

the glass-fiber filter, the membrane filter is used to collect for subsequent analysis pollutants such as zinc, asbestos, boron, and silicates. Impactors of different designs are used to measure fractions of suspended particulates of various particle sizes in the respirable range.

PERCEPTION OF AIR POLLUTION

Improved surveillance networks are now providing an increasingly rich array of air-quality data to professionals and planners. The question that then ought be asked is the nature of public perceptions of the pollution problem, and especially the ability of people to discriminate among different levels of pollution intensity. Some evidence about awareness and perception has been provided in one recent study of Toronto, Canada, undertaken by Auliciems and Burton (1970). These authors drew their evidence on public awareness of air pollution in Toronto from two recent surveys. A study made in 1967 by Peter A. Barnes, then a student in the Department of Geography at the University of Toronto, involved the interviewing of 200 households randomly selected from areas immediately adjacent to pollution recording and monitoring stations. These respondents were interviewed by Barnes and others in person. The second study was conducted in 1969 by Brian Shepherd for Pollution Probe, an action-oriented citizens' group based at the University of Toronto. The Shepherd study involved interviewing 214 respondents by telephone.

Barnes' respondents were presented with a list of ten local problems and asked to rate each according to their degree of "satisfaction" on a five-point scale. The question was asked with reference to both the respondent's own neighborhood and the city in general. The results are listed in Table 4.7. Air pollution clearly ranked as the number-one problem perceived in both the neighborhoods and the city. Forty-five percent of the respondents described the air-pollution problem as very unsatisfactory in Toronto; a further 42.5 percent said it was moderately unsatisfactory. Water pollution was ranked fifth for the city—behind air pollution, traffic congestion, juvenile delinquency, and noise.

Shepherd's respondents were read a list of "areas of political importance" and asked how the government should rate each item. In one case air and water pollution were not listed separately, but "pollution control" headed the list, with 82.3 percent of the respondents classifying it as extremely important. Detailed figures are listed in Table 4.8. When respondents were asked to indicate which type of pollution they were most concerned about, the largest group, 37.4 percent, chose an answer stating that all types of pollution are equally important. Among three individual types of pollution, however—air, water, and soil—air pollution was ranked highest with 27.6 percent, compared with a close 24.3 percent for water pollution (see Table 4.9).

The two surveys also addressed the question of particular sources of pollution. Nearly half of Shepherd's respondents (45 percent) could not name a specific source of pollution. About one in four respondents (27 percent) could name a source for air pollution, and these included vehicle exhausts (13 percent) and smoke from factories and apartments (5 percent). In the Barnes survey sources of pollution were suggested. Of the eight possible sources listed, automobiles headed the list.

What accounts for this demonstrably high degree of public awareness about the air-pollution problem in Toronto? To what extent is it due to the severity of the problem itself as indicated in instrumental measurements of pollutants on direct sensory experience, and to what extent do the mass media play a role?

TABLE 4.7

Awareness of problems relating to Toronto[a]

Order of Presentation	Area of Concern	Toronto		Neighborhood
		Very Unsatisfactory	Very and Moderately Unsatisfactory	Very and Moderately Unsatisfactory
5	Air pollution	46	88.5 (1)[b]	60 (1)
7	Traffic congestion	38.5	73 (2)	39.5 (2)
4	Juvenile delinquency	29.5	72 (3)	38.5 (3)
6	Noise levels	20.5	56 (4)	37 (4)
10	Water pollution	27	39.5 (5)	26.5 (6)
9	General congestion of population	12.5	27.5 (6)	18.5 (7)
1	Availability of recreational areas and programs	6.5	22 (7)	35 (5)
2	Employment levels	6	14.5 (8)	13.5 (8)
3	Garbage collection and disposal	3.5	12.5 (9)	9.5 (9)
8	Racial problems	1	11.5 (10)	4.5 (10)

[a] Q: How would you rate each of these for Toronto? How would you rate your own neighborhood in terms of these problems?
[b] Indicates rank.

Physiological Perception of Pollutants

For many large cities, the broad cause-and-effect relations of air pollution may be represented by schematic diagrams such as Figure 4.5, in which, for example, sulfur dioxide may directly cause health effects, or may also reach sufficient concentrations to become an odor nuisance, or may through oxidation and combination with suspended water droplets form sulfuric acid, which in turn may produce material, vegetation, or physiological damage.

But the complexity of these interrelations is apparently poorly understood and seldom perceived. While pollutants may be variously perceived at any stage following emission, the strongest stimuli in Toronto apparently are provided by the visible particulates such as smoke, vehicle exhaust gases, reduced visibility by haze, and the soiling of buildings, cars, and clothing by deposited matter. What is critical in this is that the visually most readily perceived particles are least likely to constitute health hazards, owing to their relatively easy elimination from the human system; rather, they are simply a soiling nuisance. As in most North American cities, the unburnt gaseous exhaust emissions of motor vehicles must be considered a major source of pollution. However, owing to the absence of conditions in Toronto which lead to the formation of smog, the hydrocarbons are not perceived as a health danger, but in view of their aromatic properties, they are classed instead as odor nuisances. The accompanying discharge of the highly poisonous carbon monoxide is of course imperceptible, since the gas is both colorless and odorless, and since physiolo-

TABLE 4.8

Awareness of Problems Concerning the Government[a]

Order of Presentation	Problem	Percentage of Respondents Regarding Problem as . . .	
		"Extremely Important"	"Extremely Important" Plus "Important"
3	Pollution control	82.3 (1)[b]	100 (1)
8	Inflation	58.6 (2)	90.4 (4)
4	Housing	55.6 (3)	92.1 (2)
9	Health and welfare	45.4 (4)	91.3 (3)
5	Unemployment	43.0 (5)	89.8 (5)
2	Indian affairs	43.0 (5)	87.9 (7)
6	National unity	42.5 (7)	84.5 (8)
1	Northern Ontario	29.4 (8)	89.3 (6)
7	Tourist development	13.2 (9)	67.4 (9)

[a] Q: I am going to read you a list of areas of political importance and would like you to tell me how "important" you feel the Government should rate each item.
[b] Indicates rank.

TABLE 4.9

Concern for types of pollution[a]

Order of Presentation	Problem	Percentage of Respondents . . .	
		"Most Concerned"	"Least Concerned"
1	Air pollution	27.6	10.3
2	Water pollution	24.3	4.2
3	Soil pollution	0.9	36.5

Air and water pollution equally important	8.0%
All pollution is equally important	37.4%
Other combinations	1.8%

[a] Q: Of the three following types of pollution, which are you most concerned about? Least concerned about?

gical impairment may not be recognized until the onset of such acute symptoms as headache, dizziness, nausea, fainting, and so on.

Apart from hydrocarbons and carbon monoxide, the most serious toxic and corrosive gaseous pollutants monitored in Toronto are oxides of sulfur (SO_2) and nitrogen (NO_2), and oxidants. The perception of gaseous matter depends mainly upon the sense of smell, which may, or may not, precede physiological damage. As illustrated by Figures 4.6 and 4.7, biological impairment (and material deterioration) is related to the duration of exposure to a pollutant, and it is possible that serious damage may eventuate from very low and imperceptible concentrations.

The determination of olfactory threshold levels of the atmospheric pollutants presents difficulties, owing not only to possible additive, antagonistic, potentiation, and synergetic combinations of the substances but also to the individual variability and state of health of the perceiver. However, an inspection of Table 4.10, which shows the existing concentrations of the major pollutants in Toronto, together with determined olfactory threshold levels and lowest observed values of physiological effect, suggests that the gases can only very rarely be perceived by the primary sensory mechanisms. Thus given the nature and concentrations of the pollutants in Toronto, it is paradoxical that direct sensory perception of the contaminants is related more to the visual and olfactory stimuli of the less hazardous pollutants.

The argument above implies that, in the absence of very unusual atmospheric conditions, the citizens of Toronto are actually unable to perceive differences between the degrees of pollution by the continuously monitored gases. This supposition is supported by an earlier study in Buffalo in which correlation between the degree of sulfation (not much different to that found in Toronto) and subjective perception showed important inconsistencies. In Barnes's survey there were also indications of people's inability to perceive the toxic gases in the present concentrations. Responses to the question "In your opinion, is air pollution worse in any particular season?" indicated summer as the most polluted season, although maximum concentrations of sulfur dioxide occur in the winter

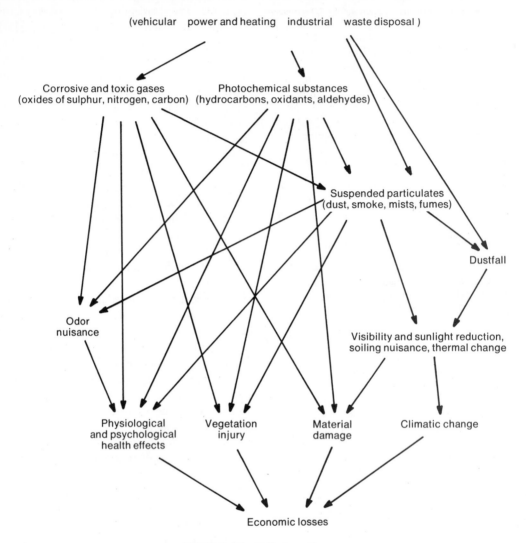

FIGURE 4.5.   Pollution effects.

months with a pronounced minimum in summer (Table 4.11). The concentrations of nitrogen dioxide and the oxidants do not appear to be seasonal, but the aromatic hydrocarbons and the deposition of particulate matter peak in spring. Similar results were recorded in St. Louis, where it was pointed out that awareness of pollution may be more related to people's seasonal behavior than to actual pollution concentrations.

There is additional evidence of incongruity between physiological perception of air pollution and what people report. The Barnes survey respondents were asked to indicate which of six specific effects of air pollution affected them personally. The responses (Table 4.12) are sur-

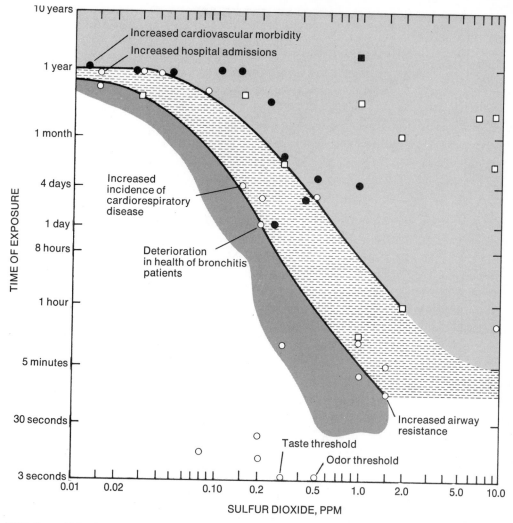

KEY: O, morbidity in man; ●, mortality in man; ◻, morbidity in animals, ◼, mortality in animals, shaded area, range of concentrations and exposure times in which deaths have been reported in excess of normal expectation; dashed area, range of concentrations and exposure times in which significant health effects have been reported; speckled area, ranges of concentrations and exposure times in which health effects are suspected.

FIGURE 4.6. Effects of SO_2 on health.

prisingly strong. That 56 percent of the respondents are personally affected by particulate matter is credible. So is the report that 21 percent can identify poor visibility or haze. But in a city that is not subject to photochemical smog and where it is highly unlikely that the toxic gases have even rarely achieved sufficient concentrations to induce irritation of the mucous membranes, it is surprising to note that 30 percent of the respondents reported experience of respiratory irritation and 29 percent irritation of the eyes which they attributed to air pollution.

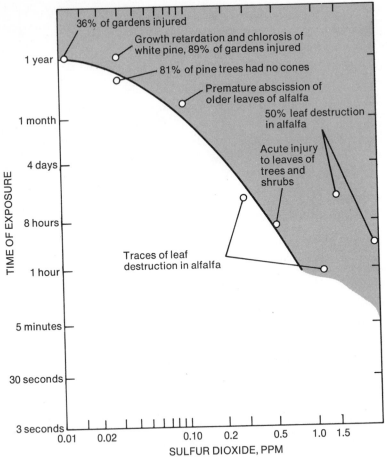

FIGURE 4.7.   Effects of SO₂ on vegetation (after Stern).

KEY: Shaded area, range of concentrations and exposure times in which injury to vegetation has been reported, white area, range of concentrations and exposure times of undetermined significance to vegetation.

These results were probably obtained by the procedures Barnes used. If, instead of naming six effects, the interviewer had simply asked: "In what ways are you personally affected by air pollution?" the responses probably would have been significantly lower. Nevertheless, the fact that respondents are willing to say that they suffer irritation of the eyes or respiratory tract, and to attribute this to air pollution, indicates again the high degree of public awareness and suggests again that it is the result of factors other than or in addition to direct sensory experience.

The Communications Media

It seems clear that the statements of experts as reported in the media and the rising level of journalistic accounts have been major forces contributing to the growth of public awareness and concern, rather than any increase in the problem itself, or some change in people's ability to discriminate different physiological impacts. In some cases the media have been accused of irresponsible reporting likely to cause undue public alarm. A well-known case in point

TABLE 4.10

Gaseous concentrations in central Toronto,[a] threshold and physiological effect levels[b] (ppm)

Pollutant	Olfactory Threshold Level	Physiological Effect Level	Mean Worst Month	Mean Year	Maximum in Year	Number of Hours in Year	Exceeding ppm
SO2	0.5	0.3	0.13	0.07	0.88	37	> 0.4[c]
			0.07	0.05	0.50	3	> 0.4[d]
			0.17	0.10	1.15	112	> 0.4[e]
NO2	0.1	0.3	0.05	0.04	0.22	2	> 0.2
CO	—	2.7	4.15	3.04	15.00	2648	> 4.0
Oxidants	0.2 (in smog)	0.3 (in smog)	0.03	0.02	0.13	0	> 0.15
Hydrocarbons	Various	?	4.14	2.10	15.00	4	> 10.0

[a] Department of Energy and Resources Management (1969).
[b] From various sources in *Air Pollution*, edited by Stern (1962).
[c] Average of five stations. [d] Least polluted station. [e] Most polluted station.

TABLE 4.11

Seasonal awareness of pollution and concentrations

	Spring	Summer	Fall	Winter
SO2 deposition, mean ppm/month (20 stations)	18.8	7.9	15.7	24.7
Hydrocarbons, mean ppm/month	3.3	1.0	0.7	1.7
Dustfall, mean tons/sq. mile/month	31.4	24.2	22.8	23.8

	Percentage of Respondents Who Observed no Seasonality	Percentage of Respondents Who Judged Pollution Worst According to Season			
Toronto	24.5	16.5	31.0	17.0	11.0
Neighborhood	40.5	11.0	25.0	14.0	9.5

is the Canadian Broadcasting Corporation's television program *Air of Death*, which led to the establishment of a special independent inquiry by the Ontario Government into the fluorosis poisoning in the vicinity of the Erco plant near Dunnville, Ontario. The program itself was subsequently the subject of an inquiry by the Canadian Radio and Television Commission.

Since there appear to have been no studies of air pollution in Toronto prior to 1967, it is not possible to chart with any accuracy the growth of public concern. It seems safe to assume, however, that it has followed closely the growth in newspaper coverage. Figure 4.8 shows the increase in number of newspaper items on an annual basis from 1958 to 1969 for air and water pollution in the Toronto *Globe and Mail*. For comparative purposes a similar curve is shown

TABLE 4.12

Reported effects of air pollutiou in Toronto[a]

Order of Presentation	Effect	Percentage of Respondents Identifying Ill Effects	
1	Particulate matter/dust	56.5	(1)[a]
6	Odor	54.5	(2)
3	Discoloring of buildings, laundry, etc.	33.2	(3)
5	Respiratory irritation	30.0	(4)
4	Irritation of eyes	29.5	(5)
2	Poor visibility or haze	21.5	(6)

[a] Q: Are there any ill effects of air pollution that affect you personally?
[b] Indicates rank.

for the *New York Times*. Referring to the nature of pollution coverage by the press, Ken Lefolii has recently stated: "In the media, pollution has the top of the charts all to itself, number one in the magazines, number one on television, number one in the papers." Much higher than that it is not possible to go.

The Consequences of Awareness

As a result of the high degree of public awareness of air pollution in Toronto the general public has begun to take action. A citizens' organization has been formed called GASP (Group Action to Stop Pollution). This organization has focused most of its attention on air pollution. So far however, it has been inclined to take a legalistic approach and has become neither a mass movement nor notably activist.

Quiet diplomacy does not characterize the activity of another Toronto group, however, called Pollution Probe. Established in early 1969 and based at the University of Toronto, this group has attacked a number of pollution problems. A minor storm was created about the use of diazinon by the Metro Parks Department in

the summer of 1969, when a "public inquiry" was held by Pollution Probe into the death of a number of ducks found by Probers on Toronto Island. Pollution Probe activities have included a mass procession and funeral service for the Don River, and publication of the phosphate content of particular brands of detergents, which was followed very quickly by an announcement by the federal minister of energy, mines and resources, that phosphates would be banned from detergents in Canada by 1972. Probe activities also played a role in the Ontario Government decision in November 1969 to ban the use of DDT Recently Probe has been attacking the air pollution problem, specifically the sulphur dioxide emitted by Ontario Hydro's Hearn Generating Station. Dramatic Probe advertisements on air pollution have also been reaching the general public in the *Toronto Telegram*.

In addition to joining and supporting the activities of GASP and Pollution Probe, it appears from the surveys reported above that Toronto citizens are anxious to do more and see more done about the problem. The Shepherd survey asked about the appropriate use of penalties against polluters. The results are listed in

TABLE 4.13

Suggested penalties against polluters in Toronto[a]

Penalty	Percentage of Respondents Preferring as	
	First Action	Eventual Action
A warning	55	–
A token fine	14	1
A stiff, substantial fine	24	37
Closing down the polluting operation	6	58

[a] Q: Which penalties against polluters would you support as a first action? Which of these is the strongest measure you would not accept as unreasonable for eventual action?

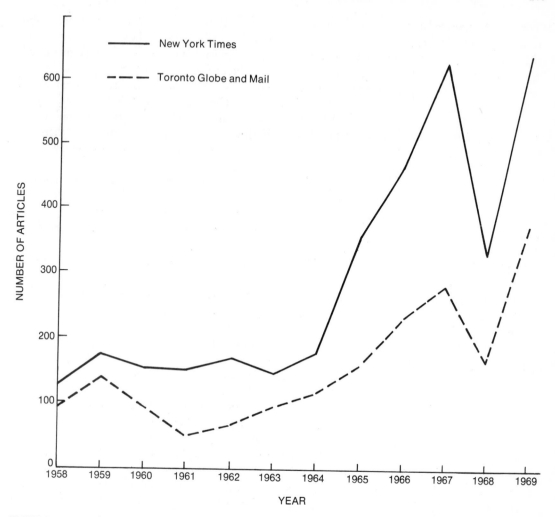

FIGURE 4.8. Annual totals of combined air- and water-pollution articles appearing in the *New York Times* and *Toronto Globe and Mail*, 1958–1969.

Table 4.13. While 55 percent would prefer a warning as the first government action, as many as 37 percent thought that action should begin with a fine, and 58 percent thought that eventual action should involve closing down the polluting operation.

The Shepherd survey also asked about willingness to pay. Recognizing the limitations of this type of question in which the respondent only has to *say* what he is willing to do with no immediate fear of actually having to do it, it is interesting to compare Toronto responses with those in a recent U.S. national opinion poll run by Gallup for the National Wildlife Federation. The U.S. question asked about the willingness to pay increased taxes to improve natural surroundings. The Shepherd survey question was specifically directed to pollution control in

Toronto. As indicated in Table 4.14, the distribution of responses in Toronto was more extreme than the U.S. national sample. In Toronto there were both more people unwilling to pay and more people willing to pay a moderate or large

TABLE 4.14

Suggested financial contributions in Toronto and the U.S.[a]

	Percentage of Respondents Willing to Pay	
	Toronto	U.S.
None or noncommittal	41	27
Small amount ($10 or less)	12	51
$10–$40	14	–
Moderate or large amount ($40+ in Toronto $50+ in U.S.)	29	22

[a] Q: (In Toronto) Considering the problem of pollution and that in the final analysis the public, you, pays for it either in taxes or cost of goods and services, how much money in total do you think you yourself would be willing to contribute per year to eliminating pollution?

(In U.S.) How much would you be willing to pay each year in additional taxes earmarked to improve our natural surroundings?

amount. Even with the high degree of public awareness, 41 percent in Toronto were unwilling to pay or were noncommittal. On the other hand, 29 percent of Shepherd's respondents did say that they would pay $40 or more annually. In Toronto 58 percent thought that the polluter should bear the costs, 23 percent thought the government should pay, and 15 percent supported a shared-cost arrangement.

Implications for Public Policy

Toronto citizens, like citizens elsewhere, thus were shown in the Barnes and Shepherd studies to be highly aware of air pollution. They were getting organized and they were anxious for

something to be done. They even were willing to pay. Their awareness, however, was generated to a considerable degree by the mass media, and the potentially most dangerous pollutants were not those that can be readily detected by the senses. The problem was seen as more serious for the city as a whole than for a person's neighborhood. Under these circumstances there was some danger that the sense of urgency would decline, that the crisis would pass, and that the public would again become apathetic. The consequences would probably be that little would be done to curb the growth of the problem, and a steady decline would take place toward future disaster.

The development of successful policies for environmental quality control depends on the understanding of an *educated* and *informed* public. Given the limitations of physiological perception and media-induced mass movements, it is important therefore to develop ways of communicating complex scientific information in a form that can be readily understood, yet does not oversimplify. Generation of unjustified alarm and inducement of unwarranted complacency are equally to be avoided. The introduction of an air-pollution index in Ontario in April 1970, after the Shepherd study, thus provided Auliciems and Burton the opportunity to assess in a scientifically controlled manner the effect of such information on public attitudes to air pollution (1972).

The Ontario index was based on sulfur dioxide and particulates on the assumption that these two pollutants are the most significant in Ontario and act synergystically to affect the health of the population (Shenfield and Frantisak, 1970). By reference to epidemiological studies (Lawther, 1958) and levels of pollution observed during major episodes in London, New York, and Osaka a scale was constructed and critical values selected at 32, 50 and 100. An index value of 32 marked the *advisory level;* lower values were considered acceptable. If meteorological conditions were expected to remain adverse for at least six more hours, managers of significant sources of pollution would be advised to curtail operations. *First* and *second alert levels* were set at 50 and 75, and at each level Ministerial Orders to cut back operations were issued. The *episode threshold level* was set at an index value 100, and managers of all sources of pollution could be ordered to cease emissions entirely.

The index was thus to be used in conjunction with weather forecasts primarily as an air management tool. When the capacity of the atmosphere to absorb and diffuse pollutants is high, no action is taken. Thus, without imposing unnecessary costs upon society for pollution abatement, the capacity of the atmosphere to absorb effluents is used and the public health is protected. It should be noted, however, that the index does not measure "air quality" but only sulfur dioxide and particulates. The index values are based on observations at one location only, and the averaging time of 24 hours means that short-run peaks are not reported.

During its first year in Toronto, from April 1970 to April 1971, the index exceeded 32 on ten occasions and 50 once. It is now the practice of the Ontario Air Management Branch to issue air-pollution index values four times daily in Toronto, Hamilton, Windsor, and Sudbury. The media refer to the index value frequently as part of a weather report or forecast. A typical statement on a Toronto radio station might be:

> The temperature in downtown Toronto is 32°F; at the airport, 25°F. The air-pollution index for Toronto is 18; for Hamilton, 28.

To determine the effects of the index, three "waves" of interviews were conducted at monthly intervals prior to the introduction of the index in Windsor and Sudbury. These were followed by a second series of three "waves" after the index had been put into operation. London

(Ontario) and Ottawa were used as control cities in order to take account of changes in public attitudes and awareness resulting from factors other than the index.

In Windsor, no significant differences in the level of public concern were found. In Sudbury, a significant *decline* occurred over a period of five months. A similar decline also occurred in one of the nonindex control cities (London). The index seems to have had little effect on the level of public concern compared with other prevailing influences, at least in the short term.

Misconceptions about the meaning of the index were apparent. Asked about the applicability of the index to their neighborhood, 40 percent of the respondents living between five and ten miles from the index station in Toronto replied affirmatively, although in fact considerable differences in index values do occur over distances as small as half a mile. Some confusion was created by radio and television broadcasts of values on a different index scale from Buffalo and Detroit. Asked about personal response to high readings, approximately 10 percent stated that cars could be left at home. This would substantially decrease carbon monoxide emissions, but would have no significant effect on the index because of the way it was constructed.

The index appeared to be readily accepted by many people, and its continued use as an informational device and a management tool seemed assured to Auliciems and Burton. When the current wave of concern with environmental quality declines, they felt that the repeated reporting of the air-pollution index might help to maintain public awareness. The index also strengthened government control measures directed at public and private sources of pollution and involved considerable cooperation with industry. The performance of the index was such that the development of other indices of environmental quality and the improvement of this one were recommended.

APPENDIX TO CHAPTER 4
MAJOR AIR POLLUTANTS*

Description and Sources	Effects	Abatement and Control Methods
ARSENIC AND ITS COMPOUNDS A brittle, very poisonous chemical element. Major sources are: smelters processing gold and copper; cotton ginning and the burning of cotton trash; use as pesticide; combustion of coal.	ON HUMANS, ANIMALS AND PLANTS: Arsenic is extremely poisonous. Arsenical dusts may produce dermatitis, bronchitis and irritation of the upper respiratory tract. Use of medicines containing arsenic has produced growths and cancers of the skin. The relationship of arsenic to other types of cancer, particularly lung tumors, is uncertain. Herbivorous animals have been poisoned after eating plants contaminated with arsenic compounds.	1. *Use of air cleaning devices to remove particulates from smelters and cotton gins.* Equipment must operate at temperature low enough (100°C) to condense arsenic fumes. Electrostatic precipitators Cooling flues Bag houses, especially those using wet scrubbing vacuum pumps instead of fabric filters. 2. *No methods available to control emissions produced by burning cotton trash.*
ASBESTOS General name given to a variety of fibrous minerals. Products made of asbestos are virtually indestructible. Major pollutant is a dust composed of asbestos fibers. Major sources are: asbestos mines and factories; the wearing away of brake linings, roofing, insulation and shingles; fireproofing of buildings with sprayed asbestos applications.	ON HUMANS AND ANIMALS: May cause chronic lung disease or cancer of the lung and pleural cavity.	IN MANUFACTURING: *Ventilation* through fabric sleeve filters; *carrying out some operations* (such as spinning and weaving of asbestos fabrics) *as wet processes* to eliminate dust. IN TRANSPORTATION: *Use of plastic-coated bags to transport asbestos.* IN CONSTRUCTION: *Use of insulators* to enclose the work area when asbestos fireproofing is blown onto steel frames. This technique is not completely effective. IN MINES AND MILLS: *No information available.*
BARIUM AND ITS COMPOUNDS A slightly malleable metal. Most important pollutant is in solid particle form. Major sources are: industrial processes involved in the mining, refining and production of barium and barium-base chemicals; use of barium compounds as a fuel additive for the reduction of black smoke emissions from diesel engines (producing micro-sized particles in vehicle exhaust).	ON HUMANS: Inhalation of barium compounds can cause baritosis, a nonmalignant lung disease characterized by fibrous hardening.	1. *Use of conventional air-cleaning devices to remove particulates:* Bag filters Electrostatic precipitators 2. *No information available on control of diesel vehicle exhaust.*

*Based on information contained in documents published by the EPA, HEW, and from reports prepared by Litton Industries, Inc., under EPA contract.

Description and Sources	Effects	Abatement and Control Methods

BERYLLIUM AND ITS COMPOUNDS

A hard metallic element which forms strong, hard alloys with several metals, including copper and nickel. Major pollutant is beryllium dust.

Major sources are: industrial plants engaged in the extraction, refining, machining and alloying of the metal; combustion of coals containing small quantities of beryllium; proposed use of beryllium as an additive in rocket fuels. During the 1930s, use of beryllium in production of fluorescent lamps was a major source of pollution.

ON HUMANS AND ANIMALS:

Inhalation of beryllium or its compounds can cause a bodywide systemic disease, with pulmonary damage of major concern. The acute form occurs as a chemical pneumonitis, with inflammation of the respiratory tract. Chronic beryllium disease, which differs clinically from the acute form, has also caused severe respiratory damage. Bone and lung cancers have been produced experimentally in animals, and malignant tumors have been recorded in cases of human beryllium disease.

ON PLANTS:

There is some evidence that beryllium in soils is toxic to plant life.

1. *Use of conventional air-cleaning devices:*

a. For wet chemical processes: scrubbers, venturi scrubbers, packed towers, organic wet collectors, wet cyclones.

b. For dry processes: conventional bag collectors, reverse-jet bag collectors, electrostatic precipitators, cyclones, unit filters.

2. *Discontinuance of use of beryllium in fluorescent lamp tubes.*

BORON AND ITS COMPOUNDS

A nonmetallic chemical element which occurs only in combination with other elements (as with sodium and oxygen in borax). Most important pollutants are boron dusts and borane fuel.

Major sources are: use of borane (a compound of boron used as a high-energy fuel for rocket motors and jet engines); combustion of petroleum fuels which contain boron as an additive; burning of coal which contains boron; manufacturing processes employed to produce boron compounds (which are used as water softeners and in the manufacture of soap, enamels, glass and pottery).

ON HUMANS AND ANIMALS:

Inhalation of boron compounds as dusts can be moderately toxic, causing irritation and inflammation but no permanent injury. Inhalation of a borane fuel can be highly toxic; it produces signs of severe central nervous system damage, and high concentrations can cause death after relatively short exposure.

ON PLANTS:

Kills plants if applied in more than minute quantities.

1. *Prevention of accidental spilling of fuels.*

2. *Reduction or elimination of boron additives in vehicle fuels.*

CARBON MONOXIDE

A colorless, odorless, tasteless gas, about 97 percent as heavy as air.

U.S. emissions in 1966: 101.6 million tons.

The major source (60 percent of total emissions in 1966) is gasoline-powered motor vehicles; other sources are industrial (10 percent), including foundries, petroleum refineries and kraft pulp mills; burning of solid wastes (7.5 percent), forest fires, structural fires, burning banks of coal refuse and fires in underground coal mines or coal seam outcrops.

ON HUMANS:

When this gas enters the bloodstream, it interferes with the ability of the blood to transport oxygen, thus impairing the functioning of the central nervous system.

At high concentrations it kills quickly.

At concentrations of 100 parts of carbon monoxide per million parts of air (100 ppm), most people experience dizziness, headache, lassitude and other symptoms of poisoning. Concentrations higher than this occasionally occur in garages, in tunnels or behind automobiles in heavy traffic.

FROM MOTOR VEHICLE SOURCES:

1. *Factory installation of emission control systems on new-model vehicles* (in effect since 1968 models of autos and light trucks, beginning with 1970 models of buses and heavy-duty trucks). These are of two types:

a. Crankcase ventilation systems, in which exhaust vapors are routed back into the fuel induction system and burned in the engine. These devices remove primarily hydrocarbons.

b. Exhaust emission control systems, which operate either by injecting air

Description and Sources	Effects	Abatement and Control Methods

Exposure to 30 ppm for eight hours or 120 ppm for one hour may be a serious risk to the health of sensitive people (those suffering from impaired circulation, heart disease, anemia, asthma or lung impairment). In six U.S. cities where EPA measured carbon monoxide inside motor vehicles in traffic, averages ranged from 21 to 39 ppm.

Animal experiments indicate that carbon monoxide exposure is a traffic safety hazard. Exposure to levels of carbon monoxide commonly found in traffic may have effects on the driver similar to those resulting from alcohol or fatigue—reduced alertness and a decrease in the ability to respond properly in a complex situation, with resultant impairment of driving ability.

Susceptibility to carbon monoxide poisoning is increased by high temperature, high altitude, high humidity and the use of alcoholic beverages or certain drugs, such as tranquilizers.

into the exhaust system (thereby changing the carbon monoxide into carbon dioxide) or by reducing the quantity of carbon monoxide coming out of the engine cylinders. The latter is accomplished by designing engines which have improved air-fuel mixing and distribution systems and by tailoring ignition systems to furnish the best degree of control.

These devices can be effective in meeting emission standards for carbon monoxide and hydrocarbons, and preliminary studies indicate that they are also effective in reducing nitrogen oxides. EPA now tests manufacturers' prototype models, to determine whether federal emissions standards for carbon monoxide and hydrocarbons are met.

2. *Application of exhaust emission control devices on pre-1968 model cars and trucks* (of special significance in Appalachia, where many used vehicles are on the roads). These devices are currently being developed by various automobile manufacturers and are designed to improve the ignition process and to cut down on the emission of carbon monoxide, hydrocarbons and nitrogen oxides by diminishing the amount of fuel delivered to the engine. NAPCA is currently testing three such devices.

3. *Modifying vehicle fuel*, changing its volatility, hydrocarbon type and additives. Under consideration: liquefied petroleum gas, liquefied and compressed natural gas.

4. *Changing the power source for vehicles*. Under development: automatic gas turbine, steam engine, electric drive, free-piston, and Stirling stratified-charge engines.

5. *Better inspection and maintenance of vehicles*, including governmental certification of maintenance and inspection personnel to protect the public from mechanics who inadvertently increase pollution from exhausts because of incorrect or incomplete work.

Description and Sources	Effects	Abatement and Control Methods
		6. *Substitution of public for private automobile transportation.*
		7. *Planning of freeways and traffic control systems* to minimize stop-and-go driving.
		8. *Planning for emergency actions* to reduce vehicular emissions during periods when unfavorable weather conditions create an air pollution emergency.
		FROM STATIONARY SOURCES (INDUSTRY, POWER PLANTS, FIRES)
		1. *Good practice.* Proper design, application, installation, operation and maintenance of combustion equipment and other systems.
		2. *Change of fuel or energy source.* Change from oil and coal to gas, nuclear power or hydroelectric power, which can be centrally generated at installations where carbon monoxide emission can be controlled.
		3. *Change of waste-disposal method.* Use of sanitary land fill to replace open burning; treatment of burning coal waste piles.
CHLORINE GAS Chlorine is a dense, greenish-yellow gas with a distinctive, irritating odor. It is noted for its very strong oxidizing and bleaching properties. Although not flammable, it can support combustion, and many materials and metals can burn in a chlorine atmosphere—sometimes with explosive violence. Major sources are: industrial preparation, particularly the process of liquefaction before use or storage; use of chlorine in the chemical and pulp and paper industries; leakage in storage or transportation.	ON HUMANS: Low concentrations can cause irritation of the eyes, nose and throat; larger doses can cause damage to the lungs and produce pulmonary edema, pneumonitis, emphysema or bronchitis. Incidental chlorine leakage has caused injury and death to humans and animals. ON MATERIALS: Corrosion.	1. *Removal of residual gases which remain after liquefaction.* Liquid scrubbers (using water, alkali solutions, carbon tetrachloride or brine solution). Solid absorbents such as silica gel. 2. *Shunting untreated residual gases to other in-plant operations for direct use* (for example, chlorination of hydrocarbons).
CHROMIUM A very hard metal which has a high resistance to corrosion and is best known for its use as a decorative finish in chrome plating. Important pollutants are the chemical chromium compounds. Possible sources are: industries which	ON HUMANS: Inhalation of chromium compounds may produce cancer of the respiratory tract. Workers in the chromate-producing industry have experienced deaths from cancer of the respiratory tract at a rate 28 times greater than the	*Use of conventional air cleaning devices to remove particulates:* Bag filters. Precipitators. Scrubbers (including mist eliminators and inhibitors).

Description and Sources	*Effects*	*Abatement and Control Methods*

use chromium in electroplating and in the manufacture of chemicals and stainless and austenite steels; coal burning; use of chromium compounds as fuel additives, corrosion inhibitors, pigments and tanning agents.

normal rate. Exposure to airborne chromium compounds may also produce dermatitis and ulcers on the skin.
ON MATERIALS:
Chromic acid mists discolor automobile and building paints.

FLUORIDES

Compounds of the element fluorine. May occur in the atmosphere as solid particles (sodium and calcium fluoride) or as highly irritant and toxic gases (for example, hydrofluoric acid) which are usually found in the atmosphere in extremely low concentrations.

Major sources are industrial plants (phosphate fertilizer, aluminum metal, brick and tile, steel), the firing of some types of rockets and combustion of coal.

ON HUMANS:
Fluorides are highly active and extremely irritating to exposed surfaces of the body. In amounts emitted by industrial plants in several areas of the U.S., fluorides cause eye irritations, nosebleeds, inflammations of the respiratory tract and severe difficulties in breathing.
ON ANIMALS:
Fluoride emissions settle out of the air onto local pastures, building up toxic doses in the grass and other forage for cattle. When the cattle eat this forage, they develop fluorosis, an ailment which causes crippling skeletal changes, including the softening of gums, wearing away of teeth and malformation of bones and joints.
ON PLANTS:
Fluorides cause withering of shrubs and damage to flowers and citrus groves. Low concentrations of fluorides damage gladioluses, pine, apricots, prunes and azaleas.

IN MANUFACTURE OF PHOSPHATE FERTILIZER AND PROCESSING OF ANIMAL AND POULTRY FEED:
Use of scrubbers. Wastewater accumulates in ponds, where lime treatment may prevent evaporation into the air.
IN ALUMINUM MANUFACTURE:
Use of air-cleaning devices (cyclones and electrostatic precipitators with scrubbers).
IN STEEL MANUFACTURE:
Partial control through use of air-cleaning devices to remove particulates.
IN BRICK AND TILE MANUFACTURE:
No devices now used. Could use scrubbers.
IN GLASS MANUFACTURE:
Little or no control today. Some smaller furnaces use scrubbers and bag houses.
IN COAL COMBUSTION:
Little or no control at present. Could use electrostatic precipitators in combination with scrubbers to remove particulates.

HYDROCARBONS[a]

Compounds of hydrogen and carbon. Major polluting hydrocarbons are those which result from the incomplete combustion of fuels and the evaporation of fuels and industrial solvents. Polluting hydrocarbons exist in the air primarily as gases (including methane, ethylene and acetylene); others, including cancer-inducing agents such as benzo-a-pyrene, are solid particulates.

U.S. emissions in 1966: 31.5 million tons.

The American Chemical Society esti-

ON HUMANS:
Most hydrocarbons are toxic only at relatively high concentrations. A considerable number of hydrocarbons, including benzo-a-pyrene (a substance found in cigarette smoke), have produced cancer in laboratory animals. One study indicates that, in terms of this substance, breathing city air is the equivalent of smoking from 7 to 36 cigarettes a day, depending on the degree of concentration.

Even at very low concentrations, certain types of hydrocarbons (particu-

FROM MOTOR VEHICLE SOURCES:
Same as for carbon monoxide. Emissions resulting from evaporation of gasoline from fuel tanks and carburetors can be limited by storage of the vapors (within the engine itself or in a carbon canister which adsorbs the fuel vapors) and then routing the vapors back to the engine, where they will be burned. Federal standards controlling these emissions will be in effect beginning with 1971 vehicle models.

FROM STATIONARY SOURCES:

[a] Including organic solvents.

Description and Sources	Effects	Abatement and Control Methods

mates that most (approximately 85 percent) of all hydrocarbons in the air are emitted from natural sources (forests, vegation and the bacterial decomposition of organic matter).

The major man-made source of hydrocarbons is the processing, distribution, marketing and use of petroleum. The hydrocarbons in vehicle exhausts, which result from the incomplete burning of gasoline in the internal combustion engine, accounted for over half of the man-made hydrocarbon emissions in 1967. Other important sources were the evaporation of industrial solvents and incineration of waste.

larly the olefins produced during incomplete combustion of fuel) react with sunshine to produce photochemical oxidants, which are the toxic and irritating compounds in smog. The effects of these compounds are described in a separate section of this table.

1. Design equipment to use or consume completely the processed materials.

2. Use materials which have a higher boiling point or are less photochemically reactive.

3. Use control equipment to reduce emissions.

4. Stop open burning of waste by use of multiple-chamber incinerators or disposing of waste in sanitary land fills.

HYDROGEN CHLORIDE

A colorless gas with a strong, pungent and irritating odor. Because of its high solubility in water, the gas is readily converted into hydrochloric acid fumes and droplets in the air or when inhaled into the lungs.

Major sources are: the commercial use and production of the gas and the acid; burning of paper products and fossil fuels (coal and oil); manufacture of chemicals (hydrochloric acid is a byproduct).

ON HUMANS:

Inhalation causes coughing and choking, as well as inflammation and ulceration of the upper respiratory tract. Irritation of the eye membranes is also common, and exposure to high concentrations can cause clouding of the cornea. Erosion of teeth may also result.

ON MATERIALS:

Hydrochloric acid is extremely corrosive to most materials.

ON PLANTS:

Both the gas and the acid damage the leaves of a great variety of plants.

1. *Use of water-absorption facilities* which convert the gas to hydrochloric acid:

Water scrubbing systems.

Rotary brush scrubbers.

Ejector venturi scrubbers.

2. *Use of dry solid adsorbents.*

3. *Addition of basic salts* (such as sodium carbonate) to coal before burning.

LEAD

A metallic element which is a natural constituent of soil, water, vegetation and animal life, and is taken into the body in water and food as well as in air. Most air pollutants are in the form of aerosols, fumes and powders.

The major source of airborne lead in urban areas is the exhaust from gasoline-fueled vehicles. (Lead is added to high-octane gasoline motor fuels to cut down on engine knock.) Other man-made sources are manufacturing (lead additives for gasoline, lead processing and the manufacture of lead products), combustion of coal (as in dry-bottom power plants which use pulverized coal), transfer and transportation of leaded gasoline, use of pesticides and

ON HUMANS AND ANIMALS:

Lead is a cumulative poison. One form of lead poisoning damages the brains of young children and may cause death. Other forms cause severe malfunctioning of the alimentary tract (loss of appetite, constipation, colic), general weakness and malaise and impaired functioning of the nervous system, with resulting weakness, atrophy and sometimes paralysis of the extensor muscles of the forearm. Auto exhaust containing lead was found to increase the concentration of lead in the bones of mice.

FROM VEHICLE SOURCES:

Reduction or elimination of lead in fuel; use of particulate traps on vehicle exhausts.

FROM LEAD PROCESSING AND THE MANUFACTURE OF LEAD PRODUCTS:

Control of operating conditions (temperature and timing); use of conventional air-cleaning techniques (bag house filters, scrubbers, electrostatic precipitators).

FROM COAL COMBUSTION:

Use of electrostatic precipitators.

FROM MANUFACTURE OF LEAD ADDITIVES FOR GASOLINE:

Use of water scrubbers and bag house filters.

Description and Sources	*Effects*	*Abatement and Control Methods*

the incineration of refuse. Natural sources include silicate dusts from soils and particles from volcanoes.

FROM TRANSFER AND TRANSPORTATION OF LEADED GASOLINE:
Use of vapor recovery systems; reduction or elimination of lead in gasoline.
FROM USE OF PESTICIDES:
Use of pesticides which do not contain lead; improved techniques of pesticide use.
FROM INCINERATION OF REFUSE:
Use of sanitary land fills instead of incineration.

MERCURY AND ITS COMPOUNDS

A heavy metal which is liquid at ordinary temperatures, has high specific gravity and high electrical conductivity.

Major sources are: the mining and refining of mercury; industrial applications (mercury-arc rectifiers, mercury precision casting); laboratory equipment and instruments (spillage creates droplets which vaporize); agricultural use of mercury compounds as pesticides (now declining).

ON HUMANS AND ANIMALS:

Mercury and most derivatives are lethal to man, animals, and plants. Inhalation can cause acute mercury poisoning, which may be fatal or cause permanent damage to the nervous system. Russian experiments with animals indicate that chronic exposure to mercury vapor may cause a chronic form of mercury poisoning which is difficult to diagnose because the symptoms (exaggerated emotional response, gum infection and muscular tremors) are ambiguous and frequently appear long after exposure.

FOR APPLICATIONS WHICH USE MERCURY AT NORMAL TEMPERATURES:
1. *Proper ventilation in work areas.*
2. *Cleaning up spilled mercury* (sweeping with special vacuum cleaners or chemical treatment).
3. *Use of nonporous material* for floors, working surfaces and protective clothing.
FOR APPLICATIONS WHICH USE MERCURY AT HIGH TEMPERATURES:
1. *Condensing mercury vapors* by:
Cold-water-jacketed condensers.
Impregnated charcoal.
Water scrubbers.
2. *Conventional control of pesticides* (see pesticides).

NICKEL AND ITS COMPOUNDS

A grayish-white metallic element— hard, tough and markedly resistant to oxidation and corrosion—which forms a variety of alloys with other metals. Major pollutants are nickel dust and vapors.

Major sources are: plants producing nickel alloys (including stainless steel), catalysts and chemicals; aviation and automobile engines burning fuels containing nickel additives; burning coal and oil; nickel plating facilities; incineration of nickel products.

ON HUMANS:

Inhalation may cause cancer of the lung, cancer of the sinus, other disorders of the respiratory system and dermatitis.

1. *Use of conventional air-cleaning devices.*
Bag filters.
Precipitators.
Scrubbers.
2. *Decomposition of gaseous emissions at high temperatures,* forming nickel (which can be removed as a particulate) and carbon monoxide.
3. *No control methods currently available for vehicle engine exhausts.*

Description and Sources	Effects	Abatement and Control Methods

NITROGEN OXIDES

Compounds of nitrogen and oxygen. Most significant pollutants are two gases:

nitric oxide, a colorless gas which is relatively harmless but which usually converts in the atmosphere to the more dangerous nitrogen dioxide;

nitrogen dioxide, a gas which is normally brownish-red in color and which is produced during the burning of fuels and, to a lesser extent, during chemical processes. In the presence of sunshine, nitrogen oxides act as the trigger for the photochemical reactions which produce smog (see hydrocarbons and photochemical oxidants).

U.S. emissions in 1966: 16.7 million tons.

Most nitrogen oxides are the result of fuel combustion. Nearly half come from the use of fuels in transportation, particularly gasoline in the automobile. The second largest source (40 percent) is the burning of fossil fuels (coal, oil and natural gas) in generating electric power and space heating.

ON HUMANS AND ANIMALS:

Little is known about the direct effects of nitrogen oxides at levels commonly found in polluted air (1-3 ppm). At 13 ppm, they may cause eye and nose irritation. Animals exposed to 10-20 ppm showed damage to lung tissue and increased susceptibility to infection.

Major effects result from the substances formed when nitrogen oxides (in combination with hydrocarbons, discussed above) are exposed to sunlight, forming photochemical smog (see photochemical oxidants).

ON PLANTS:

Nitrogen oxides restrict growth and cause injuries similar to those caused by sulfur dioxide.

FROM MOTOR VEHICLES SOURCES:

Same as for carbon monoxide. Emissions standards for new vehicles were to be effective beginning with 1973 models. Preliminary studies indicate that the exhaust emission control systems and devices used to control emissions of carbon monoxide and hydrocarbons may also be effective against nitrogen oxides.

FROM STATIONARY SOURCES:

1. Modification of combustion methods.

2. Substitution of electricity for oil, coal, and natural gas fuels.

3. Substitution of sanitary land fills for open burning of solid waste.

4. Relocation of power generating stations to remote places.

5. Burning nitrogen oxide gases to reduce them to elemental nitrogen.

6. Scrubbing with caustic substances.

7. Addition of urea to nitric acid to prevent release of nitrogen oxides.

ODOROUS COMPOUNDS

Offensive smells which provoke people into complaining about air pollution. Hydrogen sulfide is a major offender.

Major sources are: kraft paper mills; animal-rendering plants; chemical plants; petroleum refineries; metallurgical plants; diesel engines; sewers and sewage treatment plants.

ON HUMANS:

Nausea, headache, loss of sleep, loss of appetite, impaired breathing, allergic reactions and emotional disturbances.

ON PROPERTY:

Discouragement of capital improvements, damaged community reputation, stifling of community growth and development, decline in property values, tax revenues, payrolls and sales.

1. *Combustion.* Incineration at the source.

2. *Absorption.* Used when odorants are soluble in water. Various devices (including spray towers, cyclone scrubbers, trays) bring vapor into contact with liquid.

3. *Adsorption.* Activated charcoal commonly used.

4. *Masking or counteracting odors.* Usually uses synthetic compounds with a pleasant smell.

5. *Dilution with air.* Requires favorable weather conditions.

6. *Source elimination.* Use of low-sulfur fuels.

7. *Removal of particulates which carry odors.* See particulates.

8. *Chemical control.* Oxidation or combination may change odorous to nonodorous compounds.

9. *Biological control.* Use of organisms which control sewage odor by oxidizing the odorous gases.

Description and Sources	Effects	Abatement and Control Methods

10. *Containment.* Covers on fuel tanks, sewage ponds and other open storage areas.

ORGANIC CARCINOGENS

Carbon compounds which cause cancer in experimental animals, and which are therefore suspected of playing a role in causing human cancer, particularly cancer of the lung. (This category includes some of the hydrocarbons discussed earlier in the table.) Most frequently studied is benzo-a-pyrene, a substance also found in cigarette smoke.

Major source is the incomplete combustion of matter containing carbon. Heat generation (burning coal, oil and gas) accounts for more than 85 percent; refuse burning, motor vehicle exhaust and industrial processes account for 5 percent each.

ON ANIMALS:

Certain organic compounds, especially benzo-a-pyrene, have been found to increase tumor incidence in experimental animals. In addition, animal studies indicate that other carbon compounds may encourage or slow the development of malignant tumors.

Same as for hydrocarbons.

PARTICULATES

Any matter dispersed in the air, whether liquid or solid, that has individual particles smaller in diameter than 500 microns (approximately 1/50 of an inch). Particulates may remain airborne from a few seconds to several months. The category includes some compounds which are not solid or liquid while in industrial stacks, but which condense when dispersed into the regular atmosphere. Included are: aerosols (solids and liquids of microscopic size which are dispersed in gas, forming smoke, fog or mist), visible particles (such as fly ash, metallic particles and dust), fumes, soot (carbon particles impregnated with tar), oil and grease. Particulates are responsible for grime.

U.S. emissions in 1966: 28.6 million tons.

Of the total volume of particulates in the U.S. in 1966 (28.6 million tons), nearly one-third (primarily fly ash from coal combustion) was produced by plants generating electric power and

Some particulates are directly harmful—they contain poisonous or disease-producing substances (for example, hydrocarbons, arsenic, asbestos, beryllium, fluorides and lead, which are described in this table).

Other particulates multiply the potential harm of irritant gases. For example, sulfur dioxide (a pollutant described in this table) is a gas which is highly soluble in water, and if inhaled by itself it will dissolve relatively harmlessly in the upper respiratory tract. But sulfur dioxide is rarely inhaled alone; when it is adsorbed on particulate matter, it will penetrate deep into the lung, where it can cause damage to lung tissue.

Still other particulates speed chemical reactions in the atmosphere, and these reactions may produce much more harmful substances than the ingredients that went into them. For example, certain particulates speed the conversion of sulfur dioxide to sulfuric acid.

FROM MOTOR VEHICLE SOURCES:

Same as for carbon monoxide. See also lead and boron. Research on particulate emission control is being conducted by EPA. It has not yet been determined whether emission control systems (described under carbon monoxide) are effective in removing particulates from vehicle exhaust.

FROM STATIONARY SOURCES (INDUSTRY, POWER PLANTS, FIRES):

1. *Use of air-cleaning techniques and devices* by industry and power plants to remove particulates:

Inertial separators or gravitational settling chambers.
Cyclones.
Bag houses and fabric filters.
Electrostatic precipitators.
Scrubbers and venturi scrubbers.

2. *Control of construction and demolition* (including grading of earth, paving roads and parking lots, sandblasting, spray painting). Hooding and venting

Description and Sources	Effects	Abatement and Control Methods

space heating. Another one-fourth of the total came from industrial sources—dust, fumes, smoke and mists which arise from fuel combustion and the loss of materials or products into the atmosphere. Slightly more than one-third of the total particulates are the result of fires—incineration of refuse, forest fires, and man-made fires. In the transportation category, the major source of particulates is the automobile exhaust, which is characterized by an extremely large number of fine particles, including lead. Diesel-fueled vehicles are particular offenders, producing approximately ten times as much particulate matter per gallon as gasoline-fueled vehicles.

to air pollution control equipment; wetting down working surfaces with water or oil.

3. *Disposal of solid waste by sanitary land fill, composting, shredding and grinding* rather than incineration.

PESTICIDES

Economic poisons used to control or destroy pests that cause economic losses or adverse human health effects. Includes: poisons to kill insects, weed and brush, fungi, rodents, molluscs, algae, worms; repellents; attractants; plant growth regulators.

The primary source of pesticides in the air is from the application process; a certain amount of drift is unavoidable even under ideal conditions. Pesticides can evaporate into the air from soil, water, and treated surfaces, and pesticides contained in dust from the soil can enter the air and be transported for considerable distances before falling back to the earth. Plants manufacturing pesticides also produce pollutant emissions.

ON HUMANS:

One class of insecticides (the chlorinated hydrocarbons, which include DDT) may cause poisoning in humans; in mild cases symptoms include headache, dizziness, gastro-intestinal disturbances, numbness and weakness of the extremities, apprehension and great irritability. In more severe cases, fine muscular tremors appear, and these may lead to convulsions or death from cardiac or respiratory arrest. Another category of insecticides (the organophosphates) cause loss of appetite, nausea and headache, followed by vomiting, abdominal cramps, excessive sweating and salivation. A large dose will cause gastrointestinal symptoms and bronchial secretion that may be accompanied by pulmonary edema. In severe cases, convulsions, coma, and death may occur.

Weed killers may cause irritation of eyes and gastrointestinal disturbances; they have caused liver and kidney injury in experimental animals.

Fungicides cause allergic dermatitis, irritation of the mucous membranes and kidney damage.

1. *Control of pesticide drift during application:*

Improved application equipment and methods;

Improved formulas for pesticides (increased use of large oil-based droplets rather than dusts);

Wider distribution and use of weather data in area where pesticides are to be used.

2. *Control and abatement during production:*

Enclosure of grinding, mixing, packing and filling operations;

Venting of solid emissions through bag houses and cyclones;

Venting of liquid emissions through liquid scrubbers.

Description and Sources	*Effects*	*Abatement and Control Methods*

PHOTOCHEMICAL OXIDANTS

Chemical compounds which are the major components of smog and which are formed when hydrocarbons and nitrogen oxides (discussed above) are exposed to sunlight. Most significant oxidants are ozone and PAN (peroxyacyl nitrates).

Sources are the same as those for hydrocarbons and nitrogen oxides.

ON HUMANS:

The most common effects are eye irritation and difficulty in breathing, particularly for people already suffering from respiratory disease.

At levels commonly found in city atmospheres, ozone causes irritation of mucous membranes in nose and throat. At somewhat higher levels, it causes coughing, choking and severe fatigue. At relatively high levels, such as those occurring during severe photochemical smogs, ozone interferes with lung function for the duration of exposure and up to 24 hours beyond, and causes bronchial irritation, slight coughing and soreness in the chest. At these high levels, ozone also reduces visual acuity and causes recurrent headache, fatigue, chest pains, difficulty in breathing and wheezing. Long-term exposure to ozone shortens the lives of experimental animals.

Preliminary studies indicate that PAN causes eye irritation and has the same effects on lung function as ozone.

ON PLANTS:

Photochemical oxidants cause lesions in the leaves of plants, thereby causing a serious decline in agricultural crops (particularly citrus and leafy vegetables) in California and along the eastern seaboard from Boston to Washington,

See hydrocarbons and nitrogen oxides.

Effects (cont.)

D.C. Ozone is toxic to field and forage crops (such as tobacco), leafy vegetables, shrubs, fruit and forest trees (particularly conifers). PAN is toxic to many species of field crops (spinach, beets, celery, tobacco, peppers, endive, Romaine lettuce, swiss chard and alfalfa) and to several ornamental plants (petunias, snapdragons, primroses, asters and fuchias).

ON MATERIALS:

Ozone damages textiles, discolors dyes and accelerates the cracking of rubber. Stressed rubber has cracked after less than an hour's exposure to ozone in concentrations lower than those commonly reached in metropolitan areas.

ON VISIBILITY:

Photochemical smog can reduce visibility to as low as a quarter of a mile. In Los Angeles, where smoggy days are commonplace, visibility frequently is less than three miles, which is considered the minimum visibility for safe operation of airplanes.

RADIOACTIVE SUBSTANCES

Substances which give off radiant energy in the form of particles or rays as a result of the disintegration of atomic nuclei. Major pollutants are radioactive gases and particulates (dust, fumes, smokes and mists).

Atmospheric radiation arises from both natural sources (rocks, soils and cosmic rays) and from artificial sources (nuclear explosions and the nuclear industry in general).

World population received a significant dose of radiation as a result of nuclear weapons testing (an average of

ON HUMANS AND ANIMALS:

Radiation causes leukemia and genetic effects. Since the genetic effects of various amounts of radiation cannot always be determined, many scientists accept the belief that there is no safe level of exposure, i.e., no threshold below which there is no danger of biological damage to humans.

1. *Limiting emissions of radioactive pollutants:*

In uranium mining: wet drilling, underground drainage and clearing away ore;

In nuclear reactors: use of closed-cycle coolant systems and maintenance of high coolant purity;

In nuclear testing: choice of ideal meteorological conditions.

2. *Containment:*

   a. Completely containing pollutant so it does not escape into the atmosphere by use of hermetically sealed tanks and closed-cycle process systems.

Description and Sources	*Effects*	*Abatement and Control Methods*
5–10 percent higher than the levels of natural radioactivity), resulting in contamination of food and soil. Experience to date has shown that, although there is a potential for radiation release from all facets of the nuclear industry, the amount of radiation reaching the general public from the nuclear industry is insignificant when compared with the natural radiation dose. However, because of projected expansion of nuclear industry, there is evidence that Krypton-85, which is released from nuclear fuel reprocessing, may be a problem. The U.S. Atomic Energy Commission has established maximum permissible concentrations for radionuclides that can be released from nuclear plants.		*b.* If an accident allows fission product to escape from reactor, isolating the polluted air in a reactor containment building. 3. *Dispersal.* Diluting pollution by mixing with air in stacks. 4. *Site location.* Choosing localities where possibility of excessive radiation dose to general population is minimized (depends on type of installation, meteorological factors, distribution of population). 5. *Removal of particulates and gases:* *a.* Filtration: roughing filters, absolute filters, bag filters, deep-bed sand filters. *b.* Centrifugal collection (cyclones). *c.* Electrostatic precipitators. *d.* Wet collection: wet filters, viscous filters, packed towers, cyclone scrubbers, venturi scrubbers. 6. *Adsorption and chemisorption.* Use of activated carbons, silica gels, and chemicals based on soda lime. 7. *Absorption.* Removing gases that react chemically with scrubbing liquid or are highly soluble in it. Uses water or a weak alkaline solution; produces radioactive waste water. 8. *Delay for decay.* Retaining gases in tanks until radioisotopes have decayed. Effective for short-lived isotopes. 9. *Physically or chemically locking radioactive wastes into solid forms* which can easily be stored, monitored and protected.
SELENIUM A chemical element found in soils (particularly in the Midwest) and fuels. Major pollutants are a solid (selenium dioxide), which turns to acid in moist environments, and a gas (hydrogen selenide). Major sources are: combustion of and fumes from refinery waste; incineration of trash, particularly paper products which contain minute quantities of selenium.	ON HUMANS: Selenium compounds in the air cause irritation of the eyes, nose, throat and respiratory tract; prolonged exposure may cause gastrointestinal disorders. ON ANIMALS: Swallowing selenium compounds may cause cancer of the liver, and is known to produce pneumonia and degeneration of liver and kidneys.	1. *Installation of good ventilation systems* in fuel refineries and incinerators. 2. *Use of personal protective equipment* by workers (safety goggles, respirators). 3. *Use of conventional air-cleaning devices* to remove particulates: Wet scrubbers. Electrostatic precipitators. 4. *Burial of solid waste.* 5. *Dilution of liquid wastes* by washing them away.

Description and Sources	*Effects*	*Abatement and Control Methods*

SULFUR OXIDES

Chemical compounds of sulfur and oxygen. The most significant pollutants are:

sulfur dioxide, a colorless gas, which has a pungent and irritating odor at concentrations above 3 ppm and which can be tasted at concentrations from 0.3 ppm to 1 ppm in air. In the atmosphere sulfur dioxide is partially converted to sulfur trioxide.

sulfur trioxide, a gas which combines with water in the atmosphere to form sulfuric acid, or with other materials in the atmosphere to form various sulfate compounds.

U.S. emissions in 1967: 31.2 million tons.

Nearly three-fourths of the sulfur oxides emitted in the U.S. in 1967 resulted from the burning of sulfur-bearing fuels in order to produce electric power and space heating. (Coal combustion alone accounted for more than 60 percent of total emissions.) Industrial processes, primarily smelting and petroleum refining, accounted for most of the remainder.

ON HUMANS:

Sulfur dioxide gas alone can irritate the upper respiratory tract. If it is adsorbed on particulate matter, or if it is converted into sulfuric acid, it can be carried deep into the lungs, where it can injure delicate tissue.

Prolonged exposure to relatively low levels of sulfur dioxide has been associated with an increase in the number of deaths from cardiovascular disease in older persons.

Prolonged exposure to higher concentrations has been associated with an increase in respiratory death rates and an increase in complaints by school-children of cough, mucous membrane irritation and mucous secretion.

Very heavy concentrations of sulfur oxides (as in the four-day October 1948 air disaster in Donora, Pennsylvania) cause cough, sore throat, chest constriction, headache, a burning sensation of the eyes, nasal discharge and vomiting. During the year following the disaster, 20 people died in Donora, where the normal mortality would have been two.

ON PLANTS:

Damage to or death of trees and plants may occur as far as 52 miles from smelters discharging large amounts of sulfur oxides, and levels routinely observed in U.S. cities are damaging to plants. The plants most sensitive to sulfur pollution are those with leaves having high physiological activity—alfalfa, grains, squash, cotton, grapes, white pine, apple and endive.

ON MATERIALS:

Sulfur oxides attack and destroy even the most durable of materials. Steel corrodes two to four times faster in urban and industrial areas than it does in rural areas, where much less sulfur-bearing coal and oil are burned. Sulfur pollution also destroys zinc, silver and palladium (used in electrical contacts), paint pigments and fresh paint (thus delaying drying), nylon hose (which can be destroyed during a lunch hour

1. *Change from high-sulfur coal and oil to low-sulfur fuels or electricity.*

2. *Removal of sulfur from fuel before use.* For coal, cleaning techniques (crushing and flotation); for fuel oil, catalytic treatment with hydrogen or blending with low-sulfur distillate oils.

3. *Increased combustion efficiency.*

4. *Removal of sulfur oxide from fuel gases by:*

Reaction with calcined limestone, then removal by fly ash control devices or wet scrubbers;

Reaction with alkalized alumina, followed by recovery of sulfur (which has commercial value);

Catalytic oxidation to sulfuric acid (which has commercial value).

5. *Dispersion by use of tall stacks.* Limited by local meteorological and topographic conditions.

Effects (cont.)

in a high-sulfur atmosphere), and stone buildings and statuary.

Cleopatra's Needle, a famous sculpture from ancient Egypt, has deteriorated more in the 90 years since its arrival in New York City than it did during the more than 3,000 years it spent in Egypt. The corrosive action of the sulfur oxides is accelerated by the presence of particulates and water.

ON VISIBILITY:

When high concentrations of sulfur oxides are coupled with relatively high humidity, visibility goes down because of the formation of sulfuric acid, which scatters light. Reduced visibility is a hazard to land, water and air transportation.

Description and Sources	Effects	Abatement and Control Methods
VANADIUM AND ITS COMPOUNDS A rare malleable metal. Major sources are: vanadium refining industries; alloy industries; power plants and utilities using vanadium-rich residual oils.	ON HUMANS AND ANIMALS: Vanadium is toxic to humans and animals. Human inhalation of relatively low concentrations has resulted in inhibition of cholesterol synthesis; chronic exposure to environmental air containing vanadium has been statistically related to mortality rates from heart diseases and certain cancers. Exposure to high concentrations results in observable effects on the gastrointestinal and respiratory tracts.	ABATEMENT AND CONTROL METHODS 1. *Use of additives* (such as magnesium oxide) when burning high-vanadium content oils to reduce the quantity of small particulates emitted. 2. *Use of conventional air-cleaning devices to remove particulates:* Cyclones and other centrifugal collectors. Electrostatic precipitators.

CHAPTER *5*

managing the air resource

With air pollution increasing as a problem, the combination of growing public awareness and protest, better surveillance, and improved knowledge of air-pollution meteorology has produced a succession of attempts to develop more comprehensive systems of air-pollution control.

Perhaps the most spectacularly successful legislation has been the British Clean Air Act of 1956 (Burton et al., 1972), although even in its success the case illustrates the complexity of ecological relationships in cities and the difficulties inherent in air-resource management. Further, it is difficult to evaluate the direct effects

of this legislation on air quality in the sense that technological change, particularly changes in the consumption of certain fuels, may have had an impact on air quality whether or not the legislation had been passed (Auliciems and Burton, 1973). As we noted at the beginning of the previous chapter, for many decades the atmosphere over the United Kingdom deserved its reputation as one of the most polluted in the world. Substantial reductions in the smoke content of the atmosphere have occurred over the past fifteen years since the passage of the Clean Air Act. In the act, the attack was focused consciously on domestic heating through coal fires,

Materials are included from:
    Ian Burton, Douglas Billingsley, Mark Blacksell, and Geoffrey Wall, "A Case Study of Successful Pollution Control Legislation in the United Kingdom," paper presented to the International Geographical Congress, Montreal, 1972. Begins on page 124.
    Kenneth R. Woodcock, *A Model for Regional Air Pollu-*

tion Control Cost/Benefit Analysis, TRW Systems Group, McLean, Virginia 22101 (prepared under Contract PH 22-68-60, U.S. Environmental Protection Agency). The report can be obtained from the National Technical Information Service, U.S. Department of Commerce, 5285 Port Royal Road, Springfield, Va. 22151 (accession number PB 202 353). Begins on page 128.

which had constituted the main source of smoke in the atmosphere. "Smokeless zones" were established by local authorities; in these zones the burning of ordinary bituminous coal for domestic heating was prohibited. Thus the legislation made a frontal attack on the coal fire, widely regarded as an integral part of the British way of life. The act provided payments to individual households of 70 percent of the reasonable cost of converting to heating systems that are smokeless. In practice this meant switching to smokeless solid fuel such as coke, or to oil, electricity, or gas.

Interesting features of the legislation were that it required changes on an individual household basis of long-practiced habits and thus it was as much a behavioral change as a technical innovation. Also, the act was permissive. Local authorities were not required to adopt a plan for smoke control but were encouraged to do so by the central government, which contributed to the expense in a cost-sharing arrangement. The central government would pay 40 percent of the costs of conversions. The local authority normally contributed 30 percent and the individual householder bore the remaining 30 percent himself, plus any other improvements he might wish to make at the time "in excess of the expenditure which would have been reasonably incurred in doing what was reasonably necessary . . . ."

Prime targets for smoke control were the so-called "black areas." These were based on the criteria of population density (1,000 persons and over per square mile), main industrial concentrations, and fog frequency [average of 30 or more occurrences of fog per year at 9: 00 A.M. with visibility less than 1,000 yards (1,006 meters) period 1934–43]. Some 325 local authority jurisdictions were on the list of black areas, and by 1971 all but 20 had begun to adopt smoke-control programs. Some 82 other local authorities not in black areas have also adopted smoke-control programs.

The rate of progress in adopting the programs varied considerably among authorities. Most rapid progress and success was made in London. By the end of 1968 over 60 percent of all the premises in Greater London and over 50 percent of its total acreage was covered by smoke-control orders. The total cost of conversions to smokeless fuels in the London Boroughs has been approximately 15 new pence (or 38 cents U.S.) per head per annum. At the same time, smoke concentrations have fallen since 1958 by 80 percent in central London, hours of sunshine in December have increased by 70 percent, and winter visibility has increased threefold. The infamous killer smogs appear to have been completely eliminated.

Progress has not been so rapid in the northern cities. Edinburgh, for example, has made slow headway. The target data for completion of smoke-control programs runs into the 1980s for many local authorities, and some places have a target data of 1990. Also, the rate of adoption of smoke-control orders has been slowed by shortages of solid smokeless fuels, which have even made it necessary to suspend temporarily the fuel regulations in some designated smokeless zones. In some coalfield communities, the adoption of smoke-control programs is being actively resisted by local leaders.

The success of the Clean Air Act in reducing smoke concentrations seems attributable to three major factors. First, it happened to coincide with a trend toward central heating and a switch away from coal to other fuels. In the relatively affluent Britain of the 1960s many householders were thinking about converting to central heating anyway. Official encouragement and the availability of financial assistance undoubtedly accelerated the trend. Second, the permissive nature of the legislation placed major responsibility for initiative at the local level. The local councils were able to gauge the receptivity of the affected population with considerable accuracy, and instead of becoming a mandatory imposition from Whitehall, the adoption of smoke-control programs became for some a measure of civic pride and progressiveness.

A third and possibly fortuitous set of factors involved the changing pattern of atmospheric variables themselves. The period in question appears to have been one of greater atmospheric turbulence with fewer and shorter occurrences of temperature inversions. Thus the better-ventilated atmosphere over the major cities may have helped the process of smoke abatement, giving an appearance of greater success than can in fact be ascribed to the legislation alone. On the other hand, it is not beyond the bounds of possibility that reductions in smoke brought about by the Clean Air Act have themselves contributed to a greater degree of atmospheric turbulence, thus illustrating the complexity of the man-nature interface in cities.

AIR-POLLUTION CONTROL IN THE UNITED STATES

Progress has been less rapid in the United States. The first Federal legislation concerned exclusively with air pollution was enacted in July 1955, a year earlier than Britain's Clean Air Act, but it did not provide for action. Instead, it simply authorized $5 million annually to the Public Health Service of the Department of Health, Education, and Welfare for research, data collection, and technical assistance to state and local governments. The Clean Air Act of 1963 came only after substantial pressures for action. This legislation provided grants to air-pollution agencies for control programs (with special bonuses for intermunicipal or interstate areas), and it provided for the first time Federal enforcement authority to attack interstate air-pollution problems.

In October 1965 the Clean Air Act was amended to permit national regulation of air pollution from new motor vehicles. The first standards were applied to 1968 models. These standards were tightened for 1970 and 1971 model cars, and even more stringent standards were announced for 1973 and 1975. Finally, in November 1967, the Congress passed the comprehensive Air Quality Act, which set in motion a new regional approach to establishing and enforcing Federal-state air-quality standards; it provided that air-quality control regions must be designated; air-quality criteria must be promulgated which describe the harmful effects of an air pollutant on health, vegetation, and materials; control-technology documents must be issued showing availability, costs, and effectiveness of prevention and control techniques; the states must set standards limiting the levels of the pollutant described in the criteria and control-technology documents; and, finally, the states must establish comprehensive plans for implementing the standards, by setting specific emission levels by source and a timetable for achieving compliance. It should be noted, however, that the changing energy situation may rearrange stated priorities.

In 1970 came the so-called Clean Air Amendments. The new Environmental Protection Agency was to set air-quality standards for the entire nation, rather than relying on the individual states. Each of the 50 states was to develop plans to implement EPA's national ambient air-quality standards, which were to include new stationary sources for pollutants such as asbestos, cadmium, and beryllium.

The first step called for in the 1970 amendment was accomplished in April 1971, when EPA established primary and secondary standards for six of the most widespread air pollutants—particulate matter, sulfur oxides, carbon monoxide, hydrocarbons, oxides of nitrogen, and photochemical oxidents (see Table 5.1). Later in 1971 the Department of Health, Education and Welfare issued documents on lead, fluorides, and polynuclear organic compounds.

The Clean Air Amendments called on the states to develop plans to achieve, within three years after their approval by EPA, primary standards to protect public health. Secondary

TABLE 5.1

National primary and secondary ambient air-quality standards

Pollutant	Primary Standards	Secondary Standards
Sulfur oxides	(a) 80 micrograms per cubic meter (0.03 ppm) —annual arithmetic mean. (b) 365 micrograms per cubic meter (0.14 ppm) —maximum 24-hour concentration not to be exceeded more than once per year.	(a) 60 micrograms per cubic meter (0.02 ppm) —annual arithmetic mean. (b) 260 micrograms per cubic meter (0.1 ppm) —maximum 24-hour concentrations not to be exceeded more than once per year, as a guide to be used in assessing implementation plans to achieve the annual standard. (c) 1,300 micrograms per cubic meter (0.5 ppm)—maximum 3-hour concentration not to be exceeded more than once per year.
Particulate matter	(a) 75 micrograms per cubic meter—annual geometric mean. (b) 260 micrograms per cubic meter— maximum 24-hour concentration not to be exceeded more than once per year.	(a) 60 micrograms per cubic meter—annual geometric mean, as a guide to be used in assessing implementation plans to achieve the 24-hour standard. (b) 150 micrograms per cubic meter— maximum 24-hour concentration not to be exceeded more than once per year.

Pollutant	Standards (no distinction between primary and secondary)
Carbon monoxide	(a) 10 milligrams per cubic meter (9 ppm) —maximum 8-hour concentration not to be exceeded more than once per year. (b) 40 milligrams per cubic meter (35 ppm) —maximum 1-hour concentration not to be exceeded more than once per year.
Photochemical oxidants	160 micrograms per cubic meter (0.08 ppm) —maximum 1-hour concentration not to be exceeded more than once per year.

TABLE 5.1 (Continued)

Hydrocarbons	160 micrograms per cubic meter (0.24 ppm) —maximum 3-hour concentration (6 to 9 A.M.) not to be exceeded more than once per year.
Nitrogen dioxide	100 micrograms per cubic meter (0.05 ppm) —annual arithmetic mean.

DEFINITIONS: *ambient air:* the portion of the atmosphere, external to buildings, to which the general public has access.
national primary ambient air-quality standards: levels of air quality which the Administrator judges are necessary, with an adequate margin of safety, to protect the public health.
national secondary ambient air-quality standards: levels of air quality which the Administrator judges necessary to protect the public welfare from any known or anticipated adverse effects of a pollutant.

SOURCE: Rules and Regulations: Title 42—Public Health; Chapter IV—Environmental Protection Agency; Part 410 —National Primary and Secondary Ambient Air Quality Standards. Published in: *Federal Register*, Vol. 36, No. 84, part II, Friday, April 30, 1971, Washington, D.C.

standards—to safeguard aesthetics, vegetation, and materials—are to be achieved within a reasonable time. The states submitted their plans in early 1972, and in May 1972 EPA approved 14 plans and partially approved 41 plans, covering all states. At the same time, a Federal district court ruled that EPA could not approve a plan that would permit deterioration of air-quality standards in areas where the air is now cleaner than the standards set by EPA, thus establishing the principle that the national air-quality standards set *maximum* levels of pollution only in those cases where the air is of a quality less than the standards; for air of better quality, the higher standard must obtain.

An important feature of the Clean Air Amendments was the establishment of strict emission standards for automotive pollutants, and the requirement that 1975 standards for new-car emissions of carbon monoxide and hydrocarbons should be 90 percent below the 1970 standards, a requirement extended to nitrogen oxide by 1976. To further curb auto-mobile pollution, in February 1972 EPA issued proposed regulations to require the general availability of lead- and phosphorus-free gasoline by 1974.

The urgency and forthrightness with which EPA has demanded that new automobiles comply with its emission standards are called for by the situation. Data on present levels of pollution in our urban environment, the projected increase in urban traffic in the years ahead, and the performance of pollution-control systems under actual driving conditions make it clear that even applying stricter standards in 1975 will only prolong the downward curve in vehicle emissions until the middle 1980s. After that, carbon monoxide levels will again rise because of the sheer number of automobiles on the roads and highways. Hence, EPA is also concerned about finding alternatives to the present internal combustion engine, but this will require rather dramatic new technological breakthroughs or stringent controls upon the highly-valued personal mobility of Americans.

Similar problems afflict the attempt to develop strict standards for the sulfur oxides, one of the most difficult classes of air pollutants to control. Because of their toxicity and pervasiveness, they are among the most dangerous air pollutants to human health and are clearly the most harmful to vegetation, buildings, and materials. Their potential increase is tied to their chief source, the burgeoning electric power industry, which almost doubles its output every ten years.

At present about 65 percent of the energy for generating electricity stems from coal; gas, oil, and hydroelectric sources account for about 34 percent; and nuclear energy the remaining 1 percent. By 1980, 22 percent of the total installed electric power capacity is expected to be nuclear. By 1990 it will be 40 percent. However, by far the greatest source of energy is now, and for the rest of this century will continue to be, the burning of coal and oil. The amount of coal used for power by the year 2000 will be four times greater than it is today.

A number of alternatives are available to control sulfur oxide pollution over the next decade. Switching fuels is possible, but only when an alternative, low-sulfur fuel is available. Most coal near the nation's centers of population and power demand is high in sulfur. Low-sulfur coal not only is far away but also commands a higher price for use as coke by domestic and foreign steelmakers. North Africa and other areas are rich in low-sulfur oil but are limited by low production and refinery capabilities. Oil import quotas bar it from certain areas of the midwest and the west coast, although the oil may be imported to other areas of the United States. The United States will probably continue to rely primarily on residual oil from the Western Hemisphere—and that oil will have to be desulfurized before it is used. Natural gas carries an insignificant sulfur content, but it is the scarcest of fossil fuels, and most of it is being conserved for nonpower purposes.

Sulfur can be separated from coal and oil, but the processes are costly, and some are not fully developed technically. Methods to remove sulfur from the stack gases after the fuel is burned are under development. However, none of these processes is yet in large-scale use, and the costs are not yet known. Some of the stack-control processes recover sulfur or a sulfur by-product, which can be sold to help offset costs. Some are also being evaluated for their potential in reducing pollution from nitrogen oxides. Again, new technologies may be needed, and the tradeoffs involved in any control program are of great complexity, directly or indirectly affecting every corner of American society and every citizen.

THE IMPLEMENTATION PLANNING PROGRAM

The Air Quality Act of 1967 and the Clean Air Amendments of 1970 set up a framework for air-resource decisions at the regional level. The Act provided for the establishment of air-quality control regions (over 240 AQCR's are now in

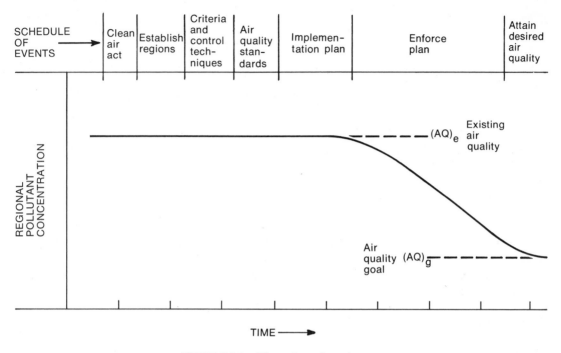

| SCHEDULE OF EVENTS ➡ | Clean air act | Establish regions | Criteria and control techniques | Air quality standards | Implementation plan | Enforce plan | Attain desired air quality |

FIGURE 5.1.   The path to clean air.

existence), utilization of air-quality criteria and control-technology documents to set standards, and preparation of implementation plans for attaining these standards. This idealized path to the attainment of clean air is shown in Figure 5.1.

The core of the contemplated planning procedure, the Implementation Planning Program (IPP), is illustrated in Figure 5.2. The heart of the IPP is an atmospheric diffusion model, which predicts ambient concentrations of pollutants from sources. Input to the model is in the form of an emission inventory, which lists the major sources of pollutants and gives detailed engineering parameters for the sources of pollution and the emissions generated. Emission contributions from sources that cannot be identified individually are aggregated to form area sources. Meteorological data are included on wind speed, wind direction, mixing depth, and other phenomena characterizing the transport mechanism whereby pollutants are transmitted from sources to receptors.

To improve the accuracy of the diffusion model, a calibration procedure is used to compare predicted pollutant concentrations with measured air-quality values. The procedure adjusts for errors in the diffusion model which result from inaccuracies in the mathematical diffusion equation, inaccurate source-emission and meteorological data, irregularities in the topography of the region (which the model assumes to be a flat plain), and other deviations. The Atmospheric Diffusion Model thus predicts the concentration and distribution of pollutants for the AQCR with reasonable accuracy.

Before regional emission-control strategies are tested, a Control Cost File is prepared by the computer. Each major source (i.e., point source) is assigned all control devices which may reasonably be used for reducing emissions from that source. For particulate emissions, control devices generally take the form of emission-control equipment applied externally to the polluting process. For sulfur dioxide emission, either low-

INPUTS

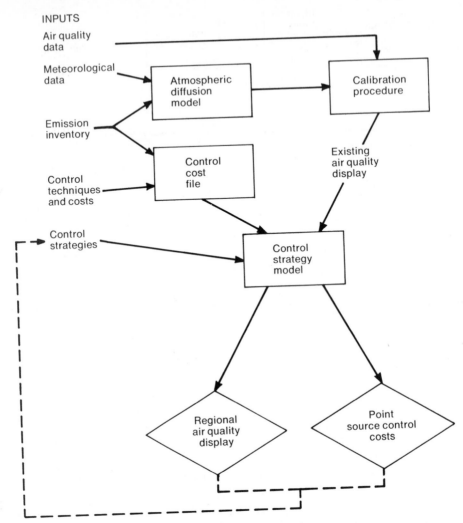

FIGURE 5.2.   Implementation planning program.

sulfur fuel substitutions or fuel-gas desulfuriza-tion techniques are entered into the file. The Control Cost File thus takes the form of a list of all point sources and the appropriate control devices for each, with each alternative device representing a different level of control efficiency for a given source.

The IPP model is used to evaluate the effec-tiveness of alternative control strategies for a region. A control strategy is a combination of

emission-control standards for specific cate-gories of emission sources. Different emission standards are normally applied to three major source categories: solid waste disposal, industrial processes, and fuel combustion. An additional emission standard uniformly reduces the emis-sions from area sources by a specified amount.

When the effectiveness of a control strategy is analyzed, the Control Strategy Model applies the designated emission standards to each of the point sources in the AQCR. The reduction in emissions from point sources generally lowers the pollutant concentrations within the region. The Control Strategy Model recomputes the pollution concentration distribution and calculates the emission-control costs for sources affected by the emission standards. The most significant output of the Control Strategy Model is a regional display of pollutant concentrations and an estimate of the annual control cost for all sources in the region which must comply with the control strategy.

The IPP model is now being used to evaluate emission-control strategies in, for example, the District of Columbia portion of the National Capital Interstate Air Quality Control Region (NCIAQCR) and the Metropolitan Cincinnati Interstate Air Quality Control Region (MCIAQCR).

Figure 5.3 illustrates the existing ground-level particulate concentrations in the NCIAQCR as predicted by the calibrated Atmospheric Diffusion Model. In this region, the goal of the implementation plan was to attain an annual arithmetic average of particulate concentrations of 86.6 $\mu g/m^3$ as an interim standard and 65.2 $\mu g/m^3$ as a long-term standard. In testing the acceptability of a strategy, the IPP model was used to make sure that the annual average concentration did not exceed the long-term air-quality standard at any point in the AQCR.

To meet the standards, a control strategy for reduction of the particulate concentrations was required. The isopleths in Figure 5.3 indicate

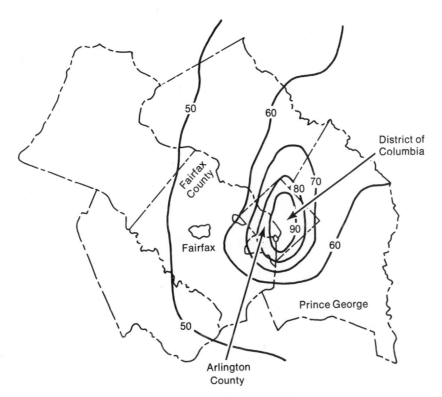

FIGURE 5.3. Existing ground-level particulate intensities in the NCIAQCR as computed by the verified diffusion model.

TABLE 5.2

Particulate control strategies–National Capital Interstate Air Quality Control Region

Strategy Number	Point Sources		Area Sources		Control Cost		Maximum Receptor ($\mu g/m^3$)
	Percent Reduction	New Emission Rate (tons/day)	Percent Reduction	New Emission Rate (tons/day)	$ × 10^6	$/ton Removed	
		(84.7)[a]		(75.6)[a]			
1	36.3	54.0	18.0	62.0	0.5	47	107.7
2	87.4	10.7	51.4	36.7	13.9	514	92.2
3	62.2	32.0	47.5	39.7	4.0	210	90.0
4	52.7	40.1	48.6	38.9	4.4	267	76.0
5	86.4	11.6	51.4	36.7	11.8	471	69.4
6	78.2	18.4	51.4	36.7	11.6	489	69.7
7	76.0	19.9	51.4	36.7	11.6	489	69.7
8	36.3	54.0	36.3	48.2	0.5	47	89.8
9	41.0	50.0	18.6	61.6	0.6	44	81.8
10	77.0	19.5	51.4	36.7	11.6	489	70.0
18	70.4	25.0	51.4	36.7	10.8	498	68.2

[a] Existing conditions based on the 1969 inventory collected for the NCIAQCR and the validated diffusion model.

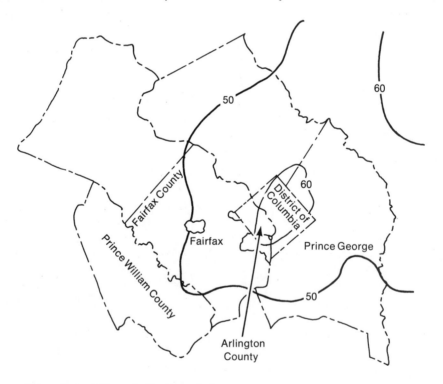

Note: Annual Concentrations in $\mu g/m^3$

FIGURE 5.4.   Predicted particulate intensities after enactment of the proposed emission-control strategy in all political jurisdictions.

that annual average intensities above 90 $\mu g/m^3$ were observed in the NCIAQCR. Concentrations of up to 107.7 $\mu g/m^3$ could be expected within this 90-$\mu g/m^3$ isopleth (the 100-$\mu g/m^3$ isopleth was too small to be drawn on the map). Analytical results for ten control strategies are presented in Table 5.2. The reduction in emissions from point and area sources is indicated, as well as the control cost expected and the pollutant concentrations at the maximum receptor in the region. Strategy 18 was selected for the District of Columbia, on the basis of (1) control costs, (2) expected air quality (which, within experimental error, approximated the air-quality standard), and (3) the assumption that the emission-control technologies required to meet the strategy were technically feasible and economically reasonable. Particulate levels expected after the application of the proposed control strategy are illustrated in Figure 5.4.

ECONOMIC ANALYSIS FOR EFFECTIVE AIR-RESOURCE PLANNING

At face value this appears to be a very reasonable way of going about the planning process. The Implementation Planning Program's procedures are, however, deficient in several respects. In particular, they do not take into account either the economic effects of pollution control or the relationship of control costs to benefits derived. Regional policies are being established on the basis of an examination of pollution sources and related control technologies, specific pollutants and emission rates, ambient air quality in the region, and effects of air quality on the receptors. Since economic considerations are not included, potential impacts on the regional and national economy are not being evaluated. Nonetheless, such effects as changes in fuel prices, added production costs, and increased cost of electrical power may influence such other facets of life as unemployment, inflation, and the balance of payments.

These factors should be included in any comprehensive planning procedure.

The basic economic issues involved in air-pollution control may be portrayed as in Figure 5.5. When all relevant tangible and intangible effects are considered, primary concern is directed to the marginal cost of control and the marginal benefits (that is, the marginal reduction in air-pollution damages), which are functions of regional pollution intensities. The goal of the decision-maker is to reduce pollution intensities to the level where society's welfare is maximized. This condition exists at the intersection of the marginal-cost and marginal-benefit curves in Figure 5.5.

Analysis of the economic aspects of the problem calls for appropriate economic tools. In particular, welfare economics may be applied in the form of cost/benefit (C/B) analysis, as a means of evaluating social well-being within a region. The procedures for air-pollution C/B analysis are not unlike those used in other public investment decisions, including water-resource analysis, although measurement of the extremely subtle effects of air pollution greatly complicates the analysis.

Application of Economic Theory and Cost/Benefit Analysis

Cost/benefit analysis may be effectively applied in determining the optimum allocation of resources for a public project or program. Such an application is analogous to the use of financial or investment analysis by the private sector to evaluate corporate or private ownership investment projects. The analytical problem in the private sector is much less complex, since market prices are available by which to measure the flow of costs and benefits over time. In the public sector, governments invest funds and make decisions where the forces of supply and demand break down (that is, where the economy alone does not provide the degree of well-being desired by the society).

There is no marketplace where the exter-

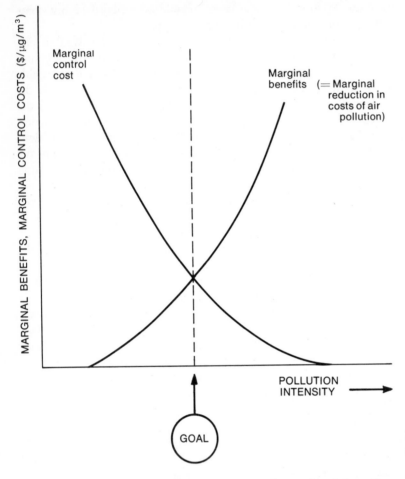

FIGURE 5.5. Air pollution efficiency analysis.

nalities created by emission sources are corrected by the inherent demand of the receptors for clean air. When regional governments attempt to solve the problem, they are forced to consider causes and effects outside the marketplace and are left with no means for readily evaluating the costs and benefits of an investment decision or public program. C/B analysis of public programs is thus complicated by problems associated with both the measurement and the evaluation of effects.

Cost/benefit analysis has long been used to evaluate public programs. Prest and Turvey (1965) trace the development of C/B analysis from 1844, the year in which Dupuit's classic study of the utility of public works appeared in France. Dupuit's treatise represented a highly significant breakthrough in economics. Cost/benefit analysis first achieved prominence in the United States, however, where it was found to be particularly applicable to navigation problems. The River and Harbor Act of 1902 required a board of engineers to report on the desirability of river and harbor projects under consideration by the Army Corps of Engineers, taking into account the benefits to commerce and the cost. Under the New Deal in the 1930s the idea of a broader social justification for projects developed. The Flood Control Act of 1936 authorized Federal participation in flood-control schemes "if the benefits to whomsoever they may accrue are in excess of the estimated cost." Other agencies soon accepted the concept of C/B analysis, and in 1950 an interagency committee produced the "Green Book," which attempted to codify and agree on general analytical principles. C/B analysis flourished in the 1960s, initially through Department of Defense acceptance of the planning-programming-budgeting (PPB) system and later as a result of the late President Johnson's desire that this tool be utilized throughout the government. It has since been applied to numerous socially oriented programs in such areas as urban renewal, transportation, and health.

The analytical structure presented in this section combines systems analysis and C/B analysis to provide a formal structuring of causes and effects associated with the air-pollution control problem. Such a framework provides a means for maximizing the utility of research findings and drawing attention to parameters not previously considered in the decision-making process. The approach can be used to identify future research needs and to prevent misallocation of resources. Finally, a computerized tool for C/B analysis offers opportunities to gain further knowledge by examining the interrelationships between relevant factors through trial and error or through sensitivity analysis.

Theoretical Considerations

The social costs of air-pollution control affect the individual, the corporate sector, and the public sector. Individual costs represent an incremental portion of consumption benefits. Such costs might take the form of annual incremental costs of products that are altered for air-quality purposes (i.e., fuels for home heating, gasoline for automobiles, and so on) or annual incremental costs of activities which replace activities that are outlawed by air-pollution control regulations (e.g., the cost of solid waste removal

and disposal when backyard burning is prohibited).

The corporate sector feels the impact of air-pollution control costs through emission-reduction activities, air-quality monitoring, and research and development on process innovations or pollution controls. The impact of these costs may be passed on to the individual in the form of an increase in the price of the goods and services marketed. Without emission control, the cost of air pollution is transferred to the community in the form of damages represented by external diseconomies (negative externalities), since the costs are negative benefits and are external to the firm. The justification for air-pollution control is based on the premise that it is socially cheaper to control emissions at the source (i.e., to increase the internalities) than it is to bear the cost of a polluted air resource (i.e., to live with the externalities).

Public expenditures for pollution control are associated with (1) enforcement of individual and corporate control activities, (2) reduction of emissions from public facilities, (3) regional and nationwide monitoring of pollution concentrations, (4) research and development on new control techniques and instruments, and (5) research on air-pollution effects. When evaluating the cost of air-pollution control to the public sector, allocation of annual revenues at the federal, state, and local levels of government must be measured. The impact of these costs is felt by the individual in the form of increased taxes.

Social benefits, like social costs, have an impact on the individual, the corporate sector, and the public sector. The social benefits to be measured in C/B analysis are the technological or "real" effects which alter the total production possibilities and total welfare opportunities for consumers in the economy. The economic effects of air pollution may be grouped as follows:

1. *Direct effects*—the direct and immediate externalities borne by the receptor.

2. *Adjustments (indirect effects)*—effects which induce persons and firms to make certain adjustments in order to reduce the direct impact of the pollutants.
3. *Market effects*—effects realized through the marketplace as a result of the adjustments made.

Figure 5.6 illustrates the manner in which the individual feels the effects of air pollution. A structure of the type shown in Figure 5.6 is required as a starting point for classification of the major costs and benefits of emission-control strategies.

In discussing the effects of public programs, a major economic distinction is drawn between pecuniary effects and technological effects. *Pecuniary effects* are the result of changes in relative prices in the economy. They involve a redistribution of goods and services among people. *Technological effects* (also called "real" effects) alter the total production possibilities or total welfare possibilities for consumers in the economy. These effects are termed "economies" when they are favorable and "disecon-

omies" when they are unfavorable. Thus, manpower training programs produce real benefits for trainees insofar as they increase the workers' productive capabilities. Once the trainee is part of the training program, the benefits are classified as internal real benefits or economies ("internal" because the effects are borne by the firm that does the training). Air and water pollution are classic examples of external real economies. These effects are classified as "external" because they are borne by persons other than those who caused the pollution. They are considered "real" because production or consumption opportunities elsewhere in the economy are reduced, since polluted water is a detriment to other uses of water (i.e., commercial, drinking, swimming, and so on).

The concepts of pecuniary and real effects would be applicable, for example, to a shift in output from firms which liquidate because of excessive costs of air-pollution control to firms which supply control equipment. The resulting

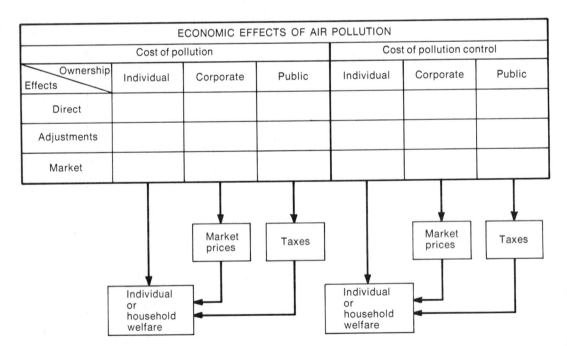

FIGURE 5.6.   Structuring the economic effects of air pollution.

increase in revenues to the suppliers of control equipment is a pecuniary effect (i.e., a redistribution). The important consideration is that only a shift within the economy exists, without an increase or decrease in the productivity of the economy as a whole (assuming a market economy without serious imperfections).

Technological effects are felt by firms which must purchase hardware, switch fuels, install monitoring devices, or perform research. When the responsibility for pollution control is placed upon the pollutant emitter, costs are internalized and measured on the balance sheet of the firm, instead of being passed along as an externality to the community. Such costs are felt as a net decrease in productivity for the total economy, since the same quantity of product is being produced at an increased cost. This decrease in net productivity is a relevant social cost for C/B analysis.

Like social costs, effects are identified as either pecuniary or technological in the evaluation of social benefits. For example, air-pollution control may reduce demand for certain products and services in some sectors of the conomy (e.g., window washing, house painting), thus causing a shift in output from these sectors to the rest of the economy. The reduction in revenues for the sector in which demand is reduced and the corresponding increase in demand and in revenues for the rest of the economy are pecuniary effects. The net increase in aggregate consumption or aggregate production benefits which the society realizes from improved air quality represents a technological effect and a social benefit. For example, as an individual becomes more productive (because of improved health or enhanced psychological attitude) or as he derives more satisfaction from a given income (i.e., through increased welfare or income utility), social benefits for society increase accordingly.

Another concept employed in C/B analysis is that of the so-called "secondary effect" of a project. As the term is generally used, such effects represent the external pecuniary effects. They include the results of changes in demand for particular resource inputs used by the project and the accompanying changes in income of the resource owners. The results of changes in the demand pattern for particular outputs as well as the accompanying changes in incomes of their sellers, as the initial beneficiaries spend their added income and the initial cost-bearers reduce their spending, are likewise considered to be secondary effects. Such "respending" is essentially a by-product or side-effect of a project and does not reflect any increase in the economy's total productive capability, since such increases are already counted in the real benefits. Secondary effects reflect shifts in relative demand patterns which produce increased income for some persons and decreased incomes for others.

Secondary benefits thus represent the values added by incurring secondary costs in activities stemming from or induced by the project (i.e., indirect contributions of public investment to aggregate consumption). The principal sources of secondary benefits are:

1. Departures from competition in the further processing of goods and services produced by means of public project outputs.
2. Changes in consumption sufficient to produce changes in the price of consumer goods.
3. External economies associated with public projects.
4. Private investment induced by public projects.

It is common in C/B analyses to distinguish between costs and benefits that are "tangible" and those that are "intangible." Tangible effects can be measured and priced for decision-making purposes; intangible effects cannot. In other words, tangible effects include those for which, at a particular point in time, data are available whereby the effects may be assessed a value placed on them. But obviously, what is tangible or intangible, measurable or nonmeasurable, is less a matter of what is abstractly possible than it is of what is pragmatically feasible at reasonable cost. What is intangible today because of data limitations may be tangible tomorrow as a result of research efforts aimed at quantification of effects. To cite an example, in the Middle Ages and earlier it must surely have been argued by some that one's feeling of warmth or cold was intangible, unmeasurable, and so on. Fortunately, Gabriel Fahrenheit did not agree.

The concept of intangible and tangible effects is of great importance in air-pollution control. Since most of the effects of a polluted atmosphere are now considered intangible, qualitative considerations will influence decisions concerning the development of a regional air-resource plan. For decision-making purposes, such intangible effects must be identified and ranked according to their importance. As planned research efforts are implemented, more data will become available and additional air-pollution effects may be quantified.

The use of C/B analysis to determine the economic efficiency of alternative control strategies is illustrated in Figure 5.7. The graph shows one way of plotting pollution and control cost curves for a hypothetical Air Quality

Control Region (AQCR). These theoretical curves are based on the control costs and pollution damage costs for five increasingly stringent emission control strategies (S_A through S_E). As the stringency of the control strategies increases, there is a corresponding reduction in the regional pollution intensities.

Costs of pollution damage and control are determined for each strategy (e.g., $CC_{(E)}$ and $CP_{(E)}$ for strategy S_E). Above the two cost curves is a "total cost to society" curve, which is a summation of control and damage costs. The marginal cost of control increases as control efficiency increases, and the marginal cost of pollution increases as pollution intensity increases, as shown in Figure 5.1. The minimum cost to society thus corresponds to the intersection of the control-cost and cost-of-pollution curves.

Control costs, and benefits are illustrated in Figure 5.8. The control-cost curve in this illustration is identical to that in Figure 5.7. The benefits curve represents the differences, in pollution costs under existing conditions (S_0) and under various emission-control strategies.

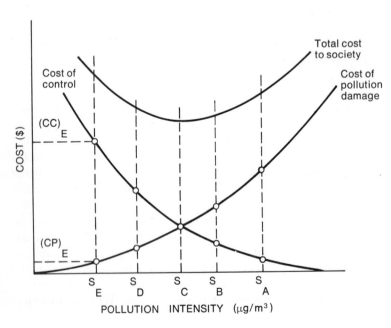

FIGURE 5.7. Structuring the economic effects of air pollution.

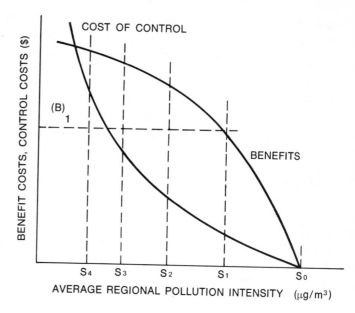

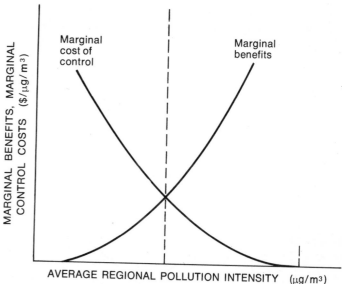

FIGURE 5.8. Cost of control and benefits.

The benefit, B, for strategy S_1, for example, is the difference between pollution costs under strategies S_0 and S_1. The optimum welfare condition for society is represented by strategy S_2, where the absolute difference between benefits and costs reaches its maximum value. From the lower graph it is evident that for strategy S_2 marginal benefits equal marginal costs. This condition of marginal welfare, referred to in economics as the "Pareto optimum," exists when one more dollar spent on improving the welfare of one individual necessarily detracts from the welfare of another. Thus under strategy S_2 if one dollar more is spent on the control of emissions, benefits valued at less than a dollar will be gained. On the other hand, if one dollar less is spent on control, more than a dollar's worth of benefits will be lost.

This concept is further illustrated in Figure 5.9, where the abscissa represents "tons of emissions removed" (under various emission-control strategies) rather than "regional pollution intensity" (this change reverses the location of the marginal-cost and marginal-benefit curves.) As in Figure 5.8, the Pareto-optimality condition exists where welfare is maximized.

As Figure 5.9 indicates, the goal of the air-resource decision-maker is to remove the Pareto-irrelevant damages, since for these, the benefits derived from pollution control will be less than the costs of controlling the pollutants. For maximum efficiency it is important that a pollution-control policy provide for removal of Pareto-irrelevant damages only. Benefits under the Pareto-optimum strategy are represented by quadrangle *AECB*; the cost of pollution control

by triangle *BEC*. The net benefit to society is thus represented by triangle *AEB*. In other words, it is desirable to internalize the Pareto-relevant externalities (i.e., by making the polluting sources pay the control cost) without infringing upon the Pareto-irrelevant externalities; that is, it is desirable to control pollution at the source up to a point where the next dollar spent on pollution control is equal to the resulting incremental social benefits obtained by the community.

The shaded area under the marginal control cost and marginal benefit functions in Figure 5.10 represents total air-pollutant disposal cost to society at the maximum-welfare condition. This total cost may be reduced once the maximum-welfare condition has been obtained (see Figure 5.11). Through technological advances in air-pollution control systems, society will experience an effect that may be portrayed as a shift of the marginal control-cost curve to the right. Such advancement is a classical case of a

FIGURE 5.9. Pareto-relevant and Pareto-irrelevant externalities.

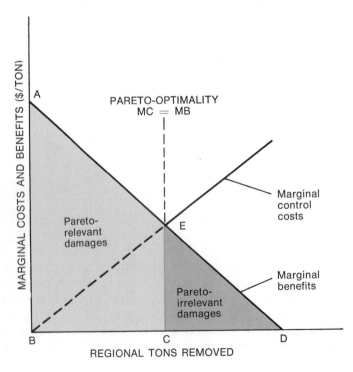

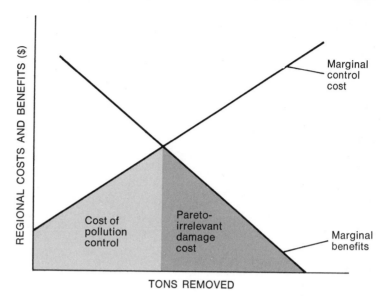

FIGURE 5.10. Relevant costs of air-pollution disposal.

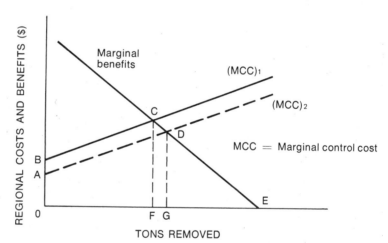

FIGURE 5.11. Reduction of the relevant costs of air-pollution disposal.

technological effect. Society benefits by a more efficient mode of operation—that is, a net increase in productivity.

Application of Cost/Benefit Analysis

The aim of C/B analysis is to maximize the present value of all benefits less that of all costs incurred, subject to specified constraints. In air-pollution control, C/B analysis can be employed to compare the social costs and bene-fits resulting from a potential air-resource policy with those to be expected from a continuation of the existing level of effort (the "base alternative"), as shown in Figure 5.12. After defining the project life (the period of time over which costs and benefits will be measured), the costs and benefits of alternative air-resource policies are computed and discounted back to the base year for purposes of comparative analysis. The resulting data may then be used in the evaluation of alternative policies.

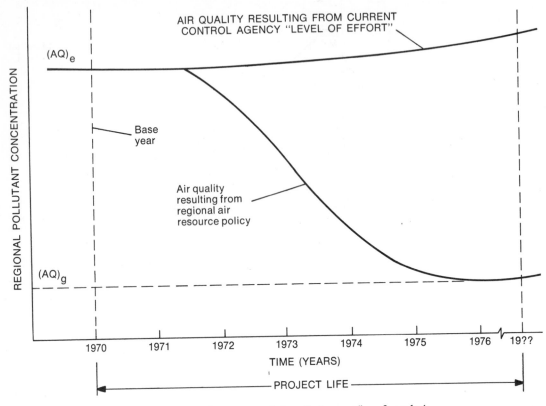

FIGURE 5.12.   The concept of air-pollution cost/benefit analysis.

Determination of the project life is an important factor in the design of a C/B analysis study, since various costs and benefits are frequently realized at substantially different points in time. Project life is estimated rather subjectively, on the basis of an assessment of such factors as physical lifespan, technological change, shifts in demand, and emergence of competing products. For water-resource projects involving the construction of dams, project life may be defined as 50 or 100 years for dams that are expected to perform for 150 years. In air-pollution planning, a shorter project life is desirable because of the following factors:

1. Frequent changes in air-resource requirements.
2. Rapid depreciation of control equipment (15 years or so).

3. Obsolesence of current control equipment because of technological innovations.
4. Rapid technological and conceptual changes throughout the relatively new field of air-resource management.

A simple flow diagram of the C/B model and its relation to IPP is shown in Figure 5.13. A general description of the model will serve as an introduction to the C/B system.

Two outputs of IPP now being used in regional air-quality decision-making are: (1) point-source control costs, (2) air-quality display (as previously cited). Point-source control costs are estimated for each identified pollution source with particulate or sulfur dioxide emission rates greater than 24 tons per year (the commonly accepted cutoff point). The control costs are

IMPLEMENTATION PLANNING PROGRAM (IPP)

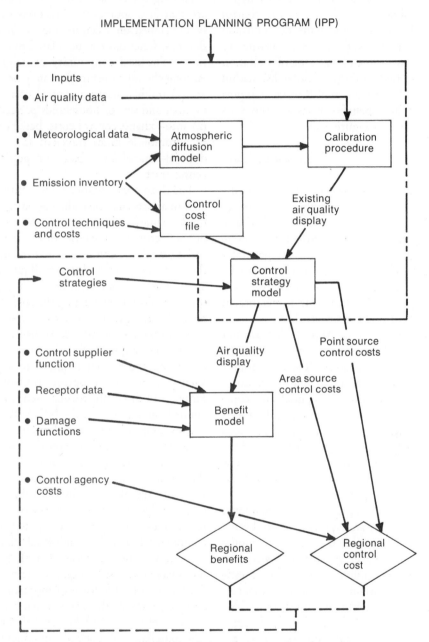

FIGURE 5.13. Regional air-pollution cost/benefit model.

calculated on a source-by-source basis by hypo-thetically applying to each source the control system needed to comply with the emission strategy under investigation. The air-quality display is a two-dimensional plot of pollution concentration (in the form of isopleths) within an AQCR. The outputs of IPP serve as inputs to the costs and benefits parts of the C/B Model, as shown in Figure 5.13.

Estimates of Costs

The IPP model computes the expected emis-sion-control costs for both public and private sources. Control technologies are hypothetically applied to point sources as a basis for the cost-estimating procedures. These costs are generally acceptable for C/B analyses, but they must be supplemented by area source-control costs and control-agency costs, to provide a measure of the total costs of pollution control.

Emission sources in an AQCR that are not considered point sources are represented in the IPP model as area sources. The area-source category includes residential and small com-mercial fuel combustion, residential and com-mercial solid waste, automobiles, and process sources not large enough to be identified as a point source. Area sources are not identified in-dividually in the IPP model, and emission-con-trol cost estimates are not prepared for these sources in the existing planning process.

The task of identifying control techniques and control costs for area sources has not been a high-priority item. As C/B analysis techniques are developed, however, greater emphasis must be placed on determining rigorous cost esti-mates for all important sources. The resources invested in such cost estimates must, of course, be weighed against the benefits derived. Since cost estimates for point sources alone are inadequate for regional C/B evaluations, it appears the expenditure of resources in develop-ing a cost-estimating procedure for area sources is justifiable.

Among the considerations that seem relevant are that area source-cost functions should thus be developed on a census tract or grid basis so that cost functions can be related to characteris-tics of the local community or neighborhood. Among the relationships that may be developed are (1) residual heating control costs, based on number and size of households per census tract; (2) auto-exhaust control costs, based on number of automobile miles traveled; (3) solid waste disposal-control costs, based on population per census tract.

The third cost category which must be evalu-ated in a C/B analysis is the cost associated with implementation of the control program by the public sector. For purposes of the analysis, con-trol-agency costs can be taken as an allocation of the control-agency budget for all jurisdictions in an AQCR for control of the specific pollutants under analysis. In evaluating the cost of a specific control strategy, the relevant control-agency costs are the incremental costs determined from the budget required for the current level of effort and the budget required to support the agency under the proposed control strategy. Figure 5.14 shows the format used for reporting control-agency costs in the NCIAQCR.

Most of the current air-pollution control legis-lation is based on the concept of controlling pol-lutant emissions through direct regulation (in the form of an emission standard). The Tax Reform Act of 1969, on the other hand, in-cludes inducements in the form of a provision for a five-year write-off on pollution-control equipment installed in industrial plants which were in operation on December 31, 1968. Some states have likewise recognized the need for and desirability of some form of mechanism to help companies absorb the heavy initial control costs. Such relief generally takes one of three forms. The purchaser of control equipment may be allowed to accelerate the depreciation write-off (over a period of one to five years) for income-tax or franchise-tax purposes. Purchases of pollu-tion-abatement equipment may be exempted

Jurisdiction	1970 Budget* ($)		Budget for Compliance** ($)	
Pollutants	Total	SO$_x$ & Part.	Total	SO$_x$ & Part.
Maryland				
● Montgomery Cty.				
● P. Georges Cty.				
State of Virginia				
● Arlington Cty.				
● Fairfax Cty.				
● Loudoun Cty.				
● Prince William Cty.				
● Alexandria City				
● Fairfax City				
● Falls Church				
District of Columbia				
Total				

*Current "level of effort."

**Budget needed to support air resource program for an identified control strategy.

FIGURE 5.14. Accounting for control-agency costs.

from sales and use taxes, or pollution-abatement installations may be exempted from property taxes.

In C/B analysis, it is important to include the social costs to the public sector which result from financial incentives, credit subsidies, and other inducements for private-sector emission control. When air-pollution control strategies in a region are based on direct regulation, the social cost of the inducement is not substantial (but should nonetheless be evaluated). When tax write-offs, direct payments, and other forms of financial inducements are utilized, the social cost to the public sector is substantial. More intensive study of such schemes is recommended.

Estimation of Benefits

The social costs of air-pollution control include all economic effects resulting from the allocation of resources to administration, research, enforcement, measurement, and implementation in connection with the control of pollutant emissions. Social benefits, on the other hand, are those increases in welfare which result from improved air quality. To measure the benefits resulting from the application of control strategies, a *benefit model* may be developed (see Figure 5.15). The benefit model determines damage costs by relating air-quality data to *receptor data* and to *damage functions* which express the social value of air quality effects on receptors. The difference in air-pollution damage cost between existing air quality and the control-strategy air quality is the value of the strategy "benefit."

The control-supplier function, also shown in Figure 5.15, is a relationship which predicts the stimulus to the regional economy resulting from the demand for air-pollution control equipment and services.

To put the benefit model in perspective, a flow diagram of a C/B model (without the control-supplier function) is presented in Figure 5.16. As illustrated, control-strategy air quality is first related to receptor information (census-tract data). Damage is determined for each census tract by means of a damage function which expresses damage cost as a function of air quality and census data. The regional damage cost is computed by summing overall census tracts in the AQCR.

The design of the benefit model is described in the following sections.

Receptor Data

In C/B analysis, the consequences of government policies are traced back to the fulfillment of individual (or household) wants. This rule of C/B analysis is the determining factor in the selection of census-tract information to describe air-pollutant receptors.

IPP now includes procedures for relating air-quality data (as calculated by the atmospheric-diffusion model) to census tracts. The typical atmospheric-diffusion model is currently designed to compute air-pollutant concentrations

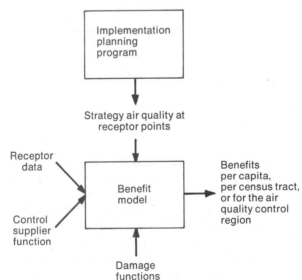

FIGURE 5.15. Benefit-model design.

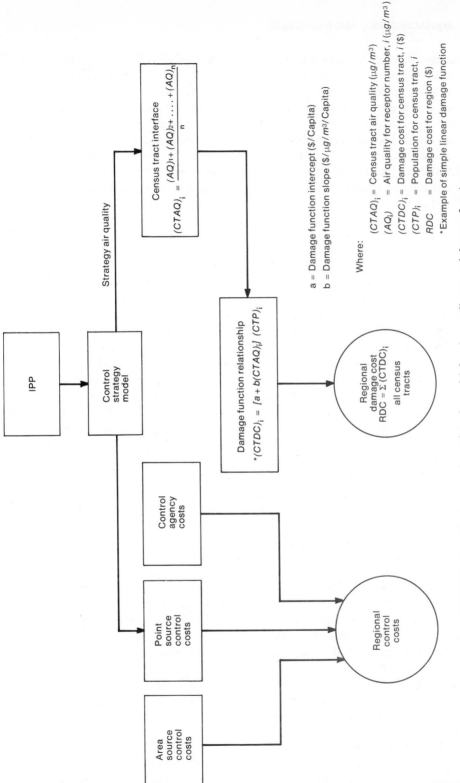

FIGURE 5.16. Cross-sectional cost-benefit model for given pollutant and damage function.

at approximately 250 receptor points (located on a grid) within an AQCR. It is a relatively simple procedure to select specific receptor points to represent each census tract. Each census tract is identified by one or more receptor points which represent that tract. The computer then calculates a simple arithmetic average of the pollutant concentrations at the receptor points. This average is referred to as the "census-tract air quality" (CTAQ).

Damage Functions

Damage functions are the most complicated and least clearly defined inputs to the benefit model, owing to the lack of knowledge of the cause-and-effect relationship between air pollutants and receptors and the current inability to place a value on the effects.

In an economic sense, supply and demand exist for air quality just as they do for goods and services in the private sector. In the private sector, price is a function of the effects of supply and demand for goods and services in the marketplace. Since there is no marketplace for the air resource, the price of clean air will depend upon society's willingness to pay for improved air quality.

In Figure 5.17, a parallel is drawn between the demand for goods and services in the private sector and that for air quality in the public sector. An air-pollution damage function is in essence a demand function for air quality, an aggregation of the citizens' willingness to pay for a collective good. Willingness to pay for air quality is the damage-function expression that is applicable to C/B modeling. Individuals may pay, for example, to avoid such damages as corrosion of materials and soiling of property. Many people likewise prefer to avoid intangible air-pollution effects which are detrimental to aesthetic pleasure or which produce general sluggishness.

In C/B analysis, the consequences of government actions are all traced back to the fulfillment of wants of individuals. Individuals feel the effects of air pollution directly and indirectly in the form of (1) actual outlays; (2) reduction in income, health, or satisfaction; (3) complete foreclosure of some opportunities.

In practical terms, a damage function represents a dose-response relationship in which the damage cost is the price an individual (or individuals) will pay to avoid the response. Damage functions are expressed in the form of a rate (i.e., value of damage allocated over a fixed period of time). Figure 5.18 shows the variables which may be used in measuring the rate of damage. The valuation of damage is expressed as the cost factor K.

Identification of Air-Pollution Effects

Air-pollution effects may be categorized as follows: (1) *direct effects*—the direct and immediate externalities borne by the receptor; (2) *adjustments* (indirect effects)—effects which induce persons and firms to make certain adjustments in order to reduce the direct impact of the pollutant; (3) *market effects*—effects realized through the marketplace as a result of adjustments made to reduce the direct impact of pollutant concentrations.

Air-pollution effects are felt by the individual, the corporate sector, and the public sector. (Refer back to Figure 5.6.) Effects realized by the corporate sector are passed along to the consumer in the form of price increases. The effects of air pollution on the public sector are likewise usually passed along to the taxpayer in the form of increased taxes. Figure 5.19 gives examples of effects on the individual, the private sector, and the public sector. Benefits to the individual are divided as follows: (1) effects relating to the individual's person (i.e., health, welfare, productivity, etc.); (2) effects relating to property owned by the individual.

Assessment of Air-Pollution Effects

Once the effects have been identified, the next step in developing damage functions is to assess

● Demand functions can be determined for goods and services in
the marketplace, that is . . .

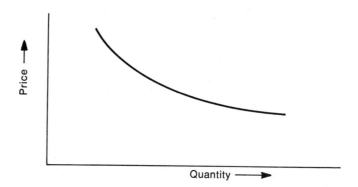

● A damage function may be considered an air quality demand function . . .
that is, a "willingness to pay" for quality of the air resource
(as compared to quantity of product) . . .

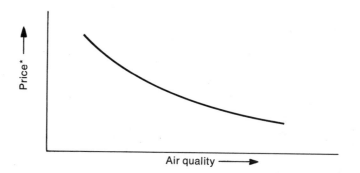

FIGURE 5.17. What is a damage function?

*The price one is willing to pay to have improved air quality

the magnitude of these effects. This procedure requires an analysis of the chemical reactions between pollutants and receptors, as well as a determination of the physiological, pathological, psychological, and other effects of the pollutants on living organisms. The dose-response relationship between pollutant and receptor must also be examined. As is indicated in EPA's criteria documents, the analyst must be concerned with the following factors: intensity, chemical composition, mineralogical structure, absorbed gases, coexisting pollutants, physical state of pollutant (solid, liquid, gaseous).

In addition, the characteristics of the receptor must be evaluated. Relevant characteristics include: physical characteristics, individual susceptibility, state of health, rate and sight of transfer of receptor.

The measurement of pollution effects is greatly complicated by the fact that such effects are quite subtle and vary according to both pollutant concentration and duration of

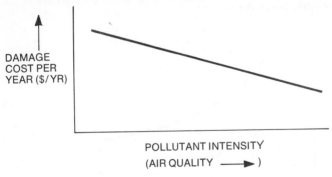

POLLUTANT INTENSITY

(AIR QUALITY ⟶)

RATE OF DAMAGE

$$D = f[\, a, t, AQ, RC, PP \,]$$

where:

   D = Damage per period of exposure.
   a = Concomitant conditions, such as temperature, pressure, humidity, etc.
   t = Exposure duration (ie, 1 year)
  AQ = Pollutant intensity
  RC = Receptor characteristics
  PP = Properties of pollutant

ANNUAL DAMAGE COST

$$C = (K)(D) = g[\, K, a, t, AQ, RC, PP \,]$$

where:

   K = Cost per unit damage
   C = Damage cost per period of exposure

FIGURE 5.18. Damage function—a rate.

exposure. Degree of exposure is expressed in terms of dosage (duration of exposure times pollution concentration). Because of changing atmospheric conditions the pollutant concentration to which an individual is exposed varies significantly over a relatively short period. In addition, numerous pollutants affect receptors, and the aggregate mix of pollutants at any one location is constantly changing. As human beings move from place to place in the course of a day, they are exposed to an even greater variety of combinations of pollutants. Finally, the effects of pollutants on health and property remain unclear, owing to the lack of a full understanding of synergistic phenomena. Much additional research is needed if the total effects of air pollution are to be determined.

Evaluation of Air-Pollution Effects

The third and final task in the process of producing a damage function is an evaluation of the effects which have been identified and assessed. Problems arise, of course, in placing a price on effects such as those outlined above. Welfare economists consider the value of social benefits (i.e., the individual's willingness to pay). In preparing damage functions, the analyst is faced with such complex problems as determining society's willingness to pay when society itself is unable to clearly identify the effects of

SOCIAL BENEFITS $= B_t = B_h + B_p + B_i + B_u$

Where:

B_h = INDIVIDUAL HEALTH BENEFITS
- INCREASED NET AGGREGATE PRODUCTIVITY BENEFITS FROM ENHANCED:
  - JOB PERFORMANCE
  - PRODUCTIVE LIFE SPAN
  - ALERTNESS, PSYCHOLOGICAL SATISFACTION, ETC.
- INCREASED NET AGGREGATE CONSUMPTION BENEFITS FROM REDUCED:
  - MEDICAL CARE
  - PREVENTIVE MEDICINE, ETC.

B_p = INDIVIDUAL PROPERTY BENEFITS
- INCREASED NET AGGREGATE PRODUCTIVITY BENEFITS FROM PROPERTY, I.E.,
  - MATERIALS
  - ANIMALS
  - VEGETATION
  - LAND, ETC.
- INCREASED NET AGGREGATE CONSUMPTION BENEFITS FROM REDUCED PROPERTY MAINTENANCE, I.E.,
  - LAUNDRY
  - AUTO WASHING
  - WINDOW CLEANING, ETC.

B_i = PRIVATE SECTOR BENEFITS
- NET AGGREGATE PRODUCTIVITY BENEFITS OF GOODS AND SERVICES PURCHASED FROM THE PRIVATE SECTOR RESULTING FROM PRICES WHICH DO NOT INCLUDE THE COST (TO THE FIRM) OF:
  - CLEANLINES
  - PROPERTY DISUTILITY
  - INCREASED WORKER PRODUCTIVITY, ETC.

B_u = PUBLIC SECTOR BENEFITS
- NET AGGREGATE PRODUCTIVITY BENEFITS OF PUBLIC SECTOR SERVICES DUE TO COSTS TO THE GOVERNMENTS FOR:
  - CLEANLINES
  - PROPERTY DISUTILITY
  - INCREASED WORKER PRODUCTIVITY, ETC.

FIGURE 5.19. Social benefits resulting from air-pollution control.

- WHY IS THERE A VALUATION PROBLEM? ---- BECAUSE THERE IS NO MARKET WHERE SUPPLY AND DEMAND FOR THIS PRODUCT (THAT IS, QUALITY AIR) DETERMINES A PRICE

- HOW THEN IS A PRICE PLACED ON SUCH A PUBLIC GOOD? ---- THE MEASUREMENT RULE USED IS AS FOLLOWS:

  ESTIMATE WHAT THE USERS OF THE PUBLIC PRODUCT ARE WILLING TO PAY ---- SUCH A MEASUREMENT IS CALLED A "SHADOW PRICE"

- HOW ARE SHADOW PRICES DETERMINED?

METHOD #1   CONSIDER THE PRODUCT AS AN IN-TERMEDIATE GOOD AND THEN ESTIMATE THE VALUE OF THE MARGINAL PRODUCT OF THE GOOD IN FURTHER PRODUCTION, THAT IS, ASSUME THE USER IS A PRODUCER AND THEN ASK: BY HOW MUCH DOES THE PUBLIC OUTPUT INCREASE HIS INCOME?

METHOD #2   MEASURE THE COST SAVINGS OF THE PUBLIC SERVICE, THAT IS, THE REDUCTION IN THE COSTS THAT THE INDIVIDUAL WOULD HAVE INCURRED IF THE PUBLIC SERVICE WERE NOT SUPPLIED.

METHOD #3   ESTIMATE DIRECTLY THE USERS PRICES BY APPEAL TO MARKET INFORMATION, THAT IS, LOOK FOR NEAR SUBSTITUTES FOR COLLECTIVE CONSUMPTION.

FIGURE 5.20. How to value air-pollution effects.

air pollution, or attempting to determine the value which society places on one of a number of synergistic effects resulting from air pollution, cigarette smoking, natural oxidation, and so on. The need to evaluate the aesthetic consequences of air pollution further complicates matters, since such effects are perceived by the individual on both the conscious and subconscious levels.

The task of evaluating public undertakings involves working in the absence of market prices for most analytical inputs and outputs. The job of the analyst is to develop values for inputs and outputs which are consistent with those found in the marketplace.

The price placed on a public good is referred to as a "shadow price." Margolis (1957) states that "the process of forming the shadow values is made difficult not only because of market limitations, but also because there is no widespread agreement on the basis for generating social values. Should one try to aggregate the preference of people in a society or should one attempt to rely on the preferences of program planners or administrators?" Margolis also argues that it is the willingness to pay for government outputs which signifies their values.

The purpose of evaluating air-pollution costs and benefits is to assist the decision-maker in determining a policy. Shadow prices are utilized so that the effects of a public program (as it affects society) can be evaluated in monetary terms (i.e., on the basis of a common unit for comparing effects). Shadow prices are useful means of expressing utility, but unless the decision-maker is confident of the monetary values assigned to the effects, little is gained through the analytical process.

The question of how shadow prices are determined is, of course, highly relevant. Margolis discusses techniques for estimating "willingness to pay." Figure 5.20 summarizes the shadow-pricing problem and identifies three methods of determining shadow prices. The literature on the analysis of public expenditures contains theoretical discussions of this topic.

Types of Air-Pollution Damage Functions

The damage function developed by Wilson and Minnotte (1969), for the Washington D.C., metropolitan area is presented in Figure 5.21. The damage function relates per capita annual soiling cost to concentrations of suspended particulates. The authors utilized the results of air-pollution statistical studies in the Washington, D.C., area conducted by Irving Michelson. Michelson's study used responses to a questionnaire to determine the frequency of certain household cleaning chores in areas of high and low air pollution within the metropolitan area. Wilson and Minnotte applied shadow prices to the "frequency of cleaning" function determined by Michelson. Method 3 (Figure 5.20) was utilized; that is, the prices of cleaning services in the private sector were determined and then applied to the specified chores identified by Michelson. The soiling-damage function was utilized to estimate savings (benefits) from reduced soiling for residential households. Studies of a similar nature have been conducted in Kansas City and the Ironton-Ashland-Huntington metropolitan area. The procedures used in developing the damage functions were those previously outlined in this section (identification, assessment, and evaluation).

On the basis of a statistical analysis, economists Anderson and Crocker (1970), have determined a negative correlation between particulate and sulfur dioxide concentrations and residential property values. The authors evaluated the combined effects of suspended particulates and sulfur dioxide (as measured by sulfation) on residential property in the following Census Bureau classifications: (1) owner-occupied; (2) renter-occupied, gross rent; and (3) renter-occupied, contract rent. The most significant independent variables which affect property values were identified and are shown in Figure 5.22. It should be noted that sulfation rate and suspended particulate concentration are included as significant variables. The statistical results of the Anderson

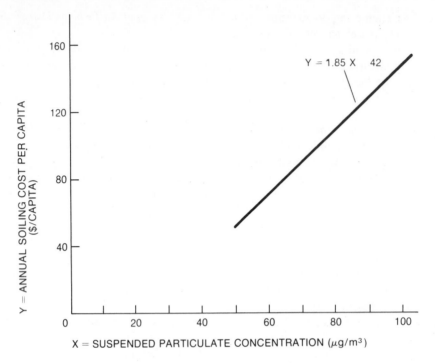

FIGURE 5.21.   Example damage function for direct effects (from Wilson and Minnotte, 1969).

PROPERTY-VALUE FUNCTION:

PV = f (a, PSN, PPT, MFI, DLP, OLD, NWT, DIS, MRM)

Where property value is quantified for each census tract as:

Type I: median property value—owner-occupied
Type II: median property value—owner-occupied—75 percent or more single-family dwellings
Type III: median gross rent—renter-occupied
Type IV: median contract rent—renter-occupied

The independent variables of significance are as follows:

  a = constant
PSN = annual arithmetic mean sulfation
PPT = annual arithmetic mean suspended particulates
MFI = median family income
DLP = percent of living units dilapidated
OLD = percent of houses over twenty years old in 1959
NWT = percent of housing occupied by nonwhites
 DIS = distance of census tract from central business district
MRM = median number of rooms in housing unit

FIGURE 5.22.   Example damage function for market effect. See Table 5.3 for quantitative results. (From Anderson and Crocker, 1970.)

TABLE 5.3

Regression results of Anderson-Crocker study for the Washington, D.C., SMSA

Dependent ╲ Independent	Regression Coefficients			
	Type I	Type II	Type III	Type IV
Const.	3.3901 (0.4012)	1.1617 (0.5622[a])	0.2428 (0.4441[b])	0.4705 (0.3859[b])
ln (PSN)	−0.0712 (0.0222)	0.0010 (0.0270[b])	−0.0905 (0.0239)	−0.0727 (0.0207)
ln (PPT)	−0.0610 (0.0318[b])	−0.1698 (0.0509)	0.0049 (0.0316[b])	−0.0302 (0.0275[b])
ln (MFI)	0.7677 (0.0447)	0.9970 (0.0587)	0.5109 (0.0492)	0.4650 (0.0431)
ln (DLP)	0.0044 (0.0059[b])	0.0113 (0.0079[b])	0.0121 (0.0055[a])	−0.0054 (0.0048[b])
ln (OLD)	−0.016 (0.0103)	−0.0213 (0.0107[a])	−0.0606 (0.0125)	−0.0408 (0.0108)
ln (NWT)	0.0251 (0.0064)	0.0321 (0.0080)	−0.0043 (0.0066[b])	−0.0124 (0.0058[a])
ln (DIS)	−0.0582 (0.0158)	−0.0312 (0.0097)	−0.0216 (0.0152[b])	−0.0111 (0.0132[b])
ln (MRM)		0.9064 (0.1948)		
R^2	0.6966	0.7897	0.6963	0.7549
S^2	0.0222	0.0179	0.0181	0.0136
T	275	121	218	218

[a] Not significantly different from zero at the 0.01 level.
[b] Not significantly different from zero at the 0.05 level.

and Crocker work for the Washington, D.C., SMSA are presented in Table 5.3.

The benefits measured by the Wilson/Minnotte and the Anderson/Crocker damage functions represent only a small portion of the "benefits" that are desired by society. The Wilson/Minnotte function measures only the direct effects of soiling resulting from suspended particulates. Numerous other direct effects have been identified for particulates as well as other pollutants. The Anderson/Crocker functions estimate only the market effects resulting from society's preference to reside in cleaner rather than dirtier air. The market effects result from the conscious and subconscious perception of direct effects. The impact of the effects and adjustments are reflected in the values of properties as established in the marketplace.

Application of Air-Pollution Damage Functions

Damage functions are generally expressed in relation to number of households (or population) and pollution concentration. In the C/B model, damage functions are applied to each census tract in an AQCR to determine the census-tract damage cost. The sum of the damage costs for all census tracts in an AQCR determines the AQCR damage cost.

The damage estimates of the direct effects of pollution are estimated as a function of particulate and/or sulfur dioxide concentrations for the base alternative (i.e., the existing condition) as well as for predicted concentrations under a given emission-control strategy. Social benefit is considered to be the difference between the damages from the base alternative and damages after application of the control strategy (see Figure 5.23). The social benefits from market effects are the differences between the annualized household property values under the two strategies (also shown in Figure 5.23).

Development of Damage Functions

There is a dire need for additional research on the effects of air pollution. As an interim measure, however, the development of methods which transform available data into useful damage functions can be tested. One of the advantages of a C/B simulation tool is that it

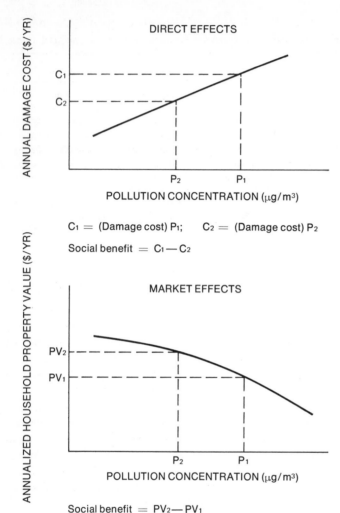

C_1 = (Damage cost) P_1; C_2 = (Damage cost) P_2

Social benefit = $C_1 - C_2$

Social benefit = $PV_2 - PV_1$

FIGURE 5.23.   Application of damage functions.

may be used in sensitivity analyses to determine the reasonableness of proposed damage functions. Brainstorming sessions can be useful in determining how the damage functions are to be created. A modification of the Delphi procedure may also be applicable as a means of estimating "personal preferences."

Many different approaches can be taken in the development of damage functions. The analyst may look at damages to individual classes of receptors (pinto beans, electrical contacts, guinea pigs, or whatever) and then aggregate these damages by means of statistical techniques in order to project total damage costs. Another approach is to use analytical techniques in the development of "comprehensive damage functions" based on the best available data.

Many questions arise in evaluating methodologies for the development of damage functions. Must all effects be identified and evaluated, or can knowledge of specific effects be the basis for decision-making? Can a comprehensive damage function be developed as a function of personal income, residential location, occupation, health

TABLE 5.4

Example data for the development of damage functions for health effects

Disease	Pollution Reduction	Expected Annual Saving ($ millions)
All respiratory diseases	50%	1,222
Cardiovascular diseases	50%	468
Cancer	50%	390
Total		2,080

SOURCE: Lave and Seskin (1970).

status, or other variables? Can health data such as those obtained by Lave and Seskin (see Table 5.4) be used in the development of broad-based health functions? Can "personal preference" be defined on the basis of intensive surveys and congressional polls (i.e., do such polls indicate willingness to pay for solutions to society's problems)? How can sociologists, psychologists, economists, and statisticians contribute to a comprehensive study of damage functions?

Such questions must be examined in relation to the air resource decision-making process and the needs of the decision-maker.

Use of the Cost/Benefit Model to Develop Emission-Control Standards

If C/B analysis can be used to evaluate the economic effects of an emission-control strategy in AQCR, it is reasonable to assume that it can be applied in the development of emission-control standards (or regulations). Emission standards have thus far been based on engineering analyses of sources and available control technology. The allowable emission rate is frequently expressed as a function of process or boiler size. So that no firms will be placed in an advantageous or disadvantageous economic position relative to other competitive firms, emission standards are generally applied uniformly to all sources in a region (i.e., all firms bear the same burden).

Such emission standards are generally promulgated and applied without regard to the planning objectives of the AQCR, however. Emission standards currently tend to be economically inefficient because they are uniformly applied to all sources in the AQCR. For critically located sources, such emission standards are needed to satisfy air-quality standards. For sources in other locations, such emission standards may be too stringent, as will be seen in the following example.

Particulate concentration distributions in the NCIAQCR before and after application of emission standards are shown in Figures 5.24 and 5.25. A cross-sectional view of pollution concentration relative to geographical location is presented in Figure 5.26. The upper and lower curves in Figure 5.26 represent pollutant concentrations before and after enactment of an emission-control strategy, respectively. The criterion for determining the acceptability of an emission-control strategy is that air quality at any point in the region must meet or surpass the proposed air-quality standard.

Owing to the uniform application of emission standards, the same level of control is required for sources affecting the pollution concentration in areas outside the center city as is required for sources affecting the center city. Since the long-term standard is based on the removal of all identifiable effects which lower the welfare of society, it may be asked whether there is a need for further reduction in pollutant concentrations at the perimeter of the region (that is, whether "nondegradation" is essential when existing pollutant concentrations are far below levels at which effects are observed or welfare decreased). The sources are being treated equitably, but the receptors are not. An economically inefficient solution thus exists.

This situation can be illustrated as in Figure 5.27, where source equity (i.e., uniform application of emission standards for all sources in an AQCR) is plotted as a function of receptor equity (i.e., equal pollution concentration ex-

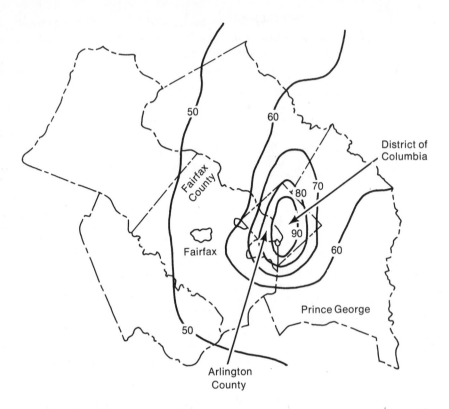

FIGURE 5.24.   Existing ground-level particulate concentrations in the NCIAQCR as computed by the verified diffusion model (annual intensities in $\mu g/m^3$).

posure for all receptors). The curve shows situations in which the condition of source equity is matched by receptor inequity and vice versa (source inequity and receptor equity). Position A on the curve corresponds to a situation involving source equity and receptor inequity. Such a situation is further shown in Figure 5.28. A hypothetical situation for position B is shown in Figure 5.29.

The current application of emission standards is represented by position A. Position B is typical of an emission standard based on geographical location in the AQCR. Figure 5.30 illustrates such an emission standard, with control being more stringent in Zone W than in Zone X and so on (an example of such a regulation would be the prohibition of automobile traffic in the

central city). An emission standard which varies with geographical location within an AQCR is likely to be more economically efficient for society since, relative to a uniform standard, there is a control-cost saving with a negligible reduction in benefits. The practicality of emission standards such as the one illustrated in Figure 5.30 should be determined. There is likewise the need to reexamine the basis for developing emission standards. If an urban growth objective is to enhance the quality of the downtown area through commercial development and construction of middle-income residences, and at the same time to relocate industry outside the center city, then emission standards based on a policy oriented toward position B would be compatible with regional goals.

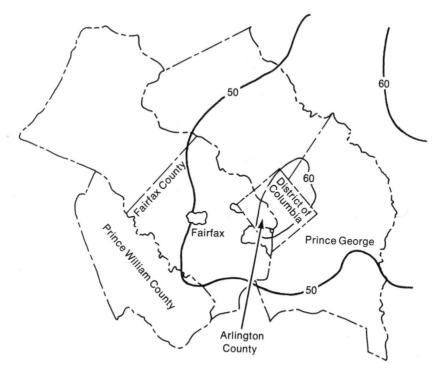

Note: Annual Concentrations in $\mu g/m^3$

FIGURE 5.25. Predicted particulate concentrations after enactment of the proposed emission-control strategy in all political jurisdictions (annual intensities in $\mu g/m^3$).

The foregoing presentation has been designed to indicate ways in which cost/benefit analysis can be used to examine new policy alternatives. The model is likewise useful as a means of evaluating existing policies. The important contribution made by the development of the C/B model is the ability to look at benefits (and damages) relative to specific geographical areas in an AQCR.

Analysis of the Distribution of Benefits

The C/B model is capable of evaluating the distribution of effects on the sources and receptors. Equity evaluation of air-pollution control costs to firms affected is important in a competitive economy. The distribution of benefits resulting from cleaner air must likewise be evaluated for purposes of urban planning, land use, and so on. Some equity evaluations which are possible with the C/B model are:

1. Compare the absolute pollutant concentration to income. Although benefits (measured in dollars) are not being considered here, the relationship between actual air quality and income class will be valuable to a regional decision-maker who evaluates long—term air quality trends and is cognizant of air-pollution interim. Essentially the relationship in question is:

$$I \quad f(AQ) \qquad \text{where } I = \text{income.}$$

This relationship can be measured for existing conditions as well as under alternative regional control strategies.

2. Compare the change in air quality resulting from a

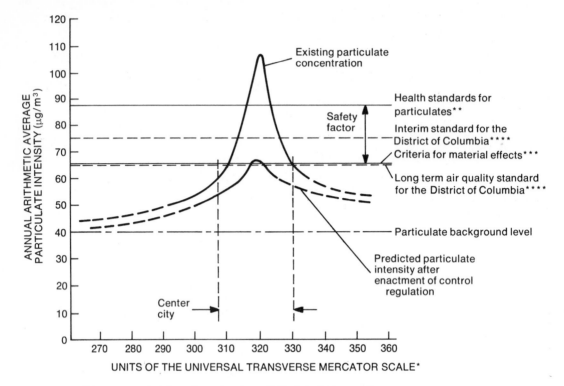

*Measurements taken along the plane 4305 of the Universal Transverse
Mercator Scale.
**Annual Geometric Mean = 80 μg/m³.
Annual Arithmetic Annual Mean = 86.8 μg/m³.
***Annual Geometric Mean = 60 μg/m³.   Annual Arithmetic Mean = 65.2 μg/m³.
****Standards proposed under procedures established by the Air Quality Act
of 1967. The National Primary and Secondary Air Quality Standards of
the Clean Air Amendments of 1970 would also apply.

FIGURE 5.26.   Predicted air-quality improvement in the NCIAQCR.

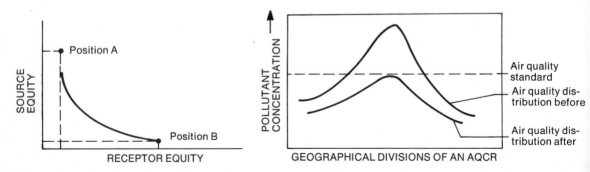

FIGURE 5.27.   Source equity vs. receptor equity.   FIGURE 5.28.   Source equity (position A).

FIGURE 5.29. Source equity (position B).

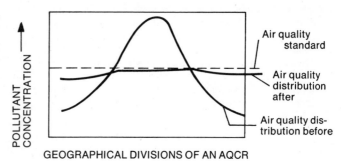

FIGURE 5.30. An emission standard based on geographical location.

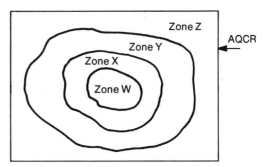

- Emission standard in zone W more stringent than in zone X; zone X standard more stringent than zone Y; and so forth

regional control strategy to income class. This comparison answers the question: What improvement in air quality was obtained for each income class? The relationship is as follows:

$$AQ = g(I).$$

The change in air quality can be measured in two ways:

(a) Absolute improvement in air quality (e.g., $\mu g/m^3$), where:

$(AQ)_A = (AQ)_b - (AQ)_a,$
$(AQ)_A$ = absolute change in air quality,
$(AQ)_b$ = air quality before strategy,
$(AQ)_a$ = air quality after strategy.

(b) Relative improvement in air quality (e.g., percent), where:

$$(AQ)_R = \frac{(AQ)_b - (AQ)_a}{(AQ)_b},$$

$(AQ)_R$ = relative change in air quality.

3. Comparison of benefits (in dollars) resulting from a regional control strategy to each income class, i.e.,

$$B = f(I).$$

4. Comparison of benefits per income (i.e., B/I) resulting from a regional control strategy for each income class, i.e.,

$$(B/I) = g(I).$$

This procedure will measure the improvement in aggregate consumption and productivity benefits resulting from a given strategy for each income class. This is the most significant measure for equity analyses, since it relates the importance of benefits to individual consumption levels (i.e., an additional dollars worth of well-being for an individual earning $10 per year is far more significant than an additional dollars worth of well-being for an individual earning $10,000). These data may be presented as follows:

Income ($)	Benefit ($)	Benefit Income (%)
2,000	80	4
4,000	120	3
.	.	.
.	.	.
.	.	.
25,000+	500	2

5. Analysis of benefits and benefit/income ratios for nonwhite (NWT) and white (WT) sectors of a regional population. The procedure used could be as follows:
   - Divide census tracts into WT and NWT, where a NWT tract is defined as one having 50 percent or more nonwhite residents.
   - Develop comparative data on these tracts, as follows:

I ($)	WT (B) ($)	NWT (B) ($)	WT (B/I) (%)	NWT (B/I) (%)
2,000	90	70	4.5	3.5
4,000	110	130	5.5	6.5
.	.	.	.	.
.	.	.	.	.
.	.	.	.	.
25,000	600	400	400	1.6

6. Analyses for an entire region as well as by individual political jurisdiction.

The Region and the Nation

A flow diagram of the C/B model as used directly in decision making is illustrated in Figure 5.31. But even this model is limited in scope. The resulting estimates of control costs and benefits derived from the direct utilization of the model are not reflected as impacts on the economic activity of the region or the nation. The reallocation of resources in the economy, which is expected from an air-pollution control policy, is not reflected in the C/B model. Impacts on such economic indicators as employment, capital investment, regional income, value added, and others are not measured. Air-pollution policies have an effect on such indicators on the region and the nation and should be evaluated.

To measure the impacts of control policies on the economy, the control-cost and benefit estimates from the C/B model must be evaluated in a series of economic models. CONSAD Research Corporation has developed an economic-model system for this purpose (see Figure 5.32). The CONSAD model system has been designed to determine the economic effects of air-pollution policies on regions and the nation. The economic-model system currently consists of two major components: a regional economic model (applied to 100 of the nation's AQCRs) and a national input/output (I/O) model (see Figure 5.33). The regional economic model determines the effects of air-pollution control costs and benefits on an open regional economy. The national I/O system is introduced to serve the role of the external markets (provide interregional feedback) for the regional economy, and also to measure the structural change of the national economy upon air pollution control to the 100 AQCRs. The economic-model system measures effects of air-pollution strategies in terms of changes in unemployment, value added, income, and other measures of economic activity.

In this way, C/B analysis can be used in a variety of public policy investigations, determining, for example:

1. Regional economic changes expected to result from application of various emission standards to major polluters.
2. Regional economic effects expected to result from reduction of industrial damage and growth in air-pollution equipment industries.
3. Changes in regional output, investment, employment, income, and consumption associated with various emission standards.
4. Fiscal effects of regional implementation of air-quality control programs. Such effects include the tax-base impacts of economic change and the rate of achievement of emission standards specified in the implementation plan.
5. Statistical indicators, including industry-specific ratios of air-pollution control costs to total investment and to value added in production.

Conclusions

Figure 5.34 illustrates the air-resource decision-making process and the role of economic analysis in evaluating the ability of alternative solutions to satisfy planning objectives. The combined procedures of economic, cost-benefit,

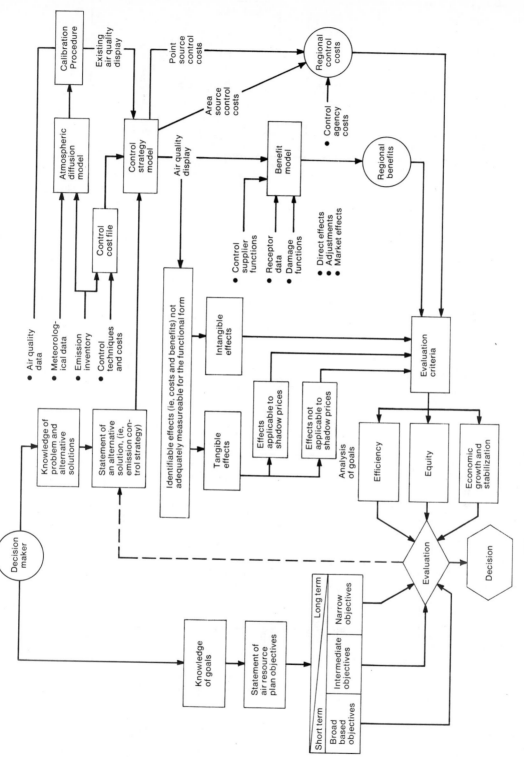

FIGURE 5.31.   Direct application of C/B model in strategy analysis.

163

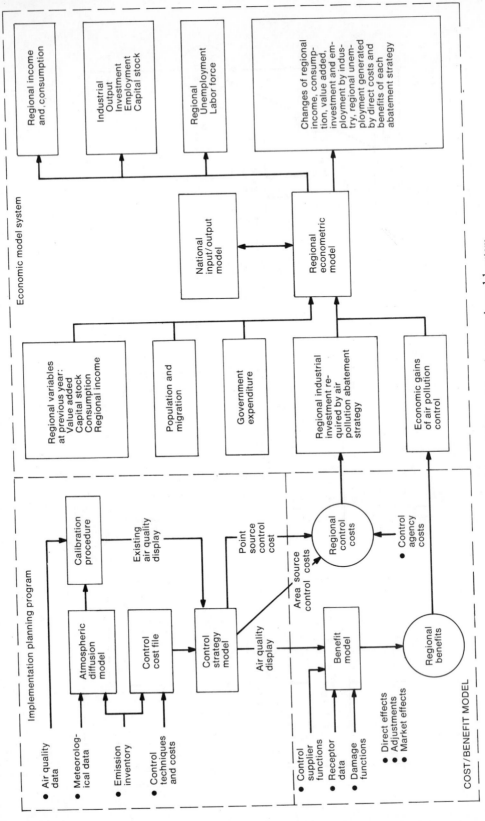

FIGURE 5.32. Use of C/B model with economic model system.

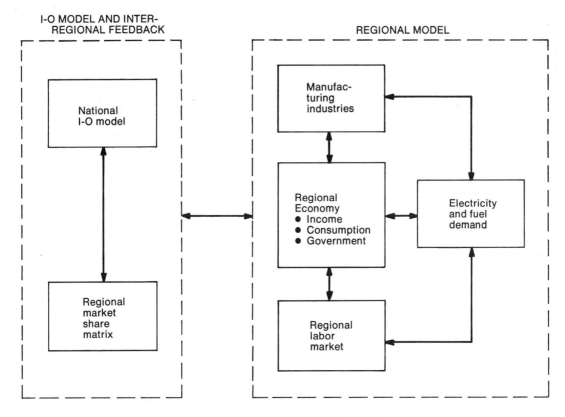

FIGURE 5.33.   Major components of the model.

and systems analysis that have been described ultimately are directed toward the development of social and economic indicators (evaluation criteria). These indicators form a basis for evaluating goals in the following categories:

1. *Economic efficiency*—increased welfare for the region, i.e., increased aggregate income and productivity.
2. *Economic redistribution*—the desirable distribution of benefits among income classes.
3. *Economic growth and stabilization*—stability of employment and regional product, as well as growth in regional income, employment, and other economic indicators.

The welfare indicators which are used in the evaluation of goals may be consistent with certain regional planning objectives and detrimental to others. Another role of the decision-maker is to determine which of the regional objectives

are most important in relation to both short-term and long-term goals.

Finally, to meet the primary and secondary air quality standards that are set, the air-resource planner must establish policies in the following areas:

1. *General stringency of control.* How efficient must emission control be in order to optimize the welfare of the region relative to the air-resource and other urban goals?
2. *Compliance schedule.* How quickly can the region move toward the optimum-welfare condition, taking into account the welfare of the regional economy?
3. *Inducement approach.* What combination of emission regulations, emission taxes, land-use planning, product laws, and so on represents the most efficient and equitable approach in reaching the desired objectives?
4. *Locational aspects.* What is the most efficient and

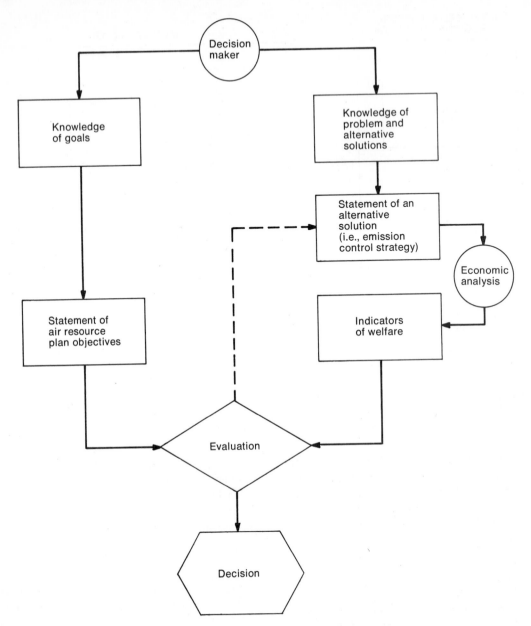

FIGURE 5.34.   Air-resource decision-making process.

equitable manner in which emission limitations can be applied relative to geographical location in the AQCR?

Effective air-resource planning will require more sophisticated tools to answer these questions than have thus far been available, and this is why the highest priority should be given to research directed to many of the questions raised as we discussed the format of C/B models for evaluation of air-quality programs.

CHAPTER 6

the nature of water pollution

Chapters 4 and 5 dealt with the nature of air pollution and with the use of modern cost-benefit analysis in air-resource management. In a similar way, Chapters 6, 7, and 8 will deal with water pollution, the measurement of water-quality trends, and water-resource management.

Few laymen quite appreciate the quantities of water and of water-borne effluents involved in the "metabolism" of a modern city. As noted in Table 1.1 earlier, a city's metabolic requirements include the materials and commodities needed to sustain the urban dweller, but its metabolic cycle also involves the residues and wastes of daily life. The average city dweller uses daily 150 gallons of water, four pounds of food, and 19 pounds of fossil fuels. This is converted into roughly 120 gallons of sewage (which assumes 80 percent recovery of the water input) and four pounds of refuse (which includes food containers and miscellaneous rubbish). One consequence in these areas is an emerging water shortage. Uncontrolled, another result can be water pollution.

Throughout history, impure water has been a leading cause of fatal disease in man; such waterborne diseases as typhoid fever and dysentery were still common in the United States less than a century ago. In 1900 the U.S. death rate from typhoid fever was 35.8 per 100,000 people. If such a rate persisted today, the deaths from typhoid would far exceed those from automobile accidents. But by 1936 the rate had

This chapter draws from:
Nancy B. Hultquist, "Water Pollution as an Aspect of Dynamic Urbanism," Technical Report No. 4, Institute of Urban and Regional Research, University of Iowa, Iowa City, Iowa, 1971. Begins on page 169.
M. Gordon Wolman, "The Nation's Rivers," *Science*, Vol. 174 (November 1971), pp. 905–918. Begins on page 173.

been reduced to 2.5 per 100,000 and today the disease is almost unknown in the U.S.—as a result of improvements in the quality of drinking water.

In underdeveloped nations, on the other hand, where many cities are still without adequate water supplies, waterborne diseases are among the leading causes of death and debility. In Central and South America more than a third of 75 million people living in towns or cities with a population of more than 2,000 are without water service. Similarly, in India about a third of the urban population of 80 million are without an adequate water supply. As a result, Calcutta is the endemic center of cholera for all of Southeast Asia.

It was the great typhoid epidemics that swept London in the mid-nineteenth century that underscored the peril of water pollution and launched the first organized steps to combat it. Until very recent times this stress on preventing waterborne disease in the interests of public health was the major thrust of efforts to maintain or improve the quality of the environment. Indeed, most Americans have acted, until recently, as though their rivers and lakes had an infinite capacity to absorb wastes. Pollution was considered the price of progress. Not until 1948 was the first comprehensive Federal water-pollution control legislation enacted, and the first permanent legislation was not passed until 1956. The original overriding concern was with human health, and almost all state water-pollution programs were carried on by state health departments.

Water-pollution control legislation and programs have now been broadened to embrace a host of environmental concerns, including recreation and esthetics, culminating in the Federal Water Pollution Control Act Amendments of 1972. Epidemics due to waterborne causes are largely of the past, and health efforts have broadened to include more sophisticated concern for the effects of small amounts of toxic chemicals on humans and other forms of life. Indeed,

today the attack on water pollution is directed at eight categories of water pollution in the United States:

1. Domestic sewage and other oxygen-demanding wastes.
2. Infectious agents.
3. Plant nutrients, particularly nitrogen and phosphorus.
4. Organic chemical exotics, particularly insecticides, pesticides, and detergents.
5. Other mineral and chemical substances from industrial, mining, and agricultural operations.
6. Sediments from land erosion.
7. Radioactive substances.
8. Heat.

All these are the results of man's activities, and, with the possible exception of the fifth and sixth on the list, are being produced largely within the large metropolitan complexes that generally are located along the coasts, the Great Lakes, or the main stems of America's rivers.

Three reasons, besides the changed nature of the health problem, help explain the broader environmental concern of today: first, the growth of industries and cities has multiplied pollution in most waterways; second, demand for outdoor recreation has grown in a society increasingly affluent and leisure oriented; and third—a thread running through all the others—is man's inexplicable affinity to water. Whether it is the pleasure he derives from a fountain, the mood of a walk along the lake shore, the relaxation of fishing, or his identification with majestic water bodies—the Danube, the Great Lakes, or San Francisco Bay—man has found tranquility and inspiration in his appreciation of water. But the current condition of many of our lakes and rivers makes appreciation impossible.

Pollution problems exist in all parts of the United States, particularly in the northeast and in the Great Lakes region. In these areas, which have experienced tremendous urban and industrial growth over the past century, there was, at least until recently, inadequate investment in the construction of treatment plants. Now a long backlog of needed construction has accumulated. Specific sources of pollution, besides the ordinary municipal and industrial wastes, affect certain areas. Acid mine pollution is common in the coal-mining states of Appalachia, and saline pollution occurs in the irrigation areas of western states.

In some areas of the country, remedial programs have succeeded in raising the levels of water quality. However, population and industrial growth, higher water quality demanded by the public, and the increasing severity of certain types of pollution—for example, oil spills and increased algal blooms in lakes—all mean that Americans have only begun to tackle the problem.

URBANIZATION AND WATER POLLUTION: THE ROLE PLAYED BY NATURAL PROCESSES

The water resource of an area is a very complex system involving many natural processes whose interrelationships are not entirely known. Thus, we have much still to learn about the way in which natural processes intervene between some of the hydrologic effects of increasing urbanization discussed in Chapter 3 and the location, nature, and intensity of water pollution.

A problem of perception arises, too. One of man's first steps in "developing" an area is, for example, to drain its swamps. But swamps perform an important role in improving the quality of the water flowing through them (Wharton, 1970), as well as acting as natural reservoirs that help maintain seasonally steady flows of water. The southern river-swamps, for example, appear to have the ability to clean pollutants from water by acting like "giant kidneys." These systems collect deposits of silt, organic materials, and toxic chemicals, which can be utilized by the biotic community. The swamp acts as a vast ion-exchange bed, and, in conjunction with the moving stream water, the swamp apparently provides a natural hydro-geo-biological water-treatment function. Regarding the lack of systematic research on the value of swamps, Wharton (1970) writes:

> It would seem hazardous to do anything to a stream system which appears to be able to treat water used by man or industry, or which can indirectly prevent contamination of food sources. It should be clear at this point that while a great deal of research is needed, neither the man-made reservoir, farm pond or channeled stream, nor any combination of these man-made modifications, can substitute for the functions of the natural stream and swamp in the maintenance of water quality.

This simply serves to emphasize what was said a moment ago: the water resource of an area is a very complex system whose relationships are not entirely known, and man's perceptions may be at odds with the physical facts. Thus, it is necessary that we begin by discussing those natural subprocesses and effects of pollution about which there is a reasonable body of knowledge: the oxygen cycle and eutrophication, along with the known effects of nutritional, bacterial and viral pollutants, dissolved and suspended solids, and heat.

Organic Wastes and Biochemical Oxygen Demand

Natural organic wastes such as vegetation decompose by bacterial action. Bacteria attack wastes dumped into rivers and lakes, using up oxygen in the process. Thus organic wastes are measured in units of biochemical oxygen demand (BOD), the amount of oxygen needed to decompose them. Expressed most simply, BOD is defined as "the amount of oxygen that is needed by any unit volume of water to oxidize all organic matter within it" (Grava, 1969).

Certain aerobic bacteria which require free oxygen will break down organic matter to

TABLE 6.1

Bacterial reactions in water pollution[a]

Aerobic Reactions	Anaerobic Reactions
Carbon, C $\longrightarrow$ CO$_2$ + carbonates + bicarbonates	C $\longrightarrow$ organic $\longrightarrow$ CH$_4$ $\longrightarrow$ CO$_2$
	acids methane
Nitrogen, N $\longrightarrow$ NH$_3$ $\longrightarrow$ HNO$_2$ $\longrightarrow$ HNO$_3$	N $\longrightarrow$ amino $\longrightarrow$ NH$_3$ + amines
ammonia nitrous nitric	acids
acid[b] acid[b]	
Sulfur, S $\longrightarrow$ H$_2$SO$_4$	S $\longrightarrow$ H$_2$S + organic S compound
sulfuric acid[b]	
Phosphorus, P $\longrightarrow$ H$_3$PO$_4$	P $\longrightarrow$ PH$_3$ + organic P compound

[a] These reactions are given in Klein (1962), pp. 37–38; Although somewhat dated, his book is an excellent introductory source on the causes of river pollution and on the nature of the various kinds of pollution and their effects on the rivers.
[b] Neutralized by bases present.

relatively harmless, stable, and odorless end products in well-diluted oxygenated water. This process allows the stream to recover naturally from the effects of small pollution loads and is sometimes described as "self-purification." The oxidation reactions which occur are represented on the left side of Table 6.1. When excessive pollution by organic matter causes depletion of the dissolved oxygen, the remaining organic and dead fish are acted upon by a different set of bacteria which do not require free oxygen. Anaerobic bacteria utilize combined oxygen in the form of nitrates, sulphates, phosphates, and organic compounds. The anaerobic decomposition of organic matter results in a different set of end products, among which methane and hydrogen sulfide are quite objectionable. The reactions are shown on the right side of Table 6.1. Putrefication is the general term applied to an anaerobic decomposition of organic matter and is one of the more easily recognized indicators of water pollution in its advanced stages.

Table 6.2 illustrates the difference between two urban land uses using a five-day BOD measure in Chicago (American Public Works Association, 1969). When dissolved oxygen falls below a certain critical level (in the case of many

fish about 5 ppm), mortality may occur. If the waste loads are so great that large amounts of oxygen are spent in their decomposition, certain types of fish can no longer live in that body of water. A pollution-resistant, lower order of fish, such as carp, replaces the original fish population. The amount of free oxygen in a water body is therefore one of the best measures of its ecological health.

Obviously, BOD is increased by the addition of raw sewage to lakes and rivers; in fact, it is increased by any ingredient which may utilize oxygen. In this respect, increasing urbanization is particularly critical. Recall the hydrological effects of increasing urbanization outlined in

TABLE 6.2

BOD concentration of storm water held in selected catch basins

Land Use	BOD in mg/liter
Commercial	225
Commercial	160
Commercial	150
Residential	50
Residential	85

SOURCE: Modified from p. 85, American Public Works Association (1969).

Chapter 3: increased volume and speed of storm-water runoff; increased peak flows and flooding; increased sediment loads and decreased ground-water recharge (Turk, 1970). A recent study of Lubbock, Texas, revealed that storm-water drainage had an average BOD concentration equivalent to secondary sewage treatment effluent (Brownlee et al., 1970). Urbanization quite obviously reduces water quality.

Eutrophication and the Role of Nutritional Pollutants

The limit of the natural processes just discussed is called eutrophication—most commonly associated with the dying of lakes. All lakes go through a natural cycle of eutrophication, but normally it takes thousands of years. In the first stage—the oligotrophic—lakes are deep and have little biological life. Lake Superior is a good example. Over time, nutrients and sediments are added; the lake becomes more biologically productive and shallower. This state—the mesotrophic—has been reached by Lake Ontario. As nutrients continue to be added, large algal blooms grow, fish populations change, and the lake begins to take on undesirable characteristics. Lake Erie is now in this eutrophic stage. Over time, the lake becomes a swamp and finally a land area.

The rate of eutrophication is directly related to the amount of nutrients introduced into a body of water. The nutrients can consist of sediment, organic matter, or chemicals which accelerate algal growth. When the algae die, oxygen is used up. The temperature usually changes because turbidity prevents light penetration to the lower water levels. Photosynthesis is prevented, and fish are forced to rise to warmer waters to obtain oxygen. Some species of fish cannot stand the shock of warmer temperatures, so often the better species are replaced by carp, suckers, or other less desirable types. Ultimately, even these die.

Natural drainage contains nutrients and would create eutrophication over a long period of time, but urban drainage accelerates eutrophication (Weibel, 1969). A wide range of nutrient materials is introduced to water courses, as shown in Table 6.3. These arise from normal

TABLE 6.3

Constituent concentrations found in the runoff from an urban area in Cincinnati, Ohio, July 1962 through July 1964[a]

Constituent	Range in Values	Mean Storm Values
Turbidity (J.u.)	30–1,000	176
Color (C.u.)	10–460	87
pH	5.3–8.7	7.5
Alkalinity (mg/l)	10–210	59
Total hardness (as CaCO₃) (mg/l)	19–364	81
Chloride (mg/l)	3–428	12
SS (mg/l)	5–1,200	227
VSS (mg/l)	1–290	57
COD (mg/l)	20–610	111
BOD (mg/l)	1–173	17
Σ N (mg/l)[b]	0.3–7.5	3.1
Inorganic N (mg/l)	0.1–3.4	1.0
Hydrolyzable PO₄ (mg/l)	< 0.02–7.3	1.1
Organic chlorine (mg/l)₄[c]	0.38–4.72	1.70
Coliform organisms (number per 100 ml)	2,900–460,000	—

[a] January and February 1963 not included.
[b] Arithmetic sum of the four forms of nitrogen.
[c] From eleven storms, August 1963 to February 1964.

stream runoff as well as from the combined-sewer overflows which occur in many cities during peak-flow periods (Table 6.4). Sewage is by far the largest urban contribution to eutrophication, even though much sewage is treated in some manner (Table 6.5).

Among the chemicals introduced to water bodies, nitrogen and phosphorus are the most significant nutritional pollutants, along with potash. Nitrogen comes from a variety of sources: both sewage and fertilizer contain nitrogen. Decomposition of organic matter produces other nitrogen forms—for example,

TABLE 6.4

Nutrients in urban street drainage
(Seattle, Wash. May–Nov., 1959)

Type of Street	Antecedent Rainfall in Inches (one week)	Nitrogen (mg/l)		Phosphorus (ppb)	
		Total Kjel. N	Nitrates	Sol.	Total
Residential	0.0	6.68	0.65	14	166
Major highway	0.0	9.06	2.24	54	352
Major highway	0.0	7.45	2.80	72	404
Arterial street	0.0	8.01	0.52	14	81
Residential	0.55	0.39	0.02	70	98
Major highway	0.55	0.91	0.03	08	21
Arterial street	0.55	0.22	0.12	20	21
Residential	0.78	2.78	1.10	16	154
Arterial street	0.78	1.43	0.29	10	108

SOURCE: Modified from Sylvester (1960).

TABLE 6.5

Nutrients in sewage

Nutrient	Concentration, ppm
Nitrogen	20– 50
NH_3	7– 40
NO_3	0– 4
NO_2	0– 0.3
Organic	3– 42
Carbon	66–176
Soluble phosphorus	1– 13
Potassium	13– 44

SOURCE: Bartsch (1961), using data from Fitzgerald and Rohlich (1958).

oxidation to nitrites and nitrates. The latter, in concentrations exceeding 10 mg/l, are dangerous to small babies, causing a condition called methemoglobinemia ("blue babies"). As early as 1947 Sawyer found that inorganic nitrogen exceeding 0.3 mg/l and inorganic PO_4 exceeding 0.03 mg/l are threshold levels for algal blooms (excessive production). Interestingly, in the Lubbock study, the nitrogen runoff samples of one storm ranged from less than 1.0 to 13.6 mg/l (Brownlee et al., 1970).

Water temperature affects the amount of dissolved oxygen and therefore influences life processes of aquatic organisms such as fish. While there are exceptional environments (for example, the Okefenokee Swamp, which supports fish and other biotic life in water temperatures exceeding 95°F), the more common environments are those in which fish generally do not withstand water temperatures in excess of 86°F, or if they do, the reproductive process is precluded.

Temperature plays a vital part in chemical and biochemical reactions. Self-purification of streams is affected by the water temperature, since bacterial action is much faster at higher temperatures than at lower ones. Streams will recover from the effects of organic pollution more rapidly in warmer months than in winter. However, a heavy pollution load is more likely to deoxygenate a stream, since warm water contains less dissolved oxygen than cold water. Anaerobic decomposition is accelerated in warmer water and thus is more likely to occur when hot effluents are discharged into a stream. The harmful effects of heat, therefore, can be linked to its influence on the processes previously discussed as well as to its direct effect on aquatic life.

Dissolved and Suspended Solids

Among the dissolved solids that pose pollution problems and health threats are pesticides and herbicides, salt and detergents. Suspended solids include sediments and street litter.

Pesticides and herbicides are used in gardens and lawns in residential areas, particularly in the suburbs, and runoff contains considerable amounts of these chemicals and their residues (Viessman, 1969). The pesticides are carried to the water by soil particles. It has been shown that there is a strong binding characteristic between pesticide residues and soil particles

(Lichtenstein, 1966). Pesticides at the present time are not generally a direct threat to humans, but the chief hazard is chain feeding and residue concentration from plankton, to fish, to fish-eating birds, to bird-eating birds (Chesters and Konrad, 1971).

In northern cities large quantities of salt are used for snow control. This can be an appreciable pollutant from street drainage (Veissman, 1969). Typical applications vary widely, from 100 to 2,000 pounds per lane mile, yet several states may apply as much as 20 tons per lane mile (APWA, 1969), potentially increasing the salinity of water supplies.

Some detergents used to contain ABS (alkyl benzene sulfonate) which does not break down. It therefore could travel long distances causing foam in streams (Swenson and Baldwin, 1965). The sight problem has been corrected by the use of the new chemical called LAS (linear alkylate sulphonate), but pollutants now exist in the form of phosphates from detergents still on the market.

The major sources of suspended material from urban areas are sediment yield and street litter. In a Chicago street-sweeping survey the amount of street refuse for 18 hand-swept test areas over a 10-week period in 1967 ranged from 0.5 lb to 8.0 lb/110 ft of linear feet per day. The average amount of street refuse for the test areas was 2.4 lb/day/100 ft of curb for single-family area, 3.5 lb/day/100 ft of curb for multiple-family areas, and 4.7 lb/day/100 ft of curb for commercial areas (American Public Works Association, 1969). The components of street litter from the sweeping were, in order, dirt (65 percent), rock (10 percent), paper (7 percent), smaller amounts of glass, wood, and metal, and extremely variable amounts of vegetation (APWA, 1969). The Chicago study suggests that street litter can add significantly to the impact of urban areas on water quality. However, the study also highlights the need for systematic studies of these effects in terms of city size, location, functions, and climatic factors.

Bacterial and Viral Pollutants

Along with nutrients, bacteria and viruses are introduced to water bodies and constitute actual or potential health hazards rather than contributing to eutrophication. Coliform and streptococcus are among the bacterial pollutants contributed by humans, land mammals, and birds. A criterion of 10/liter of coliform is used as a maximum for United States bathing waters by the Water Pollution Control Administration (Viessman, 1969). Yet in studies of storm runoff in Seattle, Pretoria, and Stockholm, the average coliform count was 117,000/liter (see also Table 6.3).

Treatment with chlorine has eliminated most bacteria problems with water supply. However, viruses have become a source of concern to public health officials (Herfindahl and Kneese, 1965; Vadjic, 1968). Periodic outbreaks of gastroenteritis (intestinal flu) and hepatitis may be caused by waterborne viruses. Such viruses can also cause polio, meningitis, rashes, and the grippe. Viruses commonly get into water through inadequate treatment of sewage. Testing procedures for viruses are difficult to carry out, and knowledge of effects of the relatively small numbers of viruses in water supplies is limited. Nevertheless, viral pollution is not believed to be extremely serious unless introduced directly to groundwater through fractures or dissolution channels. Studies have shown that earth, sand, and gravel result in rapid confinement or filtering of the organisms (McGauhey, 1967). But flood waters will introduce such pollutants to the water system and add a health hazard associated with storm runoff from urban areas.

APPRAISAL OF TRENDS IN WATER AND RIVER QUALITY

An important question of definition is raised by the foregoing: Given the many possible pollutants and their effects on BOD and on human health and satisfaction, exactly how should one measure water pollution to be able to assess the need for pollution control, to estimate the benefits to be derived from a particular course of action, and to evaluate the effects both of continued urban development and of control mechanisms on pollution?

Such were the questions addressed by M. Gordon Wolman (1971) in the first systematic survey of water-quality trends in the United States ever attempted. Wolman pointed out that definitions of water pollution are often subjective. Thus pollution is sometimes defined as any impairment of water which lessens its usefulness for beneficial purposes, or anything the public does not like, or even that which is getting worse. Each implies both a value judgment and a subjective perception of the resource. Because such definitions do describe public attitudes toward environmental quality, they provide incentives to public action.

To evaluate alternative ways of combating observed or perceived conditions of water and river deterioration, however, requires objective measurements that describe the perceived conditions and can be related to technological and other measures appropriate to management of the water resource. Over the years, in assessing water and river quality, a number of parameters have been observed which might provide objective criteria that could be used to study trends in the condition of the nation's rivers. Two principal questions can be raised about these observations: (1) whether there are measurable trends in the observed data and (2) whether the variables being measured are those that provide the best measure of the perceived condition or qualities in which the public or society at large may be interested. The rest of this chapter will focus on these two issues.

Relatively few studies of the quality of the nation's rivers have been directed toward determining changes in specific parameters over long periods. This is not surprising, because a number of obstacles interfere with adequate

statistical analysis. First, hydrologic records in the United States are relatively short. There are few continuous records for periods as long as 50 or 60 years. Second, techniques of observation and of analysis have changed over the years. Analytical techniques, in particular, have become more sophisticated, and routine measurements of exceedingly small quantities of contaminants are now possible which, only a few years ago, were considered impractical. Thus some comparisons reflecting changes in techniques of detection rather than real trends may be misleading.

Third, changing the location or frequency of observations of water quality may distort the record. Observations of water quality are often made in the vicinity of metropolitan areas adjacent to the intakes of city water supplies. From time to time the intakes are moved to avoid sewer outfalls. While the intake may be moved upstream only a few hundred yards, the new record differs completely from the previous record, which was essentially monitoring the relation between the quality of the river and the inflow from the outfall.

Fourth, adequate comparisons of specific variables related to water and to river quality require systematic correlation with hydrologic behavior. Such correlations are rarely available.

Fifth, a knowledge of the "natural background" or temporal variability of a given parameter is often essential in detecting and measuring a trend. Statistically, a trend cannot be discerned unless it is possible to discriminate between the variability of the phenomenon as it might occur unaffected by the influences that one wishes to measure, in this case so-called pollution, and the variability normally associated with diurnal, annual, and significant secular climatic variations that occur in the hydrologic record over any period of time. Lastly, explanation of changes in water-quality parameters requires a knowledge not only of the natural background but of the economy and land use of the area.

It was not possible for Wolman's survey to overcome all of these difficulties. He did, however, find a limited number of variables for which assessments of trends could be made. These are largely transport characteristics: dissolved oxygen, dissolved solids, biochemical oxygen demand, suspended sediment, *p*H, and temperature. What was not assessed were other characteristics of water quality associated with the river or river site: the variety and associations of stream and shoreline biota; site characteristics such as channel morphology, bottom conditions, trash, and shoreline vegetation.

What do the data on the transport characteristics show? Available examples of each will be discussed in turn.

Dissolved Oxygen

Dissolved oxygen, expressed as a percentage of saturation, for the Hudson River between Troy, New York, and the Battery below New York City, was measured in the summer of 1933, many times in the interim, and in August of 1965. A comparison between the summer data for 1933 and a curve drawn for 22 to 24 August is shown in Figure 6.1. The comparison indicates that dissolved oxygen in the Hudson River in 1965, despite the fact that flow in 1965 was quite low, is roughly the same over most of this length as it was in 1933, except in the vicinity of the metropolitan area below Albany and Troy. There the summer curve shows a lower

sag in 1965 than was apparent in 1933. Observations of the river made at a number of intervals between 1933 and 1965 show wide variations in dissolved oxygen in this reach, with the winter curve showing considerably less sag than the summer curves both for 1933 and 1965. The data in Figure 6.1, as well as curves for the interim period (available from the New York State Health Department), suggest that, despite large increases in population in the New York metropolitan area as well as in the vicinity of Albany and Troy over much of the length of the river, roughly 100 miles (160 kilometers), the dissolved oxygen has remained essentially constant.

Of perhaps even greater interest are figures for dissolved oxygen at the narrows and the upper bay of New York Harbor (Figure 6.2). Data for the period 1909 to 1931 show the decline in the dissolved oxygen from 1909 to 1931. Phelps (1934) noted, however, that much of the decline in the dissolved oxygen actually took place between 1909 and 1920, as shown by the distribution of points on Figure 6.2. Three later points are shown for the years 1955, 1960, and 1965 from the Public Health Service report of 1965. In themselves, the three points cannot be used, of course, to define a trend, but it appears that there has been little or no change in dissolved oxygen between 1930 and 1965.

On a stretch of the nation's largest river, the Mississippi River at Minneapolis-St. Paul, dissolved oxygen has remained approximately

FIGURE 6.1. Comparative levels of dissolved oxygen in the Hudson River in 1933 and in 1965.

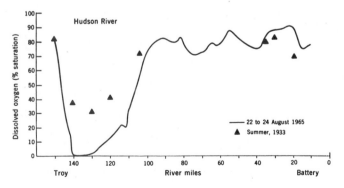

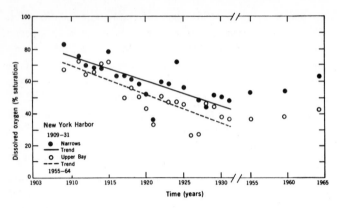

FIGURE 6.2. Comparative levels of dissolved oxygen in the vicinity of New York Harbor. Note the broken scale 1933–1955. All points are averages of summer values. (Data and curves 1909–31 from Phelps, 1934.)

constant since 1938 in the reach below the metropolitan area (Figure 6.3). Between 1932 and 1938 dissolved oxygen increased as a result of construction of sanitary works, including major sewage-treatment plants. The cost of these facilities including treatment plants ($4.8 million) and intercepting sewers ($11.6 million)

totaled $16 million between 1934 and 1937. Oxygen levels attained in 1938 have been substantially maintained to the present time with the construction of additional treatment facilities between 1963 and 1966 at a cost of $27 million, as the population in the Twin Cities areas has grown from about 250 thousand to 1.5 million

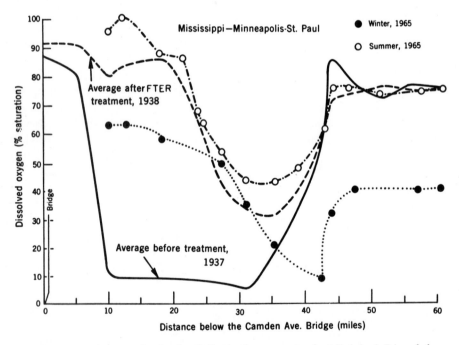

FIGURE 6.3. Comparative levels of dissolved oxygen in the Mississippi River below Minneapolis-St. Paul. The winter data represent a survey during January, February, and March. The summer data were obtained during July, August, and September.

TABLE 6.6

Approximate populations and expenditures on major works including sewage treatment, interceptors, and pumping stations in several regions

River	Region	Population	
		Year	Numbers
Hudson	New York metropolitan	1930	7 million
		1964	11.3 million
	Albany-Schenectady-Troy	1930	127,000
		1965	697,000
Mississippi	St. Paul-Minneapolis	1940	796,000
		1964	1.6 million
Potomac	Washington, D.C., metropolitan	1930	487,000
		1940	908,000
		1967	2.6 million
Delaware	Philadelphia metropolitan	1950	3.6 million
		1960	4.3 million
Ohio	Basin area	1950	17.6 million
	Municipal		9.3 million
	Municipal		11.3 million

River	Expenditures ($106)	Period	Item
Hudson	12	1963–68[a]	Sewers only
	180	1968–70	Sewers only
	1400	1965–76	Treatment plants
Mississippi	16.4	1934–37	Treatment plants and sewers
	27	1963–66	Treatment plant
	3.3	1968	Annual operation and maintenance
	33	1969–71	Treatment plant
Potomac	60	1950–60	
Delaware	300	Since 1946	
Ohio	1000	1952–61	

[a] Per year.

(Table 6.6). Not shown in the comparison in Figure 6.3 are the effects of projected expenditures to 1971, which include an additional $33 million to reduce the biochemical oxygen demand by 90 percent. The low value of the dissolved oxygen for the winter periods is presumably related to the frozen condition of the river. A mean of the two curves suggests that the dissolved oxygen level has remained approximately the same over the last 30 years.

While below Philadelphia on the Delaware River the oxygen-sag curve falls to levels of 5 percent saturation or less, in a limited reach for the period 1950 to 1963 some miles above Philadelphia and at central Philadelphia dissolved oxygen fluctuated around a value of 75 percent saturation, remaining essentially constant.

Where dissolved oxygen has been maintained in waters adjacent to major metropolitan centers, it has required large expenditures on sewers and on sewage treatment works to accommodate large increases in population (Table 6.6). The "Red Queen" process of running to stay in place, illustrated in St. Paul and in part of New York, may not be viewed as progress by some, but may still be viewed as an accomplishment often unrecorded in the current popular literature. The Potomac estuary in the vicinity of Washington, D.C., presents a different picture. Here the impact of large metropolitan growth on a relatively small river and sluggish estuary is evident. In contrast to the Mississippi, the Hudson, and the Delaware, the relative size of the metropolitan population of Washington, as contrasted with the flow of the river, has placed a burden on the capacity of the river which is insufficiently compensated by sewage treatment works built in the area. Despite expenditures upward of $70 million from 1938 through 1965, in recent years dissolved oxygen during the summer months has retreated to the position occupied by similar curves in 1932 before major treatment works were installed in 1938 (Figure 6.4). The oxygen-sag curves for 1954 to 1967 and for 1960 to 1967 for consecutive minimum flows of 28 days show declines below the figures for 1932 before major treatment works were installed. While major improvements in treatment processes and in the volume of wastes that can be treated are planned for the metropolitan area of Washington, the demands on the river, posed by sewage and other wastes, have exceeded the assimilative capacity of the Potomac, so

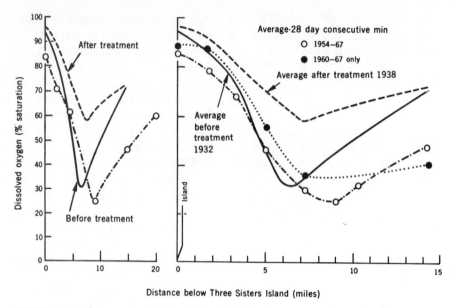

FIGURE 6.4. Comparative levels of dissolved oxygen summer flows, Potomac River below Washington, D.C., 1932, 1938, 1954–67 inclusive, and 1960–67.

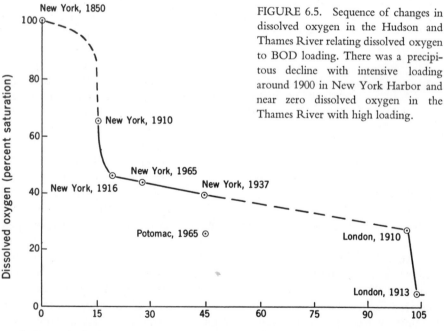

FIGURE 6.5. Sequence of changes in dissolved oxygen in the Hudson and Thames River relating dissolved oxygen to BOD loading. There was a precipitous decline with intensive loading around 1900 in New York Harbor and near zero dissolved oxygen in the Thames River with high loading.

that there results a burgeoning algal population with associated odors and esthetic problems.

Torpey (1967) has suggested that the dissolved oxygen in such major estuaries as the New York Harbor and the estuary of the Thames in London was controlled primarily by organic activity associated with nutrients promoting the growth of algae. Torpey's curve, reproduced in Figure 6.5, indicates that, in estuaries such as these, the dissolved oxygen declined rapidly once the input, expressed as biochemical oxygen demand (BOD) per acre of surface per day (1.0 pound per acre is equivalent to 1.12 kilograms per hectare) exceeded a specific threshold. He suggested that the rapid decline in dissolved oxygen occurred in a range of instability associated with large organic loading. This range or zone for New York appears to be defined roughly for the period from 1890 to 1916. Thereafter, a kind of plateau was maintained in the dissolved oxygen as a result of the production of oxygen by algae. Despite a large increase in population, from 1937 to 1965 loading decreased as a result of the installation of sewage-treatment works. Gould (1968) noted, however, that, while the pollutional load "decreased about 38 percent, the saturation deficit of dissolved oxygen decreased only 11 percent." If the data are applied to the Thames estuary at London, Torpey's estimate (Figure 6.5) shows a dissolved oxygen in the Thames in 1910 of approximately 25 percent saturation, whereas in 1913 the figure was near zero or approximately 5 percent. The precipitous decline from 1910 to 1913 represented another zone of instability accompanied by wide fluctuations in dissolved oxygen.

In contrast to the figures for the dissolved oxygen in New York Harbor and the Thames, dissolved oxygen in the Potomac River at Washington, approximately 25 percent saturation at a loading rate of approximately 45 pounds of BOD per acre per day, falls well below the general curve defined on the basis of the New York Harbor and the Thames (Figure 6.5) data. This may result from the fact that the flushing time of the Potomac, including the effect of the relatively small river flow, is considerably longer that that either for New York Harbor or for the Thames in London. Torpey (1967) analyzes these and the historical relationships for the Hudson and the Thames. The curve represents a complex of hydrodynamic, chemical, and organic interactions and hence cannot be simply generalized to other estuaries. A comprehensive paper on the Hudson by Howells et al. (1970), for example, points out the complexity of the relation between biota and nutrients and the potential for rapid deterioration in oxygen levels and organisms despite the fact that "serious fouling and deoxygenation have so far been avoided for most of the river." Ketchum (1969) also notes the very high phosphorus concentration in the Hudson estuary.

Whether or not the curve suggested by Torpey is indeed a general phenomenon remains to be verified. However, Torpey (1967) and later Gould (1968) have pointed out that, if the postulated "plateau" in dissolved oxygen does indeed exist in a number of estuaries, large increases in sewage treatment works could have a relatively small impact on the dissolved oxygen of such estuaries controlled by biological activity where treatment levels still operated within a range of dissolved oxygen represented by the "plateau" from roughly 30 to 40 percent saturation. Large expenditures of funds for treatment works might be reflected in only modest improvements in the quality of the water as measured by dissolved oxygen. Thus the effort to reverse a trend may be exceedingly difficult in reaches subject to the complex biological phenomena likely to be found in a number of rivers in critical estuaries on the coasts of the United States.

Inability to understand the precise causes of the changes in a parameter such as the dissolved oxygen also poses problems from the standpoint of the evaluation of alternatives directed toward the improvement of river quality. Because of the magnitude of the expenditures required to correct the conditions of such estuaries and rivers, it becomes imperative that understanding be improved to the point where returns per dollar invested can be more easily evaluated if the public is to be able to choose those alternatives which it feels are worth the expenditures required.

Dissolved Solids

While information on the dissolved solids carried by rivers in the United States is more extensive than that for the dissolved oxygen or other parameters, few examples of comparative changes over a period of time have been analyzed which include controls of hydrologic variation as well as accurate measurements of dissolved materials. Curves relating streamflow and dissolved solids for the Passaic River at Little Falls, N.J., in the New York-New Jersey metropolitan area show a progressive increase in dissolved solids from 1948 through 1955 to 1963. At a discharge of 200 cubic feet per second (5.7 cubic meters per second), for example, the dissolved load has increased from approximately 130 parts per million (ppm) in 1948 to 150 ppm in 1963 (Anderson and Faust, 1965). The significance of changes in flow in relation to dissolved load, however, is suggested perhaps by the increase in dissolved load between the years 1945 and 1960 on the Delaware River at Trenton (McCarthy and Keighton, 1964). An increase in concentration is confounded by a decline in annual discharge in the same period. Records since 1964 suggest a reversal if not a downward trend in concentration of dissolved solids.

Analyses of long-term trends in dissolved materials for several rivers and a station in Lake Michigan constitute one of the most extensive analyses of such records thus far published (Table 6.7). Beginning in the late nineteenth century, although the records are broken in places, the data show significant increases in chloride, sulfate, nitrate, and total dissolved solids at specific sites on the Illinois, Mississippi, and Ohio rivers and in Lake Michigan. Increases since about 1900 range from about 50 percent in total dissolved solids to 300 percent in chlorides, amounts that must be viewed as significant despite the absence of controls for variations in discharge and the broad scatter in the values of each of the variables.

Acid waste from coal mines has long been recognized as a pollutant in the eastern United States where underground and open-pit mining have been pursued. In some instances the amount of acid appears to be directly related to the rate of coal production. However, despite repeated efforts at mine sealing, particularly during the 1930s, relatively little reduction in acidity can be seen in rivers affected by discharge from mines. Thus, from 1947 to 1965 the sulfate concentration in the Schuylkill River at Berne, Pennsylvania, has remained constant despite installation of control measures particularly in effluents from active mines (Biesecker et al., 1968).

An increase in salinity is associated with return flows from major irrigation projects in the western United States. For example, it is estimated that the weighted average concentration of 501 ppm at Lee Ferry on the upper Colorado River is higher by 238 ppm as a result of man's activities (Iorns et al., 1965).

An illustration of changes in the concentrations of dissolved organic matter is provided in a brief record on the Illinois River (Sullivan and Evans, 1968). Before about 1955 synthetic detergents posed major problems in streams in many if not most regions here and abroad. The early "hard" detergents were not readily degradable by organisms within the streams. Before detergents were introduced, background levels in the Illinois River were about 0.5 milligram per liter measured as methylene blue active substance.

From 1959 to 1963 all of the detergents were alkyl benzene sulfonate (ABS). Betweeen 1963 and 1965, ABS was being replaced by linear

TABLE 6.7

Long-term observations, dissolved solids (Illinois; data from Ackerman et al., 1970).

	Chloride		Sulfate		Nitrate		Total Dissolved Solids	
Year	Amount (mg/liter)	Year	Amount (mg/liter)	Year	Amount (mg/liter)	Year	Amount (mg/liter)	
Lake Michigan off Waukegan								
1861	0.6 to 1.7	1900	5	1900	1.0	1861	136	
1897	3.0	1926	14.4	1924	1.3			
1969	7.7	1969	25.7[a]	1930	0.5			
				1969	1.0[a]	1969	160	
Illinois River at Peoria								
1889	33			1900	6.2	1895	318	
1898	21.5	1907	46.6	1945	10.0	1900[b]	240	
1908	15[b]	1945	100	1952–62	Decline			
1968	50[c]	1968	120	1968	16	1968	417	
Mississippi River at Alton								
1898	8			1900	4	1889	181	
1925	13			1920	7	1897	220	
1969	27[d]			1931	4.2			
				1969		1969	329	
Ohio River at Cairo								
1910	11			1910	2.5 to 4.1			
1913	15			1915–20	3.5			
1919	10	1951	45	1950	3.5	1954	176	
1966	23.6	1966	61.4	1966	5.4	1966	219	

[a] Rise since 1948.   [b] Increased dilution.   [c] Rise after 1950.   [d] Rise after 1960.

alkylate sulfonate (LAS), a more rapidly biodegradable detergent. By 1965 to 1966 LAS was the sole surfactant in the Illinois River. From 1959 to 1965 mean monthly concentrations ranged from lows of about 0.4 mg/liter to a maximum of 9 mg/liter. During the winter the concentrations exceeded 0.6 mg/liter. By 1965 to 1966 concentrations of surfactants ranged from about 0.2 to 0.3 mg/liter. In general, high concentrations were associated with high input, although monthly mean flow rates were somewhat higher in 1965 to 1966.

The detergent case illustrates the reversibility of certain pollution effects, in this case a reversibility achieved as a result of the compulsory introduction of a new material. The new products did not eliminate phosphorus from the river systems, but surfactant levels in the Illinois River decreased from 1959 through 1966 even though the amount of detergent used was increasing at a rapid rate. Similar results were obtained in Germany and elsewhere in Europe.

Perhaps the best set of analyses of trends in river quality—albeit over a relatively short period—is for the Ohio River for the period since the introduction of the major cleanup efforts inaugurated by the creation of the Ohio River Water Sanitation Commission (Orsanco). During this period efforts to maintain the quality of the Ohio River have been successful in that the levels of a number of indicators have remained roughly constant from 1952 to 1964 (Figure 6.6). Sulfate concentrations exceeded the standard at two points roughly 18 percent

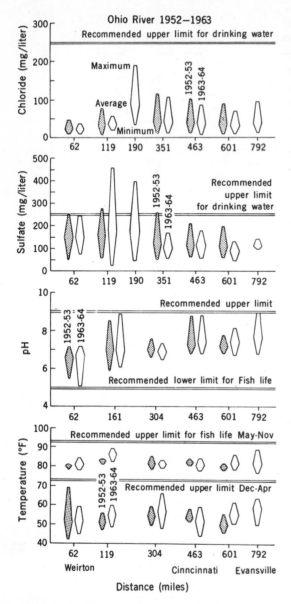

FIGURE 6.6. Comparative levels of selected ions, pH, and temperature in the Ohio River from 1953 to 1963.

at Cincinnati. Regression lines relating flow and chloride concentrations showed significant differences at all flows. However, these statistical analyses apparently show smaller increases in chlorides in this reach of the river than are suggested by the more limited data shown for the Ohio at Cairo, Illinois, in Table 6.7. Chloride concentrations are lower today than in 1952 at many points, with the exception of the reach below the confluence of the Muskingum which contributes large amounts of chloride into the main river. Limited chloride control has been achieved in part by scheduling the rate of chloride discharge in accordance with the capacity of the river and the desired quality objectives.

In the Ohio high pH at mile 16 and at mile 161 is attributed to the presence of considerable growth of algae (Orsanco, 1965). Throughout the river, temperatures are about the same as they were a decade earlier, and nitrate concentrations have remained constant at roughly 1.5 to 12.3 mg/liter for the past 12 years. In addition, phosphate (PO_4) levels have remained at approximately 0.06 to 1.15 mg/liter since measurements were first taken in 1954. Canalization of the Ohio and construction of dams up to 50 feet (15 meters) high have altered the oxygenation pattern along the river. Where sedimentation occurs in some pools, algae growth has occurred and reoxygenation is slowed at the greater depths. In contrast, higher detention times have reduced the amounts of coliform bacilli present.

In addition to the improvements in control and treatment of industrial wastes, more than $1.2 billion has been spent on sewage treatment works for municipalities, and now 99 percent of the urban population of the Ohio River Basin is served by sewage treatment facilities. Of the total expenditure, $300 million has been spent in the Ohio Valley. Cleary (1967) estimates that, "... a price tag of $100 per capita would represent a fair average expenditure to cover the cost of treatment works, interceptor sewer installation, site purchase, and the associated engineering and legal fees." At places—

of the time. A detailed study by Orsanco (1957) showed that in the 40-year period between 1914 and 1952 to 1954 chloride concentrations increased 50 percent at Weirton and 60 percent for example, Cincinnati—the river has improved sufficiently to permit the establishment of very large recreation facilities, including large marinas and many pleasure boats. In any event, the fact that the river has been rehabilitated for use in a number of places and that a number of measurable parameters have remained constant despite a fourfold increase in population from 1952 through 1963 (Table 6.6) illustrates the possibilities of maintenance and, perhaps, enhancement of river quality.

Sediment

The concept of sediment as a pollutant is of relatively recent origin. Even during the 1930s, when problems associated with soil erosion and the need for soil conservation were first clearly faced—although the importance of reservoir sedimentation was recognized—emphasis was placed on the value of the land lost to production rather than on the offsite effects of erosion and sedimentation.

Problems posed by sediment as a pollutant are primarily a function of climate, associated with vegetation and land use. The significance of geologic erosion has not always been appreciated. Early predictions that Lake Mead behind Boulder Dam would fill within a period of 50 years, in part because of accelerated erosion due to overgrazing, gave way after detailed study (Thomas, 1954) to estimates of 350 to 400 years. It was also recognized that the accelerated erosion resulting from poor land use, while of major consequence to husbandmen and to the local landscape, represented a minor contribution on top of an already high rate of erosion characteristic of semiarid regions. Where sediment yields are normally high in the middle west and southwest, the effects of man have probably not exceeded the effects brought on by the vicissitudes of nature (Ruhe and Daniels, 1965).

In the eastern United States, sediment yields have varied from about 100 tons per square mile

per year (166 tons per square kilometer) or less in presettlement time (Table 6.8) to 600 to 800 tons per square mile per year where land is in crops. In contrast, in metropolitan regions undergoing development construction, activities increase sediment yields to rates of 1000 to 5000 tons per square mile or higher. Upon completion of construction, an urbanized cover of concrete, asphalt, and rooftops reduces sediment yields to levels probably less than those of forested areas before settlement. For the most part, then, sediment as a pollutant in the eastern United States is principally a function of land use. The association of sediment pollution with urban expansion in the humid east concentrates the problem in major population centers—centers often adjacent to estuaries.

In the western United States, changes in the sediment load have been associated not only with changes in land use, but perhaps even more significantly with regulation of streamflow by impoundments. The effect of large reservoirs that may trap as much as 99 percent of the inflowing sediment is illustrated by data from two sampling stations in the Colorado River (Figure 6.7). The annual sediment load of the Colorado River at Grand Canyon upstream from Lake Mead fluctuates widely from year to year; in some instances variations are four- to sixfold. In contrast, the station at Topock, Arizona, 115 miles downstream from Boulder Dam, accurately reflects the effects of the major impoundment. Closure of Boulder Dam took place in 1933. Thereafter, the annual suspended load at Topock declined progressively during the period of record shown here to virtually zero in 1939. On the Mississippi, a significant change in the average annual sediment load of the river over a long period of time did not occur until the advent of major regulation of the Missouri main stem (Jordan, 1965). Reduction of sediment downstream from major reservoirs has often resulted in progressive degradation in the reach below the dam and in some instances in redeposition well downstream.

TABLE 6.8

Sediment yield from drainage basins under different land use, eastern United States

Drainage Area (sq mi)	Yearly Sediment (tons/sq mi)	Land Use	Characterization
		Broad Ford Run, Maryland	
7.4	11	Forested: entire area	Presettlement
		Gunpowder Falls, Maryland	
303	808	Rural: agricultural 1914–43; farmland in county 325,000 to 240,000 acres	Intensive agriculture
	233	Rural: agricultural 1943–61; farmland in county 240,000 to 150,000 acres	Urban fringe rural
		Building site, Baltimore, Maryland	
0.0025	140,000	Construction: entire area exposed	Undergoing construction
		Little Falls Branch, Maryland	
4.1	2,320	Construction: small part of area exposed	
		Stony Run, Maryland	
2.47	54	Urban: entire area	Urban

Whether river regulation enhances or degrades river quality depends in part on details of operation as well as on the purposes of regulation. Clear water may reduce the cost of water treatment, provided that the water does not require the addition of solids for filtration. The clarity of the water may also increase algae production. Changes in gradient may result in sluggish flows preventing rapid dilution of waste from outfalls, and flow regulation may enhance growth of riparian vegetation. In that more than 150 major reservoirs have been constructed throughout the middle west and western United States on virtually every major river, one can expect changes in river sedimentation and in water quality in all of these rivers. In some instances, regulation of the flow will provide additional water for downstream reaches which will lead to the availability of water for dilution of wastes and hence, in the classical sense, a decrease in the probability of pollution.

In others, the results may be exceedingly complex.

Sediment in the Schuylkill River in Pennsylvania has been significantly reduced by a major effort begun in 1950 (Biesecker et al., 1968). The reduction of sediment transported to tidewater reversed a trend in the Schuylkill initiated in the middle of the nineteenth century with the development of coal mining in the basin. The annual discharge of suspended sediment has been reduced about tenfold at Landingville in the upper basin, and downstream at Philadelphia a threefold reduction has been achieved (Table 6.9). While the program for coal-mine reclamation and control has been unable to reduce the sulfate concentration in the river (see above), it took roughly two years at the upstream station for the accumulative curve of sediment yield to show a progressive reduction, and the effects of the program were felt downstream at Philadelphia roughly three to

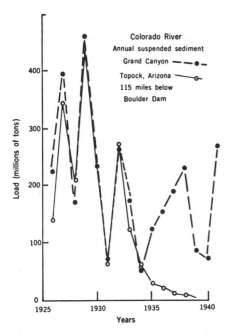

Colorado River
Annual suspended sediment
Grand Canyon — — ● —
Topock, Arizona ——○—
115 miles below
Boulder Dam

FIGURE 6.7. Variability of annual suspended sediment load on the Colorado River and reduction in sediment load after closure of Hoover Dam in 1933 as reflected at Topock, Arizona, in contrast to upstream station at Grand Canyon.

five years later. The total cost of the sediment-control program—including the cost of three major desilting basins, the operating and maintenance costs required to remove accumulated sediment, and the costs of channel restoration involved in dredging 24 million cubic yards (18.5 million cubic meters) of fine sediment or culm associated with coal-mine wastes—was originally estimated at $26 million. Actual expenditures have probably been higher. This record on the Schuylkill River indicates again that reclamation is possible where the requisite control procedures exist and where society is willing to bear the cost.

Temperature

The use of water for cooling in industrial processes (particularly the large quantities de-

manded by modern power-generating stations), the increase in the numbers of impoundments, and the recognition that water-temperature changes are associated with land use have all stimulated concern for the potential effects of higher temperatures in river water. Some examples of the magnitudes and effects of these changes have been documented.

In Long Island streams (Pluhowski, 1970) urbanization produced changes in runoff and in temperature through changes in infiltration, in clearance of vegetation from the channel, in small impoundments in different reaches, and in land use adjacent to the channel. These changes have been accompanied by significant alterations in the temperature regime. On the forested Connetquot River, for example, the variability of both winter and summer temperatures is exceedingly small. On East Meadow Brook, which drains an urban watershed (Table 6.10), variations in temperature are large. Only a small length of channel of East Meadow Brook is bounded by shade trees, in contrast to the virtually continuous shade on the Connetquot. In addition, between 1937 and 1962 direct runoff increased by 270 percent on the urban watershed. Thus a seasonal temperature range on East Meadow Brook of 28°F (15.6°C) contrasts with 17°F (8°C) on the Connetquot, and mean temperatures in June 1967 were 6°F (3.3°C) higher on the urban stream. Removal of brush and trees along streams in the absence of urbanization was shown by Brown and Krygier (1970) to increase the average maximum monthly temperature by 14°F (7.8°C) and to increase the annual maximum temperature from 57° to 85°F (14° to 30°C).

Analysis by Jaske and Goebel (1967) of the effect of the large reservoir system on the Columbia River indicates that temperature variability has decreased with an accompanying small decrease in mean temperatures in upstream reaches of the river. However, below Hanford, Washington, no decrease in the mean tempera-

TABLE 6.9

The effects of the restoration on sedimentation in the Schuylkill River

Location	Drainage Area (sq mi)	Trap Efficiency of Desilting Basin (%)	Average Annual Suspended-Sediment Discharge[a]			
			Before Restoration		After Restoration	
			Tons	Tons/sq mi	Tons	Tons/sq mi
Landingville[b]	133		609,000	4,580	51,800	390
Desilting basin: Auburn	157	91				
Auburn	157		581,000	3,700	4,700	30
South Tamaqua[b, c]	65.7		679,000[d]	10,000	62,400	950
Desilting basin: Tamaqua	67	86				
Desilting basin: Kernsville	340	49				
Schuylkill River at Berne	355		1,260,000	3,550	14,000	39
Schuylkill River at Philadelphia (Manayunk)	1,893		1,750,000	920	656,000	350

[a] Based on long-term flow duration and transport curve for indicated period.
[b] Above desilting basin system.
[c] Called little Schuylkill River.
[d] Calculated by subtracting suspended-sediment discharge at Auburn from Berne.

TABLE 6.10

Temperature variations and watershed characteristics of Long Island streams showing the effect of urbanization (data from Pluhowski, 1970)

Item	Rivers	
	East Meadowbrook	Connetquot
Drainage (sq mi)	31	24
Character	Urban	Forested
Vegetation along stream	Low	High
Temperature (°F):		
Five-station mean		
June	66	60
January	42	42
Variation along stream		
June	10	0.5
January	2.0	1.0
Maximum range	17	28
Mean discharge (ft²/sec)	~16.6	~38.8
Runoff	270%[a]	3%[b]

[a] Direct runoff increase 1937–1962.
[b] As storm water, which was 3 percent of the total discharge.

ture is apparent. Thus, the effect of the reservoirs has been to reduce temperature variability, much as flow variability is reduced by regulation. These observations of course do not describe the local effects of release of cold water—for example, from the bottom layers of stratified reservoirs, an effect seen downstream from a number of reservoirs in the southeastern United States.

The effects of urbanization and of reservoir regulation, while ubiquitous and perhaps growing as the urban areas grow, are probably small in contrast with the potential for temperature rises posed by heated discharges of cooling water from power plants. For this reason, the potential effects of such discharges have received much attention, and there have been several reviews of the subject (Jensen et al., 1969).

A few illustrations are given here from the experience of the Tennessee Valley Authority (TVA) because they are suggestive of the nature and magnitude of the problem. The Widow's Creek steam plant on the Tennessee River, for

TABLE 6.11

Thermal effects: some TVA power plants

Total Capacity (Mw)	River-Flow (ft³/sec)	Velocity (ft/sec)	Cooling Water Discharge (ft³/sec)	Temperature Increase (°F)		Effect on Aquatic Life
				Maximum (°F)	After Mixing (°F)	
Widows Creek, Guntersville Reservoir						
540	47,000	1.75	2,200	10.3	1	Diversity and abundance same above and below
Colbert, Pickwick Reservoir						
800	55,000	0.9	1,900	12		Discharge to Cane Creek; no significant effect on bottom organisms
Paradise, Green River above dam						
1,380	1,300	0.25	550	11 (controlled)		Relative abundance of fish reduced; Summer periphyton growth rate down; winter, some rise; Recovery 15 miles downstream; Slime growth greatest near plant

example, has a capacity of 540 megawatts and the river has a flow of 47,000 cubic feet per second (Table 6.11). The cooling-water discharges in a characteristic plume with higher temperatures at the surface decreasing in intensity with distance and with depth. The maximum temperature difference at the discharge point is 10.3°F (5.7°C), and a temperature elevation of about 1°F (0.6°C) exists at a distance of about one mile downstream from the plant. At three plants, as Table 6.11 shows, the maximum increase in temperature is from 10° to 12°F (5.6° to 6.7°C). At the Paradise plant on the Green River, essentially a pool, the maximum temperature is actually controlled by operation of the plant so as not to exceed the value shown.

Of particular interest is the response of the biota as observed at three sites reported in Table 6.11. On the Green River, at the Paradise plant, the temperature of the river water rises rapidly to about 98°F (37°C) immediately below the outfall. Initially the temperature rise is associated with a marked decline in zooplankton volume, but there is subsequent progressive re-

covery in the downstream direction. Recovery of all the biota is complete approximately 15 miles downstream from the plant (Table 6.11).

These few examples of temperature changes associated with cooling-water discharges do not support a conclusion that major biota degradation will automatically accompany such discharges. Indeed, under some circumstances, the effects of thermal effluents on aquatic life appear minimal (Merriman, 1970). However, where mixing appears to be limited and where the flow capacity of the river is low, a number of changes in aquatic life have been observed, including growth of epiphytic organisms on submerged surfaces near the plant, some reduction in the seasonal abundance of fish, especially in summer periods close to outfall areas, and a change (increase) in the growth rates of some species. Beyond a relatively limited perimeter, temperature increases after mixing appear to be of the order of 1° to 5°F (0.5° to 3°C), the amount obviously influenced by the volume, location, temperature differences, and mixing characteristics encountered at each locality. While such results may not be unexpected, it is important to note that, in some instances, regulations have established upper bounds of temperature that may not be exceeded.

While temperatures on the Connecticut, the Ohio, and the Columbia rivers appear to show little change over the past decade, rivers in urban areas and those subjected to large thermal effluents have apparently experienced some increase in temperature. That trends are exceedingly difficult to detect is suggested by preliminary study of mean temperatures for July and August on the Delaware River at Trenton from 1945 to 1965. Mean temperature corrected for discharge variations apparently increased 1.2°F (0.7°C). However, the great variability in the temperature indicates that the apparent trend is not statistically significant. Although discerning a trend in water temperature is difficult, evaluating potential biological effects is even more difficult. Unfortunately, empirical studies, which up to now suggest relatively modest effects on the biota, do not help to establish the level at which cumulative heating may exceed a biologically significant threshold. Such studies suggest simply that, in a number of places, if a threshold exists, it has not yet been exceeded.

Radioactivity

Radioactive materials have been released to the waters of the country from bomb testing in the atmosphere, from mining and milling, and from the use of radionuclides in industry, research, and commerce. For example, concentrations of strontium-90 in rivers, as measured at 128 stations in the United States, rose from a low in 1960 of less than 1 picacurie per liter to almost 4 pc/liter late in 1963 after a period of weapons testing (Water Pollution Surveillance System, 1963). (Drinking-water standards permit a maximum concentration of 10 pc/liter.) From the cessation of testing in 1963, the level returned to about 1 pc/liter by late 1965.

For the mining industry a particularly interesting illustration is provided by a study of changes in gross alpha and beta radioactivity in a reach of the Colorado River in the vicinity of two mills (Morgan, 1959). Samples of water, algae, and mud from the bed of the river were taken above and below two milling sites. As Figure 6.8 shows, gross beta radioactivity rises rapidly immediately downstream from each site. The magnitude of the rise is greatest in the algae, and successively less in the mud and in the drinking water. Thus the relative concentration in the biota is highest and the beta activity is greater than the alpha. The increased radioactivity of the water exceeds that permitted by the drinking-water standard of 1000 pc/liter at one location immediately downstream from a mill. Concentrations of beta activity in the algae decline more slowly and over a greater distance than they do in either the water or the bottom mud. While absolute amounts are low, the river travels 50 miles before the concentrations of radioactive materials are reduced to the background level.

No comprehensive figures are available which can be used to appraise the total content or extent of radioactive materials in the rivers of the country or the magnitude of changes in radioactivity in past decades. Data are available at several industrial locations, however.

Studies of the uptake of these nuclides by water, bottom mud, plankton, fish, and vascular plants indicate that removal of strontium-90 from the water is very limited in the Mohawk River downstream from the Knolls Atomic Power Laboratory. However, the amounts of cesium-137, zirconium-95, and strontium-90 in the bottom muds decrease by several orders of magnitude in a pool at a distance of about 2 miles, and at locations 12 to 15 miles downstream concentrations were lower by factors of 10 to 100 as compared to maximum values at the outfall (Friend et al., 1965). Cesium concentrations in algae also declined in the downstream direction.

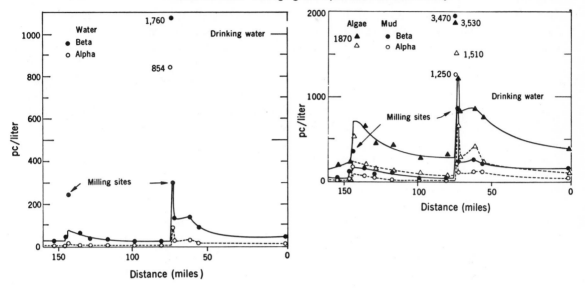

FIGURE 6.8.   Radioactivity in water, mud, and algae in the Colorado River at and downstream from milling sites. Solid symbols are beta activity, open symbols alpha. Note broken scale. Values of especially high points are given beside the symbols. Drinking water standard is also shown.

On the Clinch and Tennessee river systems in the vicinity of Oak Ridge National Laboratory concentration of most radionuclides in bottom muds declined downstream by 4 or 5 orders of magnitude over a distance of 20 to 50 miles, except in reservoir deposits near dams. Quantities of radioactive materials in bottom muds of the Clinch River are directly related to the deposition of fine-grain sediments, particularly clay minerals, just as radioactivity is associated with fine sediments in the Columbia River below the source locations and above McNary Dam (Nelson and Hanshold, 1970). On the Clinch River, according to Carrigan (1969), "during 19½ years of waste disposal 64 percent of the stream bed has become covered with radioactive sediment, and in the 22-mile-long reach, at least 20 percent of the cesium-137 and rare earths released to the river are retained in the bottom sediment." Present levels are not a hazard. Whether retention poses an eventual hazard depends both on future releases, now

declining, and on maintenance of safe disposal practices. Concentration in fish has generally followed the food chain, with highest concentrations in plankton feeders and the lowest in game fish. Concentration factors for strontium-90 in fish ranged from 10 to 100.

These examples confirm the fact that industrial activities are increasing the burden of radioactivity on specific rivers. Under existing controls, hazardous levels are not experienced at most sites. The extent to which such materials may accumulate or be dispersed in the river environment is a function of the half-life of the radionuclides, absorption by biota, and the rate of transport of sediments. Work remains to be done on the long-term relations among these variables, including the role of benthic organisms in concentrating radioactivity from both inorganic and organic sediments. Because radioactivity is carried upward in the food chain and because of the long half-life of many radionuclides, continuing vigilance appears warranted. Such vigilance should be coupled with recognition that thus far processes have not apparently resulted in widespread spatial dispersion of high concentrations of radionuclides in rivers.

Pesticides

Expansion of pesticide use is a post–World War II phenomenon, and warnings of potential damages beyond the point of application were issued in the 1940s. By 1962, a sampling program of 101 stations revealed DDT in 32 samples from nine rivers in the United States. Subsequent studies have added to the number of locations at which pesticides have been observed in river water and to the knowledge of modes of dispersal and accumulation. Schafer et al. (1969) reported detectable quantities of dieldrin in 40 percent and of endrin in more than 30 percent of 500 samples of finished water derived from the Mississippi and Missouri rivers. Smaller amounts of other pesticides were also found.

Because of the extensive agricultural enterprise in California, approximately 20 percent, as has been estimated, of all pesticides used are applied in that state. Thus the careful documentation of pesticide distribution in some California rivers by Bailey and Hannum (1965) provides an excellent illustration of the relation between heavy pesticide application and its behavior in river systems. Where pesticide applications are heavy, such as in the southern San Joaquin and Imperial valleys, concentrations are correspondingly high in river waters (Table 6.12). For the Sacramento River system as a whole, high values of 0.229 micrograms per liter in the San Joaquin near Vernalis, 120 miles above Golden Gate, decline to 0.110 μg/liter at Antioch 66 miles downstream. The decline continues to San Francisco Bay because of inflow dilution, including tidal flushing and uptake by aquatic organisms and sediments. Concentration decreases at a rate of about 0.0016 μg/liter per mile. Pesticide concentrations in sediment exceeded those in water 20 to 100 times, concentrations being proportionally higher as the sediment becomes finer. Even on the Feather River, at an upstream station where water samples averaged only 0.009 μg/liter, the average of ten samples of sediment contained a concentration of 24 μg/liter.

In contrast to the high concentrations observed in the agricultural areas of California, lighter applications in forestry suggest more rapid disappearance of the pesticide with surface and river runoff. On several experimental sites in Oregon, for example, endrin from endrin-coated Douglas fir seed was detected in stream-flow two hours after seeding and during a high

TABLE 6.12

Pesticides in California rivers

Area	Application Rate (pound/acre)	River	Location	Pesticide Concentration (μg/liter)	
				Water	Mud
Sacramento Valley	0.75–1.0	Feather	Nicolaus Bridge	0.009	24
		American	Sacramento	0.120	
		Sacramento	Walnut Grove	0.113	94
Southern San Joaquin Valley	1.25 DDT	San Joaquin	Vernalis	0.229	31
	2.40 other	San Joaquin	Antioch	0.101	212
Imperial Valley	1.25 DDT	Alamo		0.421	
	2.40 other				

flow six days later. The total, however, amounted to only 0.12 percent of the endrin used, and during the storms later in the year concentrations averaged 0.02 μg/liter (Marston et al., 1969). The results were roughly similar in a study of concentrations of the herbicide amitrole sprayed on a forested watershed. Immediately below the site a maximum concentration of 155 parts per billion, measured 30 minutes after application, decreased to 26 ppb after two hours, and none was detectable after five days. Similarly, no amitrole was detected at a station 1.8 miles downstream.

Although the association of fine-grained sediments and pesticides has been established, studies in the lower Mississippi River area failed to show significant concentrations at predictable dispositional loci, but rather concentrations were low and dispersed and no build-up was observed where pesticides were derived from farm use. Concentrations were greater near manufacturing and formulating plants (Barthel et al., 1969).

Many of the very high concentrations of pesticides experienced in rivers or streams resulting in major fish kills, for example, have been associated with direct discharges, spills, or direct spraying from the air to the watercourse. The number of fish kills from pollutants, about 400 to 500 per year (FWPCA, 1960-1968), has changed relatively little since reporting began. For other pollutants, as well as pesticides, however, each year is characterized by one or more excessive or exceedingly high mortalities associated with a particular accident. Statements such as

> The dam of a temporary slush pit broke and its contents (sodium chloride and/or bentonite, a drilling mud) entered the creek 100 yards from the well site. The pollution gave the creek a "milky" appearance and traveled the entire 39 miles as a "slug"... (1,200,000 fish).

or

> Potato field north of a creek was sprayed by plane.

> ... Area is stocked with trout.... Water appeared normal, no other damage apparent (600,000 fish) (FWPCA 1960–1968).

in the reports of fish kills clearly indicate that the increase in manufacturing industries and ubiquitous use of insecticides is inevitably accompanied by accidents during manufacture and application of the product. In general, industrial and municipal activities account for about 50 to 75 percent of the reported fish kills and insecticides for only about 10 percent. The total number of reported incidents does not appear to be large, but presumably the number of accidents will continue to be some proportion of the total volume of use. While active campaigns promoting more careful handling will tend to reduce accidents, if increasing use of highly toxic products continues, one can expect increasing reports of the presence of pesticides as well as increasing numbers of significant fish kills from specific accidents.

Pesticides of different composition, of course, behave quite differently. Thus DDT with a lower solubility in water is likely to be found in sediments or biota and at lower concentrations in the river water itself. In addition, a number of the phosphorus compounds are degradable and short-lived in contrast to the persistent life of chlorinated hydrocarbons. In many ways, the chlorinated hydrocarbons pose much the same problem as radioactive materials do; they are persistent and concentrations increase from water, to sediment, and thence to biota with progressively higher concentrations higher in the food chain.

Experience shows that biota in river systems may be decimated by biocides. Effects of specific doses will depend not only on the strength and composition of the biocide, but on the seasonal and feeding cycles of the organisms. At the same time, populations may readily recover, either by drift or from remnant resident populations (Hynes and Williams, 1962). In contrast, subtle or delayed effects of pesticides accumulated in sublethal doses in various organisms have also been documented and may pose continuing hazards so long as persistent pesticides continue to be used. There is some evidence that public concern with the effects of such pesticides may be leading to a reduction in their use in the United States. However, even with marked reduction in use, many years may elapse before residuals accumulated in soils, vegetation, and other organisms are flushed to rivers and, in turn, disappear from the river systems themselves. With improved detection systems for pesticides, their reported presence in river water, bottom muds, or biota may continue to increase for some time to come. Thus, while one might suggest that thus far the magnitude of the effect of biocides on rivers has been quite limited, little can be said on the distribution and long-term alterations which may accompany increased use of biocides.

Trash and Debris

In the eyes of many, trash and debris are ubiquitous features of rivers and bays, particularly in metropolitan regions. Photographs of tires, market carts, tangled lumber, and tin cans commonly appear in newspapers and magazines. While sequential sets of ground or aerial photographs which might provide a record of changes in the quantity of debris at a given site are unavailable, paired photographs at two points in time are graphic but not quantitative. There is reason to believe, however, that debris may be one of the most significant elements influencing the public's perception of pollution.

The inner harbor of the port of Baltimore (north branch of the Patapsco River) includes an area of about 1000 acres (400 hectares). A principal tributary, Jones Falls, drains 46 square miles, of which about 20 are in urban land uses. Several large storm drains also empty directly into the harbor.

From 1961 through 1969 approximately 600 tons of debris per year were removed from the inner harbor by the debris recovery program.

While a marked increase appeared from about 300 to 600 tons between 1963 and 1964, data are insufficient to define a significant trend. (The estimated cost of removal is roughly $15 per ton.) Observations suggest that Jones Falls, the storm drains, illegal disposal of dunnage, and rotting derelicts are the principal sources of debris. Monthly figures show that the maximum tonnage usually occurs in the summer months and is presumably related to rapid runoff from intense storms. This is corroborated by limited data from a trash boom sometimes in operation on Jones Falls. In one September storm at least 7 tons of debris were trapped by the boom, and it is estimated that an equal amount escaped earlier when the boom failed. Each of several smaller storms contributed 4 tons of debris, and in one event 52 tires were retrieved. Observations of urban rivers in Baltimore suggest that individual reaches may contain many cubic yards of debris per city block (Wolman, 1967). This material appears to be periodically flushed to the estuaries by large storm flows.

Comparable quantities of debris (150 tons in 6 months) are being retrieved from the Potomac River near Washington, D.C., and doubtless equal and larger amounts from other areas (Wolman et al., 1957). Data for the establishment of trends are not available. Of more importance, it may well be that volumes and weights are particularly inadequate as measures of the impact of debris on pollution.

Conclusions

All measures of growth whether population, gross national product, waste loads, or demand for recreation suggest that demands on the country's water resources are increasing at a rate that exceeds the rate of installation of waste treatment facilities (Figure 6.9). Presumably these demands constitute the customary measure of "pollution" and the basis for prophecies regarding the condition of the resource and its future

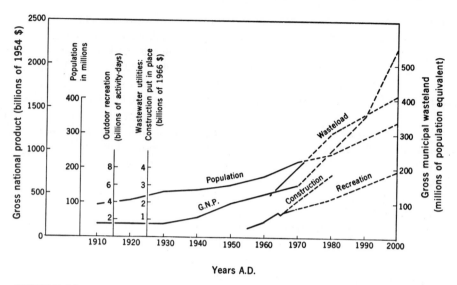

FIGURE 6.9.   Measures of demand on water resources including gross national product, population, municipal waste loads, and outdoor recreation, as compared with proposed construction of waste-water utilities to parallel waste loads. Estimated construction expenditures should approximate $4 to $5 billion per year. Actual expenditures approximately $1.5 billion per year.

prospects. Pressures posed by population and growth must have an effect on the river systems, which, even with regulation, have finite assimilative or carrying capacity for wastes of different kinds. At the outset, then, one might assume, even in the absence of proof, that the very large increase in society's activities should have recognizable consequences. Unfortunately, what the foregoing examples suggest is that it is easier to estimate the potential demand on a river system than it is to measure the effect. Certainly many rivers of the United States, such as those in Illinois, Colorado, and other places cited here, are not as they were 70 years ago. Nevertheless, while we "know" that conditions must be getting worse, we are hard pressed to determine precisely the relation between the pressures posed by society and the responses of the river system.

To a large extent observations of the condition of river systems have been confined to measures of the quality of the flow itself and exclude descriptions of the bed, banks, and environs of the river. In some instances the parameters observed—for example, dissolved oxygen or coliform organisms—are surrogates for broader effects of greater interest. Although useful, they provide only partial measures of the river's capacity (Downing and Edwards, 1968). Thus in the Hudson River, while it can be shown that the change is exceedingly small since 1922, we have some reason to believe that dissolved oxygen inadequately describes accumulating sludge on the bottom of the river as well as increasing growth of algae. Many years ago Henderson (1969) demonstrated that a portion of the Shenandoah River was virtually devoid of life despite high oxygen levels and other quality standards of the water. Intended to surmount this disability, current attempts to quantify biological observations may not in fact do so unless they are associated with true biological surveys (Hynes, 1964). Observation programs continue to emphasize measures of water quality to the virtual exclusion of measurements of river quality (Langford and Davis, 1970).

Observational programs appear to be particularly weak with regard to the detection of subtle initial changes from a natural to a polluted condition. This is not to suggest that no such observations are being made—for example, on wild rivers—but rather that there is no systematic program for the detection of initial changes.

The initiation and progression of change are often considered impossible to prevent and inexorable in character. This leads further to the view that virtually all changes from a pristine to a used condition are irreversible. Such does not appear to be the case. Experience on the Ohio River described above, the reversal of changes in surfactant concentrations in the Illinois River, and the marked reduction of sediment in the Schuylkill River illustrate that it is possible to reverse or to improve the conditions of some rivers with respect to important pollutants. Fish may migrate rapidly to formerly polluted areas when either industrial shutdowns or large cleanup programs occur. The Thames River near London is reported to have fish for the first time in many decades as a result of a major pollution-control program. Indeed, a brief report suggest "that the condition of rivers in England and Wales . . . may well have improved since 1958" (Owen et al., 1970).

Because the evidence up to now does indicate that the pressure on the water resources posed by population and industrial growth significantly exceeds the rate of investment in control facilities, much higher cost must be incurred if even a rough parallelism between development and control is to be achieved. More important, the kind of technology that will be needed is not only more expensive, but may be distinctly different in kind from secondary treatment that is now projected for most municipal areas.

Even if treatment or pollution control were to maintain parity with pollution pressure,

there is good reason to believe that many would continue to hold to the definition: "pollution is that which is getting worse." In the eyes of the beholders (Davis, 1971), the sights and smells of rivers today may be considered unsatisfactory, and while the "quality" of the rivers may be unchanged, they will be viewed as being polluted and becoming more so, as the interests of those living in more crowded areas turn toward rivers to satisfy their recreational and esthetic needs. Many observers have noted historic changes in values in the environment, and there is reason to believe that these play no small part in the current scene (Lowenthal, 1968).

The paucity of information and the handful of investigators concerned with evaluating trends in the quality of the rivers of the United States suggest some specific conclusions. First, none of the observational programs were designed specifically to measure the quality of rivers or the river environment. The sampling programs emphasize the measurement of specific characteristics primarily related to water use by industry and municipalities. The new National Water Quality Network should improve on this single objective orientation (Sayers, 1971). Few observational programs combine the necessary hydrology with measurements of water quality, river characteristics, and biology. While some long-term observations exist, the lack of coordinate observations makes long-term comparisons virtually impossible. For this reason, one must resort to the selected or case method described here.

In addition, as Dworsky and Strandberg (1967) emphasize, interpretation is "the vital part of the task of water quality assessment." Such interpretation requires the knowledge and skill of analysts familiar both with the data and with the changing characteristics of the land use and economy of the drainage basin. The new emphasis on quality of the environment demands continuing assessment and interpretation.

A second conclusion from the available data

suggests that surrogate measures of river and water quality as well as a multiplicity of measurements of easily measured parameters may shed little light on the dynamics of the processes active in river systems; hence, such measures may be of limited use in estimating the likelihood of reversing specific observed trends in the absence of a knowledge of their causes. Additional attention must be given to the measurement of parameters related to models of river behavior and to estimates of inputs based on budgets of materials derived from industrial outputs and land use.

Third, while hydrologists have long been concerned with variability of the flow of natural rivers, because of the difficulty of observation much less attention has been given to the variability of biological activity as well as physical variability associated with natural variations and cycles in rivers. Many measurements of biological effects are done during low and summer flows when measurement is easy, organisms often flourish, and concentrations of various substances in the flow are high. The effect of winter flow on the growth of slimes on the bottom of rivers, for example, and the special significance to the flora and fauna of periodic floods are not well documented. Significantly, however, among the most common trends in river management is the progressive regulation of flow through the provision of storage. Conceivably, regulation rather than pollutants alone may have the most far-reaching effects on the character of many river systems. To date, observations have not been designed to measure these effects.

Because the demands on the waters of the rivers of the country are increasing, the concept of threshold and irreversibility must be studied on (1) pristine waters to disclose the nature of the initial, presumably biological, changes which take place and (2) specific rivers where large-scale control or cleanup programs have been initiated. It may well be that observations designed to detect "polluters"—that is, observations designed to support the enforcement of standards—may not in themselves provide satisfactory measures of thresholds, trends, or reversals of trends. If one is to judge the effectiveness of the expenditure of large sums of money, observational tools must be designed to evaluate the response of the rivers to these expenditures.

CHAPTER 7

water-resource management

Several things should be said to amplify the discussion of water pollution in Chapter 6. Two are of real significance: water-pollution problems do increase with size of city (Table 7.1); and although pollutants are produced by many sources, the principal contributions to water pollution in urban areas come from industrial and municipal wastes.

INDUSTRIAL WASTES

The more than 300,000 water-using factories in the United States discharge three to four times as much oxygen-demanding wastes as all the sewered population of the United States. Moreover, many of the wastes discharged by industry are toxic. Table 7.2 shows the amount of water consumed by various industries and the pollution loads, before treatment, that they produce. The output of industrial wastes is growing several times faster than the volume of sanitary sewage.

Although there is as yet no detailed national inventory of industrial wastes, indications are that over half the volume discharged to water comes from four major industry groups—paper, organic chemicals, petroleum, and steel.

Selections are integrated from:
Federal Water Quality Control Administration, *Delaware Estuary Comprehensive Study*, Preliminary Report and Findings, Philadelphia: FWQCA, July 1966. Begins on page 204.
Walter E. Westman, "Some Basic Issues in Water Control Legislation," *American Scientist*, Vol. 60 (November–December 1972), pp. 767–773. Begins on page 228.
A. Myrick Freeman, III, and Robert H. Haveman, "Residual Changes for Pollution Control: A Policy Evaluation," *Science*, Vol. 177 (July 1972), pp. 322–329. Begins on page 237.

TABLE 7.1

Incidence of water-pollution problems for
metropolitan areas, 1965

Metropolitan Area Population Size in 000	Total Number of Areas in Group	Areas with Pollution Problem	Fraction with Pollution Problem
<100	21	8	0.381
100–<250	78	46	0.590
250–<500	56	35	0.625
500–<1000	35	25	0.714
1000–<2500	22	17	0.773
>2500	7	6	0.857

SOURCE: U.S. Geological Survey, Water Data for Metropolitan Areas, by William J. Schneider, Paper 1871, 1968. A metropolitan area was counted as having a pollution problem whenever the source stated there was a problem with municipal-industrial waste disposal, or that waters were polluted.

The greatest volume of industrial wastes is discharged in the northeast, the Ohio River Basin, the Great Lakes states, and the Gulf Coast states. Lesser, but significant volumes are discharged in some areas of the southeast and the Pacific Coast states.

Most industrial water waste can be curbed—and much has been—by treatment and by designing production processes that minimize waste. For example, the average waste from modern sulfate pulp and paper plants is only 7 percent of what it was in the older sulfite process. Treatment processes are now available for most industrial wastes. Their total estimated costs, as a percentage of gross sales by all industry, are well under 1 percent, although costs are much higher for some industries. Also, many industrial wastes—those from food processing, for example—can be treated efficiently (after pretreatment in some cases) in municipal waste-treatment systems.

Because treatment is feasible, the Federal Water Pollution Control Act Amendments of 1972 have launched a major attack on the na-

tion's water-pollution problems, as we shall see later. Some industrial pollution, however, presents difficult abatement problems. The trend toward using and shipping complex chemical products has greatly increased the possibility of releasing wastes in the environment. Many of these new chemicals are very difficult to detect and to control, and it may be that too little caution and study preceded the processing and marketing of some of them.

Small amounts of heavy metals can be a problem. For example, little attention has been given, until recently, to mercury, although separate incidents of mercury poisoning had occurred in Japan and Sweden. Currently, levels of mercury above Food and Drug Administration standards have been discovered in more than twenty states with the result that, in many of them, sport and commercial fishing has been curtailed. The Federal government has collected data on the sources of mercury discharge—mainly chemical plants—and has sought court action against eight firms. The Council on Environmental Quality is coordinating long-term federal agency efforts to spell out the danger and develop remedial programs.

Many authorities believe that waste heat looms as one of the most serious types of future water pollution. The chief source of thermal pollution today is the electric power industry, which requires tremendous amounts of water for cooling. Other sources include petroleum, chemical, steel, and pulp and paper processing. The heaviest users are listed in Table 7.3.

The best single indicator of future potential for thermal pollution is the predicted increase in the generation of electricity. The electric power industry is growing at a rate of 7.2 percent annually, virtually doubling every ten years. This trend is expected to continue, as Table 7.4 shows.

The principal use of water in steam-electric generating plants is for condenser cooling. The amount of water necessary depends on plant

TABLE 7.2

Estimated volume of industrial wastes before treatment, 1964[a]

Industry	Waste-Water Volume (billion gallons)	Process Water Intake (billion gallons)	BOD (million pounds)	Suspended Solids (million pounds)
Food and kindred products	690	260	4,300	6,600
Meat products	99	52	640	640
Dairy products	58	13	400	230
Canned and frozen food	87	51	1,200	600
Sugar refining...	220	110	1,400	5,000
All other	220	43	670	110
Textile mill products	140	110	890	N.E.
Paper and allied products	1,900	1,300	5,900	3,000
Chemical and allied products	3,700	560	9,700	1,900
Petroleum and coal	1,300	88	500	460
Rubber and plastics	160	19	40	50
Primary metals	4,300	1,000	480	4,700
Blast furnaces and steel mills	3,600	870	160	4,300
All other	740	130	320	430
Machinery	150	23	60	50
Electrical machinery	91	28	70	20
Transportation equipment	240	58	120	N.E.
All other manufacturing	450	190	390	930
All manufacturing	13,100	3,700	22,000	18,000
For comparison: Sewered population of United States	5,300[b]		7,300[c]	8,800[d]

[a] Columns may not add, due to rounding.
[b] 120,000,000 persons times 120 gallons times 365 days.
[c] 120,000,000 persons times 1/6 pound times 365 days.
[d] 120,000,000 persons times 0.2 pound times 365 days.
SOURCE: Data derived from T. J. Powers, National Industrial Waste Assessment, 1967.

efficiency and the designed temperature rise within the condensers. The temperature rise of cooling water condensers is usually in the range of 10° to 20°F, with the average rise about 13°F. Large nuclear steam electric plants require about 50 percent more condenser water for a given temperature rise than late model fossil-fueled, steam-electric plants of equal size. However, the development of advanced reactors, such as the fast breeder, will essentially eliminate the difference between nuclear and fossil-fueled plants. It is estimated that by 1980, cooling operations by the electric power industry will require the equivalent of one-fifth of the total fresh-water runoff of the United States.

MUNICIPAL WASTES

The second source of urban water pollution is municipal waste and sewage. The story of attempts to deal with the problem is a long one. One of the first methods used to dispose of sewage was the cesspool—a covered pit dug in the ground. In England this pit was lined with impervious material and had to be cleaned out at

TABLE 7.3

Use of cooling water by U.S. industry

Industry	Cooling Water Intake (billions of gallons)	Percent of Total
Electric power	40,680	81.3
Primary metals	3,387	6.8
Chemical and allied products....	3,120	6.2
Petroleum and coal products	1,212	2.4
Paper and allied products	607	1.2
Food and kindred products	392	0.8
Machinery	164	0.3
Rubber and plastics	128	0.3
Transportation equipment	102	0.2
All others	273	0.5
Total	50,065	100.0

SOURCE: Federal Water Pollution Control Administration, *Industrial Waste Guide on Thermal Pollution*, September 1968.

TABLE 7.4

U.S. electric power: past use, future estimates

Year	In Billion Kilowatt-Hours
1912	12
1960	753
1965	1,060
1970	1,503
1975	2,022
1980	2,754
1985	3,639

SOURCE: Federal Water Pollution Control Administration, *Industrial Waste Guide on Thermal Pollution*, September 1968.

intervals. In the United States the cesspool was lined with pervious material to allow the liquid to leach slowly into the soil. When the cesspool was filled with solids, it was abandoned and a new one dug. It was rarely advantageous to remove the solids from the old cesspool, since by the time the pool was filled, the ground had become so clogged with leaching solids that it could no longer absorb liquids. Today, cesspools are considered dangerous because of the relative ease with which they pollute groundwater supplies.

The septic tank was developed by an Englishman named Cameron and his associates in 1896. The septic process involves biological action similar to that which disposes of animal waste in nature. Bacteria work in the absence of oxygen to convert a portion of the organic matter in the sewage to liquids. In the process gases are given off, such as carbon dioxide and methane. The effluent from the tank is then transferred into the ground through a seepage pit or leaching bed. Typically, this is a "field" of several narrow trenches arranged in a finger pattern about three feet below ground level. Septic effluent can become a public nuisance if by some means it reaches the surface.

Failure of a septic system is usually related to subsoil conditions. If the soil is impermeable, the effluent will not leach into the ground but will find its way to the surface in back yards or into basements. If the soil is only slightly permeable, septic-tank effluent will sometimes cause it to clog and become impermeable. In very permeable soils the septic effluent may flow through too quickly to allow adequate filtering and biological action before it reaches some undesired location. To function efficiently, septic tanks require periodic removal of the sludge and scum. With disease spreading among urban populations and a developing awareness of microbiology, around 1875 growing attention was given to the public treatment of sewage. One method was to use raw sewage in land irrigation. As with cesspools and septic tanks, however, this method tends to clog the soil, and it also requires a large disposal area. A second technique involved the removal of large solids by sedimentation. In Europe, experimentation with this second method centered on the use of chemical precipitation to settle solids. On the North American continent the use of screening devices was more common. Neither of these processes was fully satisfactory in the removal of disease-carrying bacteria.

Today, most municipal waste-treatment systems are aerobic; that is, they introduce air into the sewage to induce oxidation. The plants, however, handle more than just domestic wastes from homes and apartments. On a nationwide average, about 55 percent of wastes processed by municipal treatment plants comes from homes and commercial establishments and about 45 percent from industries. Less than one-third of the nation's population is served by a system of sewers and an adequate treatment plant. About one-third is not served by a sewer system at all. About 5 percent are served by sewers which discharge their wastes without any treatment. And the remaining 32 percent have sewers but inadequate treatment plants. Of the total sewered population, about 60 percent have adequate treatment systems. The greatest municipal waste problems exist in the areas with the heaviest concentrations of population, particularly the northeast.

Three levels of treatment are employed in municipal plants. *Primary* treatment is a simple gravity process that separates and settles solids in a big tank. Such primary plants provide BOD removal levels of 25 to 30 percent. *Secondary* treatment is a biological process that speeds up what nature does in natural water bodies. In the activated sludge process used by many large cities, bacteria and air are mixed with sewage to accelerate decomposition of wastes. The other secondary treatment process—the trickling filter—involves spraying wastes uniformly over a rock bed. Bacteria formed on the rocks, in the presence of air, accelerate decomposition of wastes. Good secondary treatment plants remove 90 percent of measured BOD. That does not mean that 90 percent of total oxygen-demanding wastes are removed, but only the part that is measured by certain laboratory tests.

Advanced waste treatment, often called *tertiary* treatment, involves a wide variety of processes tailored for specific treatment needs. For example, one advanced waste treatment process is lime-alum precipitation, which removes 80 percent of phosphates from waste water, compared to an average of 30 percent in normal secondary treatment. Other processes, using carbon adsorption and sand filtering, remove up to 99 percent of measured BOD.

The waste loads from municipal systems are expected to nearly quadruple over the next fifty years. Even if municipal and industrial waste loads are cut substantially through treatment, pollution problems will continue to plague densely populated and highly industrialized areas where the capacity to assimilate waste is exceeded.

Among other municipal waste problems that will grow more apparent as conventional treatment reduces gross pollution loads are those caused by storm or combined sewers and by nutrients. Many cities have combined sewers, which discharge raw sewage along with street runoff directly to streams when treatment systems become overloaded during storms or thaws. Even where sewers are separated, pollution from storm-sewer discharges carrying a variety of wastes from the streets is possible. Although combined sewer problems exist in most regions of the country, the most severe are centered in the northeast, midwest, and to some degree the far west.

Municipal wastes contribute the major load of usable phosphates and significant amounts of nitrates to water bodies. Already nutrient pollution has led to a strict requirement for very high treatment levels for waste discharges to the Great Lakes and several other areas. Secondary treatment plants remove an average of 30 percent of the phosphorus and up to 20 percent of the nitrogenous materials, although with modifications higher levels of treatment are possible. In many places treatment levels approaching 100 percent will probably be necessary—especially if the phosphate content of detergents is not reduced.

LEGISLATIVE DEVELOPMENT

The first temporary water-pollution control legislation in the United States was not enacted until 1956. The Federal Water Pollution Control Act of 1956 authorized planning, technical assistance, grants for state programs, and construction grants for municipal waste-treatment facilities. Amendments followed in 1961, which among other things extended Federal enforcement authority and increased construction grant authorizations.

In 1965 more amendments established the Federal Water Pollution Control Administration as successor to a program previously in the Public Health Service of the Department of Health, Education, and Welfare. The Administration was transferred to the Department of the Interior in May 1966. The most important provisions in the 1965 act called for the establishment of water-quality standards and implementation plans for clean-up of all interstate and coastal waters.

The Clean Water Restoration Act of 1966 provided more Federal money for building treatment facilities. The Water Quality Improvement Act of 1970 provided tighter controls over oil pollution, vessel pollution, and pollution from Federal activities and broadened the earlier laws in other respects.

This progressive legislative development culminated in the Federal Water Pollution Control Act Amendments of 1972, which mandated a sweeping Federal-state campaign to prevent, reduce and eliminate water pollution. Two general goals were proclaimed for the United States:

1. To achieve, wherever possible, by July 1, 1983, water that is clean enough for swimming and other recreational uses, and clean enough for the propagation of fish, shellfish and wildlife.
2. By 1985, to have no discharges of pollutants into the nation's waters.

The goals were set within the framework of a series of specific actions that *must* be taken, with strict deadlines and enforcement provisions, by Federal, state, and local governments and by industries. While most responsibility for eliminating water pollution still resides in the states, the framework of a new national program was provided, with supervision of the States by the Environmental Protection Agency, and the Federal control responsibility was extended from interstate waters to all U.S. waters. The Federal government was granted power to seek court injunctions against polluters creating health hazards or endangering livelihood, and Federal aid to local governments to build sewage-treatment facilities was provided.

The specifics of the 1972 Amendments relate to industrial and municipal pollution, the setting of water-quality standards, licensing discharges into the nation's waters, and to the enforcement provisions.

Industrial Pollution

The law set deadlines for actions to control water pollution from industrial sources:

1. Industries discharging pollutants into the nation's waters must use the "best practicable" water-pollution control technology by July 1, 1977, and the "best available" technology by July 1, 1983.
2. EPA must issue guidelines for "best practicable" and "best available" technologies for various industries by October 1973. The guidelines can be adjusted by several factors, including the cost of pollution control, the age of the industrial facility, the process used, and the environmental impact (other than on water quality) of the controls. EPA also has to identify pollution-control measures for completely eliminating industrial discharges.
3. By May 1974 new sources of industrial pollution must use the "best available demonstrated control technology." This will be defined by EPA in the form of "standards of performance" for various industries no later than May 1974. Where practicable, EPA may require no discharge at all of pollutants from new industrial facilities.
4. Discharges of toxic pollutants will be controlled by effluent standards to be issued by EPA no later than

January 1974. EPA is required to provide an ample margin of safety in setting effluent standards for toxic pollutants. EPA is also empowered to prohibit discharges of toxic pollutants, in any amount, if deemed necessary. EPA had already established, under earlier water-pollution control legislation, strict limits on the discharge of such toxic pollutants as lead and mercury. The new law strengthened control of toxic pollutant discharges.

5. Discharge into the nation's waters of any radiological, chemical, or biological warfare materials or high-level radioactive waste was prohibited.

6. Any industry that discharges its wastes into a municipal treatment plant was required to pretreat its effluent so that the industrial pollutants do not interfere with the operation of the plant or pass through the plant without adequate treatment. This requirement takes effect no later than May 1974 for new industrial sources of pollution and no later than July 1976 for existing industrial facilities.

7. The law also authorized loans to help small businesses meet water-pollution control requirements. The loan program is designed for firms that would be likely to suffer "substantial economic injury" unless they receive financial assistance to comply with the law. EPA was required to issue regulations for the loan program in April 1973. The loans will be made by the Small Business Administration, after EPA certification of the proposed controls.

Municipal Pollution

The law also provided for more Federal aid to local governments and set deadlines for stronger control measures:

1. Federal construction grants of up to $18 billion were authorized between 1972 and 1975 to help local governments build needed sewage-treatment facilities, with payment to extend over a nine-year period. However, half these funds were withheld in 1972–73 by the Nixon administration.

2. An additional $2.75 billion in Federal grants was authorized to reimburse local governments for treatment plants built earlier in anticipation of Federal aid.

3. The Federal share of the cost of local treatment facilities is now 75 percent, with state and local governments paying the balance. The maximum federal share was 55 percent under previous legislation. The law also established an Environmental Financing

Authority to help state and local governments raise their share of the cost of treatment facilities.

4. In order to qualify for a Federal construction grant, sewage-treatment plants approved before June 30, 1974, must provide a minimum of secondary treatment. After that date, Federal grants may be made only to plants that will use "best practicable" treatment.

5. All sewage-treatment plants in operation on July 1, 1977—whether or not built with the aid of a Federal grant, and no matter when built—must provide a minimum of secondary treatment. Exception: A plant being built with the help of a Federal grant that was approved before June 30, 1974, must comply with the secondary-treatment requirement within four years, but no later than June 30, 1978.

6. Also by July 1, 1977, all sewage-treatment plants must apply whatever additional, more stringent, effluent limitations that may be established by EPA or a state to meet water-quality standards, treatment standards, or compliance schedules.

7. All publicly owned waste-treatment plants—whether or not built with the aid of a Federal grant, and no matter when built—will have to use "best practicable" treatment by July 1, 1983.

8. Areawide waste-treatment management plans are to be established by July 1976 in urban industrial areas with substantial water-pollution problems. Federal grants of up to $300 million are authorized between 1972 and 1975 to help areawide agencies develop and operate integrated water-pollution control programs.

9. In order to be eligible for a Federal construction grant after July 1976, a waste-treatment plant in one of these urban industrial areas must be part of, and in conformity with, the areawide plan.

Water-Quality Standards

The law continued and expanded the water-quality standards program initiated under earlier legislation. Water-quality standards define, of course, the uses of specific bodies of water—such as public water supply, propagation of fish and wildlife, recreation, and agricultural and industrial water supply. The standards also include "criteria" based on those uses and a plan to implement and enforce the criteria. The standards must protect public health and welfare and enhance water quality. The new standards program will operate as follows:

1. Water-quality standards previously established by states for interstate waters, subject to EPA approval, remain in effect unless they are not consistent with the objectives of the old law.
2. The states must now also adopt water-quality standards for intrastate waters and submit them to EPA for approval by April 1973. EPA is required to set standards for intrastate waters if the states fail to do so.
3. If a state finds that the use of "best practicable" or "best available" controls are not adequate to meet water-quality standards, more stringent controls must be imposed. To this end, the states must establish the total maximum daily load of pollutants, including heat, that will not impair propagation of fish and wildlife. EPA will identify pollutants for which maximum daily loads might be set.
4. EPA is required to submit a report to Congress by January 1, 1974, on the quality of the nation's waters. The report must identify water bodies that, in 1973, met the 1983 goal of water quality adequate for swimming and for the protection and propagation of fish and wildlife. The report must also identify water bodies that might achieve the 1983 goal by 1977, 1983, or any later date. The report will also include an inventory of sources of water pollution.
5. The states are required to submit to EPA similar reports each year on the quality of bodies of water within their borders. The first report is due by January 1, 1975.
6. EPA is required to submit the state water-quality reports to Congress each year, along with its own analyses, beginning no later than October 1, 1975.
7. At least once every three years the states must hold public hearings to review their water-quality standards and, if necessary, update the standards subject to EPA approval.

Permits and Licenses

The 1972 law also established a new system of permits for discharges into the nation's waters, replacing the 1899 Refuse Act permit program. No discharge of any pollutant from any point source is permitted without a permit, and publicly owned sewage-treatment plants and municipally controlled discharge points as well as

industrial discharges must obtain permits. The permit program operates as follows:

1. Until March 1973, EPA or a state with an existing permit program deemed adequate by EPA was able to issue permits for discharges. State permits issued during that period were subject to EPA veto.
2. EPA had to issue guidelines for state permit programs by the end of 1972 and was to approve by March 1973 state permit programs that meet those guidelines.
3. After a state permit program goes into effect, EPA will retain the right, unless waived, to review and approve any permit that affects another state. EPA will also have authority, unless waived, to review proposed permits to determine whether they meet the requirements of the new Federal legislation.
4. A state's permit program is subject to revocation by EPA, after a public hearing, if the state fails to implement the law adequately.
5. The Army Corps of Engineers retains authority to issue permits for the disposal of dredge-and-fill material in specified disposal sites, subject to EPA veto of disposal sites if the discharge will have an adverse effect on municipal water supplies, fishery resources, or recreation.
6. Disposal of sludge from sewage-treatment plants into water bodies or on land where it affects water quality is prohibited except under a permit issued by EPA. After EPA establishes regulations for issuing sludge-disposal permits, a state may take over the permit program if it meets EPA requirements.
7. Anyone applying for a Federal license or permit for any activity that might produce discharges into the nation's waters must obtain certification from the state involved that the discharge will be in compliance with the new law. States must give public notice of all applications for certification and may hold public hearings on certification applications.
8. If a certification by one state will result in a discharge that may affect water quality in another state, a public hearing must be held by the Federal agency that issues the license or permit, if requested by the second state. If the permit or license will result in discharges that are not in compliance with water-quality requirements, the license or permit cannot be issued.

Enforcement

The law eliminates the earlier time-consuming system of abatement conferences and hearings to compel compliance with water-pollution control regulations. Stringent enforcement machinery, with heavy penalities, now exists to speed compliance with the law. For example:

1. EPA has emergency power to seek an immediate court injunction to stop water pollution that poses "an imminent and substantial endangerment" to public health, or that endangers someone's livelihood.

2. Polluters must keep proper records, install and use monitoring equipment, and sample their discharges.

3. EPA has the power to enter and inspect any polluting facility, to check its records and monitoring equipment, and to sample its discharges. A state may assume this authority if approved by EPA.

4. Except for trade secrets, any information obtained by EPA or a state about a polluter's discharges must be made available to the public.

5. EPA may enforce permit conditions and other requirements of the law by issuing administrative orders that are enforceable in court, or by seeking court action.

6. Penalties for violating the law range from a minimum of $2,500 to a maximum of $25,000 per day and up to one year in prison for the first offense, and up to $50,000 a day and two years in prison for subsequent violations.

7. Any citizen or group of citizens whose interests may be adversely affected has the right to take court action against anyone violating an effluent standard or limitation, or an order issued by EPA or a state, under the law. Any citizen or group also has the right to take court action against EPA should EPA fail to carry out mandatory requirements of the law.

8. The 1972 law extends the oil-pollution control, liability, and enforcement provisions of earlier legislation to other "hazardous substances." These are defined as substances that "present an imminent and substantial danger to the public health or welfare, including, but not limited to, fish, shellfish, wildlife, shorelines, and beaches."

9. Finally, to assist in enforcement as well as to measure the effectiveness of the water-pollution control program, a national surveillance system to monitor water quality will be established by EPA in cooperation with other Federal agencies and state and local governments, to extend the present 20 percent coverage of the nation's streams provided in the past by the Federal Water Quality Administration, the U.S. Geological Survey, and the states into a complete monitoring and surveillance network.

STANDARD SETTING: THE CORE OF WATER-RESOURCES POLICY

Clearly, the process of standard-setting lies at the core of the planning and control system envisaged in the Federal Water Pollution Control Act Amendments of 1972. How are such standards set, given the broad goals relating to swimming, aquatic life, and the banning of discharges? What are the issues that arise in standard setting?

To answer the first question, the next section reproduces part of a planning report on the Delaware Estuary completed by the Federal Water Quality Control Administration in 1966 (preserving intact all of the "federalese" that characterizes such reports) to illustrate what is involved in both development of standards and in related cost-benefit analysis. This example of the "classical" approach in the United States is followed by a discussion of the assumptions implicit in standard-setting of the kind illustrated (the "technological"), as well as some of the differences that arise if, as with the 1972 Amendments, an alternative "ecological" view is used.

The Delaware Estuary Study: Determination of Objectives

According to the planning report issued by the Federal Water Quality Control Administration in 1966, the process of establishing water-use and water-quality objectives for the Delaware Estuary was as follows: first to investigate all feasible water uses; second, to determine water-quality criteria to assure these uses; and last, to assign water-quality goals to the various sections of the estuary according to where the uses were designated. The controlling factor in this procedure was the feasibility of making reaches of the estuary suitable for each of the uses.

Literally thousands of combinations of uses versus location could have been investigated for the estuary; but obviously a different approach had to be worked out to limit the number of alternatives. The method was to elicit a realistic range of water-use objectives from the people of the region as represented on a Water Use Advisory Committee (WUAC). Through this committee, discussions were held concerning possible swimming areas, desirable fishing locations, community desires on withdrawal of water from the estuary, and industrial desires as to water use. The committee was also asked to suggest quality criteria for the various water uses.

Based on this work of the WUAC, the alternatives were reduced to five sets of possible water-use and associated water-quality objectives. Even among these five objectives, different combinations of uses could be devised. It was felt, however, that the five objective sets ranging from maximum feasible enhancement of the river under present technology down to maintenance of present levels of use and quality would provide a sufficient span so that a final set of use/quality objectives could be chosen. The final objective need not be any one of the individual sets but could be composed of various features from each of the objective sets. For each set, the costs were evaluated and the benefits were described and, where possible, also quantitatively evaluated. Hence, through a healthy decision-making process taking full advantage of all available technical information throughout the discussions, a final set of use/quality objectives could be established. The information flow in this process is depicted in the diagram in Figure 7.1.

Thus, the water-use and water-quality goals used in the development of a water-pollution control program for the estuary were ascertained through a technical, quasi-political

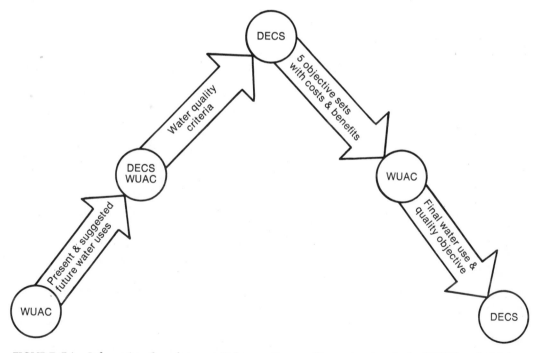

FIGURE 7.1. Information flow between Delaware Estuary Comprehensive Study (DECS) and Advisory Committees.

decision-making process involving the community of water users and water-pollution control administrators in the region.

The five water use/quality objective sets that resulted are as follows:

Objective Set I. This set represents the greatest increase in water use and water quality among all of the objective sets. Water-contact recreation is indicated in the upper and lower reaches of the estuary. Sport and commercial fishing was set at relatively high levels consistent with the makeup of the region. A minimum daily average DO goal of 6.0 mg/liter is included for anadromous fish passage during the passage periods. Thus anadromous fish passage is included as a definitive part of the water-quality management program. Fresh water inflow control will be necessary to repulse high chloride concentrations to Chester, Pa., thereby creating a potential municipal and industrial water-supply use.

Objective Set II. The area of water-contact recreation is reduced somewhat from that of objective set I (OS-I). A reduction in dissolved oxygen (DO) is considered to result in a concomitant reduction in sport and commercial fishing. DO goals for anadromous fish passage remain as in OS-I. Chloride control would be necessary to prevent salt-water intrusion above the Schuylkill River.

Objective Set III. This set is similar in all respects to OS-II except for the following three changes. First, the specific DO criteria for anadromous fish passage is not imposed. However, substantial increases in anadromous fish passage will result from the treatment requirements imposed to control DO during the summer assuming that the waste load reductions are carried out during the anadromous fish run periods. Second, a general decrease in the sport and commercial fishing potential is imposed through a lowering of the DO requirements. Third, the quality at points of municipal water supply were reduced.

Objective Set IV. This set represents a slight increase over present levels in water-contact recreation and fishing in the lower reaches of the estuary. Generally, quality requirements are increased slightly over 1964 conditions (OS-V) representing a minimally enhanced environment.

Objective Set V. This set represents a maintenance of 1964 conditions, i.e., a prevention of further water-quality deterioration.

The water uses protected by each objective set are presented graphically in Figure 7.2. This chart indicates the sections of the estuary for which the various water uses were considered. The associated water-quality goals for each objective set were selected on the basis of the designated uses in each section or group of sections. The most stringent criteria were selected where several uses were designated for the same section.

In all, twelve primary parameters were considered in the development of these objective sets:

1. Dissolved oxygen (DO) (mg/liter).
2. Chlorides (mg/liter).
3. Coliform bacteria (no. of organisms/100 ml).
4. Turbidity (turbidity units).
5. pH (pH units).
6. Total alkalinity (mg/liter).
7. Phenols (mg/liter).
8. Synthetic detergents (mg/liter).
9. Total hardness (mg/liter).
10. Temperature (mg/liter).
11. Floating debris, oils, grease.
12. Toxic chemicals.

The ranges and values of these parameters for each objective set are presented in Tables 7.5 to 7.9.

One general feature of these goals is that in no case is the objective for a water parameter less than present conditions. A noteworthy point is that each objective set specifies the reduction of floating oils, grease, debris, and potentially toxic chemicals to negligible levels. Another important feature is that levels of quality parameters specifically designated for seasonal water-use activities may also vary with the season. This is the case for parameters associated with water-contact recreation and anadromous fish passage.

Thus each objective set consists of a number of water uses designated at various locations in the estuary. Associated with each of these uses is a list of water-quality goals which, if achieved, will satisfy the quality needs of the water uses.

After the costs and benefits of the five objective sets were evaluated, the WUAC began the

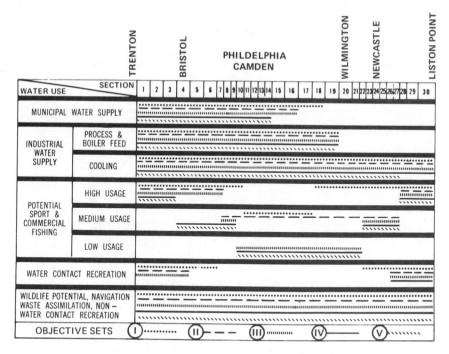

FIGURE 7.2. Water uses for objective sets I–V.

task of deciding on a final recommendation. This work required numerous meetings, discussions, and correspondence involving all members of each of the four subcommittees. If a member was not able to attend a subcommittee meeting, he was informed of all decisions and asked to make comments by letter. In the final analysis, each subcommittee chairman was able to arrive at a consensus which represented the general attitudes and desires of his group. The members of the WUAC then met and arrived at a consensus of OS-III as the committee's final recommendation.

During the final phases of the decision-making process, efforts were made to further clarify the differences between objective set II, objective set III, and present conditions (OS-V). One major concern was the deletion of anadromous fish passage as a definitive part of the water-quality management program in OS-III. Most persons agreed that a substantial increase in anadromous

fish passage would result from OS-III with the control of DO during the summer period. However, a more quantitative description of the differences between OS-II and OS-III with respect to anadromous fish passage was desired.

At this point, an intensive investigation of the waste-control programs of OS-II and OS-III as related to anadromous fish was carried out. The analyses utilized a time-varying computer simulation model of the estuary to forecast the DO profiles and time series under various flow conditions for oxygen-demanding loads for OS-II, OS-III, and OS-V. The analyses considered the passage period, the distribution of passage over time, and the estimated survival rates at different DO levels for both male and female fish. The results are shown in Figure 7.3 and summarized in Table 7.10.

Figure 7.3 shows that under present waste-loading conditions (OS-V) the estimated survival 24 out of 25 years is at least 20 percent; once out

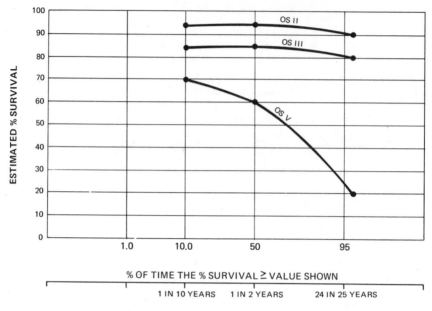

FIGURE 7.3.   Estimated total (male and female) upstream shad passage for OS-II, III, and V (present conditions).

of every two years at least 60 percent; and once out of ten years at least 65 percent. Under the waste-loading conditions envisioned for OS-III the estimated survival 24 in 25 years would be at least 80 percent; i.e., once in 25 years the survival would be less than 80 percent. This reveals that the estimated maximum difference of total shad passage between OS-II and OS-III is about 10 percent expected survival for both the 24-in-25-years case and in 1-in-10-year flow. A substantial increase in potential shad passage will occur with OS-III over OS-V. This increase in percent survival amounts to 60 percent for 24 out of 25 years.

Evaluating Alternative Programs to Achieve the Delaware Estuary Objectives

Given specification of the objectives, attention turned to the methods by which water quality might be improved. These include: (1) limiting effluent discharge to the estuary by requiring reduction of wastes before discharge, (2) piping of the wastes to a place or places where the discharges will have a reduced economic and/or social effect, (3) flow regulation, (4) removal of benthic sludge deposits, (5) in-stream aeration, and (6) control of storm-water discharges.

A successful comprehensive program to achieve a particular water-use and water-quality objective set might incorporate several of these possibilities but in the final analysis should depend primarily on reduction of waste at the source since this has a higher assurance of successful control. Piping of wastes creates chloride-control problems by diverting flow from the estuary and engenders new pollution problems in the discharge area. Maintenance of minimum flows has important chloride-control effects but does not significantly alter summer average dissolved-oxygen levels. However, transient releases of significant amounts of freshwater inflow can be beneficial in specific instances.

TABLE 7.5

Water-quality goals for objective set I

Quality[a,b]	Trenton	Bristol	Torresdale	Philadelphia Camden	Chester	Wilmington	New Castle	Liston Point
Section	1 2 3	4	5 6 7	8 9 10 11 12 13 14 15 16	16 17 18	19 20 21 22	23 24 25 26 27	28 29 30
Dissolved oxygen[c]	6.5		6.5	5.5 4.5	4.5 5.5	5.5 6.5	6.5 7.5	7.5
D.O.[i] 4/1–6/15 and 9/16–12/31	6.5							6.5
Chlorides[d]					50 250			
Coliforms (no./100 ml)	5,000[e]				5,000[e]	5,000[f]		5,000[f]
Coliforms 5/30–9/15	4,000[e]		4,000[e]	5,000[e]	5,000[e]	5,000[f]	4,000[e]	4,000[e]
Turbidity (Tu)	Natural levels + 30							Natural levels + 30
Turbidity 5/30–9/15			Natural levels	Natural levels + 30		Natural levels + 30	Natural levels	
pH[g] (pH Units)	6.5–8.5			6.5–8.5		6.5–8.5		6.5–8.5
pH[g] 5/30–9/15		7.0–8.5			7.0–8.5		7.0–8.5	
Alkalinity[g]	20–50		20–50	20–120			20–120	
Hardness[h]	95		95	150	150			
Temperature[g] (°F)	Present levels							Present levels
Phenols[h]	0.001				0.001	0.01		0.01
Syndets[h]	0.5				0.5	1.0		1.0
Oil and grease	Negligible							Negligible
Toxic substances	Negligible							Negligible

[a] mg/l unless specified. [b] Not less stringent than present levels. [c] Summer average. [d] Maximum 15-day mean. [e] Maximum level.
[f] Monthly geometric mean. [g] Desirable range. [h] Monthly mean. [i] Average during period stated.

209

TABLE 7.6

Water-quality goals for objective set II

Quality[a,b]	Trenton	Bristol	Torresdale	Philadelphia Camden	Chester	Wilmington	New Castle	Liston Point
Section	1	2 3 4	5 6 7	8 9 10 11 12 13 14	15 16 17 18	19 20 21 22	23 24 25 26	27 28 29 30
Dissolved oxygen[c]	5.5		5.5	4.0	4.0	5.0	5.0	6.5
D.O.[i] 4/1–6/15 and 9/16–12/31	6.5							6.5
Chlorides[d]				50	250			
Coliforms (no./100 ml.)	5,000[e]		5,000[e]	5,000[f]				5,000[f]
Coliforms 5/30–9/15	4,000[e]	4,000[e]	5,000[e]	5,000[f]			5,000[f]	4,000[e]
Turbidity (Tu)		Natural levels + 30					Natural levels + 30	
Turbidity 5/30–9/15	Natural levels		Natural levels + 30				Natural levels + 30	Natural levels
pH[g] (pH Units)	6.5–8.5		6.5–8.5					6.5–8.5
pH[g] 5/30–9/15	7.0–8.5		6.5–8.5				6.5–8.5	7.0–8.5
Alkalinity[g]	20–50		20–50	20–120			20–120	
Hardness[h]	95		95	150	150			
Temperature[g] (°F)		Present levels					Present levels	
Phenols[h]	0.001		0.001	0.005	0.005 .01			0.01
Syndets[h]	0.5		0.5	1.0				1.0
Oil and grease, floating debris	Negligible							Negligible
Toxic substances	Negligible							Negligible

[a] mg/l unless specified. [b] Not less stringent than present levels. [c] Summer average. [d] Maximum 15-day mean. [e] Maximum level.
[f] Monthly geometric mean. [g] Desirable range. [h] Monthly mean. [i] Average during period stated.

TABLE 7.7

Water-quality goals for objective set III

Quality[a,b]	Trenton	Bristol	Torresdale	Philadelphia Camden	Chester	Wilmington	New Castle	Liston Point
Section	1 2 3 4	4 5	5 6 7 8 9	10 11 12 13 14 15 16	16 17 18 19	20 21 22	22 23 24 25 26	26 27 28 29 30
Dissolved oxygen[c]	5.5		5.5 3.0			3.0 4.5	4.5 6.5	6.5 6.5
Chlorides[d]				50	250			
Coliforms (no./100 ml)	5,000[f]							5,000[f]
Coliforms 5/30–9/15		4,000[e]	5,000[f]				5,000[f] 4,000[e]	
Turbidity (Tu)		Natural levels + 30						Natural levels + 30
Turbidity 5/30–9/15		Natural levels	Natural levels + 30				Natural levels + 30 Natural levels	
pH[g] (pH Units)		6.5–8.5						6.5–8.5
pH[g] 5/30–9/15		7.0–8.5	6.5–8.5				6.5–8.5 7.0–8.5	
Alkalinity[g]		20–50	20–50 20–120				20–120	
Hardness[h]		95	95 150		150			
Temperature[g] (°F)		Present levels				Present levels		
Phenols[h]		0.001	0.001 0.005		0.005 0.01			0.01
Syndets[h]		1.0						1.0
Oil and grease		Negligible					Negligible	
Floating debris		Negligible					Negligible	
Toxic substances		Negligible					Negligible	
	1 2 3 4	5	6 7 8 9	10 11 12 13 14 15 16	17 18 19	20 21 22	23 24 25 26	27 28 29 30

[a] mg/l unless specified. [b] Not less stringent than present levels. [c] Summer average. [d] Maximum 15 day mean. [e] Maximum level.
[f] Monthly geometric mean. [g] Desirable range. [h] Monthly mean.

TABLE 7.8

Water-quality goals for objective set IV

Quality [a,b]	Trenton	Bristol	Torresdale	Philadelphia Camden	Chester	Wilmington	New Castle	Liston Point
Section	1	2 3 4	5 6 7	8 9 10 11 12 13 14 15 16	17 18 19	20 21 22	23 24 25 26 27 28	29 30
Dissolved oxygen [c]	4.0		4.0	2.5		2.5	3.5	5.5
Chlorides [d]				50 250				
Coliforms (no./100 ml)	5,000 [f]							5,000 [f]
Coliforms 5/30–9/15	5,000 [f]						5,000 [f]	4,000 [e]
Turbidity (Tu)		Natural levels + 30					Natural levels + 30	
Turbidity 5/30–9/15		Natural levels + 30			Natural levels + 30			Natural levels
pH [g] (pH Units)		6.5–8.5		Present levels	Present levels		6.5–8.5	6.5–8.5
pH [g] 5/30–9/15		6.5–8.5		Present levels	Present levels		6.5–8.5	7.0–8.5
Alkalinity [g]		20–50		Present levels			Present levels	
Hardness [h]		95		95 150				
Temperature [g] (°F)		Present levels			Present levels			
Phenols [h]		0.005		0.005 0.01				0.01
Syndets [h]		1.0						1.0
Oil and grease		Negligible					Negligible	
Floating debris		Negligible					Negligible	
Toxic substances		Negligible					Negligible	

[a] mg/l unless specified. [b] Not less stringent than present levels. [c] Summer average. [d] Maximum 15-day mean. [e] Maximum level. [f] Monthly geometric mean. [g] Desirable range. [h] Monthly mean.

212

TABLE 7.9

Present water quality for objective set V

Quality[a,b]	Trenton	Bristol	Torresdale	Philadelphia Camden	Chester	Wilmington	New Castle	Liston Point
Section	1 2 3	4 5	6 7	8 9 10 11 12 13 14 15	16 17 18 19	20 21 22	23 24 25 26 27 28	29 30
Dissolved oxygen[c]	7.0		5.8	1.0		1.0	4.2	7.1
D.O.[h] 4/1–6/15	10.0	8.9	8.7	5.8	4.9	4.3	5.3	7.7
D.O.[h] 9/16–12/31	9.0	7.6	6.0	0.9	4.5		8.1	9.5
Chlorides[d]			50	100, 250, 400	1,340	2,400		
Coliforms (1000/100 ml) — Max.	22	16	280	864, 490	460, 760	150	170	9.0
Coliforms (1000/100 ml) — G.M.	2.6	2.7	6.8	25, 63	66, 51	22	7	0.7
Coliforms[e] (1000/100 ml)	23	25	40	110, 380	300, 280	73	26	8.7
Turbidity[e] (Tu)	139	78	110	112, 105	83, 130	120	83	75
Turbidity[e] 5/30–9/15	23	28	29	24, 22	24, 27	27	37	43
pH[f] (pH Units)	7.0–8.2		6.9–7.6	6.6–7.4		5.5–7.2	5.2–6.6	6.1–7.0
pH[f] 5/30–9/15	7.0–8.7		6.9–7.6	6.6–7.3		6.4–7.0	5.6–7.6	6.1–7.8
Alkalinity[f]	25–51		33–46	34–50		13–41	4–25	10–49
Temperature[f]	35.6–86.0		34.7–86.0	37.4–84.2		34.7–84.2	35.2–83.8	
Phenols[g]	0.01	0.02	0.03	0.04, 0.03	0.05, 0.05	0.06		
Syndets[g]	0.20	0.24	0.32	0.41, 0.67	0.87, 0.94	0.90		
Hardness[g]	83			122	467			

[a] mg/l unless specified. [b] 1964 "Present conditions." [c] Summer average. [d] Maximum 15-day mean. [e] Maximum level. [f] Present range. [g] Monthly mean. [h] Average during period stated.

TABLE 7.10

Estimated total (male and female) upstream shad passage

	Minimum Percent Survival		
Recurrence Interval	1 in 10 Years	1 in 2 Years	24 in 25 Years
Objective Set			
OS–II	95	95	90
OS–III	85	85	80
Present: OS–V	65	60	20

Little is known of the practicability of the in-stream aeration of an estuary. The size of the operation may cause difficulties in terms of other uses of the estuary (i.e., navigation, recreation) and in any event would only improve DO without improving other water-quality parameters. In-stream aeration can be considered, however, as a transient supplement to effluent waste removal. Sludge removal and stormwater overflow control also fall into the category of supplemental control measures to be considered in conjunction with effluent control.

There are many ways of controlling the discharge of waste to the estuary to satisfy a specified water-quality objective. The problem is to choose a scheme that balances the apparent equity of the solution to the individual waste discharger, the economic cost to the region, and the means of administering the water-quality management program. Several different categories were investigated. All relate primarily to the control of waste sources to improve DO. If the control scheme to meet a specific DO objective did not meet all other variables (e.g., bacteria), separate control procedures (e.g., disinfection) were then imposed. The control programs investigated were:

1. *Uniform treatment.* Each waste discharger must remove the same percent of the "raw" load (the load before any waste reduction).
2. *Zoned-uniform treatment.* The estuary is divided into a series of zones and a uniform treatment level (same percentage reduction of the "raw" load) is found for each of the zones that will satisfy the DO goal at least cost to the region.
3. *Municipal-industrial category.* A uniform treatment level is found for all municipalities and another is found for all industries that will satisfy the DO objective at least cost to the region.
4. *Cost minimization.* This program computes the amount of waste to be removed at individual effluent sources so as to secure the DO objective at least cost to the region.

In all of these programs it was assumed that no source will discharge any more waste than is presently being discharged and that all sources which are now below primary treatment (35 percent) removal will be raised to at least that level.

Forty-four industries and municipalities, comprising approximately 97 percent of the 1964 carbonaceous oxygen-demand waste discharge to the estuary, were included in the evaluation of the alternative programs. The underlying systems on which these analyses were based are for steady-state flows of 3000 cfs at Trenton. Some additional estimates were made for flows of 4000 and 6000 cfs at Trenton. Best estimates of the decay, reaeration, and diffusion rates as well as other physical parameters were supplied by extensive investigation of the physical system. Waste loadings were based on the best estimates available and for the most part were based on actual sampling data. Estimates of costs to reduce waste loadings to the estuary were supplied cooperatively by most of the major dischargers. The dischargers were requested to reflect load increases for about a ten-year period (1975–1980) by estimating the cost of treatment to maintain certain levels of discharge through that time period.

Table 7.11 shows the estimated costs (construction cost plus the present value of operation and maintenance costs at a 3 percent discount rate and a 20-year time horizon) to reach the DO objectives under each of the alternative control programs. Table 7.12 shows the waste-reduction

TABLE 7.11

Summary of total costs (estimated in millions of 1964 dollars) of dissolved-oxygen objectives[a, b]
Flow at Trenton = 3,000 cfs

Obj. Set	Uniform Treatment			A-Zoned			B-Zoned			Municipal Industrial Category			Cost Minimization		
	Cap.[f]	O&M[g]	Total	Cap.	O&M	Total	Cap.	O&M	Total	Cap.	O&M	Total	Cap.	O&M	Total
I	180	280 (19.0)[c]	460[d]	180	280 (19.0)	460	180	280 (19.0)	460	180	280 (19.0)	460	180	280 (19.0)	460
II	135	180 (12.0)	315[e]	125	150 (10.0)	275	105	145 (10.0)	250	135	180 (12.0)	315	115	100 (7.0)	215
III	75	80 (5.5)	155[e]	55	75 (5.0)	130	50	70 (4.5)	120	75	45 (3.0)	120	50	35 (2.5)	85
IV	55	75 (5.0)	130	40	50 (3.5)	90	40	40 (2.5)	80	50	30 (2.0)	90	40	25 (1.5)	65

[a] Costs include cost of maintaining 1964 conditions.
[b] Costs reflect waste load conditions projected to 1975–1980.
[c] Annual operation and maintenance costs in millions of dollars/year.
[d] HISEC-TER (92–98 percent removal) for all waste sources for all programs. Includes in-stream aeration cost of $20 million.
[e] OS-II and OS-III for all programs include $1–2 million for either sludge removal or aeration to meet goals in sections 3 and 4.
[f] Capital costs.
[g] Operation and maintenance costs, discounted to present value at 3 percent—20 years.

requirements for reaching the DO objectives. The A-zone configuration is exactly the same as the present Delaware River Basin Commission zones in the estuary; zone A-1 extends from Trenton, N.J., to Pennypack Creek, zone A-II extends from Pennypack Creek to the Pennsylvania-Delaware state line, and zone A-III from the state line to Liston Point, Delaware. The B-zone configuration divides zone A-II into two zones: zone B-I extends from Trenton, N.J., to Pennypack Creek, zone B-II from Pennypack Creek to the confluence with the Schuylkill River, zone B-III from the Schuylkill to the Pennsylvania-Delaware state line, and zone B-IV from the state line to Liston Point, Delaware. These zones are shown on the map in Figure 7.4.

Since the waste-removal programs were based on DO improvement, the pH and bacterial objectives were not met in all cases. The additional cost of neutralization and chlorination in these cases was also calculated. However, the cost of additional reservoir storage for flow regulation to control chloride levels in the estuary is not included. Table 7.13 shows the total costs of the alternatives when the costs of chlorination and pH control are added.

The DO objective for objective set I can be reached only by 92–98 percent removal of all carbonaceous waste sources plus in-stream aeration and dredging of sludge deposits at an estimated cost of 460 million dollars. However, estimating the cost of removal above the 85–90 percent level is difficult, since only pilot tertiary treatment-plant data exist. Thus a program recommending 92–98 percent removal would require additional work on large-scale advanced treatment processes and costs.

TABLE 7.12

Summary of waste-reduction requirements to meet dissolved-oxygen objectives (percent removal based on 1964 waste loads)
Flow at Trenton = 3000 cfs

Obj. Set	Uniform Treatment		A-Zoned		B-Zoned		Municipal Industrial Category		Cost Minimization	
	No. of Waste Sources Involved	Minimum[a] Treatment (Computed % Removal)	No. of Waste Sources Involved	Minimum[a] Treatment (Computed % Removal)	No. of Waste Sources Involved	Minimum[a] Treatment (Computed % Removal)	No. of Waste Sources Involved	Minimum[a] Treatment (Computed % Removal)	No. of Waste Sources Involved	Treatment[b] Range (Computed % Removal)
I	22M-22I[c]	HISEC-TER (92-98%)[d]	22M-22I	All Zones HISEC-TER (92-98%)[d]	22M-22I	All Zones HISEC-TER (92-98%)[d]	22M-22I	HISEC-TER (92-98%)[d]	22M-22I	HISEC-TER (92-98%)[d]
II	22M-22I	HISEC-TER[e] (90%)	1M-1I	A-I-SEC[e] (85%)	1M-1I	B-I-SEC[e] (85%)	22M	Municipal HISEC-TER (90%)	15M-16I	PRIM to TER[e] (35-98%)
			14M-14I	A-II-HISEC-TER (90%)	5M-4I	B-II-SEC (85%)	22I	Industrial HISEC-TER (90%)		
			4M-6I	A-III-SEC (85%)	9M-10I	B-III-HISEC-TER (90%)				
					4M-6I	B-IV-SEC (85%)				
III	15M-20I	SEC[e] (75%)	1M-1I	A-I-SEC[e] (85%)	1M-1I	B-I-SEC[e] (85%)	17M	Municipal SEC (85%)	9M-10I	PRIM to SEC[e] (35-85%)
			11M-14I	A-II-SEC (80%)	2M-4I	B-II-INT-LS (70%)	16I	Industrial HIPRIM (45%)		
			4M-4I	A-III-HI-PRIM-LI (50%)	7M-10I	B-III-SEC (80%)				
					4M-4I	B-IV-HI PRIM-LI (50%)				

	Sources [c]	Treatment level [a,b]
IV	14M-19I	INT-LS (70%)
	1M-1I	A-I-SEC (85%)
	9M-14I	A-II-INT-LS (70%)
	0M-1I	A-III-PRIM (35%)
	1M-1I	B-I-SEC (85%)
	5M-4I	B-II-SEC (80%)
	7M-7I	B-III-INT-LS LS (60%)
	0M-1I	B-IV-PRIM (35%)
	17M	Municipal SEC (80%)
	5I	Industrial PRIM (35%)
	7M-10I	PRIM to SEC (35-85%)

[a] Minimum treatment required by solution but not below present treatment level.
[b] Treatment range is for all 44 sources. Sources not in solution remain at present level.
[c] M = municipal waste source, I = industrial waste source (total number of sources used = 44).
[d] Also requires additional control measure such as stream aeration.
[e] Requires aeration or sludge removal to meet DO goal in sections 3 and 4.

217

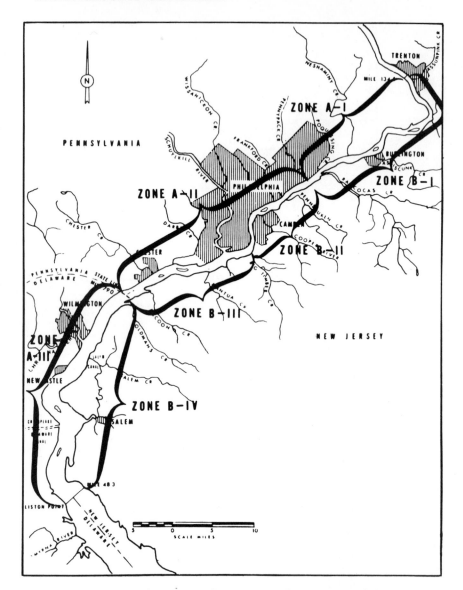

FIGURE 7.4.   A-zone and B-zone configuration used for evaluation of alternative programs.

The costs of attaining the other objective sets differ, owing to the type of program used. In OS-II and OS-III about 1 to 2 million dollars were necessary for stream aeration in some upper sections to cope with natural undesirable quality conditions. Many sources would have to make improvements to keep their present level of discharge, as is required for objective set V. This cost is approximately 30 million dollars. Five sources must raise their treatment to primary

TABLE 7.13

Estimated total costs of objective sets (millions of dollars)
Flow at Trenton = 3,000cfs

OS		Uniform	A-Zoned	B-Zoned	Municipal-Industrial	Minimization
I	DO Cost[c]	460	460	460	460	460
	Bact.	30	30	30	30	30
	Total	490	490	490	490	490
II	DO Cost[c]	315	275	250	315	215
	Bact.	20	20	20	20	20
	Total	335	295	270	335	235
III	DO Cost[c]	155	130	120	120	85
	Bact.	20	20	20	20	25[a]
	pH	—	15[b]	15[b]	25[b]	25[b]
	Total	175	165	155	165	135
IV	DO Cost[c]	130	90	80	90	65
	Bact.	15	15	15	15	20[a]
	pH	—	15	15	15	15[b]
	Total	145	120	110	120	100

[a] To meet bacterial goals, additional chlorine dosages needed by several sources not in DO program.

[b] To meet pH goals, pH control needed by several sources not in DO program.

[c] Other water-use goals (except chlorides) assumed to be met by DO, pH, and bacterial control measures. Chloride goal requires freshwater flow regulation. Meeting the phenol goal for OS-I in sections 18–22 may require supplemental phenol control measures. All DO costs include $30 million cost of maintaining OS-V.

treatment at a total cost of 10 million dollars. These costs of maintaining existing conditions are included in the tables.

Studies of these alternatives at different steady fresh-water inflows showed changes in costs as the flow increased. Under certain water-quality objectives and types of waste-reduction program the cost of achieving the DO goal was higher at 6000 cfs than at 3000 cfs. This is basically due to a "shift" in the DO profile, requiring certain waste sources to remove additional amounts of waste load at a subsequent additional cost.

If an assured high level (90–95 percent survival) of anadromous fish passage is desired, while all other water uses are satisfied by OS-III quality goals, DO levels must be raised to OS-II goals approximately six months of the year. It is

estimated that for 50 percent of the years, this requirement could be met by fresh-water inflow controls. At most, the level of this augmentation would be about 10,000 cfs for 30 days. The other 50 percent of the years, the DO objectives could be met in either of two ways: (1) in-stream aeration at an estimated total cost (OS-III, B-zone + assured anadromous fish passage) of 145 million dollars or (2) by requiring waste-reduction facilities that are sufficiently flexible to enable operation at OS-II levels during the critical periods and at OS-III levels during the rest of the time at a cost (OS-III, B-zone + assured anadromous fish passage) of 195 million dollars.

The cost of piping wastes out of the study area was also investigated. Two problems are apparent in the design. The first is that not enough is known of the Delaware Bay environment to assure that the piping of wastes to that area would not create new pollution problems; thus more time and money would have to be spent to determine the outfall location. An undesignated area off the coast of New Jersey was therefore used for design purposes.

Second, when ocean disposal is considered, a pipeline would divert flow from the estuary which would normally help control chlorides. This would result in an additional cost for chloride control in the form of additional storage in upstream reservoirs. Table 7.14 presents the capital costs for chloride control as well as for piping of all wastes to the ocean. No estimates have been made of additional costs incurred by the increased pollution load in the ocean disposal area.

TABLE 7.14

Capital costs for attainment of objectives
(millions of dollars)

Obj. Set	Estimated Diverted Flow[a] (cfs)	Piping of Wastes Out of the Estuary			Waste Removal at the Source
		Piping	Chloride Control[b]	Total	
I	1200	125	40	165	180
II	1150	120	35	155	115
III	800	90	25	115	50
IV	650	65	20	85	40

[a] It is assumed that industrial waste streams will be separated to allow cooling water to return to the stream.
[b] Estimated capital cost of additional storage necessary to counteract effects of diverted flow.

Table 7.14 indicates that for OS-IV, III, and II, waste reduction at the source appears to be less costly on a capital-construction basis. For OS-I, the piping alternative becomes more attractive than waste reduction at the source. This is a reflection of the relatively high treatment costs to achieve 92–98 percent removal of oxygen-demand material.

In many regional studies, economies of scale may be obtained by having many small waste dischargers send their wastes to a more efficient regional treatment plant. To a large extent this has already been carried out in that part of the Delaware amenable to consolidation. On the Pennsylvania side, all of the City of Philadelphia, some surrounding municipalities, and many industries along the river in the area, comprising 40 percent of the waste discharges to the estuary, are served by the City of Philadelphia's three treatment plants. The Wilmington-New Castle County waste-treatment plant serves all of the Wilmington metropolitan area and the major portion of New Castle County. The refineries clustered around the Schuylkill and along the Pennsylvania side may, because of the nature of their wastes, find it difficult to discharge to a municipal plant or even to a regional industrial waste-treatment unit. The many small communities in the residential complex around Camden, N.J., and in the vicinity of Marcus Hook and Chester, Pa., would benefit from a regional treatment plant. The industrial waste discharges consist of a relatively few large waste sources at some distance from one another, thus precluding a regional industrial treatment plant.

Rough estimates of the total cost (including capital and operation and maintenance) of reaching the various DO objectives by mechanical aeration based on the scale-up of pilot plant data are shown in Table 7.15.

TABLE 7.15

Estimated total cost to reach DO objectives by mechanical aeration

Objective Set	Cost (millions of dollars)
I	70
II	40
III	12
IV	10

It should be noted that this meets DO objectives only, and additional expense would be necessary to meet other parameter objectives. Since a large-scale in-stream aeration such as would be required for the Delaware has never been attempted, considerable study would have to be devoted to the feasibility of the size of the system that is required. It is anticipated that some problems may also develop in interferences with navigation and recreation as well as the creation of nuisance conditions (foaming, etc.).

If the waste loadings to the stream that are prescribed for each objective set are held constant, that particular objective set will always be maintained. For a particular water-quality objective set, the allowable waste discharges vary with the type of a waste-reduction program chosen to obtain a solution. Some average estimates, however, can be computed; these are shown in Table 7.16. The geographical distribution of the allowable load is extremely important in achieving the specific objective.

TABLE 7.16

Average allowable carbonaceous oxygen demand

Objective Set	Discharges per Day
V	950,000
IV	520,000–670,000
III	450,000–520,000
II	150,000–220,000
I	100,000

Obviously, if the total load were all discharged in one location, an entirely different water-quality response would result than if the load were equally distributed along the length of the estuary.

The costs shown in Table 7.11 for achieving the various objectives show estimates of costs of maintaining these discharges for the time period up to 1975–1980. Estimates of future loadings based on economic projections show a substantial increase in waste production in the estuary. To maintain the objective under these increased waste loadings will increase the program cost. To maintain the objectives from 1975 to 1985, it

is estimated that the region would have to spend an additional 5.0 to 7.5 million dollars per year.

By 1975, overall treatment levels to maintain OS-IV would approach 80 percent, for OS-III about 90 percent, and for OS-II 93 percent. By 2010, the estimates of waste loadings before treatment or reduction are so large that 96–99 percent waste removal will be necessary to maintain the objectives. An estimate of the treatment costs for that time would be misleading for several reasons. First, as waste-removal requirements to meet the necessary levels of discharge become more stringent and expensive, alternatives such as piping of wastes out of the critical areas (see Table 7.14), water recycling and reuse, and in-stream aeration may become more economically feasible alternatives. Second, some industrial waste sources faced with discharge limits might turn to in-plant changes, adopt more efficient processes made possible by advanced technology, or perhaps shift production to products which create less waste load in their manufacture.

Thus, the means by which the objective selected will be maintained will be largely a function of the future economic alternatives. At present the reduction of waste at the sources appears to be the least expensive and most feasible alternative. By 1985–1990 additional treatment to maintain an objective may be more expensive than some other schemes, and a new look may be needed at the various alternatives available at that time.

Benefits of the Alternative Programs

Intuitively, numerous benefits are derived from water-quality enhancement programs. These are realized by a more economic utilization of natural resources, preservation of fish and wildlife, and protection of the region's health and welfare. The value placed upon such general items rests on the judgment of society at large. These intangible items, in essence, provided the impetus for the comprehensive study of the Delaware Estuary. Therefore, one of the basic goals of the Delaware Estuary Study was to better define and quantify the benefits of enhancing water quality in the Delaware Estuary.

Quantification of the benefits is an essential part of any engineering feasibility study. However, in the water-pollution control field, the "state-of-the-art" is new, and much methodology is currently being formulated. The Delaware Estuary Study did proceed, however, with an analysis of quantifying the benefits for several water uses and for each of the objective sets. It was not expected that *all* the benefits could be quantified: certain intangibles will always remain, calling for value judgments based on the costs of achievement and the qualitative social goals of improvement in quality.

For example, in several complex areas, such as water-treatment technology, until further basic research is done which correlates the physico-chemical treatment procedures with the quality of the raw water sources, the benefits will remain unquantifiable. The major source of municipal supply that may benefit from improved quality is the Torresdale Water Treatment Plant of Philadelphia. The fact that this plant is able to produce a potable water from an estuarine source of the present quality at a relatively low cost obscures the benefits picture for water supply. It is probable that the net monetary benefits in terms of dollar savings in treatment costs at Philadelphia's Torresdale Plant will be relatively small at the alternative levels of water-quality enhancement. What may result, however, after pollution abatement is carried out, will be a reduction in the taste and odor problems and therefore an increase in Philadelphia's ability to produce a more palatable drinking water.

The estimation of industrial water-quality benefits is a complex process influenced by many factors. Among industrial plants, variations in operating policy, type of construction, method of water use, and degree of water treatment must all be considered.

In an attempt to account for these factors, information was obtained from the major water-using industries along the estuary. Data were received on the cost effect of variation of dissolved oxygen and chloride levels in the intake water. These two variables were found to be the most important quality parameters to industrial water users. In most industrial plants, the chain of cause-and-effect relationships linking river water and monetary savings had not been previously quantified. In spite of the difficulty of such estimates, a number of positive replies were received; many of the nonzero responses were in the petroleum-refining, chemical-industry, and paper-products categories. Other industries, such as the electric power utilities, indicated no effect for the quality characteristics.

The information supplied by these industries was used to compute statistical estimates of benefits (or costs) for the major water-using industries, including those unable to determine their own cost response. For this latter group the annual benefit (dollars per year) was considered to depend on the following variables:

1. Dissolved oxygen or chloride level, each a function of the objective set.
2. Location.
3. Quantity of estuarine intake water.
4. Industrial type.
5. Type of use.

In terms of location, benefits (or costs) are considered to accrue only in those areas of the estuary exhibiting significant dissolved oxygen increase or chloride depression. These areas are determined primarily by the objective sets.

Response-surface analyses were carried out to obtain the statistically best estimate of annual benefit given the input variables for any industry. The total benefit in annual terms is then the sum of individual industry values, where some are based on original interview data and others on the statistical estimates derived from the response surfaces. In all cases the benefits (costs) represent a dollar value which would accrue as a result of steady-state (long-term) conditions. The inputs are assumed to be relatively stable at the levels indicated by the objective sets over a number of years, with the exception of water use. The latter experiences a secular increase over time projected, as shown in Figure 7.5. The estimated present (1964) values of the benefits (costs) of achieving new dissolved oxygen levels are shown in Figure 7.6. It will be noted that increased DO results in increased cost (or negative benefits). This is primarily due to increased corrosion rates at the higher oxygen levels.

The benefits derived from chloride control were not related as such to a pollution-abatement program. Rather these benefits would result only if the required flows were released from proposed Corps of Engineers' reservoirs. Thus chloride costs and benefits cannot be compared

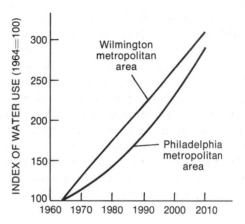

FIGURE 7.5.   Index of industrial self- supplied water use from surface sources.

to other costs and benefits contained in this report. It is estimated in a report by the Federal Water Pollution Control Administration to the Corps of Engineers entitled, "Water Quality

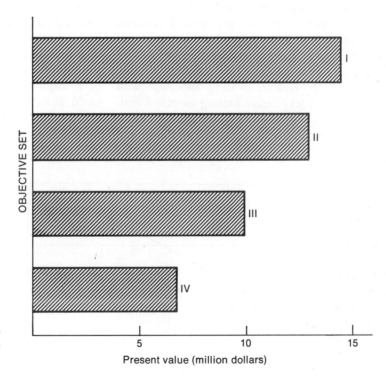

FIGURE 7.6. Industrial dissolved-oxygen incremental negative benefit (cost) in 1964 dollars.

Control Study—Tocks Island Reservoir— Delaware River Basin," June 1966, that a minimum regulated flow of about 4000 cfs at Trenton would meet the chloride goals of objective sets II and III. This flow would be achieved under the present up-basin reservoir plan and would result in a benefit to industrial water users of almost $4 million per year. An additional 2200 cfs (to a total minimum regulated flow of 6200 cfs) would be required to meet the chloride goal of OS-I. It is estimated that this would have a direct new quantifiable benefit of $2 million per year over and above the $4 million per year of OS-II and OS-III.

The quantifiable monetary benefits associated with increasing recreational possibilities in the Delaware Estuary were estimated as part of a cooperative study by the Delaware Estuary Study and the Bureau of Outdoor Recreation (BOR) and through a contractual study being carried out by the Institute for Environmental Studies (IES), University of Pennsylvania.

The general types of recreational activities considered include swimming, boating, and sport fishing. Recreational boating was further broken down into three subuses: (a) pleasure boating, (b) pleasure boating associated with fishing, and (c) pleasure boating associated with fishing and water-contact recreation. The benefits of other activities such as picnicking and sightseeing result from an improved aesthetic surrounding and are nonquantifiable. Sport fishing for shad in the Delaware Basin above Trenton, N.J., was also included, since the quality of the estuary directly affects the supply of this activity.

The analyses estimated the net dollar benefits that would accrue in the 1975–80 period from increased recreational possibilities for each of the objective sets over present conditions. This was accomplished in general by (1) estimating the total recreation demand in the Delaware Estuary region by applying average national participation rates to the region's present and projected population, (2) estimating the maximum capacity of the estuary under each of the objective sets, (3) estimating the part of the total demand expected to be fulfilled by the estuary, and (4) applying monetary unit values to the estimated total participation demand in the estuary to arrive at total estimated recreation benefits.

Figure 7.7 presents the estimated present and projected recreational demand in terms of "activity-days" in the Delaware Estuary region. These results show a substantial demand for these types of recreational activities. The analyses have also shown that the estuary has the capacity of a major potential recreation resource and could absorb much of this total demand if water-quality conditions were improved and recreational parks, facilities, and access routes constructed.

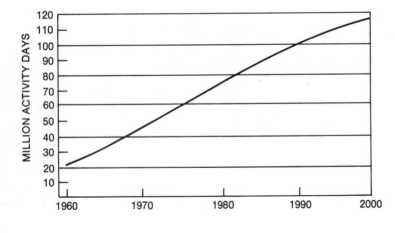

FIGURE 7.7. Estimated future recreation demand in the Delaware Estuary region.

The monetary benefits derived from increased recreational usage for each objective set depended on several factors and assumptions. The difficulty in specifying these factors is a result of the present state-of-the art in describing recreational benefits. Thus to avoid specifying a simple monetary value, which may be misleading, a range of values was computed. As additional information is generated by the Institute of Environmental Studies, better estimates of the recreational benefits will be available. However, it is expected that any new estimates will remain within the range of benefits reported herein.

The maximum and minimum values of the range of recreational benefits to 1975–80 were computed on the following basis:

1. *Water-contact recreation benefits*
   MAXIMUM: For the maximum net benefit for OS-I thru IV, negligible gross benefits are assumed for OS-V on the basis that no authorized water-contact reaction occurs in the estuary. Present quality conditions restrict improvement and construction of recreational facilities and access routes by Federal, state, and local agencies.
   MINIMUM: Water-contact recreation benefits are assumed to accrue under OS-V in an area of marginal water quality in the lower estuary.

2. *Boating-capacity estimates*
   MAXIMUM: 4 activity days per boat.
   MINIMUM: 2.5 activity days per boat.

3. *Monetary value per activity day* (based on guidelines presented in the document prepared by the Ad Hoc Water Resources Council, "Evaluation Standards for Primary Outdoor Recreation Benefits")
   MAXIMUM: 25 percent of usage per activity day. @ $5.00
   75 percent of usage per activity day. @ $1.25
   MINIMUM: 25 percent of usage per activity day. @ $3.00
   75 percent of usage per activity day. @ $0.75

In accordance with other economic calculations made in the study, the 1975–80 recreation benefits in terms of 1964 dollars are reported as Present Values calculated with an interest rate of

TABLE 7.17

Estimated recreational benefits (1975-1980) in millions of dollars (present value)

OS	Net Benefits[a]		Net Marginal Benefits	
	Max.	Min.	Max.	Min.
I	355	155		
			35	20
II	320	135		
			10	10
III	310	125		
			30	10
IV	280	115		

[a] Net benefits above OS-V.

3 percent and a time horizon of 20 years. The results of the analyses are presented in Table 7.17 and depicted on Figure 7.8. Benefits were ascertained by subtracting the value for OS-V from the gross values of the other objective sets. The net marginal benefits are of special importance, since they show the change in benefits between objective sets.

A study was also made to define and quantify the benefits that would accrue to the commercial fishing industry. Although the estuary proper no longer supports a substantial commercial fish harvest, its water quality does influence commercial fish production in adjacent areas.

For shad and other migratory fish, the estuary serves as a passage between their spawning grounds in fresh water and their primary habitat in the sea; it is a place of temporary residence possibly once or twice in a lifetime. For the menhaden the move is from the ocean into the lower portion of the study area, where they grow substantially during their two-to three-month stay. Finally, the study area is important to the large number of other species which spend most of their lives therein and are considered permanent residents.

When calculating benefits, a given species was considered to be benefically influenced by improved water quality if it must depend on water

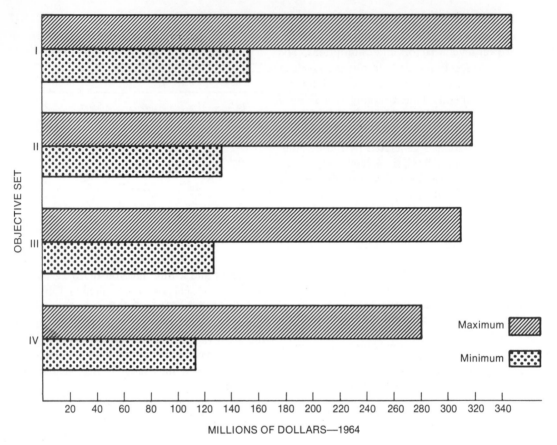

FIGURE 7.8.   Present value (1964) of recreation benefits from demand satisfied by the Delaware Estuary.

within the study area for survival at some period in its life cycle. The commercial fishery attributable to the study area contains three components: the menhaden, the shad, and a composite group of all other commercially harvested species. It is assumed that an increase in the volume of good-quality water will support an enlargement of the above fish populations, which, in turn, will be reflected in greater commercial fish harvests.

Menhaden are the basis of the largest commercial fishery in the United States. The Delaware and southern New Jersey fishing industry averages about $4,000,000 annually, of which approximately $1,400,000 is attributable to fish

from the Delaware. Virtually all menhaden caught are reduced to fish meal, condensed solubles, or oil. Most of the meal and condensed solubles are added to swine or poultry feed where they supply vitamins, minerals, and growth factors. Menhaden oil is used in paints, varnishes, and soaps and is also shipped to Europe, where it is used in manufacturing margarine.

As the water quality improves with each objective set, the volume of water inhabitable by menhaden will also increase. For this estimate, it was assumed that the dollar value of the catch attributable to the Delaware River would increase in proportion to the volumetric increase

TABLE 7.18

Estimated net commercial fishing benefits (present value, millions of dollars)

		Shad			Total	
	Menhaden	Unsuccessful Fishway	Successful Fishway	Other Finfish	Minimum	Maximum
OS-I	7.4	1.3	4.0	.3	9	12
OS-II	7.4	1.3	4.0	.2	9	12
OS-III	3.7	1.1	3.3	.2	5	7
OS-IV	1.9	.9	2.5	.1	3	5

in inhabitable water. The results are presented in Table 7.18.

Shad fishery benefits were calculated under two primary considerations: (1) the suggested fishway at the proposed Tocks Island Dam will not be successful, (2) the fishway will be successful or alternative spawning grounds will evolve. The proposed Tocks Island Dam will probably by a hindrance to the normal migration of shad to and from the principal spawning areas above the dam site. Because of this obstacle, it is the general opinion of biologists that shad spawning success will be considerably reduced in the Delaware River. When developing estimates of the shad fishery under the water-quality conditions represented by the different objective sets, the following items were considered: probable size of the attainable harvest, the effect of good fishery management, research into anticipated markets, opportunity to develop new markets, water quality under various flow and waste-load combinations, time of year and duration of the annual shad migration, and the dissolved oxygen tolerance of shad. The estimated value of the annual commercial shad harvest is given in Table 7.18.

In the final category of commercial fisheries are all the remaining species that are harvested on a commercial basis, such as croaker, striped bass, weakfish, blue fish, and white perch. The value of these fish caught within the study is quite small—of the order of $12,000 annually.

With pollution-abatement programs, new areas of good-quality water will be available and in turn should produce fish. The increased volume of good-quality water under various objective sets is reflected in the anticipated harvests for "other finfish" as given in Table 7.18.

It was anticipated that commercial fishing within the study area will be quite limited, primarily because of competing uses such as recreational boating, sport fishing, commercial shipping, and waste disposal. However, with improved water-quality conditions the lower portion of the study area will increase in value for its two most important functions: (1) a nursery area for juvenile fish and (2) an area with a very high production of aquatic organisms which serve directly and indirectly as food for fish which are harvested in abundance elsewhere.

Another type of benefit will result from the effect of the preceding quantifiable direct benefits on the regional economy. These benefits include (1) "induced" benefits that are realized by new or expanded activities in the region and, (2) secondary benefits that are realized by a large number of trade and service industries. These extra benefits are estimated to be in the range of at least 15 percent of the direct quantifiable benefits.

Numerous other uses, it was felt, would be improved as a result of increased water quality. The water-quality levels presented in the four objective sets would reduce the rate of delignification, corrosion, and cavitation of piers, wharfs, buoys, bridge abutments, and boat engines and hulls. Debris, silt, oils, and grease that settle and block channels and intake devices and clog cooling systems in boat engines would be reduced substantially. The dollar benefits attributable to these effects, however, remain undefined.

Another important benefit of increased water quality would be an improved aesthetic value of the river. Part of these benefits are reflected in the estimates of increased recreational value. However, these estimates do not include the increase in value of property adjacent to the estuary that will occur by providing a water course that is more aesthetically pleasing; nor do the quantifiable benefits include the enhancement of parks and picnic areas adjacent to this watercourse.

The benefit analyses above can be summarized as follows:

For objective set IV, which represents a relatively slight increase in water quality, the range of estimated increase in quantifiable benefits is 120 to 280 million dollars. As the objective is raised to set III, the estimated range in benefits is 130 to 310 million dollars. A further increase in water quality to objective set II results in a relatively small increase in benefits—140 to 320 million dollars. Finally, the water uses that are associated with objective set I are estimated to have a range of quantifiable benefits of 160 to 350 million dollars. Further insight is gained from these figures when the marginal benefits of achieving one objective set over another are compared to the marginal costs.

To go from OS-IV to OS-III would result in 10 to 30 million dollars in additional benefits, whereas the additional cost as reported in Table 7.13 of achieving OS-III over OS-IV is about 35 million dollars (assuming a cost minimization management procedure). An additional 10 million dollars in benefits would accrue if OS-II is achieved over OS-III; whereas 100 million dollars in additional expenditures would have to

be made. To obtain OS-I over OS-II, 255 million dollars more would have to be spent to obtain a 20- to 30-million-dollar increase in benefits.

It is apparent that once the water quality reaches a threshold level at which several important legitimate activities may or are assumed to occur, only a small amount of new benefits will result with any additional increase in water quality. For example, once the bacterial standard for water-contact recreation is obtained so that swimming and water skiing will be authorized, no further quantifiable benefits will result if the bacterial levels obtained are less than the standard. The important factor is that beaches and facilities may be improved and constructed and recreational usage will increase. What does result with lower bacterial levels in this case is a safety factor in obtaining and maintaining the goals; this, however, remains unquantifiable.

Another factor to be recognized is that quantifiable benefits are related not only to water quality (i.e., areas that may be used for a particular activity) but also the demand for a particular use. In other words, in certain cases the estuary under the objective sets has much more capacity than demand. It is assumed that for all water uses, no quantifiable benefits will accrue from unused capacity. Thus, there are no sport-fishing benefits unless there is a fisherman, no industrial benefits without water being pumped, no swimming benefits without a swimmer, and no boating benefits without a boater.

WATER-POLLUTION CONTROL VIA STANDARD-SETTING: TECHNOLOGICAL VS. ECOLOGICAL GOALS

In the view of many ecologists, the kind of standard-setting and cost-benefit analysis illustrated in the foregoing section involves the application of one of two internally coherent but mutually antipathetic philosophies, the *technological* and the *ecological*. Westman (1972) points out that although differences about water-quality standards are at face value simply an expression of different opinions as to the goals being sought, the controversies are usually rooted in fundamentally different methods of conceptualizing the nature and behavior of pollutants.

At their broadest, the goals sought in environmental policy may be classified into three groups:

I. *Economic*
   National economic efficiency
   Regional economic development
   Income redistribution
II. *Environmental*
   Minimum disruption of natural environment
III. *Social*
   Political equity
   Prestige
   Acceptability
   Well-being of people

The economic objectives include national economic efficiency, regional economic development, and income redistribution. National economic efficiency refers to the need to derive a net benefit from a water-resource program on a national scale. Emphasis in this case is placed on efficient use of federal funds. Regional economic development emphasizes resource development as an incentive to long-range improvement of a region's economy. These investments do not necessarily have to be efficient from a national standpoint. The third goal, income redistribution, while similar to regional economic development, emphasizes the short-range improvement of a region and involves the transfer of income from region to region.

The environmental objectives include minimum disruption of natural environment (preservation), environmental quality, aesthetics, and control of the natural environment. The preservation objective maintains that the "natural environment" should be maintained in its "original" state. The environmental-quality objective strives for optimum quality of the

natural environment. In this case, certain standards of quality can be met through manipulation of the environment. This stands in contrast to the preservation objective, which aims at the "primeval status quo." Aesthetics is a vague objective, the subjective expression of some value which is a measure of "good taste," such as the desire to avoid channelized rivers because of their sterile appearance. The final objective—controlling the natural environment—emphasizes man's role as the conqueror of natural forces. The major value perceived is that of manipulating nature for man's personal needs.

Social objectives include political equity, prestige, acceptability, and well-being of people. Political equity is generally a goal sought in allocating resource projects among competing political jurisdictions. It is necessary to reduce conflict to a minimum by giving each jurisdiction its proper share. Resource projects often serve as a source of prestige for a particular political unit. It is frequently of consequence for a state to possess a superlative resource project— say, the world's highest dam. Often planners will consider a pragmatic goal, acceptability, since it is a basic component of implementation. The final objective, the well-being of people, is an omnibus purpose which serves to protect interests that have no voice in decision-making and to provide general social equity.

The array of goals in a broad sense points out several interesting facts. The range, to begin with, is really quite large. Each goal represents a set of values which decision-makers can adopt. Further, these goals are all unique on the same scale: each represents a distinctive point of view.

Another consideration is the need to discriminate between similar-sounding goals. As pointed out previously, the differences between regional economic development and income redistribution are quite significant from an economic point of view. Similarly, the three similar-appearing goals of preservation, environmental quality, and aesthetics all represent distinct viewpoints. The first is concerned with strict *preservation* of a "natural" condition, the second with *maintenance* of certain arbitrary standards, and the third with *compliance* with a third set of values emphasizing beauty, open space, and so on.

A final consideration is ambiguity regarding goals. Although the economic goals are generally thought through reasonably well, there is a great deal of confusion regarding environmental and social goals. There are tendencies to consider the various alternative environmental goals in one package. This is true of social goals as well. Even in studies concerned with alternative goals, such ambiguities arise.

Underlying these different goals is the difference in philosophy alluded to earlier.

In Westman's view, the technologist defines goals in terms of *uses* to which a stream is to be put by man—e.g., irrigation, industrial processing, swimming and boating, drinking-water supply, maintenance of sport fishing, support of wildlife of interest to hunters or birdwatchers. By contrast, the ecological viewpoint seeks the restoration and maintenance of the *physical, chemical, and biological integrity* of the waterways. The ecologist assumes that if this "balance of nature," approaching the pristine state, is restored and maintained, the water will be clean enough for all of man's desired uses. Table 7.19 summarizes the major differences between the technological and ecological points of view.

The technologist will argue that the level of cleanliness of water sought by the ecologist will be "unnecessarily high" for many desired uses and therefore is an unnecessarily costly goal. The ecologist will reply in turn that, in fact, pollution of our waterways has set streams on a sliding path towards degradation and destruction, at the cost of billions of dollars in fish kills, lost recreational sites, tourism, hunting and fishing licenses, increased costs to clean up water for drinking or industrial use, and less tangible or as yet unknown costs to public health and welfare. The crux of the ecologist's retort is that once we start polluting our streams, we cannot control

TABLE 7.19

Alternative approaches to key legislative issues in water-pollution control

Legislative Issue	Technological Approach	Ecological Approach
Water-quality goal	Use to which water body is to be put by man	Restoration and maintenance of physical, chemical, and biological integrity of water bodies
Mode of treatment of pollutants	Removal of materials by sewage treatment (physical filter); liquid remainder placed in water body (assumes assimilative capacity of water body)	1. Recycling of liquid materials by land disposal (living filter) 2. Elimination of discharge into waters, based on nonreliance on assimilative capacity 3. Land-use controls for nonpoint sources of pollution
Mode of classification of pollutants	Physical and chemical parameters as they are affected by the control technology (e.g. settleable solids, suspended solids)	Chemical and biological parameters as they affect the biology of the stream (e.g. nutrients, nonnutrients, toxic substances, pathogens)
Mode of monitoring the success of pollutant removal	In-plant monitoring of effluent	Biological monitoring in stream
Legal point of control	Ability to meet water-quality standards based on use	Achievement of integrity of water body by elimination of discharge; application of best available technology before discharge

the level or manner of destruction wrought, and our costs of rehabilitating the water bodies for man's use will continue to accrue; by contrast, a stream existing close to its natural state has the ability to maintain its own health, without the help of technology but with the aid of an ancient and continuing history of evolutionary adaptation to restore equilibria (homeostasis). In terms of the depreciation costs of maintenance of this "health" on a stable basis over a long period, a system which repairs itself is clearly the least expensive to man.

This controversy is flared by contrasting judgments as to what is the natural "assimilative capacity" of waters for pollutants. Traditionally, the technologist has assumed that aquatic ecosystems have the capacity to digest, degrade, and ultimately cause to disappear, the pollutants placed in them. The ecologist, on the other hand, will point out that no materials placed in the waters disappear, and all additions to a water body change it to a greater or lesser extent. A functional definition of assimilative capacity in the ecological context would be that resilience in a natural water body which ensures that any changes in the aquatic ecosystem resulting in a physical, chemical, or biological change in a a pristine water body will be of a temporary nature, such that by natural processes, within a few hours, days, or weeks, the aquatic ecosystem will return to a state functionally identical to the original.

An example of a compound that comes closest to being "assimilated" in the technologist's sense would be a pure carbohydrate such as sucrose (sugar): given adequate dissolved oxygen, aerobic bacteria, and proper sediment conditions, sucrose is capable of being completely digested in aquatic ecosystems into carbon dioxide and water. These are perhaps the most harmless end products possible, since both are natural components of surface waters. Yet even with this paradigm, the ecologist could well point out that the digestion has occurred at the cost of the stream's dissolved oxygen and has increased the dissolved CO_2 levels available for photosynthesis and the growth of algae and diatoms, which will in turn further compete with fishes for the limited supplies of dissolved oxygen. This shift in O_2/CO_2 balance will be compensated to some extent by physical processes in the stream, since O_2 and CO_2 exchange between water and air is dictated by physicochemical principles of solubility, and incorporation during turbulence. CO_2 balance is also mediated by equilibria between gaseous CO_2 in water and carbonate and bicarbonate molecules in precipitated or dissolved phase.

However, the steady state, or amount of CO_2 and O_2 dissolved in water, which will exist when equilibrium is restored, will be influenced in part by the amount of CO_2 or O_2 introduced by the bacterial respiration of sucrose. That is, despite the existence of homeostatic mechanisms to restore the *equilibrium* of CO_2 and O_2 in water, biological activity acting on introduced material is capable of shifting the steady-state *level* of reactants and products present when the new equilibrium is achieved, by the familiar chemical principle of mass action. The only way to guarantee that equilibrium will be maintained at the original steady-state level is to recycle the materials that are present and neither add nor take away a net amount of material.

When the concept of "assimilative capacity" is examined in relation to any more complex pollutant, such as phosphate detergent or mercurial pesticide, still other limitations to the concept emerge. In the case of a phosphate detergent, for example, the detergent is eminently digestible, "biodegradable," but the elements and compounds into which it is degraded are plant nutrients. If phosphorus is a limiting element to growth of the phytoplankton in a lake or estuary, its introduction after assimilation of detergents will accelerate the eutrophication which we have seen to cause such havoc in terms of reducing dissolved oxygen contents of waters, clogging water bodies with plant growth, suffocating fish and other animals, and preventing aerobic degradation on the lake bottom. The phosphorus will never disappear: as an element, it can be broken down no further, and wherever a particular molecule may be in the cycling of nutrients—in the sediment, in the water, or in biological tissue—it is contributing to the increase in the resource base of the ecosystem, which stimulates the increased biomass and productivity of the system.

In the case of a mercurial pesticide, the mercurial portion is not a nutrient but a toxic material; whether it lodges first in sediment, water, air, or tissue, it will reenter and recycle through all these phases, never to "disappear" (Peakall and Lovett, 1972). The organic portions of the pesticide and detergent will be degraded to the extent that oxygen is available, and at varying rates of time, depending on their molecular structures and the size of the preexisting microbial community. The degradation will induce a set of changes comparable to those discussed above for sucrose.

The ocean may serve as a sink for these materials, but only to the extent that the materials are not then recycled via wave droplets into clouds, to fall as rain onto land and streams once again (Frost, 1969). To the extent that the ocean does serve as a repository for these wastes, it is itself an aquatic ecosystem subject to increasing pollution and degradation. If what technologists have meant by "assimilative capacity" has been the transfer of pollution from fresh water to estuaries and oceans, we scarcely have here a concept to be relied on to protect our biosphere. In fact, the estuaries themselves, which serve as major spawning areas for both freshwater and marine organisms, have in recent years shown an increasing toll from this misinterpretation of "assimilative capacity" (U.S. Department of Interior, 1970).

Heat has occasionally been suggested as a pollutant that can be harmlessly assimilated outside a certain "mixing zone." It should be clear that in stratified bodies, even if the heat is returned to a water layer identical in temperature to the effluent, the width of the stratum of that temperature will be expanded, to the detriment of those organisms that cannot tolerate or do not thrive at that temperature. In streams, mixing zones have been permitted—zones where a higher temperature in a limited area near the outfall pipe is diluted downstream to an ambient level. While the stream is demonstrating an "assimilative" capacity to the extent that it dilutes the heat, not only is the total heat content (and temperature) increasing for a fair way down the stream, but frequently a thermal barrier to fish migration is created at the mixing zone (not to mention the in-situ organisms which are killed). Furthermore, the change in solubility of gases induced by the temperature change further affects the biological repercussions in the system, and changes occur in resistance to disease and poisoning (Cole, 1969; Westman, 1972).

The concept of "assimilative capacity" has been essential to the technologist's human-use approach to water-quality standards. If one is to classify the upper reaches of an estuary for industrial use (including oil discharge from tankers) and the lower portion for fishing, as is done in Galveston Bay, for example, one must assume that the bay has the capacity to assimilate the waste oil before it reaches the shellfish beds, an assumption which denizens of the Houston region have come to question. (About half of Galveston Bay is now closed to oyster harvesting because of pollution; Carter, 1970). Similarly, to allow industrial processing in the upper reaches of the Mississippi and swimming in the lower reaches is to assume an assimilative capacity.

This kind of assumption is made throughout any use-classification system for streams, almost invariably without a detailed foreknowledge of the fate of the pollutants in the stream. In fact, the difficulty of predicting the fate of pollutants in a water body is a condition which is likely to be with us for a long time to come. In the ecological schema, little or no reliance is placed on the assimilative capacity of streams, leading directly to the conclusion that discharge of pollutants into waters must be eliminated if integrity is to be restored and maintained.

In terms of waste treatment, it becomes the technologists's goal to "treat" pollutants in a way that will diminish their damaging properties to the level at which the stream's "assimilative capacity" can cause the remainder to disappear. On this premise, sanitary engineers have designed physical, chemical, and "biological" methods of waste pretreatment: physical methods most commonly involve tanks to allow materials to settle and filters to sort larger solids; chemical methods involve adding materials to cause precipitation of certain compounds for disposal as sludge, and chlorinating to kill bacteria; "biological" methods consist mainly of producing a culture of bacteria which can digest organic matter under artificially aerated conditions, rather than allowing the same process to proceed in sediments in lake or stream, where aeration is usually not as good and where dissolved oxygen levels will consequently be depleted. The end products of treatment are a liquid containing varying amounts of nutrients, pesticides, hormones, and other substances that have escaped precipitation or digestion, and large amounts of sludge. Even the best tertiary treatment is limited in its extent of nutrient removal (Table 7.20), and most treatment methods do

little to remove certain organically active materials such as female sex hormones excreted in the urine of women on the pill (Tabak and Bunch, 1970), orthonitrochlorobenzene (Middleton, 1959), and viruses (Berg et al., in press).

By contrast, since it is a necessary corollary of the ecological approach that discharges into waters be eliminated, emphasis is placed on returning liquid wastes to the land in a spray-irrigation system (Elazar et al., 1972; McGauhey and Krone, 1967; Schwarz, 1959). Table 7.20 highlights the relative efficiency of such a scheme versus advanced waste-treatment technology. The "living filter," as this system is sometimes called, basically consists of returning nutrient-laden wastewater to the land to irrigate crops and forests. Wastewater which infiltrates below the plant-root zone is captured in drainage tiles and monitored for water quality. The water may then be retreated or, if sufficiently clean, discharged into a stream.

From urban areas, it is necessary to transport the wastes by pipeline 100 miles or more to farm

TABLE 7.20

Comparison of efficiency of waste treatment and disposal methods

Treatment Method	Biological and Chemical Oxygen Demand (BOD & COD)	Suspended Matter	Percentage Removed Bacteria	Viruses	Phosphorus (13)	Nitrogen (13)	Heavy Metals (16) (cadmium, chromium, etc.)
Primary treatment:							
Fine filters (screens)	5–10	5–20	10–20	0			
Settling tank	25–40	40–70	25–75	0	0–10	0–?	0
Secondary treatment:							
Trickling filters	65–95	65–92	90–95	0–?	10–70 (14)	50	0–10
Tertiary treatment:							
Advanced chemical treatment	65–95 (98[a])	80–95 (98[a])	90–98 (99[a])	0–(90?) (14)	60–98	85	99
Soil filter (land disposal, 12)	90–95 (98[a])	85–95 (98[a])	95–98 (99[a])	100? (18)	98	85	99[b]

[a] Environmental Protection Agency estimates, 1971.

[b] This is a possible maximum; toxic materials could accumulate in the crops or be lost to groundwater. Synthetic organic toxic materials are likely to be less well adsorbed by land than metals, since they evaporate to air more easily.

fields and to arrange for storage tanks when ground is frozen. Furthermore, water quantity and quality must be adjusted before spraying to ensure that the liquid medium is appropriate in amount and composition for plant growth. This means that in practice wastewater destined for land disposal must be pretreated by mechanical means to sort out solids and remove toxic materials. It will not ordinarily need tertiary treatment for nutrient removal, however, since the nutrient composition can be adjusted by dilution and supplementation with appropriate nutrients. Land disposal achieves the recycling of nutrient materials, since most of the nutrients (such as those in human feces) come from plants and animals that have extracted nutrients from the soil.

The land, like the water, has differing capacities to degrade, adsorb, or otherwise respond to different pollutants. Thus, land disposal offers particular advantages for the disposal of nutrients and viruses, since the latter are capable of being killed on certain soils (Bauer Engineering, 1971; Westman, 1972) (see below), and nutrients can be taken up by crops rather than contribute to algal growth and eutrophication in waterways. Toxic materials, however, require treatment or recycling before wastewater is applied either to the land or the water, in order to avoid the dangers of buildup of the materials in soil or sediment, and of bioaccumulation of toxic levels of these materials along the food chain. Nonnutrients, such as relatively inert suspended solids, are poorly assimilated by either land or water; the degree of pretreatment necessary for nonnutrient pollutants before disposal, and the optimum medium (land or water) for disposal, varies in different cases.

Both land and water disposal involve use of waste-treatment plants at some state, resulting in sludge accumulation. Ideally, this sludge will also be returned to the land as humus or mulch. If the sludge contains toxic materials, it may have to be treated for their removal; if the extracted toxicants are not sufficiently pure to be resold, the only sump remaining for them is burial. Some localities are using sludge to recondition stripmined areas (Sosewitz, 1971; Nephew, 1972), but at present most sludge is sold to local nurserymen, placed in landfill sites, or made into a water pollutant by dumping out at sea.

In addition to the disposal of municipal and industrial wastes, any approach to water-pollution control must consider the nonpoint sources of pollution: pollutants which do not come from a localized outfall pipe. In this category fall agricultural and silvicultural runoff (eroded soil, fertilizers, and pesticide runoff); urban and construction runoff (oil, lead, and asbestos from roads, eroded soil, excess water from sealed surfaces); mining runoff (drainage from mines, filtrate from ore spoil heaps); and saltwater intrusion due to reduction of freshwater flow from irrigation, groundwater extraction, diversion, or other means. As yet the technologist has not addressed himself to control of these sources, which are estimated to account for one-half or more of current water pollution in the United States (U.S. Senate Public Works Committee, 1971).

The ecological approach to these nonpoint sources of pollution basically involves land-use controls: better soil conservation practices on farms, avoidance of clear-cutting of forests on slopes, rapid revegetation of mined areas and liming of acid-forming underground mines, provision of drainage ditches and storage tanks for water from roads and house tops, and avoidance of excessive extraction of water from freshwater tables within precarious reach of saltwater tables beneath them.

Inherent in the technological approach to pollution control is a viewing of pollutants in terms of the ways in which they are treated by control technology. Thus in Table 7.21 it may be noted that the classical parameters which have been used in this approach to classify pollutants have been physical and chemical ones, derived from the size of pollutants (what filters they go

TABLE 7.21

Alternative classifications of some effluent parameters characteristic of the technological and ecological approaches[a]

Technological

Dissolved solids[b]
Suspended solids[b]
Settleable solids[b]

Ecological

Nutrients: elements or compounds which are composed exclusively of one or more essential elements and which exist or can be shown to be transformed in the receiving water within one week into forms that are part of the natural cycle of assimilation and release of substances from the biota in the receiving water. "Essential elements" means C, O, H, N, S, Cu, Mg, Mn, Ca, P, Zn, K, Fe, Cl, B, Mo, Si, Na.

Nonnutrients: elements or compounds, or combinations thereof, which either are not composed wholly of, or will not be transformed within one week, into nutrients that are essential to the natural cycle of receiving waters (e.g. dyes, plastics, some petrochemicals and ore tailings).

Pathogens: any organism capable of causing infection or disease (e.g. bacteria, viruses, amoebae).

Toxic substances: those materials or combinations of materials (nutrient or nonnutrient) which upon exposure, ingestion, inhalation, or assimilation into any organism, either directly from the environment or indirectly by ingestion through food chains, will cause death, disease, behavioral abnormalities, cancer, genetic mutations, physiological malfunctions (including malfunctions in reproduction), or physical deformations in such organisms or their offspring (e.g. methyl mercury, DDT, dioxins). Most materials have toxic effects only at certain concentrations. For enforcement purposes, it is useful to designate the particular materials which, due to man's activities, are likely to reach concentrations at which they have destructive effects.

[a] Distinction is between physical and biological properties of pollutants; other parameters may be common to the two approaches.
[b] Determined by particle size, shape, and charge.

through and whether they settle). BOD and COD (chemical oxygen demand) occupy intermediate positions in this regard in that, while they reflect oxygen consumption within an artificially aerated culture, their significance is in direct relation to the oxygen demand of the aquatic system into which the effluent is put. Thus BOD and COD can appropriately be used in either the technological or ecological approach, provided they are not assumed to be the sole characteristic of a pollutant that will have biological effect.

Coliform count has long been viewed as a rather crude indicator for the presence of pathogens; *E. coli* is an ordinarily harmless bacterium of the human intestine. Its presence in water is a marker of the presence of human excrement, indicating the possibility that other human parasites, of possible pathogenicity, may be present. Ideally, a more intensive search for pathogens would be carried out as well.

The value of the ecological classification of pollutants is its orientation toward the effect of the pollutants on organisms in the stream. All nutrient pollutants, for example, will contribute to the resource base of the ecosystem, and many at some point in the development of the ecosystem may become the nutrient limiting the growth of dominant organisms. This category thus bears direct relation to the potential of the pollutant to accelerate eutrophication. Nonnutrients are more likely to have a physical effect: fibers covering estuary bottoms and smothering fish eggs, for example; but equally importantly, the nonnutrients represent a category of pollutants of unknown future activity. Perhaps some will be proven toxic as they change form with time. The definition of toxic substances must be considered in relation to the concentration in which the substance is active in water. Thus "exposure" to a toxic pollutant is intended to mean exposure at a concentration which is, or could potentially occur, in a receiving water as a result of current additions of pollutants by man, directly or indirectly, and which will produce the undesirable effects listed in the definition (Table 7.21) at that concentration.

It is important that pathogens be examined more broadly to include viruses. Hepatitis is the main viral-type organism to persist in streams and accumulate up food chains. Between 1961 and 1970 thirty outbreaks of hepatitis in the United States were associated with water systems (Surgeon-General Jesse Steinfeld, pers. comm.). Soil types of fine texture have been reported (Bauer Engineering, 1971) to adsorb and detoxify viruses effectively when they have been sprayed with wastewater of pH 6 to 9, an acidity range in which viruses are positively charged. If this property of soils proves to apply to a wide range of viruses, land disposal of viruses would represent an improvement over existing technology, which relies principally on chlorine and storage time of the water to detoxify viruses, and which does not detoxify all viruses.

Obviously, whichever approach is used, certain physical parameters of importance to water use will have to continue to be measured—e.g., heat, turbidity, salinity, BOD-COD, pH. It is mainly the distinction between filtration properties that requires emphasis.

It follows from the effect-of-treatment-plant approach to pollutant classification that monitoring of the success of pollutant removal will be accomplished by testing the effluent for turbidity, pH, BOD, and so on before discharge. The ecological approach, on the other hand, must emphasize the effect that BOD, nutrient concentrations, toxic substances, and so on will have on the integrity of the stream. In this way biological monitoring of the health of organisms in the stream, representative of each level in the food chain, becomes essential.

This monitoring would involve such live tests as swimming speed, rate of response to stimuli, heartbeat rate (Cairns et al., 1970; Shirer et al., 1968), and such analyses as tissue analysis for accumulation of toxic materials. The sampling should include every trophic level from algae to predatory birds that eat fishes from the stream. This approach can, of course, be supplemented by standard biological assays in flow tanks with measured amounts of effluent (McKee and Wolf, 1965), but such a technique is not suitable to detect longterm, cumulative effects of pollu-

tion on stream integrity. Sampling would ordinarily also include tests for stream pH, turbidity, and so on. In this way sampling would reveal the extent of nonpoint source pollution as well.

It has been the logical conclusion of the technological approach that pollution must be regulated in such a way as to protect the water quality of a stream for its desired use. That is, an effluent is judged in violation of statutes if its component pollutants will deleteriously affect the stream's biota, turbidity, and so forth. Herein, indeed, lies the ultimate pitfall of the technological method: it requires pollution-enforcement officials to have the unassailable ability to predict the effect that an effluent will have on the ecology of a water body. This is a task which has so far escaped the abilities of the most expert aquatic ecologists: there is simply not enough known about the workings of nature—the size, flow rate, and seasonal fluctuations of streams; the effect of chance storms; the biological functioning, requirements, and tolerances of all the species in the stream, and their interactions; the composition of sediments and their potential chemical interactions with foreign substances; the rate of dissipation of heat—to make a legally tight judgment. Compound this with the task of predicting the interactive and cumulative effects of hundreds of separate effluents along a major river, and the administrator is faced with a task that simply cannot be accomplished with our present knowledge. In fact, with the large element of chance events involved, it may be argued that the effects will never be perfectly predictable. But if you cannot predict whether the placement of 200 outfalls on the stream will still maintain a water quality suitable for irrigation, how can you regulate the composition and quantity of effluent permitted to be discharged to a stream designated for this use?

In the case of the ecological approach, the dilemma persists. The water-quality goal is to achieve the physical, chemical, and biological integrity of the stream. It is assumed that the only stream with that property is one at or close to the pristine natural condition. Thus in a strict sense, elimination of discharge is the only permissible strategy. To allow anything short of that is to battle with the uncertainties of relating effluent composition to its effects on water quality.

The U.S. Congress, in attempting to follow the ecological approach, ruled in its 1972 Amendments that the discharge of pollutants from point sources must be eliminated by 1981. Facing the reality, however, that economic and technical factors might prevent the achievement of this goal within the time allotted, it was necessary to provide some interim basis for regulation until closed-cycle systems for industry, land-disposal of liquid wastes, and burial of sludge by municipalities could be instituted at a reasonable cost. Not wanting to return to the difficulties of a water-use criterion, the Senate chose to rely on a system man does know a great deal about—his own technology.

In hearings before the U.S. Senate in 1970 and 1971, senators were told that closed-cycle technology was now available for all major industrial processes. It was ruled that by 1976, industry must use the "best practicable" technology, and by 1981 the "best available" technology for treatment of effluents before discharge. The terms "practicable" and "available" refer to differences in the current use of the technology. "Practicable" refers to the average of the best performers in industrial category; "best available" to the best performer in the industry.

This approach eases the burden of enforcement considerably. Administrative agencies know with a good deal of precision what technology is available for effluent treatment and can require national standards, industry by industry (with some adjustment for plant size) on an unequivocal basis. The Amendments provide that the technology must be updated at least every five years if systems for complete elimination of discharge continue to be unavailable. Furthermore, the government will continue to develop and demonstrate its own technology, as a goad to private pollution-technology firms.

RESIDUALS CHARGES AS AN ALTERNATIVE TO STANDARD-SETTING

The "technological" and "ecological" approaches are alternatives only within the context of the standard-setting approach to effluent control. There are alternatives to standard-setting, too, and among these, the one that has been discussed most is the assignment of residuals charges.

The essence of this approach is the levying of taxes or charges on wastes (residuals) discharged to the environment, to create economic incentives for pollution control. As Freeman and Havemen (1972) note, until recently only academic economists espoused this position, but in the 1971 report of the Council on Environmental Quality, the White House endorsed residuals charges as an alternative pollution-control strategy.

At an abstract level the logic of the argument in favor of residuals charges is impeccable. Even at the practical level of policy implementation, the case for such a strategy appears very strong indeed. Yet despite the increasing interest in the concept and the growing support for specific proposals, the public debate has been clouded by confusion and misconceptions. This has allowed some assertions questioning the efficacy, feasibility, and effectiveness of residuals charges to gain an unwarranted degree of acceptance.

To dispel what they perceive as the "confusion," Freeman and Haveman compare the residuals charge strategy with the relevant alternative, direct regulation of discharges through permits backed by an administrative and judicial enforcement system. The regulation-enforcement strategy is the relevant alternative because it is the mainstay of the 1972 Amendments.

The case for the economic incentives or residuals-charge strategy rests on the acceptance of two primary propositions. The first is that, in a market economy, prices play a major and valuable role in the allocation of resources to uses that will be of highest value. The second is that degradable environmental resources, unlike most other resources, are now outside the scope of the market system, and the uses to which they are put are not subject to the guidance of prices.

Economic theory teaches that, given certain assumptions and conditions, markets can solve efficiently or optimally the problem of allocating scarce resources. The ideally functioning market system provides information and signals to economic decision makers. These signals are the prices of goods and resources. The information they convey concerns the relative gains and costs of using the resources at hand in different ways. Market prices reflect the marginal valuation or willingness to pay for goods on the part of consumers. Costs reflect the value of resources in alternative uses. In the idealized system, the competition for profits leads to an expansion of the production of goods to the point where their prices equal their marginal or incremental costs of production. Thus the amount people are willing to pay for a good equals the value of the resources used in producing it—no more, no less. No more, because producers would otherwise expand output in order to capture the excess of value over cost. No less, because with losses the resource owners would be induced to shift their resources to uses of higher value.

In the case of environmental resources, however, the price signals are absent. Land, labor, and capital have their prices. But environmental resources—public watercourses, the atmosphere, and public lands—have no price because no one owns them. As a result, these resources are treated by everyone as free goods. When scarce resources are made available at a zero price, and with no nonmarket control of their use, they are overused and abused. The "freeness" of the resource results in there being no incentive for the population to economize on the resource or to allocate it to the use of highest value.

Hardin called this the "tragedy of the commons" (1968). In his apt example of the communal grazing land, each herdsman would introduce more cattle as long as there was any grass left. Since he did not own the pasture land, the herdsman would reckon only the costs to himself of letting in more cattle and would ignore the costs he imposed on other herdsmen as well as the long-term damages that would be caused by overgrazing. The historical solution to the common grazing problem, at least in western societies, has been the division of land and the establishment of rights of ownership so that markets and prices would control and ration the use of land.

The atmosphere and our watercourses are the modern equivalents of the commons. To the dischargers the use of the atmosphere and watercourses is free. The availability of environmental resources to users at a zero price results in their overuse and pollution.

When a common property resource, such as the air or water, is being overused, there are two possible solutions. Hardin suggested that the solution was mutual coercion, mutually agreed upon by the majority. The appropriate pattern of usage would be determined by some political process and implemented· by some nonmarket means, the police power of the state being relied on to carry out the plan. The licensing of television broadcasting stations and issuing of permits for discharges into navigable waterways are examples of this approach. In essence, this solution is the regulation-enforcement strategy of the 1972 amendments. The other alternative is to reproduce the effect of private markets by charging a price or fee to those who would use the common property resource. The fee or price would then allocate or ration the resource. Grazing fees per head of cattle on federal lands, stumpage fees for timber cut in national forests, admission fees to national parks, and residuals charges are all examples of the economic incentives approach to managing common property resources.

Under a system of residuals charges, people discharging wastes are required to pay the government a certain sum for each unit of wastes discharged. Dischargers are led to compare the cost of using the environment for waste discharge—as reflected to them by the residuals charge—with the cost of handling their waste-disposal problems in some other way. The choice of means for dealing with the waste is left to the discharger. And he has a wide range of options. He may treat the waste, recycle it, store it, or find methods of production which reduce the volume of waste generated (Kneese and Bower, 1968, especially chaps. 4 and 8). His only guide is the relative costs of alternative procedures, one of which is dumping the waste untreated into the environment.

People generating wastes will reduce their discharges to the environment as long as the marginal cost of doing so—the marginal cost of waste treatment (or recycling, or waste storage)—is less than the price or marginal cost of discharging the waste to the environment. The higher the residuals charge the greater the incentive to seek alternatives to direct discharge, and the smaller the flow of wastes to the environment. In this way environmental resources can be brought back into the economic system. The incentives which induce efficiency in the use of labor, capital, and land can also effect a more efficient allocation of environmental resources.

Policy proposals cannot be evaluated effectively in a vacuum. Any given policy can best be evaluated by comparing it with the relevant alternatives—one of which is to do nothing. The relevant comparison is between a residuals charge strategy and the regulation-enforcement aspects of the present strategy for controlling air and water pollution. This strategy, as embodied in federal and state law, consists of, first, the establishment of ambient air- and water-quality standards and, second, the use of the police power of the state to bring about a reduction in discharges sufficient to attain these standards.

Given the establishment of quality standards, this approach can best be viewed as a two-step process in which regulations are established and compliance with them is enforced. In establishing regulations, the public authority must determine the maximum allowable total discharges for a river stretch or an air basin, consistent with the attainment of the quality standard. Then the authority must, in some way, allocate this total among all dischargers. This allocation will determine the terms of the licenses or permits that will be held by all dischargers and that will specify the maximum allowable discharges or standards of effluent or emission quality. In enforcing the regulations, the authority must undertake surveillance of dischargers so as to detect violations and must initiate judicial or quasi-judicial proceedings to compel compliance or to impose sanctions (such as fines and jail sentences) when violations are detected.

The ideal situation for performance of a system of regulation and enforcement is one in which there are no violations whatsoever. In practice, the number of violations (whether or not detected) depends on the cost of compliance with the regulations, the penalties associated with being caught in a violation, and the probability of being detected in violation and having the penalties imposed. All these factors must be considered in assessing the effectiveness of any regulation-enforcement system.

If the residuals-charge strategy is to be taken seriously, a satisfactory answer must be provided for the question of what the appropriate charge would be on a particular pollutant. The basic logic of the residuals-charge proposal suggests one answer: the charge should equal the marginal or incremental damage caused by the pollutant, as measured in dollars (Kneese and Bower, see chaps. 5 and 6). This logic is described as follows.

When wastes discharged to the environment impair its use for other purposes—for example, life sustenance or recreation—there is, in principle, a willingness on the part of the affected individuals to pay to avoid these adverse effects. This willingness to pay is the monetary measure of the damages or costs of pollution. Efficiency in the allocation of environmental resources requires that these damages be equated with the costs of their being avoided at the margin. Because people discharging wastes minimize their own costs by equating their marginal costs of waste reductions with the residuals charge, a charge equal to the marginal pollution damages will lead to the efficient allocation of the environmental resource. The reduction in environmental damages associated with a one-unit reduction in discharges will just equal the incremental cost of obtaining that reduction. Where marginal environmental damages exceed marginal waste reduction costs, further reductions in discharges are called for and will be induced in the dischargers as they respond to the charge set equal to marginal damages.

If monetary damages are to be the basis for establishing residuals charges, estimates of these damages must be available. Although economists are making progress in estimating some forms of pollution damages in dollar terms, sufficiently reliable information for setting residuals charges on this basis is not now available nor is it likely to be in the near future.

The first misconception regarding residuals charges is the belief that such charges can be implemented only if the magnitudes of the damages are known in terms of dollars. Fortunately, the economic logic of the residuals-charge strategy provides an alternative means of determining the charge that should be imposed—one which is consistent with present legislation and which utilizes available or readily obtainable information.

Under present environmental policies, the federal government has required states to establish standards or minimum acceptable levels for air and water quality. For any such standard there is a maximum permissible rate of discharge of residuals which is consistent with that standard. An appropriate residuals charge, if set high enough, can induce dischargers to limit their discharges to this maximum amount. In economic terms the standard establishes a maximum supply of permissible discharges, and the price (residuals charge) must be set high enough to ration this fixed supply among those who wish to make discharges. In other words, there is a market clearing price or charge which will equate the quantity of discharges demanded with the fixed supply implied by the standard (Dales, 1968).

The response of dischargers to the charges imposed depends on the marginal costs that they will incur if they reduce their residuals by treatment and other means. If the public authority responsible for setting residuals charges knows the marginal-cost schedules of dischargers, it can readily calculate the appropriate residuals charge. The charge must be set at the marginal cost of waste reduction at the level of control required to attain the standard.

Although information on the costs of reducing wastes is far from perfect, we do have some data. A number of studies have been conducted on the basis of cost estimates obtained for engineering designs of waste-reduction methods. While such estimates are not accurate for all dischargers, they do permit analysts to make reasonable projections of the responses of representative dischargers to a charges system, and to estimate the appropriate charges. Even if the marginal cost of treatment is not known with accuracy, the appropriate charge can be discovered by observing the responses of dischargers when they are presented with alternative charges. If an initial charge fails to attain the quality standard, the charge should be raised until the standard is met (Hass, 1970). An added benefit of this approach is that it generates valuable information on the minimum costs of attaining different standards of environmental quality under various environmental conditions and for different types of wastes.

The charge most frequently uttered against an economic incentives strategy is that it allows those with financial means to buy their way out of effective environmental control. To those offering this criticism, the idea that polluters can purchase the right to degrade the environment through the exercise of economic power has appeared to be both vulgar and a fatal policy flaw.

The "license to pollute" cliche should be laid to rest once and for all. First, it must be recognized that residuals charges are no more a license to pollute than are the allocation of permits issued under a regulation-enforcement strategy. In both approaches it is recognized that some use of watercourses for residuals absorption is appropriate. In both approaches, the quality standard of the stream will be attained if the policy is properly implemented. The residuals-charge strategy will achieve the desired reduction in discharges by raising the polluter's cost of discharging; the use of permits will achieve the desired reduction by enforcing the rules implied by license provisions.

With a means of enforcing effluent standards, the license to pollute is, in effect, awarded to the discharger free of charge. The discharge permit is treated as a "right" which is assigned to the polluter by the public. With a residuals-charge approach, however, the discharger must pay by the pound for each unit of waste which is released into the environment. He must, in essence, compensate the public for the right to make use of the environment for waste discharge. In this context, the labeling of the residuals-charge strategy as a "license to pollute" makes sense only if the effluent-standards approach is also so regarded and if the required payment of the charge fails to induce dischargers to search for measures of discharge control or treatment in order to reduce liability to the charge. Indifference to the residuals charge is not consistent with human behavior as it is revealed in business.

Representatives of industry have argued that residuals charges would cripple industry's ability to finance pollution-control equipment. Industry, it is claimed, is already spending as much as is possible on efforts to control pollution.

The vacuousness of this position is evident from several perspectives. First, by implication this assertion contends that economic incentives—prices and costs—fail to influence business decisions and behavior. Observed behavior verified by empirical estimates contradicts this contention. For example, when firms purchase labor-saving capital equipment in response to rising wages, they are demonstrating their responsiveness to economic incentives. It is interesting that, in other contexts, the role of economic incentives in achieving efficiency has been regarded as of primary importance by business decision makers.

Second, this position suggests that the main effect of any decrease in profits would be to reduce expenditures for residuals abatement or treatment. Without appropriate incentives, it is probable that businesses do afford investments in pollution control low priority. After all, with little effective penalty for discharging wastes, the return on abatement investments will not be high. It is the purpose of a residuals-charge policy to alter these priorities and to remove pollution-control efforts from their dependence on some notion of social responsibility.

Finally, if continued discharge is made costly through a residuals-charge policy, abatement investments will become profitable and, as with profitable labor-saving investments, industry will find the financial resources to undertake these activities.

Although industry expects to spend 4.9 million dollars on pollution control in 1972, this figure is only 5.3 percent of all planned capital expenditures. A doubling in the amount of spending for pollution control could be accommodated with only a 5.6 percent reduction in other capital spending. It is not that financial resources are unavailable; rather, what is lacking is the incentive to use more of these resources for pollution control.

The practice of imposing sewer (or user) charges on those who discharge wastes to municipal sewer systems is now well established and generally accepted. The municipality accepting the wastes for treatment renders a service and incurs real costs which must be covered by revenues. Some have argued that although user charges are reasonable, residuals charges are not, because in the latter case no service that entails cost is rendered.

The argument is invalid. Although there are some differences, the cases of user charges and residuals charges are alike in two essential respects. First, in both cases a service of value is rendered to those who discharge wastes. In one case this service is provided by a system constructed and operated by human beings and employing labor and capital; in the other case the service is provided by a natural system. Second, the use of both systems for waste disposal entails real social costs. In one case, these are the opportunity costs of the labor and capital utilized in treating the wastes; in the other case the costs are imputed damages in the form of recreation opportunities foregone, medical costs incurred, and longevity sacrificed. It is the existence of these costs and the absence of any institutions for imposing these costs on those who use the environment for waste disposal which make pollution a problem for public policy.

On a somewhat different level, the issue here is a legal one involving property rights. Because the ownership rights in the environment are not well defined, it is argued that residuals charges are not legitimate. Dischargers are, in effect, asserting that they have a right to the assimilative capacity of the environment and, therefore, should not have to pay anyone else for its use.

While the question of ownership of environmental resources has not been finally resolved in the law, the thrust of recent legislation and case law is in opposition to the position outlined above. These legal developments have tended to assert public ownership in the common property resource. The recent passage of laws containing licensing requirements supports this view. And a residuals-charge policy would simply assert that what the public has the right to give away through licenses it can also charge a price for.

In order to impose residuals charges it must be possible to measure residuals flows directly or to estimate their magnitudes by accurate indirect means. For a residuals-charge system to provide appropriate incentives to dischargers, the bill paid by the discharger must vary directly and closely with the composition and quantities of wastes actually discharged. Several observers have argued that because accurate monitoring of residuals flows is not practical, a residuals charge is not a feasible alternative (Robertson, 1970, 1971). However, the argument will not stand closer inspection.

In order for any pollution-control strategy to be effective in controlling or restricting discharges to some maximum amount, information must be obtained on what is being discharged. For example, if an effluent licensing system is to be strictly enforced, the policing agency must be able to measure discharges accurately, continuously, and at reasonable cost in order to detect and take action on violations of the license terms. Fortunately, for most of the more significant and ubiquitous pollutants the measurement technology is available and its cost is reasonable relative to the other costs and benefits associated with pollution control.

While both a residuals-charge strategy and a regulation-enforcement approach have identical requirements for information on rates of discharge, they differ in their requirements for information regarding the costs of reducing waste discharges. Under a regulation-enforcement system, the objective is to issue licenses which restrict discharges sufficiently to attain the environmental quality standard. The total allowable discharge could be allocated among licenses in an infinite number of ways. No information is required on the costs borne by the dischargers in order for them to meet the standard. For the residuals-charge system to achieve precisely the desired environmental quality, a charge structure must be established that will induce individual dischargers to reduce their effluents. To ascertain the appropriate charge, policymakers should be able to estimate the costs of such reduction incurred by individual dischargers.

However, the capacity to achieve precisely a desired environmental quality is only one of several criteria that might be used to evaluate policy. A further relevant factor is the total cost to society of achieving the standard. Although any set of permitted discharges can achieve the standard, only that set of license allocations which equates the marginal costs of waste reduction of all dischargers will achieve the standard at minimum total cost. Departures from this rule are likely to raise total costs substantially. For example, studies have shown that the imposition of requirements for uniform treatment may entail total costs which exceed the minimum costs by a factor of 2.

A residuals-charge strategy has the virtue of leading automatically to the achievement of any given reduction in discharges at the lowest possible cost. This is because each polluter will reduce his discharge to the point at which the cost of reducing it by one more unit is just equal to the residuals charge imposed—the equal marginal cost condition for cost minimization. For that charge to be selected which will exactly attain the target, however, information must be available on the costs of reducing discharges at all sources.

In sum, in the absence of perfect knowledge concerning the costs of waste reduction, a regulation-enforcement system can achieve the quality standard but at a total cost which is likely to be substantially above the minimum attainable. Under similar circumstances, the residuals-charge system will achieve pollution reduction at minimum cost, but will necessitate some iterative (trial-and-error) experimentation with

charges in order to find the exact charge at which the quality standard is attained (Hass, 1970). Because of inefficiencies due to temporarily unstable charge structures, total costs may be somewhat above the minimum. However, increases in total costs due to temporary instability in charges are not likely to be as large as the cost of the inefficiencies that are built into the regulation-enforcement system.

Defendants of the present regulatory-enforcement strategy have repeatedly stated that residuals charges would be administratively too complex to be workable. This position stems from a fundamental misconception of the regulatory-enforcement process. It is in the American tradition to create regulatory agencies to deal with problems caused by malfunctionings in the economic system. The existence of agencies such as the Interstate Commerce Commission, Federal Power Commission, and Food and Drug Administration is sufficient to convince most people that the problems for which these agencies were created are being dealt with successfully. But a careful analysis of the evidence shows that this is rarely the case (MacAvoy, 1970).

The naive view of the regulatory process is that an agency establishes rules and regulations to govern the behavior of the regulated and to further the public interest. The threat of sanctions is deemed to be sufficient to deter violations; but if any occur, violators are quickly brought to justice. The reality is quite different. The enforcement of regulations is essentially a political process entailing bargaining between parties of unequal power (Holden, 1966). In this process the real issues are camouflaged in technical jargon, and the regulators are largely protected from political accountability for their actions. The regulatory agency and the interests they regulate bargain over the regulations to be set. They bargain over whether violations have occurred and if so who was responsible. They bargain over what will be acceptable actions to correct infractions. And in the rare instances where the bargaining process breaks down and the conflict moves to the courts for resolution, the judicial system seeks reasonable accommodation and acceptable compromise. Only rarely is it forced by the flow of events into making either/or choices. At every stage of this multi-level bargaining process those being regulated have a lot at stake, while the public interest is diffuse, poorly organized, and poorly represented. Predictably the bargains struck favor those being regulated. The upshot is that the more numerous the decisions and the further removed they are from elective politics, the less likely it is that these decisions will serve the public interest.

The regulatory-enforcement approach to pollution control suffers from all these faults. In the case of the efforts made by the federal government to control air pollution, this is amply documented (Esposito, 1970). The history of federal enforcement of regulations aimed at the control of water pollution is no better. On the basis of past experience with the regulatory process, it would seem that the burden of proof of its effectiveness should lie upon those who advocate its continued application to the problem of pollution control. Freeman and Haveman believe that the residuals-charge strategy will be administratively simpler and more effective than regulation; and the point can be made relatively easily.

In order to evaluate this claim, it is first necessary to specify the characteristics of a residuals-charge system. Given that environmental quality standards have been set, a single per-unit charge would be levied on each of the prominent harmful substances found in effluents or emissions. Each discharger would be responsible for monitoring his discharge, reporting its composition and quantity to the public authority, and making the appropriate payments. There is an obvious comparison with the system of reporting and paying corporate income taxes. As in the case of the income tax, rules and standards of accuracy for measurement would have to

be specified and audits for compliance would have to be undertaken. Dischargers would be required to install and maintain the required monitoring equipment, subject to audit and calibration for accuracy by the authorities. Information on discharges and payments would be recorded and made available for public scrutiny.

With such a system there is little room for administrative discretion and bargaining. The primary decision is the actual charge to be imposed, and this decision is a significant and highly visible one. There is also a clear performance criterion by which one can judge whether the rate of charge is satisfactory. If environmental quality standards are being met, the rate is high enough; if not, the rate should be raised. Finally, while the history of regulation suggests that the zeal and effectiveness of the regulatory agency diminish over time, the effect of a residuals charge is durable. It remains effective unless the real cost of a fixed charge is eroded by inflation or unless there is an explicit political decision to remove it.

The conclusion with respect to administrative feasibility is a strong one: a residuals-charge system poses no unique or particularly difficult administrative problems. Rather it is an administratively simple strategy which avoids many of the pitfalls of the regulation-enforcement approach and leaves less room for powerful interests to gain special advantages through low-visibility negotiations with the regulatory agency.

It has also been suggested that effluent charges are administratively cumbersome because the optimal charge structure must vary over the seasons and with variations in the stream flow or meteorological changes (Robertson, 1970). It is seldom recognized, however, that these same factors dictate the variability over time in the terms of the discharge permits issued under the regulation-enforcement strategy. Residuals-discharge permits should allow higher discharges during periods of high assimilative capacity while calling for reduced discharges (or perhaps no discharges at all) during critical periods of low stream flow or atmospheric temperature inversion. A license system with a constant maximum allowable rate of discharge is no better or worse in this respect than a residuals-charge system where the price is constant all the year round. Seasonal and other variations can and should be included in either strategy.

The arguments examined by Freeman and Haveman did not, in their view, form a strong case for rejecting the residuals-charge strategy—indeed, quite the opposite. Considering the failure of the current regulation-enforcement approach and, in particular, its political and administrative difficulties, a new environmental strategy which minimizes reliance on regulation-enforcement and which emphasizes the use of economic incentives to achieve changes in behavior seemed to the economists desirable on practical as well as theoretical grounds.

CHAPTER *8*

assurance of municipal water supplies

Alongside the problem of water-*quality* maintenance and improvement, there is the associated problem of the adequacy of municipal water *supplies*. The two may be linked through recycling and renovation of wastewaters for municipal purposes. Let us turn to an examination of this case, because it raises a variety of underlying perceptual and behavioral issues and will permit a whole range of alternatives in water management to be examined.

As Johnson (1971) notes, the problem of supplying water for municipal use is becoming increasingly difficult in the United States, and this trend is expected to continue into the foreseeable future. According to recent estimates of the Water Resources Council, several regions in the United States may experience critical problems of water shortage compounded by water-quality deterioration unless suitable measures are taken. Under certain conditions, the optimal solution to increasing municipal demands and reducing water-quality deterioration may rest with wastewater renovation. Advanced waste treatment could lower the amounts of pollutants discharged to prescribed levels, and the resultant high-quality effluent could be made available on-site for municipal use. The prospective use of renovated wastewater for municipal supply must therefore be evaluated against the range of technical, economic, and social factors which may affect its usage.

The problems associated with prospective municipal water "shortages" are not unique to any area in the country. The differential distribution of water supply and demands in space and time has resulted in both seasonal and annu-

---

This chapter relies upon:
  James F. Johnson, *Renovated Waste Water*. Department of Geography Research Paper No. 135, University of Chicago, 1971, pp. 3–23 and 160–166. Begins on page 247.

al shortages for municipal uses in many parts of the United States. Rapidly increasing urbanization in the southwest has severely taxed that area's permanent water supplies, and the more humid midwest and northeast have been subject to periodic water shortages in spite of apparently adequate resources. Several large-scale projects have been proposed for the southwest, where emphasis has been on quenching that area's growing thirst with interbasin transfers, in spite of their questionable economic efficiency. The problem is of an equally serious nature in eastern cities such as New York, where the water "shortages" caused by the declining reservoir levels in the drought of 1965–66 could have been averted through the use of water from the Hudson River.

In these and other situations, there has been a manifest tendency to meet increasing municipal demands through conventional alternatives such as the transport of water from distant sources. At the same time, inefficiency of municipal usage and deterioration in the quality of supplies has added to the seriousness of local situations. Much of what has been wrong with past approaches to more efficient water management lies in the failure of water planners to recognize the integrated nature of water systems and the impact which each alteration of the water in these systems has upon subsequent uses and users. Greater emphasis has been placed upon the procurement of water than upon the most efficient use of supplies.

Completely renovated municipal sewage effluent in some instances could supply cities at a lower cost than conventional sources, and the impact of using such an alternative could be profound. For instance, a community that would return 80 percent of its initial water withdrawal to its system for reuse could cumulatively increase the utility of this water supply fivefold. This being so, it may be fruitful to examine the position of renovation within the framework of municipal water-supply and water-quality management systems. The range of alternatives for

coping with problems of municipal water supply and water-quality deterioration are discussed in order to assess the relative status of wastewater renovation. Because of the variation in environmental conditions throughtout the country, the practicality of these alternatives may vary considerably in different situations. This discussion does not attempt to specify the practicality of these alternatives; rather, it seeks to lay out the options available to communities for solving their water-supply and wastewater problems.

WATER SUPPLY

Several possible approaches are available to cope with growing municipal demands for water. Options available to any community would vary considerably throughout the country and may involve various combinations of these alternatives. These include (1) bearing shortage or pollution, (2) transporting distant sources and storing untimely sources, (3) increasing the overall water supply, (4) changing water quality, and (5) changing water use (Table 8.1). The alternatives may be outlined with a view to showing the distinctive role of water reuse; each has its distinctive effects upon the water system.

Bear Shortage or Pollution

Theoretically, the community has available to it the "no action" alternative of bearing shortage or pollution of its present water supply without seeking other alternatives—but whether such an option is viable is questionable. A decision to bear shortage would invoke consumer self-restraint; there is no guarantee of the effectiveness of this alternative and no measure with which to support most efficient use. Over the long run, the most productive uses would be competing for water with marginal uses without benefit of any effective market mechanism to

TABLE 8.1

Alternative for meeting increasing demands

Goals	Approaches	Techniques
Bear shortage or pollution		
Use available supply	Storage	Reservoirs
		Storm catchment
	Transport	Aqueducts
		Ground pumpage
		Motive transport
Increase overall supply	Precipitation inducement	Cloud seeding
	Increase and capture snow- and ice-melt	
Change water quality	Treat influent	Freshwater purification
		Desalination
	Treat effluent	Advanced waste treatment
Change water use	Reduce use	Price curbs— metering
		Restricted use
		Recycling
	Curb waste	Evapotranspiration reduction
		Seepage reduction
	Alter distribution	Dual supply lines
		Directed pipelines
		Bottled water

foster efficiency. One of the more obvious drawbacks to such an alternative would be in the probability of diminished residual supply for fire protection, which would most likely be reflected in the higher cost of insurance.

Likewise, the probable community response to the bearing of increased pollution may render it infeasible.

Available Supply

Man conventionally has turned to the storage and transport of high-quality waters in order to satisfy municipal demands. This practice continues today, even where lower-quality sources are available at a more favorable cost. Whether the solution to increasing municipal demands lies in the construction of larger *reservoirs* and more distant *aqueducts* is the subject of considerable debate. As construction costs and interest rates increase, such alternatives become impractical in comparison with nonstructural alternatives. Nevertheless, these schemes continue to dominate the imagination of many planners. Projects such as the Cannonsville reservoir to supply New York City, the Feather River project to supply Southern California, and the Central Arizona project have been subject to severe criticism; yet, other and more elaborate schemes appear to be in the offing. Perhaps the use of *underwater flexible piping* may be an alternative in coastal areas. One study has indicated that substantial cost savings would be realized in using this method rather than the inland route to transfer water from northern to southern California.

Groundwater pumpage has been a popular mode of municipal water supply wherever possible, owing to its generally high quality and low production costs. Because ground aquifers are spread thinly and are slow to recharge, increasing urban demands have resulted in diminishing groundwater levels in many areas. Where wells must extend to continually deeper aquifers, the production costs are likely to increase rapidly. This increase would result from lower yields, increased power and equipment requirements, and higher chloride content. Unless technological advances can improve the efficiency of deep-well drilling, it is likely that heavier urban demands upon localized groundwater sources will have to be met by supplementing with other sources or by aquifer recharge.

Motive transport has been considered for solving municipal water problems, although generally in remote locations. Tank trucks, railroad cars, and tanker vessels all have been used for this purpose, but they usually have not been designed for the job and their costs are high. Motively transported water generally has been used only where other alternatives are not available, whether due to emergencies such as drought or contamination or because of remote location. It is unlikely that this alternative will be considered by communities where other alternatives are available, especially considering the risk posed by possible failure of delivery.

Increase Overall Supply

Increasing municipal demands also may be met through increasing the overall supply of available water. This can be accomplished through precipitation inducement or through snow- or ice-melt. Precipitation inducement is a highly complex alternative, and little is known of the potential consequences. One study has indicated that while it would be more economical than conventional alternatives in some locations, it may not be as suitable elsewhere. The present limitation appears to be primarily a physical one. Its prospective use is complicated by potential litigation involving both on-site and off-site damages. Such damages could grow out of (1) conflicting weather requirements of property owners, (2) unanticipated destructive effects such as floods, and (3) deprivation of benefits of natural weather such as off-site reduction in precipitation.

Snow-melt is an important source of water supply, particularly in the west. Because storage is dependent upon regional climate, it is thought by some to be beyond the control of man. Snow accumulation can have a significant effect upon the general availability of water, seasonal low stream flows, and direct evaporation. At present, the practicality or physical capability of supplying additional demands through this alternative has not been determined; perhaps future technology will lead to its more efficient utilization. The harnessing of water contained in *ice masses* also warrants further consideration. However, it appears that the distance between massive glacial deposits and municipal demands would inhibit any such project. One interesting scheme proposed by John Isaac would offer a partial solution to the growing water demands of Los Angeles by towing icebergs from the Antarctic. However, there is some doubt whether such an alternative is physically viable.

Change Water Quality

The alternative that appears to offer the greatest potential for meeting future water needs is improving the quality of polluted waters. Major cities generally are located near or help generate vast quantities of low-quality water. Considering the trend to increasing costs for fixed capital projects such as reservoirs and aqueducts, alternatives geared to the continual refinement of purification technology and concomitant cost efficiencies would appear to be attractive.

More attention should be given to forms of catchment that are less spectacular. Paved surfaces and even roofs provide potential for meeting future demands. Low-quality waters are available as saline or brackish supplies from which inorganic material need be removed, surface supplies in which organics pose the main problem; or as sewage effluent from which organics and possibly inorganics need be removed.

The purified product of *low-quality surface water* is used throughout the country, although to a lesser extent where higher-quality supplies are even remotely available. The use of these polluted waters is mostly the result of deterioration of a once-clean supply. It is likely that many water managers would opt for transporting clean waters to cities if the choice were open to them, in view of such recent expansion as that of Detroit to Lake Huron. Although the monetary costs of increasing supplies through treatment of polluted sources are less than for most transport-oriented alternatives, it is likely that costs in terms of aesthetics and hygienic risk may offset this in many situations.

The use of *desalinized seawater* has received considerable attention and should add measurably to available supplies in coastal areas once treatment costs are reduced. Apparently desalinized water bears no stigma to prospective domestic users, owing to the inorganic rather than organic pollutants. It is likely that this source will be viewed as a practical alternative for meeting future demands, especially in coastal areas with limited freshwater supplies. Its value to inland areas is quite limited by high transport costs. For instance, a study of the feasibility of transporting desalinized seawater to augment the flow of the Colorado River indicated that the transport cost would be several times that of desalination.

The use of *renovated municipal sewage effluent* would be competitive with both transport- and treatment-oriented alternatives, although the problems of aesthetics and hygienic risk associated with organically polluted sources may be an inhibiting factor. Because of its lower pollutant load, secondary sewage effluent would be less expensive to "desalinize" than brackish or saline water. With the rising costs of construction-oriented purification alternatives, it is likely that the use of renovated wastewater would be practical in a number of situations. This is especially true where high waste-treatment requirements reduce the marginal cost of providing a potable product.

Change Water Use

Municipal demands also could be met more effectively by changing the way in which water is used. This can be accomplished by reducing the amount used, by curbing waste, or by altering the distribution system in order to gear water quality to usage.

Reduction in use could be accomplished by metering or pricing curbs, use restrictions, or recycling. Both *metering* and *pricing curbs* have been found to be effective means of lowering municipal water demands, although not generally employed by water managers for this purpose. Several major cities, including New York and Chicago, do not meter their water supplies,

instead charging a flat rate. The practicality of metering must be weighed according to installation and computation costs versus the increased utility of available supplies. One study indicated a 40 percent drop in per capita water consumption in Boulder, Colorado, from 1960 when only 5 percent of the city was metered to 1965 when it was fully metered. Another study indicated that the quantity of water demand for residential uses, particularly sprinkling, is affected by the price charged. Howe (1968) suggests that even the magnitude of maximum-day demands responds to price charges, and this could be used by management for either increasing or decreasing average- and maximum-day demands.

Restrictions on use have been employed for temporary water shortages, but not as permanent measures. Temporary restrictions on lawn-watering, car-washing, and other peak uses could substantially reduce peak loading but tend to be unpopular. Such restrictions in some instances might not act in the interest of economic efficiency, in that they might penalize those users or uses that are willing and able to pay the marginal cost.

In response to the growing scarcity of available water and the increase in associated production costs in certain situations, some industrial users have begun to *recycle* water. The recycling of water for cooling and certain types of processing that have low-quality requirements is especially valuable in arid regions where the cost and quality of fresh water is too high for the needs of these uses. Perhaps more industries would gear operations to recycling if the cost of purchasing water reflected marginal production costs as it should, rather than the distribution costs that encourage large-volume usage. Nonetheless, recycling warrants serious consideration for satisfying some of the future municipal demands.

Increased municipal demands also could be satisfied in part by reducing the amount of water wastage through evaporation, transpiration, and seepage. Evaporation can be lessened by covering water surfaces, whether by chemical or structural measures. Hexadecanol has been applied to water surfaces in reservoirs as a monomolecular film and found significant in *reducing evaporation*. However, its use is not physically practical at present because it can be broken down by wind and wave action. Evaporation losses in open conduits account for some 20 percent of water flow in some parts of the southwest. In spite of high costs, complete closure may be practical in areas of high potential evaporation that face future water scarcity. Other methods such as design of reservoirs to obtain low area-to-volume ratio, alteration of the thermal stratification of water in reservoirs, and selective withdrawal of warmer water from stratified reservoirs may be practical alternatives in certain situations.

Increased water yields also may be realized by *reducing transpiration* from vegetation, although municipalities may have little control over the most substantial sources of transpiration losses. In the arid southwest, for instance, the maintenance of irrigation agriculture with nearly 100 percent evapotranspiration losses ignores the economic value of water for alternative municipal and industrial uses. Unfortunately, the political factors in water development may far outweigh economic factors in such situations. Still, certain communities can increase water yields substantially through more effective watershed management. As one example, elimination of ground and forest vegetation through chemical application added 190,000 gallons of water per acre in a Newark, N. J., watershed.

Seepage is a problem in both the import and distribution of municipal water supplies. The *lining of conduits* with concrete or other impervious materials would remove the seepage losses in the import of water, but the costs may be considerable. Seepage within the distribution system also is a serious problem owing to the cracking of pipes, and losses may run from 10 to 20 percent. Where water production

costs are high and seepage losses considerable, the isolation and repair of breaks may prove to be a practical alternative for meeting a portion of increasing demands. In fact, the hygienic risk posed by seepage inflow may be sufficient reason itself for greater concern with *pipeline repair*.

Another means of meeting increased municipal demands would be to alter the distribution system in order to make more efficient use of the range in quality of alternative water sources. The increased production costs for obtaining a high-quality water may not be compatible with the needs for certain uses which can utilize a low-quality product at reduced costs. The supplying of valuable high-quality water for certain industrial and domestic uses and for fire protection may not be the wisest allocation of the resource under conditions of increased scarcity. Distribution systems that allow for some greater degree of choice may improve this efficiency. Alternative means of distribution include dual supply lines, directed pipelines, and bottling.

Dual supply lines would direct two water supplies of different quality to the consumer. In such a system, lower-quality water could be used for lawn watering or flushing of wastes—uses that account for nearly one-half of residential demands. Although the costs may be excessive in presently developed areas, dual systems warrant serious consideration in newly developing areas. However, the risk associated with potential error in cross-linkage of supply lines may act as a constraint upon serious consideration of this alternative.

Directed piping of nonpotable water merits serious consideration in terms of both economic efficiency and public acceptance. It is likely that water could be directed to high-demand industrial conglomerations at low cost, especially where distances between supply and demand are minimal. Also, public reaction would not be a factor, because potential linkage with domestic systems would be nil. It has been over two decades since U.S. Steel at Sparrows Point began using Baltimore's sewage effluent; perhaps the time has arrived for broadening the scope of directed piping to provide a partial solution to increasing industrial demands.

Uses requiring potable-quality water account for a small share of residential demands. Therefore, it may be worthwhile considering a distribution scheme incorporating *bottled water*. In recent years, sales of bottled water have increased tremendously, and a range of products and distribution modes has developed. This results from apparent dissatisfaction with municipal supplies. Mass distribution of bottled water could be an effective means of freeing municipal piped supplies from the inhibiting requirements of potability.

WATER QUALITY

Several alternatives are available to communities to stem the increasing deterioration of water by municipal sewage effluent and to increase the wastable municipal supply. Essentially these involve two steps, collection and disposal (Table 8.2). Approaches to increase the efficiency of collection are (1) extension of sewerage pipelines, and (2) preventing storm runoff from causing combined-system overload. Approaches to minimize the effect of sewage disposal include (1) concentrating disposal in specific watercourses, (2) utilizing stream purification, (3) utilizing soil purification, and (4) increased sewage treatment.

Collection

Collection involves the transfer of wastes from one location to another and is not necessarily remedial to the system as a whole. Nevertheless, much of the water-quality deterioration in developing urban areas today grows out of the inability to collect and treat municipal wastes adequately. Urban fringe areas often

TABLE 8.2

Alternatives for reducing water-quality deterioration

Goals	Approaches	Techniques
Increase collection efficiency	Centralize waste water operations	Extend sewerage facilities
	Prevent overburden from storm runoff	Separate storm and sanitation sewers
		Temporary diversion and storage
Minimize effect of disposal	Selective pollution	Assigned waste channels
	Utilize stream purification	Flow augmentation
		Temporary waste withholding
		Effluent dispersal by pipeline
	Utilize soil purification	Land disposal— spreading
	Withholding waste	Increased waste treatment

lack the refined treatment facilities necessary to cope with rapidly increasing waste loads. Pollution of water resources may result from the discharge of raw waste into surface streams as well as oversaturation of septic systems. Much of this pollution could be stemmed by *extending municipal sewerage facilities* to outlying areas. However, dispersion of urban settlement can make such sewage collection an expensive matter, and the problems of intercommunity politics and "equitable" service charges may severely inhibit such schemes.

Another factor that has a substantial impact on water quality is the design of collection systems with respect to storm runoff and municipal waste. At present, most systems combine both storm and sanitation sewers, and serious pollution is caused by overloading of the system during heavy storm runoff. This pollution results from the diversion of untreated sewage along with storm waters into receiving watercourses.

Alternative solutions would be either separate storm and sanitation sewers, or diversion and temporary storage of storm water.

Separate storm and sanitation sewers are quite expensive because of the construction and renewal costs involved. Present research indicates that dual sewer systems are practical in some circumstances, such as newly developing urban areas. The prospects for using storm runoff as an alternative source of water supply also should be considered. In areas already developed, *temporary storage of storm water* may be a more practical solution than dual sewer systems. Two schemes presently under study appear to be of practical value for particular situations. These are the use of deep caverns for storm waste storage at Chicago and the use of inflatable bags at Washington, D.C., Sandusky, Ohio, and Cambridge, Maryland.

Waste Disposal

Communities generally have used nearby watercourses as convenient means of waste disposal. The capability of flowing waters to assimilate low-volume waste loads probably reinforced the perceived practicality of this choice. Where flows are less adequate, wastes generally are disposed of on land, utilizing the capability of soils to purify percolating waters. However, water and soil purification capabilities are limited, and communities have supplemented these with treatment systems based on similar principles. In most of these schemes, man adjusts the variables of flow and waste discharge in an attempt to optimize purification capabilities. Alternatives are (1) diversion to assigned waste channels, (2) streamflow augmentation, (3) temporary withholding of wastes, (4) dispersal of effluent by pipeline, (5) land disposal, and (6) increased waste treatment.

One approach to the problem would be to *designate particular channels for waste transport* and allow deterioration therein. Two factors support such a system. First, it may not be in the interest of economic efficiency to attempt to bring all watercourses up to habitable quality, especially those which are well entrenched in industry. It may be that the cost of waste treatment would be far greater than the benefits of water-quality improvement. In addition, such a channel may provide for regional waste disposal and may be economically practical on these additional grounds. However, it is worth noting that the inequitable distribution of benefits and costs to uses along the channel such as recreation may render such an alternative politically infeasible.

The conventional regional approach to reduction of water-quality deterioration has been *flow augmentation* of the stream. Flow augmentation distributes the flow of the water course evenly through a series of catchment dams, thereby maintaining levels suitable for maximum dilution of wastes throughout the year. This is generally practical where seasonal irregularities in low flow can be adjusted, but it should not be considered as a solution independent of other schemes. For instance, Davis (1966) has demonstrated that flow augmentation as a singular means of pollution abatement is much more costly than a combined approach with increased waste treatment.

The *temporary withholding of wastes* during periods of low streamflow also is geared to the variable assimilation capacity of the watercourse. This is generally practical where critical low flow is of short duration, but it would not be economically practical over longer periods.

Still another means toward optimizing the assimilation process is the *dispersion of effluent* by pipeline along a watercourse. One study found this to be a practical alternative to other forms of water-quality management. In each instance, however, the use of the watercourse as a cleansing agent passes the cost of purification on to other users. These costs are most evident in the reduction of recreational and aesthetic pleasures derived from the water course.

The *disposal of treated sewage effluent on land* is

a relatively common practice in arid environments such as the southwest that do not afford sufficient volumes of water flow for assimilation. Although this may remove the direct threat to intermittent flowing streams, care must be exercised to insure against pollution of the groundwater resources. Increased urbanization and waste loading would necessitate either increased discharge acreage or increased pretreatment if the quality of groundwater resources is to be safeguarded.

The most effective long-range alternative for restoring water quality, and that which minimizes disbenefits to downstream users, appears to be *increased waste treatment*. This includes the primary stage of solids removal, the secondary stage of biological purification, and advanced chemical techniques where warranted. Increased treatment would free greater stretches of the watercourse for various types of recreation, fish and wildlife uses, and aesthetic pleasure than would other alternatives. On the other hand, the problem of ultimate waste disposal is yet unresolved, and a continuing effort must be made to determine the best disposal sites and mode of transport.

WASTEWATER RENOVATION

The optimal solution to the problems of municipal water demands and water-quality deterioration may rest with wastewater renovation. Sewage effluent would be purified through advanced waste treatment, and this high-quality water would be made available onsite for municipal use. The idea of reusing water is neither new nor unique; the seemingly radical element is the degree and proximity of reuse. It is estimated that over 40 percent of the U.S. population reuses water that has been used for some domestic or industrial purposes including power cooling, and 60 percent of the population reuses water that has been used upstream. In some instances where the water-supply intake of one city lies immediately downstream of the sewage outfall of another, or where tidal influence returns the flow of a city's effluent to its water supply, water systems currently do use waste water.

As waste-treatment requirements increase in order to stem the growing deterioration of our waters, the quality of treated effluent will increase accordingly. On the basis of standards currently being used, as we noted earlier, municipalities discharging into streams will be required to provide a minimum of secondary treatment, and in some cases tertiary treatment. Also, there is growing awareness on the part of state governments of the need to provide for more stringent regulation of intrastate streams. As a result, treated effluent in many cities will be suitable for nonpotable municipal uses and with additional treatment would be suitable for the home.

Practicality of Use

The practicality of using renovated wastewater for municipal water supply varies with environmental conditions. In particular, it is tied closely to the quality of effluent discharged by the community and the availability of suitable alternative sources of supply.

Increasing waste-treatment requirements that limit the discharge of organic wastes and nutrients will result in the availability of a high-quality product effluent for many communities throughout the United States. In many instances, both in humid and arid environments, this effluent may be less expensive for satisfying particular urban demands than alternative sources of supply. This should become more obvious in the near future in view of the growing scarcity of good reservoir sites, the increasing costs of construction-oriented alternatives, and the growing competition for state and federal funds necessary for the construction of many of the larger projects.

The use of renovated wastewater, on the other hand, should become relatively less expensive in time, owing to the refinement in purification technology and the increasing sewage-treatment requirements. The nature of this use could vary considerably, depending upon the different water-supply conditions throughout the United States. In water-scarce areas, such as the southwest and the Great Plains, it may be more practical for communities to consider direct aquifer recharge with renovated wastewater for municipal supply. On the other hand, advanced waste-treatment requirements in the midwest and northeast may make it more practical for many communities in these regions to consider at least directed piping of renovated wastewater to satisfy concentrated high-volume demands, such as for industrial usage.

Greater emphasis is needed at the national level to assure a coordinated management of water-quality control and water supply. At present, various agencies are charged with specific tasks within each of these two problem areas. In particular, more effort is needed to classify, describe, and analyze the resource situations most amenable to advanced waste treatment. Present efforts are piecemeal, apparently being limited to the funding of separate operations in particular communities, apart from any ordering by regions or conditions of environmental stress. The water-resource agencies concerned with this problem need first to improve the methods of classifying environmental situations in the United States according to the nature of resource deterioration, the alternatives available to improve the quality of these resources, and the immediacy with which these programs should be put into action. From this, it would be possible to describe more accurately the regions where high-quality effluent may be available for meeting future municipal and other water demands.

Technical and Institutional Factors Affecting Reuse

The use of renovated wastewater appears to be considered by many water managers as a desperation alternative, one more appropriate for consideration in arid environments. A reversal of thinking is required if renovated wastewater is to be considered when it is the most economical alternative rather than when it is the "only" economical alternative. Planners and managers should recognize that several alternative methods are available by which to use renovated waste water—namely: direct reuse; aquifer recharge; directed piping to high-volume users such as industry; and, possibly, systems in which bottled water is distributed for potable usage. Study has indicated that while the use of renovated wastewater at Tucson may be of more apparent practicality, it also is likely to be of practical value to communities in more humid regions of the country, such as Indianapolis and Philadelphia.

Consideration of renovated wastewater as a practical alternative may be constrained by the organization of water agencies in a community or region. In order to incorporate the use of renovated wastewater into municipal water planning in an efficient manner, administration of supply and disposal should be effectively coordinated. In communities where separate agencies are responsible for water supply and waste disposal, an effort should be made to establish liaison between them in order to make efficient use of renovated wastewater. The situation is most critical where agencies are wholly segregated—for example, where a community has a private water utility and a public sewage-disposal agency.

This may be asking too much of most communities. Nevertheless, renovated wastewater is going to be an integral part of municipal water management in the relatively near future, and we should be concerned that communities use this source wisely at the most opportune time. Because of the constraints created by the lack of administrative linkages and inadequate information flows, water-management officials may not consider the use of renovated wastewater in spite of its possible value. Federal agencies involved, therefore, should consider creation of information services which could take an active role in both disseminating information and providing technical expertise.

Consumer Attitudes toward Renovated Wastewater

The issues of whether or not the municipal use of renovated wastewater is technically feasible or economically practical lose relevance if officials responsible for water management preclude the consideration of such alternatives. Both water analysts and community water-management officials have expressed concern that consumers would not accept the use of renovated wastewater because of certain aesthetic and hygienic constraints. In fact, however, consumer attitudes are found to vary considerably according to differential perceptions of their resource situations, and certain personal factors. Perhaps the most significant finding is that some of the factors which may affect the economic practicality of using renovated wastewater, namely the adequacy and quality of water-supply sources, also are associated with individual attitudes toward renovated wastewater.

The perceived adequacy of water-supply sources to meet anticipated future demands showed a significant association with consumer acceptance of possible community consideration of renovated wastewater. Because the scarcity of alternative sources, or the cost of developing them, may signal the need for communities to consider renovated wastewater, it is important for managers to be aware that the perceptions of these conditions also may be reflected in more favorable public support. There also is a significant association between consumer perception of the quality of the present water-supply source and attitude toward use of renovated wastewater as reflected in willingness to pay. Where communities consider it economically practical to supplement a source of low organic quality with renovated wastewater, it is important again for managers to be aware that perception of these conditions by the public may be reflected in more favorable support.

Certain personal factors also show significant associations with attitudes toward renovated wastewater. In particular, the associations of education and knowledge of renovated wastewater with consumer attitudes may signal the possible importance of both general education and specific information programs in the prospective adoption of such innovations. Educational level shows a rather strong association with both acceptance of community consideration of renovated wastewater and the willingness to drink the product. As educational levels increase in the future, consumer attitudes may be even more favorable toward renovated wastewater, especially in view of the continually increasing public familiarity with technological achievements. There also is a significant association between knowledge of renovated wastewater and willingness to drink the product. In view of the apparent importance of both education and knowledge of the product, consideration should be given to the possible value of information programs as social guides concerning the acceptance of renovated wastewater.

Future Directions for Research

It seems clear that officials responsible for the management of municipal water supply should give greater attention to understanding consumer attitudes relevant to these and other water decisions. In fact, a greater understanding is needed of both consumer and manager attitudes, especially as they relate to one another. In such work, it may be profitable to proceed to obtain a better understanding of community acceptance, rather than that of consumers alone. This would provide officials with an appraisal of the validity of their perceptions concerning consumer attitudes and goals relevant to both the specific issue of renovation and the broader area of water management. Presumably such in-depth analysis could be extended to cover a cross section of environmental conditions in order to observe whether public-official relationships would vary with these conditions.

Community acceptance, however, falls short of community adoption. The controversy over fluoridation has left its mark in cautioning against the assumption that the one assures the other. In spite of generally favorable reactions accorded to fluoridation, it met rather resounding defeats when put to public referenda. A range of factors appeared to contribute to the defeat of fluoridation referendums. Research on issues like fluoridation may provide the basis for comparison of an innovation which, as yet, is relatively unpublicized. Much needs to be done toward evaluating the weight of factors in the fluoridation issue as they relate to the pro-spective adoption of renovated wastewater for municipal water supply.

Among the most significant points in favor of subsequent research on the renovation issue is the opportunity it provides for the meshing of disciplines. Technically, it serves to combine the often separate subsystems of water supply and water-quality control. To the social and behavioral sciences it offers the opportunity to observe the range of psychological, social, economic, and political impacts associated with the radical concept of ingestion of a product of human waste. Hopefully, subsequent research will lead not only to a better understanding of factors surrounding the prospective community acceptance and adoption of using this valuable resource, but also to a refinement in the techniques of water-resource management.

CHAPTER *9*

solid-wastes management

The question of wastewater renovation discussed in Chapter 8 links closely to that of the pollution of both land and water associated with disposal of solid wastes. Solid wastes—refuse in the streets, litter on beaches and along roadsides, abandoned autos on isolated curbsides and in weeded vacant lots, rusty refrigerators and stoves in backyards, thousands of dumps—can be seen scarring many parts of the American landscape. And the less visible aspects of the problem—soild wastes in the ocean, contamination of ground water, and wasted resources—are even more critical.

Proper management of solid wastes is thus an integral part of any attempt at upgrading environmental quality. Stricter enforcement of air-quality standards has focused attention on burn-ing dumps and inefficient incinerators, many of them operated by municipal governments. Water-quality research is beginning to probe the effects of dumps and landfills on the purity of groundwater. What is clear from this research is that each effluent is an interacting part of a total environmental system. Recalling what was said in earlier chapters of this book, the most important feature of such systems is the synergistic effect that characterizes the pollutants—they combine and interact in unforeseen ways.

The principal problems associated with disposal of solid wastes have been well documented and can be divided into five areas: (1) rats, flies and other pests; (2) air pollution (smoke, fly ash, and odors); (3) unsightliness, blowing paper; (4) pollution of ground and surface waters; and

Materials are included from:
John R. Sheaffer with Berndt von Boehm and James E. Hackett, *Refuse Disposal Needs and Practices in Northeastern* *Illinois* (Chicago, Ill.: Northeastern Illinois Planning Commission, 1965). Begins on page 264.

(5) increased truck traffic. All of these problems can be minimized or satisfactorily solved by competent engineering and planning when selecting refuse disposal sites and methods of operation, making most solid-waste management strategies of essentially local concern.

For this reason, local governments have traditionally shouldered primary responsibility for solid-waste collection, processing, and disposal. Not until 1965, with passage of the Solid Waste Disposal Act, did the federal government assume a major role. Under the act, the federal government became responsible for research, training, demonstrations of new technology, technical assistance, and grants for state and interstate solid-waste planning programs. The legislation focused attention on studies to conserve natural resources by reducing waste and unsalvageable materials and by solid-waste recovery—i.e., on proper methods of residuals management. Under the act, the Department of Health, Education, and Welfare, through the Bureau of Solid Waste Management, was to administer the federal program for solid wastes from all other sources. HEW's function subsequently was transferred to EPA and became the Office of Solid Waste Management.

The Office of Solid Waste Management and the Bureau of Mines have been instrumental in promoting both technological innovations and improved methods of resource recovery, or recycling. Local governments have only limited funds, and municipal officials are timorous about interfering with refuse collection routines for fear of upsetting labor relations and public relations. Consequently, local innovation has been minimal. Even when the evidence is clear that new methods result in improvements, jealousies and fear of adverse employee relations sometimes prevent implementation. Most state governments have also avoided heavy research and experimental program funding in solid-waste management. This emphasizes the need for research and development programs to assure that once the value of an innovation is evident,

it is quickly incorporated into as many systems as possible.

WHAT MAKES SOLID WASTES

The total solid wastes produced in the United States in 1967 reached 365 billion tons, as shown in Table 9.1. Most of it originated from agriculture and livestock. Other large amounts arose from mining and industrial processes. Some 256 million tons arose from residential, commercial, and municipal uses in urban areas. Only three-fourths of this waste was collected.

TABLE 9.1

Generation of solid wastes from five major sources in 1967

	Solid Wastes Generated	
Source	Pounds/ Capita/Day	Million Tons/Year
Urban:		
domestic	3.5	128
municipal	1.2	44
commercial	2.3	84
subtotal	7.0	256
Industrial	3.0	110
Agricultural:		
vegetation	15.0	552
animal	43.0	1,563
subtotal	58.0	2,115
Mineral	30.8	1,126
Federal	1.2	43
U.S. totals	100.0	3,650

Although urban wastes from homes, businesses, and institutions make up a small part of the total load of solid waste produced, they are the most offensive and the most dangerous to health when they accumulate near where people live. Agriculture and mineral wastes, although much greater in volume, are generally spread more widely over the land. They are more isolated from population concentrations and may not require special collection and disposal. Nevertheless, as more is learned about the effects of agricultural and mineral wastes on the quality of air, water, and aesthetics, steps to curb their production and facilitate disposal seem likely.

The largest single source of solid wastes in this country is agriculture. It accounts for over half the total. The more than 2 billion tons of *agricultural wastes* produced each year includes animal and slaughterhouse wastes, useless residues from crop harvesting, vineyard and orchard prunings, and greenhouse wastes.

Herds of cattle and other animals, once left to graze over large open meadows, are now often confined to feedlots where they fatten more rapidly for market. On these feedlots they generate enormous and concentrated quantities of manure that cannot readily and safely be assimilated by the soil. Manure permeates the earth and invades waterbodies, contributing to fish kills, eutrophied lakes, off-flavored drinking waters, and contaminated aquifers. Feedlots intensify odors, dusts, and the wholesale production of flies and other noxious insects. Animal waste disposal is a growing problem because the demand for animal manure as a soil conditioner is declining. Easier handling, among other advantages, favors chemical fertilizers.

About 110 million tons of *industrial solid wastes* (excluding mineral solid wastes) are generated every year. More than 15 million tons of it are scrap metal, and 30 million tons are paper and paper product wastes; a miscellaneous bag of slags, waste plastics, bales of rags, and drums of assorted products discarded for various reasons make up the rest. The electric utility industry produced over 30 million tons of fly ash in 1969 from burning bituminous coal and lignite. By 1980 the figure could rise to 40 million tons. Currently, only about 20 percent of ash material finds any use.

In 1967, 1,126 million tons of *mineral solid wastes*, comprising 39 percent of total solid wastes, were generated in the United States—most of it from the mineral and fossil-fuel mining,

milling, and processing industries. Slag heaps, culm piles, and mill tailings accumulate near extraction or processing operations. Eighty mineral industries generate solid waste, but eight of them are responsible for 80 percent of the total. Copper contributes the largest waste tonnage, followed by iron and steel, bituminous coal, phosphate rock, lead, zinc, alumina, and anthracite. By 1980 the nation's mineral industries will be generating at least 2 billion tons of waste every year.

In 1969 Americans threw away more than 256 million tons of *residential, commercial, and municipal solid wastes*. Approximately 190 million tons were collected by public agencies and private refuse firms. The remainder was abandoned, dumped, disposed of at the point of origin, or hauled away by the producer to a disposal site.

The solid waste collected annually includes 30 million tons of paper and paper products; 4 million tons of plastics; 100 million tires; 30 billion bottles; 60 billion cans; millions of tons of demolition debris, grass and tree trimmings, food wastes, and sewage sludge; and millions of discarded automobiles and major appliances.

Waste-Generation Factors:
The Evidence from California

One of the most comprehensive surveys of solid wastes has been completed in the state of California. This survey pinpointed in great detail the sources of solid wastes and enabled waste-generation factors to be developed that allow prediction of the likely growth of solid wastes. This survey found that in 1967, total solid-waste production in California amounted to 71,502,000 tons. Of this total 32.0 percent (22,914,000 tons) was municipal waste, 48.8 percent (34,901,000 tons) was agricultural waste, and 19.2 percent (13,687,000 tons) was industrial waste. The amount of solid wastes produced by each county is listed by categories in Table 9.2, together with the ranking of each county

TABLE 9.2

Total solid-waste production in California

County	Municipal Tons/Year	Industrial Tons/Year	Agricultural Tons/Year	Annual Total Tonnage	Rank in State
Alameda	1,347,000	388,000	125,000	1,860,000	15
Alpine	< 1,000	3,000	< 1,000	3,000	58
Amador	10,000	62,000	15,000	87,000	54
Butte	90,000	114,000	456,000	660,000	30
Calaveras	10,000	84,000	11,000	105,000	53
Colusa	11,000	0	540,000	551,000	35
Contra Costa	549,000	253,000	378,000	1,180,000	21
Del Norte	13,000	372,000	33,000	418,000	38
El Dorado	40,000	318,000	19,000	377,000	40
Fresno	479,000	254,000	2,876,000	3,609,000	2
Glenn	16,000	53,000	526,000	595,000	33
Humboldt	101,000	1,802,000	250,000	2,153,000	12
Imperial	79,000	9,000	2,493,000	2,580,700	6
Inyo	12,000	1,000	11,000	23,000	56
Kern	322,000	82,000	2,117,000	2,521,000	7
Kings	60,000	15,000	1,396,000	1,471,000	17
Lake	15,000	69,000	43,000	127,000	52
Lassen	14,000	147,000	28,000	189,000	49
Los Angeles	8,985,000	1,881,000	1,779,000	12,645,000	1
Madera	41,000	107,000	635,000	783,000	27
Marin	196,000	9,000	313,000	518,000	36
Mariposa	4,000	10,000	42,000	56,000	55
Mendocino	45,000	901,000	89,000	1,035,000	23
Merced	102,000	15,000	2,101,000	2,218,000	11
Modoc	7,000	92,000	77,000	176,000	50
Mono	4,000	0	2,000	6,000	57
Monterey	240,000	73,000	777,000	1,090,000	22
Napa	74,000	6,000	140,000	220,000	46
Nevada	21,000	102,000	18,000	141,000	51
Orange	1,557,000	223,000	456,000	2,236,000	9
Placer	66,000	198,000	91,000	355,000	41
Plumas	10,000	364,000	5,000	379,000	39
Riverside	483,000	88,000	1,539,000	2,110,000	13
Sacramento	733,000	73,000	847,000	1,653,000	16
San Benito	14,000	5,000	175,000	194,000	48
San Bernardino	714,000	920,000	1,535,000	3,169,000	3
San Diego	1,559,000	107,000	741,000	2,407,000	8
San Francisco	1,071,000	122,000	0	1,193,000	20
San Joaquin	277,000	182,000	1,773,000	2,232,000	10
San Luis Obispo	95,000	8,000	457,000	560,000	34
San Mateo	589,000	99,000	29,000	717,000	29

(cont.)

TABLE 9.2 (cont.)

County	Municipal Tons/Year	Industrial Tons/Year	Agricultural Tons/Year	Annual Total Tonnage	Rank in State
Santa Barbara	245,000	39,000	328,000	612,000	32
Santa Clara	1,174,000	343,000	387,000	1,904,000	14
Santa Cruz	100,000	142,000	97,000	339,000	42
Shasta	70,000	659,000	153,000	882,000	24
Sierra	2,000	208,000	2,000	212,000	47
Siskiyou	30,000	687,000	157,000	874,000	26
Solano	173,000	41,000	511,000	725,000	28
Sonoma	167,000	216,000	915,000	1,298,000	18
Stanislaus	168,000	156,000	2,277,000	2,601,000	5
Sutter	36,000	16,000	577,000	629,000	31
Tehama	26,000	288,000	152,000	466,000	37
Trinity	8,000	260,000	2,000	270,000	44
Tulare	173,000	182,000	2,629,000	2,984,000	4
Tuolumne	17,000	310,000	8,000	335,000	43
Ventura	353,000	68,000	820,000	1,241,000	19
Yolo	77,000	31,000	769,000	877,000	25
Yuba	40,000	38,000	180,000	258,000	45
Additional Statewide		392,000		392,000	
Total[a]	22,914,000	13,687,000	34,901,000	71,502,000	

[a] The data in this and the following tables may not balance due to errors inherent in maintaining significant figures.

according to the total amount of wastes produced.

Previously, in solid-waste planning, a general rule-of-thumb factor of 4 or $4^1/_2$ pounds per person per day has frequently been quoted and has been accepted as a national average for solid-waste production. For comparison purposes, the more than 71 million tons of solid wastes produced annually in California by a population of almost 20 million persons represented a production factor of 20.2 pounds per person per day. This per capita figure breaks down into 6.5 pounds per day of municipal waste, 9.8 pounds per day of agricultural waste, and 3.9 pounds per day of industrial waste. The discrepancy highlights the need for the kind of data provided by the California study.

Municipal Wastes

The California researchers believed that larger urban centers would be likely to generate more municipal wastes than smaller centers. For this reason, the entire state's population was divided into population groupings. Waste-production factors were then established for each population density grouping for commercial, demolition, and special wastes. Each population center, whether it was an incorporated city or located in unincorporated areas, was grouped into one of the following categories:

Less than 1,000 persons
1,000 to 10,000 persons
10,000 to 100,000 persons
More than 100,000 persons

TABLE 9.3

Statewide municipal waste production in California

	Applicable Population	Waste Generation Factor	Annual Total Tonnage
Residential waste			
Countywide average	19,432,620	2.5 lb/capita/day	8,866,100
		Subtotal	8,866,100
Commercial waste			
< 1,000	1,722,770	1.5 lb/capita/day	471,600
1,001–10,000	1,928,050	2.0 lb/capita/day	703,700
10,001–100,000	8,433,500	2.5 lb/capita/day	3,847,800
> 100,000	7,348,300	3.5 lb/capita/day	4,693,700
		Subtotal	9,716,800
Demolition waste			
1,000–10,000	1,928,050	100 lb/capita/year	96,400
10,001–100,000	8,433,500	250 lb/capita/year	1,054,200
> 100,000	7,348,300	500 lb/capita/year	1,837,100
		Subtotal	2,987,700
Special waste			
Street refuse	14,412,080	120 lb/capita/year	864,700
Sewage residue	17,709,850	54 lb/capita/year	478,200
		Subtotal	1,342,900
		Total	22,913,500

In the case of metropolitan areas, the populations used were those of the cities plus high-density unincorporated surrounding areas. The populations living in other unincorporated areas were categorized by communities; scattered persons or small villages were placed in the less-than-1,000 group.

Table 9.3 presents the total amount of municipal wastes generated in California during 1967, listed by the various categories, with waste-generation factors calculated. This represents the quantity of wastes "produced"— not necessarily the quantity collected or taken to disposal sites. As indicated in the table, almost 23 million tons of municipal wastes representing 6.5 pounds per capita per day were generated in 1967. Table 9.4 identifies some of the special waste-generation factors that were found.

Industrial Solid Wastes

A very detailed analysis of industrial solid wastes was completed by the California researchers. The data on quantities of industrial solid wastes produced were determined from

TABLE 9.4

Estimation procedures and estimates of municipal wastes

Waste Source	Multipliers	Source Units	Tons/Year
Household garbage and rubbish			
Single family unit	1.42910 tons/unit/year	173,819	248,405
Multiple family unit	0.62755 tons/unit/year	106,984	70,347
City streets: leaves, litter, sweepings, and tree trimmings	42.9 lb/capita/year	758,230	16,264
Refuse collected along highway right-of-way			
Freeway refuse	8.0 tons/mile/year	62	496
County roads refuse	3.3 tons/mile/year	200	660
Sewage-treatment residue	87.1 lb/capita/year	805,930	35,098
Local parks and playgrounds	5.4 lb/capita/year	805,930	2,176
Regional parks			415
Total waste			373,861

field surveys (interviews), mail surveys, and the application of waste-production factors to employment data and production data.

When the results of the studies were assembled, it was found that during 1967 an estimated 13,687,000 tons of industrial wastes were produced in California. As shown in Table 9.5, these wastes are composed of four major groups: food processing (2,127,000 tons); lumber (7,993,000 tons); chemical and petroleum (464,000 tons); and manufacturing (3,103,000 tons). From the data, the industrial-waste multipliers shown in Table 9.6 were calculated.

COLLECTION AND DISPOSAL

Residential, commercial, institutional, and industrial solid wastes are the clearest threats to health and to the urban environment, so they are the chief target of waste-disposal strategy. Most such waste comes from urban areas and requires quick removal. It is increasing at a rate of about 4 percent a year.

Three facets of the production and discard of these growing mountains of solid-waste materials need examination: collection methods, disposal techniques, and recycling and reuse.

Collection Methods

Refuse-collection methods in most of the United States do not differ substantially from what they were when workers picked up the trash in horse-drawn wagons before the turn of the century. This lack of technological advance is particularly burdensome because up to 80 percent of the funds spent on solid-waste management goes into collecting the waste and hauling it to a processing plant or a dump. The one significant advance has been the compactor truck. These closed-body vehicles now make up a large part of the 150,000 refuse-collection trucks in the United States. With hydraulic presses, they compress waste, usually at a 3-to-1 ratio, thus saving vehicle space and cutting the number of trips necessary to cover collection routes. However, the compactor has disadvantages. Because refuse of different types is mixed and crushed, recyclables are lost or contaminated by unusable waste.

Disposal Techniques

In recent years the character of refuse has been changing because of new techniques in food packaging, in home heating, and in disposal

TABLE 9.5

Industrial solid waste production in California[a]

County	Food Processing, Tons/Year	Lumber		Chemical and Petroleum, Tons/Year	Manufacturing		Annual Total Tonnage	Rank in State
		Logging Debris, Tons/Year	Sawmill and Planing Mills, Tons/Year		Heavy, Tons/Year	Light, Tons/Year		
Alameda	151,900		16,700	11,000	155,900	52,900	388,000	7
Alpine		3,000					3,000	55
Amador		11,400	50,200				62,000	40
Butte	12,800	48,000	50,200		1,000	2,200	114,000	27
Calaveras		50,500	33,500				84,000	34
Colusa							0	58
Contra Costa	19,100			152,100	73,300	8,900	253,000	16
Del Norte		238,200	126,000			7,400	372,000	8
El Dorado		232,900	84,600				318,000	11
Fresno	121,700	88,000	16,700	6,700	13,400	7,200	254,000	15
Glenn	2,400	51,000					53,000	41
Humboldt	3,600	1,215,300	551,400		4,000	27,300	1,802,000	2
Imperial	9,000						9,000	51
Inyo						1,000	1,000	56
Kern	33,400	20,000		13,600	13,600	1,100	82,000	35
Kings	4,600			5,600		4,900	15,000	47
Lake	2,700	66,000					69,000	38
Lassen		111,000	36,300				147,000	24
Los Angeles	340,700		64,100	230,300	985,600	260,400	1,881,000	1
Madera	3,000	70,300	34,100				107,000	28
Marin	1,000				4,800	3,100	9,000	49
Mariposa		10,000					10,000	50
Mendocino	500	474,700	419,300		800	5,800	901,000	4
Merced	14,900				400	100	15,000	47
Modoc		91,800					92,000	31
Mono							0	58
Monterey	63,600			100	2,800	6,200	73,000	36
Napa	2,800				3,000	200	6,000	53
Nevada		58,800	42,900				102,000	29
Orange	86,300			3,400	105,800	27,100	223,000	17
Placer	3,300	113,200	80,800			400	198,000	20
Plumas		221,300	142,100				364,000	9
Riverside	45,000			5,000	29,200	8,400	88,000	32
Sacramento	55,100			100	9,600	8,300	73,000	36
San Benito	4,500				500		5,000	54
San Bernardino	44,000	10,000	25,300	2,000	834,800	4,400	920,000	3
San Diego	35,300			3,700	59,900	7,900	107,000	33

TABLE 9.5 (cont.)

County	Food Processing, Tons/Year	Lumber		Chemical and Petroleum, Tons/Year	Manufacturing		Annual Total Tonnage	Rank in State
		Logging Debris, Tons/Year	Sawmill and Planing Mills, Tons/Year		Heavy, Tons/Year	Light, Tons/Year		
San Francisco	60,900			2,400	45,200	13,700	122,000	26
San Joaquin	123,000		33,500	200	12,500	12,800	182,000	21
San Luis Obispo	6,000			1,000		800	8,000	52
San Mateo	19,300	23,700		5,800	45,100	4,800	99,000	30
Santa Barbara	28,300			1,300	9,100	600	39,000	43
Santa Clara	230,000			7,700	89,800	15,800	343,000	10
Santa Cruz	52,600	18,200	66,600		4,600	500	142,000	25
Shasta	400	419,900	227,600			11,400	659,000	6
Sierra		165,600	42,000				208,000	19
Siskiyou	2,100	465,400	194,800			24,500	687,000	5
Solano	39,800				1,000	200	41,000	42
Sonoma	42,200	69,300	92,200		3,700	8,900	216,000	18
Stanislaus	146,000			1,600	3,900	4,600	156,000	23
Sutter	13,800					2,700	16,000	46
Tehama	2,000	107,100	173,700			4,800	288,000	13
Trinity		217,900	42,600				260,000	14
Tulare	59,100	50,000	66,900		5,600	500	182,000	21
Tuolumne		191,700	118,700				310,000	12
Ventura	54,800			1,800	10,200	800	68,000	39
Yolo	28,600				1,800	300	31,000	45
Yuba	900	37,500					38,000	44
Multicounty	156,200	5,200	203,400	8,100	15,400	4,100	392,000	
Total	2,127,000	4,957,000	3,036,000	464,000	2,546,000	557,000	13,687,000	

[a] Quantities have not been reported for individual counties where there are less than three establishments in a particular category. These quantities have been included in the multicounty figure. Multicounty also includes companies without a fixed location within the state or with a significant number of employees in more than one county.

A blank represents no waste generated or less than three establishments located in the county.

itself—notably the advent of the household garbage grinder. The significant effect of these new techniques has been to change the composition of refuse, reducing the proportions of wet garbage and ash and increasing the relative amounts of paper.

At least six methods are currently used or could be used to dispose of refuse. They are:

1. Swine feeding of the garbage portion.
2. Open dumping (which accounts for 77 percent of all collected solid wastes, at 14,000 dumps).
3. Sanitary landfill.
4. Incineration (accounting for 10 percent of domestic solid wastes; 300 municipal incinerators account for half the tonnage burned).
5. Composting.
6. On-the-site disposal.

TABLE 9.6

Industrial multipliers

No.	Title	Small Firms		Large Firms		Annual Waste: All Firms			
		Total Employment	Annual Waste Volume per Employee (cu yd)	Total Employment	Annual Waste Volume per Employee (cu yd)	Volume per Employee (cu yd)	Densities (lb/cu yd)	Pounds per Employee	Tons per Employee
		1	2	3	4	5	6	7	8
19	Ordnance and Accessories	—	—	29,499	4.476	4.476	294.4	1,317.7	0.65885
203	Canning and Preserving	—	—	—	8.977	8.977	1,240.0	11,131.4	5.5657
20	Other Food Processing (Except 203)	920	20.961	4,306	8.720	10.875	885.8	9,633.1	4.81655
21	Tobacco	—	—	—	—	—	—	—	2.49365
22	Textiles	—	—	—	—	—	—	—	0.52575
23	Apparel	98	35.360	623	2.077	6.601	159.3	1,051.5	0.52575
24	Lumber and Wood Products	455	48.492	217	—	48.492	894.5	43,376.1	21.68805
25	Furniture and Fixtures	385	86.877	—	—	86.877	464.0	40,310.9	20.15545
26	Paper and Allied Products	570	65.442	1,535	37.440	45.022	557.0	25,077.3	12.53865
27	Printing, Publishing, and Allied	1,744	25,230	1,923	7.252	15.802	1,671.0	26,405.1	13.20255
28	Chemicals and Allied	701	18.348	937	—	18.348	895.0	16,421.1	8.21075
30	Rubber and Plastics	173	28.583	653	18.854	20.892	148.2	3,096.2	1.54810
31	Leather	—	—	—	—	—	—	—	2.49365
32	Stone, Clay, Glass, and Concrete	960	29.235	1,696	5.260	13.926	2,601.5	36,228.5	18.11425
33	Primary Metals	—	4.443	—	—	—	—	—	6.7300
34	Fabricated Metal Products	1,259	21.214	1,304	13.206	17.140	785.3	13,460.0	6.7300
35	Nonelectrical Machinery	2,838	17.909	5,805	11.401	12.862	650.3	8,364.2	4.18210
36	Electrical Machinery	2,337	16.645	37,814	7.333	7.875	756.5	5,957.4	2.97870
37	Transportation Equipment	557	14.348	4,183	24.580	23.378	290.3	6,786.6	3.39330
38	Instruments	825	8.943	926	NA	8.943	562.9	5,034.0	2.51700
39	Miscellaneous Manufacturing Industries	317	5.946	149	NA	10.493	475.3	4,987.3	2.49365

Swine Feeding

The feeding of garbage to swine was at one time a very profitable method of refuse disposal in the United States. A survey undertaken in 1930 reported that 38 percent of the 557 American cities with over 4,500 population disposed of their garbage by feeding it to swine.

The feeding of raw garbage to swine led to outbreaks of vesicular exanthema among farm animals which resulted in substantial economic losses to agricultural interests. The state of Illinois, to cite one example, enacted legislation in 1953 requiring that "all garbage ... shall before it is fed to swine ... be thoroughly heated throughout ... to destroy the virus of vesicular exanthema or of any other disease transmissible to swine from garbage." This requirement reduced considerably the number of "piggeries," for small operations could not afford the equipment needed to cook garbage. Also, many of the piggeries in built-up areas came to be regarded as nuisances, and public opposition caused them to discontinue their operation.

To look at a particular urban example, there are 22 licensed garbage feeders in the Chicago metropolitan area. At least 15,000 tons of garbage are consumed by them each year, from a variety of sources (Table 9.7). This is a volume of refuse equal to that which would be produced by approximately 30,000 inhabitants, or less than one-half of one percent of the population of northeastern Illinois. It is apparent that swine feeding is insignificant in the overall disposal picture. It does deserve attention, however, because of its health and nuisance aspects.

There are two general types of swine-feeding operation. First, a few large scavengers use swine feeding either as an exclusive method of disposal or as one of several methods. These firms are usually paid fees for collecting the refuse. In addition, they are able to realize other revenue from the sale of swine and fertilizer. The major profits, however, come from the collection service. Since only the edible garbage can be consumed by hogs, the other materials contained in the refuse must be disposed of in other ways.

In the second group are small operators who feed swine to supplement their incomes. This group consists largely of farmers who are able to use the hog manure as fertilizer and sell the fattened swine at the local stockyards.

The feeding of cooked garbage to swine may be considered an economically desirable method of disposal. However, the problems of cooking the refuse and separating the garbage from the inedible materials are major obstacles. Also, after separation, about one-third of the collected refuse (by weight) still remains to be disposed of by means other than swine feeding.

The low nutritive content of common refuse, coupled with the social stigma attached to garbage-fed pork, eliminates this method as an acceptable means for the disposal of large volumes of municipal refuse. Small feeding operations, however, are likely to continue using garbage from special sources such as hotels, hospitals, military bases, schools, and other large institutions.

Open Dumping

An open dump is an area where refuse is dumped and allowed to remain exposed to the atmosphere. In addition, rodents and flies have easy access to the refuse. Open dumping is still frequently practiced, but it is not a desirable method of refuse disposal for other than inert material.

Open dumps vary in degree of offensiveness. Those which are "worked" (in which bulldozers are used periodically to level and compact the refuse) are more tolerable than those which use no equipment. National surveys have shown that more than 50 percent of American cities with over 2,500 population dispose of much of their community refuse in "unworked" open dumps.

Some open dump sites are swampy or filled with water and present a deplorable picture of smelly refuse floating on water that has become sour and stagnant. The probability of groundwater contamination is especially high at these sites where refuse is continually saturated. Those parts of the dumps that are above water are infested by vermin and are often aflame, giving rise to air pollution and serious odor problems. Such conditions need not be tolerated, since satisfactory conditions generally can be achieved at relatively minor costs through the application of existing knowledge.

There is urgent need for a program that will result in refuse-disposal operations that are not objectionable. One desirable step would be to convert all open dumps to sanitary landfills and to close all of those that cannot be so converted. The very existence of open dumps makes it extremely difficult to gain approval of new sanitary landfills, because the unfavorable public image of open dumps is projected to any proposed new sites.

TABLE 9.7

Licensed swine feeders in Northeastern Illinois

License No.	County	Swine Fed Annually	Tons of Garbage Fed Annually	Source of Garbage	Estimated Length of Average Haul
1562	N. Cook	1,400	2,550	Evanston Area & Great Lakes Naval Station	14 miles
1611	N. Cook	125	90	2 restaurants in Winnetka	25 miles
1613	N. Cook	NA	NA	NA	NA
1633	N. Cook	25	55	Several collection points	7 miles
1567	S. Cook	200	60	Several collection points	3 miles
1568	S. Cook	NA	NA	NA	NA
1571	S. Cook	NA	NA	NA	NA
1658	S. Cook	65	275	Chicago S. side hotels	15 miles
1660	S. Cook	16,000	7,800	Loop hotels, restaurants	22 miles
1661	S. Cook	NA	NA	Chicago loop	35 miles (1 trip per week)
1664	S. Cook	80	NA	Hospital, restaurants in Dyer, Indiana	9.5 miles
1669	Chicago	175	50	NA	60 miles
1558	Kane	70	10	Several collection points	7 miles
1569	Lake	600	300	Several collection points	20 miles
1570	Lake	80	80	NA	1 mile
1612	Lake	NA	NA	NA	NA
1614	Lake	2,000	2,500	Great Lakes Naval Station	17 miles
1615	Lake	700	1,100	Great Lakes Naval Station	10 miles
1659	Lake	30	30	Great Lakes Naval Station	10 miles
1677	McHenry	1,000	780	McHenry County Dairies	7 miles
1560	Will	50	30	Wilmington Widows Home	2 miles
1584	Will	35	35	Wilmington	2 miles
Totals:		22,635	15,745		

SOURCE: Survey by Northeastern Illinois Metropolitan Area Planning Commission, July 1961.

Sanitary Landfill

Sanitary landfill is a nuisance-free method of refuse disposal characterized by competent and continuing engineering planning and control. Sanitary landfills do not produce ground- and surface-water pollution, nor is there burning of any kind. Refuse is compacted and covered each day with six inches or more of earth cover material. The earth cover also is compacted to provide a tight seal that will do the following:

1. prevent flies from laying eggs on the refuse or rodents from invading the fill;
2. seal in odors;
3. prevent rain water from entering the fill;
4. minimize the blowing and scattering of refuse;
5. prevent the emergence of adult flies that have been bred in the refuse, and
6. provide a surface on which trucks can operate.

The operation and maintenance of sanitary landfills requires equipment that can satisfactorily perform the various operations of excavation, compaction, and cover needed by the quantities of refuse that are dumped at the site. When desired grades are achieved, the fill is topped with a final cover of at least two feet of earth (but preferably four to eight feet) to seal in odors.

Although sanitary landfills can be used to "reclaim" waste lands for parks and recreational areas or as sites for construction, they need not be confined to such waste lands. Communities that do not have any low areas, swamps, or pits to fill can use sanitary landfills to add relief to relatively flat land, and with proper landscaping the completed fills can enhance the aesthetic appearance of the community.

Many reports discuss the merits of sanitary landfills; yet it is difficult to convince the public of the validity of such claims, since the concept of the open, uncontrolled dump is so firmly entrenched. Countless problems beset public officials who attempt to show that there is a distinction between open dumps and sanitary landfills. The stigma attached to open dumps generally is projected by the public to all types of refuse disposal, even those which create neither nuisance nor health problems.

Central Incineration

Space requirements for refuse disposal can be reduced substantially by incineration. Unlike common fuels, refuse is physically heterogeneous and therefore requires special incinerators. High-temperature burning (at 1,400°F) is required to prevent smoke and odors which result from incomplete combustion. In addition, control devices are necessary to reduce the amount of dust and fly ash discharged from the stack. Even a properly designed incinerator will give off smoke and odors if it is overloaded or improperly operated. Some incinerators in the metropolitan area are operated above their design capacity.

In northeastern Illinois, to return to the Chicago case, incineration takes place almost exclusively in large central incinerators. The rated capacity of the ten incinerators in the metropolitan area ranges from 180 to 1,200 tons per 24-hour day. All of the large plants are relatively new. Capacity is related to the size of the area that can be economically served, and this in turn is determined by the cost of transporting refuse to the site of the incinerator. Another factor controlling the size of incinerators is the amount of truck traffic that can be handled efficiently at the site.

In the past, incinerators of less than 100 tons per 24 hours capacity had been operated by a number of municipalities. These have all been abandoned except two. The other municipalities have, for economic reasons, either contracted with private scavengers for refuse collection and disposal or else continued with municipal collection, but with disposal transferred to sanitary landfills or privately owned incinerators. Because incinerator operation requires the service of competent, trained personnel, it has been the practice of the Illinois Department of Public Health to discourage the use of incinerators by small communities to which such personnel are not readily available.

Cook County appears to be unique in the country in having three large incinerators built and operated solely by private interests. Plans to construct several more are under consideration. This situation reflects, in part, the inaccessibility of existing disposal sites and the intense public opposition to the opening of new sites.

There are several relatively small, cone-shaped, prefabricated incinerators in the metropolitan area, two of which are publicly owned. The absence of refractories to hold heat in this type of installation makes it impossible to maintain temperatures constantly high enough to completely burn noxious gases and particulate matter. Incinerators of this kind are little more than enclosed bonfires and are major contributors to air pollution. They are not suitable for disposing of large amounts of municipal refuse.

Although incinerator plants are generally located in manufacturing districts, they can be designed as handsome structures on attractively landscaped sites. In Evanston the municipal incinerator is situated in the central business district and has not been a cause of complaint. Street patterns (as they affect truck traffic), the availablity of utilities, the water supply for wet scrubbers, and zoning performance standards all influence the location of an incinerator. In addition, a central location within the area of collection is desirable. Where available, sewage treatment-plant effluent can be used in wet scrubbers, thereby conserving the potable water supply. Also, sewage sludge can be dried or burned by heat given off by incinerators, as provided for at some locations.

Properly operated incinerators produce a stable ash and residue amounting to 5 to 35 percent of the volume of incoming material, depending on its nature. Usually the ash cannot be disposed of on the incinerator site, and transport to a disposal site is necessary. The use of railroads

or barges should be considered for large incinerators, since in many instances truck traffic is considered a greater nuisance than the possible smoke, fly ash, or odor from the incinerator.

Land requirements for incinerators are modest. A plant of 400 tons per day capacity can be fitted on a three-acre parcel, though a larger site is necessary if shrubbery and trees are desired to screen the plant from view, or if traffic and truck storage are problems. Operational standards contained in zoning ordinances generally limit the emission of particulate matter to a given amount per acre of site per hour, and this might make it necessary to have sites larger than those necessary to accommodate the physical plants. Where large sites are provided, it is usually planned to dispose of some of the residue on the property.

Composting

Composting involves the decomposition of refuse, through bacterial action, into a humus-like material similar to peat moss in appearance and application. This appears to be a desirable solution, for it results in a usable product—a soil conditioner and fertilizer. Although in other countries composting has been an important means of refuse disposal for many years, this method has not been widely used in the United States. One plant is located in Norman, Oklahoma; a second plant in Phoenix, Arizona, is currently undergoing test runs.

One reason for the small number of composting operations in this country is that it has not been easy to find a market for compost here. Farming in the United States is generally less intensive than in European and Asian countries, which have fewer acres of arable soil per capita.

The rich prairie soils of northeastern Illinois produce high yields per acre, making it extremely difficult to sell compost there. This can be confirmed by the experience with sewage sludge, which is a better fertilizer than compost. The Metropolitan Sanitary District of Greater

Chicago produces 200,000 tons of sludge per year, much of which cannot be readily marketed.

Composting does not produce atmospheric emissions, nor does it create a water-pollution problem.

In areas where there is need for fill to raise the ground level, compost, although more expensive, may be preferred to raw refuse as fill. In some areas markets can be found for materials that must be removed from the refuse before composting, such as rags, metals, glass, and paper. The revenue realized from these salvaged items can defray some of the costs of a total composting and garbage operation.

On-the-Site Disposal of Refuse

There is an increasing tendency to dispose of certain types of refuse at the place of origin, or "on the site." On-the-site disposal aids in reducing the cost of refuse collection by reducing the volume that must be hauled to central disposal sites. Home incinerators and garbage grinders are the most widely used methods.

Home incinerators. The most common home incinerators in use today are gas-fired or electrically heated combustion chambers that burn refuse under controlled conditions within buildings. The wire baskets, drums, or masonry enclosures that are often used for poorly controlled backyard burning are not included.

Municipal authorities do not encourage the installation of home incinerators, because they are often improperly operated and because burning generally does not take place at temperatures that are high enough (1,400°F) to result in complete combustion. In addition, it is extremely difficult to regulate the maintenance and operation of large numbers of home incinerators. A recent survey of 20,000 of them revealed that only 1 percent met air-pollution standards. In addition, the improper installation and operation of a home incinerator can create a fire hazard. One municipality in northeastern Illinois has had three home fires that were traced to faulty installations of home incinerators. This problem, however, can be overcome by setting installation standards.

The central-heating furnace of a building does not deserve the name of "incinerator" any more than do such devices for outdoor rubbish burning as wire baskets, brick boxes, and steel drums with holes punched in the bottom by the plant handyman. Apartment buildings that burn refuse in heating-system furnaces have added considerably to the air-pollution problem. An on-the-site incinerator must be designed by a competent engineer and erected or installed with consideration for the peculiarities of the site.

Garbage grinders. The garbage portion of refuse can be processed by grinding it and flushing it through sewers to the sewage treatment plant for disposal. Most domestic grinders are permanently installed in the drains of kitchen sinks. This makes it convenient for the housewife to dispose of garbage at that part of the house in which it is most likely to be produced.

Communities which have installed grinders can reduce the frequency of collections because all easily spoiled refuse is ground and flushed away. Consequently, it is becoming increasingly popular, in small municipalities, to require garbage grinders in every house. An example is Shorewood Hills, Wisconsin, where most of the 475 grinders were bought by the village at a cost of $73,945 or $159.02 per grinder (or approximately $39.75 per person served). This cost could be amortized over a ten-year period, which is the estimated serviceable life of a grinder. Annual operating costs are estimated at $5.50 per capita, or $22.00 per family.

Garbage production in Shorewood Hills amounts to approximately 0.7 lb per capita per 24 hours. Using this figure, overall costs of the grinder operation are approximately $74 per ton of garbage ground. In addition, there would be increased costs at the sewage-treatment plant where the ground garbage must ultimately be disposed of.

Technological Outlook

Since World War II the composition of refuse in the United States has changed. Ashes, which formerly constituted a major portion of refuse, have decreased in importance as coal has been largely replaced as a fuel by gas, oil, and electricity. However, this reduction has been offset by increased amounts of paper, glass, plastics, and tin cans. Thus, there appears to be an increase in the volume of burnable material (paper and plastics) and a decrease in the volume of unburnable material such as ashes. Increased dependence on frozen and canned foods has tended to reduce the garbage fraction in refuse, and it appears reasonable to expect further reduction in the future.

In spite of many technological achievements, there is still a need for a method of refuse disposal that can process or handle all kinds of refuse. Swine feeding, incineration, composting, and on-the-site disposal can handle only certain components of refuse. To date, sanitary landfill is the only method developed that can accommodate all types; for that reason, sanitary landfill sites will be a necessary element in future refuse-disposal programs. The space required at sanitary landfills will be affected, however, by the extent to which swine feeding, incineration, composting, and on-the-site disposal are used to reduce the volume of refuse.

An additional technique which may conceivably be useful in a metropolitan area is the transfer station. Such stations and their equipment are nearly dustless and odorless in operation and can thus be located in densely populated areas, where refuse from collection trucks can be transferred to larger trucks for transportation to disposal sites. The use of transfer stations would make possible the economic use of disposal sites located on the periphery of the metropolitan area.

MULTIPURPOSE CONCEPTS IN REFUSE DISPOSAL

It may sometimes be economical to design a refuse-disposal program to serve several purposes. If the multipurpose approach can be shown to be economically feasible, it will be possible to realize additional benefits.

Land Reclamation

The concept of land reclamation has commanded a great deal of attention. Generally, the argument is advanced that sanitary landfills or dumps should be located in low areas in order to "reclaim the land" so that it can be used for some new purpose. Parking lots, parks, and other recreational areas constitute the most common use of land reclaimed by sanitary landfills or open dumps—as, for example, portions of Chicago's Grant and Burnham Parks. Generally, these areas may be utilized as little as two years after the completion of the fill. Subsequent settling of the land is usually minor and can be corrected at little expense.

If a more intensive use, such as a building site, is contemplated for a former disposal site, foundations should be carried through the fill to native soil or, if this is not practical, special footing designs should be employed to prevent uneven settlement.

Besides the problem of groundwater pollution which is discussed below, there is the fact that filling of swamps or flood-plain lands can have an adverse effect upon flood conditions. Flood control is essentially a space-allocation problem, and under natural conditions flood plains and swamps provide natural channel storage areas for surplus water. If these areas are filled, they are no longer available for flood-water storage, and space needed to accommodate flood waters can be obtained only by raising flood stages. In addition, encroachment in the channel cross section reduces the hydraulic efficiency of the waterway and may cause it to back up behind the constriction. The increased upstream flood heights may cause additional damage not only to riparian development but also to inland areas which have direct storm-sewer connections to the waterway. Although the use of sanitary landfills or open dumps is sometimes extolled as a desirable way to "reclaim flood-plain areas," care must be exercised to see that the operations are properly designed and located so that they will not cause adverse effects on flood stages.

A variation of the use of sanitary landfills to reclaim land is found in San Bernardino County, California. Here, refuse is being used to construct a 1,400-foot levee along the Santa Anna River. This compacted landfill is 250 feet wide at the base and 35 feet high, with 4 : 1 side slopes. After a final cover of 12 to 18 inches of soil, plans call for the U.S. Army Corps of Engineers to cap the landfill with concrete to withstand erosion during floods.

Heat Production

In many instances, part of the cost of operating public incinerators is defrayed by charging fees to industrial and commercial enterprises for the use of the facilities. Also, in a number of instances steam is generated and sold to nearby users. The new southwest incinerator in the city of Chicago is designed to furnish steam to two nearby industrial plants.

A limitation on the sale of steam from incinerators is that most of them operate only five 24-hour days per week, and some shut down at night. Refuse collection, also, is ordinarily on an eight-hour, five-days-per-week basis. Where incinerator fuel is not sufficient to produce steam continuously, an interruptible market for the steam must be found. An alternative would be to equip the plant with gas and oil burners to generate steam when refuse was not being incinerated.

Recycling and Reuse

The federal government has set as a goal the reduction of solid-waste volume and encouragement of reuse and recycling. The recycling of waste materials into the economy has not been widely applied in the United States. Economic considerations and the abundance of virgin resources have forestalled the development of recycling technology and markets. Primary materials producers, often with the help of tax concessions, have developed remarkably efficient technologies for removing metals and other substances from their virgin state. But meanwhile, techniques for separating and recovering waste materials remain primitive and expensive.

There are many aspects to recycling, including (1) the characteristics and the volume of the products which enter the market and eventually end up as solid wastes, (2) identification of characteristics and items most troublesome to solid-waste management, and (3) decisions on how to control their presence in refuse. Some items can be returned by consumers for reuse. Others may be sorted by householders for separate collection. Or the most economical solution may be to salvage from mixed-collection wastes.

Sorting Mixed Refuse

Much more work is needed to develop an effective way to salvage the valuable elements of collected mixed refuse. It is difficult and costly. And the instability of salvage markets has only added to the problem. The Stanford Research Institute in Menlo Park, California, has constructed a pilot scale unit in which a vertical stream of air separates mixed waste materials. After technical difficulties are overcome, this air classification process may prove an economic alternative to hand separation.

At College Park, Maryland, the Bureau of

Mines has constructed an advanced reclamation system with mechanical separators which sort metals and glass from incinerator residues. Recent technological advances there have produced a highly sophisticated process which sorts glass by color and isolates several exotic metals. It adds $3 per ton to normal collection and disposal costs, not considering any income from the sale of salvaged materials. The Bureau is now developing data for the design of commercial plants based on this process.

Auto Disposal

A number of specific components in solid wastes present particular difficulties and require special mention. Abandoned autos are one of the most conspicuous problems. On the average, 9 million autos are retired from service every year. Although statistics on the annual number of abandoned. vehicles are subject to dispute, it is thought that approximately 15 percent are abandoned on city streets, in back alleys, along rural roads, and in vacant lots throughout the nation. Most autos are abandoned because they are no longer serviceable and have little or no parts value to auto wreckers. The total number of abandoned cars in the country has been estimated between 2.5 and 4.5 million.

The 85 percent of autos that are properly turned in by their owners enter a complex recycling system, usually beginning with the auto wrecker, whose chief business is selling the parts that can be removed. Some wreckers claim to obtain 97 percent of their sales revenues from parts. The high value of junk cars for parts and their often negligible value for scrap means that wreckers have little incentive to move their inventories to scrap processors. Except when there is demand for scrap, the junk cars just pile up.

Auto wreckers eventually, however, have to move the hulks to scrap processors. Most processors, using powerful hydraulic presses, reduce the cars to small bales containing high percent-

ages of nonferrous materials—copper, upholstery, chrome, plastic, and glass. The bales are then sold to steel mills, which turn them into products which do not require high-quality steel, or pass them on to mills which have sufficient capacity to dilute their contaminants. A growing number of processors produce a higher-priced scrap through mechanical shredding and electromagnetic separation. Costs for shredding equipment, however, have limited the widespread use of this process, particularly by small scrap processors.

Steel mills and foundries are major users of ferrous scrap. In 1969, 50 percent of the material used for the production of all steel products was scrap. Six percent of that scrap was from junk autos. But changes in steel production techniques make it difficult to predict future scrap needs. Basic oxygen furnaces and electrical induction furnaces are partially replacing the open hearth furnace. The first requires less scrap; the second uses more. It is even more difficult to predict export scrap demand and the effects of new fabricating and casting processes on the scrap market.

The Council on Environmental Quality is taking the lead in recommending a bounty payment or some other system to promote the prompt scrapping of all junk automobiles. However, having reviewed the range of alternatives leading to a federal or state bounty system, the Council has concluded that under present conditions it is not practicable at these governmental levels.

Most of the systems considered by the Council would be funded by a tax on the sale of all automobiles sold in the future or the collection of a fee from all present owners and future buyers. The bounty payment would be made to the scrap processor, the auto wrecker, or the owner of the car being junked. All of those proposals would put an unfair burden on the owners of the 85 percent of autos that are properly turned over to auto wreckers, in order to take care of the remainder which are not.

Furthermore, the Council is not persuaded that the demand for auto scrap would be improved by such a system, nor that it would in fact influence the economics affecting abandonment. The resulting fund of payments would divert billions of dollars from other investments in the private economy. Administration and enforcement of the system would require excessive increases in government personnel and expenditures. The Council also determined that firm penalties against abandonment, together with improvement of state title and transfer laws, particularly for cars of low value, might substantially reduce abandonment and put abandoned vehicles more promptly into the scrapping cycle. Such laws should be strengthened.

Any attempt to solve the problem of abandoned cars, however, must consider the problems of fluctuating scrap demand, steel production technology, transportation rates for scrap, export scrap markets, availability of shredding equipment, and characteristics of the auto parts market. Otherwise, assuming abandonment could be reversed, hulks would only continue to pile up in junk yards. The Council will continue its study of these broader problems, looking toward a solution that will involve the entire auto scrapping system.

Other Items

In 1969, 43.8 billion *beverage containers* for beer and soft drinks were made in the United States. By 1980, if the trend to throwaway containers continues, 100 billion of these bottles and cans will be produced and discarded every year. Beverage containers already comprise 3.9 percent of all collected refuse, and the number is growing at a rate of nearly 7.5 percent per year—compared to 4 percent for all refuse. Bottles and cans constitute a major part of what is left in incinerators after burning. They must be hauled to land disposal sites. Each year an estimated 1 to 2 billion glass and metal beverage containers end up as litter on highways, beaches, parks, and other public areas. Severe penalties for littering have not worked in the face of the rising sales of the throwaway bottle and can, and strict enforcement of these laws has been difficult.

Paper constitutes almost 60 percent of roadside litter and is difficult to collect. Last year, 58.3 million tons of paper were consumed in the United States. Nineteen percent of this was recycled. Fifteen percent was temporarily retained or lost its identity in manufacturing processes. The remaining two-thirds—or 40 million tons—was discarded as residential, commercial, institutional, and industrial solid wastes. Typically, paper comprising 40 to 50 percent of mixed refuse is disposed of at an annual cost of over $900 million. Paper production is a multiple polluter. It crops up as a factor in timber wastes, in air and water pollution, and in the removal of organic materials from soils in managed forests. Much of the discarded paper consists of technically reusable fiber. Although the United States recycles only 19 percent of its paper, Japan reclaims and reprocesses nearly half of the paper its people use.

Plastics comprise an increasingly worrisome element in solid wastes. They are virtually indestructible, do not degrade naturally, and resist the compression plates of compactor trucks. In incinerators most plastics tend to melt rather than burn and to foul the grates. One range of plastics, polyvinyl chloride (PVC), is a new arrival in the packaging market. When burned, it produces hydrochloric acid. Although not yet widely used in the United States, in Germany it has already been blamed for increased air pollution, damage to incinerator stacks, and—in rare cases—destruction of nearby flora.

Another potential problem arises from disposing of *pesticides*. As stronger legislation and regulation of these agents takes effect, the proper disposal of undesirable or condemned commodities becomes important. Even the containers used to market pesticides may retain considerable toxicity after discard. Although there have as yet been no serious cases, concentration of these agents in sanitary landfills and open dumps could contaminate groundwater and imperil public health.

Rubber tires are just as difficult to get rid of. Burning them pollutes the air. In sanitary landfills, they defy compaction and tend to gravitate to the surface. Changing technology has lessened the use of old rubber in the manufacture of new rubber products; thus most old tires are not recycled.

The Fish and Wildlife Service and the Bureau of Solid Waste Management are investigating the use of old tires as reefs and fish havens along the Atlantic coast of the United States. The ocean bottom is sandy and relatively flat for great distances. Artificial reefs constructed of tires may promote an increase in desirable species, since many game fish require relief features such as reefs for protection and spawning grounds. If this concept proves practical, very large numbers of old tires could be turned into an important ecological side benefit.

REFUSE DISPOSAL AND GROUNDWATER POLLUTION

A consequence of prevailing modes of refuse disposal is groundwater pollution. Returning to the Chicago case, the water needs of approximately 1,500,000 persons in northeastern Illinois are supplied from the groundwater reservoir. Declining water levels in the deep sandstone aquifers have resulted in the increased use of shallow aquifers. Usually, these shallow aquifers are hydrologically connected with the surface and are subject to contamination by refuse-disposal operations.

The degree to which shallow groundwater reservoirs are provided natural protection is largely dependent upon the subsurface environment. This section will therefore discuss the geohydrologic environment and will focus specifically upon those aspects of the geologic environment that influence the occurrence and movement of subsurface waters. The intimate relation between the geologic environment and groundwater contamination makes it possible to delineate areas where the potential for contamination from refuse disposal is greatest.

Nature of Contaminants

Analyses of leachates from refuse-disposal operations have shown that both biological and chemical contaminants are present. Chemical contaminants, because they are usually in solution, travel more extensively into and through the subsurface than do bacterial contaminants. This is particularly true when the contaminants move through a granular medium, such as sand or silt. Such a medium tends to function as a natural filter bed which restricts the movement of bacterial contaminants and separates them from the percolating waters. Dissolved chemical constituents, however, are seldom removed by a "filtering" process but continue to move with the fluid. The chemical constituents will contaminate the groundwater until their concentrations are diluted to the point where their presence in the water cannot be recognized. If the geohydrologic environment is evaluated in terms of its capacity to protect groundwater sources from chemical contamination, it can be assumed that protection from bacterial contamination will also be provided.

The Geohydrologic Environment

Because the relations between the spread of biological and chemical contaminants in all geohydrologic environments are not well known or documented, it is necessary to take the conservative position that unless protection against *any* contamination of water sources is provided for, a potentially unfavorable condition exists.

In evaluating the potentiality for groundwater pollution in a particular geohydrologic environment, the following elements need to be considered: (1) the mobility of the contaminants, (2) their access to subsurface water reservoirs (aquifers), and (3) the distribution of contamination within the aquifers.

Mobility of contaminants. Contaminants are leached from refuse by the movement of water through it. During this movement, the chemical constituents are taken into solution and the biological constituents are translocated by the seeping waters. Where disposed refuse is constantly saturated by moisture in geologic environments that are hydrologically connected with subsurface water sources, a particularly undesirable condition exists. However, even the leaching of refuse by intermittent saturation constitutes a condition where there is a potential hazard of groundwater contamination.

Either intermittent or constant saturation of disposed refuse may occur as a result of: flooding with surface-water runoff during or following the placing of the fill; infiltration by rainfall; disposal of refuse directly into a saturated zone (i.e., below the local level of the water table), and addition of water to promote compaction in a sanitary landfill. Too often, the low areas or holes usually selected as refuse-disposal sites are places where the potential for intermittent or constant saturation of the refuse is greatest. The results of a study made in California demonstrate that rainfall does not penetrate and leach a sanitary landfill in that climatic environment. In the humid temperate climate of Illinois, however, the likelihood of leaching by rainfall penetration is not known. The hazard can be limited by the employment of proper disposal methods and provisions for adequate drainage.

The dumping of refuse into pits, quarries, or depressions that extend below the level of the water table permits more or less continuous saturation of the refuse and consequent leaching of contaminants. In such a case, if the water that moves through the refuse also has direct access to a usable aquifer, the hazard of contaminat-

ing groundwater sources is great. (See Figure 9.1, types A and B.)

Access to aquifers. Contaminants leached from refuse move most freely into groundwater reservoirs where earth materials of relatively high permeability are present between the source of contamination and the aquifer (types A and B, Figure 9.1.) Where these are separated by materials of extremely low permeability, such as clay or shale, the movement of contamination may be so restricted that adequate protection from contamination of water supplies can be provided (type C, Figure 9.1.)

In northeastern Illinois shallow aquifers occur in the strata of consolidated rock (bedrock) and in the unconsolidated glacial deposits, called drift, that overlie the bedrock. The shallow bedrock aquifers are dolomites (limestonelike rocks) through which water moves via networks of joints, cracks, and fissures. Because of their fractured and open nature, dolomite rock formations are widely used as sources of groundwater. For the same reason, they are particularly susceptible to contamination, the openings in the dolomite making it possible for bacterial and chemical contaminants to move considerable distances through it. Dolomite is the principal rock type of the strata of the Silurian System and the Galena-Platteville Formation and is widely distributed as the uppermost bedrock in northeastern Illinois.

The glacial drift immediately underlies the land surface almost everywhere in the metropolitan area. The drift varies in thickness and composition; in much of the area the thickness of the drift is less than 50 feet, but in some areas it exceeds 400 feet. In some locations the drift is composed partly or entirely of unconsolidated deposits of sand or gravel of sufficient thickness and permeability to constitute significant aquifers. The drift might also contain deposits consisting largely of clay or silt of such low permeability that water movement through them is slow and small in volume. Such fine-grained deposits, where present, might provide

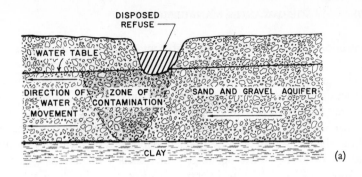

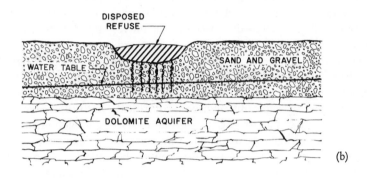

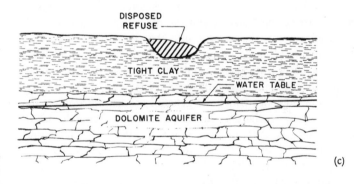

FIGURE 9.1 Effects of refuse disposal on four types of geologic environment: (a) contamination resulting from disposed refuse in direct contact with high water table; (b) unfavorable geologic environment: permeable materials between refuse and shallow aquifer; (c) favorable geologic environment: shallow aquifer separated from refuse dump by seal of tight clay; (d) diversion of groundwater flow by pumped well, with resulting diversion of contamination toward the well.

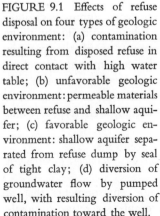

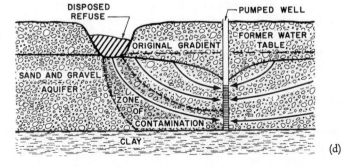

279

protection against the movement of contaminants into underlying drift or bedrock aquifers.

The granular nature of the drift serves to restrict the movement of bacterial contaminants; filtering effectiveness is related, in general, to the size of the intergranular openings through which the fluid moves. Fine-grained deposits with small intergranular openings will restrict the spread of bacterial constituents to a greater degree than will coarse-grained materials. Very coarse-grained deposits, such as gravel, might have openings so large that bacteria can move through them as freely as through fractured dolomite.

Distribution of contaminants. Once contaminants leached from refuse have reached the groundwater reservoir, distribution is controlled largely by the pattern of the groundwater movement. The general direction of movement of contaminants will be in the direction of the groundwater flow.

The natural direction of groundwater movement in a humid region such as northeastern Illinois is from the uplands toward the river valleys, with eventual discharge into the rivers and streams. In fact, a large portion of the base flow of the surface streams is supported by discharge from the shallow groundwater reservoir.

In the upland areas, which are generally areas of groundwater recharge, the water table is farther below the surface and there is a better opportunity to locate disposal sites above the local level of the water table. However, should the groundwater reservoir in these areas become contaminated, widespread and deep distribution of contaminants through it will result.

In valley areas, the water table is nearer the surface. Disposed refuse is more likely to be continuously saturated by groundwater, and the risk of contaminating the groundwater reservoir is consequently somewhat greater. Contamination is likely to be less extensive, however, since the valleys are generally areas of groundwater discharge.

The depositing of refuse in valley areas also presents a greater risk of contaminating the surface waterways. Groundwater moving laterally toward streams through the landfill can leach contaminants from refuse and introduce them into the surface water. The nearer the landfill is to the stream and the greater is the permeability of the material between the landfill and the stream, the greater is the hazard.

In places where groundwater saturation is at shallow depths, water may have to be pumped or tiled from an excavated landfill site to a nearby waterway so that refuse-disposal operations can be conducted "in the dry." Groundwater moving through the emplaced refuse to the point of pumping will leach contaminants from the refuse, with consequent direct introduction into the waterway. When pumping stops upon completion of the landfill operation, the level of saturation will rise, and continued lateral movement of ground water through the buried refuse may carry contaminants into aquifers or waterways along the line of groundwater flow.

In places where groundwater movement is upward through buried refuse, as may be the case in some marshy areas or in portions of flood plains, the possibility that contaminants might move downward into aquifers is very slight. However, drainage from such areas—through waterways, tiles, or ditches—might be contaminated.

The natural pattern of water movement can, however, be changed by pumping water from the groundwater reservoir. Pumping creates a cone of depression which results in the movement of groundwater toward the pumping center; consequently, contaminants introduced into the groundwater reservoir in an area influenced by pumpage will tend to migrate in the direction of the discharging wells (type D, Figure 9.1).

Unfavorable Geohydrologic Environments

The geohydrologic environments that are likely to be unfavorable for refuse disposal—

i.e., the areas in which there are greater probabilities of the occurrence of unfavorable environments—are as follows in environments such as those of northeastern Illinois:

1. *Areas with less than 50 feet of drift cover over dolomite aquifers.* Adequate protection from the movement of contaminants into the dolomite aquifer is most likely to be provided where a sufficiently thick cover of drift overlies the bedrock. In areas where the drift cover is less than 50 feet there is a greater possibility that contaminants will reach the aquifer. In their natural state, such areas are therefore generally considered unfavorable for refuse disposal.

2. *Areas of surficial sand and gravel aquifers.* Many of the stream valleys in the metropolitan area were discharge ways for melt-waters from the ancient glaciers. Within these valleys were deposited coarse-grained sands and gravels of sufficient thickness and permeability to be valuable groundwater aquifers. Because of their presence at land surface these deposits sometimes are used as sources of aggregate for road and building construction. Refuse disposed of in abandoned sand and gravel pits or on the surfaces of such deposits can be a source of contamination to surficial sand and gravel aquifers. In addition, where a relatively thin sand and gravel aquifer immediately overlies a creviced dolomite aquifer, both might be subject to contamination from the disposed refuse.

3. *Areas with more than 50 feet relatively permeable surficial drift.* The drift underlying the upland areas ranges in composition from predominantly clay to predominantly gravel. Where surficial deposits are coarse-grained, drift aquifers are more likely to be found at shallow depths—and the movement of contaminants from refuse-disposal sites into the aquifers is also more likely. Adequate protection does exist where the upper part of the drift which has a thickness of more than 50 feet is composed predominantly of fine-grained material of relatively low permeability and in those areas that are underlain by bedrock of low permeability in which the drift cover is thin or absent. Such conditions exist in areas underlaid by the shale bedrock of the Pennsylvania System and the Maquoketa Formation. In some places, however, the Maquoketa Formation contains aquifer units that might be subject to contamination.

*Geohydrologic Guide Lines
for Disposal-Site Evaluation*

The emphasis in these last few pages has been on the relationship between refuse disposal and the groundwater aquifers. Disposal of refuse without regard to the deleterious effect it can have on underlying groundwater reservoirs has been relatively common.

Because of the extreme variability in geologic conditions within any area, sites selected for refuse disposal should be individually evaluated as to the risk of groundwater contamination. The chief considerations in such evaluations are summarized below.

1. *Proper drainage.* Surface drainage must not be allowed to collect in the dumping area and provision should be made for immediate disposal of the moisture that collects from precipitation on the site. Also, the site must be protected against flood waters from nearby waterways. Since conditions of water saturation are probably necessary before contaminating constituents can be leached from the refuse and introduced into the subsurface, proper drainage plays a major role in safeguarding water quality.

2. *The nature and distribution of earth materials and the presence or absence of usable shallow aquifers.* The sequence, nature, and thickness of the subsurface materials should be sufficiently well established so that the probability of movement of contaminating constituents into aquifers can be evaluated. The risk of introducing contaminants into shallow aquifers is greatest at refuse-disposal sites which are in contact with permeable earth materials.

3. *The position of the local water table and direction of groundwater movement.* Disposal sites subject to constant or intermittent saturation by a high groundwater table constitute particularly hazardous environments for refuse disposal. Where groundwater movement is influenced by a center of pumping, it is possible for any contaminants that are leached from the refuse to be carried into the groundwater supply.

4. *Present and potential use of shallow aquifers.* The presence of shallow aquifers in the vicinity of disposal sites should suggest caution even if the general direction of groundwater movement is away from all areas of present or contemplated groundwater use. Pumpage of groundwater from the shallow aquifers might cause later diversion of groundwater flow from the disposal site toward the areas of discharge.

CHAPTER *10*

noise pollution
and abatement strategies

Noise is everywhere, especially in urban areas. The roar of air and surface transportation, the general din and hum of construction projects, and industrial noise all pound the ear virtually without ceasing. During the 1960s the measured amounts and extent of urban noise rose significantly, and so did the social awareness of noise and the discomfort caused by it.

The most severe noise conditions are generally encountered in the work environment. Excessive exposure to such noise for long periods is known to cause irreversible hearing loss. It is estimated that up to 16 million American workers today are threatened with hearing damage.

The worker exposed to noise during working hours must also endure high levels of noise on his way to and from work. Furthermore, at home he must listen to household appliances, noisy neighbors, and a variety of outdoor noises which surround and permeate his dwelling.

Recognition of the fact that noise is an environmental problem that affects people other than workers has been late in coming. Federal noise legislation first appeared in 1968 when Congress directed the Federal Aviation Administration (FAA) to establish rules and regulations to control aircraft noise. At the state and local level, laws tended to treat noise as a public nuisance, and enforcement was both difficult and spotty. More recently some jurisdictions, notably California and Chicago and New York City, have established new laws and ordinances that are based on noise-generating characteristics of specific equipment and, hence, are easier to enforce.

The second part of this chapter is based upon:
Martin Wachs and Joseph Schofer, *A Systems Analyst View of Noise and Urban Planning,* Discussion Paper Series No. 14, Center for Urban Studies, University of Illinois at Chicago Circle, 1970. Begins on page 289.

The Clean Air Amendments of 1970 called for the establishment of an Office of Noise Abatement and Control in the U.S. Environmental Protection Agency (EPA). The legislation also called for public hearings on environmental noise and a special report to the Congress on the problem, incorporating the results of the public hearings and other special studies. Information from this EPA report as well as extensive congressional hearings formed the basis of the Noise Control Act of 1972. This Act represents the first major Federal attempt to eliminate excess noise at the design stage of a wide variety of new consumer products. The Administrator of EPA is required to develop and publish information about permissible levels of noise and then to set noise standards for products that have been identified as major sources of noise. While aircraft noise control remains under the administration of the FAA, the law gives EPA an advisory role in formulating criteria and standards for controlling this source of noise.

Specifically, the Noise Control Act of 1972 contains the following provisions:

1. EPA is directed to develop and publish information on the limits of noise required for protecting public health and welfare as well as a series of reports to identify products that are major sources of noise and to give information on the techniques for controlling noise from such products.

2. Using the criteria thus developed, the EPA Administrator is required to set noise-emission standards for products that have been identified as major sources of noise and for which standards are deemed feasible. The law requires such standards to be set for products in the categories of construction equipment, transportation equipment (except aircraft), all motors and engines, and electrical and electronic equipment. It also grants authority to set for other products standards deemed feasible and necessary to protect public health and safety.

   EPA has authority to require the labeling of domestic or imported consumer products as to their noise-generating characteristics or their effectiveness in reducing noise. Manufacturers or importers of nonconforming or mislabeled products are subject to fines of up to $25,000 per day for each violation and to imprisonment for up to one year. Manufacturers must issue warrants that their regulated products comply with federal standards at the time of sale. They are also required to maintain records and provide information, including production samples, if requested by EPA.

3. The EPA Administrator also is to prescribe noise-emission standards for the operation of equipment and facilities of interstate railroads, trucks, and buses.

4. All federal agencies are directed to use the full extent of their authority to insure that purchasing and operating procedures conform to the intent of the law. EPA may certify low-noise emission products for purchase by the federal government.

5. The EPA Administrator is required by mid-1973 to make a comprehensive study of aircraft noise and cumulative noise exposure around airports. Using this information, EPA is to submit to the FAA proposed regulations to control aircraft noise and sonic booms. After a hearing and further consultation with EPA, the FAA may adopt or modify the proposed regulations. The FAA may reject the proposals if it believes they are unsafe, technologically or economically unfeasible, or not applicable to certain aircraft.

SOURCES OF NOISE POLLUTION

A standard measure for noise loudness is decibels on the A scale (dBA), which weighs sound intensity according to the presumed pattern of human hearing. Studies of noise perception indicate that an increase of 10 decibels, for a given tone, is perceived as a doubling of the noise level; that is, 100 decibels seems twice as loud as 90 decibels. More generally, the perceived difference in relative level of D_i and D_j can be written as $2^{(D_i - D_j)/10}$.

In decibel measurement, the zero decibel level is set at the threshold of audibility for the normal ear. The threshold of hearing at zero dBA is very low indeed, for if man's ears were any keener they would respond to the molecular motions of air particles. The sound of a whisper is around 25 dBA, ordinary conversation is 60 dBA, and and a shout around 80 dBA. Automobile traffic ranges from 50 to 80 dBA, a subway train from 90 to 100 dBA, and a jet plane at 1000 feet is over 100 dBA. At expressway speeds a single trailer truck can generate steady noise levels above 90 dBA. A line of trucks can produce noise levels of 100 dBA or more. Construction noise often reaches 110 dBA, the proverbial boiler factory can reach 125 dBA, and the decks of aircraft carriers reach 155 dBA.

Figure 10.1 depicts an approximate scale of noise levels. These, of course, are averages in a fundamentally variable noise environment, as depicted in Figure 10.2.

The most useful data bearing on noise by locale currently available were presented by the Environmental Protection Agency in the 1971 report to the President and Congress. A series of 24-hour outdoor noise recordings was made at each of 18 sites; major emphasis was on suburban and urban residential areas, but the coverage was quite broad, and it represents a preliminary cross section of the United States noise environment. The range of daytime outdoor noise levels at each of the 18 locations is presented in Figure 10.3. The locations are arrayed in descending order of their daytime "residual noise levels," defined as that reading below which 10 percent of the observations fell, and labeled the L_{90} level. The evidence was employed to estimate typical L_{90} readings for residential areas, by locale, as shown in Table 10.1.

TABLE 10.1

Qualitative descriptors of urban and suburban detached-housing residential areas and approximate daytime residual noise level (L_{90})

Description	Typical Range dB(A)	Average dB(A)
Quiet suburban residential	36 to 40 inclusive	38
Normal suburban residential	41 to 45 inclusive	43
Urban residential	46 to 50 inclusive	48
Noisy urban residential	51 to 55 inclusive	53
Very noisy urban residential	56 to 60 inclusive	58

SOURCE: U.S. Environmental Protection Agency, *Report to the President and Congress on Noise*, Dec. 31, 1971, Table 2.2.

EFFECTS OF NOISE

Noise can have many adverse effects, including damage to hearing, disruption of normal activity, and general annoyance. Extremely loud noise, such as a sonic boom, can also cause physical damage to structures.

The most common and best understood physiological effect of noise is hearing impairment—either temporary or permanent. The amount of permanent hearing loss produced by sufficient exposure to high-level noise depends on the nature of the noise, the time distribution of particular exposures, the total duration of the exposure over a lifetime, and individual susceptibility. For essentially continuous types of noise, such as that in many factories, enough research has been done to permit some statistical prediction of the risk of hearing damage. More research is needed, however, to predict damage which results from noise of a discontinuous nature.

Noise is known to produce various temporary changes in man's physiological state, in particular a constriction of the smaller arteries. This can mean a speeded up pulse and respiration rate. Some medical authorities believe that continued exposure to loud noises could cause chronic effects such as hypertension or ulcers. Startling noises elicit involuntary muscular responses. Research is still necessary to permit quantitative prediction and understanding of the extraauditory physiological impact of noise.

More research is needed on the effects of noise on performance of manual tasks. Laboratory studies paint a confusing picture: noise sometimes degrades performance, sometimes improves it. The type of task; the intensity, quality, and repetition rate of the noise; the personality and mood of the worker; and the duration of the task—all seem to interact in unpredictable ways. Workers who must devote constant attention to detail (e.g., console monitoring in quality inspection) may be more prone to dis-

Sound Source	dB (A)*	Response Criteria
	— 150	
Carrier Deck Jet Operation	— 140	
	— 130	Painfully Loud Limit Amplified Speech
Jet Takeoff (200 feet) Discotheque Auto Horn (3 feet)	— 120	Maximum Vocal Effort
Riveting Machine	— 110	
Jet Takeoff (2000 feet)		
Shout (0.5 feet)	— 100	
N.Y. Subway Station		Very Annoying
Heavy Truck (50 feet)	— 90	Hearing Damage (8 hours)
Pneumatic Drill (50 feet)		
	— 80	Annoying
Freight Train (50 feet)		
Freeway Traffic (50 feet)	— 70	Telephone Use Difficult Intrusive
Air Conditioning Unit (20 feet)	— 60	
Light Auto Traffic (50 feet)	— 50	Quiet
Living room		
Bedroom	— 40	
Library		
Soft Whisper (15 feet)	— 30	Very Quiet
Broadcasting Studio	— 20	
	— 10	Just Audible
	— 0	Threshold of Hearing

*Typical A—Weighted sound levels taken with a sound-level meter and expressed as decibels on the scale. The "A" scale approximates the frequency response of the human ear. Source: Department of Transportation.

FIGURE 10.1 Weighted sound levels and human response.

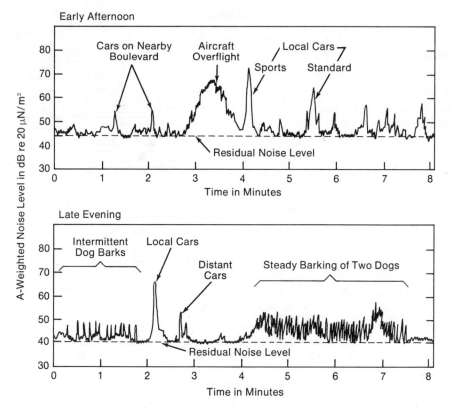

FIGURE 10.2 Two samples of outdoor noise in a normal suburban neighborhood with the microphone located 20 feet from the street curb (source: Wyle Laboratories, "Community Noise," a report prepared for the Environmental Protection Agency, 1971).

traction. Noise can mask auditory warning signals and thereby cause accidents or cause annoyance and general fatigue.

Individuals vary widely in their sensitivity to noise. A few percent of the population appear not to be bothered by noise, no matter how loud. At the other extreme, a hypersensitive few are distressed by almost any noise. Sensitivity to noise may vary considerably from day to day.

A person may be psychologically predisposed to tolerate and accept a given noise environment when he feels that the noise is an inevitable by-product of a useful or valuable service. He also tolerates it if his health is not affected and it does not generate fear. One survey of noise around an airport indicated that people's general con-

nection between noise and their fear of aircraft crashing has more effect on the degree of annoyance than does the actual level of noise.

Still another factor is the extent to which people who are annoyed by noise desire to complain and actually do complain about the noise. Complaint data clearly show, however, that new noises will prompt substantial additional response from the community if such noises are heard and identified above the noise level that already exists.

The actual physical threshold of noise-induced pain for humans has been estimated variously at 120 to 140 dBA. Prolonged exposure to levels above 90 dBA induces permanent loss of hearing, and some see the danger level for hearing

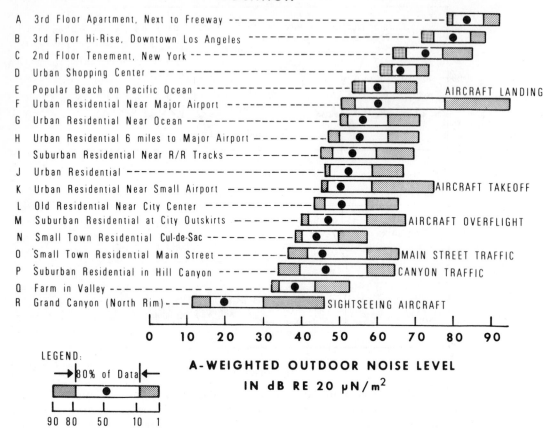

LOCATION

A 3rd Floor Apartment, Next to Freeway

B 3rd Floor Hi-Rise, Downtown Los Angeles

C 2nd Floor Tenement, New York

D Urban Shopping Center

E Popular Beach on Pacific Ocean — AIRCRAFT LANDING

F Urban Residential Near Major Airport

G Urban Residential Near Ocean

H Urban Residential 6 miles to Major Airport

I Suburban Residential Near R/R Tracks

J Urban Residential

K Urban Residential Near Small Airport — AIRCRAFT TAKEOFF

L Old Residential Near City Center

M Suburban Residential at City Outskirts — AIRCRAFT OVERFLIGHT

N Small Town Residential Cul-de-Sac

O Small Town Residential Main Street — MAIN STREET TRAFFIC

P Suburban Residential in Hill Canyon — CANYON TRAFFIC

Q Farm in Valley

R Grand Canyon (North Rim) — SIGHTSEEING AIRCRAFT

0   10   20   30   40   50   60   70   80   90

LEGEND:

→ 80% of Data ←

90 80   50   10 1

**A-WEIGHTED OUTDOOR NOISE LEVEL
IN dB RE 20 μN/m²**

FIGURE 10.3   Range of daytime outdoor noise readings for 18 locales
(source: EPA Report to the President and Congress on Noise, 1971).

loss at even lower levels. There is evidence that some workers experience hearing loss at a sustained level of 80 dBA. That noise tends to increase with city size and density is obvious but not easily documented. Some corroboration emerges from the indirect evidence of the location of major noise sources, regulatory standards, and some limited collection of data.

The sources of loudest ambient noise occur in large cities: jet airports, heavy traffic, building construction, and demolition. A New York City Task Force on Noise Control observed: "The New Yorker's day is filled with the nerve-wracking shriek and clank of the subway, the deafening cacophony of pneumatic hammers, traffic, jet planes . . . ." Regulatory standards are indicative of land-use (and density) effects. Swiss standards, for example, are shown in Table 10.2.

The rapid growth of aviation since World War II and the development of jets have created a major noise problem in airports and the areas around them. A four-engine jet at takeoff generates 115 to 120 dBA. A measure of the resulting annoyance is that about 50 of the 140 major American airports are involved with formal complaints concerning noise, including a sizable number of lawsuits. The Airport Operators

TABLE 10.2

Swiss standards for outdoor noise levels in dBA

	Basic Noise Level		Frequent Peaks		Infrequent Peaks	
Locale	Night	Day	Night	Day	Night	Day
Hospital	35	45	45	50	55	55
Quiet residential	45	55	55	65	65	70
Mixed use	45	60	55	70	65	75
Commercial	50	60	60	70	65	75
Industrial	55	65	60	75	70	80
Main road	65	70	70	80	80	90

SOURCE: Cited by Walter W. Soroka, "Community Noise Survey," American Speech and Hearing Association, Proceedings of the Conference: *Noise as a Public Health Hazard*, Washington, 1969, p. 177.

Council International estimates that by 1975, 15 million people will be living near enough to airports to be subjected to intense aircraft noise. Figure 10.4 and Table 10.3 show the compatibility of different kinds of land use with different levels of exposure to aircraft noise.

TREATING NOISE IN THE URBAN ENVIRONMENT: CONTROLLING THE LOCATION OF ACTIVITIES

Wachs and Schofer (1970) have pointed out that there are three principal alternatives open in treating noise problems: development of new technologies, careful choice and control of the location of noise sources and receivers, and direct control of noise itself. While technological innovation can be expected to be the most productive path to eliminating any problem of concomitant effects, the long time lags typically associated with invention and implementation usually lead to a search for more immediate solutions. Influencing the location of noise sources and noise-sensitive activities in urban areas represents a macroscopic approach to the problem open to the analyst.

The Problem of Tradeoffs

One of the principal tradeoffs which must be made in any urban area is between the benefits which are derived from accessibility to services and systems and the disbenefits which arise from proximity. People want to be near work, firehouses, hospitals, stores, and theaters, but they suffer when these are all in their back yards. Zoning ordinances attempt—sometimes ineffectively—to provide the collective benefits of accessible factories and business while insulating most people from their negative effects, including noise. There is heavy reliance upon public and private transportation systems to provide this accessibility without proximity, but these relatively ubiquitous systems themselves are generators of a large proportion of the noise in urban areas. Those whose residences are proximate to especially noisy transportation facilities bear a burden so that the population as a whole can live in relative isolation from the noise and smoke of industry and commerce.

There is fairly little flexibility in the design of intraurban transportation facilities which would permit the location of these facilities away from residences, thus minimizing the noise and other concomitant effects which not only disturb those residences but may also be physically harmful. To perform effectively, transportation systems must be built in network configurations which follow urban density. In fact, it is well known that dense residential development follows transportation network facilities, because the accessibility benefits outweigh the discomforts and the perceived health hazards of noise and other concomitants.

Consumer Attitudes and Perceptions

For example, attitude surveys have shown that, while homeowners recognize urban freeways as sources of noise, air pollution, and safety hazards for their children, they find it desirable to be located as close as five blocks from such

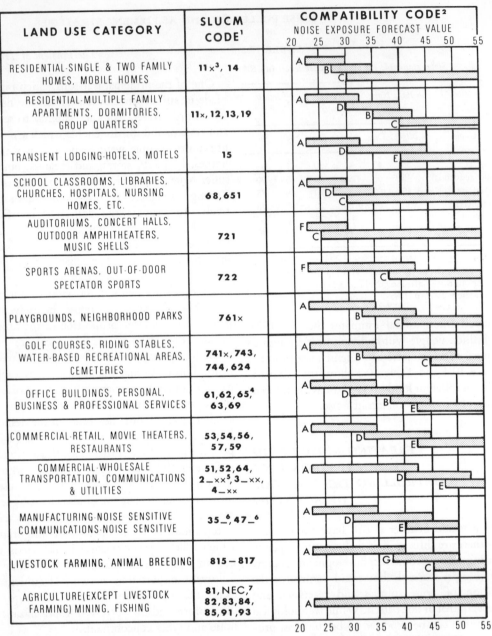

LAND USE CATEGORY	SLUCM CODE[1]	COMPATIBILITY CODE[2] NOISE EXPOSURE FORECAST VALUE
RESIDENTIAL-SINGLE & TWO FAMILY HOMES, MOBILE HOMES	11×[3], 14	A, B, C
RESIDENTIAL-MULTIPLE FAMILY APARTMENTS, DORMITORIES, GROUP QUARTERS	11×, 12,13,19	A, D, B, C
TRANSIENT LODGING-HOTELS, MOTELS	15	A, D, E
SCHOOL CLASSROOMS, LIBRARIES, CHURCHES, HOSPITALS, NURSING HOMES, ETC.	68,651	A, D, C
AUDITORIUMS, CONCERT HALLS, OUTDOOR AMPHITHEATERS, MUSIC SHELLS	721	F, C
SPORTS ARENAS, OUT-OF-DOOR SPECTATOR SPORTS	722	F, C
PLAYGROUNDS, NEIGHBORHOOD PARKS	761×	A, B, C
GOLF COURSES, RIDING STABLES, WATER-BASED RECREATIONAL AREAS, CEMETERIES	741×,743, 744,624	A, B, C
OFFICE BUILDINGS, PERSONAL, BUSINESS & PROFESSIONAL SERVICES	61,62,65,[4] 63,69	A, D, B, E
COMMERCIAL-RETAIL, MOVIE THEATERS, RESTAURANTS	53,54,56, 57,59	A, D, E
COMMERCIAL-WHOLESALE TRANSPORTATION, COMMUNICATIONS & UTILITIES	51,52,64, 2_××[5],3_××, 4_××	A, D, E
MANUFACTURING-NOISE SENSITIVE COMMUNICATIONS-NOISE SENSITIVE	35_[6],47_[6]	A, D, E
LIVESTOCK FARMING, ANIMAL BREEDING	815−817	A, G, C
AGRICULTURE(EXCEPT LIVESTOCK FARMING) MINING, FISHING	81,NEC,[7] 82,83,84, 85,91,93	A

NOISE EXPOSURE FORECAST VALUE
20   25   30   35   40   45   50   55

1. STANDARD LAND USE CODING MANUAL
2. CORRESPONDING LAND USE DESCRIPTORS ARE LISTED IN TABLE FOUR
3. X = A SLUCM CATEGORY BROADER OR NARROWER THAN, BUT GENERALLY INCLUSIVE OF THE CATEGORY DESCRIBED
4. EXCLUDING HOSPITALS
5. XX = SOME EXCEPTIONS MAY OCCUR FOR PARTICULAR OR SPECIALIZED NOISE SENSITIVE ACTIVITIES
6. DEPENDENT UPON SPECIFIC TASK REQUIREMENTS
7. NOT ELSEWHERE CLASSIFIED

FIGURE 10.4   Land-use compatibility chart for aircraft noise (source: Bolt Beranek and Newman, Inc., *Chicago Urban Noise Study*, a report prepared for the Department of Environmental Control, City of Chicago, 1970).

TABLE 10.3

Noise compatibility interpretations for use with Figure 10.4

Compatibility Code	Land-Use Descriptors
A	Satisfactory, with no special noise-insulation requirements for new construction.
B	New construction or development should generally be avoided except as possible infill of already developed areas. In such cases, a detailed analysis of noise-reduction requirements should be made, and needed noise-insulation features should be included in the building design.
C	New construction or development should not be undertaken.
D	New construction or development should not be undertaken unless a detailed analysis of noise-reduction requirements is made and needed noise-insulation features included in the design.
E	New construction or development should not be undertaken unless directly related to airport-related activities or services. Conventional construction will generally be inadequate and special noise-insulation features must be included. A detailed analysis of noise-reduction requirements should be made and needed noise-insulation features included in the construction or development.
F	A detailed analysis of the noise environment, considering noise from *all* urban and transportation sources, should be made and needed noise-insulation features and/or special requirements for the sound-reinforcement systems should be included in the basic design.
G	New development should generally be avoided except as possible expansion of already developed areas.

One of the difficulties that arise in the use of such information in design and decision is the unreliability of consumer perceptions as they are identified through purchasing decisions and attitude surveys. While such approaches allow the use of consumer preferences for guiding urban design, the average citizen may not be aware of the physiological and psychological hazards associated with the outputs of some common systems. The resident of an apartment near an expressway may be willing to smell automobile exhaust fumes, but he might not wish to expose his children to lead poisoning. Free lead from automobile exhausts, however, cannot be sensed by humans; hence choices of apartment locations do not reflect this factor. Similarly, families can become accustomed to the sound of elevated trains a few feet from their windows, but the fact that they select an apartment near such a facility does not insure that their health will be unaffected.

It becomes the responsibility of the scientist, the medical doctor, and the urban systems analyst to give fair consideration to the latent impacts of concomitant system outputs which are not reflected by patterns of market behavior or attitude surveys. Such individuals have not only the necessary skills but also the responsibility to inform the decision-makers and the public of such harmful effects, as well as to seek design and location alternatives to minimize the consequences of concomitant outputs.

Controlling the Location and Timing of Activities

Activities may be located and timed in various ways to control the effects of noise. Investigations in England have shown that people are more likely to experience annoyance due to excessive noise during the evening hours, particularly in residential areas. During the evening hours, high levels of complaint were obtained for sound levels up to 20 dB lower than those producing similar complaint levels during the

facilities; furthermore, they generally would be reluctant to move if a new freeway were to be built even closer to their homes. The tradeoff relationships representing both the desire for proximity and the concern for avoiding unpleasant concomitants have recently been measured mathematically and may now be used as design tools.

daytime. Similarly, the degree to which noise serves as an annoyance to people is related to the activities in which they are engaged; higher levels of noise appear to be more acceptable in work places and in places of commerce than in the home. This raises the possibility of planning commercial and industrial areas adjacent to or over highways and rapid transit facilities. These activities, less sensitive to noise and more prone to daytime activities, would serve as buffers between transportation noise and residences, would not be hampered by transportation noise, and would probably derive economic benefit from the accessibility provided by such locations.

This idea is quite consistent with current interest in planning for the multiple uses of freeway rights of way. Recent proposals, however, that more extensive use of such rights of way be made for residential construction seem to have some serious drawbacks as far as noise is concerned. Certain land uses, in terms of noise, are compatible with transportation facilities. These may include commercial and industrial land uses, but probably not residential land uses.

It is well known that noise is dissipated exponentially with distance from the source. For a single point source, sound level decays approximately 6 dB for each doubling of distance from the source. If the noise is produced by a line source, such as a crowded highway, the sound will decrease 3 dB for each doubling of distance. For this reason, consideration might be given to condemning strips of land wider by several hundred feet than are required by rights of way for transportation facilities. This will assure that few individual homeowners will have to bear the brunt of the noise-impact of such facilities. This course of action, however, would increase the cost of a transportation facility without changing its transportation performance. The possibility for this type of excess condemnation might be enhanced if the excess land were resold for use in ways more compatible with transportation noise than are residences.

For large, unique elements of the urban system allow greater flexibility for planning for the control of noise than do network systems. While these facilities need not be near the people or institutions they serve in terms of distance, they frequently require high levels of accessibility as measured in time and cost. Thus, for the location of new airports or heavy industry, planning can be more responsive to considerations of noise. Locations may be possible which minimize the effects of noise upon the surrounding communities while not interfering with the performance outputs of these facilities. Compatibility with surrounding land uses, and stringent controls following the construction of these facilities, can become requirements if organized pressure is effectively exerted on the political decision-makers. Near O'Hare Airport in Chicago, perhaps 200,000 people live in a 35-square-mile area which has a noise impact (based upon frequency of flyovers, runway orientation, and sound-emission properties of aircraft) judged to be uncomfortable. That these noise levels could have been anticipated at an earlier date is significant, since perhaps one-half of that population occupies residences built after O'Hare was built but before noise reached its current levels. Stringent controls could have restricted development to nonresidential uses in these impacted areas, with possible economic losses to some developers. Controls over the development of areas impacted by a third major airport for Chicago, or by major industrial facilities, will certainly involve many jurisdictions. State-level controls on development would, therefore, be required to avoid the repetition of past mistakes. Organized public and professional reactions would undoubtedly be prerequirements for such controls.

With respect to such unique entities as airports, many possibilities are raised by recent proposals for the building of major new cities where there are none today. Such a new city might be planned around an airport, with rings of industrial and commercial activities separating residences from the airport's noise and pollution and keeping residences from under the flight paths of aircraft. Such a plan could be developed for an efficient and functional city while achieving desired performance levels for the airport. As long as proposed new cities remain at the small scale of Reston, Va., Columbia, Md., and Jonathan, Minn., however, this proposed concept will remain untested.

Limitations of Zoning

Zoning regulations offer a passive mechanism for *permitting*, rather than promoting, desirable patterns of urban development. Because of its passive nature, zoning does not always bring about the most effective urban system performance. Perhaps more importantly, traditional zoning ordinances fail to encourage, and may actually discourage, the search for innovations.

For example, an inflexible regulation which prevents residences and certain noise-generating activities from being in close proximity does not provide a payoff to the designer who can produce a technology which makes these uses compatible. An industrial plant which is quiet and clean might still be prohibited from a desirable location. The result of such regulatory programs is often urban sprawl and an antiquated technology with little hope for innovation.

A more effective alternative is performance zoning. If the performance properties of a normally undesirable land use can be shown to be acceptable, the new activity may be introduced to the area. In this way, developers and locators are encouraged to solve the problems of concomitants through new technologies in order to compete for more desirable locations in the region.

Investing in Noise-Control Technology

Aside from questions of facility location planning on a regional scale, a much larger range of more microscopic responses to noise is possible. These include modifications to existing urban systems and the incorporation of technological features into new systems which will control noise levels in one or more of the four ways presented in the following paragraphs.

First, noise-generating components of urban systems could be replaced by quieter components which accomplish the same performance objectives. Quieter engines are being developed for jet aircraft, although they are more costly and deficient in performance. Quieter machinery could be adopted for industrial operations. This approach has the advantage that the costs of reducing noise are borne directly by those who generate it and by their customers. On the other hand, there is often little motivation for concern about concomitant outputs. Strong public pressures and perhaps even litigation may be necessary stimuli to action.

Second, noise generators could be insulated at the source of the noise. Sound-insulating materials could thus be required in noisy factories to prevent the noise from leaving the site. Expressways and railways could be depressed to limit their noise-transmission properties. This has proved to be an effective strategy, and yet it frequently results in unpleasant aesthetic aspects, both for the roadside resident and the drivers themselves. Problems of urban expressway planning are illustrative of the complex interactions between system inputs and concomitant and performance outputs which must be considered by the urban systems analyst.

Third, noise transmission could be reduced by interposing barriers between noise sources and receivers. Airport runways could be insulated from surrounding communities through the use of sound barriers. Urban expressway noise transmission may be reduced by structural barriers or through the use of bordering trees and shrubbery. These devices require additional space, usually secured by condemning adjacent properties; thus, they may be very costly in areas of high density. Distance alone, of course, serves as a sound attenuator, but it is highly inefficient when land costs are high. The use of barriers, expecially aesthetically pleasing ones such as shrubs, also enables us to capitalize on an interesting psychological factor relating to noise perception: people are less annoyed by traffic noise if they cannot see the road.

Finally, the reception of noise could be controlled by insulating the potential receiver. Thus, homes under aircraft flight paths could be required, by building codes, to contain special sound insulation, as do many airport hotels. Soundproofing measures can be costly, particularly when applied to existing buildings. For example, double-pane windows would typically be installed because of the considerable increase in attenuation capability they achieve over standard windows; however, they require air conditioning and special considerations for ventilation and fire escapes, resulting in noticeable cost increases. Furthermore, efforts to keep sound away from particular receivers place the burdens of action as well as cost on those who suffer rather than those who cause the problems, thus introducing the element of inequity.

Decisions on these and other solutions to the problems of noise in our urban environment will continue to be difficult. Each of these measures is costly, and the potential benefits are not well defined. Attenuation or noise reduction at the source rarely improves the performance outputs of the system causing the noise, and frequently performance is degraded. Problems of this nature are particularly acute in cases where those who suffer from the concomitant effects are not the people who benefit directly from system performance. For example, the families who live near major airports are not frequent air travelers; therefore, they will not be willing to trade better air service for more frequent noise in their homes. Furthermore, the industries which generate the noise will be reluctant to commit resources to noise reduction, since their customers will not benefit.

We have referred repeatedly to the difficulty of analyzing tradeoffs among various possible strategies for noise control. It should not be a goal to reduce the performance levels of the many complex systems necessary to urban life. To reduce the noise levels without decreasing system performance often requires large expenditures. These are frequently difficult to justify in economic terms even when medical, psychological, or aesthetic benefits can be estimated. Although it is easy to agree that lower levels of traffic noise in homes would be desirable, before funds are allocated to the reduction of traffic noise, a subjective economic decision must be made. A recent study showed, for example, that an "average" new ranch house could be sufficiently insulated from traffic noise at 1,000 feet for a cost of $1,030. With 800,000 new homes built each year in this country, this would require a total annual outlay of more than 800 million dollars. Can it be demonstrated that the benefits gained are worthy of such an expenditure?

A complicating factor arises from the fact that the incidence of the costs varies with the proposed solution, making it easy for each interest group to favor the solution which would require the costs to be borne by other groups. Should methods of residential-area traffic noise control be adopted which must be paid for by the automobile and truck owners, by the owners of residential property, or by the public as a whole? Equal reductions in noise level might be attained by vehicle modification, the insulation of residences, or the construction of noise barriers near highways. If these do achieve equal reductions in noise, and it can be demonstrated that the result is socially desirable, the efficiency expert might favor the least-cost alternative. Home owners living near highways, automobile companies, and taxpayers not directly affected would argue for different solutions, however. The systems engineer can make a valuable contribution by estimating the costs and effectiveness of such alternatives, but his analysis rarely reveals one solution as superior to all others along every possible dimension of comparison. Ultimately, such decisions must be political.

CHAPTER *11*

environmental pollution

and human health

Air, water, land, and noise pollution—all adversely affect man and his environment in many ways. They soil his home and interfere with the growth of plants and shrubs. They diminish the value of his agricultural products. They obscure his view and add unpleasant smells to his environment. Most important of all, they endanger his health. The measured health effects of pollution must be of central importance in the fight against pollution.

Table 11.1 summarizes the known effects of pollutants on plants. Are there similar demonstrable relationships between pollution and human health? What are the general correlations of environmental pollution and the physical and mental health of urban residents? To what extent can these correlations be equated with specific causal mechanisms associated with pollutants? In this chapter three separate sets of evidence are presented that cast light on these questions: (a) an analysis of the relationship between the incidence of emphysema and air pollution; (b) evidence on the relationship of mortality and air pollution; (c) an ecological statistical study of the extent to which long-term exposure to a variety of environmental chemicals is related

Materials reprinted are drawn from:

S. Ishikawa, M.D., P. H. Bowden, M.D., V. Fisher, M.D., J. P. Wyatt, M.D., "The 'Emphysema Profile' in Two Midwestern Cities in North America," *Archives of Environmental Health*, Vol. 18 (1969), pp. 660–666. Begins on page 297.

Lester B. Lave, "Does Air Pollution Shorten Lives?" Paper prepared for the Committee on Urban Economics Summer Conference, University of Chicago, September 10–11, 1970. Begins on page 302.

Richard J. Hickey, David E. Boyce, Evelyn B. Harner, and Richard C. Clelland, "Ecological Statistical Studies Concerning Environmental Pollution and Chronic Disease," *IEEE Transactions on Geoscience Electronics*, Vol. GE8 (October 1970), pp. 186–202. Begins on page 317.

TABLE 11.1

The six worst pollutants that harm plants

Pollutant	Where It Comes From	Symptoms on Leaves	Levels at Which Susceptible Plants are Injured (in parts per million)
SULFUR DIOXIDE (SO$_2$)	Burning high sulfur coal, oil, or gas for industrial or home heating, smelting, refining, and production of electric power.	**Broad-leaved plants:** White to straw-colored, dry, papery blotches at margins and between veins. Blotches may turn brown to reddish-brown on some species. Both leaf surfaces are affected. Veins normally remain green. Yellowing and gradual bleaching of surrounding tissues is fairly common. **Grasses:** Yellow to light tan or white streaks on either side of midvein. **Conifers:** Tan to reddish-brown dieback or banding of needles with yellowish borders. Heavy leaf drop may occur.	0.5 for 4 hours or 0.25 for 24 hours. In burning a ton of coal, 80 lbs. of sulfur dioxide is emitted.
FLUORIDES (HF)	Industries producing glass, aluminum, pottery, brick and ceramics, refineries, metal smelters, and phosphate fertilizers.	**Broad-leaved plants:** Yellowish mottle to reddish-brown or tan discoloration at margins and tips. **Grasses and Conifers:** Tipburn and dieback. A narrow, yellowish to dark brown band often borders the scorched areas. Injured leaves and fruits may drop early. Young, succulent growth is injured the easiest.	Fluorides are **accumulated** up to several hundred or thousand ppm. **Gladiolus** exposed 4 weeks at 0.001 ppm, or less than a day at 10 parts per billion, may accumulate 150 ppm.
CHLORIDES, CHLORINE (-CI)	Glass-making factories, refineries, refuse dumps, incinerators, spillage.	**Broad-leaved plants:** Tan-to-brown dead areas, usually near margins, tips, or between larger veins. **Grasses:** Progressive streaking toward main vein between tip and where blade bends. **Conifers:** Tipburn of current season's needles. Middle-aged or older leaves usually more susceptible than young ones. Bleaching without killing may occur, as well as tissue collapse.	2 hours at concentrations from 0.1 to 4.67 ppm. Chlorides do **not** accumulate in plant tissues after exposure.
OZONE (O$_3$)	Sunlight reacting with exhaust gases from autos, buses, trucks and planes; combustion of fuels; brought down from the stratosphere by vertical winds; electrical storms.	**Broad-leaved plants:** Red-brown to black stippling, silver or bleached straw-white flecking, mottling, or chlorosis of **upper** surface. **Lilac:** Leaves rolled and scorched at margins. Growth stunted; flowering and bud formation depressed. **Grasses:** Small dead flecks scattered on one or both surfaces; may merge to form larger dead areas. **Conifers:** Brown tipburn, or yellow to brown or reddish flecking and banding of needles. Susceptible white pines are stunted to dwarfed and yellowish.	4 to 6 hours at 0.02 to 0.04. Ozone and SO$_2$ often combine to injure plants **before** either alone would cause damage.

TABLE 11.1 (cont.)

Pollutant	Where It Comes From	Symptoms on Leaves	Levels at Which Susceptible Plants are Injured (in parts per million)
PEROXY-ACETYL NITRATE (PAN)[a]	Sunlight reacting with exhaust gases (oxides of nitrogen and un-saturated hydrocarbons) from autos and other combustion engines.	**Broad-leaved plants:** Tissue collapse on **lower** surface. Results in a glazing, bronzing, or silvering in bands or blotches. **Grasses:** Bleached, tan-to-yellow, longitudinal bands. **Conifers:** Needles turn yellow. Early maturity or senescence, yellowing, moderate to severe stunting and early leaf fall may occur.	1 hour or more at 0.01 to 0.05. Requires light before, during and after exposure. Best known in Los Angeles basin area.
ETHYLENE (H_2C-CH_2)	Exhaust gases from autos, buses, trucks, and planes. Problem in fruit, vegetable, and cut-flowers rooms and greenhouses where manufactured gas is still used.	**Broad-leaved plants:** Downward curling of leaves and shoots (epinasty), followed by early leaf and flower drop, yellowing, stunting of growth. **Conifers:** Drop of needles and young cones. New growth stunted; cone development is poor. **Certain orchids:** Dry sepal disease. **Carnation, Narcissus, Rose:** Buds fail to open ("sleepiness"). **Rose** buds may blast; flowers show color-breaking. **Snapdragon, Calceolaria:** Blooms drop (shell) early.	0.001 for 24 hours produces dry sepal in **Cattleya** orchids; 0.1 for 6 hours causes epinasty in tomato and sleepiness in carnation.

[a] Other PANS, such as peroxypropionyl nitrate and peroxybutryl nitrate, may be present in city air, producing plant symptoms indistinguishable from those caused by peroxyacetyl nitrate.

to chronic diseases, taking into account demographic, ethological, climatic, and economic variables.

THE "EMPHYSEMA PROFILE"

A high incidence of anatomic bronchitis and emphysema has been reported by several investigators in such cities as Boston, London, and St. Louis and it has been suggested to be the consequence of air pollution. Up to the present, there has been a lack of properly controlled morphological data for comparative studies of pulmonary emphysema associated with environmental effects, however. An ecological study therefore was undertaken by Ishikawa et al. (1969) to assess prevalence and severity of pulmonary emphysema utilizing a series of post-mortem lungs obtained from long-time residents in two cities: a heavily industrialized urban community (St. Louis) and a prairie-agricultural city (Winnipeg, Canada).

In this study, a series of 300 adult lungs (left side) was collected from each city through a routine autopsy service involving three general hospitals during the years 1960 to 1966. Complete hospital records including occupational and smoking history obtained from next of kin were available for the cases studied. A critical review of these records, with particular attention to smoking habits, was made by the same investigators without prior knowledge of the morphological findings in each case analyzed. Environmental and meteorological data were obtained from reports of federal and provincial laboratories.

Lungs from autopsy were inflated up to a

stable pressure of approximately 25 cm H_2O with formaldehyde solution and fixed for a few days. Multiple paper macrosections were prepared by a standardized technique. Three sections from different saggital planes were made on the lung of each autopsy case.

Each paper section was examined by hand lens and the anatomic extent of the disruptive emphysematous alteration determined by a grid system and stereoscopic method. The extent of emphysema was evaluated and was expressed as a percentage of the total lung field. For ease of discussion, this anatomic categorization has been classified under the terms mild, moderate, and severe. Mild cases were defined as having

less than 20 percent of emphysematous destruction; moderate, from 20 percent to 70 percent; severe, over 70 percent. There was no significant disagreement among investigators in reading the extent of lung dissolution due to emphysema.

Table 11.2 shows the characteristics of the study population. The age distribution for both groups was almost identical, as shown on Figure 11.1. The women numbered 96 (32 percent) in St. Louis and 93 (31 percent) in Winnipeg. The majority of the subjects were white; nonwhite represented only a minority (7 percent in St. Louis and 2 percent in Winnipeg). Any immigrants in this retrospective survey were from Europe, had arrived in North America before

TABLE 11.2

Study population for the emphysema profile

	Cases	Mean age	Women	Immigrant		Nonsmokers, percent
				Percent	Mean age migrated	
St. Louis	300	60.4	96	9	22	25
Winnipeg	300	59.2	93	20	28	26

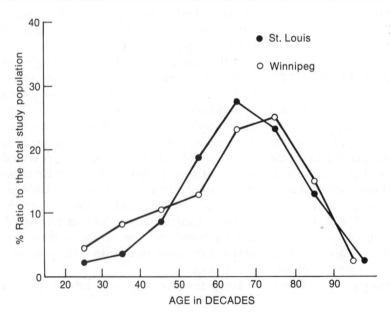

FIGURE 11.1 Age distribution of the study population.

the age of 30, and had lived approximately two-thirds of their lives in the same geographical area. From the statistical evidence, it is apparent that the immigrant group did not influence the emphysema profile.

The occupations of the subjects studied were manual laborers, farmers, and clerks and for the most part were in the low to middle socio-economic group. Miners and others having a history of prolonged exposure to chemicals or other irritants were excluded from the study.

Nonsmokers in the St. Louis cases constituted 25 percent of the total under study (12 percent in men and 48 percent in women); in Winnipeg they represented 25 percent of the total (14 percent in men and 44 percent in women). According to lifetime smoking history, individuals who had smoked more than 30 cigarettes a day continuously for at least 25 years were classified as "heavy smokers." No other specific classification of smoking habits was made because of the retrospective nature of the study. Any smoker other than categorized by us as a heavy smoker was classified as "light to moderate smoker."

Four major pollutants are commonly held to be implicated in the production of chronic lung diseases; Table 11.3 shows the amount of these

TABLE 11.3

Air-pollution emissions[a]

	Sulfur Oxides	Nitrogen Oxides	Hydrocarbons	Particulates
St. Louis	455	138	374	147
Winnipeg	36	20	62	82

[a] One thousand tons per year.

four major air pollutants discharged into the atmosphere in both cities.

St. Louis is heavily contaminated and in contrast to Winnipeg puts out thirteen times as much sulfur oxides, seven times as much nitrogen oxides, six times as much hydrocarbons,

and twice as much particulates per year. The particulates in St. Louis are mainly emitted by industry, while in Winnipeg this fallout, although high, is clearly of the nonrespirable dust type. Dust fall practically disappears in Winnipeg from November 1 till the end of March. Photochemical action of inversions is negligible.

Table 11.4 shows meteorological characteristics of the two cities. St. Louis, owing to its heat

TABLE 11.4

Meteorological characteristics

	Degree Days by Year	Precipitation (inches)	Wind Speed (mph)
St. Louis	4,699	36.8	9.3
Winnipeg	1,679	20.4	12.7

islands and much warmer temperatures, has continuous environmental inversions with a poor diffusion of pollutants; Winnipeg is much colder, the air is dry and often windy, and the land is flat; the atmosphere is unstable with excellent diffusion. With limited industrial contamination in Winnipeg, the pollutants are thus readily dispersed.

The prevalence of anatomic emphysema in similar age groups was significantly different. Figure 11.2 shows the prevalence in the two cities. There were practically no cases of emphysema in Winnipeg in subjects under the age of 50. In the late age groups, however, the curves of the two communities approach each other.

For convenience, the cases are divided into three age groups as in Figure 11.3—20 to 49, 50 to 69, and 70 and over. In the first group, there were seven times as many cases of emphysema in St. Louis as in Winnipeg. In the second group the ratio of emphysema was two to one, and in the third group 1.5 to 1.

The principal difference of the emphysema profile in the two cities rests upon the severity of the disease process. On Figure 11.4 the extent

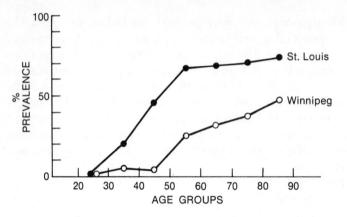

FIGURE 11.2 Anatomic emphysema based on series of 300 lungs from each city.

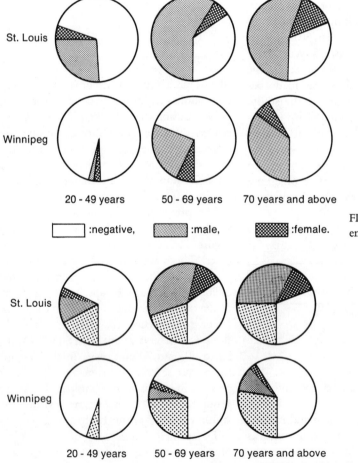

FIGURE 11.3 Prevalence of emphysema in three age groups.

FIGURE 11.4 Extent of emphysema.

of anatomic emphysema is shown for the three age groups. In Winnipeg, severe emphysema was uncommon in any age group, whereas cases of advanced emphysema were encountered in all age groups in St. Louis. In the older age groups there were six times as many cases of severe emphysema in St. Louis as there were in Winnipeg.

Anatomic emphysema in relation to lifetime smoking habits is shown in Figure 11.5. In nonsmokers there was more emphysema in St. Louis than in Winnipeg, although the degree of emphysema in the latter city was not severe. Of the smokers, there were four times as many cases of severe emphysema in St. Louis as in Winnipeg.

In Figures 11.6 and 11.7 the men and women are independently viewed. In Winnipeg, none

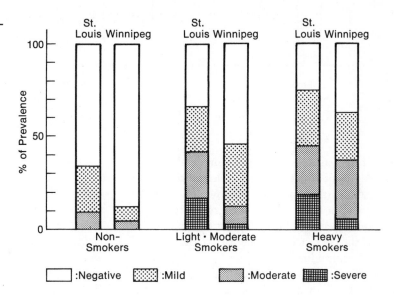

FIGURE 11.5 Emphysema profile in relation to smoking habit.

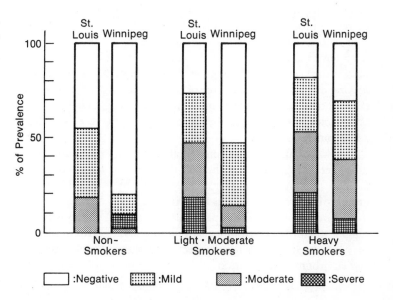

FIGURE 11.6 Emphysema profile in relation to smoking habit (men).

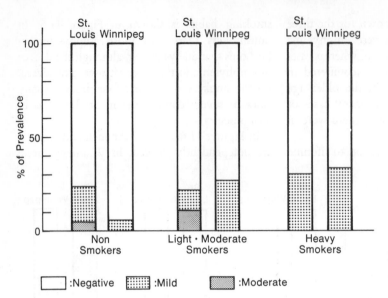

FIGURE 11.7 Emphysema profile in relation to smoking habit (women).

of the female subjects had a moderate or severe degree of emphysema regardless of the smoking habit, although more emphysema cases were found in the smokers. The general trend of the emphysema profile in both cities was a reflection of the characteristic male pattern often recorded in medical literature.

There was considerably more emphysema in St. Louis than in Winnipeg, and the anatomic emphysema was found much earlier and appeared to progress more rapidly.

In neither city were cases of severe emphysema observed in nonsmokers. From these basic observations on these two cities, which have striking differences in the degree of environmental pollution, it appears that smoking is not the only factor concerned in the development of emphysema.

The importance of environmental pollution is further strengthened by the fact that the incidence of severe emphysema in comparable groups of cigarette smokers is four times as high in St. Louis as it is in Winnipeg. These findings suggest that the development of emphysema may be related to a synergistic effect of smoking and environmental pollution.

MORTALITY AND AIR POLLUTION

As with smoking, however, establishing an association between air pollution and morbidity or mortality is a painstaking task. Other factors affecting health must be accounted for, and one must be careful to watch for subtle biases, interactions, and synergisms. As Lave (1970) has indicated, the mortality rate will depend on characteristics of the individuals in the study population, including their habits and exposures, and on the characteristics of the environment. Important factors include age (A), sex (F), genetic factors (G), nutrition— both current and cumulative (N), whether and how much he smokes (S), exercise habits (E), income (Y), race (R), the level and quality of medical care (M), occupation—including accident rate and pollution exposures (O), weather (W), air pollution—both current and cumulative (AP), and all other factors, e. These might be summarized by equation (1). Generally, the mortality rate (MR) is measured for a geographically defined group, such as the inhabitants of a city, and the explanatory variables refer to the characteristics of the city.

$$MR_g = fg(A, F, G, N, S, E, Y,$$
$$R, M, O, W, AP, e). \quad (1)$$

Observing these factors is not a straightforward procedure. For example, it is difficult to know how to measure genetic factors and how to accumulate nutrition or other effects over time. Does the effect of inadequate nutrition have less or more effect as time passes? There are many conceptual problems in measuring these variables. Certainly, the form of the functional relation is complicated.

Besides variables which are difficult to measure conceptually, some variables are unmeasured. For example, few data are collected on smoking habits in a city, while the quality of data collected on occupations in a city is quite low. Unfortunately, most of the factors in equation (1) are either unmeasured or measured badly.

If the explanatory variables were not correlated with each other (i.e., orthogonal to each other) the inability to get measures on all variables would not be important. If they were orthogonal, one could find the effect of any variable on the mortality rate by a univariate regression. However, independence is not a reasonable assumption. Air pollution is correlated both with weather and with type of industry, which in turn determines occupation mix. Poverty is associated with occupation mix, race, and age. This collinearity among explanatory variables means that univariate regressions, or simple cross tabulations (which constitute the preponderance of evidence), are not likely to produce results that one can interpret with any confidence. As a result, epidemiologists have been very critical of simple cross tabulations or univariate regressions which attempt to show the effect of air pollution on mortality.

The questions are (1) whether a particular association occurred merely by chance and (2) given that the observed association is more than a chance occurrence, is it a basis for action?

More precisely, the concern is that the association observed between A and B is not a basis for attempting to influence B by manipulating A. Children who get little to eat, especially too few vitamins and minerals, have a higher incidence of rickets. To eliminate rickets, we must find a variable that is both easy and cheap to manipulate that will prevent it. Classically, we attempted to find what "causes" rickets and then to intercede in the sequence of events. Thus, rickets is "caused" by malnutrition and the crucial variable to manipulate is the ingestion of vitamins and minerals. Note that this is not the same as concluding that children must be given a balanced diet, must eat only healthy foods, or must eat regularly. There are many ways of achieving the goal of ingesting the proper amounts of vitamins and minerals.

There has been a rather unfortunate tendency for physicians to fix on the word "cause" and attack various associations shown by correlation analysis as not having been proved to be "causal." This is taken as a reason why no attempt should be made at manipulation in order to deal with a health problem. However, as soon as the problem is stated in a decision context, the emphasis on the word "causal" can be seen to be out of proportion. While it certainly is correct that interference in a known, deterministic, causal chain is certain to lead to results, it is not generally in the public interest to hold off action until causality is established to everyone's satisfaction. In public health situations where the potential gain is high (as in stopping an epidemic) and the cost low (as in adding more chlorine to the water), no one would advocate waiting until everyone was sure that the drinking water was really the cause of the epidemic.

The point is that the level of confidence required for general acceptance of proven causality is not required in order to warrant action. For most health situations with relatively high benefits and low costs, a much lower level of confidence is called for. Thus, a prudent man would have thought seriously about giving up cigarettes long before it was generally accepted that cigarettes cause ill health.

It is difficult to establish even the level of confidence required in a decision context when a chronic disease is involved. Causes of infectious diseases are much easier to isolate than those of chronic ones; only recently have attempts been made to find the latter.

The controversy over cigarette smoking and lung cancer is an instructive example of the difficulty in finding the cause(s) of a chronic disease. Since there is a long time span associated with the development of the disease, many variables are associated with its incidence. In addition, there is no single event (such as the first cigarette) which is the "cause" of the disease. Causation becomes difficult to conceptualize, much less prove. Determining the epidemiology of a chronic disease is necessarily the tedious, needle-in-haystack process of finding whether various "plausible" associations are merely sampling phenomena. Most of the factors associated with a chronic disease will be eliminated by collecting larger samples more carefully. However, many factors will be impossible, or inordinately expensive, to eliminate.

Even in a laboratory setting it is impossible to account for all conceivable factors which might be the "true" cause of the association. After the experiment, it is always possible to suggest one or another uncontrolled factors as the "true" cause. This limitation is even more severe for evidence generated by nature. Errors of observation confound the situation, and many relevant factors are unobserved. More important, some experiments simply have not been generated by nature and so certain cross relations cannot be estimated. Note, however, that the difference between laboratory and observed data is a difference in degree, not in kind. In neither can causation be proved; in neither can all spurious factors be accounted for.

Either in the laboratory or outside in the world, the only way that causation can be established is by assumption. Formally, the correlation between A and B is spurious if we do not believe that A "causes" B, but rather that C is the real cause of both A and B. As Herbert A. Simon has pointed out, the only general way of dealing with spurious correlation is to have a maintained hypothesis about the underlying causal relation. Only by ruling out most of the possible relationships between A, B, and C can we make a statement about causality. In general, no manipulation of the data will isolate the true causal relationships between A, B, and C.

This observation that much theoretical structure is required is an important one in epidemiology, since medicine is of very limited help in providing such a theory. While no one seriously suggests that lung cancer leads to cigarette smoking, the set of possible causal factors is very large. In general, the only way that evidence can be compiled is by sampling a great many groups with a great many characteristics. The convincing evidence is that a factor, such as smoking, is associated with lung cancer under a wide variety of conditions, in a wide variety of groups of people. It is the weight of a number of studies which rules out the possibility that the association is a chance or sampling phenomenon; it is the weight of many studies in many settings which dismisses the possibility that some uncontrolled factor is the true cause of lung cancer.

However, rather than rely entirely on this sort of accumulation of studies, one can attempt careful statistical analysis. Multivariate techniques, which attempt to control for confounding factors explicitly, have much higher potential.

Basically, there are two questions to be answered. Does air pollution really shorten lives? (With the attendant question: what is the nature of the association?) How great is the effect? How many years of life are lost? (With the attendant question: what is the value of the loss?)

To answer the first question, one must control

or account for the many factors influencing health. The important factors were enumerated in equation (1). The basic data at the disposal of the analyst today are a cross section of 117 Standard Metropolitan Statistical Areas (SMSA's). Data are available on various mortality rates, on various measures of air pollution, on population density (P/m^2), and on three characteristics of the population: the proportion of 65 and older (percent 65), proportion nonwhite (percent NW), and proportion of families with income less than $3,000 in 1960 (percent poor). Some variables also are available for occupation mix and weather, but there are no data on genetic factors, smoking habits, medical care, nutrition, or exercise habits.

Of course, if the omitted variables are associated with the included ones, estimated coefficients of the included ones will be biased. Unfortunately, this is so in the analysis that follows. Smoking is known to be associated with lower class status and with age and sex. Nutrition is certainly associated with income levels. Occupation mix is certainly associated with income and pollution. Exercise patterns are probably associated with race and income. Medical care is known to be associated with race and income. These associations mean that parameter estimates will be biased, and it will be difficult to answer either of the two basic questions with absolute certainty.

However, detailed mortality data offer a way out of the problem. Mortality data are available by sex (male and female), race (white and nonwhite), and age group (less than 28 days, less than 1 year, less than 15 years, 15–44 years, 45–64 years, and older than 64). Having 24 slightly dependent variables opens the possibility of contrasting the results for different mortality rates and examining changes in particular elasticities. Contrasting these parameter estimates enables us to disentangle the various effects, thus providing more insights into the complexities of the underlying relationship.

For example, it has been reported elsewhere

(Lave and Seskin, 1970) that the estimated coefficient of "percent nonwhite" is positive and quite significant in a regression to explain the total mortality rate. There are three possible interpretations of this result: (1) Nonwhites are known to have a higher mortality rate, and so areas with more nonwhites have higher mortality rates. (2) Higher nonwhite death rates are only a part of the higher death rates; the real effect is that nonwhites directly cause the mortality rates for whites to be higher (as through, for example, higher crime rates). (3) The factors which lead to a concentration of nonwhites cause higher (or lower) death rates for both whites and nonwhites. Without additional data, there is no way of determining which of these explanations is the correct one.

However, as soon as race-specific mortality rates are available, it is possible to differentiate among these explanations. Suppose that the same regression is run with total white and total nonwhite death rates as the dependent variables. There are four possible sign combinations for the coefficient of "percent nonwhites" in explaining changes in white and nonwhite death rates: $(++)$, $(--)$, $(+-)$, and $(-+)$. The first suggests that areas with many nonwhites have high death rates for both blacks and whites; i.e., they are inherently unhealthy places. The second $(--)$ suggests (although blacks have a higher death rate than whites) that the factors which have led nonwhites to congregate in certain areas tend to lead to low mortality rates. The third pattern $(+-)$ suggests that there is some sort of war going on between blacks and whites; when there is a concentration of blacks, the death rate is high for whites and low for nonwhites and vice versa. Finally, $(-+)$ suggests that whites tend to exploit nonwhites economically when there are enough nonwhites to make exploitation profitable. The higher the percentage of nonwhites in the population, the lower the white death rate and the higher the nonwhite death rate (i.e., only in areas with a concentration of nonwhites is there a concerted pattern of nonwhites performing the more demanding and unhealthy jobs). Not only does the sign pattern distinguish among the three possible explanations listed above, but we can use it to explore the relationship in even greater detail by looking at mortality rates by age and sex.

A caveat is necessary before we accept these interpretations. Other explanatory variables in these regressions are air pollution, percent over 64, population density, and percent poor. If important variables associated with percent nonwhite are omitted or if the form of the regressions is badly specified, these interpretations might be completely incorrect. Only if we can regard the estimated parameters as being approximately correct can we regard the interpretations as justified. Elsewhere it was shown that a simple linear relation is as good as other plausible specifications. We have confidence in the correctness of the parameter estimates, although we can understand an argument that, for example, the parameter estimates are incorrect because the income variable was specified badly.

Rather than spell out all the possible relationships and their interpretation, it would be easier to present the empirical results and present only the relevant interpretations. We proceed to describe the data and results in general.

The Data

The mortality data come from two sources. The total death rate and total nonwhite death rate (for 1960) are reported in *Vital Statistics* along with total nonwhite death rates (per 10,000 live births) for infants dying under 28 days and under 1 year. Also reported are the number of persons dying (both total and nonwhite) for age categories, 0–14, 15–64, and 65 and older. To get mortality rates for these categories, we divided each by total population, since the size of the population at risk was not available. Thus, these death rates are not true age specific

rates, but only approximations. More detailed mortality rates are available in *United States Metropolitan Mortality 1959–1961*. Mortality rates for SMSA's are listed by sex and race (white, nonwhite) for 12 age groups, averaged over three years. Age groups were aggregated to get rates which correspond to previous age groupings. These mortality rates are sufficiently detailed that there are problems with small samples; this is the reason why deaths were aggregated across the three years in computing rates, rather than simply using the 1960 death rate. However, there are still SMSA's where the nonwhite population is so small that certain rates are meaningless. For this reason, three of the 117 SMSA's are eliminated in analyzing the nonwhite death rates.

Air-pollution data were collected by the National Air Sampling Network and reported in *Air Pollution Measurements of the National Air Sampling Network*. Data for 1960 were collected on suspended particulates and total sulfates. The data consisted of 26 biweekly measurements; we selected the minimum and maximum readings, as well as the arithmetic mean of the 26 readings. The limiting data source was that on air pollution. Data on both suspended particulates and sulfates were available for only 117 SMSA's.

Socioeconomic data for the SMSA's are reported in the *City and County Data Book*. This information is based on the 1960 Census. We collected data on population per square mile in the SMSA, on the proportion of the population which was nonwhite, the proportion of the population 65 and older, and the proportion of the families whose income was less than $3,000.

Measurement errors can be important in these data. For example, generally only a single location in an SMSA was used for sampling air pollution; since there are different pollution sources and various terrain, a single source is not likely to be representative of the entire area. The mortality data also entail a number of problems. For some age-, race-, and sex-specific deaths the number of reported deaths sometimes exceeded the population at risk (which was very small). Another problem is the mobility of the population. Many of the people injured by pollution migrate to less polluted places, while many rural people, with little previous exposure, migrate to industrial areas. This migration will lead to downward biases in the estimated coefficient of air pollution. Perhaps the only pure data, from the viewpoint of measured exposure, are for infant death rates, where the exposure is known reasonably accurately. However, measurement errors will not lead to biased coefficient estimates unless the omitted variables are systematically related to the explanatory variables.

Method

Linear regressions for the mortality rates reported in *Vital Statistics* have been reported previously (Lave and Seskin, 1970). A regression involving all independent variables was reported; also, insignificant variables were omitted and "best" regressions reported. These best regressions, along with the same specification for the more detailed mortality rates, are discussed below.

The regression for the total mortality rate is shown in equation (2):

$$MR_i = 19.607 + (0.041 \text{ mean } P) + (0.071 \text{ min } S)$$
$$ (2.53) \phantom{+ (0.041 \text{ mean } P) } (3.18)$$
$$+ (0.008 \ P/m^2) + (0.041 \ \% \ n\text{-}w)$$
$$ (1.67) (5.81)$$
$$+ (0.687 \ \% > 65) + e_i \qquad (2)$$
$$ (18.94)$$

where "mean P" is the arithmetic mean of the 26 suspended particulate readings, "min S" is the smallest of the 26 sulfate readings, "P/m^2" is the population density in the SMSA, "% $n\text{-}w$" is the percentage of the SMSA population who are nonwhite, "$\% > 65$" is the percentage of the SMSA population who are 65 and older, and "e" is an error term. This regression explains variations in the total mortality rate across 117 SMSA's extremely well, since 82.7 percent of the variation is explained ($R^2 = 0.827$). Each of the coefficients except population density is extremely significant, as shown by the t statistics below the coefficients, and, as expected, increases in each of the variables would lead to an increase in the total mortality rate.

The percentage of older people is the most important variable in equation (2). A ten percent increase in the proportion of people 65 and older (raising the mean from 84 to 94) is estimated to raise the total death rate 6.87 per 10,000 (from a mean of 91.3 to 98.17). If the nonwhites in the population increased by 10 percent (raising the mean from 125.1 to 135.1), it would raise the total estimated death rate by 0.41 per 10,000. If air pollution worsened and either the minimum sulfate level or mean particulate level rose by 1 microgram per cubic meter, the total death rate would rise by 0.71 or 0.041, respectively. This regression is presented in Table 11.5 along with regressions explaining the mortality rate for all nonwhites, for white males, white females, nonwhite males, and nonwhite females. The results when the total mortality rate is disaggregated in this way will be discussed in the next section.

Also presented in Table 11.5 is the regression for the under-28-day death rate per 10,000 live births. The most significant variable is the proportion of the population which is nonwhite; a one-percentage-point increase would raise the death rate by 0.98 per 10,000. Neither of the two pollution variables attains statistical significance, although increased pollution appears to have a stronger effect on this infant death rate than on the total death rate. Apparently, many factors that affect this infant death rate are not present in the regression, since only 27.1 percent of the variation is explained.

The other category of infant death rate is for children dying during their first year. Again, the percentage of nonwhites is the most signifi-

TABLE 11.5

Mortality regressions: age, race, sex-specific death rates[a]

DEPENDENT VARIABLES:	All Ages						Under 28 Days				
	Both M & F Both W & NW	NW	M-W	M-NW	F-W	F-NW	Both M & F Both W & NW	M-W	M-NW	F-W	F-NW
R^2:	0.827	0.339	0.198	0.208	0.389	0.340	0.271	0.276	0.080	0.115	0.130
EXPLANATORY VARIABLES:											
Constant	19.607	9.181	102.405	103.813	61.899	67.412	149.428	175.240	314.580	125.836	206.087
Min. part.	0.041 (2.53)	0.186 (3.53)	0.033 (1.81)	0.074 (1.55)	0.035 (2.79)	0.107 (2.82)	0.083 (1.62)	0.036 (0.75)	0.147 (0.73)	0.053 (1.34)	0.270 (1.61)
Mean part.											
Min. sulfates	0.071 (3.18)	0.106 (1.49)	0.044 (1.77)	0.071 (1.09)	0.070 (4.02)	0.191 (3.72)	0.120 (1.82)	0.026 (0.42)	−0.145 (−0.56)	0.068 (1.34)	0.344 (1.61)
P/m^2	0.001 (1.67)	−0.003 (−2.16)	0.001 (1.83)	0.001 (0.41)	0.001 (2.54)	0.001 (−0.80)					
Percent NW	0.041 (5.81)	0.148 (6.52)	0.028 (3.51)	0.101 (4.87)	−0.007 (−1.24)	0.088 (5.41)	0.098 (4.04)	−0.011 (−0.48)	0.278 (2.85)	−0.033 (−1.78)	0.254 (3.13)
Percent 65	0.687 (18.94)	0.547 (4.70)	0.034 (0.85)	0.149 (1.40)	0.023 (0.82)	0.054 (0.64)					
Percent poor							0.056 (1.45)	0.097 (2.67)	−0.368 (−2.39)	0.098 (3.31)	−0.293 (−2.29)

(cont. on p. 310)

a MEAN (AND STANDARD DEVIATION) OF EACH VARIABLE

MORTALITY RATES (PER 10,000)

	Total	White Male	White Female	Nonwhite Male	Nonwhite Female
Total:	91.3 (15.3)				Total nonwhite: 97.9 (24.8)
Total:		115.4 (7.9)	71.1 (6.3)	141.5 (20.6)	107.1 (17.9)
28 D:	187.3 (24.5)	196.9 (20.5)	148.8 (17.1)	294.5 (84.0)	233.5 (71.7)
1 yr.:	254.0 (36.4)	253.8 (27.5)	194.7 (22.3)	425.8 (113.5)	397.7 (91.7)
14 yrs.:	8.2 (1.8)	66.4 (8.3)	50.2 (6.0)	118.8 (28.7)	93.9 (22.0)
14–44:	31.6[b] (5.2)	60.9 (7.9)	32.3 (4.1)	123.6 (40.1)	85.0 (26.3)
45–64:	51.5 (14.4)	326.2 (32.2)	153.2 (18.7)	472.7 (116.6)	340.1 (98.8)
> 65:		741.4 (54.9)	501.1 (49.8)	714.1 (134.5)	533.4 (90.6)

EXPLANATORY VARIABLES

Min. particulates ($\mu g/m^3$):	45.5	(18.6)
Mean particulates ($\mu g/m^3$):	118.1	(40.9)
Min. sulfates ($\mu g/m^3 \times 10$):	47.2	(31.3)
Population Density (P/m^2):	756.2	(1370.6)
Percent NW ($\times 10$):	125.1	(104.0)
Percent 65 ($\times 10$):	83.9	(21.2)
Percent poor ($\times 10$):	180.9	(65.5)

b 14-64 death rate.

TABLE 11.5 (cont.)

Under 1 Year

	Both M & F Both W & NW	M-W	M-NW	F-W	F-NW
R^2:	0.537	0.070	0.126	0.174	0.119
Constant	185.802	231.196	379.376	162.805	251.032
Min. part.	0.365	0.129	0.578	0.293	1.125
	(2.82)	(0.93)	(1.02)	(2.76)	(2.45)
Mean part. Min. sulfates P/m²					
Percent NW	0.186	−0.069	0.447	−0.086	0.205
	(6.52)	(−2.25)	(3.49)	(−3.67)	(1.98)
Percent 65					
Percent poor	0.157	0.140	−0.206	0.162	0.118
	(3.38)	(2.82)	(−0.99)	(4.27)	(0.70)

Under 15 years

	Both M & F Both W & NW	M-W	M-NW	F-W	F-NW
R^2:	0.602	0.185	0.096	0.313	0.163
Constant	9.825	66.994	100.558	51.000	53.138
Min. part.	0.008	0.058	0.220	0.068	0.293
	(1.37)	(1.46)	(1.51)	(2.59)	(2.72)
Mean part. Min. sulfates P/m²					
Percent NW	0.003	−0.045	0.070	−0.041	0.044
	(2.11)	(−4.44)	(1.84)	(−6.06)	(1.58)
Percent 65	−0.044	−0.107	−0.042	−0.111	0.094
	(−7.42)	(−2.67)	(−0.29)	(−4.16)	(0.87)
Percent poor	0.007	0.063	0.016	0.058	0.078
	(3.38)	(4.39)	(0.29)	(6.08)	(1.95)

TABLE 11.5 (cont.)

	15–44 Years					45–64 Years			
	Both M & F Both W & NW	M-W	M-NW	F-W	F-NW	M-W	M-NW	F-W	F-NW
R^2:	0.538[a]	0.236	0.321	0.164	0.345	0.336	0.311	0.395	0.477
Constant	11.397	52.921	49.719	28.626	30.009	245.138	237.856	131.695	141.855
Min. part.									
Mean part.	0.025	0.036	0.150	0.026	0.111	0.127	0.252	0.086	0.373
	(2.82)	(2.05)	(1.73)	(2.74)	(1.99)	(1.91)	(1.00)	(2.33)	(1.99)
Min. sulfates	0.019	−0.021	0.028	−0.005	0.068	0.069	0.099	0.185	0.980
	(1.51)	(−0.87)	(0.23)	(−0.37)	(0.89)	(0.75)	(0.29)	(3.61)	(3.85)
P/m²	0.001	0.000	0.003	0.001	0.001	0.006	0.006	0.003	−0.004
	(3.19)	(0.59)	(0.96)	(1.89)	(0.89)	(3.01)	(0.78)	(2.84)	(−0.68)
Percent NW	0.034	−0.023	0.140	−0.013	0.104	0.107	0.326	−0.028	0.472
	(6.73)	(−2.35)	(2.92)	(−2.53)	(3.37)	(2.87)	(2.33)	(−1.36)	(4.56)
Percent 65	0.109	−0.062	0.033	−0.025	0.054	0.202	0.406	0.065	−0.109
	(5.31)	(−1.52)	(0.17)	(−1.14)	(0.43)	(1.31)	(0.71)	(0.77)	(−0.26)
Percent poor	0.013	0.069	0.180	0.023	0.110	0.154	0.667	−0.009	0.333
	(1.81)	(5.06)	(2.67)	(3.13)	(2.52)	(2.96)	(3.39)	(−0.33)	(2.29)

[a] 14-64 death rate.

(cont.)

TABLE 11.5 (cont.)

	Both M & F Both W & NW	M-W	65 & Older M-NW	F-W	F-NW
R^2:	0.394	0.385	0.051	0.295	0.108
Constant	52.412	698.367	679.310	470.984	499.750
Min. part.					
Mean part.					
Min. surfates	0.156	0.637	0.927	0.806	0.904
	(4.58)	(4.15)	(2.29)	(6.36)	(3.42)
P/m.²					
Percent NW	−0.066	0.103	−0.066	−0.064	−0.066
	(−6.47)	(2.24)	(−0.54)	(−1.67)	(−0.84)
Percent 65					
Percent poor					

cant variable, and a one-percentage-point increase would lead to an increase of 1.86 per 10,000 in the death rate. Poverty is also an important variable, since a one-percentage-point increase in the number of poor families would lead to a comparable (1.57/10,000) increase in the death rate. The most important pollution variable for this category was the minimum observed particulate reading. An increase of 1 microgram per cubic meter would raise the death rate 0.365 per 10,000. When the death is for the first year, rather than the first month, a much greater percentage of the variation is explained, since R^2 rises to 0.537.

Four other age-specific regressions are reported: the first is the rate among children under 15 years. This regression is quite similar to the previous one, except that the proportion of the population which is 65 and older has been added. The coefficient is negative and extremely significant. Apparently, concentrations of older people mean that children are more closely supervised. Over 60 percent of the variation is explained by this regression.

The next age specific rate is for people aged 15–64 years. (This group is broken into two parts: 15–44 and 45–64 for the sex and race specific regressions.) This regression is quite similar to that for the total death rate. The principal difference is that this age group is a bit less sensitive to the two measures of pollution. The significance of the "> 65" variable is probably due to the approximation used in computing this age-specific mortality rate.

The final age-specific rate is for people 65 and older. In this case proportion nonwhite is a significant negative influence. Again the approximation used in computing this mortality rate is probably responsible for the significance of this variable. The estimated coefficient of minimum sulfates shows that this group is quite sensitive to sulfate pollution; an increase of 1 g/m^3 would increase the death rate by 1.56 per 10,000.

Some caution must be used in interpreting these age-specific results. As noted earlier, the under-15, 15–64, and over-64 death rates are not true age-specific rates, since the population at risk was not tabulated. Instead, we had to use total population as the denominator. However, the more detailed mortality breakdowns are correct age-specific rates and can be used for comparison.

A comparison of results with the more detailed sex- and race-specific mortality rates will be presented in the next section. However, a result that should be commented on here is that R^2 falls significantly in going from the aggregated category to the sex and race disaggregation. Such a result might stem from three causes.

The first possibility is that the major explanatory power of the independent variables is lost in the disaggregation. Presumably, the reason why proportion nonwhite is such a powerful variable is that nonwhites have a higher death rate. When mortality rates are disaggregated by race, proportion nonwhite no longer has this effect. A second possibility is that the sample size for the disaggregated categories is so small that sampling variation is very important; thus, it is sampling error which is leading to the lower explanatory power. The final possibility is that the mortality rates for the disaggregated categories are three-year averages; thus, the explanatory variables, particularly the air-pollution variables, may be less accurate descriptions of the population and conditions than they are for the 1960 death rate.

This drop in R^2 is not really a fall in explanatory power nor is it important. The individual coefficient estimates continue to display magnitudes and signs which are consistent with what we would expect from the aggregated categories. This consistency is most important and reassuring.

Results

Another way of presenting the results is shown in Table 11.6, where the elasticities

TABLE 11.6

Elasticities for each explanatory variable[a]

	Both W and NW	Male		Female		All NW
		W	NW	W	NW	
MINIMUM SULFATES						
All ages	3.68	1.80	2.34	4.62	8.58	5.06
< 28 days	3.04	(0.63)	(−2.29)	2.16	6.87	
15–44 yr	2.81[b]	(−1.65)	1.04	(0.71)	(3.72)	
45–64 yr		(1.00)	(0.98)	5.69	13.44	
≥ 65 yr	14.32	4.06	6.06	7.59	7.91	
MEAN PARTICULATES						
All ages	5.29	3.33	6.15	5.80	12.09	22.32
< 28 days	5.22	(2.16)	(5.89)	4.17	13.61	
15–44 yr	9.44[b]	7.01	14.24	9.52	15.41	
45–64 yr		4.61	6.29	6.63	12.92	
MINIMUM PARTICULATES						
< 1 yr	6.53	(2.32)	6.16	6.84	14.60	
≤ 14 yr	4.41	3.95	8.42	6.19	14.16	
PERCENT POOR						
< 28 days	5.39	8.90	−22.52	11.91	−22.66	
< 1 yr	11.17	9.98	−8.71	15.07	(6.10)	
≤ 14 yr	15.76	17.18	(2.37)	20.96	14.91	
15–44 yr	7.19[b]	20.60	26.22	12.91	23.24	
45–64 yr		8.52	25.47	(−1.12)	17.64	
PERCENT ≥ 65 YEARS						
All ages	63.21	(2.49)	8.73	(2.71)	(4.32)	46.42
≤ 14 yr	−44.81	−13.54	(−2.93)	−4.16	(8.29)	
15–44 yr	29.02[b]	−8.47	(2.21)	−6.46	(5.28)	
45–64 yr		5.19	(7.14)	3.56	(−2.67)	
POPULATION PER SQUARE MILE						
All ages	0.66	0.64	(0.30)	0.99	(−0.64)	−2.53
15–44 yr	2.10[b]	(0.40)	(1.53)	1.30	(1.32)	
45–64 yr		1.44	(0.95)	1.59	(−0.85)	
PERCENT NONWHITE						
All ages	5.68	3.03	9.11	−1.20	10.88	19.36
< 28 days	6.57	(−0.69)	12.10	−2.80	13.93	
< 1 yr	9.15	−3.38	13.46	−5.50	7.53	
≤ 14 yr	4.80	−8.50	7.51	−10.22	6.01	
15–44 yr	13.33[b]	−4.76	14.52	−5.20	15.71	
45–64 yr		4.10	8.85	−2.29	17.81	
≥ 65 yr	−16.12	1.74	(−1.19)	−1.59	(−1.60)	

[a] The figures are elasticities (multiplied by 100). Where the regression coefficient was less than its standard error, the elasticity is in parentheses. These elasticities correspond to the regression coefficients listed in Table 11.5.
[b] These death rates are for 15–64 years.

(calculated at the mean) of each explanatory variable (multiplied by 100) are presented for all regressions. Coefficients which were smaller than their standard error are in parentheses. Thus, the first regression might be reinterpreted as estimating that 10 percent increases in each of the independent variables would produce the following percentage increase in the death rate: mean particulates—0.529; minimum sulfates—0.368; population density—0.066; proportion nonwhites—0.568; and proportion 65 and older —6.321.

Table 11.6 facilitates comparison of the effect of an explanatory variable on a number of dependent variables. Thus, the effect of minimum sulfates is greater on nonwhites than on whites. In looking at the detailed age breakdown, minimum sulfates has little effect on whites (either male or female) until age 65; then it is quite significant. For nonwhites, there is an effect on infants, but the effect drops off during the rest of childhood. For nonwhites, minimum sulfate begins to become important again by age 45, and it becomes much more important after age 65.

This same pattern is apparent for the effect of mean particulates, except that the effect starts much earlier in whites and is always smaller than in nonwhites. Again, with minimum particulates, it is true that women are more sensitive than men and that nonwhites are more sensitive than whites.

The variable for poverty displays an interesting pattern of elasticities. For children, females are more sensitive to poverty than are males. After age 14, however, the pattern reverses and it is men who react more directly to poverty. A startling result is that poverty seems to be good for very young black children: under 28 days, the greater the poverty, the better they fare. Such an effect would be produced if areas with concentrations of the poor had good welfare facilities. After childhood, nonwhites seem to be more sensitive to poverty than whites. Since they experience proportionally more of

the poverty, their mortality rate is much more sensitive to the amount of it.

The elasticities for population per square mile show a similar effect. As one might expect, the death rate increases with population concentration for the total and white total death rates. Living in large, concentrated cities is less healthy than living in smaller, less concentrated ones for vast numbers of reasons having to do with crime, air quality, and many public health factors. The interesting effect comes in attempting to explain the nonwhite death rate. Here the coefficient is negative, indicating that nonwhites live longer in larger cities. Apparently, such cities have programs to take care of indigents, especially nonwhite indigents.

The elasticities for the proportion of the population over 65 are somewhat difficult to interpret. So far as the total death rate is concerned, the elasticity is always positive: older people have a higher death rate, so cities with more older people have higher death rates. For the age-specific rates, negative elasticities are apparent for whites under 45 and positive elasticities for whites over 44. For children, one might expect that old people tend to serve as babysitters and so having more older people around means that children are more closely supervised. It is difficult to explain negative elasticities for white adults (aged 15–44). It is also difficult to interpret the positive elasticity for adults 45–64. For nonwhites the elasticity is always insignificant.

The basic result for proportion nonwhite was hinted at earlier. For the nonwhite death rates, both male and female, concentrations of nonwhite are associated with much higher death rates. The same result follows for each of the age-specific rates until the 65-and-older category. The effect is strongest for children under one year and then falls off for the rest of childhood. The effect of nonwhite concentration is greater for the 15–44 group than for children. However, at this point there is a divergence between males and females. For the 45–64 age group the effect on females continues to rise, while that on males falls slightly. Both rates come together in the 65-and-older class. Apparently, there is a selection process such that nonwhites living to age 65 have strong constitutions and have a long life expectancy.

Concentrations of nonwhites tend to lower the female white death rate and raise the male white rate. Both of these relationships are not consistent across all age groups. For every age group the sign for females is negative, and for all age groups through 44 years the sign for males is negative. Thus, the exploitation hypothesis seems the correct one. Concentrations of nonwhites lower the white death rate and raise the nonwhite death rate. In particular, the mechanism for white women seems to be that nonwhite women assume many of the household chores and increase the leisure of white women. For males, nonwhite males might assume the jobs which involve particularly hard labor or involve health risks, which white males under 45 would be likely to perform in other areas.

For the three categories of death rates among children, there is a striking difference between whites and nonwhites. White children have a lower death rate when there are many nonwhites around (presumably, because nonwhites are used to tend white children). Nonwhite children have a higher death rate (perhaps because they are unwatched, or just less well taken care of) when there are many nonwhites. The same effect continues into adulthood. Whites have lower death rates, but the effect is much smaller. Nonwhite adults have higher death rates, and the elasticity is quite large. At age 45, male whites exhibit a change in the pattern: concentrations of nonwhites lead to a higher death rate. Apparently, factors which lead to concentrations of nonwhites tend to increase the death rate for white males after age 45. No such effect is evident for white women: they continue to benefit from concentrations of nonwhites all of their lives.

For nonwhite males, living in an area with a concentration of nonwhites makes the greatest difference during the latter part of the first year of life. The effect then falls off and begins to rise again toward the end of childhood. The effect then falls off and begins to rise again toward the end of childhood. The elasticity is extremely large in the 45–65 group and then seems to fall off again, probably indicating some sort of selection process. Almost precisely the same pattern can be seen for nonwhite females.

From these results it therefore may be concluded that air pollution has more effect on women than men, and more effect on nonwhites than on whites. The very young and very old are most sensitive to air pollution. The indication is that mortality rates could be lowered substantially by abating air pollution. For example, lowering the measured levels of minimum sulfate readings and mean particulate readings by 10 percent would result in a 0.897 percent decrease in the total death rate. A 50 percent abatement would lower the death rate by 4.485 percent. Assuming that those who are saved have the same life expectancy as others in their cohort, a 50 percent abatement in air pollution (specifically in minimum sulfates, minimum particulates, and mean particulates) would increase life expectancy some 3 to 5 years for a newborn. As estimated elsewhere, such an abatement would reduce the economic cost of morbidity and mortality by just under 5 percent (Lave and Seskin, 1970). Thus, such an abatement is probably the single most effective way of improving the health of middle-class families. Note that this middle-class family could do something about smoking but is powerless to lower its exposure to air pollution (except by leaving the city). The importance of this improvement in health can be assessed by noting that eradicating all cancer would result in lowering the economic cost of morbidity and mortality by 5.7 percent.

Even so, there are many reasons to believe that these estimates are gross understatements of the health cost of air pollution. Chronic diseases generally involve long periods of illness. The economic costs, calculated as the sum of lost work and medical expenditures, grossly understate the amount that would be paid to achieve good health for such a chronically ill period. In addition, death may not result from the chronic illness itself but rather from one or another complication. For example, chronic bronchitis or emphysema is likely to result in death due to heart disease or pneumonia.

Perhaps the only good way to estimate the health costs of air pollution therefore would be to analyze morbidity, rather than mortality data. It seems certain that such an investigation would give a higher health cost, since no one can die of emphysema or other chronic illnesses who has not suffered them, but some of the people with chronic illnesses die from other causes. In addition, such an investigation would pick up increases in morbidity rates, such as simple respiratory diseases, which may occur long before death is a possibility. Other, much less severe, illness is known to result from air pollution but to be unrelated to mortality. For example, eye irritation is a common reaction to acute pollution; such costs will never be reflected in mortality statistics (except possibly for accidents).

ENVIRONMENTAL POLLUTION AND CHRONIC DISEASE

Hickey, Boyce, Harner, and Clelland (1970) have attempted to determine the extent to which environmental chemicals, along with other broad classes of environmental variables, e.g., demographic, ethological, climatic, and economic, are associated statistically with chronic diseases. Of equal or greater importance was the objective of investigating experimental evidence and theory in biology and biochemistry, particularly in molecular biology and ecological genetics, in an attempt to identify the mechanisms underlying the more important statistical results. Statistical correlations alone do not and cannot establish causality.

There have been a number of infamous incidents of atmospheric inversions or other stagnations in which unusually severe air pollution occurred for several days, resulting in a marked short-term rise in mortality rate, particularly among the infirm or ill. Severe episodes recorded to date include the Donora, Pa., tragedy of 1948, the episode in the Meuse Valley, and also some rather severe occurrences in London (Kotin and Falk, 1964). These short-term episodes of pollution are generally classed as demonstrating acute effects. Less severe effects of pollution may be ocular and respiratory irritation, foul aromas, and reduction in visibility due to haze or fog. It is difficult not to observe such effects.

One may reasonably inquire, however, whether long-term low-concentration levels of exposure to atmospheric pollution, which may cause relatively little irritation, discomfort, or odor, might in reality constitute a more serious health hazard than the relatively few acute episodes which have led to newspaper headlines and flurries of public health activities. If mutagens should happen to be involved, they may not be noticed by direct observation. Exposure to low levels of ionizing radiation, which is mutagenic, is not detectable by the normal physiological senses unaided. Consider normal background radiation, for example. It was observed (Hickey, 1968) that government "has a responsibility to protect the public from health hazards which are obscure as well as from hazards which are more easily recognized."

Air-quality standards, as established by various governmental regulatory agencies, are based primarily on acute effects which are difficult to detect and which, though suspected, are not yet adequately proven. It is toward the general problem of determination of health risks of long-term subacute exposure of human populations to environmental chemicals, some of which may be mutagenic, that the following sections are addressed.

Hypothesis

The central hypothesis is based on a mutagenic or radiomimetic theory of cumulative molecular degradation of deoxyribonucleic acid (DNA). The hypothesis may be stated as follows. Among the environmental chemicals to which human and other populations are exposed are certain ones which affect DNA by causing alterations in the sequence of purine and pyrimidine bases along the DNA strand or helix. Such alterations in the genetic code are alterations in the cell genotype which often, but not always, result in changes of cell phenotype.

It should be noted that not all mutations are maintained; many mutations are corrected by genetic repair mechanisms which involve repair enzymes (Brookhaven Symposia in Biology, No. 20, 1968; Strauss, 1961; Cleaver, 1968). Further, hypothesizing that there are mutagenic environmental chemicals does not, of course, presume that all chemicals are deleterious. In fact, it would be expected that some chemicals would be beneficial and might even protect vulnerable functional groups of DNA from attack by chemical mutagens. Some metals are essential to survival.

Biological Theory

In the atmosphere an equilibrium exists between NO_2 and its dimer, i.e., $2NO_2 \rightleftharpoons N_2O_4$. NO_2 is a brownish gas and is favored in the equilibrium by higher temperatures. Both dissolve in water to form equimolar portions of nitrous and nitric acids. In the more neutral body tissues and fluids, neutralization will occur with various bases such as amines or amine functional groups. Since nitrous acid is a weak acid, its neutral derivative of a weak base can undergo hydrolytic dissociation to

lead to the probabilistic occurrence of free molecular nitrous acid. This acid is a powerful mutagen (Watson, 1965) which may attack certain amine groups such as exist on the bases of DNA in such a manner that the genetic code is changed. Other amines also may be attacked. Practically all code changes are deleterious.

Thus, atmospheric NO_2 may pose a mutagenic threat to the health of populations. If the effect is mutagenic and probabilistic, mimicking to some extent the mutagenic effects of ionizing radiation, the health effects on populations, if they occur, should be demonstrable statistically in such populations in accordance with the degree of exposure to the chemical.

It is also known that various metals are bound to both ribonucleic acid (RNA) (Wacker and Vallee, 1959; Wojnae and Roth, 1964) and to DNA (Cheek et al., 1968). This metal binding may be through chelation (Seven and Johnson, 1960), perhaps involving primary amine groups of DNA and RNA. If certain metals are bound to these amine groups and involve reaction equilibria, the amine groups might be protected from attack by nitrous acid while the metal is bound. Thus some chelating metals may reduce the risk to DNA of accumulating mutations from mutagens, such as, perhaps, nitrous acid.

Until quite recently the question of the mutagenic hazard of SO_2 and its derivatives, sulfite and bisulfite, was rather unclear. Sulfites and bisulfites have been on the Food and Drug Administration list of approved food additives (GRAS) for many years, as have certain nitrites and nitrates. But in 1970 Shapiro et al. (1970) and Hayatsu et al. (1970) reported that bisulfite adds to a double bond in the nuclear structure of two nucleic acid bases, cytosine and uracil. Cytosine is found in both DNA and RNA; uracil is normally found only in RNA. They also noted that, on standing, the bisulfite derivative of cytosine was found to deaminate to form the bisulfite derivative of uracil. Thus a conversion of one base to another was accomplished. This, when it happens in DNA, is a mutation.

Another potential mutagenic aspect of these bisulfite additions is that while bisulfite is combined with cytosine, upon DNA replication the replicated DNA strand may contain code errors in the base sequence induced by the bisulfite-addition structure of the base which is different from the base itself. Watson (1965) has discussed the fact that base analogs can be powerful mutagens, citing the thymine analog, 5-bromouracil, as an example.

A number of other reports have implicated air pollutants as being involved in contributing to chronic disease mortality, particularly cancer (Stocks, 1960; Kotin and Wiseley, 1963; Kotin and Falk, 1964; Manos and Fisher, 1959). Some of these are particularly concerned with polycyclic hydrocarbons and other complex organic compounds in the atmosphere, some of which, such as benzo-a-pyrene (3,4-benzopyrene), are known to be carcinogenic (Sawicki et al., 1960).

Sawicki et al. (1960), in studies on benzo a pyrene content of the atmospheres of urban communities in the United States, estimated the number of micrograms of this compound inhaled per year from ambient air. For several representative cities figures were as follows: Los Angeles, 20; New Orleans, 26; Cincinnati, 79; Detroit, 110; and Birmingham 150. Data on annual mortality rates for cancer of the respiratory system for the standard metropolitan statistical areas (SMSA's) which include these cities are given in Table 11.7. Sawicki et al. (1960) noted in a preliminary assessment that 1950–1959 benzopyrene data and 1949–1951 mortality data for lung cancer and cancer at other sites for various cities "failed to reveal a significant relationship."

In connection with the possible health risk of inhalation of carcinogenic polycyclic hydrocarbons, it is important to note that a mammalian enzyme, benzopyrene hydroxylase (Silverman and Talalay, 1967), has evolved which metabolizes benzopyrene. Based on such observations, a comment of Lawther (1965)

may be appropriate: "Our work leads us to believe that 'classic' carcinogens such as 3,4-benzopyrene may have claimed too much attention in recent years to the detriment of the search for more sophisticated mechanisms by which lung cancer may develop."

If atmospheric SO_2 and NO_2 are mutagenic hazards to which human and other populations are exposed and if certain major chronic diseases of man, such as cancer and heart disease, are cumulative somatic genetic degenerative diseases, the genetic effects of such mutagens should be demonstrable in human populations. In those metropolitan areas or regions in which the supposed mutagenic hazards are high because of high environmental chemical concentrations, mortality rates for the presumed somatic genetic disease should be high; where the hazards are low, the mortality rates should be low. Moreover, if the theory is correct and if cancer and heart disease are in part, perhaps largely, cumulative somatic genetic diseases, then where the mortality rate for one type of cancer is high, the mortality rates for other types of cancer should also be high, and the mortality rates for some types of heart disease, such as arteriosclerotic heart disease, should also be high and vice versa.

It should be recognized that (1) since Pb, Sn, Ni, As, polycyclic carcinogens, radioactive materials, and other materials are found in urban atmospheres, (2) since high levels of all of these materials under certain high-dosage conditions are known to be hazards to health and survival, (3) since human populations nevertheless are surviving and reproducing to such an extent that population problems exist, (4) since human and other life evolved in the presence of all these materials, (5) since all of the elements exist in the earth's crust, and (6) since polycyclic carcinogens have been in the environment a very long time as they are found in coal and other geological deposits of organic origin, it seems clear that the evolved life forms including man must have become safely adapted

TABLE 11.7

Examples of the relative constancy of annual mortality from breast cancer[a] for 1961–1964 within metropolitan areas, and differences in mortality rates between metropolitan areas

| SMSA | Deaths per Year | | | | | Death Rate per 100,000 Population Based on | |
	1961	1962	1963	1964	Mean 1961–1964	Total Population	Females Only (14 years and older)[b]
Baltimore, Md.	242	242	272	255	252.8	14.64	40.30
Birmingham, Ala.	85	81	90	82	84.5	13.31	36.07
Boston, Mass.	544	572	570	556	560.5	21.65	55.66
Charlotte, N.C.	19	23	33	27	25.5	9.37	25.87
Chattanooga, Tenn.	35	31	36	41	35.8	12.62	33.83
Chicago, Ill.	1,037	1,054	1,106	1,085	1,070.5	17.21	47.54
Cincinnati, Ohio	153	210	184	222	192.3	17.94	47.80
Denver, Colo.	134	112	114	125	121.3	13.05	35.68
Detroit, Mich.	534	510	524	499	516.8	13.73	38.95
El Paso, Tex.	27	26	16	27	24.0	7.64	24.07
Las Vegas, Nev.	11	8	17	14	12.5	9.84	29.38
Los Angeles, Calif.	987	1,095	1,033	1,099	1,053.5	15.62	40.00
Newark, N.J.	335	337	333	361	341.5	20.21	51.97
New Orleans, La.	117	104	124	138	120.8	13.90	38.01
New York, N.Y.	2,094	2,158	2,144	2,236	2,158.0	20.18	50.75
Philadelphia, Pa.	690	678	748	762	719.5	16.57	44.10
Phoenix, Ariz.	54	64	87	92	74.3	11.19	32.75
Scranton, Pa.	49	45	43	49	46.5	19.83	53.88
Seattle, Wash.	160	166	143	161	157.5	14.22	39.61
St. Louis, Mo.	306	341	340	310	324.3	15.74	42.20

SOURCE: *Vital Statistics of the United States*, vol. 2 (Mortality), pt. B, annual issues. (Actual data, unadjusted for age, sex, or race.)
[a] International Statistical Classification (ISC) 170.
[b] 1960 census.

to the presence of these materials in the environment at levels existing naturally during that evolution (Schroeder, 1965). These may be considered as levels to which populations are ecologically adapted. Thus the fact that Pb, Sn, and other materials are toxic at high levels does not mean that they are toxic at all levels. Such simplistic inferences, which disregard ecological and evolutionary facts, must be avoided. Genetic systems are exceedingly complex, and it would not be surprising if ecological genetic mechanisms relating to chronic disease and senescence also proved to be highly complex.

Methods of Analysis

Since human ecology involves many environmental and other variables and since the problem is in part one of ecological statistical analysis, multivariate analysis is an appropriate research method for examining the ecological system (Morrison, 1967; Cooley and Lohnes, 1962). Computer methods are essential, considering the amount of data involved. The computer employed was the University of Pennsylvania IBM S/360 M65 and M75.

In particular, multiple regression analysis

was utilized (Williams, 1959). A standard form of this procedure is stepwise multiple regression analysis, which was used in initial studies; more recently a computer program for optimal regression analysis has been developed (Beale et al., 1967, Boyce et al., 1969 and 1970). This program identifies the combination of N variables in a larger set that maximizes the square of the multiple correlation coefficient R^2 for a given value of N. The optimal program is typically used in a sequential manner to make selections of $N = 1, 2, 3, \ldots, n$ predictors. The predictor selected for $N = 1$ may or may not be among predictors selected for $N = 2$, and those selected for $N = 2$ may or may not be selected for $N = 3$, and so on. In contrast, stepwise regression programs usually proceed in a cumulative manner, retaining previous selections.

Using the R^2 maximization criterion, one selects predictors on statistical grounds only. This selection should be influenced by (1) presence or absence of authentic biochemical relationships to the disease, (2) quality of the data (if poor enough, an authentic biochemical predictor might not be selected), (3) large covariance of a biologically unimportant predictor with an important one, and (4) random effects leading to spurious correlation.

The material involved in the general study is too extensive to include in this discussion except as excerpts. One multivariate statistical approach to studies on the relationship of chronic disease mortality rates in urban populations to concentrations of environmental air pollutant and other chemicals was reported by Hickey et al. in 1967. This report was mainly methodological. Three subsequent preliminary reports concerning cancer, heart disease, and birth defects were issued in the course of development of methods and biological-biochemical theory (Hickey, 1968; Hickey et al., 1970a and b). The material presented here summarizes a portion of the studies. Some representative examples of input data and statistical analytical

finding are given here, together with a brief discussion of the findings; some comments pertaining to problems of measurement of pollutant concentrations conclude the chapter.

Historical Statistics

The results presented here pertain to data covering relatively short time periods, generally 1957–1964 for pollution data and 1959–1961 and 1961–1964 for disease mortality data. Atmospheric-pollution data for cities in the United States are very scarce prior to 1957, and measurements on SO_2 and NO_2 commenced being taken in some quantity only in 1962.

In order to attack the problem at all, it was necessary to assume that measured pollution concentrations in these years were rather typical of the regions in which the measurements were made and that for some years prior to the measurements very similar concentrations prevailed. Such an assumption is necessary inasmuch as biological senescence is clearly a continuing process.

It might be noted that since 1900, the per capita consumption of cigarettes has increased (Public Health Service, October 1968). It is also known that air pollution has become much more serious since 1900. Further, since 1900, through advances in medicine, mortality rates for various infectious diseases have dropped considerably, and mortality rates for cancer and cardiovascular-renal diseases have risen. For example, from 1900 to 1957, annual deaths per 100,000 persons from tuberculosis dropped from 194.4 to 8.4. For influenza and pneumonia, the death rate dropped correspondingly from 202.2 in 1900 to 28.2 in 1957. For gastritis, duodenitis, enteritis, and colitis, the combined mortality rate dropped from 142.7 deaths per 100,000 persons per year in 1900 to 4.5 in 1957.

During this same period the annual mortality rate reported for malignant neoplasms rose from 64.0 to 147.9 deaths per 100,000 persons. Correspondingly, the annual mortality rate for major cardiovascular-renal diseases rose from 345.2 to 510.7 deaths per 100,000 persons from 1900 to 1957 (U.S. Bureau of the Census, 1960).

Clearly, if the risk of death from infectious diseases is reduced, the risk of death and thus the death rate for chronic diseases should be increased. The causes of increases in the mortality rates for noninfectious chronic diseases over time are obviously complex. Further study is necessary to account for the statistical relationships between chronic disease mortality rates and (1) reduced mortality risk over time to infectious diseases, (2) atmospheric pollution, (3) drinking-water characteristics, (4) demographic variables, (5) smoking, (6) increased use of drugs or pharmaceuticals, (7) ethological influences, (8) food utilization and malnutrition, (9) genetic damage by mutagens at the germinal level, and (10) other variables.

Experimental Observations; Results of Optimal Multiple Regression Analyses

The input data for the present analyses consist of (1) means of annual mean concentration values for atmospheric chemicals in micrograms per cubic meter for 38 SMSA's in the United States, along with (2) means of annual mortality rates in deaths per 100,000 persons for these metropolitan areas. The 38 SMSA's selected were determined by availability of pollution data. These chemical data were those available over the 1957–1964 period, with available annual mean concentrations for one to six years usually being averaged to obtain the mean values for analyses. The atmospheric chemicals included were Cd, Cr, Cu, Fe, Pb, Mn, Ni, Sn, Ti, V, Zn, As, NO_2, SO_2, and particulate sulfate. An added environmental chemical predictor variable also included was hardness of drinking water in ppm of calcium-carbonate equivalent for these same metropolitan areas. Other chemical data were generally too incomplete for analytical use.

The diseases of major interest are chronic ones such as cancer, heart disease, stroke, diabetes, general arteriosclerosis, and others whose mortality rates increase with increasing chronological age of the individuals. Thus, mortality rates are handled as dependent variables or criteria in the statistical analyses, while concentrations of environmental chemicals are the independent variables or predictors.

The SMSA's for which pollution and disease mortality-rate data were collected and used are listed below:

Birmingham, Ala.	New York, N.Y.
Phoenix, Ariz.	Charlotte, N.C.
Los Angeles, Calif.	Cincinnati, Ohio
San Francisco, Calif.	Cleveland, Ohio
Denver, Colo.	Allentown, Pa.
Washington, D.C.	Philadelphia, Pa.
Atlanta, Ga.	Pittsburgh, Pa.
Chicago, Ill.	Scranton, Pa.
Gary, Hammond, Ind.	Chattanooga, Tenn.
Indianapolis, Ind.	El Paso, Tex.
Des Moines, Iowa	Seattle, Wash.
New Orleans, La.	Tacoma, Wash.
Baltimore, Md.	Charleston, W. Va.
Boston, Mass.	Milwaukee, Wis.
Detroit, Mich.	Nashville, Tenn.
St. Louis, Mo.	Omaha, Nebr.
Las Vegas, Nev.	Wilmington, Del.
Newark, N.J.	Columbus, Ohio
Buffalo, N.Y.	Youngstown, Ohio

If regional environmental variables in fact exert causal influences on processes of senescence and thus on chronic diseases of senescence, it would appear essential that mortality rates for diseases associated with aging should be relatively constant for individual regional urban populations from year to year over a short term such as five years. However, these mortality rates would be expected to be different from region to region because of differences in characteristics of radiomimetic variables from region to region. In contrast, mortality rates for some infectious diseases would vary widely from year to year.

That these population characteristics are in

fact observed is indicated by representative vital statistical data for large metropolitan areas over the 1961–1964 period (Public Health Service, annually). The metropolitan populations used for computing rates were those of the 1960 census (U.S. Bureau of the Census, 1961). It is recognized that the size and composition of populations change over time. Factors such as migration, overcrowding, and income and their relationships to mortality are being included in current studies.

Tables 11.7 through 11.10 provide examples of data which tend to support the previous presumption that relative constancy of mortality occurs within regions from year to year, while differences in mortality rates occur between regions for the observed periods. The chronic-disease categories represented are breast cancer, cancer of the respiratory system, arteriosclerotic heart disease, and total malignant neoplasms. The general character of the observations is rather similar for a number of other categories of cancer and heart disease, diabetes mellitus, and certain other chronic diseases.

It would be expected that a fair degree of constancy would exist in moderately long-term pollution characteristics within individual regions for measures of annual mean concentrations of various atmospheric chemicals in micrograms per cubic meter of air. Considerable variations would be expected from hour to hour, day to day, and from season to season in

TABLE 11.8

Examples of the relative constancy of annual mortality from cancer of the respiratory system[a] for 1961–1964 within metropolitan areas, and differences in mortality rates between metropolitan areas

SMSA	Deaths per Year					Death Rate per 100,000 Population[b]
	1961	1962	1963	1964	Mean 1961–1964	
Baltimore, Md.	531	497	545	585	540	31.2
Birmingham, Ala.	147	146	161	176	158	24.8
Boston, Mass.	877	930	875	864	887	34.2
Charlotte, N.C.	36	56	69	54	54	19.8
Chattanooga, Tenn.	71	80	69	90	78	27.4
Chicago, Ill.	1,757	1,759	1,904	1,922	1,836	29.5
Cincinnati, Ohio	335	357	355	368	354	33.0
Denver, Colo.	152	177	188	195	178	19.2
Detroit, Mich.	928	1,037	1,082	1,103	1,038	27.6
El Paso, Tex.	34	44	43	42	41	13.0
Las Vegas, Nev.	22	29	37	43	33	25.8
Los Angeles, Calif.	1,704	1,709	1,919	1,933	1,816	26.9
New Orleans, La.	294	271	299	314	295	33.9
New York, N.Y.	3,415	3,557	3,624	3,719	3,579	33.5
Philadelphia, Pa.	1,247	1,411	1,357	1,503	1,380	31.8
Phoenix, Ariz.	112	178	175	187	163	24.5
Salt Lake City, Utah	55	58	57	66	59	15.4
Scranton, Pa.	64	75	86	71	74	31.6
Seattle, Wash.	265	269	281	276	273	24.6
St. Louis, Mo.	558	664	677	656	639	31.0

SOURCE: *Vital Statistics of the United States*, vol. 2 (Mortality), pt. B, annual issues. (Actual data, unadjusted for age, sex, or race.)

[a] ISC 160–64.

[b] 1960 census.

TABLE 11.9

Examples of the relative constancy of annual mortality from arteriosclerotic heart diseases including coronary disease[a] for 1961–1964 within metropolitan areas, and differences in mortality rates between metropolitan areas

| SMSA | Deaths per Year | | | | | Death Rate per 100,000 Population[b] |
	1961	1962	1963	1964	Mean 1961–1964	
Baltimore, Md.	3,751	3,712	4,098	3,834	3,849	222.9
Birmingham, Ala.	1,209	1,265	1,337	1,326	1,284	202.3
Boston, Mass.	11,384	11,415	11,609	10,280	11,172	431.5
Charlotte, N.C.	576	652	663	698	647	237.9
Chattanooga, Tenn.	562	621	648	714	636	224.7
Chicago, Ill.	21,226	22,517	23,542	23,386	22,668	364.4
Cincinnati, Ohio	3,216	3,360	3,443	3,307	3,332	310.9
Denver, Colo.	2,061	2,319	2,349	2,384	2,278	245.1
Detroit, Mich.	9,243	10,062	10,248	10,441	9,999	265.8
El Paso, Tex.	295	311	348	302	314	100.0
Las Vegas, Nev.	246	263	326	303	285	224.0
Los Angeles, Calif.	16,569	16,876	17,936	17,718	17,275	256.2
New Orleans, La.	2,512	2,675	2,770	2,738	2,671	307.6
New York, N.Y.	41,375	41,947	42,472	42,526	42,080	393.5
Philadelphia, Pa.	13,779	13,893	13,784	13,408	13,716	315.8
Phoenix, Ariz.	1,451	1,523	1,606	1,762	1,586	238.0
Salt Lake City, Utah	637	660	723	655	668	174.6
Scranton, Pa.	954	975	1,024	998	998	421.2
Seattle, Wash.	3,008	3,169	3,251	3,328	3,189	288.0
St. Louis, Mo.	6,077	6,403	6,808	6,812	6,525	312.7

SOURCE: Vital Statistics of the United States, vol. 2 (Mortality), pt. B, annual issues. (Actual data, unadjusted for age, sex, or race.)

[a] ISC 420.

[b] 1960 census.

representative atmospheric concentrations of specific chemicals such as SO_2 and NO_2, and this is in fact observed (Public Health Service, April 1969; The Resources Agency, June 1969). The annual mean pollutant characteristics within regions, however, would be expected to be influenced greatly by industrial, electric power, transportation, residential, and other characteristics of the cities or regions and also by differences in weather from year to year. Colder years obviously should result in higher fuel consumption than warmer years for the same localities.

Obviously there should be some differences in pollutant measurements in different pollution measuring stations in the same region. Such differences have been observed in the New York City area for SO_2 (Public Health Service, November 1969), with annual arithmetic mean values for nine stations for 1967 being reported as 0.14, 0.12, 0.13, 0.17, 0.12, 0.16, 0.13, and 0.09 ppm. But the New York City measures are rather typically high in SO_2, while the measures for some other regions, such as Salt Lake City, Utah, and Denver, have been reported as consistently relatively low compared with New York City and Chicago. California concentration figures for SO_2 also tend to be relatively low.

Examples of some mean annual measures of SO_2 and NO_2 in several cities over the 1962–1965 period (Public Health Service, 1962,

TABLE 11.10

Examples of the relative constancy of annual mortality from total malignant neoplasms[a] for 1961–1964 within metropolitan areas, and differences in mortality rates between metropolitan areas

SMSA	Deaths per Year					Death Rate per 100,000 Population[b]
	1961	1962	1963	1964	Mean 1961–1964	
Baltimore, Md.	2,822	2,762	2,942	2,982	2,877.0	166.59
Birmingham, Ala.	856	881	900	943	895.5	141.05
Boston, Mass.	5,936	5,893	5,665	5,360	5,713.5	220.66
Charlotte, N.C.	266	280	318	304	292.0	107.31
Chattanooga, Tenn.	380	392	388	417	394.3	139.23
Chicago, Ill.	10,696	10,458	11,074	10,907	10,806.3	173.37
Cincinnati, Ohio	2,005	2,071	1,973	2,103	2,038.3	190.18
Denver, Colo.	1,165	1,163	1,192	1,266	1,196.5	128.74
Detroit, Mich.	5,621	5,806	5,974	5,903	5,826.0	154.85
El Paso, Tex.	272	274	271	285	275.5	87.72
Las Vegas, Nev.	143	146	171	172	158.0	124.39
Los Angeles, Calif.	10,005	10,093	10,658	10,834	10,397.5	154.20
Newark, N.J.	3,151	3,117	3,174	3,314	3,189.0	188.76
New Orleans, La.	1,162	1,346	1,448	1,489	1,361.3	156.74
New York, N.Y.	21,284	21,404	21,591	22,087	21,591.5	201.89
Philadelphia, Pa.	7,711	7,826	7,851	8,121	7,877.3	181.38
Phoenix, Ariz.	780	924	932	998	908.5	136.92
Scranton, Pa.	477	502	521	494	498.5	212.55
Seattle, Wash.	1,772	1,756	1,734	1,813	1,768.8	159.75
St. Louis, Mo.	3,511	3,553	3,622	3,613	3,574.8	173.52

SOURCE: *Vital Statistics of the United States*, vol. 2 (Mortality), pt. B, annual issues. (Actual data, unadjusted for age, sex, or race.)
[a] ISC 140–205.
[b] 1960 census.

1965, and 1966) are given in Table 11.11. While there are some eccentricities, a moderate degree of consistency within regions seems evident, and a noticeable degree of variation appears between regions, particularly for SO_2. Such variation is essential, of course, to multivariate analysis. Further indications of the relative constancy of annual mean concentration for gaseous pollutants have been observed in continuous air monitoring program (CAMP) data obtained by the Public Health Service (Public Health Service, 1968). It should be noted that few NO_2 and SO_2 data were collected prior to 1962.

While there are various ways of reporting pollution data (annual arithmetic mean, annual geometric mean, percent of days above some critical level, and so on), annual arithmetic mean concentration is preferred for these analyses because (1) it is more generally available and (2) it is consistent with the radiomimetic hypothesis because of the additive nature of the effects. In radiobiology, the effects of exposure to low levels of ionizing radiation are essentially cumulative (Curtis, 1967). It is presumed that exposure to radiomimetic agents may lead to comparable effects.

Two additional examples of annual mean city measures of pollutants are given in Tables 11.12 and 11.13. The data are for particulate sulfate and Cu over the 1957–1964 period. Again, irregularities and eccentricities are evident, but a degree of consistency is also observable.

TABLE 11.11

Examples of relative constancy of annual mean concentration of NO$_2$ and SO$_2$ within city atmospheres over several years, and differences in concentration between cities over these years

City	NO$_2$ ($\mu g/m^3$)					SO$_2$ ($\mu g/m^3$)				
	1962	1963	1964	1965	Mean	1962	1963	1964	1965	Mean
Baltimore, Md.	110	110	127	117	116	104	104	100	83	98
Boston, Mass.	110	92	94	116	103	132	79	61	69	85
Buffalo, N.Y.	92	92	97	83	91	79	52	37	40	52
Charleston, W. Va.	110	92	89	82	93	27	27	24	17	24
Chattanooga, Tenn.	92	92	91	100	94	27	27	44	32	33
Chicago, Ill.	110	110	82	79	95	234	282	450	340	327
Cleveland, Ohio	110	92	105	107	104	104	104	87	89	96
Denver, Colo.	73	73	89	89	81	27	27	22	17	23
Detroit, Mich.	92	92	102	99	96	27	52	23	9	28
Indianapolis, Ind.	92	92	100	111	99	52	52	65	47	54
New York, N.Y.	152	132	171	157	153	418	391	448	374	408
Philadelphia, Pa.[a]	152	132	70	67	107	172	260	213	222	217
Pittsburgh, Pa.	110	110	116	117	113	78	104	88	89	90
Salt Lake City, Utah	73	73	89	107	86	27	27	17	12	21
San Francisco, Calif.	92	92	101		95	27	<25	42		ca.30
Washington, D. C.	92	92	67	63	83	79	79	128	120	101

[a] The marked decline in atmospheric NO$_2$ concentration in Philadelphia, Pa., as indicated by these measurements is unusual.

TABLE 11.12

Examples of relative constancy of annual mean concentration of particulate sulfate within city atmospheres over several years, and differences in concentrations between cities over these years

City	Particulate Sulfate ($\mu g/m^3$)								
	1957	1958	1959	1960	1961	1962	1963	1964	Mean
Los Angeles, Calif.	14.8	16.0	12.3		14.3	16.1	8.8		13.7
San Francisco, Calif.		6.2			8.9	6.6	6.3		7.0
Washington, D.C.		12.4			18.3	12.3	14.0	8.9	13.2
Chicago, Ill.		16.6			24.9	15.5	16.9	19.0	18.6
Indianapolis, Ind.	13.4	13.9			13.3	11.8	12.9	14.6	13.3
Des Moines, Iowa	12.3	8.8		12.4		7.9	5.8	4.9	8.7
Baltimore, Md.	14.4	15.6	20.5	16.5	19.8	19.1	19.5	18.1	17.9
Boston, Mass.		16.3			17.0	17.0	12.7	18.1	16.2
Las Vegas, Nev.		7.9			3.7			4.7	5.4
New York, N.Y.		22.8					31.3	33.1	29.1
Charlotte, N.C.	7.6	8.1						6.7	7.5
Cincinnati, Ohio		12.5			13.0	11.5	11.1	13.6	12.3
Philadelphia, Pa.		17.2	22.9		27.4	20.7	20.5	27.2	22.7
Pittsburgh, Pa.		15.1	21.6	15.0		17.3	16.5	17.5	17.2
Chattanooga, Tenn.		13.2	10.5		10.5	7.0	9.3	9.4	10.0
Youngstown, Ohio	16.8	14.5			15.1	14.3	13.3	13.7	14.6

TABLE 11.13

Examples of relative constancy of annual mean concentration of Cu within city atmospheres over several years, and differences in concentrations between cities over these years

City	Cu ($\mu g/m^3$)								
	1957	1958	1959	1960	1961	1962	1963	1964	Mean
Los Angeles, Calif.		0.28[a]		0.09	0.07	0.10	0.15		0.16
San Francisco, Calif.		0.03				0.04	0.03		0.033
Denver, Colo.		0.05				0.15	0.12	0.05	0.093
Chicago, Ill.		0.06			0.26[a]		0.06	0.04	0.105
Indianapolis, Ind.		0.10			0.09	0.09			0.093
Des Moines, Iowa		0.03		0.05		0.04		0.04	0.040
Baltimore, Md.	0.07	0.07		0.12	0.12	0.10		0.19	0.112
Detroit, Mich.		0.02				0.03	0.05	0.05	0.038
St. Louis, Mo.		0.08				0.07	0.11	0.08	0.085
Newark, N.J.			0.06		0.09	0.09		0.16	0.100
New York, N.Y.					0.11	0.11	0.13	0.10	0.113
Cincinnati, Ohio		0.04		0.11	0.08	0.06	0.05	0.06	0.067
Cleveland, Ohio		0.06				0.63[a]	0.14	0.15	0.245
Philadelphia, Pa.		0.08		0.08	0.09	0.08	0.07	0.08	0.080
El Paso, Tex.	0.23					0.37		0.39	0.33
Columbus, Ohio		0.035[b]			0.25[b]	0.56[b]			0.28

[a] These values tend to be "outliers," but should not be rejected without proper reason.
[b] This is a very unusual range of measurements. The reason for this variation is not known at present.

While the observations are somewhat erratic, it seems reasonable to assume that annual mean pollutant concentrations are fairly constant over time and rather characteristic of the localities. Water-hardness data are also used (Durfor and Becker, 1964).

In summary, the data used in the analyses reported are represented by Tables 11.7 through 11.13. Efforts are in progress to extend the data to cover more metropolitan areas, more years, and more chemicals, along with age-, sex-, and race-specific vital statistics. Also to be included are demographic and climatic variables.

Matrices of pairwise correlation coefficients *r* were computed using data for 38 SMSA's for (1) mortality rates for diseases, (2) pollution concentrations, and (3) pollution concentrations versus mortality rates. Tables 11.14 through 11.16 present these matrices. The number of disease variables actually analyzed is greater than the number of diseases shown in Tables

11.14 and 11.16. Further results will appear in other reports.

As shown in Table 11.14, the correlation coefficients are fairly high between the cancer and heart-disease categories with a few irregularities involving leukemia, cancer of the upper respiratory system, and hypertensive heart disease. High coefficients may be suggestive of a common etiology, whereas low coefficients may suggest different etiologies. However, if the true metropolitan mortality rate for a disease is relatively small, an unusually large variance may result from observations for small metropolitan areas, thereby reducing somewhat the correlation coefficient for that disease. The leukemia and upper respiratory cancer mortality rates are examples of this problem. In contrast, a large proportion of high correlations between diseases whose mortality rates are positively correlated with age suggests a largely common etiology.

	Gastro-intestinal Cancer (150–156A, 157–159)	Cancer of Upper Respiratory System (140–148)	Urinary System Cancer (180–181)	Leukemia–Aleukemia (204)	Genital System Cancer (171–179)	Breast Cancer (170)
Respiratory system cancer (160–164)	0.74	0.73	0.68	0.39	0.71	0.71
Gastrointestinal cancer		0.63	0.91	0.67	0.72	0.90
Cancer of upper respiratory system			0.55	0.27	0.58	0.69
Urinary system cancer				0.72	0.71	0.89
Leukemia–Aleukemia					0.52	0.63
Genital system cancer						0.74
Breast cancer						
Total malignant neoplasms						
Vascular lesions of CNS						
Diseases of heart						
Arteriosclerotic heart disease						
Hypertensive heart disease						
Congenital malformations						
Other bronchopulmonic diseases						
Diabetes mellitus						

Note: The parenthetical figures are the International Statistical Classification designations of disease, Seventh Revision of the

It is particularly interesting in Table 11.14 that the correlations between mortality rates for respiratory system cancer and a number of other cancer categories, including total cancer, are generally rather high, suggesting that the etiology of respiratory-system cancer may not be too different from the etiology of a number of other cancer categories. This indication is supported by a correlation coefficient of 0.83 between mortality rates for respiratory cancer and total malignant neoplasms, the former being a part of the latter. The coefficient of 0.91 between total cancer mortality rates and mortality rates for the broad "diseases of the heart" category is also suggestive of a common etiology. The common etiology may perhaps be aging or senescence or cumulative somatic genetic degeneration. The correlations of mortality with median age are also rather high, as expected.

An interpretation of these correlations is that in metropolitan regions where cancer mortality rates are high, heart-disease mortality rates are high, and where cancer rates are low, heart-disease rates are also low. These findings are consistent with the previously noted radiomimetic hypothesis. In regions where radiomimetic influences are strong, the rate of senescence should be higher than in localities where they are weak. Accordingly, the possibility that atmospheric chemicals are major causes of lung cancer must be examined very carefully. As a supplement to the cancer-heart disease correlation shown in Table 11.14, Figure 11.8 illustrates for the 38 SMSA's that as the mortality rate for cancer increases the mortality rate for diseases of the heart also increases.

Table 11.14 also demonstrates that mortality rates for cancer and heart-disease categories are highly correlated with the median age of the populations. Although the age-mortality association exists, "explaining" the relationship on the basis of the age of the population explains nothing about the mechanism of the disease and is of no value in instituting protective or

TABLE 11.14

Matrix of correlation coefficients for annual mortality rates for 38 SMSA's, 1961–1964

Total Malignant Neoplasms (140–205)	Vascular Lesions of the CNS (330–334)	Diseases of Heart (400–402, 410–443)	Arteriosclerotic Heart Disease (420)	Hypertensive Heart Disease (440–443)	Congenital Malformations (750–759)	Other Bronchopulmonic Diseases (525–527)	Diabetes Mellitus (260)	Median Age
0.83	0.30	0.74	0.71	0.50	−0.37	−0.18	0.62	0.72
0.97	0.32	0.90	0.88	0.35	−0.45	−0.26	0.70	0.88
0.69	0.31	0.60	0.59	0.38	−0.25	−0.32	0.45	0.58
0.92	0.41	0.87	0.88	0.26	−0.56	−0.18	0.59	0.83
0.68	0.32	0.58	0.69	−0.11	−0.32	0.14	0.25	0.57
0.81	0.68	0.69	0.64	0.40	−0.46	−0.09	0.51	0.65
0.94	0.40	0.82	0.80	0.36	−0.49	−0.24	0.52	0.85
	0.42	0.91	0.88	0.40	−0.50	−0.22	0.65	0.89
		0.37	0.36	0.21	−0.45	−0.08	0.12	0.34
			0.93	0.46	−0.51	−0.31	0.58	0.91
				0.21	−0.50	−0.27	0.51	0.86
					−0.29	−0.37	0.49	0.36
						0.31	−0.17	−0.52
							−0.30	−0.29
								0.50

International Lists, 1955.

preventive measures for public health. However, if the variation in mortality rates can be accounted for strictly by different population age structures, then the radiomimetic hypothesis based on environmental chemicals must be rejected. For this reason in the following analyses equations for age-sex-race adjusted mortality rates as well as total mortality rates are presented. For the adjusted rates, only the variation in specific mortality rates is investigated without regard to the variation of the age-sex-race structure of the population. In the latter, the variation in this structure is included in the hypothesis as well.

In Table 11.14, negative coefficients occurred rather generally for the relationships of various diseases with congenital malformations and with the "other bronchopulmonic diseases" category. While the theoretical bases for these observations are still under examination, a few brief notes and cautions on interpretation of these inverted relationships are necessary. Examination

of annual mortality statistics for congenital malformations for the United States shows very high mortality for the under-one-year group, with mortality declining to age about 30 years, after which there is a small increase followed by a further decline in the older age-specific groups. This trend contrasts, for example, with mortality trends for arteriosclerotic heart disease, in which mortality risk increases markedly with age.

If the congenital malformation mortality risk, which must have a very major germinal genetic component, is higher in populations with higher environmental mutagenic pressures, then there may also be higher rates of natural abortion in these more polluted regions, which would tend to lower the live birth rates. Thus the inverted mortality-rate statistics for congenital malformations as compared with rates for diseases of senescence would not be entirely surprising if, as radiomimetic hazards increase, senescence and mortality from diseases of

TABLE 11.15

Matrix of correlation coefficients for means of mean annual concentrations of environmental chemicals for 38 cities, 1957–1964

	Cr	Cu	Fe	Pb	Mn	Ni	Sn	Ti	V	Zn	NO_2	SO_2	Particulate Sulfate	Water Hardness	As
Cd	0.46	0.47	0.45	0.40	0.41	0.30	0.54	0.38	0.18	0.68	0.39	0.46	0.36	0.00	0.50
Cr		0.21	0.61	0.44	0.43	0.41	0.41	0.54	0.36	0.48	0.23	0.39	0.50	−0.09	0.17
Cu			0.33	0.27	0.26	0.10	0.17	0.36	−0.08	0.23	0.14	0.23	0.22	0.33	0.33
Fe				0.41	0.69	0.24	0.44	0.80	−0.03	0.67	0.19	0.18	0.35	0.32	0.27
Pb					0.10	0.36	0.48	0.53	0.33	0.46	0.41	0.35	0.24	−0.08	0.14
Mn						0.07	0.33	0.57	−0.13	0.65	0.06	0.17	0.42	0.15	0.50
Ni							0.44	0.18	0.76	0.34	0.57	0.45	0.63	−0.21	0.28
Sn								0.45	0.35	0.57	0.42	0.18	0.36	−0.05	0.26
Ti									0.02	0.51	0.01	0.05	0.19	0.10	0.30
V										0.10	0.43	0.52	0.64	−0.44	0.13
Zn											0.34	0.45	0.47	0.03	0.52
NO₂												0.23	0.46	−0.13	0.37
SO₂													0.60	−0.15	0.23
Particulate sulfate														−0.15	0.38
Water hardness															−0.19

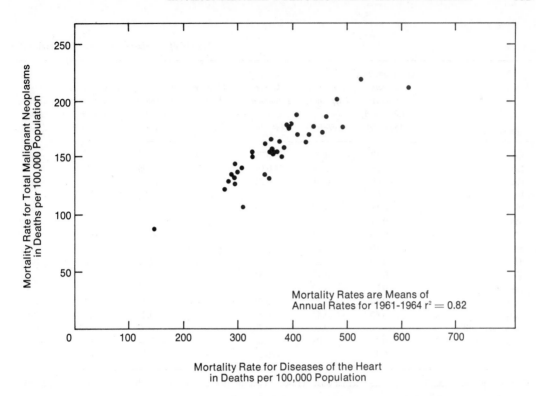

FIGURE 11.8   Mortality rates for diseases of the heart versus total malignant neoplasms for 38 SMSA's in the United States.

senescence increase, while increases in natural abortion rates would lead to reduction in birth rates. Lowered birth rates might be expected to result in somewhat parallel reductions in congenital malformation rates.

Other bronchopulmonic diseases is a category of particular interest. A major portion of this category is emphysema. While there is considerable mortality for this disease class in populations under five years of age, the major mortality is found in older age groups. But if emphysema is a disease of aging, as are cancer and heart disease, how can the negative correlation coefficients shown in Table 11.14 be explained? They cannot be explained in the manner given for congenital malformations, but they can be accounted for on a competitive mortality basis. Emphysema might be considered to be

a disease of senescence in which those individuals having progressive emphysema through biological senescence phenomena, perhaps coupled with certain genetic polymorphic problems (Liebeman, 1969), are at higher risk for contracting lung cancer than nonemphysemic individuals. If they do then develop lung cancer, they will probably die of lung cancer rather than emphysema. This competitive situation may, at least in part, explain the negative correlation coefficients. This view is supported by the fact that lung-cancer victims are very frequently found to have also been afflicted with emphysema (Hammond, 1969).

Correlation coefficients among the various chemical predictors are given in Table 11.15. With some exceptions, the coefficients are generally less than 0.5. With usual caution re-

Matrix of correlation coefficients between mean

	Gastrointestinal System Cancer (150–156A, 157–159)	Cancer of Respiratory System (160–164)	Cancer of Upper Respiratory System (140–148)	Urinary System Cancer (180–181)	Leukemia– Aleukemia (204)	Genital System Cancer (171–179)	Breast Cancer (170)
Cd	0.12	−0.20	−0.20	0.00	0.02	−0.05	−0.01
Cr	0.28	0.37	0.03	0.15	0.06	0.26	0.11
Cu	−0.09	−0.21	−0.31	−0.22	−0.22	−0.26	−0.14
Fe	0.06	0.09	−0.34	−0.05	−0.05	0.14	−0.11
Pb	0.18	0.07	−0.08	0.05	0.09	0.07	0.16
Mn	0.01	0.05	−0.25	−0.07	−0.14	0.07	−0.17
Ni	0.50	0.42	0.14	0.41	0.40	0.26	0.46
Sn	0.10	0.10	0.02	−0.06	−0.13	0.22	0.06
Ti	−0.19	−0.23	−0.54	−0.28	−0.10	−0.16	−0.33
V	0.50	0.48	0.31	0.46	0.23	0.25	0.50
Zn	0.25	0.12	−0.11	0.17	0.05	0.20	0.15
NO$_2$	0.47	0.37	0.23	0.44	0.36	0.37	0.50
SO$_2$	0.63	0.44	0.31	0.49	0.21	0.29	0.50
Particulate sulfate	0.58	0.60	0.29	0.47	0.09	0.32	0.48
Water hardness	−0.28	−0.03	−0.08	−0.35	−0.34	−0.12	−0.23
As	0.17	−0.22	−0.22	0.15	0.16	−0.03	0.04

Note: The parenthetical figures are the International Statistical Classification designations of disease, Seventh Revision of the

garding the relationship with high correlations, the data appear reasonably suitable for use in multivariate analyses.

In Table 11.16 are presented correlation coefficients between pollutant variables and disease categories. Some suggestive indicators of interesting relationships between diseases and the chemical categories, SO$_2$, NO$_2$, and particulate sulfate, are apparent. The negative relationships of several metals are also of interest. The multivariate results which follow should be examined in conjunction with these bivariate correlations.

Results of Optimal Regression Analyses

This section presents multiple regression equations based on (1) total mortality rates for SMSA populations and (2) mortality rates adjusted for age, sex, and race according to the traditional procedure. The adjustment procedure alters the observed metropolitan mortality rates to a base with a population structure of some "standard" population distribution, such as the distribution for the United States as a whole in 1960. Such adjustment, though traditional, may be scientifically invalid for ecological studies.

The procedure assumes implicitly that the members of human populations are genetically homogeneous and that the selective pressures on the various local populations throughout the vast area of the United States are uniform. It is, however, well known that all sexually reproducing populations must be genetically heterogeneous. The genetically based variation due to recombination plus mutation produces the variability on which nonuniform selection acts (Ayala, 1968; Williams, 1956; Ford, 1965). If the selective pressures vary as they can be expected to do, a genetically based metabolic defect such as a deficiency in an enzyme involved

TABLE 11.16

mortality rates for chronic diseases and annual mean concentrations of environmental chemicals for 38 SMSA's, 1957–1964.

Total Malignant Neoplasms (140–205)	Vascular Lesions of the CNS (330–334)	Diseases of Heart (400–402, 410–443)	Arterio-sclerotic Heart Disease (420)	Hyper-tensive Heart Disease (440–443)	Congenital Malfor-mations (750–759)	Other Broncho-pulmonic Diseases (525–527)	Diabetes Mellitus (260)	Median Age
0.04	−0.29	−0.01	−0.06	0.10	−0.20	−0.18	0.15	0.03
0.28	−0.01	0.29	0.11	0.40	−0.13	−0.11	0.34	0.27
−0.18	−0.37	−0.20	−0.23	−0.12	0.14	0.09	−0.02	−0.20
0.02	0.08	−0.02	−0.07	0.10	−0.04	0.11	0.09	−0.01
0.16	−0.18	0.10	0.00	0.13	−0.01	0.13	0.03	0.20
−0.03	0.05	−0.06	−0.08	0.15	−0.19	−0.14	0.16	−0.05
0.49	−0.04	0.37	0.34	0.23	−0.29	−0.20	0.35	0.36
0.09	0.08	0.01	−0.10	0.37	−0.25	−0.23	0.11	0.01
−0.23	−0.18	−0.20	−0.27	0.00	0.12	0.21	−0.23	−0.17
0.51	−0.12	0.56	0.45	0.52	−0.36	−0.36	0.32	0.50
0.21	0.04	0.08	0.03	0.11	−0.31	−0.17	0.22	0.13
0.48	0.25	0.39	0.31	0.27	−0.57	−0.26	0.29	0.40
0.56	−0.15	0.53	0.48	0.24	−0.17	−0.37	0.52	0.59
0.56	−0.00	0.56	0.48	0.52	−0.45	−0.48	0.52	0.52
−0.28	−0.14	−0.46	−0.39	−0.25	0.38	0.34	−0.14	−0.35
0.07	0.01	0.05	0.03	−0.04	−0.37	−0.25	0.01	−0.01

International Lists, 1955.

in, say, the detoxification of a pollutant chemical of environmental origin, such as sulfite or bisulfite, might be expected to result in variations in risk of somatic and germinal genetic damage due to that chemical. Such variation might be expected to produce different age structures in different areas. This question will be discussed further below.

(1) Breast cancer (ISC 170). Using unadjusted 1959–1961 metroplitan mortality data (Duffy and Carroll, 1967) and optimal regression analysis, equation (1) was estimated for mortality rate in deaths per 100,000 persons for breast cancer M_{bc}. The parenthetical international statistical classifications (ISC) numbers are those of diseases established by the World Health Organization (1957).

$$M_{bc} = -28.000 + 5.523 \ln c(NO_2)$$
$$+ 2.018 \ln c(SO_2) - 0.992 \ln c(Cd)$$
$$- 1.510 \ln c(Cu), \tag{1}$$

where $t = 4.94$ for NO_2, 4.69 for SO_2, 2.63 for Cd, and 2.06 for Cu. The R^2 value, corrected for sample size, obtained for the equation was 0.580 with a corresponding $F_{4,33} = 11.38$ (F values indicate the number of degrees of freedom in the computations). The t statistics are from the standard test for the significance of the regression coefficients and are significant at the $\alpha = 0.05$ level. The expression c(chemical) is the mean of mean annual concentrations of the chemical in mirograms per cubic meter in the atmospheres of 38 SMSA's based on data available, as noted previously.

A corresponding equation (2), comparable to equation (1), was obtained by an optimal regression analysis of the 1959–1961 breast-cancer mortality-rate data adjusted for age, sex, and race in the traditional manner:

$$M_{bc}(adj) = 4.231 + 1.932 \ln c(NO_2)$$
$$+ 0.9582 \ln c(Ni) - 1.286 \ln c(Ti), \tag{2}$$

where $t = 2.88$ for NO_2, 2.97 for Ni, and 3.93 for Ti. The corrected $R^2 = 0.563$ with $F_{3,34} = 15.02$, which is significant at the $\alpha = 0.01$ level. The t statistics are also significant at the $\alpha = 0.01$ level.

For comparison, equation (3) was obtained as in the preceding analyses using unadjusted mortality-rate data over the 1961–1964 period:

$$M_{bc} = -22.809 + 4.992 \ln c(NO_2)$$
$$+ 2.038 \ln c(SO_2) - 1.286 \ln c(Cd), \qquad (3)$$

where $t = 4.63$ for NO_2, 4.90 for SO_2, and 3.88 for Cd. For this equation the corrected $R_2 = 0.553$ with $F_{3,34} = 14.01$, which is significant at the $\alpha = 0.01$ level. The t statistics are likewise significant at the $\alpha = 0.01$ level. Comparable results were obtained on analysis of mortality statistics for females only.

(2) Lung cancer (ISC 162, 163). Using data and procedures comparable to the foregoing, the following optimal regression equation was obtained using unadjusted 1959–1961 lung cancer mortality rate data M_{lc} for the 38 SMSA's:

$$M_{lc} = -28.087 + 4.986 \ln c(NO_2)$$
$$- 2.197 \ln c(Cu) - 2.103 \ln c(Ti)$$
$$+ 5.462 \ln c(SO_4) - 0.6255 \ln c(As) \qquad (4)$$

where $t = 4.11$ for NO_2, $t = 3.05$ for Cu, $t = 3.07$ for Ti, $t = 5.96$ for SO_4 and 2.36 for As. The corrected $R^2 = 0.732$ and $F_{5,32} = 17.52$, a result significant at the 0.01 level. The t statistics are significant at the $\alpha = 0.01$ level.

Equation (5), comparable with (4), was estimated for adjusted 1959–1961 mortality data for lung cancer for the 38 SMSA's:

$$M_{lc}(\text{adj}) = 5.470 + 3.306 \ln c(NO_2)$$
$$- 2.582 \ln c(Ti) - 1.275 \ln c(As)$$
$$+ 2.507 \ln c(Mn) + 0.7177 \ln c(V), \qquad (5)$$

where $t = 3.06$ for NO_2, 3.88 for Ti, 5.19 for As, 5.17 for Mn, and 3.53 for V. The corrected $R^2 = 0.607$ with $F_{5,32} = 9.91$, which is significant at the $\alpha = 0.01$ level. The t statistics are significant at the $\alpha = 0.01$ level.

The R^2 of 0.732 for equation (4) for the unadjusted lung-cancer mortality rate indicates that about 73 percent of the variance in the lung-cancer mortality-rate criterion is explained by atmospheric concentrations of five chemicals. Such a result suggests that a major cause of lung cancer may be atmospheric pollution. This is consistent with implications of the matrix of correlation coefficients, Table 11.14, as discussed previously. The major physiological contact of human populations with the atmosphere is through the respiratory system. Highly significant results were also obtained with adjusted data, as shown in equation (5).

In equations (4) and (5) for lung cancer, NO_2 was selected as a predictor but SO_2 was not. Optimal regression equations for predicting unadjusted mortality rates for a number of other cancer categories, and also for heart disease, frequently contained both NO_2 and SO_2 as statistically significant positively correlated predictors. It is of interest to know whether one or more statistically satisfactory multiple regression equations, not necessarily optimal, may be obtained in which SO_2 is a significant predictor. Biological theory suggests that the joint NO_2, SO_2 relationship should be present for lung cancer and for the broader cancer-of-the-respiratory-system category, since the relationship is observed for other cancer categories.

To examine this question, unadjusted mortality rate data for 1959–1961 for lung cancer (ISC 162, 163) were subjected to special analysis. NO_2 and SO_2 were arbitrarily selected or "forced" as predictors, and optimal regression analysis was used to select a third chemical predictor which would maximize R^2. The following optimal equation was obtained for the prediction of unadjusted lung-cancer mortality rate M_{lc} for the 38 SMSA's:

$$M_{lc} = -21.871 + 6.516 \ln c(NO_2)$$
$$+ 1.352 \ln c(SO_2) - 3.340 \ln c(Cu), \qquad (6)$$

where $t = 4.51$ for NO_2, 2.80 for SO_2, and 3.68 for Cu. The corrected $R^2 = 0.508$ with $F_{3,34} =$

11.71, which is significant at the $\alpha = 0.01$ level. The t statistics are also significant at the $\alpha = 0.01$ level. The expected occurrence of SO_2 as a statistically significant predictor is thus established. A comparable equation using adjusted data was not acceptable because of a low t statistic for the SO_2 term. However, a result similar to (6) was obtained using unadjusted 1961–1964 respiratory-system cancer mortality-rate data.

(3) Stomach cancer (ISC 151). Analyses were carried out as for the preceding disease categories using 1959–1961 stomach-cancer mortality data. With unadjusted data the following optimal regression equation was obtained:

$$M_{sc} = -25.363 + 4.117 \ln c(NO_2)$$
$$+ 2.506 \ln c(SO_2) - 1.433 \ln c(Cd), \qquad (7)$$

where $t = 3.31$ for NO_2, $t = 5.09$ for SO_2, and $t = 3.65$ for Cd. The corrected $R^2 = 0.495$ with $F_{3,34} = 11.12$. This result is significant at the $\alpha = 0.01$ level. The t statistics are also significant at the $\alpha = 0.01$ level.

The corresponding analysis using adjusted data gave the following optimal regression equation:

$$M_{sc}(adj) = 0.9739 + 2.212 \ln c(SO_2)$$
$$- 1.010 \ln c(Cd) + 0.7249 \ln c(As), \qquad (8)$$

wher $t = 4.14$ for SO_2, 2.23 for Cd, and 2.27 for As. The corrected $R^2 = 0.349$ with $F_{3,34} = 6.07$, which is significant at the $\alpha = 0.01$ level. The t statistics are significant at the $\alpha = 0.05$ level.

(4) Arteriosclerotic heart diseases (ISC 420). Using unadjusted mortality rate data for the 1959–1961 period for arteriosclerotic heart disease M_{ahd}, a major cause of death for occidental man, the following optimal regression equation was estimated:

$$M_{ahd} = -254.90 + 71.912 \ln c(NO_2)$$
$$+ 41.336 \ln c(SO_2) - 24.225 \ln c(Cd)$$
$$- 23.140 \ln c(\text{water hardness}), \qquad (9)$$

where $t = 2.83$ for NO_2, 3.96 for SO_2, 3.02 for Cd, and 2.43 for water hardness. The corrected $R_2 = 0.474$ with $F_{4,32} = 7.21$, which is significant at the $\alpha = 0.01$ level. The t statistics for the significance of the regression coefficients are significant at the $\alpha = 0.02$ level. (Because of a data-adjustment problem for arteriosclerotic heart-disease mortality for Scranton, Pa., the results in this disease category are for 37 SMSA's, with Scranton deleted.)

An analysis on mortality data for arteriosclerotic heart disease adjusted for age, sex, and race is given in regression equation (10):

$$M_{ahd}(adj) = +7.329 + 20.339 \ln c(SO_2)$$
$$- 27.497 \ln c(Cu) + 48.399 \ln c(SO_4^=)$$
$$- 21.456 \ln c(Zn), \qquad (10)$$

where $t = 3.53$ for SO_2, 3.22 for Cu, 3.78 for $SO_4^=$, and 3.53 for Zn. The corrected $R^2 = 0.556$ with $F_{4,32} = 10.01$, significant at the $\alpha = 0.01$ level. The t statistics are also significant at the 0.01 level.

The inverse relationship of hardness of drinking water (Durfor and Becker, 1964) to mortality rate from certain cardiovascular diseases has been observed previously (Schroeder, 1965; Public Health Service, 1968).

(5) Diseases of the heart (ISC 400–402, 410–443). This broad heart-disease category contains arteriosclerotic heart disease, hypertensive heart disease (ISC 440–443), and other related categories of causes of death. Studies thus far involving comparison of adjusted versus unadjusted mortality rates have been restricted to narrow, relatively precise vital statistical categories—i.e., not over two ISC numbers.

The next multiple regression equation (11) resulted for the prediction of heart-disease mortality rate from environmental predictors using 1961–1964 mortality data. It is of particular interest because of the importance of the disease category as a cause of death and because of its similarity to equation (9) for unadjusted arteriosclerotic heart-disease mortality-rate data for 1959–1961. This equation is nonoptimal in that after 20 programmed iterations, it was not yet determined that the selections were optimal; i.e., R^2 may not have been maximized. The test statistics, however, are satisfactory:

$$M_{dh} = -258.49 + 89.001 \ln c(NO_2)$$
$$+ 51.616 \ln c(SO_2) - 28.368 \ln c(Cd)$$
$$- 29.964 \ln c(\text{water hardness}), \qquad (11)$$

where $t = 3.16$ for NO_2, 4.73 for SO_2, 3.28 for Cd, and 2.87 for water hardness. The corrected $R^2 = 0.561$ with $F_{4,33} = 10.56$, which is significant at the $\alpha = 0.01$ level. The t statistics are significant at the $\alpha = 0.01$ level.

The recurrence of the selection of SO_2, NO_2, Cd, and water hardness as predictors for both (9) and (11) is rather unlikely to have occurred by chance. It is noteworthy, in addition, that the signs of the coefficients for these predictors in both equations correspond exactly. Both equations are based on unadjusted data.

(6) Congenital malformations (ISC 750–759). It must be noted that in this mortality category the frequency of occurrence is highest among the very young, as contrasted with the cancer and heart-disease categories, for which mortality rates increase with chronologial age. Thus the regression results could be expected to be of a different character than for diseases of aging. Further, a major component of this birth-defect disease category would be expected to arise largely from germinal genetic defects rather than from cumulative somatic genetic degeneration. Germinal genetic defects would be expected to be associated with environmental mutagens, if they exist. If mutagens affect somatic cell DNA, it would seem unlikely that germinal DNA would escape the effects. Adjustment of mortality statistics for congenital malformations seems unnecessary since, for example, in 1964, in the United States as a whole there were 20,288 deaths from this cause; 14,197 of these occurred in individuals under one year of age, and 15,906 occurred in individuals under five years.

For unadjusted mortality rates over the 1961–1964 period, the following optimal regres-

sion equation was obtained for mortality rate for congenital malformation M_{em}:

$$M_{em} = 22.370 - 2.877 \ln c(NO_2)$$
$$- 0.6675 \ln c(\text{water hardness})$$
$$- 0.5937 \ln c(Zn) + 1.346 \ln c(Pb), \qquad (12)$$

where $t = 4.41$ for NO_2, 2.85 for water hardness, 2.26 for Zn, and 2.84 for Pb. The corrected $R^2 = 0.494$ with $F_{4,33} = 8.05$, which is significant at the $\alpha = 0.01$ level. The t statistics are significant at the $\alpha = 0.05$ level.

(7) Other diseases. Results for the relationships of environmental chemicals with numerous other chronic disease categories have been obtained and will be presented in other reports. Included are findings concerning cancer of various organs of the digestive system, of the urinary system, leukemia, diabetes mellitus, chronic nephritis, and others.

As an indication of the broad consistency of the findings for cancer, the following result was obtained for the total cancer category, i.e., total malignant neoplasms (ISC 140–205), using unadjusted vital statistical data for 1961-1964. The following optimal regression equation was obtained for mortality rate M_{tc} for total cancer:

$$M_{tc} = -151.33 + 40.180 \ln c(NO_2)$$
$$+ 18.843 \ln c(SO_2) - 10.120 \ln c(Cd), \qquad (13)$$

where $t = 4.29$ for NO_2, 5.22 for SO_2, and 3.52 for Cd. The corrected $R^2 = 0.554$ with $F_{3,34} = 14.08$, which is significant at the $\alpha = 0.01$ level. The t statistics are also significant at the $\alpha = 0.01$ level. The recurrence of SO_2 and NO_2 as significant positively correlated predictors for mortality rates for various categories of chronic diseases is a quite unlikely random occurrence. Functional relationships may exist.

Optimal Regression Analysis
in Predicting Median Age

Median age, a measure of age structure of populations, was subjected to optimal regression analysis in the manner used previously for chronic diseases. Median age is thus handled as a criterion. The values for the 38 SMSA's were found to vary from 22.5 to 35.8 years. Median age is influenced by birth, death, and migration variables. Regression analysis may give an indication of the possible effects of environmental chemicals on birth and age-specific death rates as they may affect median age. The effects of migration and other demographic variables have also been investigated successfully and will be reported in subsequent presentations.

Based on median-age data for 1960 for the 38 SMSA's, the following optimal regression equation was obtained:

$$\begin{aligned} \text{median age} = \ &3.493 + 2.795 \ln c(NO_2) \\ &+ 1.841 \ln c(SO_2) - 0.654 \ln c(Cd) \\ &-1.136 \ln c(Cu), \end{aligned} \quad (14)$$

where $t = 3.36$ for NO_2, 5.36 for SO_2, 2.33 for Cd, and 2.09 for Cu. The corrected $R^2 = 0.566$ with $F_{4,33} = 10.74$, which is significant at the $\alpha = 0.01$ level. The t statistics are significant at the $\alpha = 0.05$ level. The chemicals selected are the same as appeared in regression equations for various chronic diseases.

The variance of total unadjusted mortality rates for metropolitan area populations can be partitioned into two parts: (1) part due to variation of sex-age-race-specific mortality rates among metropolitan areas, (2) part due to variation in the sex-age-race distribution among metropolitan areas. The objective of the above analyses is to account for or explain statistically these two variances. Equations (2), (5), (8), and (10) are concerned with the first part of the variance as combined according to a common set of weights. Equation (14) is concerned with the first part of the variance, specifically that due to the age distribution.

Clearly, mortality rates, together with birth and migration rates, determine the age distribution of the population. Therefore, one would expect that a hypothesis that accounts for a significant portion of the variation in age-specific mortality rates would also partially explain the variation in age distribution. A complete explanation would, of course, require that migration and birth-rate variations also be accounted for. Equation (14) supports this application of the hypothesis.

The primary interest of the studies reported here is to account for variation in the total disease-specific mortality rate, which is the sum of the two parts discussed previously. Since the hypothesis being tested in these analyses contributes to both parts of the total mortality-rate variance, analysis of rates unadjusted for age and race is considered valid. Equations (1), (3), (4), (6), (7), (9), and (11)–(13) support this position.

Discussion

The recurrence of SO_2, NO_2, or both as positively correlated significant predictors for both unadjusted and adjusted mortality rates for (1) breast cancer, (2) stomach cancer, (3) arteriosclerotic heart disease, (4) diseases of the heart, and (5) total cancer does not contradict the radiomimetic hypothesis that among the environmental chemicals are some which are mutagenic and contribute to cumulative somatic genetic degeneration or disease. Thus the statistical, theoretical, and experimental evidence seem to be not inconsistent with the position that SO_2 is an environmental mutagenic hazard.

Statistical evidence, along with theoretical chemical and biological considerations, is strongly suggestive that NO_2 is also an environmental mutagenic hazard to life. The statistical findings for congenital malformations also indicate a relationship with NO_2 but not thus far with SO_2. If, at the stage of resting ova, nitrous acid can cause mutations directly, but if bisulfite acts mutagenically primarily during DNA replication, only NO_2 should be a highly significant statistical predictor for the congenital malformations mortality rate. The statistical findings are compatible with this theory.

For unadjusted lung-cancer mortality-rate data, NO_2 and SO_2 were found to be positively correlated statistical predictors. The relationship of environmental chemicals to lung cancer is being investigated further, as are the relationships to other diseases. In particular, analyses are to be run on age-specific population groups, such as for the age decade of 35 to 44 years.

It is not unlikely that individuals in different age groups are at different survival risks to environmental chemicals. One function of an essential mammalian enzyme, sulfite oxidase (Macleod et al., 1961), is to oxidize sulfite to sulfate efficiently. Based on genetic polymorphic theory, it would be expected that polymorphic variations should exist in the structure of the enzyme, with some structures functioning less efficiently than others. Some individuals would be expected whose enzymes function very poorly or not at all. Such a condition was in fact observed for an individual who dies in infancy (Mudd et al., 1967; Irreverre et al., 1967). Therefore, those individuals who are least capable of efficient oxidation of sulfite, or bisulfite, would be at maximum risk to mutagenic effects of bisulfite which exists in equilibrium with sulfite.

It would thus be expected that ecological selection pressure would occur against that group of individuals who do not oxidize sulfite or bisulfite well; the selection pressure would be a direct function of the efficiency of the enzyme clonally in the individuals and the environmental concentration of SO_2 or other bisulfite precursor. This mechanism would lead to preferential selection against the younger, more vulnerable individuals in populations. This higher mortality among the young would increase the median age of the population involved. The regression analysis for median age demonstrated positive correlation coefficients for concentrations of both SO_2 and NO_2 in the environments. Thus the statistical results in the prediction of median age are in accordance with the expectations of genetic polymorphic theory and of the radiomimetic hypothesis. In general, the statistical findings, the chemical and biological theory, the experimental evidence, and the radiomimetic hypothesis of cumulative somatic genetic degeneration appear to be compatible.

Several environmental metals have also appeared, some recurrently, as significant statistical predictors for mortality rates of the chronic diseases cited and also for median age. Chelation biochemistry, i.e., metal binding, is considered to be involved, but the details are to be discussed in other reports.

Ti occurred as a negatively correlated predictor for lung-cancer mortality rate. Schroeder et al. (1963), in a review on the biochemistry of Ti, concluded that it "is one of the few ubiquitous metals present in high concentrations on this planet upon which life does not depend." Interestingly, in the course of establishing nontoxicity of Ti for mice, they found that mature weights of experimental animals on diets containing Ti were significantly greater than weights of the controls. But Ti was found by Bernheim and Bernheim (1939) to inhibit the oxidation of cysteine to sulfonic acid. Recently Green (1968) reported that cysteine exerts a protective effect on alveolar macrophages, and Braven et al. (1967) observed that acetaldehyde reacts with cysteine, and that thiols protect against mutagenesis.

Subsequently, Fenner and Braven (1968) discussed a "thiol-defense" hypothesis concerning bronchial carcinoma and its association with cigarette smoking. They hypothesized the presence in smoke of compounds that may react with thiols, which, if not inactivated or altered, protect against mutagens and carcinogens. It is necessary to consider any atmospheric agents which may oxidize or otherwise affect cysteine, and this should include NO_2 and peroxides as well as atmospheric aldehydes and other agents. It would also seem necessary to consider bioenergetic problems which might deleteriously affect normal thiol maintenance—for example, hypoglycemia.

Harman (1961, 1966) observed that several

antioxidant-type chemicals including thiols, prolong lifespans of mice in whose diets the materials were included. Cysteine was effective, as was 2,6-di-tert-butylhydroxytoluene (BHT). The effect of Ti may be as an antioxidant or protective agent for cysteine, which deters mutagenesis. Thus, negatively correlated Ti as a statistical predictor for lung-cancer mortality would not be unexpected on this basis.

It is of interest that particulate sulfate was found to be a positively correlated predictor for mortality rates for lung cancer, for adjusted arteriosclerotic heart disease, and for the broad diseases of the heart category (Hickey, 1968). There is apparently a quite complicated relationship between sulfate, Cu, Mo, and probably other metals that influences the retention of body Cu (Underwood, 1962). Increases in sulfate, or Mo, or both in the diets of some animals have resulted in decreased retention of body Cu, while decreases in sulfate, Mo, or both have resulted in Cu accumulation. In brief, however, if increasing levels of sulfate cause reduction of cellular and body Cu levels and if Cu is chelated to and protects DNA from some mutagenic chemicals, then the positive correlation of sulfate concentration with mortality rates of some diseases related to senescence would not be surprising. The relationship of sulfate to the retention of other metals is to be examined further.

As suggested from the statistics, if a Cu deficiency existed in a human population, biochemical sites to which Cu could ordinarily bind, such as DNA, might then be filled by certain other metals, such as Cd. This is, of course, speculative. Much more examination of experimental and theoretical biochemistry is necessary.

Instrumentation Problems

Since multivariate analyses of the complex man-environment system requires extensive accurate data on environmental chemicals, high-quality reliable instrumentation is es-

sential. It is very important to obtain analytical data for precise chemical categories, such as for specific metals and for specific nonmetallic chemicals.

For example, clear separation of NO_2 and NO, and of SO_2, NO_2, and ozone, is essential. A pollutant category called "oxidants" is reported which includes anything which releases iodine in a potassium iodide reagent. Both ozone and NO_2, along with other peroxides, affect this reagent. But the enzyme, catalase, decomposes hydrogen peroxide to form water and oxygen. Other systems handle nitrite and nitrate. To examine health effects of ozone, ozone concentrations are needed, rather than ozone-NO_2-organic peroxide mixed data.

Conclusions

1. Significant statistical relationships exist between concentrations of a number of environmental chemicals, mostly atmospheric, and mortality rates for several categories of cancer and heart disease in 38 SMSA's in the United States in the samples of the data studied.

2. Significant relationships were still obtained when mortality rates were adjusted for age, sex, and race according to the usual procedures.

3. Statistically significant results were obtained in the prediction of mortality rate for congenital malformations from concentrations of environmental chemicals.

4. Statistically significant results were obtained in the prediction of median age of the 38 SMSA's from environmental chemicals using observed unadjusted age data.

5. The radiomimetic hypothesis, based on theoretical biochemical considerations, is compatible with the results of ecological statistical analyses of metropolitan data.

6. Atmospheric concentrations of several chemicals, particularly SO_2 and NO_2, recur rather consistently as positively correlated statistically significant predictors of mortality rates for major chronic diseases of senescence, such as heart disease and cancer. They are also signifi-

cant predictors for median age. NO_2 is, in addition, a significant predictor for mortality rate for congenital malformations.

7. At this point in our studies SO_2 and NO_2 seem likely to fall within the category of radiomimetic environmental chemicals. They should be considered as probably environmental mutagenic hazards to life.

8. Concentrations of certain metals, notably Cu and Cd, have appeared recurrently as negatively correlated statistically significant predictors in many regression equations for prediction of mortality rates for diseases of aging.

9. A high degree of intercorrelation exists among mortality rates for various cancer and heart-disease categories, with the exception of leukemia, in 38 SMSA's. This may suggest the concept of a rather common etiology for all, in agreement with the radiomimetic hypothesis.

CHAPTER 12

governmental programs affecting
environmental quality

By now it should be obvious that environmental externalities—pollution—arise because most decision making is highly individualistic. It is equally obvious that the only way to internalize the externalities, so that the effects of individuals' actions upon others become part of the actors' own decision-making process, is by exercise of power at some higher governmental level.

THE FEDERAL ROLE

The federal role in internalizing environmental externalities has changed over the years. As Haskell (1970) notes, federal interest in various aspects of the environment is nearly as old as the government itself. In 1789 Congress authorized the building of a lighthouse near the entrance to Chesapeake Bay to promote safe waterborne transportation. In 1802 President Jefferson approved a $34,000 appropriation for public piers on the Delaware River to promote man's use of his water environment. Since then, the federal response to environmental problems has evolved in three stages, each being added onto the last but not replacing it; few programs have been discontinued. The result is a welter of natural-resource programs and policies which can be grouped generally into those which (1) tame natural violence and exploit resources for transportation and economic

---

Selections are included in this chapter from:
   Richard N. L. Andrews, "Three Fronts of Federal Environmental Policy," *Journal of the American Institute of Planners*, Vol. 37 (July 1971), pp. 258–266. Begins on page

347.
   Merrill Eisenbud, "Environmental Protection in the City of New York," *Science*, Vol. 170 (November 13, 1970), pp. 706–712. Begins on page 368.

---

purposes, (2) conserve the quantity of resources, and (3)—only lately—conserve the quality of the environment.

Tame and Exploit

Early policies sought to put the new continent's "wild" and "hostile" nature under man's control. The purpose was to protect man physically and promote his commerce. Rivers were "improved" to facilitate waterborne transportation. Floods were controlled. Settlers overran the West and conquered it. Prairies were fenced, wild animals slain. The elimination of natural features and their replacement by a man-made environment was considered progress.

Once nature was thought to be comparatively docile, federal resource policies added an exploitative phase, beginning about 1880, to feed the industrial revolution. Nature was thought of in terms of resources for production—gold and silver, coal, iron, timber, livestock, agricultural land.

Conserve Quantity

Conservation of natural resources became federal policy under President Theodore Roosevelt, who feared for the loss of quantity. Was the nation using up too much mineral wealth, grazing land, productive soils, timber? These were rural concerns, and rural-oriented policies were developed to meet them. Roosevelt's conservation policy was to define just one allowable use for a resource and withhold it from all other uses. Development was still the central theme of policy—but to be achieved more wisely and less wastefully.

By the 1920s, significant conservation legislation began to pass both national and state legislatures. In the 1930s and '40s federal resource conservation accelerated, partly for resource protection, partly to counteract depression and to support American efforts in World War II.

Concern for quantity remained the central

theme of federal conservation policy until the late 1950s. Teddy Roosevelt's policy of limited use evolved into a conservation policy of nonuse. Particularly during World War II there was a fear of running out of low-cost raw materials. Conservation by nonuse coexisted with policies initiated earlier to exploit resources and control natural destruction.

With conservation in mind, national parks were set aside in the wide-open spaces to save some of the most spectacular of nature's wonders from exploitation. National forests were created. Restrictions were put on the depletion of resources from the public lands. Soil conservation measures were initiated to solve problems of the Great Dust Bowl of the 1930s, where topsoil blew away as a result of poor land management. At the same time coal mining and oil and gas exploration were encouraged, along with agriculture and lumbering. Flood control continued as an important fuction of the Corps of Engineers and the Soil Conservation Service.

Conserve Quality

When the quality of the air, water, and land began to worry citizens and, as a consequence, federal policy officials, the "new conservation"—the effort to conserve and restore resource quality, particularly in urban areas—was patched onto existing resource protection and exploitation programs. The initial concern for public health was soon expanded to include the interests of the conservation community in fish and wildlife species as well as aesthetic, recreation, and amenity resources of all sorts.

The "old conservation," emphasizing preservation and nonuse, proved to be irrelevant to the urban environment, where intense competition for resources requires constant use. Indeed, the urban environment theme, it has become clear, must be restoration of quality for use, reuse, and further reuse, building environmental protections into human activities.

By the late 1950s and accelerating in the 1960s,

the many urban quality problems worsened. Existing federal resource programs did not address themselves in any significant way to these problems of pollution or to the protection and acquisition of urban open spaces—those small and intermediate-sized spaces that make up the bulk of what is available in the urban environment.

Until the 1950s environmental quality management—garbage and trash collection and disposal, water supply and sewage disposal, air emissions and noise controls—was thought to be the sole prerogative of state and local governments. But as the problems worsened and it became clear that states and municipalities could not or would not act on them effectively, a federal role was established and expanded. The purpose of the federal role has always been to support and stimulate action by state and local authorities—never to supplant these authorities.

Initial Program Fragmentation

Environmental quality policy developed piecemeal. As a general perception grew that a quality problem was being inadequately treated, new federal programs and agencies were set up to remedy it.

By the end of the 1960s the fragmentation had become extreme: altogether, seventeen federal departments and independent agencies, twelve Presidential committees, commissions, and advisory bodies, and three quasi-official agencies had a part of the quality restoration effort, either directly or indirectly. Eleven coordinating bodies and units within the Executive Office of the President had been set up to coordinate the programs of these varied federal agencies. In all, 42 groups were concerned with the federal pursuit of air quality, water quality, solid-wastes management, radiation and pesticides pollution control, multipurpose open spaces, open spaces for specific purposes such as recreation and parks, and fish and wildlife protection.

To make matters worse, in the executive branch each major environmental quality program was administered separately, often in different departments. Many federal agencies began to work on each environmental problem. As public concern for pollution and noise began to grow, many resource-use agencies acquired other functions to promote environmental quality—usually research. Many agencies concentrated on just one source of damage, such as agriculture or transportation. Fragmentation produced interagency competition and reduced effectiveness.

Compounding the problem, both within agencies and in the framework of interagency competition, throughout the 1960s attempts to improve environmental quality were overshadowed by concern for environmental uses that harm the biosphere. The sponsoring agencies resisted including costs of adequate environmental protections in their programs. Thus, just as uses of the environment competed and conflicted in urban areas, so did the programs sponsored by single-mission federal agencies. The need to coordinate environmental quality programs and to include provision for protection of air, water, and land quality into other federal policies thus grew increasingly apparent. Several avenues were open to the federal government—for example, the extension of the multiple-use concept, or the issuance of executive orders, but both of these proved to be inadequate for the task.

Multiple Use

The multiple-use concept of natural-resource programs has successfully rationalized some competing uses by permitting several to coexist. However, this policy usually has been successful in rural areas. Dams and reservoirs are used to control floods, generate power, augment stream flows, and provide irrigation, water supplies, or recreation. National forests and other public lands provide timber, grazing land, minerals, and recreation. Idle farmlands are opened up to sportsmen and vacationers.

The multiple-use concept has not generally been applied to natural-resource programs in urban areas. Nor has it guided those federal programs which have had major impacts on metropolitan environments, such as transportation and housing, to ensure that public water and air supplies, recreation, and open spaces are protected.

1966 Executive Orders

Other coordinating devices have been tried. Two presidential executive orders issued in 1966 sought to resolve the most flagrant federal agency conflicts of water and air use. Executive Order 11288 (July 2, 1966) to abate and prevent water pollution from federal activities, and Executive Order 11282 (May 26, 1966) to abate and control air pollution from federal activities, both emphasized a phased pollution-abatement program at federal facilities and buildings. Primarily this meant construction of waste-treatment devices at military installations. The chief pollution-control agencies—HEW for air and Interior for water—were made the coordinating federal units. However, loans, grants, and contracts sponsored by federal agencies and performed by other organizations were not seriously included in the mandates. The agencies sponsoring these indirect activities were merely asked to examine their programs with a view to pollution control and were "encouraged" to prescribe regulation to implement such controls.

Predictably, the response to the presidential executive orders by several federal agencies concerned with environmental use was varied. Phased abatement at federal installations has for the most part been slow. At least one federal agency—the Atomic Energy Commission—judged that the executive orders gave it no authority to consider new environmental impacts, specifically thermal pollution. On the other hand, those agencies which sponsor uses requiring high quality and which bear only a small added cost for protective measures became very active in promoting clean and green resources. The latter agencies include the Fish and Wildlife Service, the Bureau of Outdoor Recreation, and the Public Health Service. Agencies that sponsor uses at the opposite end of the quality spectrum were not so receptive. Quality enhancement meant to them a substantial added cost to the conduct of their missions with little enhancement of those missions. Such agencies as the Bureau of Mines, the Department of Transportation, the Department of Defense, and the AEC are in this group. When their mission is directly enhanced by environmental quality management, considerably more attention has been devoted and more funds have been spent. Soil-erosion control and other land and water conservation measures in the Department of Agriculture are good examples of this.

Concern over mounting conflicts between federal policies and accelerating environmental deterioration prompted several federal initiatives in the year 1969–70. All were designed to coordinate the many environmental quality agencies and include resource-quality considerations in federal programs. These initiatives include a stronger executive order on air and water pollution, creation of three environmental quality coordinating bodies in the Executive Office of the President, other legal requirements enacted in the National Environmental Policy Act of 1969, the Water Quality Improvement Act of 1970, the Environmental Quality Improvement Act of 1970, and, finally, creation of the Environmental Protection Agency.

Cabinet Committee on the Environment

To coordinate all environmental concerns, President Nixon established, on June 3, 1969, by executive order, the Environmental Quality Council in the Exeutive Office of the President.

The President is chairman, the Vice President is vice chairman. Members include the Secretaries of the Departments of HEW, Agriculture, Commerce, Housing and Urban Development, Interior, and Transportation. Subsequently, the council was renamed the Cabinet Committee on the Environment.

National Environmental Policy Act of 1969

A second three-member Council on Environmental Quality was authorized by Congress in the National Environmental Policy Act of 1969, signed into law January 1, 1970. Members of this second council were appointed by the President and serve as his full-time advisors, similar to the Council of Economic Advisors for economic matters. The Council appraises current and future environmental conditions, assesses federal programs, studies issues assigned it by the President, and recommends new policies.

The 1969 Act of Congress also sets forth a statement of environmental policy. It declares "that it is the continuing policy of the federal government, in cooperation with state and local governments, and other concerned public and private organizations, to use all practicable means and measures, including financial and technical assistance, in a manner calculated to foster and promote general welfare, to create and maintain conditions under which man and nature can exist in productive harmony, and fulfill the social, economic and other requirements of present and future generations of Americans."

In addition to stating a National Environmental Policy that is to apply to all the federal government, the Act set a framework for identifying and managing the conflicts between those federal programs which restore quality and those which promote environmental exploitation. The Act:

1. Called for federal development of methods to insure

that presently unquantified environmental values will be given attention in decision-making along with economic and technical considerations.

2. Required each agency to include in every report or request for legislation and other major actions, a statement on environmental impacts, both long- and short-run, and alternative actions. Such statements were to be preceded by securing comments on this effect from all affected federal agencies, as well as state and local agencies which administer environmental standards.

3. Required each agency to review its present statutory authority, regulations and policies and procedures, and, if any prohibit compliance with the stated policy, propose to the President not later than July 1, 1971, the measures necessary to conform to the policy.

The Council on Environmental Quality was to oversee federal agencies' compliance with these requirements and to prepare an annual Environmental Quality Report for the President which is submitted to Congress.

1970 Executive Order

Then President Nixon issued a new directive, Executive Order 11507, "Prevention, Control and Abatement of Air and Water Pollution at Federal Facilities," on February 4, 1970, which superseded the 1966 presidential directives. The new order strengthened pollution controls at federally owned or leased facilities but made no attempt to cover those federal activities sponsored by loans, contracts, grants, and leases. The order was stronger than previous ones in these ways:

1. It defined the required level of pollution abatement. Federal installations are directed to comply with federal air- and water-quality standards and Atomic Energy Commission radiation requirements. If no federal standards exist, agencies must comply with any regulations that may be issued by the Secretaries of HEW and Interior on air and water pollution (HEW for air and Interior for water pollution). However, agency heads may declare their facilities exempt for national security reasons or "in extraordinary cases where it is in the national interest."

2. It set deadlines. Actions to comply with the standards were to be completed or under way no later than December 31, 1972, to comply with standards or enforcement conference deadlines. However, the Director of the Bureau of the Budget may grant time extensions if the project "is not technically feasible or immediately necessary to meet the requirements (for compliance with federal standards or regulations)."

3. It covered groundwater. Since water-quality standards are set for surface waters only, the order embraces underground waters. However, no specific pollution limits are set.

4. It set requirements for waste-treatment plant operators. They must meet state operator certification requirements or, in the absence of state requirements, guidelines which the Secretaries of HEW and Interior may issue.

5. It required authorization requests for new facilities to include pollution-control costs.

6. It provided that money appropriated for pollution controls cannot be used for any other purpose, avoiding the previous practice of diverting clean-water and clean-air funds to other uses.

7. It required water-resource development projects to be in compliance with standards and regulations. The Bureau of Reclamation, the Department of Agriculture, the Corps of Engineers, the Tennessee Valley Authority, and the United States Section of the International Boundary and Water Commission must secure a statement of the impact of the project on water quality from the Secretary of the Interior and include this view along with requests for project authorization and funding. The Executive Order makes specific for water-resource projects what the National Environmental Policy Act of 1969 required for all federal legislative requests—that a statement of the project's impact on environmental quality be included.

Environmental Quality Act of 1970

On April 3, 1970, the Water Quality Improvement Act of 1970 and the Environmental Quality Improvement Act of 1970 were signed into law. The latter Act created in the Executive Office of the President a third coordinating body, called the Office of Environmental Quality. This Office was intended to be the administrative and professional staff for the new Council on Environmental Quality. The Chairman of the Council is the Director of the Office. Its Deputy Director is appointed by the President and must be confirmed by the Senate, as are the Council members.

The law stated that "there is a national policy for the environment which provides for the enhancement of environmental quality. This policy is evidenced by statutes enacted relating to the prevention, abatement, and control of environmental pollution, water and land resources, transportation, and economic and regional development."

The Environmental Protection Agency

A final step involved substantial reorganization of the federal organizational structure for dealing with environmental problems. The Environmental Protection Agency (EPA) was officially born on December 2, 1970. It consolidated into one agency the major federal programs dealing with air pollution, water pollution, solid-waste disposal, pesticides regulation, and environmental radiation.

The agency made a rapid start. It announced a series of water-pollution enforcement actions within three weeks after its formation. In the following few months it made major moves to implement the Clean Air Act and to cancel pesticide registrations for DDT, aldrin, dieldrin, and Mirex. Internally, EPA quickly organized itself to cope functionally with related environmental programs, which was an important reason for its establishment. Three of five assistant administrators have line responsibility for the major functional areas—planning and management, enforcement, and research and monitoring. A fourth assistant administrator supervises the air and water program offices. And the fifth supervises the pesticide, radiation, and solid-waste programs. EPA's ten regional directors report directly to the administrator.

Although EPA and the Council on Environmental Quality work closely, there are significant differences between the two. The Council is a small staff agency in the Executive Office of the President. Its responsibility is to provide policy advice to the President and to review and coordinate the environmental impact and environmental control activities of all federal agencies. EPA is an operating line agency. Its responsibility is to administer and conduct federal pollution-control programs. While EPA's activities focus on pollution control, the Council's concern is with the whole spectrum of environmental matters, including parks and wilderness preservation, wildlife, natural resources, and land use.

National Oceanic and Atmospheric Administration

The National Oceanic and Atmospheric Administration (NOAA) was the second major organizational innovation of 1970. This new agency, within the Department of Commerce, consolidates the major federal oceanic and atmospheric research and monitoring programs. Both the Weather Bureau and the Coast and Geodetic Survey now operate within NOAA.

The agency monitors the impact of pollutants on the marine environment; describes changes in the oceans, estuaries, and the atmosphere; and establishes ecological base-line data and models.

Future Directions in Federal Environmental Policy

What is apparently emerging, as Andrews (1971) has remarked, is a more unified federal environmental policy that is proceeding along three fronts: control of pollution ("residuals policy"); evaluation and coordination of the impacts of federal programs on environmental quality; and planning for and controlling the uses of environmental resources to protect both developmental and conservation values. Much of this book has focused on the residuals-management aspects of pollution control, although the discussion of planning methodologies was explicitly directed to inclusion of concerns along the

second and third of these fronts. These link, in turn, to the gradual development at the federal level of a national land use policy.

A broadly conceived national land-use policy could help to meet several important needs. Comprehensive planning is needed to account for the uses of public lands and the net impacts of federal actions on the environment of the area where they occur. Steps that have been taken in the latter direction are Budget Circular A-95, which requires that each governor review all federal aid programs to his state; and the National Environmental Policy Act's requirement of environmental impact statements, which must now be included in the A-95 review. What is still needed is a policy to encourage examination of the net impacts of federal actions on an area, rather than merely project-by-project review; to shift the time horizon from the review of present proposals to the coordinated planning of future ones; and to ensure comprehensive planning of the uses of federal lands. A national land-use policy should encourage increased use of natural-process-oriented criteria for planning to supplement the present over-reliance on economic, engineering, and fiscal justifications. Such criteria—nondevelopmental uses of flood plains and steep slopes, protection of watersheds and acquifer recharge areas, and limitation of residuals-producing development to the assimilative capacity of the local environment—have been advocated for well over a decade but have rarely been implemented.

Beyond a natural land-use policy, examination of existing federal policy on the three "fronts" of environmental quality suggests six fundamental needs for future policy action.

In the area of pollution control, the most important need is for *establishment of the principle that individuals or firms should pay the full costs of their residuals.* Achievement of environmental quality, or indeed of any other social objective, is highly unlikely unless the methods that are adopted contribute to straightening out our "societal bookkeeping" by altering the economic incentives responsible for the problem. A specific action that would help is the funding of research on the damages and opportunity costs of residuals discharge to all media in each region.

Second, *flexible tools for residuals management* are needed to replace uniform emission standards, single-medium pollution control laws, and exclusive use of legal penalties as an enforcement mechanism. Important steps in this direction would be congressional action unifying the body of legislation dealing with various media and pollutants into a single systematic code for such management; encouragement of regional management approaches on the part of the Environmental Protection Administration; and enactment by the present Congress of flexible effluent taxes on specific pollutants (such as sulfur and lead) and disposal charges on solid residuals.

Third, legislation to ensure *adequate technology assessment, including* pretesting and evaluation of environmental impacts, is a necessity as increasing economic pressure is brought to bear against known or apparent pollutants. The substitution of NTA for phosphates in detergents, followed by substitution of other synthetic chemicals for NTA, provides only the most obvious example of the dangers of legislating partial solutions (such as banning one pollutant) without adequate assessment and control of potentially more hazardous alternatives. The substitution of highly toxic organic phosphate pesticides for the ecologically damaging chlorinated hydrocarbons such as DDT is another case in point.

Fourth, probably the most critical need in the whole field of environmental policy is for *development and implementation of operational environmental criteria for planning.* Extensive research is needed to determine the values of environmental resources—watersheds, ecosystems, open space, and others—for human health and welfare in both the long and the short run in various degrees of "quality" and to identify the degree to which alternative types of human modification compete with or complement these values. Immediate efforts must be made to spell out in law the best criteria presently known to environmental scientists and planners to ensure that increased use of a multiple-objective framework will enhance the rationality and responsiveness of the planning process rather than merely increase the discretionary power of planning officials.

Fifth, planners and policymakers must transcend the concept of planning as the guidance and structuring of development at the margin and begin to think in terms of *planning for the wisest uses of common property resources,* beginning with those resources that overlap jurisdictional lines, such as public lands, river basins, air sheds, and the coastal zone. Such environmental resource systems are areas of high priority for "problem shed" oriented planning and will also provide important "proving grounds" for development and testing of environmental planning criteria.

Finally, *the access of citizens to the planning processes—at all levels of government—that affect them must be increased.* This is not to say that citizens should personally make every decision. Quite obviously, there are conflicting interests, and very few decisions that modify the environment could obtain a unanimous vote; moreover, the very mechanics of attempting to actively involve citizen groups in every detail of a planning process could lead to chaos. But access must be greatly increased, and planning processes must be made more responsive to citizen priorities and preferences among competing uses of their environments.

UNITED STATES CONGRESS

Any move in the above directions resides in the willingness of the legislative branch, yet the U.S. Congress' approach to environmental quality issues has been as fragmented as that of the Executive Branch. Many committees have jurisdiction over parts of the overall problem.

In the Senate the Committees on Commerce (Merchant Marine and Fisheries subcommittee; and the Energy, Natural Resources and Environmental Subcommittee); Interior and Insular Affairs, Labor and Public Welfare; Government Operations; Finance; Public Works; Agriculture; and Appropriations consider environmental quality programs and sometimes set conflicting or overlapping policies. Some committee actions are geared to exploit resources, others to restore the urban natural environment.

Committees concerned in the House of Representatives are Government Operations (Natural Resources and Power Subcommittee); Interstate and Foreign Commerce; Merchant Marine and Fisheries; Public Works; Science and Astronautics; Interior and Insular Affairs; Agriculture; Banking and Currency; Judiciary; Ways and Means; and Appropriations. Also the Library of Congress' Legislative Reference Service has recently established an Environmental Policy Division to serve members of Congress on environmental issues and legislation.

Some members of Congress have attempted to coordinate their policy interests. In the summer of 1968 a Joint House-Senate Colloquium to discuss a National Policy for the Environment was sponsored by the Senate Committee on Interior and Insular Affairs and the House Committee on Science and Astronautics, with key members of the Public Works Committee attending. The Colloquium was itself recognition of an unwielding structural problem in Congress. From the joint meeting, the National Environmental Policy Act of 1969 emerged from the Senate Committee on Interior and Insular Affairs.

The major issues which continue to come before the Congress may be grouped under the following headings.

Policy analysis. This general category includes: identification and analysis of elements of environmental policy in laws, reports, and statements; comparison of policies for conflict or correlation; implications of policy for day-to-day living; trends in national goals and objectives—that is, quality versus productivity; and strategies for action, funding policy, and development of timetables. Policy related to population, natural resources, and environment has previously followed independent lines which are now converging.

Environmental programs. This category includes: organization and administration of government and other institutions; budgets, economics, and evaluation as to efficiency of action programs; coordination and planning for governmentwide programs. Literally everything we do affects the environment, and there is less thought of centralizing administration of programs than there is of focusing all of government on the future of environmental values.

Pollution. Pollution is interpreted to be contamination of the environment such as to inhibit some desired use. Although some parts of a pristine environment are not necessarily desirable for civilization (including swamps, volcanic emissions, burned forests, eroded soils, and desert dusts), the use of air masses, streams, and landfills as receptacles for the offal of industrial society is now a major congressional concern. Changing the use and discard habits of 150 years to a system of perpetual recycling as required by long-term ecological management is a disruptive process for individuals, municipalities, and corporations.

Agriculture. A variety of rural programs and foreign trade, as well as topics such as food and nutrition, agricultural chemicals, and agricultural wastes are involved. Agriculture may be the most radical ecological disruption perpetrated by man. Its future is now linked in the Malthusian equation to world population.

Urban conservation. The planning of land use, parks and recreation, scenic easements, and zoning are included, as is the control of noise. Major decisions in human ecology are to be made in the city where social psychological perturbations exacerbate the complex problems of plant and animal communities.

International implications. Arbitrary boundaries of local governments and the states necessitate national legislation for resolution of issues, and even larger continentwide limits may be inadequate. The United Nations conference on the human environment in Sweden in 1972 presented the first opportunity for agreements and initiatives in controlling pesticides and air pollutants and in the application of western technology in less-developed countries.

Minerals, fuels, forests, and range. Soil conservation and flood control are not novel, but early conservation measures often dictated the rules by which a continent was systematically harvested. Now we are replacing this legislation with consideration for the very long-term future. Resources are to be recovered perpetually. Fuels must be extracted, transported, and consumed without damage to environmental quality. The resources of food and fiber, air and water must be utilized at a rate which does not irreversibly destroy their restorability by natural processes. The astounding statistic that the western nations plus Japan and Russia account for 27 percent of the world's people but consume about 90 percent of its natural resources is evidence that the developed nations are the greatest threat to the environment.

Wildlife and fisheries, recreation, parks, and aesthetic values. The affluence of Americans has led directly to an appreciation of things money cannot buy. The protection of endangered species has a constituency extending far beyond those who have ever seen a whooping crane. The most immediate problem in our national parks is their preservation from their ardent and careless admirers. Politicians are now joining protest movements against intrusions of highways and industry into recreational areas—a remarkable reversal of the "chamber of commerce" viewpoint prevalent only a few years ago.

Electric power. The regulation of the production of electricity has been based on low cost to the consumer by building a large uniform load for the power plant. The resulting "energy society" now is caught between recurring blackouts (or brownouts) and the environmental consequences of more generators, including the disfiguration of the landscape by high-voltage transmission lines, thermal pollution of surface waters for cooling, air pollution by sulfur oxides and particulate matter, uncertainties of radiation from nuclear power alternatives, and the fundamental question of power-plant site location.

Population. Population is the basis of all issues in environmental quality and productivity. Too many persons are making demands on a finite environment. While the global crisis point looms and fades with temporary agricultural or engineering feats, the more tractable problem of population location and density in this country emerges for consideration. The major corridors of the northeast, Great Lakes, west coast, and Gulf coast are contrasted with the sparsely populated plains and mountains. The establishment of incentives and disincentives, even regulations, for the relocation of American citizens is a novel proposition. Planning for land use on a national scale is beginning to gain congressional acceptance. The fate of the coastal zones and consideration of the optimum use of the 700 million acres still owned by the federal government are important current issues.

THE LAW AND THE ENVIRONMENT

Following the signing into law of the National Environmental Policy Act, unprecedented development of the law relating to protection of the environment has taken place, thus adding to the executive and legislative branches of government the powers of the judiciary. There have followed: court decisions giving force to NEPA and similar federal laws, actions forcing more consideration of environmental factors in federal administrative decisions, stronger federal pollution-control laws, and a host of innovative environmental actions by the states. Together they furnish important evidence that the nation is beginning to institutionalize its concern for the quality of life.

Perhaps the most striking recent legal development has been the step-up in citizen "public interest" litigation to halt degradation of the environment. In the face of a history of administrative devisions that ignored environmental impacts and against a tide of legislative delays in developing pollution-control law, citizens concluded that they must use the courts to cure the neglect. The citizen litigation has not only challenged specific government and private actions which were environmentally undesirable; it has speeded court definition of what is required of federal agencies under environmental protection statutes. The suits have forced greater sensitivity in both government and industry to environmental considerations. And they have educated lawmakers and the public to the need for new environmental legislation.

Citizens in environmental suits have: slowed construction of a road and oil pipeline across the Alaska wilderness by requiring thorough environmental studies; prompted cancellation proceedings against the pesticide DDT; halted construction of an expressway on the banks of the Hudson River; shielded wildlife habitats in Texas and Arizona from development; suspended construction of a Corps of Engineers dam in Arkansas until NEPA was complied with; postponed highway encroachment on Overton Park in Memphis, Tenn., pending review of its necessity; and protected parts of the National Forests until it was decided whether they should be saved as wilderness areas. In this litigation, the courts have broadened the concept of a citizen's right to bring suit and the scope of court review of administrative actions.

A less dramatic development—but perhaps of more long-term significance—has been the trend in government toward tighter systems of environmental regulation. There has come with

it a greater federal recognition of the breadth of the areas needing protection. Already the progress indicates that development of the law may be as important to environmental quality as it has been, for example, to civil rights.

Federal Law

A key trend in federal legislation is the series of provisions—of which NEPA is the broadest and most important—which write environmental interests into federal government decision-making. NEPA laid down the environmental impact statement requirement in section 102(2)(C), later supplemented by guidelines from the Council on Environmental Quality. An agency proposing a major action with significant environmental impact must: describe the impact; study and describe alternatives to its proposal; obtain comments from environmentally expert federal, state, and local agencies; and make public, in advance, its environmental analysis and the comments of other agencies. This process—and the advance public response to these environmental analyses—are making federal agencies far more sensitive to the environment.

Most courts have concluded that the NEPA "102" environmental statement procedure is court enforceable at the suit of interested citizens. This provides a new basis for judicial review of federal administrative action affecting the environment. In the year and a half following enactment of NEPA, there were over twenty reported federal district court decisions involving citizen challenges to federal action under the Act. They involved, for example, federally financed highway projects, Interior Department permits for the Alaska pipeline and its related haul road, and Interior Department contract termination, a Bonneville Administration powerline, Forest Service management of National Forests, Department of Agriculture use of the pesticide Mirex against fire ants, Corps of Engineers water-resource projects, a

Corps of Engineers permit action, a Farmers' Home Administration loan, and a Justice Department grant for a prison facility. Although one decision, arising from a somewhat special set of circumstances, states that NEPA does not impose court-enforceable duties, the great bulk of district court decisions have allowed citizens to enforce the "102" procedure.

In a number of early cases the federal activities challenged had been commenced prior to the enactment of NEPA, and the question arose whether the "102" procedure applied to them. In several instances the courts held that it did, because there remained further major federal actions to which the procedure could be applied. In other instances, courts ruled that the procedure did not apply because all significant federal decisions with respect to the activity were made before NEPA took effect.

Significantly, several district-court NEPA decisions indicate that the courts will do more than just determine whether the required impact statement has been filed. They will also review whether agency compliance with the necessary analytical procedures is adequate. In this review the courts have taken evidence from the plaintiffs on the environmental impact of, and alternatives to, a proposed action. These aspects of NEPA will receive more definitive interpretation as NEPA cases move into the federal appellate courts.

NEPA has a further important effect through its requirement—in section 102(1)—that "the policies, regulations, and public laws of the United States shall be interpreted and administered in accordance with the policies set forth in this Act." That section arms federal agencies with the authority and duty to exercise their powers to promote environmental ends. In a leading case, Zabel v. Tabb, the Corps of Engineers denied a permit, on ecological grounds, to a developer who wished to fill a portion of Florida's Boca Ciega Bay for a trailer park. A federal district court held that the Corps could deny a permit only to protect navigation, which

was the original concern of the permit statute. However, the Court of Appeals for the Fifth Circuit reversed the decision, relying in part on the conclusion that NEPA "essentially states that every Federal agency shall consider ecological factors when dealing with activities which may have an impact on man's environment."

A second key case, Calvert Cliffs, involved Atomic Energy Commission responsibility under NEPA to consider environmental factors beyond radiological health and safety in nuclear plant licensing. Although AEC began applying procedures for considering environmental factors after March 1971, the federal appeals court was not satisfied. It criticized AEC for not implementing such procedures earlier and for the limitations built into them. The court ordered the Commission to conduct an environmental review of the Calvert Cliffs plant already under construction on Chesapeake Bay, for which a license had been granted.

Other agencies now include environmental considerations in exercising their regulatory authority. The Coast Guard now considers land-use and pollution factors when it reviews bridge permit requests. And the Interstate Commerce Commission considers what freight rates for scrap metal will do to the economics of recycling. The Securities and Exchange Commission is moving to require that corporate reports now include environmental information. NEPA also buttresses the President's decision to institute a Corps of Engineers permit program to enforce water-quality standards under the Refuse Act of 1899.

NEPA is the major statutory lever for environmental quality in federal government actions —but it is neither the first nor the only one.

The Congress, more and more in recent years, has enacted environmental protection laws aimed at particular federal programs. Some of these predate NEPA and served as models for its broader directives. All of them apply some safeguard against environmentally adverse decisions in specific programs. And many of the key court decisions to protect environmental values are based on them.

Section 4(f) of the Department of Transportation Act of 1966 broadly protects public parks, wildlife refuges, and historic sites against encroaching federally approved transportation projects. It prohibits such encroachment unless there is no feasible and prudent alternative and unless the project is shaped to minimize harm to the environment. The Supreme Court in *Citizens to Preserve Overton Park* v. *Volpe*, citing the strong congressional policy against encroachment upon parkland expressed in section 4(f), ruled:

> The few green havens that were public parks were not to be lost unless there were truly unusual factors present in a particular case or the cost or community disruption resulting from alternative routes reached extraordinary magnitudes.

The Fish and Wildlife Coordination Act, as amended in 1958, bars water-resource projects undertaken by a Federal Agency, or with a federal permit, from running roughshod over wildlife. It requires that wildlife be given "equal consideration" with other aspects of water-resource development. It further requires that Interior's Fish and Wildlife Service and State widlife agencies be consulted prior to project approval. In its 1970 decision in *Zabel* v. *Tabb* the Court of Appeals for the Fifth Circuit ruled in effect that a federal agency could deny or condition a permit if the action threatened wildlife. The Court observed:

> Common sense and reason dictate that it would be incongruous for Congress, in light of the fact that it intends conservation to be considered in private dredge and fill operations . . . not to direct the only Federal agency concerned with licensing such projects both to consult and to take such factors into account.

The Wilderness Act establishes a National Wilderness Preservation System of Federal lands and legally protects it against inroads.

The Act itself puts certain federal lands within the System and creates a mechanism to review further tracts in the National Forests, National Parks, and National Wildlife Refuges for the same protection. Over 10 million acres have been set aside as wilderness so far. President Nixon has recommended 3 million acres more for congressional approval. In *Parker* v. *United States*, a Federal district court barred the sale of lumber rights in a relatively untouched tract of a National Forest—until a study is completed and the wilderness character of the tract determined.

The Federal Power Act requires the Federal Power Commission to insure that any dam or related project for which it issues a license be adapted to a comprehensive plan which considers commerce, water power, and "other beneficial public uses, including recreational purposes." In *Scenic Hudson Preservation Conference* v. *FPC* local groups challenged licensing of the Storm King powerplant on the Hudson River. They argued that the EPC had failed to consider the plant's impact on the scenic beauty of the river. The Second Circuit Court held that "recreational purposes" includes conservation of natural resources and maintenance of natural beauty. It directed the EPC to reconsider the application with an eye to these factors and to possible alternatives to the project. Two years later, in *Udall* v. *FPC*, the Supreme Court gave the statute the same reading and overturned a license for the High Mountain Sheep Dam on the Snake River—because the FPC failed to consider, among other things, its impact on fish and wildlife and the relative desirability of private and federal development.

Section 1 of the National Park Service Act is another potentially important piece of environmental protection legislation. It requires that park areas be kept "unimpaired" for future enjoyment. The National Historic Preservation Act of 1966 is another. It establishes a register of historic places and requires consultation prior to any federal action potentially damaging to them. The Multiple Use-Sustained Yield Act of 1960 is still another. It directs the Forest Service to combine environmental and economic purposes in administering the National Forests.

A growing number of other environmental protection provisions have yet to go before the courts. The most recent are: section 136 of the Federal-Aid Highway Act of 1970, requiring that final decisions on federal-aid highway projects reflect environmental factors to be outlined by the Secretary of Transportation; section 16(c)(4) of the Airport and Airway Development Act, prohibiting federal approval of airport projects that hurt the environment except under stringent conditions; and section 14 of the Urban Mass Transportation Act of 1964, as amended, requiring a detailed statement of environmental impact plus public hearings prior to project approval.

The court decisions on environmental protection legislation have had and will have a much more lasting impact than merely clarifying particular legislation. *Scenic Hudson*, by placing a positive responsibility on the FPC to consider less environmentally damaging alternatives, laid a foundation for the obligation to develop alternatives imposed by NEPA. *Overton Park, Parker, Zabel* v. *Tabb, Scenic Hudson*, and *Udall* v. *FPC* confirm that courts will apply congressional expressions of environmental policy to overturn agency actions when environmental values are not adequately considered or, conversely, to uphold agency authority to take action based on these values.

Federal Pollution Control—
New Legal Techniques

New legal techniques of pollution control have accompanied tighter federal pollution-control standards. The Congress has authorized the federal government to set national standards of its own for ambient air quality and for certain emissions—moving away from the former approach in which states set standards based on federal criteria. New provisions in the air-pollution laws and other proposed pollution-control legislation signal a change in the burden of proof. Now those discharging certain materials into the environment will be required to show that their actions will not be harmful; formerly the government had to prove the danger after the fact. Federal air- and water-quality laws have been changed to place new legal restrictions on pollution from federal facilities. New legislation now permits citizens to augment government enforcement by suing polluters in federal court if they do not meet federal-state air-quality standards. Finally, the federal government is strongly backing international efforts to control marine pollution.

Citizen Checks on Agency Action

The ability of citizens and citizen groups to make their views known and to participate in government decision-making on the environment is critically important. Often individuals and groups can contribute data and insights beyond the expertise of the agency involved. In some cases, citizen groups are seeking—and making—significant changes in agency policy.

There has been a marked expansion in citizen rights to know about, to participate in, and ultimately to challenge federal agency actions, particularly those affecting the environment. This new citizen's role has evolved in many different forums. The courts have contributed—through new interpretations of such existing laws as the Freedom of Information Act and the Administrative Procedure Act. And a variety of administrative agencies have instituted procedural changes to implement NEPA.

The new openness to citizen involvement is bound to check, stimulate, and test future federal agency activities. Citizen concern cannot substitute for assumption of environmental responsibilities by government and industry.

Nor can it provide the mechanism to resolve the many policy issues involved. What it can provide, however, is quality control and "feedback."

The citizen's right to know. The Freedom of Information Act, passed in 1966, predates the upwelling of citizen environmental action. It laid down a general rule that all agency data must be available to the public, with certain exceptions, and is basic, therefore, to public availability of environmental data. The exception most likely to enter into environmental controversies permits agencies to refuse to disclose any internal papers with opinions or advice on matters of policy. But in a decision on whether the public could see a scientific report on the SST, a U.S. court of appeals held that the exemption does not protect "purely factual or investigatory reports." Factual information is exempted "only if it is inextricably intertwined with policy-making processes." Read thus, the Act should open to the public factual studies and analyses of environmental impact statements, as well as the statements themselves.

NEPA recognizes the importance of public access as a force for corrective action. It does so by requiring public availability of environmental impact statements and of agency comments, regardless of whether they contain advice on matters of policy. An Executive Order and the guidelines issued by the Council on Environmental Quality have both implemented this policy. Executive Order 11514, of March 5, 1970, directs federal agencies to maximize public information about environmentally significant programs so that the public's views can be considered. The Council guidelines generally require that draft and final environmental impact statements be available to the public for minimum periods of 90 and 30 days, respectively, before the agency acts. The guidelines also require that draft statements be made public at least 15 days before hearings. As described in Chapter 1, various channels of distribution are being set up to make the environmental impact statements and agency comments more easily available to the public.

Section 309 of the Clean Air Act, added in 1970, gives the public an additional right to information on the environmental aspects of federal action. It requires the Adminstrator of EPA to comment on any proposed legislation, regulation, or agency action affecting air or water quality, pesticides, solid-waste disposal, radiation, or noise control. These comments must be publicly available in writing at the end of EPA's review.

Together, these legal provisions greatly expand the citizen's right to the environmental information on which proposed government actions are based. Opening the decision-making process to public scrutiny should help insure that actions not responsive to the national environmental goals set in NEPA receive timely attention.

The citizen's right to participate. Citizens and citizen groups have obtained ever-increasing rights and opportunities to participate meaningfully in federal agency decision-making. The extent of participation varies considerably, depending chiefly on whether the agency determination is made formally or informally. Formal procedures are prescribed by the Administrative Procedure Act (APA) and by similar provisions in other acts. A wide variety of government decisions are made informally, without legislatively set procedures.

NEPA has enhanced the citizen's possible role, whether or not statutory formalities apply to the agency action. It ensures more detailed and easily available notice to citizens of environmental issues. It permits the public to focus on the agency's environmental findings and conclusions through the environmental impact statement.

Formal proceedings under the APA. The Administrative Procedure Act defines and prescribes procedures for two types of formal agency proceedings: adjudications and rule-making. An adjudication is a formal process in which the agency's decision must be made on the record of a hearing similar to a trial. Parties to the proceeding are allowed to submit evidence, rebut opposing evidence, and cross-examine opposing witnesses. Examples of agency adjudications are: the assessment by the Coast Guard of a civil penalty against a person who knowingly discharges oil into U.S. navigable waters, contrary to the Federal Water Pollution Control Act, and the refusal by the Environmental Protection Agency to register a new pesticide for a particular use under the pesticide laws. The agency must provide a statement of "findings and conclusions, and the reasons or basis therefore," on all issues involved. The decision can be reviewed and set aside by a court if the record does not contain substantial evidence to support it.

The public's right to participate in adjudications has received wide recognition. The APA leaves the agencies free to decide who may participate in the proceedings. Initially, agencies limited participation to persons who would be the direct objects of the agency action or regulation. Spurred by a 1966 landmark Federal circuit court decision in *Church of Christ* v. *FCC*, emphasizing agency obligations to take cognizance of a wider spectrum of public interests, the agencies that conduct APA adjudications have, by and large, considerably expanded public participation.

Rule-making is the agency process for formulating, amending, or repealing a rule. It involves major federal regulation, such as EPA's setting air- and water-quality standards. Because of the broad and pervasive nature of rule-making, participation in developing agency rules is a key opportunity for citizen input into government decisions.

The APA requires an agency generally to give advance notice of rule-making in the *Federal Register*. Then the agency must allow 30 or more days between the notice and adoption of a rule. During this time, any interested person may "participate in the rule-making through submission of written data, views, or arguments." The agency may hold an informational hearing but need not unless required by another statute. An interested person does not have to depend on the agency to initiate action. He may "petition for the issuance, amendment, or repeal of a rule." An agency's failure to act on such a petition is an "agency action" reviewable in court.

When an adjudication or a rule-making falls within section 102(2)(C)'s requirement for an environmental impact statement, NEPA strengthens the citizen's right to present relevant environmental information to the agency. It has also increased the amount of detailed environmental information that must be included in the advance notice.

Determinations made informally. Thousands of federal agency determinations take place without the formalities of adjudications or rule-making. These include the day-to-day decisions of a federal agency as well as performance of specific duties—such as consulting under the National Historic Preservation Act of 1966. The APA does not specify procedures for these decisions but merely provides for court review. Generally no law requires a public hearing, but in some instances agencies hold an informational hearing on their own initiative.

When a hearing is held, citizens may object and make suggestions. For example, an interested person may testify at the public hearings held by the Corps of Engineers for proposed water-resource projects. Agency practices, however, are not yet uniform in notifying the public of hearings.

Traditionally, citizens have had little voice in the innumerable decisions made by agencies without public hearings. In the past, Defense Department decisions on the ocean disposal of surplus munitions and many Interior Department decisions to grant mineral leases on federal lands have been made without public notice and without any means, other than by letter, for citizens to be heard.

NEPA's requirements are particularly important in informal agency decisions. Without APA proceedings or other public hearings, the environmental impact statement is the only way the public can learn of an impending action —or of the environmental issues raised. Even more important, NEPA and the Council's revised guidelines require agencies, when appropriate, to consider the comments of citizens as well as those of government agencies. Another effect of NEPA and the Executive Order which implements it is its influence on agencies to hold hearings when they would not otherwise have done so.

The citizen's right to challenge in court. One of the most striking and significant developments in environmental law is the right of citizens to take to court federal agency actions affecting the environment. NEPA and other laws require agencies to consider the environment in their actions. And citizens are now initiating lawsuits when they believe an agency has failed to do that.

The citizen's success in challenging an agency decision depends in part on a number of legal doctrines that determine the citizen's standing to bring suit. They regulate the extent to which a court may review an agency decision. They determine the evidence the court may consider beyond that developed by the agency. And they dictate whether the plaintiff must participate in the agency decision before seeking court review. Citizen suits to protect the environment are bringing evolution in all of these doctrines.

Standing. Citizens do not automatically have standing to seek review of agency decisions in court. In the past, lack of standing has been a significant impediment to a citizen's right to challenge federal agency actions. The law generally allows only persons who are "aggrieved" by agency action to seek court review. Several court review provisions give standing to "aggrieved" persons, and despite earlier uncertainty, the courts have concluded that the APA permits "aggrieved" persons to seek review of agency actions in almost every case in which a specific review provision is lacking.

The Supreme Court, in *Data Processing Service* v. *Camp*, recently held that to be "aggrieved," a person must have suffered "injury in fact" from the agency action, and the interest he seeks to assert must be an interest intended to be protected by the specific statute invoked. Environmental plaintiffs have usually been successful in meeting both requirements.

In *Data Processing*, the Court did not clearly define "injury in fact." But it did stress that the injury need not be economic but may be "aesthetic, conservational or recreational." This may mean that any responsible citizen or group may sue to protect an environmental resource, such as a recreational area, that exists for the benefit of the public.

Three U.S. Courts of Appeals, for the Second, Fourth, and District of Columbia Circuits, seem to have reached this conclusion. The Second Circuit concluded "that the public interest in environmental resources ... is a legally protected interest affording these [environmental groups] ... standing to obtain judicial review of agency action ..." on the other hand, the Ninth Circuit, in *Sierra Club* v. *Morton* (known as the *Mineral King* case), refused to permit the Sierra Club to sue to protect Sequoia National Park. It did so because neither the Club nor its members had property threatened by the action and the Club's status as an organization was not threatened. In a later decision, the Ninth Circuit refused to permit an environmental group to sue to protect San Francisco Bay on the same grounds. The court, however, did permit individual members of the organization to stay in the suit. The conflict between the courts of appeals will be resolved when the Supreme Court reviews the *Mineral King* case.

The Ninth Circuit's rule that citizen groups lack a sufficient interest to sue to enforce environmental laws threatens to leave such enforcement exclusively to government—whose actions may on occasion conflict with those laws. As the Federal District Court for Alaska has noted, denying citizen groups standing to raise environmental issues "would have the practical effect of preempting many meritorious actions, as one individual, or a small number of individuals, would have to sustain the entire financial burden of the lawsuit." The costs of effective litigation are so high that "few members of the general public will have resources or courage to face such odds for the sake of vindicating a right to which all are entitled as a matter of law."

Because environmental lawsuits are usually brought under statutes clearly intended to protect environmental values, they easily meet the protected-interest test of *Data Processing*. Citizen groups have sucessfully won standing not only under NEPA but also under the Federal Power Act, the Department of Transportation Act, the Multiple Use-Sustained Yield Act, the Wilderness Act, and federal pesticide laws. Court decisions under NEPA, which has a broadly stated environmental purpose, indicate that virtually any environmental interest falls within the protection of that Act.

Court review of agency decisions. The courts do not hesitate to review questions of law decided by federal agencies. But traditionally they have deferred to the agency for determinations of fact. As a general rule, particularly for informal decisions, the courts overturn agency "factual" findings only if they are "arbitrary or capricious." This rule makes it primarily the agencies' job to find the basic, objective facts.

Interpreting facts is a subjective process, however. And an agency's "factual" conclusions may involve weighing environmental values

against other policies important to the agency. Recognizing this, the courts have recently begun to broaden the meaning of "arbitrary or capricious." It now includes agency decisions that disregard the policies of environmental laws.

In *Overton Park*, the Supreme Court confirmed this recent trend to give greater bite to review under the arbitrary-or-capricious test. Such review "is to be searching and careful," and action should be reversed when "there has been a clear error of judgment." Although the Court also gave the reassurance that the reviewing court "is not empowered to substitute its judgment for that of the agency," its discussion indicated that court review of the facts will be exacting.

Evidence outside the agency record. In reviewing an agency's adjudication or formal rule-making, the courts are required to decide whether the agency record supports the agency action. If it does not, the action is set aside. If the agency failed to consider relevant factors, the court directs it to consider evidence and then to make a new decision. The citizen is not, however, allowed to present new evidence to the court to discredit the agency's decision.

An agency decision made without formal APA proceedings may be backed by little or no written record to explain it. So unless the court receives some evidence, it has little against which to test the agency's action. By prodding the agency to make a more complete record and by permitting the citizen to submit his own evidence, the courts are making citizen review more effective.

In *Overton Park*, the Court said that in reviewing informal agency decisions, courts must examine the "full administrative record" on which the agency acted. They cannot be satisfied with after-the-fact "rationalizations" alone. When the record does not disclose all the factors considered, the reviewing court may require the responsible officials to explain their action. The agencies thus are encouraged to produce thorough, contemporaneous written records backing their decisions.

The Supreme Court did not discuss the extent to which a plaintiff may submit his own evidence to discredit an agency action. However, in cases under NEPA the lower courts have freely admitted evidence bearing on the legality of action under the Act. For example, evidence was admitted in *Environmental Defense Fund, Inc.* v. *Corps of Engineers* to show the inadequacy of the Corps' section 102 statement in considering the danger posed for the environment by the Billham Dam project. In the recent Mirex case, the court received evidence on the fire-ant situation and determined that the Department of Agriculture's environmental study was adequate. Similarly, in *Parker* v. *United States*, the court heard evidence to show that an area was protected by the Wilderness Act until a study of its wilderness character was finished. Further litigation will define the limits of the citizen's right to introduce evidence that was not considered by the agency.

Exhaustion of administrative remedies. The citizen's expanded right to challenge federal agency decisions in court complements his right to participate in agency decisions; together, they give him a new role in shaping the environmental impact of government activity. However, the citizen may not always be free to choose the stage at which to interject his views. Generally, one who foregoes an opportunity to make his claims before an agency cannot later go into court, because he failed to "exhaust administrative remedies."

The reason for this rule is that failure to object to the agency initially deprives it of the chance to consider the objections and perhaps modify its action without judicial intervention. The exhaustion rule supports the form of decision-making created by the Congress. By permitting the agency to make a factual record, it also promotes more effective judicial review.

The exhaustion requirement applies primarily when the agency has followed formal procedures allowing for citizen participation. However, it may apply more and more to informal decisions now that citizens receive notice and can participate. An example is the recent decision in *Sierra Club* v. *Hardin*. There the Sierra Club challenged a Forest Service timber sale in the Tongass National Forest. Although it knew of the impending timber sale, the Club did not invoke Forest Service procedures for protest and review, and the court therefore refused to consider its claims. Similarly, the Audubon Society was foreclosed from challenging Corps of Engineers permits for dredging in Texas waters because it did not show that it had objected to the appropriate agencies first.

STATE AND LOCAL ACTIVITIES

States and their political subdivisions have traditionally played the lead role in environmental protection. They have led both in curbing pollution and in controlling land use. Even now, with the more direct federal involvement in environmental protection, states continue to play a vital role. State and local governments remain on the front line of essential planning, management, and enforcement.

In many instances the states serve as experimental laboratories for a variety of solutions to common problems. State innovation frequently sets a precedent for federal action. For example, California's automotive emission laws, born of acute smog in the Los Angeles basin, set the stage for the National Emission Standards Act of 1965.

Wisconsin's ban on DDT was a harbinger of similar federal action, commenced in 1969 and expanded in 1971, to cover all uses of DDT. Permit systems for pesticide use in California, Florida, Maryland, and New York established a precedent for the President's proposals for federal regulation of pesticide use.

Even organizational reform at the federal level, such as the creation of the Environmental

Protection Agency (EPA), also finds precedent at the state level. In 1967 Minnesota created a consolidated Pollution Control Agency. That same year Wisconsin formed an environmental "super department" putting resource-management and pollution-control activities under a single wing. Through creative new state approaches and national acceptance of the most successful, the federal system has profited.

Further, federal legislation is putting more and more responsibility at the state level in order to encourage comprehensive, regional efforts. For instance, the federal water-quality program traditionally has focused on the states. State responsibility for air quality has been increased by the 1970 Amendments to the Clean Air Act. Finally, in land-use regulation, long the almost exclusive province of local governments, there is widespread agreement that increased state involvement is the key to more effective controls.

Pollution Control

Many states have tightened pollution-control standards or expanded their coverage to new pollutants or activities. Many have intensified antipollution enforcement.

Inadequate data on state enforcement activities make it difficult to compare their volume or effectiveness. However, public clamor for action against violators of pollution-control standards has highlighted the weaknesses of many existing state enforcement authorities and prodded states to develop new and better mechanisms.

Air quality. A vivid example of limited enforcement authority occurred in Alabama. In July 1970 the federal government denied the state's request for financial aid for its air-quality program because the State Air Pollution Control Act failed to meet minimum requirements for such aid. Inadequate enforcement provisions were the basic reason. Then, in April 1971, after a five-day air-pollution "episode" in Birmingham, the Alabama Attorney General

filed a suit under the state's public nuisance law against thirteen major industrial companies requesting that they be given a six-month deadline to abate their pollution. The Attorney General stated that the Alabama Air Pollution Control Act could not have been invoked, since it set no applicable standards.

Residential fuel burners and incinerators. New York City's ordinance regulating the use of fuel burners and refuse incinerators in multiple dwellings was upheld by the state's highest court in November. It was challenged by more than 400 apartment-house owners. The New York City Administrative Code requires the Air Pollution Commissioner to issue operating certificates for fuel burners and incinerators. Owners must conduct such tests as the Commissioner finds necessary to determine whether the equipment meets the new standards. The law sets standards for sulfur content of fuel and requires owners to install sulfur-emission monitoring and recording devices. Once compliance dates have passed, the Commission is empowered to seal any equipment lacking a permit or emitting harmful substances. Following the court decision, the city promptly set deadlines for plans to upgrade substandard facilities. It also warned that it would use the law's enforcement authority in cases of non-compliance.

Auto emissions. Under the Federal Clean Air Act, state and local governments retain authority to regulate pollution from automobiles in use. But authority to regulate emissions from new motor vehicles is reserved to the federal government. California is an exception. Under section 209(a) of the Federal Clean Air Act, California is eligible for a waiver from EPA permitting it to establish emission standards for new motor vehicles stiffer than federal standards if needed to meet "compelling and extraordinary conditions" in that state. California, whose regulation of automotive emissions established the precedent for present federal law, has obtained several waivers since the federal law was enacted in 1965. In 1971 waivers were granted by EPA for emission standards and test procedures for various classes of vehicles in the 1972, 1973, and 1975 model years.

Indirect pollution controls. In some cases, pollution control requirements may be imposed indirectly, rather than through standards. For example, the Illinois Public Utility Commission, at the urging of the state attorney general, granted a rate increase to a large electric utility, Commonwealth Edison, on the condition that the utility take several specific pollution-abatement actions. If Commonwealth Edison fails to take the actions within the allotted time, the state may reduce the rate increase 50 percent. This is believed to be the first rate regulation in the nation to contain explicit and extensive environmental quality requirements. The requirements call for the utility to convert to cleaner fuels to protect air quality and to install cooling facilities to prevent thermal water pollution.

Water quality. Representatives of the numerous federal, state, and interstate authorities with water-pollution control enforcement responsibilities in the New York City metropolitan area have agreed to pool information and to coordinate enforcement and monitoring. This elementary step should enhance enforcement efforts, which have been hampered by fragmentated data and responsibilities.

Illinois has comprehensive legislative authority for water-pollution control enforcement. For example, the new State Environmental Protection Act permits the Illinois Pollution Control Board to force any municipality or sanitary district that has been ordered to abate water pollution to issue general obligation or revenue bonds to finance the needed treatment facilities. This provision is designed to overcome lack of funds and debt-limit problems that forestall construction of necessary sewage-treatment works in many communities.

California has also been active in water-quality enforcement. The state's new Water Quality Control Act, which took effect on January 1, 1970, sets up an arsenal of enforcement powers, including strict fines—up to $6,000 a day—against polluters. Enforcement has been vigorous, with more than one hundred direct enforcement actions taken and many waste-discharge requirements strengthened.

Phosphates. At both the state and local levels, one of the most publicized regulatory activities of the past year was enactment of restrictions on phosphate content of detergents. Cities and counties in Florida, Illinois, Maine, Maryland, Michigan, New York, Ohio, and Wisconsin have acted to limit phosphates in detergents. Several of these laws have been challenged in court by detergent manufacturers.

Solid waste. Regulation of solid-waste management practices, other than for public health protection, remains rudimentary. However, statewide and regional solid-waste planning is on the rise and is leading to increased regulatory activity—such as prohibitions against open dumps and controls over landfill practices.

In New Jersey, the Department of Environmental Protection was empowered to register all solid-waste disposal operations, to formulate a statewide waste-management plan, and to encourage regional action. It was also empowered to build disposal facilities on an experimental basis. The state plan, recently issued by the Department, recommends incineration and landfill districts.

A new Kansas law calls for limited state regulation of solid-waste management. It creates a Solid Waste Advisory Council to recommend ways to finance solid-waste systems and standards to govern the operation of disposal facilities. North Carolina has armed its State Board of Health with new solid-wastes research, standard-setting, and inspection responsibilities.

The Solid Waste Disposal Act demands that state solid-waste management plans funded under the Act include an inventory of waste-disposal facilities and a survey of problems and practices. Under the 1970 Amendments, provision for recycling or recovery of materials from waste must be included whenever possible.

Litter. Oregon passed legislation dealing with another public-arousing problem—litter by beverage containers. The Oregon law requires a deposit on all beer and soft-drink containers, 5 cents on standard-sized bottles and cans and 2 cents on small beer bottles. It also bans detachable tabs on metal cans. The law took effect in October 1972. Over forty states are considering similar legislation. In the November 1970 elections a mandatory deposit was defeated in the state of Washington. Several years ago Vermont prohibited nonreturnable beer bottles, a measure that was rendered ineffective and later abandoned after the advent of beer cans.

Noise. Comprehensive noise-pollution control is an area of increasing state and local regulatory activity. Although there are an estimated 1,500 to 2,000 state and local noise-control laws, many are limited or unenforceable. However, concern and activity in this area have been renewed. Florida recently enacted legislation authorizing its Department of Air and Water Pollution Control to establish noise standards. North Dakota has taken similar action.

In March 1971 Chicago adopted a comprehensive noise-control ordinance, which became effective on July 1. Under the ordinance, manufacturers must certify that specified types of vehicles and equipment, including construction equipment, sold in the city meet prescribed noise-emission standards. Vehicle users are also subject to noise limitations. Noise from buildings and certain noise-generating activities are also regulated.

Chicago has come up with a unique method of enforcing its new noise standards. Mobile teams, equipped with portable sound meters, will cruise the city "listening" for violations and ticketing violators.

Radiation. Legal uncertainty shrouds the future of state regulation of radioactive emis-

sions from nuclear power plants. Opinions by a federal district court in Minnesota and by the Illinois Pollution Control Board reached opposite conclusions on whether states are preempted by federal law from regulating such emissions. The federal district court held that federal radiation-control authority precludes state regulation. The Illinois Board ruled just the opposite, contending that when public health and safety—traditional state concerns—are involved, a congressional intent to foreclose state regulation must be very explicit. The Board found such an intent to be lacking in the Atomic Energy Act. The ultimate outcome of the two cases, both of which are now on appeal, will significantly influence the future of state nuclear powerplant regulation.

Reorganization

States, like the federal government, have reorganized themselves to cope with the environment. The trend toward consolidation of state pollution control programs, beginning in the late 1960s, has taken a variety of forms. The examples discussed are representative although not necessarily typical.

Prior to the reorganizations discussed below, environmental programs in most states were—and in many other states still are—scattered among several agencies, boards, and commissions. Boards and commissions, manned by government agency representatives, citizens, special-interest groups, or all of these, usually wielded considerable influence in setting pollution-control policy. Often these entities exercised powers independent of the governor, and special-interest groups sometimes dominated them.

Implementing board-established policy was generally left to one or more agencies. Most often, a state health department contained one or more units responsible for air- and water-pollution control. In some cases the water-pollution control program was lodged in a separate agency or combined with other water programs, such as water resources management. The state solid-waste management program, if any, was usually under a health department arm. Pesticides regulation was a function of the health or agriculture departments—or both. State park, recreation, fish and wildlife, and other resource programs were sometimes grouped together or were sometimes totally separate.

New York. By a statute enacted on Earth Day 1970, and effective July 1, 1970, New York State transferred most of its pollution-control and resource-management programs—the air, water, and pesticides control programs and the water resource, forest, fish and wildlife, and marine and mineral management programs— to a new Department of Environmental Conservation (DEC). Solid-waste disposal regulation, land-use planning, and noise-pollution control were also put under the Department's general purview, and it is expected that DEC will seek more specific statutory authority in these areas.

DEC is empowered to develop a statewide environmental plan and a statement of goals and strategies, to review all state agency programs affecting the environment, and to formulate guidelines for measuring the environmental values and relationships involved.

Internally, DEC is basically divided into an environmental quality (pollution-control) section and an environmental management (resource-management) section.

The act creating the DEC also created a State Environmental Board—made up of citizens and representatives of state agencies—and a citizen Council of Environmental Advisors. The Board, which replaces interagency air and pesticides boards and the Water Resources Commission, will advise the DEC Commissioner. It has veto power over environmental standards, criteria, rules, and regulations proposed by the Commissioner. The citizen Council is an advisory

body to the governor on broad environmental policy. It has specific responsibility for developing guidelines on environmental quality and economic and population growth.

Washington. The state of Washington in 1970 enacted legislation—less extensive in scope than the New York law—which consolidates environmental protection programs under a Department of Ecology (DOE). Created on July 1, 1970, DOE resulted from an across-the-board effort in the state to overhaul government structures and make them more responsive to the governor, the legislature, and the public.

DOE consolidates the water- and air-quality, solid-waste management, and water-resource programs. In contrast to New York's DEC, DOE does not incorporate other resource-management programs. Although the department is basically a pollution-control agency, programs such as pesticide control and drinking-water quality remain with the Agriculture and Social and Health Services Departments, respectively.

As in some other states that have reorganized environmental programs, a key objective was to create a strong environmental executive directly accountable to the governor while limiting the number and authority of special-interest and interagency boards and commissions that have been a hallmark of state environmental management.

Preexisting citizen or interagency boards such as the Water Resources Advisory Council and the Air Pollution Control Board gave way to an Ecological Commission to advise the DOE director. All nonprocedural rules and regulations proposed by the Director of DOE are reviewed by the Commission. The Commission has veto power over such proposals if five of its seven members disapprove.

The third element in Washington's new pollution control structure is a three-member quasi-judicial Pollution Control Hearings Board. It hears appeals from decisions of the

DOE and of local air-pollution control authorities.

One of the most significant aspects of DOE is its internal structure according to functions, such as standard setting and planning. There is no separate air-quality, water-quality, water-resource, or solid-waste component. Instead, there are two functional branches—one for administration and planning and one for public services.

Illinois. Probably the most innovative state reorganization program was adopted in Illinois. The Illinois Environmental Protection Act of 1970 transferred preexisting authorities and programs and added some new ones to three new functional entities. Resource-management programs were not affected. The Pollution Control Board (PCB) sets standards and adjudicates enforcement proceedings. The State Environmental Protection Agency (EPA) identifies and prosecutes alleged violators before the Board, issues permits, and gives technical assistance. The Institute for Environmental Quality (IEQ) conducts long-range policy planning and applied research.

Pollution-control programs—air quality, water quality, radiation control, and "land pollution control" (solid wastes)—thus were divided among three organizations. This is an atypical response to common problems that have led various other states to reorganize.

The Illinois reorganizers saw many difficulties. The State Department of Public Health (DPH) overadvised and overconsulted with polluters instead of regulating and prosecuting them. Part-time standard-setting boards—such as the Air Pollution Control Board and the Sanitary Water Board—were ineffective; they met infrequently, and some members were associated with polluting constituencies. The air-and water-quality boards were separate. Finally, the pollution-control units within DPH had to compete with other important DPH interests for money.

The framers of the Illinois reorganization plan were guided by principles in large measure different from those followed by other states. First, rather than eliminating or reducing the role of the policymaking board, Illinois professionalized it by giving it a full-time membership with staff. It also gave the board sharply defined authority for standard setting and policy development.

Second, Illinois acted upon the theory that some functions, such as prosecution and adjudication, conflict, or at least compete unfavorably, if administered by a single agency. The state also felt that long-range research and planning inevitably suffered when forced to compete for funds within an agency that must respond primarily to immediate crises and pressures. Hence, it created the independent IEQ.

Third, the Illinois approach is grounded in the belief that some duplication of responsibilities promotes a healthy competition that will maximize action against pollution. It assumes that interacting and overlapping organizations, with an involved citizenry, will "check and balance" inadequate or arbitrary action by any one organization. The Illinois Environmental Protection Agency, the Attorney General, and any private citizen all have authority to initiate enforcement proceedings. And citizens as well as the state EPA and IEQ may initiate standard-setting proceedings.

Reorganization of environmental programs such as those in New York, Washington, and Illinois, especially when linked to an expansion or streamlining of pollution-control authority, should significantly accelerate substantive progress at the state level. The varying approaches to reorganization—consolidation versus separation of functions and competitive overlap; pollution control alone versus a combination of pollution control and resource management; internal functionalization versus pollutant or media orientation—all will lend valuable comparative experience for future refinement of environmental management efforts.

STATE LAW

State governments also have responded to environmental problems with a variety of legal innovations.

Constitutional Changes

Constitutional amendments are a fundamental form of expression of legal policy. A number of states have added environmental protection provisions to their constitutions; other states are considering doing so. Some state constitutions already contain provisions dealing with conservation of natural resources. However, recent proposals focus on the individual's right to environmental protection and raise the possiblity of increased resort to the courts to vindicate that right.

New York's constitutional amendment, effective January 1, 1970, was one of the first changes. Popularly called the "Conservation Bill of Rights," it declares a state policy "to conserve and protect its natural resources and scenic beauty." It directs the state legislature to act to carry out that policy. The amendment addresses legislative responsibility more than individual rights, but another provision of the state constitution permits citizen suits to restrain its violation.

A constitutional provision adopted by the Illinois electorate in December 1970 is more directly oriented toward individual rights and obligations. Besides declaring a state policy to protect the environment, it provides that "[e]ach person has the right to a healthful environment." The Illinois amendment authorizes every person to sue to enforce this right against "any party, governmental or private." The right is subject to reasonable limitation and regulation by the state legislature.

Pennsylvania's and Rhode Island's new constitutional amendments also declare environmental "rights" in the people, but they do not expressly authorize private suits. Amendments of these several types are under consideration in a number of other states.

Experience under these state constitutional amendments is still too short to determine how well they work to protect the environment. It is unclear whether the New York amendment was intended to be enforceable by private citizens or merely a declaration of policy to be implemented by the legislature. Even where direct private enforcement is clearly contemplated, as in Illinois, the courts may take years to define the constitutionally protected rights. Despite these difficulties, support appears to be growing for writing environmental guarantees into state charters.

Environmental Statements for State Agency Actions

Since enactment of NEPA, a number of state legislatures have passed "action forcing" requirements similar to NEPA's environmental impact-statement requirement. At least four state legislatures and the Commonwealth of Puerto Rico have established such procedures.

In June 1970 the Commonwealth of Puerto Rico enacted a law directing agencies to consider the environment in their actions. It created an environmental statement procedure identical to NEPA's. The law also creates in the Governor's Office an Environmental Quality Board, which has both policymaking and regulatory authority over air and water pollution, solid-waste disposal, and other environmental problems. The law also authorizes citizen suits for violation of its regulatory provisions.

Montana enacted legislation in March 1971 that adopts the environmental statement procedure of NEPA and creates a State Environmental Quality Council. The Montana Council's role differs from that of either the Federal Council or the Puerto Rican body. Its thirteen members include the Governor or his representative, four gubernatorial appointees, and four members of each house of the state legislature. It thus serves as a joint arm of the executive and legislative branches to review and formulate state environmental policy. Legislation derived from NEPA has also been enacted in California, Washington, and Delaware and is under consideration elsewhere.

State government activities, no less than federal, have far-reaching, often unanticipated, environmental impacts. The recent state statutes are new efforts to control those consequences. Other states may be expected to make similar efforts—either by adopting the environmental statement mechanism or by developing new and as yet untried procedures.

Citizen-Suit Legislation

State legislatures, like the U.S. Congress, have moved to bolster the citizen's right to challenge activities detrimental to the environment in court. The Michigan Environmental Protection Act of 1970 is one of the most publicized of these measures. It authorizes any private or public entity to sue any other private or public entity for equitable relief from "pollution, impairment or destruction" of the "air, water, and other natural resources and the public trust therein."

Like section 304 of the Federal Clean Air Act, the Michigan Act eliminates the defenses of lack of standing and sovereign immunity. However, although the federal law provides a mechanism for private citizens to enforce antipollution standards established by government agencies, the Michigan statute takes a different approach. It directs state courts to develop a common law of environmental degradation through case-by-case definition of "pollution, impairment or destruction of the environment." Antipollution standards fixed by state agencies can be challenged. If found deficient, they may be replaced by a court-ordered substitute.

Both the Michigan Act and section 304 of the Federal Clean Air Act affirm the importance of the citizen's role before the courts. However, the Michigan Act transfers to the courts much of the standard-setting authority traditionally exercised by the other two branches of government. It thus places this authority in the branch most insulated from the elective process. In contrast, the federal provision reaffirms the role of Congress and the executive in setting standards and enlists the citizen's aid in enforcing those standards.

Legislation similar to the Michigan Act was passed recently in Connecticut. New citizen-suit statutes in Indiana and Minnesota, like the federal provision, direct the courts to look to the antipollution standards adopted by state agencies.

Invoking Nuisance Law

All states maintain programs to control air and water pollution under the Federal Clean Air Act and Water Pollution Control Act. Yet many continue to provide alternative pollution-control remedies under older, court-evoked, common-law doctrines. One of these, the law of public nuisance, has been used more and more as an antipollution tool. A public nuisance is generally defined as conduct causing "an unreasonable interference with a right common to the general public." It may be enjoined in a suit by state authorities or, in some cases, by private citizens.

Public-nuisance law arms state officials with an enforcement tool free of cumbersome pollution-control procedures. But it has certain shortcomings that limit its effectiveness. Because the concept of public nuisance is general and nonquantitative, the courts have no way to assess permissible limits of polluting activities. Rather, they must try to weigh the gravity of the harm against the social utility of the defendant's conduct. In cases involving pollution, the problem could be overcome with pollution-control standards that would serve as the measure of conduct amounting to a nuisance.

The courts now are being asked more and more to entertain public-nuisance suits brought by private citizens. Under the common law, if all members of the community suffered equally, none could sue. Their elected officials were expected to sue for them—on behalf of the state. However, very recently, there have been signs that the courts may permit private persons to sue to abate a public nuisance when only prospective relief, and not monetary damages, is sought. In a proposed study of the law on this subject, the American Law Institute has noted that this development is consistent with expanded concepts of the standing of citizen groups generally.

State Suits in the Supreme Court

The U.S. Constitution empowers the Supreme Court of the United States to exercise original (trial court) jurisdiction over "all Cases, in Law and Equity . . . between a State and Citizens of another State." The states have invoked this authority rarely on pollution matters. But growing concern about interstate pollution has triggered increased state interest in this direct resort to the Supreme Court.

In the first of several recent cases, *Ohio* v. *Wyandotte Chemicals Corp.*, Ohio sought an order to abate mercury pollution of Lake Erie by several Michigan and Canadian chemical companies. Ohio charged that this was a public nuisance. The Supreme Court declined to adjudicate the case, explaining that state courts were a more suitable and generally better equipped trial forum. The Court also implied that current state, federal, and international government efforts to deal with mercury pollution were "a more practical basis" for solving the problem than a nuisance action in any court. The Court's position on the availability of its original jurisdiction in interstate pollution matters will continue to be clarified as the court hears additional cases.

State Authority to Control Land Use

The states are growing more concerned about protecting the public interest in valuable land resources. New state laws have been passed to provide this protection. As in Maine and Vermont, these laws often increase restrictions on the way private landowners use their property. They do this under the authority of broad state "police powers" to protect the general welfare. However, the Fifth and Fourteenth Amendments to the U.S. Constitution forbid states to take property for public purposes without paying the owner "just compensation." Landowners often challenge restrictions on their rights on the basis that the regulations amount to a state "taking" of property, which requires compensation. Obviously, the states may be inhibited from pursuing new regulatory approaches if the courts too freely find the new restrictions to be a "taking" of property. The states cannot protect all critical areas and control major development if they must compensate for—or purchase—the land whose use they seek to regulate.

The Supreme Court upheld state authority to control land use through general zoning in 1926. It has not yet ruled on more modern land-use control techniques. Although some state courts have been skeptical, other recent decisions are giving fairly broad latitude to states to channel private land-use decisions along state policy lines. In 1970, for example, a California court upheld the power of the state's new Bay Conservation and Development Commission to control filling of San Francisco Bay. The Commission had refused to permit a corporation to fill submerged land that it had purchased for disposal of debris. The court rejected the corporation's claim that this refusal amounted to a taking of its property. The court stressed that the state law creating the Commission "clearly define[d] the public interest in San Francisco Bay." It held that prevention of filling was not an "undue restriction" on the landowner's property rights.

Other forms of land-use control present a similar problem. For example, some states have tried to preserve open space by requiring that subdividers dedicate a portion of each new development to public recreational use. Landowners have challenged this type of measure, also, as a taking of property. A recent decision by the California Supreme Court rejected such a challenge. The developers insisted that a city ordinance designed to preserve for park use $2\frac{1}{2}$ acres of land for each 1,000 new subdivision residents was a taking of property. The ordinance required each subdivider either to dedicate a portion of his tract or to pay a fee. The court held that because new subdivisions both increase city population and diminish available open space, the city's measure was a legitimate way to maintain a balance between population and park areas. The court implied that the ordinance would be valid even if the new park were not located near the subdivision.

Although too few to establish a trend, these decisions suggest that the Fifth Amendment permits innovative land-use control without compensation when a clear state interest exists.

THE CITIES: NEW YORK AS AN EXAMPLE

The many antipollution and environmental conservation programs come together in specific cities which have to contend with them in some interrelated fashion. An extreme case is the city of New York, described by Eisenbud (1970).

New York, by reason of its size, its geographic position in the midst of the world's most densely populated region, and decades of neglect, has been beset acutely with environmental problems. A comprehensive approach to environmental protection had been handicapped in the past by traditional organizational separation of responsibilities, with inadequate coordination among the organizational units. To provide a unified approach, Mayor John V. Lindsay created the Environmental Protection Administration (EPA) in March 1968 to consolidate former administratively separate functions concerned with environmental hygiene. With its formation, EPA became responsible for street sanitation, water supply, water-pollution control, air pollution, and noise abatement. It is an organization of more than 20,000 employees. This section deals with some of the pitfalls and successes of the program during its first two years of existence.

Air-Pollution Control

The present active program of air-pollution control began in the mid-1960s in response to widespread public interest. In 1965 Councilman Robert Low and the then mayoral candidate Lindsay began campaigns to strengthen the local laws governing air-pollution control.

A new air-pollution control law (Local Law 14) was passed by the City Council early in 1966 and mandated certain basic requirements among which were the following: (1) The sulfur content of all fuels burned in New York City would be limited to 1 percent by the 1969–1970 heating season. (2) No incinerators could be installed in newly constructed buildings. (3) All existing apartment-house incinerators were to be shut down or upgraded according to a specified timetable. (4) Emission controls were to be installed as soon as possible on all municipal incinerators. (5) All open burning of leaves, refuse, and building demolition materials would be banned within city limits.

The overall emissions of sulfur dioxide to the city's atmosphere were reduced by 56 percent by the end of 1969. This has been reflected by progressive reductions in the hourly peak concentration of SO_2 (see Figure 12.1). The annual maximum hourly concentration, which was 2.2 parts per million (ppm) in 1965, was reduced to

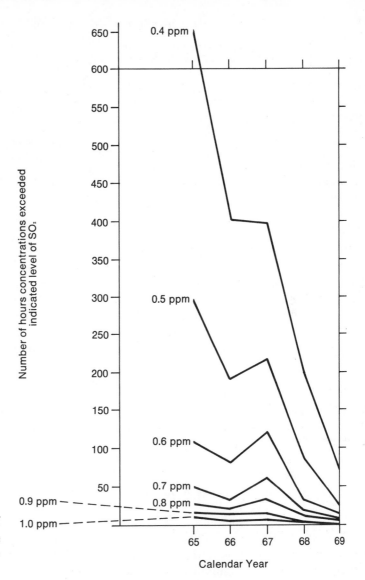

FIGURE 12.1 Number of hours the concentration of SO₂ exceeded the indicated level, 1965–1969.

0.8 ppm by 1969, and further improvement has been observed in the early months of 1970.

Dust and soot are the most annoying form of air pollution in many cities. The sources of the particulate emissions in New York City are shown in Table 12.1, which indicates that space heating, municipal incineration, apartment-house incineration, and power generation account for about 80 percent of the 69,100 tons (1 ton = 907 kilograms) emitted per year to the atmosphere as of November 1969.

During 1969, three of the city's eleven municipal incinerators were shut down, and another was scheduled to be closed as soon as alternate means of handling refuse could be arranged in the next year or two. The remaining seven incinerators are sufficiently modern so that air-cleaning equipment can be installed.

TABLE 12.1

Sources of particulate emissions to the atmosphere of New York City in November 1969

Source	Amount (ton/year)	Percent
Space heating	22,300	32.3
Municipal incineration	13,330	19.3
On-site incineration	12,690	18.4
Mobile sources	9,900	14.3
Power generation	6,400	9.2
Industrial sources	4,500	6.5
Total	69,120	100.0

The largest single source of particulate emissions to the air of New York City is space heating from about 30,000 apartment houses that burn No. 6 residual fuel oil. The black smoke that one sees curling up from apartment-house rooftops during the heating season is usually the result of improper operation of residual fuel oil boilers. Local Law 14 mandates installation of equipment modifications that will result in increased combustion efficiency and less particulate emission, and these are working well in about 1,500 furnaces where the change has been made.

The second largest source of particulates is apartment-house incinerators, about 17,000 of which were constructed between about 1947 and 1967.

The improvements required for incinerators and residual oil burners proved practical, but the apartment owners nevertheless brought suit against the city, charging that the law was unconstitutional and imposed unreasonable hardships on the landlords. This suit has stalled compliance with the provisions of Local Law 14 that pertain to apartment-house oil burners and incinerators.

The city has installed an aerometric network consisting of 38 stations that began operation in late 1968. Data from ten of the stations are telemetered directly to the laboratory; the others are manually operated. The Department of Air

Resources has also developed an alert warning system that mandates progressively more stringent steps to reduce contaminant emissions in the event of an air-pollution emergency. Should the SO_2, particulate, or CO concentrations reach predetermined values, various controls would go into effect, including reduction of municipal incineration, shifts to the less polluting fuels, and, if necessary, a gradual reduction of industrial processes, power generation, and incineration. The diminution that is continuing to take place in sulfur and particulate emissions makes it increasingly unlikely that stringent curtailment of activities will ever be necessary.

The internal-combustion engine is at present the main source of CO in urban atmospheres. The concentration of CO exceeds the air-quality target of 15 ppm near some heavily used streets, but it is not known to what extent people are exposed to these concentrations on a continuing basis. It is commonly believed that the automobile is the main source of urban pollution. This is certainly true in some localities, such as Los Angeles and certain other cities, where photochemical reactions involving components of automobile exhausts are known to contribute in a major way to the irritating smog. However, this phenomenon has been less of a problem in New York City, where the subjective complaints due to air pollution can more properly be ascribed to sulfur oxides and particulates.

Another popular misconception is that the automobile is the main polluter because its emissions are greater in quantity than any other source of air pollution. Thus in New York City in 1967 it was estimated that automobiles discharged 1.7 million tons of CO per year. The next largest pollutant was SO_2, which was being emitted to the atmosphere at a rate of 828,000 tons per year. However, SO_2 is far more noxious than CO, for which the tentative air-quality criterion in New York State is 15 ppm, as compared to about 0.1 ppm for SO_2. Thus the emissions of SO_2, though only about 48 percent of the CO emissions, are far more significant because its permissible concentration is less than 1 percent of that for CO.

The main source of CO exposure of city dwellers is apt to be cigarettes, the CO content of mainstream smoke being over 40,000 ppm. Smoking one pack of cigarettes per day is said to be equivalent to continuous exposure to 50 ppm of CO in ambient air.

As the air of our cities gradually becomes cleaner, many communities will have to answer the questions, "How clean is clean?" or "How much is clean air worth?" Unfortunately, we often lack the basic knowledge with which to answer such questions intelligently. Air pollution imposes economic losses due to soiling and corrosion and also causes health effects. Economic losses include shorter shelf life of many types of goods, higher cleaning costs, and corrosion of certain materials. The economic loss in large urban areas is thought to average $65 per person per year, but there have been no studies as to how these costs can be apportioned among the various sources of air pollution.

One could argue that every city should have the cleanest air possible. The problem is that air-pollution abatement measures cost a good deal of money, and the costs increase exponentially as the goals become more strict. The measures that must be adopted in New York City to implement the present provisions of the air-pollution control law would cost approximately $500 million within the first three years. If the economic losses due to air pollution are as high as has been estimated, this is obviously a good investment, since the city's eight million residents would receive a return on their investment of more than 100 percent per year, assuming the estimated economic loss to be $65 per capita.

The long-range prospects for clean air in New York, as in other large cities, are good, owing in part to the development of nuclear power. These plants, which are relatively pollution-free, will in time replace the fossil-fuel plants, unless the very existence of this alternative to fossil fuels causes proprietors of the latter to undertake research and development that leads to a high degree of air-pollution control. Recent developments in sulfur removal suggest that this may already be happening.

Whether the electrical generators operate on nuclear power or pollution-free fossil fuels, the central stations are destined to provide an increasing percentage of the energy needs of the community. Truly clean air will not be achieved until the thousands of inefficient individual space-heating boilers are eliminated in favor of steam or electric heat supplied from well-controlled central generating stations.

Noise Abatement

The law that established the Environmental Protection Administration specified that it should develop a noise-abatement program, the broad outlines of which were developed by a task force that spent three years preparing a thoughtful analysis of the noise problems of the city together with recommendations for the future program.

A program of noise abatement in any large city is destined to be a long and arduous one. High on the list of priorities should be construction machinery, automotive equipment, aircraft, rooftop air conditioners, sirens, horns, and subways. A model noise-abatement law, similar to the law dealing with air-pollution control, must be developed, and rules and regulations must be adopted for enforcement purposes. Finally, new technological approaches must be developed.

Some progress has already been made in New York City in a small way. From the joint efforts of the Task Force, industry, and the Department of Sanitation have come improvements now being incorporated into the city's purchasing specifications which allow a marked reduction in the noise levels from sanitation trucks. Progress has also been made in the partial quieting of diesel compressors used in construction work.

Step by step it should be possible to provide a more quiet city. However, many of the sources of noise are beyond a city's powers to control. For example, all automotive equipment is subject to state control. The acoustic standards established by New York State call for a limit of 88 decibels, 50 feet from a truck. This may be satisfactory for a throughway in the open country, but is not acceptable for a truck passing through city streets where people are located closer than 50 feet and where the sound reverberates from buildings. Accordingly, state legislation is being prepared that will mandate acoustic specifications for motor vehicles that are more appropriate for urban needs.

Aircraft noise, so troublesome to many communities, is preempted by the federal government, and the city's role is therefore limited to persuasion or such influence as can be mounted by the collected efforts of legislators from urban areas.

Water Supply

The city of New York is blessed with a supply of excellent water carried in deep rock tunnels from reservoirs located on watersheds as far away as 125 miles. The city must provide water for its own needs and is also required by state law to provide water to eight upstate counties.

The per capita demand for water has been rising steadily from about 25 gallons per day (gpd) in the early nineteenth century to more than 150 gpd at present. The demand for water by the people living in the area served by the system is now 1400 million gallons per day (mgd) and is expected to increase to 2200 mgd by 2020, at which time the extrapolated per capita daily consumption would be about 185 gpd. Present projections indicate that the demand for water will exceed the dependable yield of the present system by sometime in the late 1980s unless steps are taken to conserve the use of water.

The extent to which water can be conserved is not fully understood. Intensive educational campaigns during past periods of drought have reduced water use by about 150 mgd, but public cooperation to this extent can reasonably be expected only during periods of near emergency—not under normal conditions. In the future, water conservation should be sought by adoption of a program of universal water metering and encouragement of plumbing manufacturers to develop fixtures that use less water.

New York is almost alone among the larger cities in not having a system of universal water metering. About 170,000 meters have been installed in commercial buildings and in about 20,000 residences, but this accounts for only about 23 percent of all water accounts. Nevertheless, the per capita rate of water use is not excessive. Of the eleven largest cities in the United States, among which the per capita consumption of water ranges from 132 to 235 gpd, only three cities consume water at a rate lower than that of New York City. The reason for the wide range of per capita consumption among the various cities is not understood.

With metering, water changes could be adjusted to discourage the unnecessary use of water. Rating systems presently charge less for water as the use increases. A system must be devised that will not be punitive and will not discourage the use of water for sanitary or other purposes within reasonable limits, but that will result in increasing unit costs for water as the use increases. Before this can be done, it will be necessary to know much more than we do about the way in which water is used in the household and the minimum quantities that can be used for various purposes.

A major objective of the water-management program should be to stabilize, and possibly reduce, the per capita demand. In order to do this, one must first undertake studies designed to elucidate the reasons why the per capita demand is increasing. Second, there is a need to design plumbing fixtures that use less water. An excellent example is the toilet flush tank which in most cases uses about 6 gallons per flush. Assuming that the average person flushes the toilet four times per day (and there aren't even good data on this), this use would consume 24 gallons per day, or about 15 percent of the per capita consumption. Flush tanks are available that perform their function in a satisfactory manner with only 2 gallons per flush. The gradual changeover to more efficient tanks in the years ahead would thus reduce the per capita consumption of water by about 10 percent or more. This kind of innovation is also needed in kitchen faucets, shower baths, laundry machines, and other household or commercial plumbing fixtures.

Unless the use of water can be stabilized, additional sources of supply will be necessary in the decades ahead. Recent studies suggest that the Hudson River, which is now in the process of rehabilitation, could be used as a source of water in the latter part of this century. It will be necessary to assure that the freshwater flow is adequate to keep the saltwater tidal intrusion well below the proposed intakes presently planned for Hyde Park, and for this purpose water stored in Adirondack Mountains reservoirs would be released to the Hudson River during the dry summer months.

Water-Pollution Control

New York City currently provides some degree of secondary treatment for about 75 percent of the 1300 mgd of sewage generated. About 325 mgd of raw sewage continue to be discharged into the estuary, mainly from the west side of Manhattan. With the aid of the New York State Pure Waters Bond Issue, which provides for 60 percent reimbursement of expenditures for sewage-plant construction, a $1.2-billion program has been started by New York City which, when completed in 1975, will provide high-degree secondary treatment for all its dry-weather waste water.

When the new plants are completed, there will remain the problem that New York City, like many communities, uses combined sewers to collect both sanitary and storm drainage. The storm waters overwhelm the capacity of the sewage-treatment plants, causing overflow of untreated sewage into the estuary. This problem is particularly acute in the 30-square-mile Jamaica Bay, which drains major portions of Brooklyn and Queens and which is intended to be included in the Gateway National Park, the first national park to be located within a city. Following completion of secondary sewage-treatment facilities, a second program, not likely to be completed until the mid- or late 1980s, will provide for treatment of storm waters.

In preparation, a million-dollar ecological study of Jamaica Bay, financed by the Federal Water pollution Control Administration, has been undertaken to provide a quantitative understanding of the hydrological, biological, and chemical characteristics of the bay. A demonstration storm-water treatment plant is being built on the shore and will serve as a prototype for a ring of several additional plants that will ultimately be built on the bay's periphery. These plants will impound storm water, which will be degritted, filtered, and chlorinated before being discharged into the estuary. Additional plants of this type will be constructed in the East Bronx. It is anticipated that by the late 1980s the estuary will have been sufficiently restored so that virtually the total shoreline of New York City may be available for recreational bathing.

The purpose of estuarine pollution control is to protect the water quality for recreational purposes, seafood harvesting, and wildlife preservation. Chemical indices of pollution such as biochemical oxygen demand (BOD), concentrations of nutrient ions and toxic substances, as well as biological indicators, such as the concentration of coliform organisms, are necessary adjuncts to a water-pollution control program, but many of the standards currently in use have little basis, either theoretical or empirical, despite the fact that the standards have a fundamental influence on the design of sewage-treatment plants and their cost. In most cases there is inadequate information about the hydrological and ecological characteristics of an estuary; hence the design of water-pollution control plants cannot be optimized in relation to the nature of the receiving waters. Sewage sent to plants located in one part of an estuary may require a higher degree of treatment than that treated in a plant located elsewhere. Moreover, the location and design of outfalls may influence the treatment requirements, and these designs should be based on the characteristics of the estuary.

In the New York estuary, as in most places throughout the country, sufficient information does not exist. This is unfortunate because hundreds of millions of dollars are involved in decisions as to whether a plant should be designed, for example, for removal of either 67 or 90 percent of the BOD. There may, in fact, be no ecological or health gain in going to the higher value in one place, whereas in other cases a need for the highest possible secondary or even tertiary treatment might be indicated.

Each estuary should be studied thoroughly so that as complete as possible a mathematical model of the hydrological and biological characteristics can be developed. Such a program might take as much as ten years to complete, and it should be financed out of the appropriations for capital construction.

Bathing-water standards for saline waters are long overdue for reexamination; as in the case of certain of the air-quality criteria, there is a need for extensive epidemiological research to provide a more quantitative understanding of the relation of various amounts of pollution to the public health. Recent literature has suggested that the U.S. approach to the subject has been too conservative. The British, on the basis of studies

of the health of bathers at a number of beaches, have concluded that any beach can be used for bathing if the water is esthetically acceptable! As earlier, we are faced with the question, "How clean is clean?"

Solid-Waste Management

New York City is faced with enormous crises because of the burgeoning volume of solid waste. The streets are increasingly dirty, and the city will run out of disposal sites by the mid-1970s.

New York City's eight million people live on 6,000 miles of streets. They are joined each workday by an influx of more than two million people, approximately the population of the nation's second largest city, who come from outlying suburbs to earn their living. The rate of solid-waste generation is increasing 2 to 4 percent per year and is currently about 5 pounds per capita per day. Depending on the part of town, the cost of collecting refuse varies from $15 to $30 per ton and has increased steadily in recent years. The sanitation industry is one of the few in which wages have increased during the past decades without a commensurate increase in the productivity of labor, and it is frequently said that the only change in the technology of garbage collection is that the internal-combustion engine has replaced the horse.

The garbage can is one of the principal impediments to higher efficiency and is long overdue for replacement. Numerous alternatives are available that will make the job easier for the sanitation man, thus increasing his productivity and yielding cleaner streets at less cost. Experiments conducted during 1969 demonstrated that plastic or paper bags are an efficient and sanitary alternative and that their use should be encouraged. The main advantage is that the sanitation man is no longer required to pick up a heavy can and laboriously shake the refuse from it. Bags have been found to be popular with both the householder and the men, and their use is increasing. The cost to the householder at present is approximately 8 cents per day per bag, and this will undoubtedly decrease as the bags are made available in mass distribution.

New high-rise apartment houses are still being built with no provision for refuse handling other than the garbage can. One large housing complex was planning to use 400 cans per day. While plastic or paper bags offer a suitable alternative for private homes or small multidwelling buildings, a whole spectrum of still more efficient alternatives are available for the larger buildings. These range from containers of 1-yard capacity that can be handled manually to large 10-yard containers which are handled mechanically by special trucks. The building codes should be changed to require all future buildings to incorporate efficient methods of handling solid waste.

The federal government agreed to support a demonstration of a vacuum system for handling solid refuse within a large housing complex. The system is designed to allow the householder to drop refuse into a conveniently located hopper from which the garbage is transported pneumatically to a central location where it is then compacted and mechanically loaded for removal by the sanitation department.

Another possibility for more efficient waste handling might utilize the existing or proposed subway systems. All buildings along a subway route might drop their refuse to compactors below street grade; special subway cars would be used for hauling the containerized wastes during the night. Still another method, which might be suitable for buildings located near the waterfront, would be to transfer the refuse pneumatically (or by other methods) to hoppers that could discharge directly into barges. This would be an excellent objective at the proposed Battery Park City, which will accommodate 50,000 people and generate approximately 1,235 tons of garbage a day. There is no reason why the streets of a city should be used

for the transport of garbage if some other means can be found, especially if the alternate means are cheaper, cleaner, and more efficient.

The streets of a city become littered partly because of inefficient garbage-collection activities and partly because of the high population density and the urban lifestyle. The origins of street litter are found deeply rooted in the complex technical and social system that comprises the metropolis. Economic trends, social mores, the complexities of the criminal courts system used to enforce the sanitary laws, and vehicular traffic congestion are all part of the problem.

The scrap automobile is a case in point. Until a few years ago a scrap car could be disposed of by its owner at a price that offered incentive for him to arrange for its removal from the city streets. Changes in economics of the steel industry have altered this situation to the extent that in most parts of the city it costs more to remove a car than the car is worth. This has resulted in automobiles being abandoned on the streets of New York at an increasing rate—the total in 1969 was more than 57,000. The city has recently franchised scrap dealers to collect these cars from various parts of the city. In some cases, the scrap dealer is subsidized by the city and in others he pays the city a small price for the car. It is illegal to abandon a car in the city streets, but when the last owner removes the license plates and files off the engine number, it becomes prohibitively costly to trace him.

The nonreturnable bottle and its close relative the aluminum and steel can are another costly and offensive form of litter that owes some of its origins to the economics of our times. The beverage distributors insist that until recently a deposit bottle made as many as 30 round trips between the distributor and the customer, but that because of the indifference of the consumers to even a five-cent deposit, the number of round trips in many communities gradually diminished to as few as four or five before the bottle was discarded. This is given as the reason for the shift from deposit bottles. There is little question that the consumer prefers the nonreturnable container, as does the supermarket, some of which will no longer handle deposit bottles. The result is an enormous net increase in the volume of solid waste imposed on the city and a very considerable amount of additional litter. The nonreturnable bottle and the abandoned vehicle are examples of problems that the local community can solve only with the greatest difficulty. National policies are needed that apply uniform rules on a countrywide basis.

Vehicular congestion contributes as much to the littered appearance of streets as any other factor. Because it is prohibitively expensive to sweep streets by hand, most large cities have acquired mechanical brooms, which are effective only when the curb is clear. In New York City, alternate-side-of-the-street parking rules have been promulgated that theoretically should make it possible to sweep the curbs mechanically, but these rules are honored as much in the breach as in the observance. The basic problem is that for lack of comfortable mass transportation there are too many cars in the city. Fewer cars would make the city a far more pleasant place, would avoid the enormous economic waste of traffic congestion, and would reduce air pollution. It would, incidentally, make the streets easier to clean.

The difficulties of enforcing alternate-side-of-the-street parking rules illustrate some of the frustrations of city government. For one reason or another the New York City Police Department was unable to enforce the parking rules with sufficient stringency, and the mayor attempted to obtain authority for the uniformed Sanitation Department officers, of whom there are about 1,000, to issue summonses for parking violations. However, the state law specified that only a police officer could issue a summons. When city-sponsored legislation was introduced in Albany to make it possible for the Sanitation

Department to issue summonses, its passage failed for two consecutive years. During the third year the law was passed, and late in 1969 the Sanitation Department began to issue summonses at a rate of about 5,000 per week. However, within only a few months the new procedure, which was working very satisfactorily, was frustrated in the courts by a legal technicality. The ruling of the court in this case was so broad that it successfully blocked all the enforcement agents of the Environmental Protection Administration from issuing any summonses. No longer could the Sanitation Department officers issue summonses for littered sidewalks, nor could the the air-pollution inspectors issue summonses for violation of local air-pollution control laws. This matter has not as yet been resolved.

The Waste-Disposal Crisis

This is a major problem to New York City because its refuse disposal sites will be exhausted by the mid-1970s. Ever since colonial days the city has followed the common practice of disposing of its solid wastes by filling its lowlands, and about 11 percent of its present land area has been created in this way, including some of the most valuable commercial and recreational areas.

The largest landfill in the world is at Fresh Kills on Staten Island, but this will be completely filled by 1975. Smaller landfills in other parts of the city will also be exhausted by that time.

Data for 1969 indicate the city produced about 21,000 tons of refuse per day, of which about 7,000 tons pass through municipal incinerators before going to the landfills. A basic strategy, therefore, must be to increase the municipal incineration capacity to reduce the volume of waste and to convert the refuse to a less offensive and more manageable form. A $200-million capital program was begun, which focused on the construction of four giant incinerators; this plan would reduce the mass of refuse by about 75 percent, leaving a relatively innocuous ash that will occupy about 10 percent of the original volume.

The present generation of municipal incinerators is one of the principal sources of atmospheric particulates. However, as noted earlier, these incinerators are being equipped with air-cleaning equipment, and all new units will be provided with modern stack-cleaning devices. Since contemporary refuse has a heat value of about 5,000 British thermal units per pound, every effort should be made to dispose of the heat either for power production or for generation of steam. It is estimated that the city can in this way recover about $2 per ton of refuse burned or as much as $12 million per year. The basic economics of such heat recovery is sound, assuming that the incinerators can be built near a market for the steam, and this practice is desirable from the conservation point of view.

In the long range, one must stabilize or, better yet, reverse the rising trend in the per capita production of refuse and use of water and other resources. To accomplish this will require development of new technology, changes in people's habits, and new kinds of governmental regulation and participation. For example, New York City disposes of 350,000 tons of newsprint per year, at great cost in dollars, air pollution, and litter. From every point of view, including conservation of resources, it would be desirable to recycle this paper. If the paper were processed in a modern, pollution-free plant for reuse by the newspaper industry, the streets and skies of New York would benefit, the tax dollar would go further, distant streams would be less polluted by effluents from paper mills, and extensive woodland areas would be conserved. Other examples could be given to illustrate the ways in which our economy must close on itself to reuse the products of its industry. This objective is one of the great technological challenges of the 1970s.

Conclusion

This account of the status of environmental protection in the nation's largest city might end with some additional thoughts.

First, it should be stressed that in the long run environmental protection must go beyond pollution and must ultimately deal with other pressing problems including population control, poverty, raw-materials conservation, vehicular-traffic management, and land planning. A city that has clean air, clean streets, and clean water will not bring true quality to its citizens' way of life until these and other monumental socio-environmental problems are solved.

Second, it must be recognized that deficiencies in the political apparatus of communities have traditionally frustrated an orderly solution to complex problems, and it is hoped that this factor will not be an impediment to effective environmental rehabilitation. The elected officials, the bureaucracy of government, the unions, the community action groups, and the newspapers are important components of the social substrata from which all governmental programs must be developed and nourished. Professional environmental health specialists can define the objectives, develop the timetables, estimate the costs, and, as we have seen earlier, be given substantial sums of money with which to do the job. But factors related to the peculiar needs of the individual components of the political apparatus frequently cause apparently extraneous issues to arise. The original objectives are sometimes overlooked, and priorities become misaligned. An important function of government is to permit the development of thoroughly considered plans of action that can be implemented by professional leaders who are given authority commensurate with the responsibilities assigned to them. A community that allows itself to fail in these respects will be unequal to the ecological problems that face it.

references

ACKERMAN, W. C., HARMESON, R. H., and SINCLAIR, R. A. (1970) *Trans. Amer. Geophys. Union.* Vol. 51, p. 516.

———. (December 1969) "Some Long-Term Trends in Water Quality of Rivers and Lakes," Illinois State Water Survey, Reprint Series No. 159, paper presented at a joint symposium on Trends in Man's Environment at the National Fall Meeting of the American Geophysical Union.

AERO-JET GENERAL. (1965) *California Waste Management Study.* Report No. 3056. Azuza, Calif.

AIR CONSERVATION COMMISSION OF THE AAS. (1965) *Air Conservation.* Washington, D. C.: American Association for the Advancement of Science.

AIR POLLUTION. (1968) Commission on College Geography, Resource Paper No. 2.

AIR POLLUTION CONTROL OFFICE, ENVIRONMENTAL PROTECTION AGENCY, *A Model for Regional Air Pollution Cost-Benefit Analysis.* McLean, Va.: TRW Systems Group—Kenneth R. Woodcock.

ALLEE, P. A. (January 1970) "Inadvertent Weather Modification and Climate Change: Air Pollution and the Cloud Droplet Condensation Nuclei Concentration," *Bulletin of the American Meteorological Society.* Vol. 51, No. 1, p. 102.

AMATO, P. W. (1969) "Residential Amenities and Neighborhood Quality," *Ekistics.* Vol. 28, No. 166, pp. 180–184.

AMDUR, M. O. (September 1969) "Toxicologic Appraisal of Particulate Matter, Oxides of Sulfur and Sulfuric Acid," *Journal of the Air Pollution Control Association.* Vol. 19, No. 9, pp. 638–644.

AMERICAN PUBLIC HEALTH ASSOCIATION. (1955) *Standard Methods for the Examination of Water, Sewage and Industrial Waste.* New York: American Public Health Association, Inc.

AMERICAN PUBLIC WORKS ASSOCIATION. (1966) *Municipal Refuse Disposal.* Chicago: Public Administration Service.

———. (1967) *Problems of Combined Sewer Facilities and Overflows.* Water Pollution Control Series No. WP-20-11. Washington, D. C.: U. S. Federal Water Pollution Control Administration.

———. (1967) Research Foundation. *Problems of Com-*

bined *Sewer Facilities and Overflows.* U. S. Federal Water Pollution Control Administration.

———. (1969) *Water Pollution Aspects of Urban Runoff.* Federal Water Pollution Control Administration, Published WP-20-15.

———. (January, 1969) "Water Pollution Aspects of Urban Runoff," *FWPCA Publication No. WP-20-15,* U. S. Department of the Interior.

AMRAMY, A. (1967) "Reuse of Municipal Waste Water," *Proceedings of the International Conference on Water for Peace.* Vol. 2, pp. 421–431.

ANDERSON, D. G. (1968) *Effects of Urban Development on Floods in Northern Virginia.* U. S. Geological Survey open-file report.

ANDERSON, D. L. (September 2, 9, and 23, 1967) "The Effects of Air Contamination on Health," *Canadian Medical Association Journal.* Vol. 97, pp. 528–536, 585–593, 802–806.

ANDERSON, PETER W. and FAUST, SAMUEL D. (1965) "Changes in Quality of Water in the Passaic River at Little Falls, New Jersey, as Shown by Long-Term Data," *Geological Survey Research 1965.* U. S. Geological Survey Professional Paper 525-D, pp. D214–D218.

ANDERSON, ROBERT J. JR., and CROCKER, THOMAS D. (January 1970) "Air Pollution and Housing: Some Findings," Paper No. 264, Institute for Research in the Behavioral, Economic, and Management Sciences, Purdue University, Lafayette, Indiana.

ANDREWS, RICHARD N. L. (July 1971) "Three Fronts of Federal Environmental Policy." *Journal of the American Institute of Planners,* Vol. 37, pp. 258–266.

ANGELL, J. K., PACK, D. H., HASS, W. A., and HOECKER, W. H. (1968) "Tetroon Flights Over New York City," *Weather.* Vol. 23, p. 184.

ANTOINE, L. H. (1964) "Drainage and Best Use of Urban Land," *Public Works.* Vol. 95, pp. 88–90.

ARRHENIUS, S. (1908) *Worlds in the Making.* New York: Harper.

ATKINS, J. E. (1968) "Changes in the Visibility Characteristics at Manchester/Ringway Airport," *Meteorologic Magazine.* Vol. 97, p. 172.

ATKINSON, B. W. (October 1968) "The Reality of the Urban Effect on Precipitation—A Case Study Approach." Paper presented at W.M.O. Symposium on Urban Climates and Building Climatology, Brussels, Belgium.

AULICIEMS, ANDRIS, and BURTON, IAN. (1970) *Perception and Awareness of Air Pollution in Toronto,* Working Paper Series No. 13, Natural Hazard Research Series, University of Toronto.

———. (1973) "Trends in Smoke Concentrations Before and After the Clean Air Act of 1956." Unpublished paper, Department of Geography, University of Toronto.

———, HEWINGS, JOHN, SCHIFF, MYRA, and TAYLOR, CHRIS. (1972) "The Public Use of Scientific Information on the Quality of the Environment: The Case of the Ontario Air Pollution Index." Paper presented to International Geographical Congress, Montreal.

AYALA, F. J. (1968) "Genotype, Environment and Population Numbers," *Science.* Vol. 162, pp. 1453–1459.

BABBITT, H. C., and BAUMAN, C. H. (1958) *Sewerage and Sewage Treatment.* New York: John Wiley & Sons.

BAILEY, T. E., and HANNUM, J. R. (1965) *Proc. Amer. Soc. Civ. Eng. J. San. Eng. Div.* Vol. 93, p. 40.

BANKS, H. O., and LAWRENCE, J. H. (1953) "Water Quality Problems in California," *American Geophysical Union Transactions.* Vol. 34, No. 1, pp. 58–66.

BARKER, M. L. (1968) "The Perception of Water Quality as a Factor in Consumer Attitudes and Space Preferences in Outdoor Recreation." Unpublished Master's Thesis, Department of Geography, University of Toronto.

BARNES, PETER A. (1968) "Community Awareness and Concern with Air Quality in Toronto: A Pilot Study." Unpublished Bachelor's Thesis, University of Toronto.

BARTH, E. F., et al. (July 1966) "Removal of Nitrogen by Municipal Wastewater Treatment Plants," *Journal of the Water Pollution Control Federation.* pp. 1208–1219.

BARTHEL, W. F., HAWTHORNE, J. C., FORD, J. H., BOLTON, G. C., McDOWELL, L. L., GRISSINGER, E. H., and PARSONS, D. A. (1969) *Pestic. Monit. J.* Vol. 3, p. 8.

BARTSCH, A. F. (1961) "Induced Eutrophication—A Growing Water Resource Problem," *Algae and Metropolitan Wastes.* U.S.P.H.S., SEC TR W61-63, pp. 6–9.

———. "Settleable Solids, Turbidity, and Light Penetration as Factors Affecting Water Quality," *Biological in Water Pollution.* Transactions of the 1959 Seminar, H.E.W., Tech. Report W60-3, pp. 118–127.

———. (1968) "Eutrophication is Beginning in Lake Michigan," *Water and Wastes Engineering.* Vol. 5, No. 9, pp. 84–87.

BATHURST, VERNE M. (1965) "Soil Erosion in Urban Areas," *Soil Conservation.* Vol. 30, No. 12, pp. 274–275.

BATTIGELLI, M. (1968) "Sulfur Dioxide and Acute Effects of Air Pollution," *Journal of Occupational Medicine.* Vol. 10, pp. 500–511.

BAUER ENGINEERING INC. (1971) The Muskegon County Wastewater Management System. Chicago: Bauer Engineering, p. 16.

BEALE, E. M. L., KENDALL, M. G., and MANN, D. W. (1967) "The Discarding of Variables in Multivariate Analysis," *Biometrika.* Vol. 54, pp. 357–366.

BEEBE, R. G. (1967) "Changes in Visibility Restrictions Over a 20 Year Period," *Bulletin of American Meteorology Society.* Vol. 48, p. 348.

BEER, CHARLES G. P., and LEOPOLD, LUNA B. (1947) "Meteorological Factors Influencing Air Pollution in the Los Angeles Area," *American Geophysical Union Transactions.* Vol. 28, pp. 173–192.

BEGEMANN, F., and LIBBY, W. F. (1957) Geochim. Cosmochin. Acta. Vol. 12, p. 277.

BERG, GEORGE G. (1970) *Water Pollution*, A Scientists' Institute for Public Information Workbook. New York: Scientists' Institute for Public Information, p. 32.

BERG, GERALD. (July 1966) "Virus Transmission by the Water Vehicle, III: Removal of Viruses by Water Treatment Procedures," *Health Laboratory Science.* Vol. 3, pp. 170–180.

———, ed. (1966) *Transmission of Viruses by the Water Route.* New York: John Wiley & Sons.

———, et al. (February 1968) "Removal of Poliovirus I from Secondary Effluent by Lime Flocculation and Rapid Sand Filtration," *Journal of the American Water Works Association.* Vol. 60, pp. 193–198.

———, DAHLING, DANIEL R., BERMAN, DONALD, and WALTER, CARL. In press. "The Virus Hazard on the Missouri River." U.S. Department of H.E.W., Public Health Service. Cincinnati: R. A. Taft Sanitary Engineering Center.

BERGER, BERNARD B. (May 1960) "Public Health Aspects of Water Reuse for Potable Supply," *Journal of the American Water Works Association.* Vol. 52, p. 599.

BERKSON, J. (1955) "The Statistical Study of Association Between Smoking and Lung Cancer," *Proc. Staff Meetings Mayo Clinic.* Vol. 30, pp. 319–348.

BERNHEIM, F., and BERNHEIM, M. L. C. (1939) "Note on the action of manganese and some other metals in the oxidation of certain substances by liver," *J. Biol. Chem.* Vol. 128, pp. 79–82.

BERRY, A. E., and DELAPORTE, A. V. (1940) "Standards and Regulations for Quality of Water in Bathing Places," *Canadian Municipal Utilities (Canadian Engineering).* Vol. 78, No. 8, pp. 5–8 and 11–12.

BERRY, BRIAN J. L., and HORTON, FRANK E. (1970) *Geographic Perspectives on Urban Systems.* Englewood Cliffs, N.J.: Prentice-Hall, Inc.

BIESECKER, J. E., LESCINSKY, J. B., WOOD, C. R. (1968) *Commonwealth Penn. Water Res. Bulletin No. 3*, pp. 193.

BJERKNES, J. (1964) "Atlantic Air-Sea Interaction," *Advances in Geophysics.* New York: Academic Press. Vol. 10, pp. 1–82.

BOLT BERANEK and NEWMAN REPORT. (1964) "Judgments of the Relative and Absolute Acceptability of Actual and Recorded Aircraft Noise," Report No. 1097.

BOOKMAN, M. (1957) "Urban Water Requirements in California," *American Water Works Association's Journal.* Vol. 49, No. 8, pp. 1053–1059.

BORCHERT, J. R. (1954) "The Surface Water Supply of American Municipalities," *Annals AAG.* Vol. 44, pp. 15–32.

BORNSTEIN, R. D. (1968) "Observations of the Urban Heat Island Effect in New York City," *Journal of Application Meteorology.* Vol. 7, p. 575.

BORSKY, P. N. (1961) "Community Reactions to Air Force Noise." WADD Technical Report 60–689, pts. 1 and 2. Dayton: Office of Technical Services, U.S. Department of Commerce.

BOTTACCINI, M. R. (1968) A Preliminary Discussion of the Problem of Aircraft Noise at the University of Arizona. Unpublished manuscript.

BOWER, BLAIR, et al. (1968) *Waste Management.* New York: Regional Plan Association.

BOYCE, D.E. (January 1970) "Using the optimal regression program," preliminary discussion paper. Philadelphia: Regional Science Dept., Wharton School of Finance and Commerce, University of Pennsylvania.

———, FARHI, A., and WEISCHEDEL, R. (1969) *A Computer Program for Optimal Regression Analysis*, RSRI Discussion Paper Series, No. 28. Philadelphia: Regional Science Research Institute.

BOYD, J. T. (1960) "Climate, Air Pollution and Mortality," *British Journal Prev. Soc. Med.* Vol. 14, No. 123.

BRAMHALL, DAVID F., and MILLS, EDWIN S. (1966) "Alternative Method of Improving Stream Quality: An Economic and Policy Analysis," *Water Resources Research*. Vol. 2, pp. 355–363. (Third Quarter)

BRATER, E. F. (1968) "Steps Toward a Better Understanding of Urban Run-off Processes," *Water Resources Research*. Vol. 4, No. 2, pp. 335–347.

BRAVEN, J., BONKER, G. J., FENNER, M. L., and TONGUE, B. L. (1967) "The Mechanism of Carcinogenesis by Tobacco Smoke. Some Experimental Observations and a Hypothesis," *British Journal of Cancer*. Vol. 21, pp. 623–633.

BRAVERMAN, M. M., and THEOPHIL, C. (1965) "New York City's Air Pollution Index," *Civil Engineering*. Vol. 35, p. 64.

BRAZELL, J. H. (1964) "Frequency of Dense and Thick Fog in Central London as Compared with Frequency in Outer London," *Meteorological Magazine*. Vol. 93, p. 129.

BRESLOW, LESTER. (1962) *Air Pollution: Effects Reported by California Residents*. Berkeley: Department of Public Health, State of California.

BROOKHAVEN SYMPOSIA in BIOLOGY, No. 20. (1968) *Recovery and Repair Mechanisms in Radiobiology*. Upton, N.Y.: Brookhaven National Laboratory.

BROWN, G. W., and KRYGIER, C. A. (1970) *Water Resources Research*. Vol. 6, p. 1133.

BROWNLEE, ROBERT C., AUSTIN, T. A., and WELLS, DAN M. (1970) *Interim Report: Variation of Urban Runoff Quality with Duration and Intensity of Storms*. Water Resources Center, Texas Tech University.

BRUNNER, CARL A. (1967) "Pilot-Plant Experiences in Demineralization of Secondary Effluent Using Electrodialysis," *Journal of the Water Pollution Control Federation*. Vol. 39, Part II, pp. R1–R15.

BRUVOLD, WILLIAM H., and GAFFEY, WILLIAM R. (June 1968) "Scales for Rating the Taste of Water," *Journal of Applied Psychology*. Vol. 52, No. 3, pp. 245–253.

BUCZOWSKA, Z. (1960) "Research in the Bacteriological Pollution of Coastal Waters." *Bulletin of the Institute of Marine Medicine, Gdansk. Bulletin of Hygiene*. Vol. 35, No. 5, p. 426.

———, and NOWICKA, B. (1961) "Locating Salmonella Infection Sources of River and Bathing Beach by Means of Sewage Examination," *Bulletin of Hygiene*. Vol. 36, No. 9, p. 853.

BUDD, W. (1956) "On Intestinal Fever: Its Mode of Propagation," *Lancet*. Vol. 2, No. 694.

BUDYKO, M. I. (October 1969) "Climatic Change," *Soviet Geography*. Vol. 10, No. 8, pp. 429–457.

———. (1969) "The Effect of Solar Radiation Variations on the Climate of the Earth," *Tellus*. Vol. 21, No. 5, pp. 611–619.

BUNCH, ROBERT L., and ETTINGER, M. B. (November 1964) "Water Quality Depreciation by Municipal Use," *Journal of the Water Pollution Control Federation*. Vol. 36, pp. 1411–1414.

BUREAU of SOLID WASTE MANAGEMENT. (1970a) *Comprehensive Studies of Solid Waste Management*. Washington, D. C.,: GPO.

———. (1970b) *Mathematical Modeling of Waste Policies*. Washington, D.C.: GPO.

———. (1970c) *Solid Waste Management: Abstracts and Excerpts from the Literature*. Washington, D.C.: GPO.

BURTON, E. S., and SANJOUR, WILLIAM. (1970) "A Simulation Approach to Air Pollution Abatement Program Planning," *Socio-Economic Planning Science*. Vol. 4, pp. 147–150.

BURTON, IAN, BILLINGSLEY, DOUGLAS, BLACKSELL, MARK, and WALL, GEOFFREY. (1972) "A Case Study of Successful Pollution Control Legislation in the United Kingdom." Paper presented to International Geographical Congress. Montreal.

BURTON, IAN, and KATES, ROBERT W. (January 1964) "The Perception of Natural Hazards in Resource Management," *Natural Resources Journal*. Vol. 3, No. 3, pp. 412–441.

——, eds. (1965) *Readings in Resource Management and Conservation.* Chicago: University of Chicago Press.

CAIRNS, JOHN JR., DICKSON, KENNETH L., SPARKS, RICHARD E., and WALLER, WILLIAM T. (1970) "A preliminary report on rapid biological information systems for water pollution control." *J. Water Pollution Control Fed.* Vol. 42, pp. 685–703.

CALIFORNIA STATE WATER POLLUTION CONTROL BOARD. (1960) *Survey of Direct Utilization of Waste Waters.* Publication No. 12.

CALIFORNIA STATE WATER RESOURCES BOARD. (1956) *Water Utilization and Requirements of California.* Bulletin 2, Vol. 1.

CALLENDAR, G. S. (1938) "The Artificial Production of Carbon Dioxide and Its Influence on Temperature," *Quarterly Journal of the Royal Meteorological Society.* Vol. 64, pp. 223–237.

CARMICHAEL, L. (1954) "Science and Social Conservatism," *Scientific Monthly.* Vol. 78, pp. 372–379.

CARPENTER, RICHARD A. (June 1970) "Information for Decisions in Environmental Policy," *Science.* Vol. 168, pp. 1316–1322.

CARTER, R. W. (1961) "Magnitude and Frequency of Floods in Suburban Areas." Short Papers in the Geologic and Hydrologic Sciences, U.S. Geological Survey Professorial Paper 424–B, p. B9–B11.

CARTER, LUTHER J. (1970) "Galveston Bay: Test Case of an Estuary in Crisis," *Science.* Vol. 167, pp. 1102–08.

CARRIGAN, P. H. JR. (1969) *U.S. Geol. Surv. Prof. Pap.* 433–I, pp. 1–18.

CASSELL, ERIC J. (Spring 1968) "The Health Effects of Air Pollution and Their Implications for Control," *Law and Contemporary Problems.* Vol. 33, No. 2, pp. 197–216.

CECIL, LAWRENCE K., ed. *Water Reuse.* New York: American Institute of Chemical Engineers, 1967. Chemical Engineering Progress Symposium Series, Vol. 63, No. 78.

CHALUPNIK, JAMES, ed. (1970) *Transportation Noises.* Seattle: University of Washington Press.

CHAMBERS, LESLIE A. (1968) "Classification and Extent of Air Pollution Problems," *Air Pollution.* Ed. by Arthur C. Stern. Vol. 1, 2d ed. New York: Academic Press.

CHANDLER, T. J. (1960) "Wind as a Factor of Urban Temperatures—A Survey in North-East London," *Weather.* Vol. 15, p. 204.

——. (1961) "Surface Effects of Leicester's Heat-Island," *E. Midland Geographer.* No. 15, p. 32.

——. (1962) "Temperature and Humidity Traverses Across London," *Weather.* Vol. 17, p. 235.

——. (1963) "London Climatological Survey," *International Journal of Air and Water Pollution.* Vol. 7, p. 959.

——. (1964) "City Growth and Urban Climates," *Weather.* Vol. 19, p. 170.

——. (1965) *The Climate of London.* London: Hutchinson & Co.

——. (1966) "London's Heat Island," *Biometeorology II.* Proceedings of the Third International Biometeorology Congress, 1963. London: Pergamon Press, pp. 589–597.

——. (1967a) "Absolute and Relative Humidity of Towns," *Bulletin of American Meteorological Society.* Vol. 48, p. 394.

——. (1967b) "Night-Time Temperatures in Relation to Leicester's Urban Form," *Meteorology Magazine.* Vol. 96, p. 244.

——. (October 1968) "Urban Climates: Inventory and Prospect." Paper presented at W.M.O. Symposium on Urban Climates and Building Climatology, Brussels, Belgium.

CHANG, SHIH L. (1968) "Waterborne Viral Infections and Their Prevention," *Bulletin, World Health Organization.* Vol. 38, pp. 401–414.

CHANGNON, S. A. (1961) "Precipitation Contrasts Between the Chicago Urban Area and an Offshore Station in Southern Lake Michigan," *Bulletin of American Meteorological Society.* Vol. 42, p. 1.

——. (1962) "A Climatological Evaluation of Precipitation Patterns Over an Urban Area," *Symposium: Air Over Cities.* U.S. Public Health Service, Taft Sanitary Engineering Center, Cincinnati, Ohio, Technical Report A62–5, pp. 37–67.

——. (1968a) "The LaPorte Weather Anomaly—Fact or Fiction?" *Bulletin of American Meteorological Society.* Vol. 49, p. 4.

——. (1968b) "Recent Studies of Urban Effects on Precipitation in the United States." Paper presented at W.M.O. Symposium on Urban Climates and Building Climatology, Brussels, Belgium.

——. (1969) "Recent Studies of Urban Effects on Precipitation in the United States," *Bulletin of American Meteorological Society*. Vol. 50, pp. 411–421.

CHEEK, D. B., REBA, R. C., and WOODWARD, K. (1968) "Cell growth and the possible role of trace minerals." In D. B. Cheek, ed., *Human Growth, Body Composition, Cell Growth, Energy, and Intelligence*. Philadelphia: Lea & Febiger, Chap. 30.

CHESTERS, G., and KONRAD, J. G. (1971) "Effects of Pesticide Usage on Water Quality," *Bio Science*. Vol. 21, No. 12, pp. 565–569.

CHOW, VEN TE. (1952) *Hydrologic Studies of Urban Watersheds, Rainfall and Runoff of Boneyard Creek*. Champaign-Urbana, Ill.: Illinois University, Civil Engineering Studies, Hydraulic Engineering Ser., No. 2, p. 66.

CLARK, JOHN R. (1969) "Thermal Pollution and Aquatic Life," *Scientific American*. Vol. 220, No. 3, pp. 18–27.

CLARK, N. A., and CHANG, S. L. (1959) "Enteric Viruses in Water," *American Water Works Association Journal*. Vol. 51, No. 2, pp. 1299–1314.

CLARK, N. A., et al. (1962) "Human Enteric Viruses in Water Source, Survival, and Removability," *Proceedings, International Conference on Water Pollution Research*, London.

CLARK, W. E. (1961) "Reaction to Aircraft Noise," Wright-Patterson Air Force Base Publications ASD TR 61–610.

CLARKE, J. F. (1969) "Nocturnal Urban Boundary Layer over Cincinnati, Ohio," *Mon. Weath. Rev., U.S. Department of Agriculture*. Vol. 97, pp. 582–589.

CLEARY, E. J. (1967) *The Orsanco Story*. Baltimore: Johns Hopkins Press.

CLEAVER, J. E. (1968) "Defective Repair Replication of DNA in *Xeroderma* Pigmentosum," *Nature*. Vol. 218, pp. 652–656.

CLOUGH, W. O. (1964) *The Necessary Earth: Nature and Solitude in American Literature*. Austin, Texas: University of Texas Press.

COALE, ANSLEY J. (October 1970) "Man and His Environment," *Science*. Vol. 170, p. 132.

COLE, LA MONT C. (1969) "Thermal Pollution," *Bio Science*. Vol. 19, pp. 989–92.

COMMINS, B. T., and WALLER, R. E. (1967) "Observations from a Ten-Year Study of Pollution at a Site in the City of London," *Atmospheric Environment*. Vol. 1, p. 49.

COMMITTEE on BATHING BEACH CONTAMINATION of the PUBLIC HEALTH LABORATORY SERVICE. (1959) "Sewage Contamination of Coastal Bathing Water in England and Wales: A Bacteriological and Epidemiological Study," *Journal of Hygiene (Cambridge)*. Vol. 57, pp. 435–473.

COMMITTEE on GOVERNMENT OPERATIONS. (1970) *Phosphates in Detergents and the Eutrophication of America's Waters* (23d report). House Report No. 91–1004, 91st Congress, 2d Session.

COMMITTEE on VIRUSES in WATER. (October 1969) "Viruses in Water," *Journal of the American Water Works Association*. Vol. 61, pp. 491–494.

CONNER, W. D., and HODKINSON, J. R. (1967) *Optical Properties and Visual Effects of Smoke-Stack Plumes*. Publication No. 999–AP–39, Public Health Service, U.S. Dept. of Health, Education, and Welfare, Cincinnati Ohio.

CONWAY, M. (April 1970) "Asia: The Unnatural Rape," *Far Eastern Economic Review*. Vol. 68, No. 17, pp. 21–31.

COOLEY, W. W., and LOHNES, P. R. (1962) *Multivariate Procedures for the Behavioral Sciences*. New York: John Wiley & Sons.

CORFIELD, G. A., and NEWTON, W. G. (1968) "A Recent Change in Visibility Characteristics at Finningley," *Meteorology Magazine*. Vol. 97, p. 204.

COUGHLIN, R. E., and GOLDSTEIN, K. A. (February 1970) "The Extent of Agreement Among Observers on Environmental Attractiveness." RSRI Discussion Paper Series, No. 37.

COULOMB, J. (1970) "News Report." National Academy Science National Research Council. Vol. 20, No. 3, p. 6.

CRAIG, PAUL P. (n.d.) "Correlation Between Exposure to Atmospheric Lead and Blood Lead Levels." Research Report, Brookhaven National Laboratory, mimeo.

CRAWFORD, M. D., GARDNER, M. J., and MORRIS, J. N. (1968) "Mortality and Hardness of Local Water-Supplies," *Lancet*. Vol. 1, pp. 827–831.

CRAWFORD, T., and CRAWFORD, M. D. (1967) "Prevalence and Pathological Changes of Ischaemic Heart-Disease in a Hard-Water and in a Soft-Water Area," *Lancet*. Vol. 1, pp. 229–232.

CRIPPEN, J. R., and WAANANEN, A. O. (1969) "Hydrologic Effects of Suburban Development Near Palo Alto, California," *U.S.G.S. Open-File Report.*

CROCKER, THOMAS, and ROGERS, A. J. (1971) *Environmental Economics.* Hinsdale, Ill.: Dryden Press.

CURTIS, H. J. (1967) "Radiation and Ageing." In H. W. Woolhouse, ed., *Aspects of the Biology of Ageing,* Symposia of the Society for Experimental Biology, No. 21. New York: Academic Press, pp. 51–63.

DALES, J. G. (1968) *Pollution, Property and Prices.* Toronto: University of Toronto Press.

DARWIN, CHARLES. (1859) *Origin of Species.* First ed., London.

DAVIDSON, B. (1967) "A Summary of the New York Urban Air Pollution Dynamics Research Program," *Journal of Air Pollution Control Association.* Vol. 17, p. 154.

DAVIS, E. L. (1971) *Water Resources Research.* Vol. 7, p. 453.

DAVIS, R. K. (1966) "Planning a Water Quality Management System: The Case of the Potomac Estuary," *Water Research.* Ed. by A. V. Kneese and S. C. Smith. Baltimore: Johns Hopkins Press, p. 101.

———. (1968) *The Range of Choice in Water Management: A Study of Dissolved Oxygen in the Potomac Estuary.* Baltimore: The Johns Hopkins Press.

DAVITAYA, E. F. (1965) "O vozmozhnom vliianii zapylennosti atmosfery na umen'shenie lednikov i poteplenie klimata," *Akademiia nauk SSSR, Izvestiia Seriia Geograficheskaia.* No. 2, pp. 3–28.

DeBOER, H. J. (1966) "Attenuation of Solar Radiation Due to Air Pollution in Rotterdam and its Surroundings." Koninklijk Nederlands Meteorologish Institute, Wetenschappelijk Rapport W.R. 66–1, de Bilt, Netherlands.

DE GROOT, IDO, and SAMUELS, SHELDON W. (1962) *People and Air Pollution: A Study of Attitudes in Buffalo, N.Y.* (An intradepartmental report.)

DeMARRAIS, G. A. (1961) "Vertical Temperature Difference Observed Over an Urban Area," *Bulletin of American Meteorological Society.* Vol. 42, p. 548.

DEPARTMENT of ENERGY and RESOURCES MANAGEMENT, AIR MANAGEMENT BRANCH. (Report of November 4, 1969) *Report on Continuous Air Quality Monitoring Stations in Metropolitan Toronto During 1968,* p. 2.

DETTWILLER, I. (October 1968) "Incidence Possible de l'activite industrielle sur les precipitations a Paris." Paper presented at W.M.O. Symposium on Urban Climates and Building Climatology, Brussels, Belgium.

DILLEHAP, RONALD D., et al. (1967) "On the Assessment of Potability," *Journal of Applied Psychology.* Vol. 51, pp. 89–95.

DISEKER, E. G., and RICHARDSON, E. C., (1961) "Roadside Sediment Production and Control," *American Society of Agricultural Engineers.* Vol. 4, pp. 62–68.

———. (1962) "Erosion Rates and Control Measures on Highway Cuts," *American Society of Agricultural Engineers.* Vol. 5, pp. 153–155.

DOBROVOLNY, ERNEST, and SCHMOLL, H. R. (1968) "Geology as Applied to Urban Planning," *Proc. 23rd International Geological Congress, Prague.* Vol. 12, pp. 39–56.

DOLBEAR, F. T. JR. (March 1967) "On the Theory of Optimum Externality," *American Economic Review.* Pp. 90–103.

DOWNING, A. L., and EDWARDS, R. W. (1968) *Institute of Water Pollution Control Annual Conference.* Water Pollution Research Laboratory, Stevenage, England. Reprint No. 552.

DRONIA, H. (1967) "Der Stadteinfluss auf den Weltweiter Temperaturtrend," *Meteorologische Abhandlugen.* Vol. 74, p. 1.

DRYDEN, FRANKLIN D., and STERN, GERALD. (April 1968) "Renovated Waste Water Creates Recreational Lake," *Environmental Science and Technology.* Pp. 268–278.

DUCKWORTH, F. S., and SANDBERG, J. S. (1954) "The Effect of Cities upon Horizontal and Vertical Temperature Gradients," *Bulletin of American Meteorological Society.* Vol. 35, pp. 198–207.

DUDLEY, E. F., BELDIN, R. A., and JOHNSON, B. C. (1969) "Climate, Water Hardness and Coronary Heart Disease," *J. Chron. Dis.* Vol. 22, pp. 25–48.

DUDLEY, S. F. (November 1936) "Ecological Outlook of Epidemiology," *Proceedings of the Royal Society of Medicine.* Vol. 30, p. 57.

DUFFY, E. A., and CARROLL, R. C. (1967) *United States Metropolitan Mortality, 1959–1961.* Public Health Service Publ. No. 999–AP–39. Cincinnati, Ohio: National Center for Air Pollution Control, U.S. Public Health Service.

DUMPER, THOMAS A. (Jan.–Feb. 1966) "Impact of Urbanization on Water Development," *Journal of Soil and Water Conservation*. Vol. 21, pp. 24–31.

DURFOR, CHARLES N., and BECKER, EDITH, eds. (1964) *Public Water Supplies of the 100 Largest Cities in the United States, 1962.* Washington, D.C.: GPO.

———. (1964) "Public Water Supplies of the 100 Largest Cities in the United States, 1961." Geological Survey Water-Supply Paper 1812. Washington, D.C.: Geological Survey, U.S. Department of the Interior.

DWORSKY, L. B. and STRANDBERG, W. B. (1967) *Cornell University Water Resources Center Publication 16*, Ithaca, New York.

"EFFECTS of AIRCRAFT NOISE in COMMUNITIES." (1961) *National Academy of Sci.–Natl. Res. Council Report.*

EISENBUD, MERRILL. (November 1970) "Environmental Protection in the City of New York." *Science.* Vol. 170, pp. 706–712.

ELAZAR, DANIEL J., SCHLESINGER, JEANNE, LOCKARD, JOSEPH, STEVENS, R. MICHAEL, and STEVENS, BERNADETTE A. (1972) *Green Land—Clean Streams: The Beneficial Use of Waste Water Through Land Treatment.* Report of Center for Study of Federalism. Philadelphia: Temple University.

ELLER, J., et al. (March 1970) "Water Reuse and Recycling in Industry," *Journal of the American Water Works Association.* Vol. 62, pp. 149–154.

ESPEY, W. H., MORGAN, C. W., and MASCH, F. D. (1966) "Study of Some Effects of Urbanization on Storm Runoff from a Small Watershed," *Texas Water Development Board Report 23.* P. 109.

ESPOSITO, J. C. (1970) *Vanishing Air.* New York: Grossman.

EVELYN, JOHN. (1661) *Fumifugium: or The Inconvenience of the Aer and Smoak of London Dissipated.*

FWPCA, ANNUAL REPORTS. (1960–1968) *Pollution-Caused Fish Kills.* U.S. Department of Health, Education, and Welfare—U.S. Department of the Interior, Washington, D.C.

FAIR, GORDON, et al. (1966) *Water and Wastewater Engineering.* Vol. 1: *Water Supply and Waste Water Removal.* (1968) Vol. 2: *Water Purification and Wastewater Treatment and Disposal.* New York: John Wiley & Sons.

FEDERAL WATER QUALITY CONTROL ADMINISTRATION. (July 1966) *Delaware Estuary Comprehensive Study,*

Preliminary Report and Findings. Philadelphia: F.W.Q.C.A.

FEIG, A. M. (1968) "An Evaluation of Precipitation Patterns over the Metropolitan St. Louis Area," *Proceedings First National Conference on Weather Modification.* Albany, N.Y.: American Meteorological Society, pp. 210–219.

FELTON, P. N., and LULL, H. W. (1963) "Suburban Hydrology Can Improve Watershed Conditions," *Public Works.* Vol. 94, pp. 93–94.

FENNER, M. L., and BRAVEN, J. (1968) "The Mechanism of Carcinogenesis by Tobacco Smoke." *Brit. J. Cancer.* Vol. 22, pp. 474–479.

FERGUSON, RICHARD B. (May 1966) "Automobiles and Air Pollution," *Scientist and Citizen.* Vol. 8, p. 11.

FERMI, LAURA. (October 1969) "Cars and Auto Pollution," *Bulletin of the Atomic Scientists.* Vol. 25, No. 8, pp. 35–36.

FERRIS, B. F., JR. "Epidemiological Studies on Air Pollution and Health," *Archives of Environmental Health.* Vol. 16, pp. 511–555.

———, and WHITTENBERGER, J. L. (December 1966) "Environmental Hazards, Effects of Community Air Pollution on Prevalence of Respiratory Disease," *New England Journal of Medicine.* Vol. 275, pp. 1413–1419.

FINKELSTEIN, H. (1969) "Air Pollution Aspects of Aeroallergens." (Contract PH-22-68-25) Washington, D.C. National Air Pollution Control Administration.

FLOHN, H. (1963) *Bonner Meteorol. Abhandl. No. 2.*

FLUECK, J. A. (1968) "A Statistical Analysis of Project Whitetop's Precipitation Data," *Proceedings First National Conference on Weather Modification.* Albany, N.Y.: American Meteorological Society, pp. 26–35.

FORD, E. B. (1965) *Genetic Polymorphism.* Cambridge, Mass.: M.I.T. Press.

FREDERICK, R. H. (1964) "On The Representativeness of Surface Wind Observations," *International Journal of Air and Water Pollution.* Vol. 8, p. 11.

FREDERICKSON, H. GEORGE, and MAGNAS, HOWARD. (October 1968) "Comparing Attitudes Toward Water Pollution in Syracuse," *Water Resources Research.* Vol. 4, No. 5, pp. 877–899.

FREEMAN, A. MYRICK III, and HAVEMEN, ROBERT H. (July 1972) "Residuals Charges for Pollution Control: A Policy Evaluation," *Science*. Vol. 177, pp. 322–329.

FREEMAN, M. H. (1968) "Visibility Statistics for London/ Heathrow Airport," *Meteorological Magazine*. Vol. 97, p. 214.

FRENKIEL, F. H. (1956) "Atmospheric Pollution and Zoning in the Urban Area," *Scientific Monthly*. Vol. 82, pp. 194–203.

FRIEND, A. G., STORY, A. H., HENDERSON, C. R., and BUSCH, K. A. (1965) "Behavior of Certain Radio-nuclides Released into Fresh-Water Environments," *Ann. Rep. 1959–60 Public Health Service Environmental Health Service*. P. 89.

FROST, JUSTIN. (1969) "Earth, Air, Water," *Environment*. Vol. 11, No. 6, pp. 14–33.

GALENUS. (1944) *Galen on Medical Experience: First Edition of Arabic Version with English Translation and Notes by A. Walzer*. London: published for the Trustees of the late Sir Henry Welcome by the Oxford University Press.

GARBER, W. F. (1956) "Stream Pollution: Bacteriological Standards for Bathing Waters," *Sewage and Industrial Wastes*. Vol. 28, pp. 795–808.

———. (June 1961) "Critical Evaluation of Objectives and Standards of Bathing Water Bacteriological Quality," *Proceedings of the Rudolfs Research Conference: Public Health Hazards of Microbial Pollution of Water*. New Brunswick, N.J.: Department of Sanitation, College of Agriculture, Rutgers, The State University, pp. 463–521.

GARNETT, ALICE. (1957) "Climate, Relief and Atmospheric Pollution in the Sheffield Region," *Advancement of Science*. Vol. 13, pp. 331–341.

———. (1963) "The Survey of Air Pollution in an Industrial City: Sheffield," *Biometeorology*. Ed. by S. W. Tromp and W. H. Weihe. Vol. 2, pp. 641–647.

———, and BACH, W. (1965) "An Estimation of the Ratio of Artificial Heat Generation to Natural Radiation Heat in Sheffield," *Monthly Weather Review*. Vol. 93, p. 383.

GEORGIEVSKII, N. (1939) *Severnyi Movskoi Put*. Leningrad. No. 13, p. 29.

GEORGII, H. W., and HOFFMAN, L. (1966) "Assessing SO_2 Enrichment as Dependent on Meteorological Factors." *Staub, Reinhaltung der Luft* (In English). Vol. 26, p. 1.

———. (October 1968) "The Effects of Air Pollution on Urban Climates." Paper presented at W.M.O. Symposium on Urban Climates and Building Climatology, Brussels, Belgium.

GESNER, KONRAD. *On the Admiration of Mountains*. Translated in 1937 by H.B.D. Soule. San Francisco: The Grabhorn Press, pp. 1543–1554.

GLOCK, C. Y. (April 1956) "Church Policy and the Attitudes of Ministers and Parishoners on Social Issues," *American Sociological Review*. Vol. 21, No. 2, pp. 148–156.

GOETZ, A. (1961) "On the Nature of the Synergistic Action of Aerosols," *International Journal of Air and Water Pollution*. Vol. 4, pp. 168–184.

GOLDMAN, MARSHALL I. (October 1970) "The Convergence of Environmental Disruption," *Science*. Vol. 170, pp. 37–42.

———, ed. (1967) *Controlling Pollution: The Economics of a Cleaner America*. Englewood Cliffs, N.J.: Prentice-Hall, Inc.

GOLDSMITH, J. R. (1968) "Effects of Air Pollution on Human Health," *Air Pollution*. Ed. by Arthur C. Stern. 2d Ed. Vol. 1. New York: Academic Press, pp. 588–589.

GOLDSTEIN, G. S., and WEHRLE, P. F. (1959) "Influence of Socioeconomic Factors on Distribution of Hepatitis in Syracuse, New York," *American Journal of Public Health*. Vol. 49, p. 473.

GORDON, J. E. (1953) "Evolution of Epidemiology of Health. I: Natural History of Disease—From Hippocrates to Sydenham," *Epidemiology of Health*. Ed. by I. Galston. New York and Minneapolis: Health Education Council.

———. (1953) "Evolution of Epidemiology of Health. III: World, Flesh and Devil as Environment, Host and Agent of Disease, *Epidemiology of Health*. Ed. by I. Galston. New York and Minneapolis: Health Education Council.

GOUDEY, R. F. (February 1931) "Reclamation of Treated Sewage," *Journal of the American Water Works Association*. Vol. 23, pp. 230–240.

GOULD, R. H. (1968) *Proc. Amer. Soc. Civ. Eng. J. San. Eng. Div*. Vol. 94, p. 1041.

GRAHAM, FRANK, JR. (Sept.–Oct. 1968) "The Infernal Smog Machine," *Audubon*. Vol. 70, No. 5, pp. 30–37.

GRAVA, SIGURD. (1969) *Urban Planning Aspects of Water*

Pollution Control. New York: Columbia University Press.

GREATREX, F. B. (August 1963) *Aircraft Engineering.* Vol. I.

GREEN, C. R., and BATTAN, L. J. (1967) "A Study of Visibility Versus Population Growth in Arizona," *Journal of Arizona Academy of Science.* Vol. 4, p. 226.

GREEN, G. M. (1968) "Cigarette Smoke: Protection of Alveolar Macrophages by Glutathione and Cysteine," *Science.* Vol. 162, pp. 810–811.

GREENWALD, I. (1954) "Effects of Inhalation of Core Concentration of Sulfur Dioxide on Man and Other Mammals," *Archives of Industrial Hygiene and Occupational Medicine.* Vol. 10, pp. 455–475.

GREGORY, S., and SMITH, K. (December 1967) "Local Temperature and Humidity Contrasts Around Small Lakes and Reservoirs," *Weather.* Vol. 22, No. 12, pp. 497–505.

GUNN, R. (1964) "The Secular Increase of the World-Wide Fine Particle Pollution," *Journal of Atomic Science.* Vol. 21, p. 168.

——, and PHILLIPS, B. B. (1957) "An Experimental Investigation of the Effect of Air Pollution on the Initiation of Rain," *Journal of Meteorology.* Vol. 14, p. 272.

GUNTER, GORDON. "Pollution Problems Along the Gulf Coast," *Biological Problems in Water Pollution.* Transactions of the 1959 Seminar, H.E.W., Technical Report W-60-63, pp. 184–188.

GUTMAN, ROBERT. (October 1966) "Site Planning and Social Behavior," in R. W. Kates and J. F. Wohlwill, eds. "Man's Response to the Physical Environment," *The Journal of Social Issues.* Vol. 22, No. 4, pp. 103–115.

GUTTMAN, L., and SUCHMAN, E. (February 1947) "Intensity and a Zero Point for Attitude Analysis," *American Sociological Review.* Vol. 12, No. 1, pp. 57–67.

GUY, H. P. (1964) "An Analysis of Some Storm-Period Variables Affecting Stream Sediment Transport." *U.S. Geological Survey Professional Paper 462-E,* p. 46.

——. (1967) "Research Needs Regarding Sediment and Urbanization," *American Society of Civil Engineers Proceedings.* Vol. 93, No. HY6, pp. 247–254.

——. (1970) "Sediment Problems in Urban Areas," *U.S. Geological Survey Circular.* No. 601-E.

——, and FERGUSON, G. E. (1962) "Sediment in Small Reservoirs Due to Urbanization," *American Society of Civil Engineers Proceedings.* HY 2, pp. 27–37.

——, JACKSON, N. E., JARVIS, K., JOHNSON, C. J., MILLER, C. R., and STEINER, W. W. (1963) "A Program for Sediment Control in the Washington Metropolitan Region," *Interstate Comm. Potomac River Basin, Tech. Bull.* Vol. 1, p. 48.

HAAGEN-SMIT, ARIE J. (1966) "Atmospheric Ecology II: The Troubled Outdoors," *Interactions of Man and His Environment.* Ed. by Burgess H. Jennings. New York: Plenum Press, pp. 41–48.

HAGEVIK, GEORGE H. (1969) *Planning for Environmental Quality.* Monticello, Ill.: Council of Planning Librarians, Exchange Bibliography No. 97.

——. (1970) *Decision-Making in Air Pollution Control.* New York: Praeger.

HALDAR, A. (1950) *The Notion of the Desert in Sumero-Accadian and West-Semitic Religions.* Uppsala: A.–B. Lundequi stska Bokhandeln, p. 70.

HAMILL, L. (1968) "The Process of Making Good Decisions About the Use of the Environment of Man," *Natural Resources Journal.* Vol. 8, pp. 279–301.

HAMMOND, E. C. (1969) "Cancer Prevention and Competitive Risks," *Arch. Environ. Health.* Vol. 19, pp. 395–398.

HANEY, PAUL D. (February 1969) "Water Reuse for Public Supply," *Journal of the American Water Works Association.* Vol. 61.

——, and HAMANN, CARL L. (September 1965) "Dual Water Systems," *Journal of the American Water Works Association.* Vol. 57, pp. 1073–1099.

HANLON, JOHN (1969) *Principles of Public Health Administration.* St. Louis: Mosby. 5th Ed.

HANSEN, C. A. (April 1969) "Standards for Drinking Water and Direct Reuse," *Water and Wastes Engineering.* Vol. 6, pp. 44–45.

HANSON, L. D., SPRINGER, C. D., FARNHAM, R. S., et al. (1966) "Soils of the Twin Cities Metropolitan Area and Their Relation to Urban Development." *Minnesota University Extension Bulletin 320,* p. 40.

HARDIN, G. (1968) "The Tragedy of the Commons," *Science.* Vol. 162, p. 1243.

HARMAN, D. (1961) "Prolongation of Normal Lifespan and Inhibition of Spontaneous Cancer by Antioxidants," *J. Gerontol.* Vol. 16, pp. 247–254.

————. (1966) "Free Radical Theory of Aging: Effect of Free Radical Inhibitors on the Lifespan of LAF₁ Mice," presented at the 19th Annual Meeting of the Gerontological Society, New York, N.Y.

HARNER, E. B. (May 1969) *Air Pollution and Chronic Diseases.* Philadelphia: Institute for Environmental Studies, University of Pennsylvania.

HARRIS, E. E., and RANTZ, S. E. (1964) "Effect of Urban Growth on Streamflow Regiment of Permanente Creek, Santa Clara County, California." *U.S. Geological Survey Water-Supply Paper* 1591-B.

HARRIS, T. B. (January 1970) "Inadvertent Weather Modification and Climate Change: Evidence of the Continuing Increase of Atmospheric Carbon Dioxide," *Bulletin of American Meteorology Society.* Vol. 51, No. 1, p. 101.

HARVEY, S. C. *Heavy Metals,* pp. 943–975.

HASKELL, ELIZABETH H. (May 1970) *Quality of the Urban Environments: The Federal Role.* Washington, D.C.: The Urban Institute, Working Paper 102–6.

HASS, J. E. (1970) *Water Resources Research.* Vol. 6, p. 353.

HASS, W. A., HOECKER, W. H., PACK, D. H., and ANGELL, J. K. (1967) "Analysis of Low-Level, Constant Volume Balloon (Tetroon) Flights Over New York City," *Q. J. Roy. Meteor. Soc.* Vol. 93, p. 483.

HATCH, T. F. (1961) *The Air We Breathe.* Ed. by S. M. Farber and R. H. C. Wilson. Springfield, Ill.: Thomas, p. 115.

HAYATSU, H., WATAYA, Y., and KAI, K. (1970) "The Addition of Sodium Bisulfite to Uracil and to Cytosine," *J. Amer. Chem. Soc.* Vol. 92, pp. 724–726.

HEARD, B. E., and T. IZUKAWA. (October 1964) "Pulmonary Emphysema in Fifty Consecutive Male Necropsies in London," *Journal of Pathology and Bacteriology.* Vol. 88, pp. 423–431.

HENDERSON, C. (1969) *Progr. Fish Cult.* Vol. 11, p. 217.

HENDERSON, J. M. (December 1968) "Enteric Disease Criteria for Recreational Waters," *Proceedings American Society of Civil Engineers* (Sanitary Eng. Div.), *Journal.* Vol. 94, SA6, p. 1253.

HERFINDAHL, ORRIS C., and KNEESE, ALLEN V. (1965) *Quality of the Environment: An Economic Approach to Some Problems in Using Land, Water, and Air.* Washington, D.C.: Resources for the Future.

HERING, E. (1861–64) *Beitrage zur Physiologie.* Leipzig: W. Englemann, Vol. 5, p. 355.

HERRICK, F. H., ed. (1926) *Audubon: Delineations of American Scenery and Character.* New York: G. A. Baker & Company.

HICKEY, R. J. (November 1968) "Relationship Between Air Pollution and Health," Sec. 3. *Governmental Organization for an Air Resource Management and Control System in the Penjerdel Region.* Government Studies Center, Fels Institute of Local and State Government, University of Pennsylvania, Philadelphia, pp. 89–122.

————, (October 1969) *Environmental Pollution and Chronic Disease.* Institute for Environmental Studies and Fels Institute of Local and State Government, University of Pennsylvania, and Regional Science Research Institute, Philadelphia, p. 50.

————. (April 1969) *The Relationships Between Air Pollution and Chronic Disease Death Rates.* Final Report to the American Cancer Society; Institute for Environmental Studies, University of Pennsylvania, Philadelphia.

————, BOYCE, D. E., HARNER, E. B., and CLELLAND, R. C. (April 1970a) *Ecological Statistical Studies Concerning Environmental Pollution and Chronic Disease.* Summary in digest of Technical Papers, 2d International Geoscience Electronics Symposium, IEEE, Washington, D.C., pp. 13–1, 13–2.

————. (October 1970b) *Ecological Statistical Studies Concerning Environment Pollution and Chronic Disease.* IEEE Trans. Geosc. Electronics, Vol. GE–8, No. 4.

————. (October 1970c) *Ecological Statistical Studies of Environmental Pollution and Chronic Disease in Metropolitan Areas of the United States.* Regional Science Research Institute Discussion Paper Series No. 35, Philadelphia.

————, and HARNER, E. B. (1971) *Ecology, Ethology and Genetic Polymorphism.* MS in preparation.

HICKEY, R. J., SCHOFF, E. P., and CLELLAND, R. C. (1967) "Relationship Between Air Pollution and Certain Chronic Disease Death Rates, Multivariate Statistical Studies." *Archeology Environmental Health.* Vol. 15, pp. 728–738.

HICKS, P. M. (1924) *The Development of the Natural History Essay in American Literature.* Ph.D. Thesis, University of Pennsylvania, Philadelphia, p. 167.

HICKS, W. I. (1944) "A Method of Computing Urban Runoff," *American Society of Civil Engineers Transactions*. Vol. 109, pp. 1217–1268.

HIRSCH, A. (1883–1886) *Handbook of Geographical and Historical Pathology*. Trans. by C. Creighton. London: New Sydenham Society.

HIRSHLEIFER, J., and MILLIMAN, J. W. (May 1967) "Urban Water Supply: A Second Look," *American Economic Review, Papers and Proceedings*. Vol. 57, No. 2, pp. 169–178.

HITCHCOCK, L. B., and MARCUS, H. G. (1955) "Some Scientific Aspects of the Urban Air Pollution Problem," *Scientific Monthly*. Vol. 81, pp. 10–21.

HOBBS, P. V., and RADKE, L. F. (1970) "Inadvertent Weather Modification and Climate Change: Cloud Condensation Nuclei from Industrial Sources and Their Influence on Clouds and Precipitation," *Bulletin of American Meteorological Society*. Vol. 51, No. 1, p. 101.

HOCH, IRVING. (1972) *Urban Scale and Environmental Quality. Final Report of the Commission on Population Growth and the American Future*. Washington, D.C.: GPO.

HOCHBERG, J. E. (1964) "Perception." *Foundations of Modern Psychology Series*. Englewood Cliffs, N.J.: Prentice-Hall, Inc.

HOGAN, A. W. (1967) "Ice Nuclei from Direct Reaction of Iodine Vapor with Vapors from Leaded Gasoline," *Science*. Vol. 158, p. 800.

HOLDEN, M. JR. (1966) *Pollution Control as a Bargaining Process*. Publ. No. 9: Cornell University Water Resources Center, Ithaca, N.Y.

HOLZMAN, B. G., and THOM, H. C. S. (April 1970) "The La Porte Precipitation Anomaly," *Bulletin of the American Meteorological Society*. Vol. 51, No. 4, pp. 335–337.

HOLZWORTH, G. C. (1962) "Some Effects of Air Pollution on Visibility In and Near Cities," *Symposium: Air Over Cities*. U.S. Public Health Service, Taft Sanitary Engineering Center, Cincinnati, Ohio, Technical Report A62–5, pp. 69–88.

HOOLE, S. (1798–1807) *Select Works of Leeuwenhoek Containing his Microscopical Discoveries in Many of the Works of Nature*. London: G. and W. Nicol.

HORNER, W. W., and FLYNT, F. L. (1936) "Relation Between Rainfall and Runoff From Small Urban Areas," *American Society of Civil Engineers Transactions*. Vol. 101, pp. 140–206.

HORTON R. E. (1937) "Determination of Infiltration Capacity for Large Drainage Basins," *Transactions of the American Geophysical Union, Part II*. Washington, D.C.: National Research Council, pp. 371–385.

———. (1939) "Analysis of Runoff Plot Experiments With Varying Infiltration Capacity," *Transactions of the American Geophysical Union Part IV*. Washington, D.C.: National Research Council, pp. 693–711.

———. (1945) "Erosional Development of Streams and Their Drainage Basins, Hydrophysical Approach to Quantitative Morphology," *Geological Society of America Bulletin*. Vol. 56, No. 3, pp. 275–370.

HOSLER, C. R. (1961) "Low-Level Inversion Frequency in the Continuous United States," *Monthly Weather Review*. Vol. 89, p. 319.

HOWE, CHARLES W. (May 1968) "Water Pricing in Residential Areas," *Journal of the American Water Works Association*. Vol. 60, pp. 497–501.

HOWELLS, G. P., KNEIPE, T. J., and EISENBUD, M. (1970) "Water Quality in Industrial Areas: Profile of a River," *Environ. Sci. Technol*. Vol. 4, p. 35.

HULTQUIST, NANCY B. (January 1972) "Water Quality and Quantity as an Aspect of Dynamic Urbanism." Technical Report No. 4, Institute of Urban and Regional Research, University of Iowa, Iowa City.

HUMPHREYS, W. J. (1940) *Physics of the Air*. 3d Ed. New York: McGraw-Hill.

HUNG-CHI (1970) *Red Flag*. No. 4.

HUTCHEON, R. J., et al. (1967) "Observations of the Urban Heat Island in a Small City," *Bulletin of the American Meteorology Society*. Vol. 48, p. 7.

HYNES, H. B. N. (1964) in *Symposium on Environmental Measurement*. Public Health Service Publ. No. 999–AP–15, pp. 289–298.

———. (1969) "The Enrichment of Streams," *Eutrophication: Causes, Consequences, and Correctives*. Washington: National Academy of Sciences.

———, and WILLIAMS, T. R. (1962) *Ann. Trop. Med. Parasitol*. Vol. 56, p. 78.

IBSEN, J., INGENITO, F. E., and DEANE, M. (1969) "Episodic Morbidity and Mortality in Relation to Air Pollution," *Archives of Environmental Health*. Vol. 18, pp. 458–461.

IORNS, W. V., HEMBREE, C. H., and OAKLAND, G. L. (1965) *U.S. Geol. Surv. Prof. Pap.* 441, pp. 458–461.

IRISH, SON S. (1966) "Atmospheric Ecology I: The Confined Ambient—The Dirty Nest," *Interactions of Man and His Environment*. Ed. by Burgess H. Jennings. New York: Plenum Press, pp. 33–40.

IRREVERRE, F., MUDD, S. H., HEIZER, W. D., and LASTER, L. (1967) "Sulfite Oxidase Deficiency: Studies of a Patient with Mental Retardation, Dislocated Ocular Lenses, and Abnormal Urinary Excretion of S–sulfo–L–cysteine, Sulfite, and Thiosulfate," *Biochem. Med.* Vol. 1, pp. 187–217.

ISHIKAWA, S., BOWDEN, P. H., FISHER, V., and WYATT, J. P., (1969) "The 'Emphysema Profile' in Two Midwestern Cities in North America," *Archives of Environmental Health*. Vol. 18, pp. 660–666.

IZVESTIYA. (July 1966) Vol. 5.

JAMES, L. D. (1965) "Using a Computer to Estimate the Effects of Urban Development on Flood Peaks," *Water Resources Research*. Vol. 1, No. 2, pp. 223–234.

JASKE, R. T., and GOEBEL, J. B. (1967) *J. Amer. Water Works Ass.* Vol. 59, p. 935.

JEFFS, DONALD N., and VIIRLAND, JAAK. (Sept.–Oct. 1970) "Special Cases of Water Supply Interference Caused by Urban Development Near Toronto, Ontario, Canada," *Water Resources Bulletin*. Vol. 6, No. 5.

JENKINS, I. (1969) "Increase in Averages of Sunshine in Central London," *Weather*. Vol. 24, p. 52.

JENSEN, L. D., DAVIES, R. M., BROOKS, A. S., and MEYERS, C. D. (1969) *The Effect of Elevated Temperature upon Aquatic Invertebrates: A Review of the Literature Relating to Fresh Water and Marine Invertebrates*. Department of Geography and Environmental Engineering, Johns Hopkins University, Baltimore.

JOHNSON, JAMES F. (1971) *Renovated Waste Water*. Department of Geography Research Paper No. 135, University of Chicago, pp. 3–23 and 160–166.

JORDAN. P. R. (1965) *U. S. Geol. Surv. Water Supply Paper* No. 1802. Pp. 1–89.

KAHN, R. L., WOLFE, D. M., QUINN, R. P., and SNOEK, J. D. (1964) *Organizational Stress*. New York: John Wiley & Sons, pp. 229–232.

KARSH, ROBERT. (May 1966) "The Air St. Louisans Breathe," *Scientist and Citizen*. Vol. 8, pp. 6–7.

KATES, ROBERT W. (1967) "The Perception of Storm Hazards on the Shores of Megalopolis," in David Lowenthal, *Environmental Perception and Behavior*, Department of Geography Research Paper No. 109, University of Chicago.

KELLER, F. J. (1962) "The Effect of Urban Growth on Sediment Discharge, Northwest Branch Anacostia River Basin, Maryland," *Short Papers in Geology and Hydrology*. U.S. Geological Survey Professorial Paper 450–C, pp. C129–C131.

KELLER, W. D., and SMITH, G. E. (1967) "Ground Water Contamination by Dissolved Nitrates," *Geological Society of America*. Special Papers (Eng.), Vol. 90, p. 47.

KELLOGG, C. E. (1952) *Our Garden Soils*. New York: Macmillan.

———, and ENDERLIN, H. C. (November 1969) "What Urban Building Does to Soil and Water," *Soil Conservation*. Vol. 35, pp. 83–86.

KETCHUM, B. H. (1969) *Eutrophication*, G.A. Rohlich (Ed.) Washington, D.C.: National Academy of Sciences, p. 197.

KEUP, LOWELL E. (1968) "Phosphorus in Flowing Waters," *Water Research*. Vol. 2, pp. 373–386.

———, et al., eds. (1967) *Biology of Water Pollution*. Cincinnati: U.S. Federal Water Pollution Control Administration.

KLEIN, LOUIS. (1962) *River Pollution, Causes and Effects*. Vol. II. London: Butterworths.

KNEESE, ALLEN. (1964) *The Economics of Regional Water Quality Management*. Baltimore: Johns Hopkins Press.

———. (1962) *Water Pollution: Economic Aspects and Research Needs*. Baltimore: Johns Hopkins Press.

———, and BOWER, BLAIR T. (1968) *Managing Water Quality: Economics, Technology, Institutions*. Baltimore: Johns Hopkins Press.

KNEESE, ALLEN, and SMITH, STEPHEN C., eds. (1966) *Water Research*. Baltimore: Johns Hopkins Press.

KOCH, R. (1882) "Die Aetiologie der Tuberkulose," *Berl. Klin. Wschr.* Vol. 19, p. 221. Reprint translated by Berna and Max Pinner. (March 1932) "Aetiology of Tuberculosis," *American Review of Tuberculosis*. Vol. 25, pp. 285–323.

KOELZER, VICTOR, et al. (April 1969) "The Chicago Area Deep Tunnel Project—A Use of the Underground Storage Resource," *Journal of the Water Pollution Control Federation.* Vol. 41, pp. 515–534.

KOENIG, L. (1963) *Ultimate Disposal of Advanced-Treatment Waste:* Part 1, "Wet Oxidation"; Part 2, "Incineration." U.S. Public Health Service Publication No. 999–WP–3.

————. (1966) *Studies Relating to Market Projections for Advanced Waste Treatment.* U.S. Federal Water Pollution Control Administration Publication No. WP–20–AWTR–17.

KOHDELI, G., VALLEGIANI, L., and LUKINOVICH, N. (1954) "Influence of Economic and Social Conditions on Clinical Course and Outcome of Tuberculosis: Observations of 7,000 Cases Seen in 'Sanatorium Village,'" Ann Villagio Sanat. Sondali, 2/3, abstracted in *Excerpta Medica, Public Health, Social Medicine and Hygiene* (1956), Abstract No. 2708, Sec. 17, Vol. 2, p. 612.

KONCEK, M., and CEHAK, K. (1968) *Arch. Meterol. Geophys. Bioklimatol.*, Ser. B, *Allg. Biol. Klimatol.* Vol. 16, No. 1.

KOTHANDARAMAN, VEERASAMY. (February 1971) "Analysis of Water Temperature Variations in a Large River," *Journal of the Sanitary Engineering Division.* Illinois State Water Survey, Reprint Series No. 166. Proceedings of the American Society of Civil Engineers.

KOTIN, P., and FALK, H. L. (1964) "Atmosphere Pollutants," *Ann. Rev. Med.* Vol. 15, pp. 233–254.

————. (1964) "Polluted Urban Air and Related Environmental Factors in the Pathogenesis of Pulmonary Cancer," *Diseases Chest.* Vol. 45, pp. 236–246.

KOTIN, P., and WISELEY, D. V. (1963) "Production of Lung Cancer in Mice by Inhalation Exposure to Influenza Virus and Aerosols of Hydrocarbons," *Progr. Exp. Tumor Res.* Vol. 3, pp. 186–215.

KRATZER, P. (1956) *Das Stadtklima.* Braunschweig: Friedrich Vieweg und Sohn. (English translation available through ASTLA, AD 284776)

KRUTILLA, JOHN V. (June 1961) "Welfare Aspects of Benefit/Cost Analysis," *Journal of Political Economy.* Vol. 69, No. 3, pp. 226–235.

————. (September 1967) "Conservation Reconsidered," *The American Economic Review.* Vol. 57, No. 4, pp. 777–786.

KRYTER, K. D. (1970) *The Effects of Noise on Man.* New York and London: Academic Press.

————, and WILLIAMS, C. E. (January 1966) "Masking of Speech by Aircraft Noise," *The Journal of the Acoustical Society of America.* Vol. 39, No. 1, pp. 138–150.

KUHN, ERICH. (Spring 1959) "Planning the City's Climate," *Landscape.* Vol. 8, pp. 21–23.

"Lake Eutrophication—Water Pollution, Causes, Effects and Control" (June 1970), *Bulletin No. 22,* Water Resources Research Center, University of Minnesota.

LANDSBERG, HELMUT E. (December 1934) "Observations of Condensation-Nuclei in the Atmosphere," *Monthly Weather Review.* Vol. 62, No. 12, pp. 442–445.

————. (April-May 1937) "The Environmental Variation of Condensation-Nuclei," *Bulletin of the American Meteorological Society.* Vol. 18, Nos. 4, 5, pp. 172–175.

————. (1938) "Atmospheric Condensation Nuclei," *Ergebnisse der Kosmischen Physik.* Vol. 3, pp. 155–252.

————. (March 1940) "The Use of Solar Energy for the Melting of Ice," *Bulletin of the American Meteorological Society.* Vol. 21, No. 3, pp. 102–107.

————. (1956) "The Climate of Towns," *Man's Role in Changing the Face of the Earth.* Chicago: University of Chicago Press, pp. 584–606.

————. (1959) "Weather in the Streets," *Landscape.* Vol. 9, pp. 26–28.

————. (1960) *Physical Climatology.* 2d Rev. Ed. DuBois, Pa.: Gray Printing Co.

————. (1961) "City Air—Better or Worse," *Symposium: Air Over Cities.* U.S. Public Health Service, Taft Sanitary Engineering Center, Cincinnati, Ohio, Tech. Report A62–5, pp. 1–22.

————. (April 1967) "Two Centuries of New England Climate," *Weatherwise.* Vol. 20, No. 2, pp. 52–57.

————. (October 1968) "Micrometeorological Temperature Differentiation Through Urbanization." Paper presented at W.M.O. Symposium on Urban Climate and Building Climatology, Brussels, Belgium.

————. (December 1970a) "Man-Made Climatic Changes," *Science.* Vol. 170, pp. 1265–1268.

———. (1970b) "Metropolitan Air Layers and Pollution," *Challenge for Survival.* Ed. by P. Dansereau. New York: Columbia University Press, pp. 131–140.

———. (1970c) "Micrometeorological Temperature Differentiation Through Urbanization," *Urban Climates, World Meteorological Organization, Geneva, Technical Note No. 108,* pp. 129–136.

———. (1970d) "Climates and Urban Planning," *Urban Climates, World Meteorological Organization Geneva, Technical Note No. 108,* pp. 364–374.

———, FISCHMAN, LEONARD, and FISHER, JOSEPH. (1963) *Resources in America's Future.* Baltimore: Johns Hopkins Press.

———, YU, C. S., and HUANG, L. (1968) "Preliminary Reconstruction of a Long Time Series of Climatic Data for the Eastern United States." University of Maryland Institute of Fluid Dynamics and Applied Mathematics. Technical Note BN-571.

LANGER, C. (1963) "Ice Nuclei Generated by Steel Mill Activity," *American Meteorological Society.* Proceedings of the First National Conference on Weather Modification, Albany, N.Y., pp. 220–227.

LANGER, G., ROSINSKI, J., and EDWARDS, C. P. (1967) "A Continuous Ice Nucleus Counter and Its Application to Tracking in the Troposphere," *Journal of Applied Meteorology.* Vol. 6, p. 114.

LANGFORD, G. B. (1965) *The Great Lakes and Their Problems.* Toronto: Great Lakes Institute.

LANGFORD, R. H., and DAVIS, G. H. (1970) *Proc. Amer. Soc. Civ. Eng. J. Hydr. Div.* Vol. 96, p. 1391.

LANGNER, T. S., and MICHAEL, S. T. (1963) *Life Stress and Mental Health.* Vol. 2. New York: Macmillan.

LARSEN, RALPH I. (1966) "Air Pollution from Motor Vehicles," *Annals of the New York Academy of Sciences.* Vol. 136, pp. 275–301.

LAUSCHER, F., and STEINHAUSER, F. (1932, 1934) *Sitzungsberichte, Wiener Akad. Wiss. Math. Naturw. Kl.* Vol. 141, Abt. 2A (1932), p. 15; Vol. 143, Abt. 2A (1934), p. 175.

LAVE, LESTER B. (September 1970) "Does Air Pollution Shorten Lives?" Paper prepared for the Committee on Urban Economics Summer Conference, University of Chicago.

———. (1970) "Air Pollution Damage," *Research on the Quality of the Environment.* Ed. by A. Kneese. Baltimore: Johns Hopkins.

———, and SESKIN, EUGENE P. (August 1970) "Air Pollution and Human Health," *Science.* Vol. 169, pp. 723–733.

———. "Does Air Pollution Cause Ill Health?" Carnegie-Mellon University, Pittsburgh, Pa., Graduate School of Industrial Administration. Unpublished manuscript.

———. (1970a) "A Statistical Analysis of the Association Between U.S. Mortality and Air Pollution." Working Paper.

———. (1970b) "Air Pollution, Climate and Home Heating: The Effect on U.S. Mortality." Working Paper.

LAW, JAMES P. (1968) *Agricultural Utilization of Sewage Effluent and Sludge, An Annotated Bibliography.* Washington, D.C.: U.S. Federal Water Pollution Control Administration.

LAWRENCE, E. N. (August 1954) "Microclimatology and Town Planning," *Weather.* Vol. 9, pp. 227–232.

———. (1968) "Changes in Air Temperature at Manchester Airport," *Meteorological Magazine.* Vol. 97, p. 43.

———. (1969) "Effects of Urbanization on Long-Term Changes of Winter Temperature in the London Region," *Meteorological Magazine.* Vol. 98, pp. 1–8.

LAWTHER, P. J. (1958) "Climate, Air Pollution and Chronic Bronchitis," *Proc. Royal Soc. Medicine.* Vol. 51, pp. 262–264.

———. (1963) "Compliance With the Clean Air Act: Medical Aspects," *Journal of the Institute of Fuel.* Vol. 36, pp. 341–344.

———. (1965) "Air Pollution," *Bulletin of the New York Academy of Medicine.* Vol. 41, pp. 214–217.

LAYCOCK, GEORGE. (1970) *The Diligent Destroyers.* New York: Doubleday.

LEFOLII, KEN. (February 1970) "Will Pollution War Die?" *Toronto Daily Star.*

LEHR, E. L., and JOHNSON, C. C. (1954) "Water Quality of Swimming Places: A Review," *Public Health Reports.* Vol. 69, pp. 742–747.

LEIGHTON, A. (1961) *Photochemistry of Air Pollution.* New York: Academic Press.

LEININGER, H. V., and McCLESKEY, C. S. (1953) "Bacterial Indicators of Pollution in Surface Waters," *Bulletin of Hygiene.* Vol. 28, No. 12, p. 1076.

LENAIN, A. F. (1967) "Impact of Nitrates on Water

Use," *Journal of American Water Works Association.* Vol. 59, p. 1049.

LEOPOLD, LUNA B. (1956) "Land Use and Sediment Yield," *Man's Role in Changing the Face of the Earth.* Ed. by W. Thomas. Chicago: University of Chicago Press, pp. 639–647.

———. (1968) *Hydrology for Urban Land Planning—A Guidebook on the Hydrologic Effects of Urban Land Use.* Washington, D.C.: GPO Geological Survey Circular 554.

———, and MADDOCK, T. JR. (1954) *The Flood Control Controversy.* New York: Ronald Press.

LEOPOLD, L. B., and TILSON, SEYMOUR. (1966) "The Water Resource," *International Science and Technology.* Vol. 55, pp. 24–34.

LEOPOLD, L. B., WOLMAN, M. G., and MILLER, J. P. (1964) *Fluvial Processes in Geomorphology.* San Francisco: W. H. Freeman and Co.

LICHTENSTEIN, E. P., SCHULTZ, K. R., SKRENTNY, R. F., and TSUKANO, Y. (1966) "Toxicity and Fate of Insecticides in Water," *Archives of Environmental Health.* Vol. 12, pp. 199–212.

LIEBERMAN, J. (1969) "Heterozygous and Homozygous Alpha₁–anti–trypsin Deficiency in Patients with Pulmonary Emphysema," *New England J. Med.* Vol. 281, pp. 279–284.

LOCKE, J. (1690) *An Essay Concerning Human Understanding.* London. 1947 edition abridged and edited by Raymond Wilburn. London: Dent.

LOHR, E. W., and LOVE, S. K. (1954) *The Industrial Utility of Public Water Supplies in the United States, 1952, Part 1, States East of the Mississippi; Part 2, States West of the Mississippi.* Geological Survey of Water-Supply Papers 1299 and 1300, U.S. Department of the Interior, Washington, D.C.

LOWENTHAL, D. (1968) "The American Scene," *Geogr. Rev.* Vol. 58, pp. 61–88.

LUDWIG, F. L. (1967) *Urban Climatological Studies.* Interim Report No. 1, Contr. OCD–PS–64–201. Stanford Research Institute, Menlo Park, California (AD 657248).

———, and KEALOHA, H. S. (1968) *Urban Climatological Studies.* Final Report, Contr. OCD–DAHC–20–67–C–0136. Stanford Research Institute, Menlo Park, Calif.

LULL, H. W., and SOPPER, W. E. (1966) "Hydrologic Effects from Urbanization of Forested Watersheds

in the Northeast." Upper Darby, Pa., Northeastern Forest Experimentation Station, p. 24.

MAASS, ARTHUR. (May 1966) "Benefit/Cost Analysis: Its Relevance to Public Investment Decisions," *Quarterly Journal of Economics.* Vol. 80, pp. 208–226.

———, and HUFSCHMIDT, MAYNARD, et al. (1962) *Design of Water Resource Systems.* Cambridge, Mass.: Harvard University Press.

MACAVOY, P., ed. (1970) *The Crisis of the Regulatory Commissions.* New York: Norton.

MACIVER, IAN. (1970) *Urban Water Supply Alternatives: Perception and Choice in the Grand River Basin, Ontario.* Chicago: University of Chicago, Department of Geography Research Paper No. 126.

MACLEOD, R. M., FARKAS, W., FRIDOVICH, I., and HANDLER, P. (1961) "Purification and Properties of Hepatic Sulfite Oxidase," *J. Biol. Chem.* Vol. 236, pp. 1841–1847.

MAGILL, P. L., ed. (1956) *Air Pollution Handbook.* New York: McGraw-Hill.

MAGNUS, H. (1877) *Die Geschitchtliche Entwicklung des Farbensinnes.* Leipzig.

———. (1880) *Untersuchungen uber den Farbensinn der Naturvolker.* Jena.

———. (1883) *Uber Ethnologische Untersuchungen des Farbensinnes.* Breslau.

MALLMAN, N. and MACK, W. N. (1961) "Biological Contamination of Ground Water," *Robert A. Taft Sanitary Engineering Center Technical Report W61–5,* pp. 35–43.

MANABE, S., and WETHERALD, R. T. (1967) "Thermal Equilibrium of the Atmosphere with a Given Distribution of Relative Humidity," *Journal of the Atmospheric Science.* Vol. 24, p. 241.

MANOS, N. E., and FISHER, G. F. (1959) "An Index of Air Pollution and its Relation to Health, *J. Air Pollut. Contr. Ass.* Vol. 9, No. 1, pp. 5–11.

MARGOLIS, JULIUS. (August 1957) "Secondary Benefits, External Economies, and the Justification of Public Investment," *Review of Economics and Statistics.* Vol. 39, No. 3, pp. 284–291.

MARSH, GEORGE PERKINS. (1864) *Man and Nature or Physical Geography as Modified by Human Action.* New York: Scribner, Armstrong and Company.

MARSTON, R. B., TYO R. M., and MIDDENDORF, S. C. (1969) *Pestic. Monit. J.* Vol. 3, p. 167.

MARTENS, L. A. (1966) "Flood Inundation and Effects of Urbanization in Metropolitan Charlotte" (North Carolina). U.S. Geological Survey, open-file report, p. 54.

MARTIN, R. C. (1960) *Water for New York.* Syracuse, N.Y.: Syracuse University Press.

MARX, LEO. (November 1970) "American Institutions and Ecological Ideals," *Science.* Vol. 170, pp. 945–952.

MATEER, C. L. (1961) "Note on the Effect of the Weekly Cycle of Air Pollution on Solar Radiation at Toronto," *International Journal of Air and Water Pollution.* Vol. 4, p. 52.

MAYO, S. T. (1961) "Interactions Among Categorical Variables," *Educational and Psychological Measurement.* Vol. 21, pp. 839–858.

McCARTHY, L. T. JR., and KEIGHTON, W. B. (1964) *U.S. Geol. Survey Water Supply Pap.* 1779–X, p. 42.

McCORMICK, R. A., and BAULCH, D. M. (1962) "The Variation with Height of the Dust Loading Over a City as Determined from the Atmospheric Turbidity," *Journal of Air Pollution Control Association.* Vol. 12, p. 492.

McCORMICK, R. A., and KURFIS, K. R. (1966) "Vertical Diffusion of Aerosols over a City," *Quarterly Journal of the Royal Meteorological Society.* Vol. 92, p. 392.

McCORMICK, R. A., and LUDWIG, J. H. (1967) "Climate Modification by Atmospheric Aerosols," *Science.* Vol. 156, p. 1358.

McGAUHEY, P. H., and KRONE, R. B. (1954) "Report on the Investigation of Travel of Pollution," *California State Water Pollution Control Board Publication II.* P. 218.

——. (1967) "Soil Mantle as a Wastewater Treatment System." San. Eng. Research Lab., University of California, Berkeley. *SERL Report* No. 67–11, p. 177.

McGUINNESS, C. L. (1967) "Urbanization—Can We Live With It?" *Water Resources Bulletin.* Vol. 3, No. 1, pp. 17–20.

McHALE, JOHN. (1970) *The Ecological Context.* New York: George Braziller.

McKEE, J. E., and WOLF, H. W. (1965) *Standard Methods for the Examination of Water and Wastewater,* 12th ed. New York: American Public Health Assn., p. 769.

——. (1963) *Water Control Criteria,* 2d ed. Los Angeles: The Resources Agency of California, State Water Control Board.

McKINNEY, ROSS E., and PFIFFER, JOHN T. (May 1965) "Effect of Biological Waste Treatment on Water Quality," *American Journal of Public Health.* P. 772.

McLEAN, D. M. (1964) "Contamination of Water by Viruses," *American Water Works Association Journal.* Vol. 56, pp. 585–591.

——, BROWN, J. R., and NIXON, M. C. (1964) "Microbial Hazards of Freshwater Bathing," *Health Laboratory Science.* Vol. 1, No. 3, pp. 151–158.

McNULTY, R. P. (1968) "The Effect of Air Pollutants on Visibility in Fog and Haze at New York City," *Atomic Environment.* Vol. 2, p. 625.

MEE, T. R. (September 1968) "Microphysical Aspects of Warm Cloud." Presented at ESSA Atomic Phys. Chem. Lab. Symposium on Weather Modification, Boulder, Colorado.

MERRIMAN, D. (1970) *Scientific American.* Vol. 222, p. 42.

MESHENBERG, MICHAEL (December 1970) *Environmental Planning: A Selected Annotated Bibliography.* Chicago: American Society of Planning Officials.

METEOROLOGICAL MONOGRAPH. (1968) Vol. 8, No. 3.

MEYERSON, MARTIN, TERRETT, BARBARA, and WHEATON, WILLIAM L. C. (1962) *Housing, People, and Cities.* New York: McGraw-Hill.

MICHELSON, WILLIAM H. (1970) *Man and His Urban Environment: A Sociological Approach.* Reading, Mass.: Addison-Wesley.

MIDDLETON, F. M. (1959) "Report on the Recovery of Orthonitrochlorobenzene from the Mississippi River." U.S. Department of H.E.W., Public Health Service. Cincinnati: R.A. Taft Sanitary Engineering Center. (Unpublished.)

MIKESELL, MARVIN W. "Cultural Ecology," *Focus on Geography.* Ed. Phillip Bacon. Washington, D.C.: National Council for the Social Studies, 1970, pp. 40–42 and 50–54.

MILANKOVITCH, M. (1941) "Canon of Insolation and the Ice-Age Problem," Translation of *Kgl. Serbische Akad. Spec. Publ.* 132. Translated by Israel Program Science Translation (1969), U.S. Department of Commerce Clearing House Fed. Sci. Tech. Inform.

MILLS, C. A. (1939) "Climatic and Weather Influences

in Health and Disease," *Medical Climatology.* Springfield, Ill.: Charles C. Thomas.

———. (March 1943) "Urban Air Pollution and Respiratory Diseases," *American Journal of Hygiene.* Vol. 37, p. 131.

MITCHELL, J. M. JR. (1961) "The Temperature of Cities," *Weatherwise.* Vol. 14, p. 224.

———. (1962) "The Thermal Climate of Cities," *Symposium: Air Over Cities.* U.S. Public Health Service, Taft Sanitary Engineering Center, Cincinnati, Ohio, Technical Report A62-5, pp. 131–145.

MONCRIEF, LEWIS, W. (October 1970) "The Cultural Basis for our Environmental Crisis," *Science.* Vol. 170, pp. 509–512.

MONTEITH, J. L. (1966) "Local Differences in the Attenuation of Solar Radiation Over Britain," *Quarterly Journal of the Royal Meteorological Society.* Vol. 92, p. 254.

MORGAN, GEORGE B., OZOLINS, GUNTIS, and TAYLOR, ELBERT C. (October 1970) "Air Pollution Surveillance Systems," *Science.* Vol. 170, pp. 289–295.

MORGAN, G. M. JR. (1967) "Technique for Detecting Lead Particles in Air," *Nature.* Vol. 213, p. 58.

———, and ALLEE, P. A. (1968) "The Production of Potential Ice Nuclei by Gasoline Engines," *Journal of Applied Meteorology.* Vol. 7, p. 241.

MORGAN, J. M. JR. (1959) *A Stream Survey in the Uranium Mining and Milling Area of the Colorado Plateau, Colorado and Gunnison Rivers.* Johns Hopkins University, Baltimore.

MORRISON, D. F. (1967) *Multivariate Statistical Methods.* New York: McGraw-Hill.

MUCKEL, D. C., and SCHIFF, LEONARD. (1955) "Replenishing Ground Water by Spreading," *Water, U.S. Department of Agriculture Yearbook.* Pp. 302–310.

MUDD, S. H., IRREVERRE, F., and LASTER, L. (1967) "Sulfite Oxidase Deficiency in Man: Demonstration of the Enzymatic Defect," *Science.* Vol. 156, pp. 1599–1602.

MUNN, R. E. (October 1968) "Airflow in Urban Areas." Presented at W. M. O. Symposium on Urban Climates and Building Climatology, Brussels, Belgium.

———, HIRT, M. S., and FINDLAY, B. F. (1969) "A Climatological Study of the Urban Temperature Anomaly in the Lakeshore Environment at Toronto," *Journal of Applied Meteorology.*

———, and STEWART, I. M. (1967) "The Use of Meteorological Towers in Urban Air Pollution Programs," *Journal of the Air Pollution Control Association.* Vol. 17, p. 98.

MUSGRAVE, G. W. (1947) "Quantitative Evaluation of Factors in Water Erosion—First Approximation," *Journal of Soil and Water Conservation.* Vol. 2, No. 3, pp. 133–138.

NADER, J. S. (October 1965) "Pilot Study of Ultraviolet Radiation in Los Angeles," Public Health Service Publication 999–AP-38. U.S. Department H.E.W., National Center for Air Pollution Control, Cincinnati, Ohio.

NAMIAS, J. (November 1968) "Factors Associated With the Persistence and Termination of the Recent Northeast Drought," *Proceedings of the Fourth American Water Resources Conference,* Proceedings Series 6, pp. 582–596.

NATIONAL ACADEMY of SCIENCES. (1968) Committee on Water. *Water and Choice in the Colorado Basin,* NAS Publication No. 1689. Washington, D.C.

———. (1966) National Research Council. *Alternatives in Water Management,* Publication No. 1408. Washington, D.C.

———. (1966) *Waste Management and Control,* Publication No. 1400. Washington, D.C.

———. (1969) *Resources and Man.* San Francisco: W. H. Freeman.

"The National Air Pollution Potential Forecast Program." (May 1970) Environmental Science Service Administration. Technical Mem. WBTM NMC 47.

NEALE, J. H. (1964) *Advanced Waste Treatment by Distillation.* U.S. Department of H.E.W, Public Health Service Publication No. 999–WP-9.

NELSON, J. L., and HAUSHILD, W. L. (1970) *Water Resource Research.* Vol. 6, p. 130.

NEPHEW, E. A. (1972) "Healing Wounds," *Environment.* Vol. 14, No. 1, pp. 12–21.

NEUSSIE, V. D., and HOLCOMB. (June 1970) "Will the SST Pollute the Stratosphere?" *Science.* Vol. 168, No. 3939, p. 1562.

NISBET, R. A. (1966) Chap. III, "The Two Revolutions," *The Sociological Tradition.* New York: Basic Books, pp. 21–44.

NORCOM, G. D. (August 1925) "Relation of Water

Supply and Sewage Disposal," *Journal of the American Water Works Association.* Vol. 14, pp. 116–119.

NOURSE, HUGH O. (May 1967) "The Effect of Air Pollution on House Values," *Land Economics.* Vol. 43, No. 2, pp. 181–189.

OFFICE OF SCIENCE AND TECHNOLOGY. (1966) *Alleviation of Jet Aircraft Noise.* Washington, D.C.: GPO.

OHIO RIVER VALLEY WATER SANITATION COMMISSION. (1957) *Chloride Control Considerations for the Ohio River.* Unpublished report.

OKE, T. R. (1968) "Some Results of a Pilot Study of the Urban Climate of Montreal," *Climatology Bulletin.* Vol. 36, No. 3.

———, and EAST, C. (1971) "The Urban Boundary Layer in Montreal," *Boundary Layer Meteorology,* Vol. 1, No. 4 pp. 411–437.

OKE, T. R., and HANNELL, F. G. (October 1968) "The Form of the Urban Heat Island in Hamilton, Canada." Presented at W.M.O. Symposium on Urban Climates and Building Climatology, Brussels, Belgium.

OKITA, T. (1960) "Estimation of Direction of Air Flow from Observation of Rime Ice," *Journal of the Meteorological Society of Japan.* Vol. 38, p. 207.

———. (1965) "Some Chemical and Meteorological Measurements of Air Pollution in Asahikawa," *International Journal of Air and Water Pollution.* Vol. 9, p. 323.

OLIVER, W. (1930) *Stalkers of Pestilence.* New York: Paul B. Hoever, Inc., pp. 60–88.

OLSON, G. W. (1964) "Application of Soil Survey to Problems of Health, Sanitation, and Engineering." Cornell University Agricultural Experimentation Station, Mem. 387, p. 77.

ONTARIO WATER RESOURCES COMMISSION. (1966) *Water Quality and Pollution Control in Metropolitan Toronto Along Lake Ontario, 1964–1965.* Toronto.

ORGEL, L. E. (1965) "The Chemical Basis of Mutation," in F. F. Nord, ed., *Advances in Enzymology.* New York: Interscience Publishers, John Wiley & Sons. Vol. 27, pp. 289–346.

ORLEANS, LEO A., and SUTTMEIER, RICHARD P. (December 1970) "The Mao Ethic and Environmental Quality," *Science.* Vol. 170, pp. 1173–1176.

ORMOND, RIETTE. (1968) "San Diego County, California, Reclamation Bonanza," *American County Government.*

OWENS, M., MARIS, P., and ROLLEY, H. (April 1970) "River Quality Timely Reassurance." *New Scientist,* Vol. 46, p. 25.

PACK, DONALD H. (November 1964) "Meteorology of Air Pollution," *Science.* Vol. 164, pp. 1119–1127.

PARRY, M. (1956) "An 'Urban Rainstorm' in the Reading Area," *Weather.* Vol. 11, pp. 41–48.

———. (1956) "Local Temperature Variations in the Reading Area," *Quarterly Journal of Royal Meteorological Society.* Vol. 82, p. 45.

———. (1966) "The Urban Heat Island," *Biometeorology II.* Ed. by S. W. Tromp and W. H. Weihe. Proceedings of Third International Biometeorological Congress, Pau, France, September 1963. London: Pergamon Press, pp. 616–624.

PASQUILL, F. (1962) *Atmospheric Diffusion.* London: Van Nostrand.

PEAKALL, DAVID B., and LOVETT, RAYMOND J. (1972) "Mercury: Its Occurrence and Effects in the Ecosystem," *Bio Science.* Vol. 22, pp. 20–25.

PETERSON, E. K. (November 1969) "Carbon Dioxide Affects Global Economy," *Environmental Science Technology.* Vol. 3, No. 11, pp. 1162–1169.

PETERSON, JAMES T. (1969) *The Climate of Cities: A Survey of Recent Literature.* Durham, N.C.: National Air Pollution Control Administration.

———, and BRYSON, R. A. (1968) "Atmospheric Aerosols: Increased Concentrations During the Last Decade," *Science.* Vol. 162, p. 120.

PHELPS, E. B. (1934) "Studies of Pollution of New York Harbor and the Hudson River," *Sewage Works.* Vol. 6, p. 998.

PLASS, G. N. (May 1956) "Effects of CO_2 Variations on Climate," *American Journal of Physiology.* Vol. 24, No. 5, pp. 376–387.

PLUHOWSKI, E. J. (1968) *Urbanization and its Effect on Stream Temperature.* Ph.D. Dissertation (in preparation). Baltimore, Md., Johns Hopkins Univ.

———. (1970) *U.S. Geol. Surv. Prof. Pap. 627–D,* 1–109.

POOLER, F. JR. (1963) "Air Flow Over a City in Terrain of Moderate Relief," *Journal of Applied Meteorology.* Vol. 2, p. 446.

PORGES, RALPH. (1967) "Water Quality Management in the Delaware River Basin," *Proceedings of the International Conference on Water for Peace.* Vol. 8, pp. 47–58.

POTTER, J. G. (1961) "Changes in Seasonal Snowfall in Cities," *Canadian Geography.* Vol. 5, p. 37

PREST, A. R., and TURVEY, R. (December 1965) "Cost/Benefit Analysis: A Survey," *The Economic Journal.* Vol. 75, No. 300, pp. 683–735.

PRYDE, PHILIP R. (1972) "The Quest for Environmental Quality in the U.S.S.R.," *American Scientist.* Vol. 60, pp. 739–745.

PUBLIC HEALTH SERVICE, NATIONAL VITAL STATISTICS DIVISION, *Vital Statistics of the United States,* Vol. 2 (Mortality), pt. B. Washington, D.C.: U.S. Department of H.E.W., annual editions.

———. (1962) Division of Air Pollution, *Air Pollution Measurements of the National Air Sampling Network, Analyses of Suspended Particulates, 1957–1961.* Cincinnati, Ohio: U.S. Department of H.E.W.

———. (1962) Division of Air Pollution, *Air Quality Data, National Air Sampling Network, 1962.* Cincinnati, Ohio: U.S. Department of H.E.W.

———. (1965) Division of Air Pollution, *Air Pollution Measurements of the National Air Sampling Network. Analyses of Suspended Particulates, 1963.* Cincinnati, Ohio: U.S. Department of H.E.W.

———. (1966) Division of Air Pollution, *Air Pollution Measurements of the National Air Sampling Network. Analyses of Suspended Particulates, 1964–1965.* Cincinnati, Ohio: U.S. Department of H.E.W.

———. (1968) *Air Quality Data from the National Air Surveillance Networks, 1966 Edition,* National Air Pollution and Control Administration. Durham, N.C.: U.S. Department of H.E.W., p. 6.

———. (October 1968) *The Facts About Smoking and Health,* Public Health Service Publication No. 1712. Arlington, Va.: National Clearinghouse for Smoking and Health, U.S. Department of H.E.W.

———. (April 1969) *1967 Data Tabulations and Summaries, Continuous Air Monitoring Projects, National Air Surveillance Networks, Cincinnati,* National Air Pollution Control Administration. Arlington, Va.: U.S. Department of H.E.W. and other CAMP reports.

———. (November 1969) *Air Quality Data from the National Air Surveillance Networks, 1967 Edition,* National Air Pollution and Control Administration. Raleigh, N.C.: U.S. Department of H.E.W., p. 156.

PUSHKAREV, V. F., and LEOCHENKO, G. P. (1967) "Use of Monomolecular Films to Reduce Evaporation from the Surface of Bodies of Water," *Soviet Hydrology: Selected Papers.* Washington, D.C.: American Geophysical Union. No. 3, pp. 253–272.

PUTNAM, R. D. (1966) "Political Attitudes and the Local Community," *American Political Science Review.* Vol. 60, pp. 640–654.

QUEEN, S. A. (April 1940) "The Ecological Study of Mental Disorders," *American Sociological Review.* Vol. 5, No. 2, pp. 201–209.

RAINEY, ROBERT H. (March 1967) "Natural Displacement of Pollution from the Great Lakes," *Science.* Vol. 155, No. 3767, pp. 1242–1243.

RIDKER, RONALD G. (1967) *Economic Costs of Air Pollution, Studies in Measurement.* New York: Frederick A. Praeger.

———, and HENNING, JOHN A. (May 1967) "The Determinants of Residential Property Values with Special Reference to Air Pollution," *The Review of Economics and Statistics.* Vol. 49, pp. 246–257.

ROACH, W. T. (1961) "Some Aircraft Observations of Solar Radiation in the Atmosphere," *Quarterly Journal of the Royal Meteorological Society.* Vol. 87, p. 346.

ROBERTS, M. J. (1970) "River Basin Authorities: A National Solution to Water Pollution," *Harvard Law Review.* Vol. 83, No. 6, p. 1551.

ROSSANO, A. T. JR., ed. (1969) *Air Pollution Control. Guidebook for Management.* Stanford, Conn.: Environmental Science Service Division.

ROTHENBERG, JEROME. (1967) *Economic Evaluation of Urban Renewal.* Washington, D.C.: The Brookings Institution.

RUHE, R. V., and DANIELS, R. B. (1965) "Landscape Erosion—Geologic and Historic." *J. Soil Water Conservation.* Vol. 20, p. 52.

SAARINEN, THOMAS A., and COOKE, R. U. (October 1970) "Public Perception of Environmental Quality in Tucson, Arizona," *Occasional Papers* No. 9, Department of Geography, University College, London.

SASAKURA, K. (1965) "On the Distribution of Relative Humidity in Tokyo and Its Secular Change in the Heart of Tokyo," *Tokyo Journal of Climatology.* Vol. 2, p. 45.

SAVINI, JOHN, and KAMMERER, J. C. (1961) "Urban

Growth and the Water Regimen." U.S.G.S. Water-Supply Paper 1591-A.

SAWICKI, E., ELBERT, W. E., HAUSER, T. R., FOX, F. T., and STANLEY, T. W. (1960) "Benzo-*a*-Pyrene Content of the Air of American Communities," *American Industrial Hygiene Association Journal.* Vol. 21, pp. 443–451.

SAWYER, C. N. (1947) "Fertilization of Lakes by Agricultural and Urban Drainage," *Journal of New England Water Works Association.* Vol. 61.

SAYERS, W. T. (1971) *Environ. Sci. Technol.* Vol. 5, p. 114.

SCHAEFER, VINCENT J. (1966) "Ice Nuclei From Automobile Exhaust and Iodine Vapor," *Science.* Vol. 154, p. 1555.

———. (1968a) "Ice Nuclei From Auto Exhaust and Organic Vapors" *Journal of Applied Meteorology.* Vol. 7, p. 148.

———. (1968b) "New Field Evidence of Inadvertent Modification of the Atmosphere," *Proceedings First National Conference on Weather Modification.* Albany, N.Y.: American Meteorological Society, pp. 163–172.

———. (1969) "Inadvertent Modification of the Atmosphere by Air Pollution," *American Meteorological Society Bulletin.* Vol. 50, pp. 199–206.

SCHAFER, M. L., PEELER, J. T., GARDNER, W. S., and CAMPBELL, J. E. (1969) "Pesticides and Drinking Water: Waters from the Mississippi and Missouri Rivers," *Environ. Sci. Technol.* Vol. 3, p. 1261.

SCHELSKE, CLAIRE L., and STOERMER, E. F. (1971) "Eutrophication, Silica Depletion, and Predicted Changes in Algal Quality in Lake Michigan," *Science.* Vol. 173, pp. 423–424.

SCHMIDT, F. H. (1963) "Local Circulation Around an Industrial Area," *International Journal of Air and Water Pollution.* Vol. 7, p. 925.

———, and BOER, J. H. (1963) "Local Circulation Around an Industrial Area," *Berichte des Deutschen Wetterdienstes.* No. 91, p. 28.

SCHROEDER, H. A. (1965) "The Biological Trace Element, or Peripatetics Through the Periodic Table," *Journal of Chronological Diseases.* Vol. 18, pp. 217–228.

———, BALASSA, J. J., and TIPTON, I. H. (1963) "Abnormal Trace Metals in Man: Titanium," *Journal of Chronic Diseases.* Vol. 16, pp. 55–69.

SCHUSKY, J. (1966) "Public Awareness and Concern with Air Pollution in the St. Louis Metropolitan Area," *Journal of Air Pollution Control Association.* Vol. 16, pp. 72–76.

SCHWARZ, KLAUS. (1959) "Die Abwasserlandbehandlung als Landeskulturmabnahme, ihre Problematik und zweckmäbige Ausrichtung," *Wasserwirtschaft-Wassertechnik.* Vol. 2, pp. 620–625.

SEKIGUTI, T. (1964) "City Climate in and Around the Small City of Ina in Central Japan," *Tokyo Geography Papers.* Vol. 8, p. 93.

SEVEN, M. J., and JOHNSON, L. A. (1960) *Metal-Binding in Medicine.* Philadelphia: J. B. Lippincott.

SHEAFFER, JOHN R., VON BOEHM, BERNDT, and HACKETT, JAMES E. (1965) *Refuse Disposal Needs and Practices in Northeastern Illinois.* Chicago, Ill.: Northeastern Illinois Planning Commission.

SHEAFFER, JOHN R., and ZEIZEL, A. J. (1966) *The Water Resource in Northeastern Illinois: Planning its Use.* Northeastern Illinois Planning Commission Technical Report No. 4, p. ii.

SHAPIRO, R., SERVIS, R. E., and WELCHER, M. (1970) "Reactions of Uracil and Cytosine Derivatives with Sodium Bisulfite. A Specific Deamination Method," *Journal of the American Chemical Society.* Vol. 92, pp. 422–424.

SHELLARD, H. C. (1959) "The Frequency of Fog in the London Area Compared with that in Rural Areas of East Anglia and South-East England," *Meteorology Magazine.* Vol. 88, p. 321.

SHEPARD, P. A. (1958) "The Effect of Pollution on Radiation in the Atmosphere," *International Journal of Air Pollution.* Vol. 1, p. 31.

SHENFIELD, L., and FRANTISAK, F. (1970) "Ontario's Air Pollution Index," *Water and Pollution Control.* Vol. 108, pp. 55–58.

SHERMAN, P. (1952) *Emerson's Angle of Vision: Man and Nature in the American Experience.* Cambridge, Mass.: Harvard University Press.

SHIRER, HAMPTON W., CAIRNS, JOHN, JR., and WALLER, WILLIAM T. (1968) "A Simple Apparatus for Measuring Activity Patterns of Fishes," *Water Resources Bulletin.* Vol. 4, No. 3, pp. 27–43.

SILVERMAN, D. A., and TALALAY, P. (1967) "Studies on the Enzymatic Hydrozylation of 3,4-benzopyrene," *Mol. Pharmacology.* Vol. 3, pp. 90–101.

SLADE, D. H. (1967) "Modeling Air Pollution in the

Washington, D.C. to Boston Megalopolis," *Science*. Vol. 157, pp. 1304–1307.

SLANETZ, L. W. (June 1961) "The Detection and Use of Enterococci as Indicators of Water Pollution," *Proceedings of the Rudolfs Research Conference: Public Health Hazards of Microbial Pollution of Water*. Department of Sanitation, College of Agriculture, Rutgers, The State University, New Brunswick, N.J., pp. 200–220.

SMALL, WILLIAM. (1971) *Third Pollution. The National Problem of Solid Waste Disposal*. New York: Praeger.

SMITH, G. (1941) *Plague on Us*. New York: The Commonwealth Fund; London: H. Milford, Oxford University Press, p. 44.

SMITH, L. P. (1961) "Frequencies of Poor Afternoon Visibilities in England and Wales," *Meteorology Magazine*. Vol. 90, p. 355.

SMITH, R. C. (Jan.–Feb. 1966) "Industry's Responsibilities for Water Pollution Abatement," *Journal of Soil and Water Conservation*. Vol. 21, pp. 177–179.

SMITH, R. S., and WOOLSEY, T. D. (1952) *Bathing Water Quality and Health. II: Inland River*. Cincinnati, Ohio: Environmental Health Center.

——, and STEVENSON, A. H. (1951) *A Study of Bathing Water Quality on the Chicago Lake Front and its Relation to Health of Bathers*. Cincinnati, Ohio: Environmental Health Center.

SMITH, ROBERT. (December 1967) *A Compilation of Cost Information for Conventional and Advanced Wastewater Treatment Plants and Processes*. Unpublished report.

SNYDER, F. F. (1938) "Synthetic Unit Hydrographs," *American Geophysical Union Transactions*. Vol. 19, pp. 447–454.

SOSEWITZ, BEN. (1971) Statement on digested sludge disposal on land in the Metropolitan Sanitary District of Greater Chicago, before the Panel on Environmental Science and Technology of the U.S. Senate Subcommittee on Air and Water Pollution of the Committee on Public Works. Federal Water Pollution Control Legislation Hearings, Part 8, Serial No. 92–H18. Washington, D.C.: GPO, pp. 3687–3716; 3812–4047.

SOUTHWORTH, M. (1969) "The Sonic Environment of Cities," *Environment and Behavior*. Vol. 1, No. 1, pp. 49–70.

SPAR, J., and RONBERG, P. (1968) "Note on an Apparent Trend in Annual Precipitation at New York City," *Monthly Weather Review*. Vol. 96, p. 169.

SPIRTAS, R., and LEVIN, H. J. (March 1970) "Characteristics of Particulate Patterns, 1957–1966," National Air Pollution Control Administration Publication No. AP–61.

SPITZER, E. F. (1967) "Cities Play a Major Role in Eutrophication," report on symposium, *American City*. Vol. 82, p. 99.

SPROULL, WAYNE. (1970) *Air Pollution and Its Control*. New York: Exposition Press.

SQUIRES, P. (1966) "An Estimate of the Anthropogenic Production of Cloud Nuclei," *Journal of Tech. Atmos*. Vol. 2, p. 299.

——, and TWOMEY, S. (1960) "The Relation Between Cloud Drop Spectra and the Spectrum of Cloud Nuclei," *Physics of Precipitation*. American Geophysical Union Monograph No. 5, pp. 211–219.

STAFF of BOLT BERANEK and NEWMAN. (1964) "Development of Aircraft Noise Compatibility Criteria for Varied Land Uses." Federal Aviation Agency Publication SRDS RD–64–148.

STAIR, R. (1966) "The Measurement of Solar Radiation, With Principal Emphasis on the Ultraviolet Component," *International Journal of Air and Water Pollution*. Vol. 10, p. 665.

STANFORD UNIVERSITY AEROSOL LABORATORY and THE RALPH M. PARSONS CO. (Jan.–March 1953a) "Behavior of Aerosol Clouds Within Cities." Jt. Quarterly Report No. 3, p. 218 (AD 31509).

——. (Oct.–Dec. 1953b) "Behavior of Aerosol Clouds Within Cities." Jt. Quarterly Report No. 6, Vol. 1, p. 246 (AD 31510).

——. (Oct.–Dec. 1953c) "Behavior of Aerosol Clouds Within Cities." Jt. Quarterly Report No. 6, Vol. 2, p. 187 (AD 31711).

STERLING, T. D., POLLACK, S. V., and WEINKAM, J. (1969) "Measuring the Effect of Air Pollution on Urban Morbidity," *Archeology Environmental Medicine*. Vol. 18, pp. 485–494.

STERN, A. C., ed. (1962) *Air Pollution*. New York: Academic Press.

——. (1967) "The Changing Pattern of Air Pollution in the United States," *American Industrial Hygiene Association Journal*. Vol. 28, pp. 161–165.

STEVENS, B. H., and RYDELL, C. P. (January 1968) "Air Pollution and the Shape of Urban Areas," *Journal of the American Institute of Planners*. Vol. 34, No. 1.

STEVENS, K. N., PIETRASANTA, A. C., and STAFF of BOLT BERANEK and NEWMAN. (1961) "Procedures for Estimating Noise Exposure and Resulting Community Reaction from Air Base Operations," Wright-Patterson Air Force Base Publication WADC TN 57-10, AD 110705.

STEWART, B. A., VIETS, F. G. JR., and HUTCHINSON, G. L. (1968) "Agriculture's Effect on Nitrate Pollution," *Journal of Soil and Water Conservation*. Vol. 23, pp. 13-15.

STOCKS, P. (1960) "On the Relations Between Atmospheric Pollution in Urban and Rural Localities and Mortality from Cancer, Bronchitis, Pneumonia, With Particular Reference to 3:4 benzopyrene, beryllium, molybdenum, vanadium and arsenic," *British Journal of Cancer*. Vol. 14, pp. 397-418.

STOYER, RAY L. (1967) "The Development of 'Total Use' Water Management at Santee, California," Presented at the International Conference on Water for Peace, Washington, D.C.

STRAUB, CONRAD P. "Pollution Problems Created by Power Reactors and Other Uses of Atomic Energy," *Biological Problems in Water Pollution*. Transactions of the 1959 Seminar, H.E.W., Technical Report W60-3, pp. 33-39.

STRAUSS, B. S. (1961) "DNA Repair Mechanisms and Their Relation to Mutation and Recombination," *Current Topics in Microbiology and Immunology*. Vol. 44. New York: Springer, pp. 1-85.

STRAUSS, WERNER, ed. (1971) *Air Pollution Control, Part I*. New York: John Wiley & Sons.

SUESS, EDWARD. (1875) *Die Entstehung der Alpen*. Wien: W. Braumiller.

SULLIVAN, W. T., and EVANS, R. L. (1968) "Major U.S. River Reflects Surfactant Changes," *Environ. Sci. Technol*. Vol. 2, p. 194.

SUMMERS, P. W. (1962) "Smoke Concentrations in Montreal Related to Local Meteorological Factors," in *Symposium: Air Over Cities*. U.S. Public Health Service, Taft Sanitary Engineering Center, Cincinnati, Ohio, Tech. Rept. A62-5, pp. 89-113.

———. (1966) "The Seasonal, Weekly, and Daily Cycles of Atmospheric Smoke Content in Central Montreal," *Journal of Air Pollution Control Association*. Vol. 16, p. 432.

SUMNER, WILLIAM GRAHAM. (1959) *Folkways*, repub. of 1906 ed. New York: Dover Publications, Inc.

SUNDBORG, A. (1950) "Local Climatological Studies of the Temperature Conditions in an Urban Area," *Tellus*. Vol. 2, p. 222.

SUTTON, O. G. (1953) *Micrometeorology*. New York: McGraw-Hill.

SWAN, J. (1953) *Entire Works of Dr. Thomas Sydenham*. Edition 3, London: Printed for E. Cave, Sec. 1, Chap. 1, p. A.

SWENSON, H. A. (1964) "Sediment in Streams," *Journal of Soil and Water Conservation*. Vol. 19, No. 6, pp. 223-226.

———, and BALDWIN, H. L. (1965) "A Primer on Water Quality," United States Department of the Interior, Geological Survey.

SYDENSTRICKER, E. (1933) *Health and Environment*. New York: McGraw-Hill.

SYLVESTER, ROBERT O. (1961) "Nutrient Content of Drainage Water From Forested, Urban and Agricultural Areas," *Algae and Metropolitan Wastes*. U.S.P.H.S., SEC TR W61-63, pp. 80-87.

———. (1958) "Water Quality Studies in the Columbia River Basin," U.S. Fish and Wildlife Service Special Scientific Report, Fisheries No. 239, p. 134.

TABAK, HENRY H., and BUNCH, ROBERT L. (1970) "Steroid Hormones as Water Pollutants. I. Metabolism of Natural and Synthetic Ovulation-inhibiting Hormones by Micro-organisms of Activated Sludge and Primary Settled Sewage." *Dev. Industrial Microbiol*. Vol. 11, pp. 367-376.

TAG, P. M. (1968) "Surface Temperatures in an Urban Environment." Master's Thesis, Department of Meteorology, The Pennsylvania State University, University Park, Penn., p. 69.

TARZWELL, C. M., ed. (1962) *Biological Problems in Water Pollution*. Cincinnati: U.S. Public Health Service, 3d Seminar.

———, and GAUFIN, A. R. (1953) "Some Important Biological Effects of Pollution Often Disregarded in Stream Surveys," Purdue University Engineering Bulletin, Proceedings 8th Industrial Waste Conference. P. 33.

TAYLOR, A. W. (1967) "Phosphorus and Water Pollution," *Journal of Soil and Water Conservation.* Vol. 22, No. 6, pp. 228–231.

TEBBENS, B. D. (1968) "Gaseous Pollutants in the Air," *Air Pollution.* Ed. by A. C. Stern. Vol. 1, 2d Ed. New York: Academic Press, p. 694.

TELFORD, J. W. (1960) "Freezing Nuclei from Industrial Processes," *Journal of Meteorology.* Vol. 17, p. 676.

TELLER, AZRIEL. (1967) "Air Pollution Abatement: Economic Rationality and Reality," *Daedalus.* Vol. 96, No. 4, pp. 1082–1098.

TERRY, LUTHER L. (1966) "Environmental Health: Everybody's Business" in *Interactions of Man and His Environment,* ed. by Burgess H. Jennings and John E. Murphy. New York: Plenum Press.

THE RESOURCES AGENCY. (June 1969) *California Air Quality Data,* Vol. 1. Berkeley, Calif.: California Air Resources Board.

THOLIN, A. L., and KEIFER, CLINT J. (1960) "Hydrology of Urban Runoff," *Transactions of the American Soc. Civil Engineers.* Vol. 125, p. 1308.

THOMAS, H. E. (1954) *U.S. Geological Survey Circ. 346.* Washington, D.C.: GPO.

THURLBECK, W. M. (February 1963) "The Incidence of Pulmonary Emphysema With Observations on the Relative Incidence and Special Distribution of Various Types of Emphysema," *American Review of Respiratory Diseases.* Vol. 87, pp. 206–215.

TITLIANOV, A. (1941) *Dokl. Vses (Ordena Lenina) Akademie Sel'skokhoz. Nauk Imeni V. I. Lenina.* Vol. 6, No. 8, p. 8.

TORPEY, W. N. (1967) "Response to Pollution of New York Harbor and Thames Estuary," *J. Water Pollution Control Fed.* Vol. 39, p. 1797.

TROWBRIDGE, C. C. (December 1913) "On Fundamental Methods of Orientation and Imaginary Maps," *Science.* Vol. 38, No. 990, pp. 888–897.

TURK, L. J. (1970) "Hydrology in the Urban Environment," in *Environmental Geology,* AGI Short Course Lecture Notes, November 9–20, Milwaukee, pp. 1–18.

TYSON, P. D. (1970) "Urban Climatology. A Problem of Environmental Studies." Inaugural Lecture. Johannesburg: Witwatersrand University Press.

———, DUTOIT, W. J. F., and FUGGLE, R. F. (1972) "Temperature Structure Above Cities: Review and Preliminary Findings from the Johannesburg Urban Heat Island Project," in *Atmospheric Environ-* *ment.* Elmsford, N.Y.: Pergamon Press, Vol. 6, pp. 533–542.

U.S. BUREAU OF THE CENSUS. (1961) *Census of Population, 1965,* Vol. 1 (Characteristics of the Population), pt. A (Number of Inhabitants), table 31 (Population of Standard Metropolitan Statistical Areas in the United States and Commonwealth of Puerto Rico: 1940–1960). Washington, D.C.: U.S. Department of Commerce.

———. (1960) *Historical Statistics of the United States, Colonial Times to 1957.* Washington, D.C.

U.S. CONGRESS, REPORT OF THE SURGEON GENERAL (1962) *Motor Vehicles, Air Pollution, and Health.* Washington, D.C.: GPO.

U.S. DEPARTMENT OF HEALTH, EDUCATION and WELFARE. National Statistics Division, Public Health Service, *Vital Statistics of the United States,* Vol. II, Mortality, Part B. Washington, D.C., annual editions.

———. National Vital Statistics Division, Public Health Service, *Vital Statistics of the United States,* Vol. I, Natality. Washington, D.C., annual editions.

———. *Cost Effectiveness of Air Pollution Control Strategies.* (Course Manual, Institute for Air Pollution Training) Public Health Service, Consumer Protection and Environmental Health Service.

———. U.S. Public Health Service. *Inventory of Water and Sewage Facilities in the United States,* 1945. Paging by states.

———. (1951) *Water Pollution in the United States.* U.S. Public Health Service Pub. 64, Water Pollution Series No. 1.

———. (1956) *Municipal Water Facilities for Communities for Communities of 25,000 Population and Over, December 31, 1955.*

———. (n.d.) Division of Air Pollution, Public Health Service. *Air Quality Data, National Air Sampling Network, 1962.* Cincinnati, Ohio.

———. (1961) *Vital Statistics of the United States, 1960.* H.E.W.

———. (1962) *Analysis of Suspended Particulates, 1957–61.* U.S. Public Health Service, Publication No. 978.

———. (1962) *Drinking Water Standards.* U.S. Public Health Service, Publication No. 956. Washington, D.C.: GPO.

——. (1962) Division of Air Pollution, Public Health Service. *Air Pollution Measurements of the National Air Sampling Network. Analyses of Suspended Particulates, 1957–1961.* Cincinnati, Ohio.

——. (June 1962) Division of Air Pollution, Public Health Service. *Motor Vehicles, Air Pollution and Health.* A Report of the Surgeon General to the U.S. Congress, 87th Congress, 2nd Session, House Document No. 489, Washington, D.C.

——. (1964) Public Health Service. Advisory Committee to the Surgeon General, *Smoking and Health.* PHS Pub. No. 1103. Washington, D.C.: GPO.

——. (1965) Public Health Service. *Water Supply and Water Quality Control Study Edwards Underground Reservoir Texas.* Dallas.

——. Public Health Service. *Activities Report, July 1, 1964 to June 30, 1965.*

——. (1965) Division of Air Pollution, Public Health Service. *Air Pollution Measurements of the National Air Sampling Network. Analyses of Suspended Particulates, 1963.* Cincinnati, Ohio.

——. (1965) *Public Awareness and Concern With Air Pollution in the St. Louis Metropolitan Area.* Public Administration and Metropolitan Affairs Program, Southern Illinois University, Washington.

——. (1966) Division of Air Pollution, Public Health Service. *Air Pollution Measurements of the National Air Sampling Network. Analyses of Suspended Particulates, 1964–1965.* Cincinnati, Ohio.

——. (1967) *Economic Benefits from Public Health Services—Objectives, Methods, and Examples of Measurement.* Washington, D.C.: GPO.

——. (1967) Public Health Service. *The Health Consequences of Smoking. A Public Health Service Review.* P.H.S. Publ. No. 1696, Washington, D.C.

——. (Revised October 1968) *The Facts About Smoking and Health.* Public Health Service Publ. No. 1712, National Clearinghouse for Smoking and Health, Arlington, Va.

——. (1968) *Air Quality Criteria for Sulfur Oxides.* Washington, D.C., GPO. National Air Pollution Control Administration Publ. No. AP–50.

——. (1968) *The Health Consequences of Smoking. The 1968 Supplement to the 1967 Public Health Service Review.* P.H.S. Publ. No. 1696, Washington, D.C.

——. (1968) *Air Quality Data.* National Air Surveillance Networks, 1966 Edition. Durham N. C.: H.E.W.

——. (1969) Public Health Service. *The Health Consequences of Smoking. 1969 Supplement to the 1967 Public Health Service Review.* PHS Publ. No. 1696–2, Washington, D.C.

——. (1969) *Toward A Social Report.* Washington, D.C.

U.S. DEPARTMENT OF THE INTERIOR. (1965) Federal Water Pollution Control Administration. *The Advanced Waste Treatment Research Program, Summary Report, January 1962–June 1964.* U.S. Public Health Service Publication No. 999–WP–24.

——. (1966) Federal Water Pollution Control Administration. *Delaware Estuary Comprehensive Study, Preliminary Report and Findings.* Philadelphia.

——. (1967). Federal Water Pollution Control Administration. *Problems of Combined Sewer Facilities and Overflows–1967.* Cincinnati: Federal Water Pollution Control Admin.

——. (1967). Federal Water Pollution Control Administration. *Sewer and Sewage Treatment Plant Construction Cost Index.* Washington, D.C.: GPO.

——. (1967) *Willamette River Basin Water Quality Control and Management.* Portland: U.S. Federal Water Pollution Control Admin.

——. (1968) National Technical Advisory Committee on Water Quality Criteria. *Water Quality Criteria.* Washington, D.C.: U.S. Federal Water Pollution Control Admin.

——. (August 1968) Federal Water Pollution Control Administration. *Lake Erie Report, A Plan for Water Pollution Control.*

——. (1968) *Water Quality Control and Management, Snake River Basin.* Portland: U.S. Federal Water Pollution Control Admin.

——. (1968) *Water Quality Control Study, The Frying Pan Arkansas River Sub-basin Colorado.* Dallas: U.S. Federal Water Pollution Control Admin.

——. (1968) New York State Department of Health. *Lake Ontario and St. Lawrence River Basins, Water Pollution Problems and Improvement Needs.* Albany: U.S. Federal Water Pollution Control Admin.

——. (1968) *Advanced Waste Treatment Research. Advanced Waste Treatment, Summary Report July 1964–July 1967.* Publication No. WP–20–AWTR–18.

———. (1968) *The Cost of Clean Water*. Vol. 2. Washington, D.C.: GPO.

———. (1969) Federal Water Pollution Control Administration. *Potomac River Water Quality*. Cincinnati: U.S. Federal Water Pollution Control Admin.

———. (January 1969) The American Public Works Association. *Water Pollution Aspects of Urban Runoff*. Report No. WP–20–15.

———. (1970) *The National Estuarine Pollution Study*. Report of the Secretary of Interior to U.S. Congress. U.S. Senate Doc. 91–58. Washington, D.C.: GPO, p. 633.

———. (July 1970) Water Pollution Control Research Series, *Storm Water Pollution From Urban Land Activity*.

U.S. SENATE. (March 1970) *National Emission Standards Study*. Report of the Secretary of Health, Education and Welfare to the United States Congress in Compliance with Public Law 90–148, The Clean Air Act, as Amended, 91st Congress, 2nd Session. Washington, D.C.: GPO.

———. (January 1971) *Economics of Clean Air*. Third Report of the Administrator of the Environmental Protection Agency to the Congress of the United States in Compliance with Public Law 90–148, The Clean Air Act, as Amended, 92nd Congress, 1st Session. Washington, D.C.: GPO.

U.S. SENATE PUBLIC WORKS COMMISSION. (1971) Water Pollution Hearings. Washington, D.C.: GPO.

UNDERWOOD, E. J. (1962) *Trace Elements in Human and Animal Nutrition*, 2d ed. New York: Academic Press, pp. 85–122.

VAJDIC, A. H. (April 1968) "Viruses in Water Supplies and Their Significance in Pollution Control," Ontario Water Resources Commission, Toronto, Ontario, Paper No. 2017.

VAN ARSDOL, M. D. JR., SABAGH, G., and ALEXANDER, F. (1963) "Environmental Hazards and Social Structure in the Los Angeles Standard Metropolitan Statistical Area," University of Southern California. Unpublished manuscript.

———. (1964) "Reality and the Perception of Environmental Hazards," *Journal of Health and Human Behavior*. Vol. 5, pp. 144–153.

VERNADSKY, VLADIMIR IVANOVITCH. (1929) *La Biosphere*. Paris: Alcan.

VIESSMAN, WARREN. (1969) "Assessing the Quality of

Urban Drainage," *Public Works*. Vol. 100, pp. 89–92.

VOLZ, F. E. (1968) "Turbidity at Uppsala from 1909 to 1922 from Sjostrom's Solar Radiation Measurements," Meddelanden, Series B, No. 28. Sver. Meteor. Hydrolog. Inst., Stockholm.

WACHS, MARTIN, and SCHOFER, JOSEPH. (1970) *A Systems Analyst View of Noise and Urban Planning*. Discussion Paper Series No. 14, Center for Urban Studies, University of Illinois at Chicago Circle.

WACKER, W. E. C., and VALLEE, B. L. (1959) "Chromium, Manganese, Nickel and Other Metals in RNA," *Fed. Proc. Abst.* Vol. 18, p. 345.

WADLEIGH, C. H. (September 1967) "Agricultural Pollution of Water Resources," *Soil Conservation*. Vol. 33, No. 2, pp. 27–30, 40.

WALOGIN, HAROLD. (1968) "The Economics of Air Pollution: Central Problems," *Law and Contemporary Problems*. Vol. 33, No. 2, pp. 227–238.

WARD, W. DIXON, and FRICKE, JAMES, eds. (1969) *Noise as a Public Health Hazard*. Washington, D.C.: American Speech and Hearing Association.

WARK, J. W., and KELLER, F. J. (1963) "Preliminary Study of Sediment Sources and Transport in the Potomac River Basin." Interstate Comm. on the Potomac River Basin, Tech. Bulletin 1963–11. Washington, D.C.

WARNER, J. (1968) "A Reduction in Rainfall Associated with Smoke from Sugarcane Fires—An Inadvertent Weather Modification?" *Journal of Applied Meteorology*. Vol. 7, p. 247.

———, and TWOMEY, S. (1967) "The Production of Cloud Nuclei by Cane Fires and the Effect on Cloud Droplet Concentration," *Journal of Atm. Science*. Vol. 24, p. 704.

WASHINGTON STATE POLLUTION CONTROL COMMISSION. (1955) *An Investigation of Pollutional Effects in Lake Washington*. Washington State Pollution Control Comm. Tech. Bull. No. 18.

———. (1956) *Facts About the Seattle Sewage Problem*. Washington State Pollution Control Comm., Inf. Series No. 10.

———. (1957a) *A Reinvestigation of Pollution in Grays Harbor, 1956–57*. Washington State Pollution Control Comm. Tech. Bull. No. 21.

———. (1957b) *Pollution Investigation in Northern Puget*

Sound. Washington State Pollution Control Comm. Tech. Bull. No. 22.

WAYMAN, C., PAGE, H. L., and ROBERTSON, J. B. (1965) *Behavior of Surfactants and Other Detergent Components in Water and Soil-Water Environments.* Federal Housing Adm. Tech. Studies Pub. 532.

WEBB, W. P. (May 1957) "The American West: Perpetual Mirage," *Harpers Magazine.* Vol. 214, No. 1284, pp. 25–31.

WEIBEL, S. R. (1969) "Urban Drainage as a Factor in Eutrophication" in *Eutrophication: Causes, Consequences, and Correctives.* Washington, D.C.: National Academy of Sciences, pp. 383–403.

WEISBROD, BURTON A. (1961) *Economics of Public Health—Measuring the Economic Impact of Diseases.* Philadelphia: University of Pennsylvania Press.

WEISMAN, B., MATHESON, D. H., and HIRT, M. (1969) "Air Pollution Survey for Hamilton, Ontario," *Atm. Environment.* Vol. 3, p. 11.

WELLS, W. F. (1955) *Airborne Contagion and Air Hygiene: Ecological Study of Droplet Infection.* Cambridge, Mass.: Harvard University Press.

WESTMAN, WALTER E. (1972) "Some Basic Issues in Water Pollution Control Legislation," *American Scientist.* Vol. 60, pp. 767–773.

———. (1972) "Offshore Development: Environmental Problems of the Future," *Ecology Today.* Vol. 2, No. 2, pp. 11 ff.

———. (1972) "The Future for Land Disposal of Water Wastes." In *Water Research Foundation of Australia, Special Report.* Proc. of Symp. on Water Pollution, Brisbane, August 1972. Reprinted in *Operculum,* Vol. 2, No. 4. In press.

WHARTON, CHARLES H. (1970) *The Southern River-Swamp—A Multiple Use Environment,* Bureau of Business and Economic Research, School of Administration, Georgia State University, p. 48.

WHITE, L. JR. (1967) "The Historical Roots of Our Ecologic Crisis," *Science.* Vol. 155, pp. 1203–1207.

WHITTLESEY, D. (1956) "The Regional Concept and the Regional Method," Chap. 2 in *American Geography: Inventory and Prospect.* Ed. by Preston E. James and Clarence F. Jones, pp. 21–68.

WHYTE, WILLIAM H. JR. (1958) "Are Cities Un-American?" *The Exploding Metropolis.* Ed. by the Editors of Fortune. Garden City, N.Y.: Doubleday Anchor Books, pp. 1–31.

WHITALA, S. W. (1961) "Some Aspects of the Effect of Urban and Suburban Development Upon Runoff," *U.S. Geological Survey Report,* Lansing, Mich.

WILKINS, E. T. (January 1954) "Air Pollution and London Fog of December, 1952," *Journal of the Royal San. Inst.* Vol. 74, pp. 1–21.

WILLEKE, GENE E. (October 1968) "Effects of Water Pollution in San Francisco Bay." Project on Engineering-Economic Planning, Stanford University, Stanford, Calif., Report EEP–29.

WILLIAMS, JAMES D. and EDMISTEN, NORMAL G. (1965) *An Air Resource Management Plan for the Nashville Metropolitan Area.* U.S. Department of Health, Education and Welfare, Public Health Service, Cincinnati, Ohio.

WILLIAMS, R. J. (1956) *Biochemical Individuality. The Basis of the Genotrophic Concept.* New York: John Wiley & Sons.

———. (1959) *Regression Analysis.* New York: John Wiley & Sons.

WILLMOTT, PETER. (1964) "East Kilbride and Stevenage: Some Social Characteristics of a Scottish and an English New Town," *The Town Planning Review.* Vol. 34, pp. 307–316.

WILSON, BILLY RAY, ed. (1968) *Environmental Problems: Pesticides, Thermal Pollution and Environmental Synergisms.* Philadelphia and Toronto: J. B. Lippincott.

WILSON, J. N. (1962) "Effects of Turbidity and Silt on Aquatic Life," *U.S. Public Health Service Seminar,* pp. 235–239.

WILSON, K. V. (1966) "Flood Frequency of Streams in Jackson, Mississippi." U.S. Geological Survey open-file report.

WILSON, RICHARD D., and MINNOTTE, DAVID W. (May 1969) "A Cost/Benefit Approach to Air Pollution Control," *Journal of the Air Pollution Control Association.* Vol. 19, No. 5, pp. 303–308.

WOJNAR, R. J., and ROTH, J. S. (1964) "Metal Ions in Ribonucleic Acid: Their Nature and Interference with the Assay of Ribonuclease and Ribonuclease Inhibitor," *Biochem. Biophys. Acta.* Vol. 87, p. 17.

WOLMAN, M. G. (1964) "Problems Posed by Sediment Derived From Construction Activities in Maryland." Report to the Maryland Water Pollution Control Commission, Annapolis, Md.

———. (1967) "A Cycle of Sedimentation and Erosion

in Urban River Channels," *Geographic Annaler*. Vol. 49A, pp. 285–295, 385.

———. (November 1971) "The Nation's Rivers," *Science*. Vol. 174, pp. 905–918.

———, GEYER, J. C., and PYATT, E. E. (1957) *A Clean Potomac River in the Washington Metropolitan Area*. Interstate Commission on the Potomac River Basin, Washington, D.C., p. 63.

———, and SCHICK, P. A. (1967) "Effects of Construction on Fluvial Sediment, Urban and Suburban Areas of Maryland," *Water Resources Research*. Vol. 3, No. 2, pp. 451–462.

WOODCOCK, KENNETH R., and BARRETT, LARRY B. (February 1970) "Economic Indicators of the Impact of Air Pollution Control, Gray Iron Foundries: A Case Study," *Journal of the Air Pollution Control Association*. Vol. 20, No. 2, pp. 72–77.

WOODWELL, GEORGE M. (September 1970) "The Energy Cycle of the Biosphere," *Scientific American*. Vol. 223, No. 3, pp. 64–74.

WOOLLUM, C. A. (1964) "Notes From A Study of the Microclimatology of the Washington, D.C., Area for the Winter and Spring Seasons," *Weatherwise*. Vol. 17, p. 262.

———, and CANFIELD, N. L. (1968) "Washington Metropolitan Area Precipitation and Temperature Patterns," ESSA Tech. Memo. WBTM–ER–28, Garden City, N.Y.

WORLD HEALTH ORGANIZATION. (1969) "Health Effects of Air Pollution," *Bulletin of the World Health Organization*. Vol. 23, pp. 264–274 (seminar report).

———. (1957) *Manual of the International Statistical Classification of Diseases; Injuries and Causes of Death, 1955 Revision*. Geneva: World Health Organization.

WYATT, J. P., FISHER, V. W., and SWEET, H. C. (April 1964) "The Pathmorphology of the Emphysema Complex," *American Review of Respiratory Diseases*. Vol. 89, No. 4, pp. 533–560.

ZEISS, H. (1942–1945) *Seuchen-Atlas, Herausgegeben in Auftrag des Chefs des Wehrmachtsanitativesens*. Gotha: Justus Perthes.

index

Abortion, natural, 329–31
ABS (alkyl benzene sulfonate), as water pollutant, 79, 173, 180–81
Acid mine pollution, 169, 180
Administrative Procedure Act (APA), 355–57
AEC, *see* Atomic Energy Commission
Aerobic bacteria, 169–70
Aerobic respiration, 28
Agricultural waste, 259–60
Air of Death (television program), 105
Air pollution, 3, 81–166
  executive orders on, 344, 345–46
  health and, 297–340
    chronic disease and, 317–40
    emphysema profile, 297–302
    mortality and, 302–17
  heat island and, 51
  major pollutants, 110–23
  management of, 124–66, 359, 360–61
    economic analysis for, 133–66
    Implementation Planning Program, 128–33
    in New York City, 360, 368–71
    in United Kingdom, 124–26
    in United States, 126–33
  meteorology of, 86–96

Air pollution (cont.)
  meteorology of (cont.)
    application of, 91–92
    atmospheric transport, 91
    future problems in, 95–96
    horizontal turbulent diffusion, 90–91
    urban pollution and, 92–95
    vertical turbulent diffusion, 87–90
  perception of, 99–109
    communications media and, 104–6
    consequences of, 106–8
    implications for public policy, 108–9
    physiological, 100–104
  radiation and, 54–55
  from solid waste disposal, 268, 271, 272
  sources of, 85–86
  surveillance systems for, 96–99
  in U.S.S.R., 11–12
  visibility and, 52, 54
"Air Pollution Potential Forecasts," 93–94, 95
Air Quality Act (1967), 126, 128–29
Air Quality Control Regions, *see* AQCR
Aircraft
  noise from, 287, 288–89, 290, 292–93, 294
    legislation on, 283, 284